Encyclopedia of Earth Myths

Also by Richard Leviton

Seven Steps to Better Vision

The Imagination of Pentecost: Rudolf Steiner and Contemporary Spirituality

Brain Builders! A Lifelong Guide to Sharper Thinking, Better Memory, and an Age-Proof Mind

Weddings by Design: A Guide to Non-Traditional Ceremonies

Looking for Arthur: A Once and Future Travelogue

Physician: Medicine and the Unsuspected Battle for Human Freedom

The Healthy Living Space: 70 Practical Ways to Detoxify the Body and Home

What's beyond That Star: A Chronicle of Geomythic Adventure

The Galaxy on Earth: A Traveler's Guide to the Planet's Visionary Geography

The Emerald Modem: A User's Guide to Earth's Interactive Energy Body

Signs on the Earth: Deciphering the Message of Virgin Mary Apparitions, UFO Encounters, and Crop Circles

ENCYCLOPEDIA OF EARTH MYTHS

An Insider's A-Z Guide to Mythic People, Places, Objects, and Events Central to the Earth's Visionary Geography

RICHARD LEVITON

Cover design by Steve Amarillo

Hampton Roads Publishing Company, Inc.
1125 Stoney Ridge Road
Charlottesville, VA 22902

434-296-2772
fax: 434-296-5096
e-mail: hrpc@hrpub.com
www.hrpub.com

If you are unable to order this book from your local
bookseller, you may order directly from the publisher.
Call 1-800-766-8009, toll-free.

Library of Congress Cataloging-in-Publication Data

Leviton, Richard.
Encyclopedia of earth myths : an insider's a-z guide to mythic people, places, objects, and events central to the earth's geography / Richard Leviton.
p. cm.
Summary: "An A-Z look at cultural tales from around the world that reflect the true spiritual nature of the planet and our relation to it"--Provided by publisher.
ISBN 1-57174-333-2 (7 x 9 : alk. paper)
1. Mythology--Encyclopedias. 2. Earth--Mythology--Encyclopedias. I. Title.
BL312.L48 2005
202'.4--dc22

2005019902

ISBN 1-57174-333-2
10 9 8 7 6 5 4 3 2 1
Printed on acid-free paper in the United States

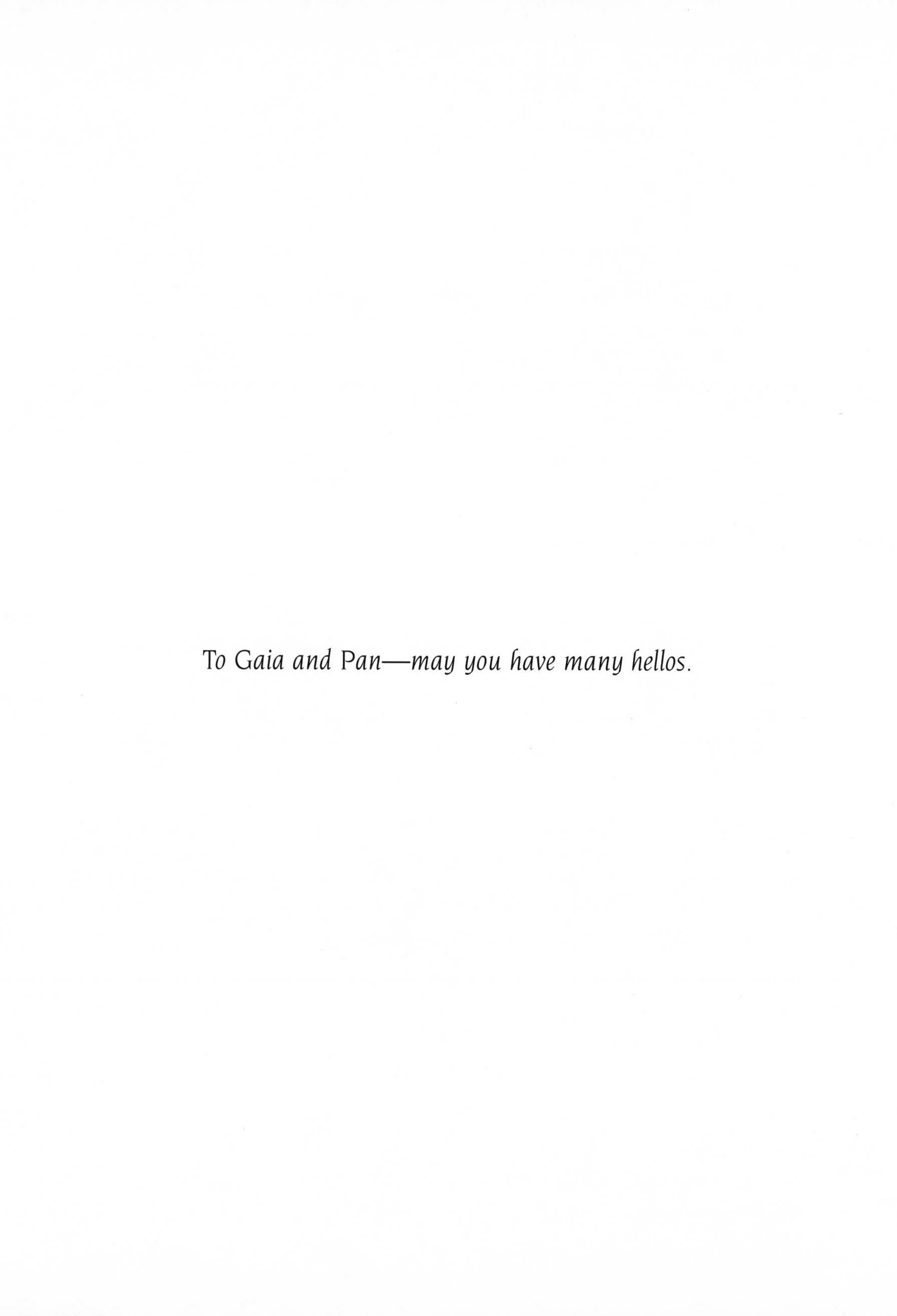

To Gaia and Pan—may you have many hellos.

Contents

Introduction

We can thank the depth psychologist C. G. Jung and the mythographer Joseph Campbell for refreshing our cultural interest in symbolism and myth and how both relate to the psyche, even illuminate it. But now it's time to take things a step further. As Campbell once commented, we need a new myth of the Earth.

The Jungian interpretation of symbolism and myth is not the edge of the world. It is but the edge of a dimension, a layer of truth. The next layer or horizon is the clairvoyant interpretation of myth and symbolism, the focus of this encyclopedia. One of the rich discoveries of this approach is to see that many, if not all, of the world's myths, culled from a variety of different cultures, say something profound about Earth. They are myths about Earth. They are clues to a secret about our planet, and they are portals into that secret realm.

What is the secret? That Earth has a soul. That Earth has a subtle body, a spiritual body, an energy body, a Light body, a mythic body, a visionary geography—there are many ways to say it. This is what it is:

Picture Earth as seen from space in the familiar NASA photographs as a lovely blue-white planet. Think of all the sacred sites you have seen pictures of, or visited, or even know of. Picture the physical features at these sites: stone circles, stone rows, pyramids, artificial hills, caves, temples, labyrinths, massive stone ruins or single standing stones, cathedrals, pagodas, shrines, mountains.

Each of the planet's many thousands of sacred sites has another aspect not ordinarily seen by the physical eyes yet able to be seen through clairvoyance. Each site has a temple of Light in the same place as the physical feature, or sometimes it is bigger. A temple of Light is one of many possible ways to point to a structured subtle space created for human interaction and illumination.

Here is where the world's myths are helpful because they provide a descriptive language for this unsuspected terrain of Light temples at sacred sites. Myths speak of Grail Castles, Sun temples, residences of the gods, Celestial Cities, dragon caves, golden apples, fairyland doors, Cosmic Eggs, hollow hills. To clairvoyant perception, these mythic terms are all maps to Earth's secret. If we take myths literally but at a clairvoyant level, they suddenly reveal a whole new terrain around us, what I call Earth's visionary geography—a landscape of visions. Visions of what? Of interactive Light temples, all part of Earth's secret.

This book looks at 153 items from the myths of 21 different cultures and interprets them in terms of what they reveal about Earth's visionary geography. Valuable knowledge about the planet's secret soul life and energy body is embedded in the myths around us. It's as if clues about Earth's visionary geography have been scattered in all cultures, awaiting our retrieval and decoding. It's just a question of how to decode them accurately.

Each entry shows how something considered mythic, such as a person, god, place, object, or event, actually illuminates something central to the esoteric makeup of the planet.

In most cases, an Earth myth also reveals

something important about human consciousness because the remarkable fact about Earth's sacred sites and their subtle Light temples is that they are individually and collectively reflections of us, of how our consciousness, generically, is put together and works. So decoding an Earth myth contributes to our self-knowledge.

But there is yet another crucial aspect to this arrangement. The Earth actually depends on our informed interaction with it through the sacred sites. It's a question of reciprocal maintenance. Sacred sites are not with us just to provide vacation opportunities. They are part of the planet's anatomy and physiology, and we are the physicians who are supposed to keep Earth's body in good trim.

This is more than environmentalism; this is tending to Earth's soul life. The Earth maintains and nurtures us physically; we are supposed to maintain the planet spiritually, contributing our spiritual light and presence back to the planetary system as a kind of food. Not much of this is happening today, largely due to the fact that few people are aware of the arrangement, and those who sense it probably lack the vocabulary to describe it and the protocols to interact with it.

It didn't used to be this way. For the most part, indigenous peoples following traditional ways contributed what was needed from the human realm to Earth. The Hopi of the American Southwest, for example, speak of how they were instructed by the god Masauu at the start of their residence on Earth in how to live correctly on the planet. They called it the Hopi Life Plan, and when they followed it, their lives prospered. The rains came, the crops grew, and the gods looked favorably upon their existence.

This knowledge for the most part has been lost in Western culture. But not lost forever; it is still all around us in the myths we take for granted, or dismiss as "fairy tales," or interpret only symbolically, not realizing they are living doorways into another realm of reality, both human and planetary.

So think of this encyclopedia as a guided tour through a layer of Earth reality whose existence you might not have suspected before. It's also an interactive tour. Each entry will send you to numerous related topics; follow the threads to related topics as a way of navigating the hologram of Earth's visionary geography.

Travel the Earth myth from its earliest days (see Dreamtime, Zep Tepi, and Hurqalya) to recent events (Ghost Dance, Harmonic Convergence) to things foretold for our future (Antichrist, Earth Changes, Ragnarok). Meet the actual spiritual beings behind the mythic façade of such characters as Pan, Gaia, the Fairy Queen, Fisher King, the Cyclops Polyphemus, Ganesh, and the Minotaur.

Get a new perspective on key events or figures in human history, such as the Fall of Man, Garden of Eden, Lucifer, Prometheus, Mephistopheles, and the Tower of Babel. Or appreciate a new, geomantic perspective on certain traditional festival days, such as Candlemas (evening of February 1 through February 2), Michaelmas (September 29), and the Wild Hunt (Winter Solstice Eve, December 20).

We are dealing with a hologram, a unified, living visionary reality overlapping our familiar physical world, in which everything is related to everything else. Follow dragons to dragon-slayers to dragon eggs to the glass mountain the dragons defend and the gods or spiritual beings who live inside these crystalline citadels and the rainbow-planked bridge you first must cross to get to the glass mountain.

The *Encyclopedia of Earth Myths* is also a practical tutorial for a new subject: the Earth. We may have thought we knew the Earth, in physical terms, but this is virtually a new planet we're being introduced to here. The planet's celestial aspect has always been here, but culturally we have entirely forgotten that. For a foundation in the model of the planet's visionary geography, try reading these entries first: Brigit's Mantle, Dreamtime, Eriu, Floating Bridge of Heaven, Hollow Hill, Holy Mountain, Hurqalya, Land of Milk and Honey, Navel of the World, Yeti, and Zep Tepi.

You may never perceive a myth or walk on the Earth in the same way again.

ADAM

The created container for human individuality before separation into genders, one capable of bearing the highest spiritual principle called the *Aleph* within the blood and physical matter of the body.

Also known as Adam of Light, Adapa, First Man.

Description: Adam is well known to the world as the first male human being created by God in His image in the Garden of Eden, and mate to Eve, the first woman. He found his first wife, Lilith, too wild and feral to be a suitable mate. Adam's name is traditionally interpreted to mean red or ruddy.

Adam is credited with having named the creatures God created. Genesis recounts how Adam stood by passively while Eve got them expelled from Paradise by tempting him to eat the forbidden fruit, presumably a golden apple, from the Tree of the Knowledge of Good and Evil.

In the Gnostic scriptures, Adam is called Adam of Light, described as the luminous man of blood. One document, called the Apocryphon of John, says that 365 angels contributed to the creation of Adam, one making the spine, another the arteries, and so forth, so that Adam was a composite of this range of angelic input. Adam lived to age 930, fathering, with Eve, Cain and Abel; he was buried on Mount Hebron or possibly Golgotha, "the place of the skull" in Jerusalem. Judaism says that after death humans must go through the Cave of Machpelah, Adam's domain, as he was the first human to die, before reentering Eden.

Explanation: The biggest obstacle to understanding Adam is taking Genesis literally in fundamentalist terms. It is a complex symbolic narrative written in Qabalistic code, based on the Hebrew, or earlier Aramaic language.

There are three most important facts about Adam. First, Adam was not the first male, but rather the archetypal, pregenderized container into which the soul was placed, later differentiated into male and female aspects. Second, Adam must be interpreted in terms of Qabalistic code (called gematria) to make sense of the concept: It means the *Aleph (A)* immersed in the blood *(DAM)*. Third, there were two Adams because humanity has been generated twice: The first Adam did in fact marry Lilith, one of the Edomites (see Kings of Edom) later removed or aborted from Creation; the second Adam was the Supreme Being's second, successful attempt to create a balanced human.

Lilith was Adam's first "wife" in the sense that "she" was the first attempt to blend or "marry" the physical-emotional aspects of being a human (the soul in matter, run amok ultimately) with the pure spiritual container, Adam.

In Hebrew, *Aleph* is the first letter of the 22-letter alphabet and is considered the container for the highest spiritual principle in existence. Blood, expressed as *dam* (you can see that to say that Adam means only red or ruddy misses the complexity of the matter), is the human physical body and all its molecular, organic, living processes. The intent with Adam was to enable the highest point of Spirit to survive and flourish within a material form. This is beyond self-aware consciousness; the Aleph is about God consciousness.

The name Adam also can be written as the number 1440. In Hebrew gematria, the letters each have a number equivalent; the final zero can be dropped or added with no distortion of the basic meaning. In this case, Adam refers to the 144,000 who will one day stand with the Lamb (Christ) on Mount Zion (in Revelation). These 144,000 individualized humans, or Adams, will earn their place beside the Christ (more precisely, in Christ consciousness) by virtue of spontaneously opening their Emeralds, the heart within the heart chakra. The Emerald, in myth, was the gift of the gods' fire that Prometheus gave to humanity.

The *Aleph* immersed in the blood of humanity is the starting point for this process, much as the Star of Bethlehem guided the Magi to the newborn Christ. In essence, the outer Star and the inner *Aleph* are identical (see Garuda). The Harmonic Convergence of August 1987 at which millions of people gathered at sacred sites was an early gathering and attunement of the 144,000 of Adam.

The Gnostic elaboration of the angelic contribution to the human makeup (Adam's body) means the macrocosm (galaxy and spiritual worlds) is copied in the microcosm (Adam and human being). This is the basis of the Hermetic axiom "As above, so below," and makes an alignment in consciousness with both possible.

Adam, as a being created by 365 angels, is templated on Earth in the form of a geomantic feature called a landscape zodiac (see White Cow). This is a hologram of the galaxy expressed as a flattened star map across the landscape. The culmination of the zodiac—that is, what you get when all the stars in it are illuminated, the inverse of the 365 angels who made Adam—is a cosmogonic figure variously called an Albion, Ymir, P'an-Ku, and Purusha. Adam is the inner Albion within each human accessed through its outer expression in the landscape zodiac.

See also: Albion, Emerald, Fall of Man, Garden of Eden, Garuda, Golden Apple, Harmonic Convergence, Kings of Edom, Prometheus, Purusha, Tree of the Knowledge of Good and Evil, White Cow, White Sow, Yggdrasil, Ymir.

AGHARTA

A name to describe the actual alternate human civilization inside Earth, limited in numbers but advanced in consciousness and technology, maintained by Gaia, the Earth's Spirit, as a fallback position.

Also known as Agartha, Agarttha, Agharti, Hollow Earth, Land of Advanced Races, Symmes' Holes, Subterranean World.

Description: The term *Agharta* comes from Buddhism and denotes a presumed subterranean civilization inside the Earth, presumed to be hollow. Some theorize that Agharta was colonized millennia ago by fleeing survivors of the continent and civilization of Atlantis as it was being destroyed. One legend has it that Agharta was colonized by humans leaving the surface many thousands of years ago, led by a holy man who guided the group underground. Human residents of Agharta are postulated to be at a higher stage of civilization, technological development, even spirituality than humans living topside, and Agharta is presumed to be the source of some of the UFOs sighted around the Earth.

In the seventeenth century, two prominent European scientists put forward the theory of a Hollow Earth. Dr. Edmond Halley (the comet was named after him) said that beneath the Earth's crust was a hollow void and that all planets are hollow. Leonard Euler, a mathematician, said there is a central Sun inside the Earth that lights a "splendid" subterranean civilization. In the early nineteenth century, John Symmes, an American lay researcher, proposed that the Earth comprises four concentric spheres with wide openings to the center of the Earth, which were later dubbed Symmes' holes. Speculation about a hollow Earth has continued since then.

Some strands of the Buddhist belief about a hollow Earth include the theory that in the cities inside the planet where millions of humans live is the seat of the Supreme Ruler of the Empire or King of the World. He controls Earth from Agharta by way of secret tunnels that connect the subterranean world with a primary outpost topside, possibly in Tibet, and possibly known as Shambhala. A variant of this theory says Agharta is a highly secret and advanced center of esoteric initiation, the true center of world government, and an impregnable fortress of the world's wisdom, connected by many tunnels with Shambhala. Agharta is also described as a subterranean kingdom beneath the landmass of Asia, connected to all the planet's continents by tunnels and passageways; this description tends to blur the distinctions between Agharta and Shambhala.

Speculation on Agharta and the Hollow Earth has been relegated in mainstream perception to the disrespected fringes of New Age belief, but some specific entrances (Symmes' holes) have been proposed, including Mount Shasta, California (which gives access to Telos, an Aghartan city); Mammoth Cave in Kentucky; somewhere in Matto Grasso, Brazil; Mount Epomeo, Italy; and Kathmandu, Nepal (said to have many concealed entrances into the mountains), among others.

Lending credibility to the subject is the longstanding and widely held belief among Native Americans that their ancestors originally arrived on the surface of the Earth by climbing up ladders, stairs, and tunnels from inside the Earth where they once lived. These emergence points on the surface of the planet are generally called *sipapuni* and are reflected in the traditional cosmological design of the kiva, a partly submerged round ceremonial space used by some tribes, especially the Hopi and the Anasazi.

Explanation: Included in the planet's visionary geography are 360 actual, physical entrances to the inside of the Earth. I call them *sipapuni* in honor of the Native Americans who sincerely and against Western ridicule stand fast in their claims to the existence of such. Inside the Earth, there is indeed a civilization of humans, though in smaller numbers than usually put forward: about 17,000.

The Navajo of the American Southwest, for example, say they emerged into the Fifth World (our present physical reality and landscape) from the Fourth World inside the Earth by climbing up a pole and emerging at its top onto an island in a lake surrounded by four snow-peaked mountains. They say this is in the San Juan Mountains of southern Colorado, and call it *Hadzinaí* or *Ni-ho-yos-tsá-tse* ("Place of Emergence" or "Land Where They Came Up").

If this legend is taken literally, which is plausible geomantically, that means some tribes of Native Americans were originally Hollow Earth dwellers.

The humans inside the Earth on occasion come through the *sipapunis* to visit our civilization, or at least observe it, and some humans topside on occasion go down to visit theirs, known variously (topside) as Agharta or Telos. The humans inside are, demonstrably, at a more sophisticated stage of evolution and consciousness; some of the UFOs observed topside come from inside the Earth. On other occasions, representatives from both human civilizations meet topside.

The purpose of a second human civilization inside Earth is to give Gaia, the Spirit of the planet, a fallback position if topside humanity severely compromises either its own conscious development or the viability of organic life on the planet and the Earth itself (as by the detonation of nuclear bombs in an all-out war).

Selected locations of *sipapuni* include Truckee, California; Salt Cave, Grand Canyon, Arizona (the Hopi emergence point); Hessdalen, Norway (a prime UFO anomaly site); Frijoles Canyon, Bandelier U.S. National Monument, (near) Los Alamos, New Mexico; Kluskap's Cave, Cape Dauphin, Cape Breton, Nova Scotia, Canada; and Mount Balsam Cone, Waynesville, North Carolina.

See also: Gaia, Shambhala.

ALBION

An expression of the cosmic totality of humanity over time, expressed in multiple copies on Earth with a landscape body made of stars.

Also known as Adam Kadmon, Anthropos, Eternal Man, Fallen Man, Gayomart, Grand Man, Humphrey Chimpden Earwicker (HCE), Manzasiri, Microprosopus, P'an-Ku, Primordial Man, Purusha, Universal Man, Ymir.

Description: Albion is an ancient name for the island of Britain after a fabled aboriginal giant who first conquered the island and named it after himself. But in the poetic vision of William Blake (*Jerusalem* and *The Four Zoas*), it is the name for the "Ancient Man," an Ur-human, like a cosmological model for all humanity, as in Emanuel

Swedenborg's Grand Man. Albion, Blake says, is the Eternal, Fallen Man, the father of all humankind, the Patriarch of the Atlantic continent. His wife is Brittannia, the folk-soul image for the country.

Blake's Albion is forlorn and despairing, having turned his back on the "Divine Vision" and in turn on his own progeny, his sons and daughters, which are usually interpreted as the tribes, races, and groupings of humanity.

Blake gave Albion a geomantic aspect, saying his giant form covers all the British Isles, with his right elbow leaning on Ireland and with London between his knees. However, all the "Starry Heavens" have departed the limbs of Albion, Blake says, suggesting that the island's sacred sites somehow had lost potency. Blake was the chief of the British Druids from 1799 to 1837, and it is not surprising that he would make this esoteric link between Albion, the spirit of the land, and the variety of holy sites laid upon it (or him). Blake prophesied that one day Albion would arise from his fallen state and once again hear the "Voice Divine."

Explanation: Albion is an expression templated across the Earth of the original archetypal design and composition of the Human, known in Qabala as Adam Kadmon. All the stars, constellations, and celestial beings and intelligences that on a macrocosmic level contributed to the creation of the original container for consciousness, variously called Anthropos, Eternal Man, Purusha, and others, is expressed microcosmically on Earth as Albion. Conveniently, for easy reference, Albion's name can be read as *A Light Being in Our Neighborhood.*

Albion's "home" is threefold: Around and within the entire planet is one Albion; within each of the 12 major geometric divisions of Earth's energy body lies an Albion; and within each of the planet's 432 landscape zodiacs (miniature interactive hologram of the galaxy—see White Cow, White Sow) is an Albion.

The three levels of Albion on Earth are also containers for the totality of human conscious and unconscious life and existence since the inception of the Earth. The planetary Albion and the 12 Albions have never awakened in the history of the Earth, but in the twenty-first century it is likely they will, one by one.

James Joyce, in his mythopoeic *Finnegans Wake,* calls Albion HCE, a protean character whose name keeps morphing throughout the tale (Here Comes Everybody, Humphrey Chimpden Earwicker). All of Dublin is HCE's body.

Albion represents several important things for humanity. For one, Albion is the point of consciousness that experiences the creation of duality out of the Tree of the Knowledge of Good and Evil. As such, Albion is an aspect or emanation of Lucifer, Lord of Light, and the ultimate embodiment of this Tree. Each landscape zodiac is templated on Earth like an apple cut in two; Albion is thus split in two as well and is reunited only when a zodiac is illuminated.

Albion is also akin to the Christ in that he is the unperfected, unreleased, and unawakened Christ of the Earth waiting to fulfill his destiny. He may fulfill his destiny in cooperation with the human, angelic, and elemental kingdoms.

For another, Albion is a hologram of the Light-Bearer, Lucifer, in his original state of divine glory, brought to Earth, and templated as the fulfillment and culmination of the awakening of the stars within landscape zodiacs. As Adam Kadmon is above in the galaxy, the total sentient expression of all the stars and constellations, so is Albion the same on Earth, with the added content of the archives of human experience on Earth since humanity's beginning.

At the middle level of the 12 Albions, each is part of a larger subdivision of Earth's surface in terms of geometric grids (pentagons). These are called Albion Plates, and each, though with different influences and astrological filters, is a microcosm of Earth's full array of geomantic features.

Geomantically, the Albion at any of the three

levels is a complex Earth-energy feature, consisting of 81 chakras (subtle consciousness centers) and many other compatible geomantic features. Albion is awakened through sustained human interaction and illumination of these features. These are the Starry Heavens Blake refers to as having departed the limbs of Albion; when Earth's visionary geography is remembered, reclaimed, and reactivated, those Starry Heavens will return to Albion's mighty limbs. Never in the history of the Earth has Albion been awake, so it will be a major event.

It is most likely that the second-level Albion, which overlies the British Isles, Portugal, Spain, and most of France, will awaken first of the 12 in the twenty-first century; this, in turn, will prod the single global Albion to awaken.

See also: Adam, Purusha, Tree of the Knowledge of Good and Evil, White Cow, White Sow, Ymir.

ANCIENT OF DAYS

An aspect of the Supreme Being expressed as a vast cosmic time reckoning that encompasses the duration of all Creation.

Also known as Ancient One, Antecedent of Time, Atum, Bendigeidfran (Bran the Blessed), Brahma, Head of Days, Kronos, Macroprosopus, Mimir, Osiris, Primal Aion, Urddawl Ben (Venerable Head), Vast Countenance, White Head, Zervan.

Description: Ancient of Days is a term used in Judaism, and especially in Qabala and the Zohar, to refer to the Supreme Being (God) by way of a complex symbolism of all aspects and functions of the divine Face, even beard hairs.

The Ancient of Days has a face whose appearance is vast and terrible, Judaic tradition says. The brightness of his face shines into 40,000 worlds; within his skull exist 13,000 myriad worlds; and the vastness of his countenance extends into 370 myriad worlds. Inside his hard skull bounded on four sides are 9,000 myriad worlds; from the subtle air of the skull 150 myriad worlds expand outward; also inside the skull are 50 gates of understanding, and one million conclaves and assemblies.

Thirteen fountains of excellent oil flow down upon the Ancient of Days' massive beard in 22 parts. From the individual beard hairs hang many thousand, innumerable worlds, all dependent on the perpetual flow of grace and light from the Ancient of Days.

If the Ancient of Days were to close his eye even for a moment, everything in existence would disappear. He has two eyes, but one is turned away from Creation, the other focused upon it. His open, holy eye is the guardian and subsistence of all things. The Ancient of Days, in a garment white as snow, sits on a Throne that is like a fiery flame and has wheels of burning fire.

Classical authorities such as Dionysius the Areopagite defined the Ancient of Days as both the eternity and time of all things prior to the advent of eternity, time, and days. Qabala says it is God as He is in Himself.

Explanation: The Ancient of Days is perhaps more easily understood by viewing him from a different cultural guise, as Brahma the Creator in Hinduism.

Hinduism has an elaborate time reckoning for cosmic existence based on Days and Years of Brahma. Brahma's size is measured in time, and all aspects, events, and the duration of cosmic, galactic, solar, planetary, and ultimately human biological time is calculated as portions of Brahma's vast extent.

One Day of Brahma (called a *kalpa*) is 4.32 billion human years and consists of 1,000 four-age periods, each lasting 4.32 million years. The four-age periods are known as yugas: *Krtayuga* (Golden Age), lasts 1,728,000 years; *Tretayuga* (Silver Age), lasts 1,296,000 years; *Dvaparayuga* (Copper Age), lasts 864,000 years; and *Kaliyuga* (Iron Age), lasts 432,000 years. Each successive age is defined as an epoch of less divine light and greater darkness and ignorance. Our current epoch within Brahma is the *Kaliyuga*, a dark time.

Creation exists during the Day of Brahma, then all the worlds dissolve during the Night of Brahma. During this Night, all the enlightened sages, the Seven Rishis, the Manus (world regents for time spans of 306,720,000 years), the minor gods, and Brahma, Vishnu, and Shiva (the major gods), all ascend to a higher sphere to preserve cosmic life and wait for the dawn of the next Day of Brahma.

This is the archetype of all Flood myths and all expressions of Noah's Ark, survivors of the Deluge, landing spots after the Flood, and repopulations of the world. When the Day of Brahma begins again, all the gods return to the lower spheres to resume their cosmic activities, though usually under new names for the new epoch. The Manu, regarded by humans as the mythical progenitor of the world or a secondary creator, becomes regent of the world for a *manvantara*, which is 71 four-age periods, or 306,720,000 years. Various myths remember this august figure as Noah, Deucalion, Yima, or Ziusudra-Utnapishtim, or as the Rich Fisher King, Lord of the Grail Castle.

One Year of Brahma consists of 360 Days and Nights of Brahma, or 155,520,000,000 years, and Brahma's entire life span is 100 such years, or 311,040,000,000,000 years. This is how old the Ancient of Days is. The full extent of the life of Brahma (36,000 divine Days) is called a Mahakalpa, and the Flood that comes at the end of his 100-year life is called Mahapralaya (great dissolution).

With most of the other equivalent names for the Ancient of Days, such as the Egyptian Osiris, the Greek Kronos, the Welsh Bendigeidfran (Bran the Blessed), the vast age of the deity is implied but not elaborated. With the Zoroastrian-Persian description of Zervan, we do find the immense time factor.

Zervan is Persian for "time." As the time-god, Zervan is four-headed (as is Brahma) and represents wisdom, power, light, and divinity. He is the father of *Ahura Mazda* (the radiant golden light) and *Ahriman* (his dark adversary). Zervan has two aspects: *Zervan akarana,* uncreated, infinite Time; and *Zervan daregho-khvadhata,* the Time of Long Dominion or Finite Time, lasting 12,000 divine years or 4,320,000 human years which is 1,000 four-age periods in Brahma's time.

So Zervan is both Time without limit and Time which is long to rule ("Sovereign Time of the Long Period"), paralleling the Vedic formulation of Days and Nights of Brahma. Zervan akarana is akin to the subtle Vedic concept of *Parabrahm* ("Beyond Brahma") which means the infinite, supreme, absolute, impersonal, timeless first principle, the Infinite Brahma with no attributes.

Another, more abstract, expression of Time is the Gnostic Primal Aion of the Unbegotten, Unknown Father. In the Gnostic view, the 30 Aions exist with the Primal Aion inside the Pleroma, a container of absolute light before Time.

For an expression of the immanence of the Ancient of Days in our world in multiple expressions of a severed divine head, see Bran the Blessed.

See also: Bran the Blessed, Fisher King, Flood, Grail Castle, Manu.

ANTICHRIST

An energy overlay, called the dark grid, imposed upon Earth's original, spiritually infused Light body or visionary geography for the purposes of defeating the unfoldment of Christ Consciousness in humans.

Also known as False Christ, Lawless One, Man of Lawlessness.

Description: In general terms, the Antichrist is a concept briefly outlined in the New Testament to refer to the archenemy of the Christ on Earth, to a spirit being who would, at the End of Time or as Apocalypse approached, be increasingly activated and active in the human world, opposing the Christ. The term *antichristos* from the Greek literally means against or instead of the Christ.

The Antichrist is described as the prince of all Christ's enemies, the usurper of Christ's name and rights, the leader and probable inspirer of all those who deny the Incarnation of the Christ as Jesus. The Antichrist is sometimes given an animal or beastly symbolism, such as a seven-headed red dragon or serpent, and as the archetypal "man of sin" he will pretend to be Christ, sit in God's sanctuary, and even claim to be God. The Antichrist is not Satan, but gains his authority from the Prince of Evil.

The Antichrist will deny that Christ ever incarnated in Man, that Jesus was the carrier of the Christ, and will deny all the doctrines attributed to the Christ during His presence on Earth and all the moral implications of those teachings. The Gospels report Jesus warning his disciples against "false Christs" arising among them.

The false Christ or Messianic pretender-denier will exhibit a contempt of all religious law and will be known as the "man of lawlessness, the lawless one." He will make exclusive claims to embody deity, will deceive many by wonders and seeming miracles, and will oppose all other religions.

The Antichrist will fool many, but will eventually be slain by the true Christ. All of this will take place, the New Testament suggests, in the End Times, the days before Judgment Day or the Apocalypse, in the Last Hour before the Second Advent and the "Day of the Lord" after a great apostasy in humankind has taken place. The Antichrist might be expressed through a single human or perhaps through a series of Antichrist embodiments.

The actual human-based identity of the Antichrist has been variously attributed. In the fourth century A.D., Cyril of Jerusalem said the Antichrist will be a magician who takes control of the Roman Empire, claims to be Christ, deceives the Jews by claiming to be the Son of David, rebuilds the Temple of Jerusalem under these false pretences, and persecutes the Christians. Post-Reformation Protestants sometimes identified the Pope in Rome with the Antichrist.

The twelfth century A.D. Cathars, Christian "heretics" who prospered for a time in southern France, said that the Catholic Church was an imposter and a false Church constructed by the God of Evil, master of our world, to masquerade as the true Christian church with great material wealth and power while the true Christian impulse was underground.

Many interpretations of the Antichrist have been introduced into Western culture in recent decades. In the widely popular Left Behind series of Christian Fundamentalist novels, the authors personified the Antichrist as a scheming charismatic world leader named Nicolae Carpathia who in the wake of planetary disasters following the Rapture (in which the Christian Elect are physically removed from Earth by Christ) uses subterfuge, murder, and deception to gain control of the United Nations and then the world government, all media, and religions through his Global Community forces.

Another interpretation suggests that the Antichrist will inaugurate a period of great tribulation at the end of history and be connected with a mighty empire much like a revived imperial Rome that will dominate politics, religion, and business, until Christ's world-changing return.

Explanation: To understand the Antichrist, you must turn everything inside out. The Antichrist is the opponent of the Christ, but is Christianity the embodiment of the Christ and is today's perception of the Christ actually valid?

The cleverest ruse used by Satan is to hide in plain sight in the guise of its opposite—the Antichrist disguised as the Christ, like the wolf among the sheep. The Antichrist calls out vociferously in the name of Christ, pointing out the infidels, alarming us against the coming Antichrist, and we miss the truth.

Even more effective is to promote the expectation of a single figure embodying the Antichrist, an attitude the Antichrist fosters. That way we fail to perceive a globally encompassing spirit of the Antichrist already here. The Antichrist is present today on Earth as a pervasive influence, and has been since the time of Atlantis, thousands of years ago.

As a planet of polarities and dualities, Earth has a Light body and a Dark body. The Light body is the glorious array of Earth's visionary geography, its terrain of sacred sites, all receptors for spiritual light and wisdom. Different cultural terms such as Hurqalya, Dreamtime, and Zep Tepi describe this. The Earth's Light body or grid is a wondrous array of higher consciousness supports, inspired by the Christ for the upliftment of all human souls.

The planet's Dark body, or dark grid, is a pathology anchored into the original and fundamental Light body like a cancerous growth. It is like a black, irregular growing mass of tendrils and anchor points, a dark octopus with a thousand snaking arms encasing the Earth, rooted into numerous geomantic sites and political power points, such as the world's major seats of national government and religious authority; for example, Washington, D.C., London, and Rome—possibly each the "mighty empire" like a revived Rome as modeled by some interpreters.

Similarly, many holy sites have infusions of dark grid or Antichrist energies, such as Glastonbury, England; Jerusalem, Israel; and Sedona, Arizona. At such places, the dark grid energies intermingle, pollute, or even overpower the Light grid inputs and generally tend to confuse or disorient visitors.

Just as an octopus can squirt a black inklike substance to confound its enemies, so the dark grid infuses the Earth with the energies, dispositions, and agenda of the Antichrist: atheism, materialism, literalism, patriarchalism, scientific imperialism, rationalism, control, mechanization, militarisim, competition, domination, skepticism, hatred of matter, disregard for the Earth, anticlairvoyance, and many other qualities of similar ilk.

The dark grid pumps these Antichrist energies throughout the planet and humanity, and the Antichrist flows through matter.

These potent qualities are the opposite of actual Christ Consciousness, which involves, in part, fraternal love, freedom, tolerance, insight, clairvoyance, independent cognition, love for matter, forgiveness, compassion, among others. The Light grid supports the unfoldment of these qualities across the Earth in a context of freedom, choice, independence, and interdependence.

Ironically, and shockingly, those parties who are most vocal about the imminence of the Apocalypse, Second Advent, Judgment Day, and the terrifying arrival of the Antichrist are actually the present-time embodiment of the Antichrist. For example, the extreme Christian Right that now dominates American politics and, increasingly, U.S. culture, is arguably the current expression of the Antichrist.

The struggle to dominate humanity and the unfoldment of its higher consciousness abilities and the permeation of Earth with spiritual Light has been intensively under way since the time of Atlantis. The Atlantean continent disappeared, and the reality of its former existence is now relegated to the sarcastic sidelines of consensus reality and history, but it still exerts a powerful influence on the United States (like a placenta still feeding its fetus) through various geomantic connections and grid networks still in place.

The Antichrist is probably the most important Earth myth to understand today, the one with the gravest possible consequences for the future—the survival—of our planet and humanity. Just as the Light grid has annual days of renewal, such as Epiphany, January 6, when the cosmic Christ focuses Christ Consciousness through the planet, so does the dark grid have its days of renewal of its input, notably every January 17.

The dark grid overlay on Earth's original Light body or grid was not an imposition by powerful outside forces. It is something that *humanity* grew over time by its own free-will choices, although most of these choices were heavily influenced by Antichrist concerns.

Since the dark grid overlay, or the slow-motion incarnation of the Antichrist in Earth's energy field, has been put into place essentially through free will, humanity can through the same free will, more wakefully applied, remove it.

Clairvoyant investigation suggests that the dark grid will be removed entirely from Earth by about 2100 A.D. In the United States, it will be removed from west to east, significantly easing up from the West Coast to the Rocky Mountains during the first half of the twenty-first century, then eventually being eradicated after great resistance from the remainder of the United States.

See also: Candlemas, Dolorous Stroke, Dreamtime, Earth Changes, Ghost Dance, Harmonic Convergence, Hurqalya, Klingsor, Mephistopheles, Michaelmas, Ragnarok, Wasteland, Zep Tepi.

ANUBIS

The watchdog of the galaxy, known as the Underworld, and associated with the star Sirius in the constellation Canis Major (Greater Dog).

Also known as Al Kalb al Jabbar, Anpu, Anup, Apuat, Caball, Canis Major, Cerberus, Dog of the Giant, Dog of the Sun, Dormarth, Garm, Guardian of the Dwelling, Keeper of the Mother's Gate, Upawet, Vastospati, Wepwawet, Xolotl.

Description: In Egyptian myth, Anubis is the jackal-headed god who guides souls after death through the 12 stations and gateways of the Duat, or Underworld. This is described in detail in the classic text, the *Book of Coming Forth into the Day* (mistranslated as the *Egyptian Book of the Dead*). Anubis is usually depicted as having a man's torso and a black jackal's head.

He was also known, in earlier texts, as *Apuat, Upawet,* or *Wepwawet,* which means "Opener of the Ways," referring to his role on behalf of souls of opening the successive ways or stations through the Duat. Usually, Anubis's parentage is given as Ra, the Sun-god, but sometimes he is the son of Nephthys and Osiris.

Anubis is the Greek rendering of the Egyptian Anpu or Anup. Among the common Egyptians, Anubis was the deity who presided over embalming rituals and to whom one placed pleas for intercession in mortuary prayers for the dead.

He has many epithets: Anubis is "Foremost of the Westerners," which refers to his role as leader or psychopomp of the dead; "Lord of the Sacred Land," indicating his supremacy over the desert lands where the necropoli were usually situated; "He Who Is Upon His Sacred Mountain," referring to the jackal god perched on heights overseeing the burial of the dead; and "Lord of the Mummy Wrappings," highlighting his involvement in embalming rituals.

His cult center in Middle Egypt was known by the Greek name Cynopolis, "City of the Dogs." In ritual processions, the image of Wepwawet as "Leader of the Gods" went before the King and other gods. (Some Egyptian scholars claim Wepwawet is a different jackal-headed god from Anubis and not merely an earlier form, and assign his major cult centers to Asyut in Middle Egypt, also known as Zauty or Lykopolis "Wolf City," and to Abydos.)

Anubis also ushered in the newly dead to the Judgment Halls of Osiris in Amenti, the Land of the Dead. The place is also called the Hall of Maat (the personification of truth and cosmic order). In this function, he was "Lord of the Hallowed Land" and "Chief of the Dwellers of the West" (most cemeteries were situated west of the River Nile), and the faithful companion to Osiris.

Sometimes Anubis is awarded equal stature with Osiris and even adjusts the weight scales in which the heart of the deceased is weighed for goodness and impurity; he does this in the company of 42 sternly silent gods.

When Osiris was cut into 14 pieces by his perfidious brother, Seth, and placed into a lead chest, Anubis watched over it as *Khent Sehet* in the place of purification, for which he was known as "Governor of the Hall of the God."

Anubis's role in Amenti is similar to the Greek Cerberus, the three-headed dog of the Underworld, servant to Hades, Lord of the Dead. Anubis is acknowledged under different names in other myths: The ancient Germans and Norse had a terrifying hound called Garm who guarded the entrance to Niflheim, a primordial land of frost and darkness. Among the Aztec there was Xolotl, the dog-god who accompanied the Sun in his journey under the Earth; Xolotl was known as the God of Death and the Setting Sun, a human-headed dog.

The Celtic Underworld god and Lord of Annwn, Gwynn ap Nudd, had a pack of white dogs with red ears, and their leader and Gwynn's faithful servant was Dormarth, which means "Death's door."

Then of course there is Canis Major, the great star-filled Hound of Heaven whose brightest star is Sirius. Sirius has been called the Eye of Anubis (Anubis being Canis Major), the Keeper of the Mother's Gate, the shape-shifting dog of the Great Goddess, whose cauldron was the galaxy of stars that Sirius-Anubis unwaveringly guards. Arab astronomers knew Sirius, our galaxy's brightest star, as *Al Kalb al Jabbar,* the Dog of the Giant (the nearby constellation Orion), and the earlier Sumerians knew Canis Major as Dog of the Sun. Often in mythic references Sirius the Dog Star and Canis Major the Dog are seen as one.

The Hindu myths about Sirius are most revealing. There the Dog and the bright star are known as Rudra, an early form of Shiva (mostly equivalent to Hades), and the constellation as *Mrgavyadha,* the Hunter of the Antelope (Orion).

Rudra shoots an arrow at Orion and releases sperm from the god's testicles. This sperm dribbles down to Earth (cosmic space and matter, not the planet) and collects as the Lake of Sperm. Rudra becomes its protector, for it is really the totality of Light that will manifest through the billions of galactic stars.

The constellation Orion to the Vedic astronomers was Prajapati, Lord of Creatures and the Cosmic Father; the Egyptians saw Orion as Osiris's home. Although it is initially confusing (in terms of gender identifications with functions), the Egyptians equated Sirius with Isis (Sothis), wife to Osiris.

Rudra (Sirius) becomes the *Vastospati,* the protector of the *Vastu,* another name for the Lake of Sperm, but here emphasizing it as a dwelling or house. Sirius-Rudra will forevermore be the protector of the stars, the guardian of the sacred galactic order, Lord of the Dwelling, the Watcher of the House of Varuna, described as a lofty cosmic structure with one thousand gates. He is always on duty, ever vigilant, guarding the gates that lead into and out of the galaxy.

Explanation: It is perhaps an easier approach to understanding Anubis's role by starting with what he does within Earth's visionary geography, most particularly with a feature called landscape zodiacs (see White Cow, White Sow). These are interactive holograms of the galaxy templated on the landscape.

On Earth, the galactic hologram is cut in two and laid out on the land like two halves of an apple with a tiny bit of skin still connecting the halves. Constellations of the Northern and Southern Hemisphere sky are within the halves; the standard 12 houses of the ecliptic (the apparent annual path of the Sun through the signs of the zodiac) appear on the perimeter of both halves—they appear twice.

One half is called the physical ecliptic, the other the etheric, depending on whether the landscape zodiac is situated in the Northern Hemisphere (physical ecliptic) or Southern Hemisphere (etheric). A total of 122 additional constellations are templated within the two zodiac halves, including that of Canis Major.

To interact successfully with the landscape zodiac, you start with Canis Major and, in effect, befriend the Dog and request his guidance. From a shamanic or psychic viewpoint, you may have some kind of visionary encounter with the Dog, as a dog spirit or in some other form. If you do not make it past the Dog (accept his guidance), you will be refused entry into the whirling wheel of stars, or what the ancients called the Mother's Cauldron. The Dog (Anubis, and all his other names) is your psychopomp to the landscape zodiac, its workings, and purpose. On a limited level, you are experiencing various signs of the zodiac as outside you, to make it easier to understand how they work within you and possibly to balance, lessen, amplify, or transmute their effects. On a larger scale, you are walking through the various parts and processes of your cosmic Self, spread out before you as a visionary temple in many parts and with many spirit guides.

The Dog not only guards the zodiac, but he is one's tutor in its nature. The dozen or so principal stars of Canis Major, including Sirius at his throat, are templated within the total landscape zodiac, and one may profitably spend much time meditating on these in the landscape before proceeding further into the cauldron of stars.

In interacting with the constellations this way, you are getting a head start on what you will have to do when physically dead. Rudolf Steiner, the Austrian clairvoyant and founder of Anthroposophy, explained that in the after-death state you find yourself in a vast stellar environment in which all the parts and processes that comprise the embodied human are now laid out before you as a living, and perhaps at first strange, environment. You see the throat and heart as clusters of stars and Star gods, which is why astrology says, for example, the constellation Leo rules the heart and Taurus (Pleiades) the throat. This cosmic array of your human body parts in their archetypal state as components of the galaxy the Egyptians called the Duat or Underworld.

The term "Underworld," used in many myth systems besides the Egyptians, is inherently confusing because it limits the nature and function of this domain to how it appears to the newly deceased humans and leaves out its cosmic qualities. A better translation of Duat than "Underworld" is "Place of Morning Twilight," a realm in which darkness is yielding to morning light. Another term the Egyptians used is *amentet*, "the Hidden Place," personified by a beautiful goddess, the Lady of the West (Nut) who receives the Sun into the mysterious region within her (Duat). A third is *neterkhert*, "the divine under place."

The Duat was also described as being inside the star-filled body of the Sky goddess Nut; she was depicted as a feminine form arched over the Earth, her body filled with stars and all the Star gods. The Duat was her interior space.

On the cosmic level, the interior, private, mysterious space of Nut is called the Round Table; it is a concentrated expression of the Duat and its gods. Here Ra the Sun-god meets with the guardians of the 12 gateways. The outer skin of Nut is the rest of the Duat, the great expanse of stars and constellations. In many myths about the Sun-god, including that of Ra, he is said to transit two realms: from sunrise to sunset (Day), and sunset to sunrise (Night). We could say the Day transit is the outer aspect of Nut, the Night is the interior, Round Table.

On the terrestrial level, this twofold nature of the Duat is expressed in the splitting of the landscape zodiac into physical and etheric halves. If you are in the Northern Hemisphere, then its stars comprise the physical part because you can actually see them at night; those you cannot see in the Southern Hemisphere comprise the etheric half because they only affect you subtly.

The physical half is the Day transit of Ra in the Duat, the skin of Nut; the etheric is the Night side, the interior of Nut with the concentrated Round Table.

At either level, cosmic and terrestrial, Anubis is the soul's guide through this system. There is even a terrestrial counterpart to the Eastern Horizon, the place in the Duat where Ra leaves the Night journey and comes upon dawn. This is the little "apple skin" left connecting the two halves; it is a junction point or bridge between the physical and etheric halves of the landscape zodiac.

The Duat (and the terrestrial versions, the landscape zodiacs) is an Underworld in spatial terms only from the viewpoint of higher, earlier levels of Creation, such as the Cosmic Egg and the Black and White Eyes of Horus. From our human and planetary viewpoint, it is most definitely the Upper World, a higher dimensional plane requiring clairvoyance to perceive while alive. It is, again from the embodied human vantage, a Land of the Dead, an Amenti or Hades, but that is seeing only a portion of it and understanding just a little of its function.

Ultimately, Anubis is identical with the variously named Lord of Fire and the Underworld, including Hades, Shiva, Rudra, and Sirius, and the Dog or jackal-headed god form is only symbolic of its guardian-watcher function drawn from human perceptions of dogs and what they do best. Anubis, as the Dog-Star Sirius, guards our galaxy just as Shiva-Rudra dances before the circle of flames, because the circle of flames (see Trickster) is the fire-rimmed galactic envelope.

You may encounter Anubis through any of the planet's 432 landscape zodiacs or at the Earth's primary grounding point for Sirius (through the dome network—see Holy Mountain) at Karnac, an extensive array of stone rows in Brittany, France.

See also: Black Eye of Horus, Cosmic Egg, Green Knight, Round Table, Trickster, Underworld, White Cow, White Eye of Horus, White Sow.

ANUNNAKI

Enlightened beings sent by the Great White Brotherhood to supervise the geomantic features of Sumer, one of Earth's early Lands of Light.

Also known as Anuna, Anunnakku, Igigi, Lords of the Flame, Lords of Wisdom, Solar Fathers (Pitris).

Description: The term *Anunnaki* refers to a collective of deities in Sumer (later called Mesopotamia, in today's Iraq). It was written variously as *a-nuna-ke-ne* or *a-nun-na,* and generally is translated as those of "princely or royal blood." It also means those who came to Earth from Heaven—humanity's early gods.

The Anunnaki, whose numbers are given differently as 7, 50, 300, or 600 (or sometimes as 300 in Heaven and 600 in the Underworld, thus 900), are all under the direction of An (or Anu), the principal Sky god based at Uruk (Erech) where his temple was *E-anna,* "House of An." It was known as the pure sanctuary, the hallowed, alluring place, the House for his descent from Heaven. One cuneiform text speaks of the *anunna eridu ninnubi,* "the Fifty Anunnaki of the city Eridu," and elsewhere they are called the "fifty great princes."

Anu's cuneiform sign was *dingir,* which meant Heaven, and he was understood to be the chief and creator of all the gods. He was known in Sumer as *lugal kur.kur.ra,* which meant "King of the Lands," and as *an gal,* "the Great An." He conferred kingship (called *anitu,* "Anu-ship") as the ultimate divine imprimatur for human leaders; Anu was the supreme source of authority, government, and order in both the human and spiritual worlds. His spouse was called Antu, and while Anu and Antu primarily lived in the celestial abode, he came down periodically to Uruk to his temple to officiate in godly matters.

Anu had two sons, Enlil and Ea (or Enki), who established themselves in their respective centers in Sumer and managed the affairs of Earth and humanity.

The Anunnaki are executive gods, ones who get basic things done, though answering to the trio of original high gods. They were credited, for example, with building the Girsu temple and the city of Babylon in Sumer, and they were said to have been on Earth before and during its creation and organization, enduring hardships such as having to eat grass to survive.

They were based in the *E-ninnu* at the temple of Nirgirsu at Lagash from which they worked as protective and interceding gods. None were ever individually named and they were always referred to as a collective in the Sumerian cuneiform texts. Probably due to their continuous presence there, Sumer (also written as Shumer) was known as "the Land of the Ones Who Watch." In Sumer, the gods were always observing, monitoring, and directing.

Igigi, another name attributed to the Anunnaki, has the same nuance, and is usually translated as "They Who Turn and See," suggesting observation.

Explanation: The Anunnaki represent a delegation from the Great White Brotherhood, based in the constellation Ursa Major (Great Bear), sent to Earth to develop and oversee one of the planet's early Lands of Light, Sumer. In composition, they were roughly comparable, though not identical, to the Tuatha de Danann, the delegation of enlightened beings sent to Ireland.

They are called, esoterically, Lords of the Flame, Solar Fathers, or Lords of Wisdom because they helped humanity develop the *Manas,* the mind principle and discernment in consciousness, represented by the image of fire or a flame.

The geomantic situation in Sumer was markedly different from that in Ireland. While Ireland was an insular landmass with a specific evolutionary agenda (to cultivate pre–Fall of Man conditions in planetary matter), Sumer was a concourse for celestial visitors coming and going from its numerous stargate terminals.

Stargates are an esoteric feature in Earth's visionary geography, more subtle to apprehend than most other features, set in the fifth rather than fourth dimension of the planet's energy body. Stargates are transportation devices that move people, objects, and materials from a point on Earth to another planet almost instantaneously. Some go to planets related to key stars, others to planets convenient to accessing entire constellations. In all, there are a little more than 2.2 million stargates on Earth, affording the planet total galactic connection.

The region between the Tigris and Euphrates Rivers in today's Iraq, once the epicenter of Sumer, is rich with stargates, even today, though they are not in use. Sumer was one of Earth's original Lands of Light primarily because of the rich array of operational stargates in such a relatively small area. Visitors from other planets (star systems) regularly came and went via Sumer's stargates, as did selected humans and the "gods," the adepts from the Great Bear.

At Sumer's peak, it was a galactic culture planted on Earth, and the planet enjoyed regular and cordial contact with many other civilizations in the galaxy.

As with the Tuatha de Danann, whose name means "People of the Goddess Danu," Sumer's galactic concourse was commissioned by the Supreme Being and executed through the Great White Brotherhood at Ursa Major, the Great Mother Goddess of the galaxy's stars and people. The various references to the high commissioning agent (God) as An or Anu (the father aspect) or Danu or Dana (the mother aspect) or Antu (An's female spouse) reflect the ultimate imprimatur.

The Anunnaki were sent to Sumer on Earth to create, sustain, and oversee the operation of the numerous light forms (geomantic features) in that landscape that would make higher consciousness states in embodied humans possible. They would remain, for a time, as benevolent Observers, as the Ones Who Watch.

Other Lands of Light in the earliest days of Earth included Mycenae in the Peloponnesus of Greece and An (or Annu: Heliopolis), near today's Cairo in northern Egypt, and, in fact, the entire Nile Valley. Myths of various cultures remember this pristine though antique time of Light on the land with the gods resident through terms such as the Aboriginal Dreamtime, the Egyptian Zep Tepi ("First Occasion"), and the Persian Hurqalya ("Celestial Earth").

These terms refer to the time on Earth *before* the Fall of Man, the Flood, the expulsion from Eden, and the Tower of Babel—all mythic codes signifying the first round of humanity, living on Earth in a time relatively free of the limitations later imposed on the second round of humanity through the numerous geomantic features of Earth's visionary geography.

The Anunnaki and the other differently named delegations of gods from the occult hierarchy in Ursa Major were present in their respective Lands of Light to supervise the development, unfolding, and expression of human higher consciousness through interaction with refined geomantic features such as stargates. It was part of first humanity's gift from above to have sufficiently expanded and sophisticated consciousness to be able to use the stargates.

See also: Dreamtime, Einherjar, Fall of Man, Garden of Eden, Glass Mountain, Holy Mountain, Hurqalya, Marduk, Seven Rishis, Tower of Babel, Tuatha de Danann, Zep Tepi.

ARGONAUTS

The seven major chakras and their seven aspects, totaling 49, under the tutelage of Orpheus, making 50, in a mystical initiation process that inducts one into the golden Halls of the Time Lords in Ogygia.

Also known as Chakras, Chakra Template, 50 Gates of Wisdom, Minyae.

Description: Apollonius's *Argonautica,* written in the third century B.C., is one of the classic travel myths of the ancient world, a story that takes place before the Trojan War and the Labors of Herakles.

Jason is dispatched by King Pelias of Iolcus on a seemingly impossible mission so as to remove him as a threat to Pelias's kingship. Jason is to travel from Iolcus to distant Colchis on the Black Sea (in today's Republic of Georgia) to obtain in whatever manner he might the Golden Fleece of King Aeetes, ruler of the fabulous kingdom of the Sun (he was the son of Helios, the Greek Sun god). King Pelias does not want the Fleece; he wants Jason removed from the picture.

Like Odysseus, Jason is favored by the Olympian goddess Pallas Athena. She designs a suitable boat for his journey, called the Argo; she secures the timber for it from Pelion; and she gets Argus, the 100-eyed guardian of Myceanae in the Peloponnesus to build it for him. The mast is a special beam cut from the oaks of Dodona, known as the oracular seat of Zeus; Hera, Zeus's Queen of Heaven, will speak through the beam to Jason during the voyage, offering guidance. The Olympian archer-god Apollo will be the Argonauts' guide.

Jason selects various heroes to accompany him, all immortals, either sons or grandsons of the gods. Some are first-generation gods themselves, such as Orpheus with his enchanting lyre and the Dioscuri Castor and Polydeuces (or Pollux, the twins of the constellation Gemini). Nearly all of the Argonauts are not especially famous in Greek myth; Herakles starts out as a member, but leaves the voyage early on.

The number of Argonauts starts at 54; five are lost or die, and a few more join. Generally, accounts round off the crew number to 50.

The voyage is successful: Through bravery, bravado, trickery, magic, and good fortune, Jason obtains the Golden Fleece and makes it home to Iolcus. Along the way, the Argonauts encounter many mythic places, monsters, and creatures of ancient lore, such as the Harpies, the giant Talos, and a dragon. Ironically, nothing further is written of Jason or the Golden Fleece after this.

Explanation: The tale describes an initiation process under the auspices of the Orphic Mysteries, having to do with accessing the august Hall of the Time Lords. It is set at Colchis, an ancient Mystery center and site of esoteric training. Much of the detail and adventures of the *Argonautica* are window dressing to provide an outer façade for the great initiation that is the heart of the story.

Jason is a human of high spiritual development, working under the auspices of two Olympian gods, Apollo and Athena, who are actually Ray Masters of the Great Bear (see Seven Rishis), representing the blue and indigo Rays. Even today, major initiations are always supervised by one or more Ray Masters.

Jason (as any human undergoing this initiation process) could also count on the benevolent guidance of the male and female aspects of the Supreme Being.

The ship Argo is a metaphor for Jason's process of awakening and balancing his seven major chakras or energy-consciousness centers and their seven aspects. This totals 49 energy centers, and the Argo could be seen now as Jason's chakra column from root (groin) to crown (top of head), seven spheres with seven smaller spheres around each, all vibrating at different rates, colors, and sounds.

The 50 Argonauts are the chakra constituents of Jason's consciousness array. Apollonius used the term *Minyae* to describe the Argonauts, since they all came from the same region and folk-soul origin, founded by a hero called Minyas.

From the Judaic mystical tradition in the Zohar, we get the same idea through different words. The Zohar speaks metaphorically of a palace created by God that has 50 mystic gates. Forty-nine of these gates are found on the four sides of the palace, but the fiftieth is not. It is the mysterious gate, and is elsewhere. All 50 gates have one lock, with only a tiny insertion spot for the key.

Qabalists speak of the 50 Gates of Binah. Binah is a name for the third Sefirah, or Light vessel, in the Tree of Life diagram of reality, and the residence of the Great Mother, the Divine Feminine, and the female aspect of God.

The specificity of Colchis as the goal of the Argonaut's journey corresponds to the fact that in ancient days Colchis was a Mystery initiation center, a place to which aspiring candidates for initiation journeyed from all over.

Orpheus is the mysterious fiftieth gate with the key that unlocks them all. He was a member of the angelic order called Nefilim, a group commissioned by the Supreme Being to work with humanity on several projects (such as inculcating a higher threshold of consciousness in the body) and to teach them the Mysteries, and he was the Lord of the Underworld, or the lower astral plane.

He was famous for his skillful, enrapturing use of his lyre, a nine-stringed harp said to have been made by his half-brother, Apollo. As Pythagoras would demonstrate later in Greek history, Orpheus knew that sounds could modulate the vibrations of chakras and their subaspects and create concord among them.

So he attuned and unified the 49 different sound vibrations of Jason's chakras. As Apollonius tells the story, often Orpheus calmed the crew with his lyre and song, such as after a dangerous passage or battle, or he led them in reverential songs to the gods or put them into mystical contemplative states. We can picture Orpheus and his lyre standing in the pineal gland in the center of Jason's head and his sixth chakra. When the Argo was built, that is, when Jason's 49 chakra vibrations were in harmony and "rowing together," then the Argonauts could approach Colchis.

The ship Argo, or the initiation process of chakra harmony, will convey Jason *through* the Golden Fleece. First he has to overcome, or gain the permission of, the Dragon of Ares that guards the Golden Fleece near King Aeetes' palace. The dragon is the same as Apophis, the monster of the deeps who assaults (guards) the Sun-god Ra's Boat of Millions of Years, and the Beast-Sorath, who guards the Time Line of the solar system, galaxy, and universe for the 104 Time Lords.

Admittedly, this is a big picture. Jason is given passage by the Dragon of Ares (Apophis, Beast-Sorath) to approach the Golden Fleece. This is a mathematical matrix (the Magic Square of the Sun, whose numerical total is 666) expressing and embodying the Time Line (the orderliness of the flow of Time) and a translocator device, something like a wormhole or stargate into a new place.

This new place is variously called King Aeetes' land of Aeaea, the golden Halls of Ogygia, the Halls of Kronos, Ra's Boat of Millions of Years, or the Hall of the Time Lords. These are 104 celestial beings, including Aeetes and his sister, Circe, who lives on the island of Aeaea, and numerous subsidiary helpers, who oversee the orderly progression and rationality of Time's progression and events.

Thus the initiation process (the ship Argo) conveys the initiate Jason (the balanced, activated composite of the 50 Argonauts or chakra components) into the Halls of the Time Lords for elucidation of the Sun, Time, and their mysteries.

Those who wish to experience the Argo within themselves may benefit from meditation at a Chakra Template (see Forest of Bliss). Many thousands of these energy copies of the chakra array are present in Earth's visionary geography and of a size suitable for interaction in the form of walking and seated meditation. Selected locations include Iona, Scotland, and Benares, India.

At Iona, you get a double immersion in the Argonautica Mystery. In addition to a Chakra Template that runs the length of the island (about three miles), Iona is the dome (see Holy Mountain) for Canopus, the star that is the rudder or keel of the Argo Navis, a massive Southern Hemisphere constellation.

Canopus, our galaxy's second brightest star and the source of a silver lightline to the Earth, is for us the prime Mother star in our galaxy. Hera, the mythical name for the female or Mother aspect of the Supreme Being (Zeus), may be accessed easily through Iona, just as Jason was able to hear her from the mast.

Insofar as all the named figures in the *Argonautica* are immortals or gods, the story's interpretation can be raised a notch to be a galactic account of star beings in search of the essence and fountainhead of galactic time and life. In this guise, the Argonauts are the parents or cosmic originals of the 50 human chakras.

We can also interpret this myth in terms of the 50 star beings (what the ancient Chaldeans called the great Star-Angels, or Spirits of the stars) whose harmony *creates* the Argo Navis, which then sails toward the Halls of the Sun, but not just the Sun of our solar system—rather, what metaphysical tradition calls the Great Central Sun (*Raja* Sun or King Star) of the entire galaxy, the mysterious, hidden center, Kronos, around which, presumably, all solar systems revolve.

See also: Beast of the Apocalypse, Forest of Bliss, Golden Fleece, Hitching Post of the Sun, Holy Mountain, Orpheus's Lyre, Seven Rishis.

ASURA

The aborted first attempt to create humanity with free will in bodies, now bound in an intermediate realm between our physical reality and the next, and awaiting release and redemption by a forgiving humanity.

Also known as Afrits, Antigods, Djinn, Kings of Edom, Raksasas.

Description: In the Vedas, the Asura are the antigods, the warring adversaries of the gods (the Sura, from *svar,* "to shine"). The antigods are older than the gods, but both were the progeny of Prajapati, Lord of Creatures, and struggle with each other for dominion of the worlds.

Some scholars derive Asura from the root *as* which means "to frighten away." In the beginning, Prajapati awarded the gods and Asura speech, both true and false, but the Asura rejected the truth, while the gods elected true speech. The Asura are seen as the gods' dark side, exercising their power at night, while the gods exercise theirs in the day.

Early Vedic references to Asuras portray them as lords, leaders of a fighting force, wielding a magical power called *maya,* and of an uncertain status between human and gods. One of the many types of Asuras described in Vedic tradition are the *nivata-kavacas* ("wearers of impenetrable armor"), the *pisacas* ("eaters of raw flesh"), and *raksasas* ("night wanderers"). Ravana, a ten-headed monster who wanted to rule the universe, was the chief of the Raksasas, and thus King of the Asuras; he ruled them from his opulent residence called Lanka on Mount Trikuta, presumed today to be somewhere on the island of Sri Lanka.

The Asura live in mountain caves, inside the Earth, in the infernal regions, and have their own cities of which at least three are named, built by their magician-architect, Maya.

They are godless enemies of the gods whom the gods' leader, Indra, slays with his *vajra* weapon, a kind of thunderbolt, in a cataclysmic battle between the gods and Asuras on Earth in primordial days. The Asuras have coverings of different colors, use metal nets, roam the world at will assuming large or small shapes, and are the demonic enemies of Agni, the Fire god.

The antigods delighted in the play of life energies through the senses, in all that drew humans away from the path of gaining full consciousness. Their name says it all: Asura, meaning "delight" *(ra)* in "life" *(asu)*. According to the *Mahabharata,* India's vast epic saga, the Asuras multiplied and became proud, vain, quarrelsome, and shameless; they were liars and preferred to exercise their power at night. They broke the law, neglected the sacrifices, and failed to visit the holy places to purify themselves spiritually. They tortured living creatures, generated confusion, challenged the gods, and were animated by passion and rage, evidencing no trace of obedience to divine law, or even recognition of it.

Explanation: The Asura were the first breed of humans created, then aborted and removed from the world, because of character defects that later became clear. They were one of two prototypes (the other was the Yeti) before humanity as we know ourselves today emerged. The Asura were given free will, psychic freedom, and full access to the formidable psychic powers *(siddhis)* that go with activating the seven chakras. The Asura's combination of free will and power, in the context of "delight in life," as their name states, led to excesses, destruction, and a destabilization of the world so that they had to be removed.

The Asura were bound into the Earth at 3,496 Lucifer Binding Sites, geomantic nodes around the planet in which Lucifer was also imprisoned. The Asura live trapped between this world and the next and await their release and redemption by humanity, who must forgive them their excesses as these led to a diminishment (or impediments to attaining) in the cognitive range and psychic access awarded us, the second generation of humanity.

The Hindu descriptions are apt, for I have seen the Asura at a Lucifer Binding Site (Lincoln Cathedral, Lincoln, England). They appeared to be ten feet tall, broad, thick, large, and so full of celestial light that their chakras emitted an energy field so strong and thick it could be mistaken for armor. Their appearance was slightly monstrous by today's standards: The men were bearded and fierce-eyed, and their bodies seemed to combine features both apelike and human, primitive and celestial. Their divine wildness, their feral freedom, was obvious. They had the freedom but not the balance in consciousness needed to wield it with wisdom and judiciousness and were a threat to physical creation.

See also: Djinn, Fall of Man, Kings of Edom, Lucifer, Raksasas, Ravana.

ATLAS

A great Star-Angel, the intelligence of Polaris, the Pole Star, maintaining the stream of light and consciousness into the galaxy from beyond.

Also known as Axis Mundi, Cosmic Mountain, Dhruva, Enlil, Grahadhara, Polaris, Sacred Pole, Shu, Taane-mahuta, Tane, World Mountain, World Tree.

Description: In Greek myth, Atlas was a Titan, one of the primordial Creator gods before the Olympians. Zeus, chief of the Olympians, commanded him to uphold the entire heavens on his shoulders or head and hands, ostensibly as punishment for defying the younger gods. Greek myth says Atlas, whose name means "very enduring" or "the enduring one," stands near the fabled Gardens of the Hesperides in the far west or was turned to stone and became Mount Atlas.

Greek myth is not clear as to whether Atlas is the guardian of the world pillar separating Earth from Heaven or is the immobilized pillar itself.

In more general mythic terms, Atlas has the same function as the *axis mundi,* the "axis of the world," the support that holds up the heavenly firmament and threads through the many worlds between Earth and Heaven. Shamans would climb this "sacred pole" to visit the various dimensions of reality above Earth.

Explanation: The geomantic reality of the

Atlas myth is easier to see through his other cultural guises. To the Egyptians, he was Shu, son of Ra the Sun god, who separated Geb, the Earth, from Nut, the Sky, because they were so close together there was no room for humans to walk around standing up. Shu maintained the division of these two primary regions with his upraised arms, and his name means "He who holds up." By separating Earth and Heaven, Shu made it possible for light and space to exist, for Heaven to be above and Earth below.

To the Sumerians, he was Enlil who parted the previously inseparable male sky and female Earth, thereby making room for the creation of humans, plants, and animals. In Polynesian and Maori myth, Atlas is Taane-mahuta, the Forest god, who lifts Rangi, the Sky-Father, off of his wife, Papa, the Earth.

The activity of Atlas, Shu, and Enlil is further illumined by the Hindu description of Dhruva, a Sky god associated with the star Polaris in Ursa Minor.

Dhruva was appointed by Vishnu (the Hindu equivalent of the Christ) to be the *grahadhara,* the pivot of the planets and stars, as a reward for his unfaltering, steadfast spiritual devotion to him. He would be the highest devotee of Vishnu among all the stars, an exemplar for all the others to follow. Where the Hindus said Dhruva's devotion was focused on Vishnu, the Egyptians said it was on Ra.

Both names in this case refer to the cosmic Christ, the great Sun within the Sun or Great Central Sun, and in terms of the galaxy's stars, he is the Logos, the rationality that pervades and coheres the galaxy's great star fields. Dhruva would be the portal for the Logos to enter and permeate the galaxy and its star beings.

The chariots of all the planets (heavenly spheres or dimensions) and all the constellations and stars would be attached to Dhruva by "aerial cords." This would keep them in their proper and allotted orbits, revolving around Dhruva. By aerial cords, we can usefully substitute threads or beams of light from Polaris.

Essentially the same is said, though in more abstract astronomical terms, of the star Polaris in the Little Dipper of Ursa Minor (the Lesser Bear)—the Pole Star. This star was called the Navel of the Earth (Greeks); the Stake (Laplanders); the Iron Peg (Turks); Great Imperial Ruler of Heaven (Chinese); the Nail (Syrians); Northern Axle, Spindle, or Pin (Arabic). Consistent with this, to the Vedic astronomers, Dhruva was the Immovable, the Motionless.

The story of Atlas is a complex geomantic picture. First, it refers to a primary thread of stellar light from Polaris directly to the Earth. It is received at the crown chakra of a global etheric being called Albion (see Albion), whose head (picture his body wrapped around the planet, his feet touching his head) is at Mount Meru, a celestial residence of the gods holographically present on Earth (though phase-shifted out of our physical reality) near southern New Zealand.

Second, this pattern is repeated 12 times across the surface of the Earth. Picture the Earth with 12 geometrical windows (each a five-sided pentagon), laid over it, side by side. These are called Universe Domes (see Holy Mountain). Over each, picture a massive half sphere, hundreds of miles across and half that high. At the topmost center part on the inside of that dome is the same thread of pure light from Polaris, beaming straight down to the land.

Both of these are expressions of Atlas holding up the world. To clairvoyant vision, it may seem that Atlas is standing on his head, or that his head is a great fountain spuming on Earth and his feet are at the "top" of the galaxy, at Polaris.

Dhruva's steadfast devotion to Vishnu can be interpreted in terms of the Pole Star, seen as a spiritual being, a great Star-Angel, at the apex of the hierarchy of Star gods, who is in constant contact with, even immersion in, the great Logos of the galaxy—Christ (Vishnu)—who transmits—*knows*—the reason for existence.

Third, there is a time reference to all of this in terms of Earth's history. The time when

Heaven intermingled so intimately with Earth that there was no separation was the time before most of Earth's visionary geography was installed. This period is known as Dreamtime, Zep Tepi ("First Occasion"), and Hurqalya.

This pertained to the terraforming epoch of the gods on Earth (see Anunnaki, Brigit's Mantle, and Floating Bridge of Heaven) before humanity's advent, and to the short-lived time of the first version of humanity under conditions of total freedom (see Asura). This period is referred to as the Garden of Eden.

The Sky had to be separated from the Earth at the Fall of Man (whose astronomical correlate was the inception of the Precession of the Equinoxes due to the tilting of Earth's axis 23 degrees). This is the time when second humanity was created and placed on Earth under conditions of comparative psychic and spiritual limitation compared to first humanity. Limitation meant less automatic and intimate intermingling of Heaven and Earth.

The mechanism whereby these Saturnian limitations were imposed on human consciousness was the installation of the majority of Earth's visionary geography, an assortment of nearly a hundred different geomantic features.

Heaven was pulled away from Earth in the sense that the immediacy of contact and intermingling was reduced a notch; material reality was set a notch further away from the spiritual dimensions so as to ground second humanity better. Where, before, first humanity had stargates amongst them (actual transportation devices from Earth to other planets in Earth's fifth-dimensional layer), second humanity had domes (energy canopies that were holograms of individual Star gods, present in Earth's fourth-dimensional layer).

The Dhruva beam of light (or pillar, nail, spindle, axis, pivot, stake) was the mechanism that both maintained the separation and still infused Earth with light from the highest source and a reliable, perpetual connection with that.

Yet at the same time, as the shaman's ascent of the sacred pole implies, the Polaris pillar threads the dimensions and star layers from the Logos down to the physical Earth, enabling human consciousness to ascend progressively up through these layers on the mystical or shamanic journey from Earth to Heaven.

Picture the 12 Universe Domes as giant round tents pitched over the land. Aerial cords (threads of light) go down from the inside top from Polaris, beaming like a great spotlight, to numerous constellations and stars depicted on the inside domed surface. These constellations are embodied in the form of massive domes (though smaller than the Universe Domes) each enclosing a hologram of the galaxy called a landscape zodiac (see White Cow, White Sow).

The spotlight at the top of the great tent is the star closest to the Logos or Christ, and, without ever moving, he (Atlas, Dhruva, Shu) transmits that exalted, pure light and spiritual intimacy to all the stars inside the tent and to Earth (in 13 places) as a ceaseless spiritual stream. This is mighty Atlas, or Atlas's pillar, holding up the world on his upraised hands and shoulders.

More deeply, this is Atlas-Dhruva perpetually infusing Earth with the spiritual stream from Vishnu, making it possible for humans to have room to move and stay connected. Atlas-Dhruva is the guardian of this stream or pillar, and is the pillar itself, insofar as it is the steady stream of his star essence into the planet.

See also: Albion, Anunnaki, Brigit's Mantle, Dreamtime, Fall of Man, Floating Bridge of Heaven, Garden of Eden, Holy Mountain, Hurqalya, White Cow, White Sow, Zep Tepi.

AVALON

One of eight Celestial Cities available to human interaction through multiple portals on Earth, this paradisal realm is the home of the mythic golden apple, a container and experience of cosmic wisdom.

Also known as Blessed Isle, Emain Macha,

Floating Island of Aeolia, Gandhavati, Garden of the Hesperides, Isle of Apples, Isle of Apple Trees, Fortunate Isle, the Lake, Land of Women, Summer Country, Summerland, Venusberg, Wonderland.

Description: Traditionally, Avalon is described as a Celtic fairyland paradise ruled over by Morgan le Fay, chief of the fays of faëry, and her eight sisters, all of whom are superb healers. A minimally described figure named King Avalloch (or Evelake) is the father of these nine women and king of Avalon.

The land is beautiful, its weather always pacific, and it is rich with white-blossomed apple trees whose fruits are golden; hence, Avalon (Insula Avallonis, Isle of Avalon) is often called Isle of Apples. Often Glastonbury in Somerset, England, is equated with Avalon or linked in some way with it, perhaps as the mystic portal into this otherwise otherworldly but alluring Celtic domain.

When King Arthur is mortally wounded, Morgan le Fay, chief of the nine fays of Avalon (and his sister or half-sister), conducts the dying Arthur on the mystic barge across the Lake into Avalon for healing or a long sleep in the hills.

In early Christian accounts (or myths), Saint Collen reputedly looked through Glastonbury Tor straight into Avalon. He saw Gwynn ap Nudd, king of the fairies, and his faëry host, dancing merrily in a grand, beautiful palace.

Avalon is described in other myth systems and given other names, though the qualities are essentially the same. In Teutonic myth, it is the Venusburg, a sybaritic grotto dedicated to the pagan love goddess, Venus, deep inside a mountain. The Germanic hero, Tannhäuser, enters the Horselloch, or Cave of Venus, through the Horselberg (Horsel Mountain) in Thuringia, Germany. Inside he is enticed by lascivious dancing nymphs scattering rose petals.

The people of Norcia, Italy, called the mountain fairy realm *Monte della Sibilla,* "The Sibyl's Mountain," and local legend has it that Sibilla and her witches live in the mountain caves where they enchant young girls to dance with the devils on Mount Vettore. Knights who sojourned with the seductive Sibilla in her grotto, enjoying her music, love, and feasting for longer than a year, would never be able to leave, but would remain deathless and ageless, feasting in abundance, revelry, and voluptuous delights in the witch's cavern.

In Greek myth, you have the Nine Muses, born addicted to beautiful song, who pass through the night, wrapped in clouds, their wonderful voices audible as they process up Mount Helicon; they sang so intoxicatingly, the Earth echoed their luscious songs, the stars stopped moving, rivers ceased flowing, and the mountain itself swelled in rapture as if to reach Heaven, so the Greek poets said.

Explanation: To start with, the name itself, Avalon, is a mantric key that, if chanted for perhaps 20 minutes for three days running, will facilitate your entrance into Avalon. *Avalon* is a key that opens the door to the astral plane. Avalon is sometimes referred to as the Summer Country, to some extent, due to that realm's perpetual summerlike, Edenic quality, where the weather is always mild, blossoming flowers proliferate, and ripe golden apples hang on the trees.

Even better, chant Avalon at any of the 144 entrances to this Celestial City or the 144 copies of this Celestial City provided for in Earth's visionary geography. Selected locations include: The Tor, Glastonbury, England; Monticello, Charlottesville, Virginia; Teach Cormaic, Hill of Tara, Ireland; Montserrat, Spain. You will encounter a landscape angel guarding each Avalon gateway, and this benign being will, in effect, check your credentials for entry.

In the tale of Saint Collen, even though, as a cleric, he didn't like what he saw, nonetheless he saw through the portal right into the astral Avalon, thus leaving us a useful example and tool of how to see through the dimensions.

Avalon is also the name of the place where the golden apples, richly described in myth, may be had. There are 47 authentic golden apples, one per Avalon, and 97 illusory ones, found in 97 Avalons; or, just as correctly, of the 144 gateways into the one Avalon, only 47 of the 144 apple trees have genuine golden apples. Discerning the real from the illusory is part of the fun of visiting Avalon.

Some of the illusory quality of Avalon and the sybarism of the Venusberg are captured in the alternate term, Summerland. Metaphysical sources say this name refers to the first three subdivisions of the astral plane and is the plane of illusion. Summerland appears to be a blissful land, but it is made of the inhabitant's wishes, with their dislikes omitted; all of it is a self-created pleasure world made by disincarnate beings out of their own thoughts and wishes.

Within Avalon, or the entire astral plane, is a Celestial City, a concentration of its essence and splendors within a contained structure. Celtic myth alludes to a King Avalloch, King of the Summer Country, and Hindu myth says that Gandhavati, one of eight Celestial Cities, is a domain of Air ruled by Vayu, the Lord of Air, wind, movement, the seven breaths and seven winds, and prana. His is the realm of inspiration, mirroring the Muses of Mount Helicon.

His Greek counterpart is Aiolus, whose name means "the mobile" and whose responsibility is the eight winds. His domain is called the Floating Island of Aeolia where he lives with his 12 children who perpetually enjoy the feasts and music in Aiolus's halls. Odysseus spent a month there, says Homer.

You may find Avalon within yourself by visiting your heart chakra. Technically, the heart chakra has two parts: an outer, called *Anahata,* which has 12 petals or vibratory fields (like Aiolus's 12 dancing children), and an inner, *Ananda-kanda,* which has eight and which contains the Garden of Eden. The wind God's attribution to Avalon is appropriate, for the element of air and the quality of movement are assigned to the *Anahata;* the name itself, which means "the not-struck sound" alludes to the music of Avalon and its variations.

The reference to Morgan le Fay and her eight faëry sisters of Avalon pertains to the fact that Avalon embodies the nine spheres of Light and consciousness said by Qabalists to be the second of four Trees of Life. This model says reality consists of four connected Worlds, each with ten spheres of Light, called *Sefiroth*; these Worlds are abstractly modeled as Trees of Life that look like three vertical pillars, connected by lines and balls of light. The Tree closest to our material world is called *Yetzirah* ("Formation") and it refers to the astral plane or, in Celtic language, the Lady of the Lake's *Lake,* the sea of stars.

Morgan and her eight sisters, actual spiritual adepts, each represent, embody, protect, and transmit one of the spheres of Light and consciousness in this Yetzirah Tree of Life, or the Lake of Avalon, on behalf of those who enter. In practical terms, the nine sisters *are* the Yetzirah Tree of the Summer Country.

See also: Garden of Eden, Golden Apple, House of Atreus, King Arthur, Lady of the Lake, Morgan le Fay, Peaches of Immortality, Rhinegold, Valkyries.

AZHI DAHAKA

The Persian perception, tilted toward the monstrous-demonic, of the bound Lucifer after the failure of the first generation of humans.

Also known as Bevarasp, Biourasf, Dahak, Lucifer, Ravana, Zahhak, Zohak.

Description: In ancient Persian lore, Azhi Dahaka is a three-headed monster who eats humans. He has three mouths, six baleful eyes, a thousand senses, and is a bane to the world, a fiendish Drug (a demon), the strongest of all Drugs, in fact, that the evil spirit Angra Mainyu (also known as Ahriman) created to oppose the material world.

One of Azhi Dahaka's worst offenses was to try to steal the Divine Glory (also called Kingly Fortune, Farr, and *Xvarnah*), the rightful possession of every Persian king and understood as a kind of mantle or nimbus of celestial light, the pure luminescence and radiance given to all spiritual beings at their conception. Only those Persian kings who did not stray from the righteous path were allowed to keep the Divine Glory as authentication of their legitimacy to be king. When the Divine Glory departed King Yima, for example, it fled in the shape of a bird.

Azhi Dahaka is finally defeated by the hero Thraetaona (also known as Fariydun, Faridu, Fredun), who imprisons the monster inside Mount Demavand (in northern Iran, near Tehran) where he will remain captive until the end of time. Another account has Thraetaona subdue the monster with his *gurz,* a cow-headed mace, then bind him in chains to a rock on the Sun-exposed flanks of the great mountain. There he will moan in thirst and misery until world's end.

Since then, the occasional volcanic rumblings of the mountain (Mount Demavand is an 18,603-foot presumed-extinct volcano) are the groans of Azhi Dahaka, and the sulfurous vapors noted around the peak are his mournful exhalations.

Explanation: Azhi Dahaka is the Persian perception of Lucifer, Lord of Light and prime benefactor of the first round of humanity, but in the Persian description he is seen after his apparent repudiation and limitation.

Lucifer, a unique archangelic being under commission by the Supreme Being, facilitated the gift of self-aware consciousness and freedom to the first generation of humans. In his Greek guise as Prometheus, this gift of consciousness was symbolized by the Titan's theft of the gods' fire for which he was punished by Zeus by being chained to Mount Caucasus and exposed to the elements.

The first generation of humanity abused its God-granted gifts and was aborted, forcibly removed from physical reality by the angelic realm. As Lucifer had invested a portion of his angelic essence in humanity and the Earth, that celestial essence had to be reduced and its range of expression limited for a time. This was symbolized by his being bound mercilessly on a high mountain.

The demonic-monstrous qualities exhibited by Azhi Dahaka (which are seen equally vividly in two other Lucifer guises, as Tezcatlipoca and Ravana) were added on to Lucifer in retrospect to remind the second-generation humans of the consequences of their forebears' abuse of freedom. In effect, Lucifer got all the blame and became vividly demonized in the Persian imagination, partly also to create a cultural bogeyman to prevent second-generation humanity from even approaching the wild freedom possessed by their ancestors under Lucifer's aegis.

Mount Demavand is specifically credited as the site of Azhi Dahaka's imprisonment because it is one of 3,496 places on Earth where Lucifer's potency is grounded, curtailed, or in the process of being freed. These geomantic features are called Lucifer Binding Sites; their function is to regulate the amount of Luciferic consciousness that can enter the planet, understood as a living conscious being, and human consciousness.

This regulation has both global and local aspects. In some areas, Lucifer's consciousness is severely restricted, such as at Mount Demavand; in other locations, it is present in the full glory of Lucifer's arrival on Earth; and in a few sites, Lucifer is being unbound and freed by human consciousness interacting with the Lucifer Binding Sites. Persian lore says Azhi Dahaka will remain captive at Mount Demavand until the end of the world, but, realistically, he will be bound only until humanity can allow some of his essence back into our planetary reality.

Thraetaona is a cultural guise for Merlin, a unique planetary mentor charged by the Supreme Being with both binding and unbinding Lucifer.

The Divine Glory, or *Xvarnah,* is a representation of the soul and its wisdom overshadowing and permeating the king. It is not stolen by Azhi Dahaka; rather, as Lucifer, Lord of Light and the Light-Bringer, it is awarded to the king by Lucifer. It is the glorious, beautiful light of the soul and the illumination of its wisdom, expressed as a feminine quality, like the Moon, to the King's Sun. It is simplistic to express this dynamic in terms of Moon-intuition and Sun-rationality, but this does capture an elementary aspect of the relationship.

This is both an inner and outer allegory: The authentic God-mandated solar King of people in the world needs the light and wisdom of the soul to be complete just as in inner, alchemical terms, rational consciousness needs the illumination of the intuition and Moon aspect of the soul. Lucifer, seen in his true guise and function, awards the Divine Glory to kings, men and women alike.

The story of Azhi Dahaka stealing the King's Divine Glory is found in other myths: In the Celtic myths, Meleagaunt abducts Guinevere, King Arthur's Queen; in the Hindu *Ramayana,* Ravana abducts Sita, Rama's consort; in Homer's *Iliad,* Paris abducts Helen, the immortal wife of King Menelaus; and in the Persian, Azhi Dahaka abducts (steals) the Divine Glory of King Yima.

Meleagaunt, Ravana, Paris, and Azhi Dahaka are all expressions of Lucifer in which his actual role, the bestower of the Divine Glory—the knowledge-rich soul in all its beauty and the essence of Beauty itself—is reversed, and he is portrayed as the abductor of it. The *Xvarnah* is an abstract expression of it whereas Guinevere, Sita, and Helen are feminized, human forms of the Divine Glory.

Probably the oldest and purest version of it is Sri, the White Goddess (also called Laksmi), the goddess of beauty and fortune, who emerged on a white lotus blossom from the Ocean of Milk when the gods churned it at the beginning of Time. Other expressions of Sri, as the primordial beauty and fortune of the knowledge-bearing soul, include the Judaic Shekinah (the feminine aspect of God) and the Gnostic Sophia (goddess of wisdom).

See also: Asura, Djinn, Guinevere, Kings of Edom, Lucifer, Merlin, Peacock Angel, Prometheus, Quetzalcoatl, Raksasas, Ravana, Tezcatlipoca.

BALOR OF THE EVIL EYE

The Irish perception of an Elohim, a member of an angelic order, in transient human form as an intimidating giant.

Also known as Balar, Yspaddaden (Welsh).

Description: In Irish myth, Balor Beimean ("Balor of the Mighty Blows") was an ill-spirited giant, presumed king of the Fomorians, early invaders of Ireland, who lived at Balor's Hill. He had one eye in the center of his forehead and another at the back of his head; the latter was evil and through it Rays of venom could strike people dead or at least petrify them with a single glance.

Understandably, he was also known as *Bailcbheimneach,* "Strong-Smiting," and *Balar Birug-derc,* "Balar Piercing-Eyed."

Most times he kept this deadly eye, called *Suil Bhalair* ("Balor's Eye"), covered by his long hair unless he had enemies he wished to destroy. This eye had a polished ring in it (to keep it closed by weighing it down) that was so heavy it took four humans to lift it. Irish legend says he got this evil (or magical) eye from the Druids, whose ceremonies he watched. The evil fumes from their potions settled on his eye, turning it venomous. Once when the eye got knocked out of its socket and rolled over the ground, 28 Fomorian warriors who saw it only for seconds were slain instantly.

The Fomorians at one time held dominance over the Tuatha de Danann, Ireland's original benevolent gods, and exacted a yearly tribute from them. Balor sneeringly collected the tribute at his citadel called *Dun Bhalair* on Tory Island; in fact, he was said to have oppressed all of Ireland with his cruelly high taxes.

Balor had a daughter named Eithne whom he kept imprisoned in a crystal tower *(Tur Bhalair)* atop Tor Mor on Tory Island, off the northwest coast of Ireland, in County Donegal. He kept her in captivity because a prophecy said she would birth the man who would kill him.

A chieftain named MacKineely (or Cian), with the help of an elf with magic, snuck into the castle, impregnated the daughter, and snatched up the *Glas Gaibleann.* The latter was a magical white (or green) cow of an endless supply of milk originally belonging to him but stolen by Balor who kept her at Port na Glaise ("Green Cow Port"). MacKineely or Cian mac Cainte, a hero of the Tuatha, fathered four sons by Eithne; Balor killed three of these, but the fourth was Lugh Lamfhota ("the Long-Handed"), and he survived.

Balor eventually got his revenge and killed MacKineely, but then his son killed Balor by thrusting a hot iron rod into his baleful eye. Another version of the story says Lugh the Irish Sun god, on behalf of the Tuatha, slew Balor with a slingshot (or a magical spear), driving the baleful eye back through his head.

Balor waged war on the Tuatha and defeated them at the Battle of Mag Tured (Moytura), killing hundreds with a single glance from his eye. But at the subsequent second Battle of Mag Tured, Lugh waited until Balor's eye was tired and finally closed; when it started to reopen, he blinded the defenseless giant.

When the giant fell—Balor was said to be enormous—27 men standing nearby were crushed beneath him. When Lugh cut out the evil eye, even then its power was such that it split and shattered all the boulders in its vicinity.

Explanation: Balor the Evil Eye is an Elohim in giant human form. The Elohim are an order of angels assigned by the Supreme Being to be prime creators of organic life, realms of consciousness, and humanity on Earth and throughout the universe. Under commission, they temporarily assumed human form, though their bodies were, from our perspective, giant, averaging 18 feet tall.

For a time, they lived on Earth in its early days setting up much of its megalithic structures, such as stone circles, Cyclopean stoneworks, and certain artificial hills such as Silbury Hill in Wiltshire and Glastonbury Tor in Somerset, both in England, among many examples.

Cosmically, the Elohim were the Titans, the antecedents of the Olympian gods, led by Zeus, who "overthrew" them just as the Tuatha de Danann did eventually. Overthrow means that the divine energy and its structures (being implemented by the Elohim as a support for matter and organic life) had moved down to the next lower hierarchical level; the potent creative powers of the Elohim in the physical domain were no longer needed, their work done; and the next echelon of celestial beings working on behalf of Earth could take over, gods like Lugh Lamfhota.

One of the Elohim is remembered as Balor, while the Elohim as a group are recalled as the Fomorians (or Fomhoire), the mysterious first inhabitants of Ireland. Irish myth tends to remember these as monsters ill-disposed to people. Sometimes they are depicted as demonic giants with one eye, one leg, one arm.

It is revealing that Eriu, the national egregor or watcher-angel for Ireland (see Eriu), took as her husband a Fomorian king named Elatha; their son became high king at Tara, the seat of Irish royalty (near Dublin and Newgrange). Esoterically, this means the Irish egregor's consciousness was aligned with the Elohim and supported their geomantic, terraforming work in Ireland's early days.

Many myths report human encounters with solitary one-eyed giants of ill intent, such as Odysseus with Polyphemus, a Cyclops ("Round-Eyed"), and David and Goliath (his single eye quality is not emphasized). The Celtic King Arthur had to overcome a "great giant" at Saint Michael's Mount in Cornwall. This fierce giant had been devouring many of the people and generally ravaging the land. Another giant, named Gargantua, lived at Mont-Saint-Michel in Brittany, a similar peak at sea's edge in northwestern France across the English Channel. In fact, the peak's original name was Mont Gargan, "Mount of the Giant Gargan."

The single eye of the Cyclops or the Evil Eye of Balor is a distorted, somewhat fearful human perception of the Elohim's unremitting divine vision. It is the pineal and pituitary gland fused into one All-Seeing Eye. The single eye connotes unitive vision, their unseverable connection with God. In the case of the Elohim, it also represents the power of their creative potency: Demonstrating its Medusa-like destructive power is a negative way of suggesting the extreme virility of its positive aspects for creating reality from directed light.

Often, the further human memory grew from the interactive reality with the Elohim as giants on the Earth the more they became demonized and the relationship was pictured as adversarial and combative. The Elohim, equipped with the Eye of God, became over time Balor of the Evil Eye, dangerous and up to no good. Where once humans would have tried to assimilate some of that unitive consciousness embodied in the single eye, later they sought to extinguish it.

A middle-ground picture of the human-Elohim interaction is the story of David and Goliath. He defeated the giant, but the important thing, usually overlooked, is that he thereby acquired Goliath's sword. Turn the story around and you get the meaning more easily: The Elohim (Goliath) instructed David (the human initiate) in the protocols of the Word-Sword, the focused mental-psychic power of word and light—the creative powers of the Elohim—to generate reality.

Tory Island is one of many Elohim nodes in the Earth grid. Consider it a meeting place and audience chamber for human-Elohim exchanges. The crystal tower is occult code to denote the dimensional divide between human physical reality and Elohim angelic reality. The Elohim used Tory Island as an outpost from which to maintain and adjust aspects of Earth's energy body. Other Elohim nodes are found at Burrowbridge Mump near Glastonbury, England, where they did early genetic engineering adjustments on humanity, and Sicily.

See also: Cyclops Polyphemus, Eriu, Giants, Tuatha de Danann, White Cow.

BEAST OF THE APOCALYPSE

A celestial being appointed by God to guard the Time Line and the Sun god's passage through the reservoir of Time.

Also known as Apep, Apophis, the number 666, Sorath, Sun Demon, Sun Spirit.

Description: The biblical book Revelation refers to a Beast as the epitome of evil and with an identifying mark of the number 666, the number of Man. For many centuries, the Beast has been the *bête noire* of Christianity, a fearsome, duplicitous, utterly dangerous, and foul creature to be avoided at all costs. The Beast and his number 666 have correspondingly been associated with evil, Satanism, black magic, witchcraft, and other forms of negative occultism.

The Beast is also feared for the possibility of his branding humans on the right hand or forehead with his terrible sign, the Mark of the Beast. Christian belief holds that, if one wears this mark, entry to Heaven will be denied. The advent of the Beast is further associated with the imminent return of Christ; in some respects, the Beast is considered the same as or an aspect of the Antichrist.

Explanation: The Beast is possibly one of the most misunderstood and perhaps deliberately distorted Christian symbols ever devised. It has nothing to do with evil, Satanism, negative or black occultism, or any of the other pejoratives thrown at it for the last two thousand years. It is only a Beast in the sense that a terrifying appearance helps it accomplish its legitimate task, in the same way that, for example, in Tibetan Buddhism, astral beings called Heruka charged with protecting the Dharma (the ways and beliefs of Buddhism) present themselves as wrathful.

The Beast is a celestial being appointed by the Supreme Being to guard the Time Line, that is (to put it mythically), the mandated and regulated passage of the Sun god's chariot through the vast extent of cosmic time, some 311 trillion years.

The number 666 refers to the Sun and, in medieval occult terms, to the Magic Square of the Sun, a mathematical template. Each of the seven planets, including the Sun and Moon, was assigned a sacred Magic Square. For the Sun, the Magic Square contains 36 numbers arranged in six equal rows; each line (for example: 6, 32, 3, 34, 35, 1) totals 111, and all six lines add up to 666. According to the sixteenth-century esotericist Cornelius Agrippa, the Magic Squares came to humanity as revelations from God to show the divine order of celestial numbers.

Despite the near hysteria about the number 666 and its connection to black magic, it is also the prime number of the Archangel Raphael. His number of allotted manifestations is 666 and his activities pertain to the Fire element.

The numbers are also written in Hebrew, generating an evocation or mantric matrix used in magic and angelic summoning. The number 666, in the Magic Square system, refers to Sorath, the Spirit of the Sun. Sorath is distinguished from the Sun god per se, such as Helios, Surya, Shamash, or Ra.

The relationship between Sun Spirit and Sun god is clear in the Egyptian depiction of Ra (or Re) the Sun god in his solar barque and the interference of the monster Apep (called Apophis) and other fiends and monsters. Ra travels with other deities (including Maat, Thoth, Horus, and others unnamed) in his solar boat; they help him navigate and make a successful passage from the eastern sky to the entrance to the Underworld at sunset. Ra even had two pilot fishes called Abtu who swam before the solar barque.

Egyptian myth says that every day Ra navigates the celestial ocean in his *mandjet,* or day barque, from sunrise to sunset; then at night, he traverses the Underworld *(Duat)* in his *mesketet* or evening barque, from sunset to sunrise. He is always accosted by the serpent Apophis, his archenemy, but, with the help of his colleagues, Ra overcomes him and journeys successfully to the sunrise.

Apophis is traditionally interpreted as the great adversary of the Sun god, one who stands for dissolution, darkness, entropy, and nonbeing. Apophis has existed from or even before the beginning of time, generated in the waters of Chaos before the Creation brought order to the unorganized primeval mass. His assaultive roar was said to be terrifying, echoing through the Underworld. Every night, Apophis hypnotized Ra and his fellow travelers, and it was only the steadfast Seth who resisted the hypnotism to push Apophis back with a spear.

As with many myths, the meaning is revealed when it is inverted. Apophis is not Ra's enemy; Apophis is the guardian of the Time Line. Apophis is Ra's God-appointed protector.

The passage of the Sun god through the stations of the day and night is classically depicted in Vedic thought as a vast circular time reservoir divided into equal 360-degree units called Cattle of the Sun or *kalpas.* Each is a specific duration of cosmic time (864 billion years) consisting of a cosmic day and cosmic night; 360 such Days (or kalpas) total 311 trillion years, the Sun's full circuit.

This circuit through the 311 trillion years of cosmic time is the time line that Apophis (Sorath, the Beast) guards. One could picture this time line as the groove in which one of the Sun god's chariot wheels rides around the perimeter of the cosmic Sun; the other wheel rides in the center of the Sun.

Even though the myth of Ra and the other Sun gods depicts their movement in daily planetary terms, as sunrise to sunrise, the myth also has meaning at the cosmic level and refers to the periods of creation and dissolution (called *Pralaya* or "Flood") in which the solar barque moves through a cosmic day of 432 billion years and a night of the same duration, both totaling 864 billion years.

Apophis is depicted as fierce, unrelenting, possessed of a world-terrifying roar because he needs it to guard Ra against the "monsters and fiends" of the cosmos who seek to disrupt the regulated passage of time—the time line. Apophis is the unpopular enforcer of the forward passage of the Sun god's chariot.

Possibly one reason for his cultural demonization (as Sun Demon, Antichrist) is to intimidate people sufficiently to keep them away from him and the time line. Another possible reason is that the human collective unconscious blames Sorath for imposing the constraints of Time on physical existence. Sorath is a "bad" being because he is seen, by way of cultural memory, as our jailer.

The celestial beings who accompany Ra in his solar barque are the Time Lords. In the Greek myth of the Sun god Helios, the collegial relationship is expressed in terms of progeny: Helios has sons (Aeetes, Perses, Phaethon) and daughters (Circe, Pasiphae), but the meaning is the same: They are Time Lords.

The Time Lords rule time through the fourth dimension. They consist of a central council of 104 Lords who operate in the dimension of Time, that is, Ra's solar barque and its passage. Each of these has many subsidiary Time Lords who report to them and work under their discretion. Sorath, at least metaphorically, is the fierce, scary, wrathful "guard dog" of the Time Lords to protect the time line against manipulation, distortion, grandfather paradoxes (i.e., going back in time and killing your grandfather), and other interferences.

See also: Argonauts, Cattle of the Sun, Flood, Golden Fleece, Hitching Post of the Sun.

BEHEMOTH

A filtered perception of the Ofanim, a prime angelic family whose activities encompass all realms of Creation and sentient life.

Also known as Behemoth of the Thousand Mountains, Behemoth upon a Thousand Hills, Eagle, Ganesh, Garuda, Phoenix, Simurgh, Thunderbird, Ziz.

Description: Behemoth is a huge beast described in the Book of Job and usually understood to be a hippopotamus, though some said it was an elephant. He was created by God at the beginning of time but was destined to be served to the righteous at the End of Days. Thus he is tied to the start and finish of time.

The term *behemot* is the plural of the Hebrew *behemah* (meaning "beast" or "cattle"), thus Behemoth means beast or animal. Behemoth, to the early Jews, was king of the land beasts, just as Leviathan, a huge whale, was king of the fishes and Ziz, a magical, gigantic bird, was lord of all avian species. He was considered the male partner and equal in strength to the female Leviathan, also primordially created by God.

According to legend, only the male Behemoth was created, but not the female. This was to prevent any more Behemoths being born because the one that existed devoured all the grasses produced from one thousand mountains every day (they grew back overnight).

The Zohar explains that the "grasses" Behemoth eats every day are actually angelic beings whose lives are ephemeral in contrast to Behemoth's and who were created on the Second Day of Creation to be food for Behemoth who is "fire consuming fire." Grass has no permanence, says the Zohar, and is meant to be eaten as food, and Behemoth consumes it just as an ox consumes the grass.

Behemoth also drank all the water that flows in the River Jordan in a year in a single swallow. Thus God assigned to him the sole use of a stream from Paradise called Yubal. If he had any offspring, surely they would destroy the world in a matter of days; thus he was prevented from ever mating with his kind.

Often he was referred to as Behemoth of the Thousand Mountains or Behemoth upon a Thousand Hills. Behemoth was so vast in size that the huge desert of Dendain (or Dudain, probably the Dudel Desert near Jerusalem) extended only across his upper body. Yet the Book of Enoch says the desert is Dunayin, is invisible, and lies east of the Garden of Eden. Behemoth was also described in the Book of Job as the chief of the ways of God, implying a close working relationship with the Supreme Being. The Book of Job declares that Behemoth's force is in his navel or belly area.

Behemoth lives among the lotuses of swamps. His task on Earth is to keep the lion, leopard, and bear at bay so that the gentler beasts can safely raise their young. He has a set of fierce horns, his bones are like tubes of bronze, his limbs like iron rods, says the Book of Job, and his outstanding size and strength were God's revelation to Job of the majesty of His divine power, which is fitting since the Book of Job says Behemoth was the first of God's works or creations.

After the Messiah comes, the Day of Judgment is concluded, and the righteous (or chosen) dwell in Heaven enjoying what is called the Messianic or eschatological feast, they will feed on the delicious flesh of Behemoth and Leviathan as a reward for their life travails. Hebrew lore says Behemoth and Leviathan will be locked in mortal combat, killing each other, before the feast.

In medieval Christianity, Behemoth became equated with Satan; and his voracious, unbelievable appetite and grotesque elephantine form (he was given a protruding potbelly and was said to waddle on his two back legs) were put forward to prove he was the great tempter of humanity, encouraging humans to indulge in a variety of gluttonous sins, and therefore was best avoided.

Behemoth's domain is the delights of the belly, inspiring people to commit the vice of overindulgence, as the Christians put it. He is the infernal watchman who presides over gluttonous banquets, and he is renowned for the power of his voice, said to be Hell's demonic singer. Legend holds that, at the summer solstice in the month of Tammuz (Hebrew calendar), Behemoth's strength peaks and he rears up on his hind legs and lets forth a fearful, awesomely loud, disturbing roar.

Explanation: Behemoth is a somewhat distorted view of the angelic family called Ofanim (from the Hebrew *ofan,* for "wheels"). The ancient Vedic seers had a clearer perception of the Ofanim in their elephant-god form as Ganesh, the benevolent, merry remover of obstacles and son of Shiva, and as Airavata, Lord Indra's Mount, and one of the treasures of the Ocean of Milk.

Even the distortions in the elephant perception are meaningful. Behemoth's belly is swollen and protruding because he is full of the Star. One of the Ofanim's epithets is Blazing Star, a reference to their concentrated manifestation as a single, miniscule star of intense, blazing light found in the human form just above the belly button. An elephant with a potbelly is a way of showing the potency of the star in its supernova or intensely illuminating form.

The gluttonous aspect, the insatiable appetite, the devouring of the grasses of a thousand mountains every day and the daily draining of the River Jordan is again apt. Here we find an equivalent Hindu perception in the god form of Garuda, the celestial bird-mount of Vishnu, the Hindu perception of Christ.

Garuda is called Eater of Snakes; the Snakes are souls with awakening kundalini, and the eating is a consuming of the elevated consciousness, but it's more like a coparticipation in it. The Toltec perception (popularized by Carlos Castaneda) of the great black enigmatic Eagle who eats the shaman's awareness is another expression of the same, though painted in bleaker, more resistant tones.

The Ofanim work in a reciprocal relationship with all sentient life, especially humans, in which they stimulate and digest expanding consciousness.

The Zohar equates the grass of the thousand mountains with the angelic orders Behemoth eats. The actual situation is that the Ofanim are regarded as the teachers and mentors of the other angelic families; metaphorically, they do not so much "eat" the other angelic orders (grasses) as act as spiritual fertilizer. Yet it could be said they consume the angelic grasses in the sense that their scope of activity and frame of awareness greatly exceed most of the other angelic orders, and thus the level of consciousness of the other angelic orders is subsumed in the greater field of the Ofanim. Just as the Ofanim stimulate and digest human consciousness as it awakens, so they spark and "consume" the God-given awareness of the angelic families.

The cosmic plethora of sentient and angelic life is accurately though metaphorically depicted as the ever-renewing grasses on a thousand mountains.

The Ofanim were among the first angelic orders to be created, at the beginning, or, in the Hindu time model, in the earliest Days of Brahma.

Thus, based on their age, scope of awareness, and the intensity of the light they emit, the elephantine image and appellation as the largest of beasts are both apt. They are prodigies of celestial awareness and even though they can be a miniscule point of light, brighter than the brightest star ever registered by scientists, their activities encompass an estimated 18 billion galaxies, making them, in terms of their effective outreach, monstrously large beings. The Ofanim describe themselves as the agents through which the Supreme Being moves through existence. Another name for this is the Wheels of the Merkabah, God's Chariot.

Their vast size is also connoted by the fact that they are capable of 40.3 million manifestations, which means they can be in 40.3 million different places at the same time. Opanniel *YHVH* is said to be the Prince of the Ofanim: He has 16 faces, four on each side; one hundred wings on each side of his body; and 8,466 eyes. This means Opanniel, on behalf of the Ofanim, can see what is going on from 8,466 different perspectives.

Yet another nuance to their size is that Judaic lore says that the Ofanim's light is so bright it illuminates *Arabot*, the Seventh Heaven, God's dwelling place.

One interpretation of their roar that echoes through the cosmos is their signature mantric sound or call, *WAW*, as transcribed from the Hebrew. *Waw* (or *vav*) is the sixth letter of the Hebrew alphabet and connotes connection. This is the power to connect Heaven and Earth, spirit and matter, and all 22 of the individual creative powers used in Creation (the Hebrews see their alphabet as living, cosmic powers instrumental in creating reality).

The link between Behemoth and its marine mate, Leviathan, a cosmic dragon, is found in Hindu lore. Leviathan, in Hindu lore, is Sesa-Ananta, a thousand-headed primordial dragon commissioned by Brahma (God) to support the world ("Goddess Earth") on its many heads and keep the world stable.

Brahma gave Sesa-Ananta a helper in this task: the fair-winged bird Garuda. Garuda is one of the many guises of the angelic order called Ofanim, and it's relevant here because, as said, Behemoth, Leviathan's mate and future rival, is a filtered perception of the Ofanim who in Hindu perception were Ganesh, the benevolent, merry elephant god. Thus the Ofanim (as Behemoth) work collegially with Leviathan and have done so since the beginning of Creation.

Their age is approximately 60,480,000,000 human years, equal to one Week of Brahma (4.32 billion years [one Day of Brahma] + 4.32 billion years [one Night of Brahma] = 8.64 billion years), sufficient time to gain the wisdom attributed to them in their Behemoth form.

Hebrew lore says that Behemoth (the Ofanim) will be the food for the righteous at the Messianic banquet at the End of Days. The flesh to be consumed will be the cumulative, expanded consciousness Behemoth has eaten throughout humanity's sojourn on Earth; the reservoir of the angelic consciousness it has consumed from the other 39 angelic orders; the awareness swallowed from its activities in 18 billion galaxies since the beginning of time; and from its sheer ontological essence of being older than almost everything else in existence—it is a precious, rich morsel of God essence older than all the stars, planets, and galaxies.

Those interested in tasting the "flesh" of Behemoth (the Ofanim) sooner than the Messianic banquet may do so any time they choose. The Ofanim, accessed as a tiny point of brilliant light just above the navel, are the portal to a vast world of psychic experiences and spiritual nourishment. As Garuda, Vishnu's celestial mount, they are the emissaries (Star of Bethlehem) of the Christ, and of the human experience of Christ Consciousness and the birth of the Christ Child.

See also: Dragon, Ganesh, Garuda, Hanuman, Leviathan, Phoenix, Simurgh, Thunderbird, Vocub Caquix, Ziz.

BIFROST

An image of the perpetual extension of the 14 Ray Masters and their color emanations from the celestial realm into the physical human world.

Also known as Aesir-Bridge, Asbru, Bilröst, Rainbow Bridge.

Description: In Norse myth, Bifrost is the bridge connecting Mitgard (Middle-Earth) on the ground with Asgard, the residence of the gods called Aesir, in the celestial realms, mythically said to be far away in the sky.

Bifrost means "quivering road" or "swaying road to Heaven" (from the Old Norse *bifa,* which means "shake, sway") and is described as a rainbow bridge. Bifrost is also translated as "the fleetingly glimpsed rainbow" or "the multicolored way," and sometimes as *Asbru,* "Aesir-Bridge," the privileged bridge into Asgard. Bifrost rises from Earth and terminates in the sky at a dwelling called *Himinbjorg* (Old Norse for "Heaven's castle" or "Heaven protection").

Another term for the bridge connecting Earth and Heaven is *Bilröst.* It was made by the gods with great skill and knowledge; comprised of three colors (it burns with fire), it is the best of bridges, and it will break at Ragnarok.

To get onto Bifrost you must pass by or through Himinbjorg, and this is Heimdall's residence, the Aesir's ever-wakeful guardian of the Rainbow Bridge.

Heimdall keeps the bridge open for the Aesir who every day ride out of Asgard and across Bifrost and into Mitgard to assemble for decisions at *Urdarbrunnr,* Urd's Well, the home of the three Norns (or Fates) who weave the destiny (fate or karma) of humans at the base of the World Tree called *Yggdrasil.*

Explanation: Although it may seem appealing to interpret Bifrost as a poetic reference to the rainbow, this is not the case. Bifrost is an emanation of the particular residents of Asgard, known to the Norse as Aesir, the Sumerians as Anunnaki, the Greeks as the gods of Mount Olympus, and to esotericists as the 14 Ray Masters of Ursa Major, the constellation of the Great Bear, seat of the Great White Brotherhood, a conclave of enlightened adepts who govern the galaxy.

The Ray Masters are known in various myths and metaphysical systems as particular well-recognized gods, such as Athena, Apollo, and Aphrodite, or El Morya, Kuthumi, and Saint Germain. Their function is to manage the differentiation of pure white light into a double rainbow spectrum of 14 rays, such as scarlet and pink, emerald green and light green, rich blue and pale blue.

Each of these color Rays represents a fundamental theme in consciousness and a stream of consciousness evolution with one Ray Master as its chief. Formerly humans, the Ray Masters long ago transcended human status through lengthy initiations to assume this larger role within the cosmos and human and planetary evolution. Asgard (also known as *E-Kur,* Glass Mountain, Crystal City) is their prime residence; though in another dimension and existing in the far future (roughly 3000 A.D.), it may be accessed by humans through clairvoyance.

The Ray Masters, and their numerous affiliate adepts within their given Ray (see Einherjar), supervise human initiations according to one's soul affiliation to a particular ray. They also are involved in the esoteric government of the Earth and humanity's conscious evolution, and coordinate with the larger and primary Great White Brotherhood headquarters on our planet and known as Shambhala, though existing in a different dimension from ours (see Shambhala).

Bifrost is essentially the Ray emanations of the 14 Ray Masters radiating out in all directions from the Crystal City. Picture it this way: Inside the Crystal City, the Ray Masters each have their own one-fourteenth spatial division of residence.

Saint Germain, for example, Master of the Lilac Ray, has a section, and we could reasonably construe this as being lilac-hued; this lilac division radiates out from the Crystal City into Mitgard, our Middle-Earth, forming one-fourteenth of the Rainbow Bridge. From other divisions of the Crystal City emanate orange, green, scarlet, purple, and gold rays, each from one Ray Master, thus forming Bifrost.

It is tempting to picture the Rainbow Bridge as we know physical bridges, that is, as a straightforward, linear bridge from point a to b and of a certain width. Bifrost is more of a double rainbow spiked collar around the Crystal City, with color Rays going out in all 360 degrees, each Ray occupying about 25 degrees. It is accurate to say Bifrost is made of the 14 Ray Masters themselves, in extension.

If your soul is on the Scarlet Ray, for example, your optimal point of entry into the Crystal City would be on the scarlet portion of Bifrost.

When the Aesir of Asgard ride out across Bifrost for their daily meeting at Urd's Well, we could picture this as the 14 Ray Masters and their Ray affiliates (Ascended Masters and adepts under their Ray tutelage) riding out of the Crystal City in all directions at once, rather than as a galloping storm of gods on their celestial steeds riding across a narrow planked bridge.

Further, we can picture the Ray Masters as *perpetually* riding forth from Asgard, sending their Rays (themselves) out into Middle-Earth every day, every minute. That means that information, consciousness, and attention are always moving out of Asgard, that is, from the Great Bear and a select branch of the Great White Brotherhood, from the future and another dimension, into our physical world.

Each of the Ray Masters represents a stream of cosmic experience, but Bifrost, consisting of the 14 Rays, offers to humanity the full spectrum of universal experience, the blended Ray of all the themes of cosmic consciousness.

The Ray Masters riding out of Asgard for Urd's Well and the deliberations of the Norns is a metaphoric way of saying the Ray Masters are intimately involved in human consciousness evolution, the soul's plan for each incarnation, the working out of karma (fate or destiny), and sequential initiations of individual humans. Yet Urd's Well also refers to another geomantic feature, called Valhalla (see Da Derga's Hostel and Valhalla), an amphitheater-size assembly place for the Great White Brotherhood, especially suited for interaction with humans.

One of the prime focuses of this information is the Christ Mystery, and the opportunity for interested humans to receive initiation into this subject.

You will find a Bifrost wherever there is a Crystal City or Asgard, as they are interdependent geomantic features in Earth's visionary geography. Selected locations include Uluru at Alice Springs, Australia; Cathedral Rock in Sedona, Arizona; Mount Shasta, California; the Tor at Glastonbury, England; Mycenae, Greece; and Monticello, Charlottesville, Virginia.

See also: Da Derga's Hostel, Einherjar, Glass Mountain, Heimdall, Seven Rishis, Shambhala, Valhalla, Wild Hunt.

BLACK EYE OF HORUS

An aspect of the Christ Consciousness, seen through the Egyptian psychic filter and templated on Earth as 1,080 Silver Eggs.

Also known as Eye of Osiris, Harwer (Haroeris), Horus the Elder, Moon Eye, Silver Egg, udjat, wadjet, wedjet.

Description: Horus, the Egyptian falcon god and considered the Face of Heaven, has two Eyes and two guises. As Horus the Younger, he is *Heru-pa-khart*, the Sun (associated with Ra [or Re], the Sun god), the White Eye (his right); as Horus the Elder he is *Heru-ur*, the Black Eye (his left) called *wedjet (wadjet or udjat)*, associated with the Moon and the wisdom god, Thoth.

Horus in general is the son of Isis and Osiris. At Heliopolis, he was known as *Harakhtes,* "Horus of the Horizon," while at Edfu he was Horus the *Behdetite,* the celestial falcon god or hawk-winged Sun disk. One of the oldest of Egyptian gods, Horus's name probably derives from *her,* which means "the one on high" or "the distant one," references to the soaring flight typical of a hunting falcon. As an all-seeing falcon, Horus's right eye was the Sun, his left the Moon, giving his long-range sight a celestial cast. Some interpreted his speckled breast feathers as representative of the stars, and his wings in downsweep were the windy sky.

Once Horus the Younger grew up, he became known as Horus the Elder. He was finally able to combat his archenemy, Seth, who had beleaguered him even as an infant. In his battle with the dark god Seth to avenge the latter's perfidy in arranging for the death of his father, Osiris, Horus became known as *Hor Nubti,* "Horus of Gold." In the conflict, Horus lost his left eye, the Moon or Black, but it was restored by Isis and was thereafter called wadjet, "Healthy Eye."

But it's also told that Seth pulled out Horus's left, Black Eye and flung it beyond the edge of the world. Then Thoth, wisdom god and guardian of the Moon, retrieved it from the outer darkness, though he found it in pieces. He reassembled Horus's eye so that it formed a full moon, and gave it back to him.

Egyptian myth says Horus the Elder battled Seth for 80 years until achieving victory, then he was inducted into the tribunal of the gods as the Lord.

Explanation: Horus the Elder is an aspect of the Christ, the ancient wisdom principle as seen through the Egyptian mythic-psychic perception. His association with Thoth, god of wisdom and the Moon, is apt, for Thoth (the Greek Hermes) was one of the prime educators and initiators in the ancient world.

The falcon imagery is also apt, for the Christ (Logos) is the far-seeing one. In the Hindu perception, Christ as Vishnu the Pervader, this is even more clear: Vishnu pervades all of spacetime, permeating all of space with his consciousness.

Seth, as Osiris's brother, in actuality was less an enemy to Horus than a benefactor. Often the myths need to be inverted to understand their meaning. Osiris is an expression of the Supreme Being and, in effect, Horus's spiritual father. Seth did not destroy Horus's wisdom eye; he gave it to him so that Horus, son of Isis and Osiris, could better see his Father.

The wedjat is the Eye of Horus that looks upon the Father and His Mysteries. In fact, the wedjat is the Eye of Osiris (the male aspect of God) seeing through Horus, as the Sun or White Eye is the Eye of Isis (the female aspect of God) seeing through Horus. Thus Horus's Eyes transmit both aspects of God.

This also means Horus, with both Eyes, has insight into the Sun and Moon gods and their temples, as templated across the Earth as Sun Temples (see Hitching Post of the Sun) and Moon-Soma Temples (see Fountain of Youth).

Horus's White, Sun Eye is represented in Earth's visionary geography as 666 Golden Eggs that birth the Christ Child, or Horus the Younger. Horus's Black, Moon Eye is represented as 1,080 Silver Eggs that birth Christ as Horus the Elder.

The Silver Child, Horus the Elder, is the inner aspect of Horus and is also the other aspect of the Golden Child, Horus the Younger. When the silver and gold aspects come together through landscape activation, then the all-seeing aspect arises as a contribution to human collective consciousness from the Earth.

Selected locations of the Silver Eggs include the Chapel of the Holy Cross, Sedona, Arizona; Cheops Pyramid, Giza Plateau, near Cairo, Egypt; the Tor, Glastonbury, Somerset, England; Cadmeia, Thebes, Greece; and Edfu, Egypt.

Hatching Horus the Elder from the Silver Egg means grounding, opening, activating, and releasing the "bird" inside the egg. It may be done, sometimes, in a few days, or it may take months or regular visits. One has to "hatch" something equivalent within oneself and, additionally, one must acquire a crystalline shaft from the realm of the Ray Masters of the Great Bear, needed to activate Horus.

This domain, a Celestial City and City of Light, is known variously as Asgard, Mount Olympus, Cedar Forest, and Glass Mountain, and is an aspect of Shambhala, the Earth's seat of esoteric government, set a thousand years in the future.

At places where Horus has been "hatched," the inner temple of wisdom (Thoth's knowledge) becomes accessible through that site, and he may induct us into the old, eternal Mysteries. Horus is Elder because as Christ he is before the Earth and our Creation; this is apparent in the Hindu myth of Horus as Vishnu, who, in between cycles of creation and dissolution of the world, dreams atop the coiled mass of Sesa-Ananta, the cosmic dragon, afloat upon the primordial Sea.

Vishnu is all that remains from the dissolution of the world at the time of Pralaya (in the West, the Flood), which is to say his consciousness is eternal. Horus the Elder, as the falcon god, flies outside all spacetime frameworks, and he can transport us into these realms too, to that undying point before and after Creation, if we wish and are prepared for it.

See also: Cosmic Egg, Fountain of Youth, Glass Mountain, Hitching Post of the Sun, Seven Rishis, Shambhala, White Eye of Horus.

BRAN THE BLESSED

An expression of the Supreme Being's immanence in the world by way of an all-seeing severed head in the landscape.

Also known as Ancient of Days, Atum, Bendigeidfran, Brahma, Face of God, Kronos, Macroprosopus, Mimir, Osiris, Primal Aion, Urddawl Ben (Venerable Head), Vast Countenance, White Head, Zervan, Zeus.

Description: The myth of a severed divine head has multiple expressions in world mythology. Bran the Blessed, son of Llyr (Lord of the Sea), as told in the Welsh *Mabinogion,* is crowned king of the Island of Britain, but he is also a colossus. He was so big he was never contained in a house or a ship; he was often mistaken for a moving mountain, and when his host had to cross the sea to Ireland, he laid himself down across the water as a bridge.

At the end of the battle of the Isle of the Mighty (Britain) against Ireland, Bran ordered his head to be cut off. He told his retinue to carry it to *Gwynfryn* (the White Mount) in London and bury it with its face looking toward France. It would, in this way, protect the nation, as long as it remained buried. However, his retinue had to make a few stops on the way with *Urddawl Ben* (the Noble Head), which sang and told stories and endlessly entertained his company.

Bran's headquarters were in Harlech, in the northwest of Wales, and through his severed head, he entertained his company for 80 years there with constant feasting and a boundless supply of drink and merriment. It was known as the Assembly of the Noble (or Wondrous) Head. Then they spent 80 years in Gwales in Pembroke (Wales), then they made it to London and buried his head at the White Mount.

Explanation: Bran the Blessed is an expression of the Supreme Being's immanence in the human world on Earth by way of a geomantic feature called the Crown of the Ancient of Days. Bran is one of many expressions of the Supreme Being's aspect of Time or extreme antiquity, better understood through the Judaic name Ancient of Days and the cosmic time reckoning of Hinduism's Brahma.

There are 72 locations around the Earth where Bran's severed head is present as an interactive geomantic feature; 12 are large and primary versions, and 60 are smaller, secondary versions. Gwynfryn in London is Primrose Hill, and the Noble, Wondrous Head of Bran is one of the Crowns.

Other Crown locations somewhat correspond with myths of divine severed heads. Golgotha

(Hill of Skulls) in Jerusalem is one. Abydos in Egypt; Banaras in India; Sacsaywaman in Cusco, Peru; Mount Ida in Turkey; and Sodorp Church in Vinstra, Norway, are more of the Crowns of the Ancient of Days.

The head of Osiris was buried at Abydos in Egypt. Mimir's Well at today's Vinstra, Norway, was where Odin, the Norse high god, went regularly for consultation with the wise Mimir, whose severed head was at or was the well. Originally, Brahma had five heads, but Shiva cut one off, carried it around India as a begging bowl, and finally planted it in Banaras at *Kapalamochana Tirtha* ("Where the Skull Fell"), thus equipping Banaras with a major point of numinosity.

During the Trojan War, Zeus, the chief god of the Greek Olympians, brooded at Mount Ida in Turkey, about 20 miles from the war. His head was not severed, but his presence, via Homer's descriptions, was represented by his gaze. It's as if all of Mount Ida is the all-seeing, all-directing head or consciousness of Zeus. In Peru, all of Cusco is said to be the landscape body of a puma, and its Speckled Head is at Sacsaywaman, a site also marked by massive stacked stones.

As for size, the 12 primary Crowns may appear to be the size of the mountains they inhabit or overlie, so that, for example, all of Mount Ida is the Crown, while the smaller Crowns, such as the one at the Rotunda on the Lawn at the University of Virginia at Charlottesville, seems about 30 feet across and high.

There are small Crowns at Harlech and Gwales in Wales, both "party" sites for the Bran's retinue in the Hospitality of the Wondrous Head. The entertainment of the Noble Head is the all-encompassing, beatific presence of the Supreme Being looking into our world, seeing everything at once, and giving us an opportunity to participate in the Presence and, as it were, regard the divine Face.

One vivid image for the Vast White Countenance, another name for Bran given by a Qabalist mystic, is to imagine a massive human-like head rising out of a calm sea to fill the space above the horizon completely and see the Face also reflected in the waters. The Crown may resemble a white marble human head on a platform, the face upward toward a domed ceiling resembling a crown. You can only see the head in profile, but light flashes out in all directions at once from its eyes, and the Rays penetrate all 360 degrees of the space around it for miles.

This geomantic feature with 72 copies can also be called the Face of God.

See also: Ancient of Days, Manu.

BRIGIT'S MANTLE

A higher dimensional terraforming energy employed by the Earth-shaping "gods" from the star Canopus to impart the silver feminine-Mother current into the Earth at a very early period of manifestation.

Description: In an old Irish myth called "The Earth-Shapers," the Tuatha de Danann, Ireland's primordial gods, contemplate the newly formed Earth enveloped by blackness and chaos and dark hissing waters filled with monsters. Present are Midyir the Haughty, Aenghus, the Dagda, Nuada, Ogma, and Brigit. The Dagda is the chief of the Tuatha and Brigit here is the Mighty Mother of the gods, the presumed Dana or Danu of the Danann, for *Tuatha de Danann* means the "Followers of the Goddess Danu." Usually Brigit is a goddess among the Tuatha.

Brigit is called Flame of Two Eternities, Shepherd of the Star-Flocks, Flame of Delight, Mother of All Wisdom, Mother of the Stars, and Battle Queen. She towered to the Heavens and her mantle swept the ground like a mist.

The Tuatha, though observing Earth, are present in a celestial realm the Irish called *Tir-na-Moe,* the "Land of the Living Heart." Brigit sings a song, then says it is what she heard the Earth singing and that she was dreaming of beauty. That the Earth dreamed and sang of beauty was to Brigit the sign the Tuatha should prepare the

Earth for life. Brigit will drape her silver mantle over it.

Midyir dives into the seething turmoil of the chaotic Earth bearing Lugh's fiery Spear of Victory, one of the Four Jewels the Tuatha bring to Earth as gifts from their holy and otherworldly cities. Midyir whirls the Spear until it becomes a wheel of fire and destroys all the monstrous life within the blackness.

He announces he has made a place for Brigit's Mantle, which she now spreads out over the Earth. It unrolls like a silver flame, or like the incoming sea with little silver flames at the foremost part of the waves. Aenghus flies down to stand in the Mantle and it becomes a drifting silver mist; when the other Tuatha stand in the mist, it is as if they are in an altered reality and are among dream images.

The Dagda spreads green fire from the Cauldron of Plenty to make the Earth green, then Aenghus scoops hollows out of the green Earth to make lakes and mountains. The Tuatha dispatch further signs of the monstrous first life. Brigit plants Midyir's Stone of Destiny at a specific place in the landscape. It sinks into the ground, music arose, the rivers and lakes fill with water, and the Earth seems to laugh with pleasure.

Finally, Brigit lifts her mantle of silver mist to reveal a beautiful island of green grass, hollows, and heights. The Tuatha, delighted, pledge to be the Earth's artificers to fashion everything there to be beautiful, as beautiful as things are in the Land of the Silver Fleece, one of the names for their heavenly realm.

Brigit announces that the name of this new land is the White Island and Island of Destiny, but it will also henceforth be known as Ireland.

Explanation: This is an ancient memory of how the gods terraformed the planet to make it suitable for human habitation. This is a time in the planet's life that preceded the installation of its visionary geography, itself a fundamental design aspect of the Earth. Although the White Island is revealed to be Ireland, the terraforming process and the focus of this myth originally were global in effect.

The Earth is a designer planet, created on demand by the "gods," a consortium of angels, extraterrestrials, and enlightened sages under commission of the Supreme Being. It has a complex array of sacred sites that comprise its visionary geography, and all of its 100+ features (with multiple copies of each) keep the Earth and human consciousness in living alignment with the galaxy.

This geography was installed, activated, regulated, and primed over a 27-million-year period, a primordial time in which the gods were present on Earth and the archetypes underlying all myths were living realities. Egyptian myth recalls this as Zep Tepi, the "First Occasion," and, among the Australian Aborigines, this is the Dreamtime. The terraforming with silver flame happened in the earliest phases of the 27 million years of the Dreamtime, earlier, in fact, than the installation of most of the visionary geographic features.

The planet has an umbilical cord that consists of two strands. Both insert into the Earth at Avebury stone circle in Wiltshire, England, but they originate from two sources: A silver strand comes from Canopus, the galaxy's second brightest star, and the bright star in the keel or rudder of Argo Navis; a golden strand comes from Sirius, the galaxy's brightest star, in the throat of Canis Major (Dog).

From a human perspective, Canopus is the seat of the Mighty Mother for Earth, and Sirius the seat of the Dagda, the chief of the gods, or Mighty Father. Through these two stars, directly "plugged" into the Earth, the ultimate Mother and Father aspects of the Supreme Being (God) influence our planet and life.

Brigit or, as she is known by her other Celtic names: Danann; Dana; Danu; Anu; or Dan, an Old Celtic word for "knowledge"; or Ana from the Old Irish *anai,* "wealth," is the Mother working through the feminine star, Canopus. She is Mother of the Stars and Shepherd of the Star-Flocks because, as the second brightest of the Milky Way's millions of stars, she is one of their two leaders. Her followers, the Tuatha, were more like colleagues working with her silver energy.

Canopus is the source of the primary feminine current of consciousness for the planet and humanity, a silver flame, just as Sirius is for the masculine, manifesting as a gold flame. Brigit's Mantle refers to the permeation of the planet by this silver flame, the essence of the Canopean Mighty Mother. It is both a one-time terraforming influence and a permanent Flame of Delight in the Earth.

The Canopus line completely encircles Earth, starting and ending at Avebury; the same is true of the Sirius line, though they are perpendicular to each other. Brigit's Mantle can be pictured like this: Visualize a silver ribbon encircling Earth; it exudes silver light in all directions, like a sea filling in shallow spaces; the planet is enveloped—painted—in this silver mist-flame.

The silver mist-flame is the thought substance of Brigit; it permeates, subdues, and organizes Earth's physical matter, until then, chaotic and irrational. Brigit already has a mental picture of the final result, the allocation of the landscape features, rivers, lakes, mountains, and continents. The Mantle is like a magic blanket that shapes physical matter in accordance with her idea.

It is also a master template for a planet's Light grid, that is, the totality of the array of visionary geographic features and all their interconnections. The Mantle is like a primary engineering blueprint in holographic form laid on the land so as to summon up, as if magically, the diversity of geomantic features.

To access or even see the silver flame or Brigit's Mantle today is a matter of penetrating in consciousness to at least the fifth dimension, to a realm two cognitive levels from our ordinary perceptual domain of physical matter. This is probably what the Irish meant by *Tir-na-Moe,* the "Land of the Living Heart," a place remote from human experience yet in contact with the Earth.

The Irish myth called this the "Land of the Silver Fleece"; some of the Tuatha are said to have the radiance of the Silver Fleece about them or to wear cloaks as if spun of fine silver mist. Certain harpers in their company were said to wear mantles of silver mist. Basically, it's silver light from Canopus, the Mother, and gold light from Sirius, the Father. Both represent permanent imprints in Earth's matter and a continuous influence or rain from above.

In summary: The Mother aspect of the Supreme Being (Brigit, Dana, Danu), working through Canopus (Tir-na-Moe) in the Milky Way galaxy, sends a silver current straight from Canopus to Avebury, where it is grounded then sent oroborically around the planet. The silver flame-mist (Brigit's Mantle) then under supervision of other gods (the Tuatha, or extraterrestrial higher dimensional beings) irradiates the entire planet like a spreading sea, permeating the inchoate proto-matter with the template of the desired landscape.

Brigit's Mantle has an application at the individual human level, a mark of recognition, grace, and initiation from Brigit, the Divine Mother. Irish myth speaks of people robed in silver mist or wearing beautiful silver cloaks. Brigit can infuse a person through the core of their being with a pure silver shaft of light; this then forms a silver cloak around the person's auric field, amplifying clairvoyance and facilitating perception of reality in the fifth dimension, particularly of the Earth's vast though quiescent stargate network (see Land of Milk and Honey, Rising Rock).

See also: Dreamtime, Floating Bridge of Heaven, Hollow Hill, Hurqalya, Rainbow Serpent, Tuatha de Danann, Zep Tepi.

CAMALATE

An esoteric training and initiation academy, founded 26 times in different cultures, for men and women seeking individuation and wholeness in the context of unifying humanity, Earth, and cosmos.

Also known as Arthur's Palace, Camelot.

Description: Camalate is the name given to King Arthur's residence and headquarters for his Round Table of Grail Knights. Archeologists are not completely certain where the British King Arthur's Camalate was located, but leading contenders include Winchester, Caerleon-on-Usk (Wales), and, the most likely, South Cadbury Castle, 12 miles from Glastonbury in Somerset.

One of the earliest published references to Arthur's Camalate was by John Leland, the British antiquarian in 1542. He said that at the south end of the church of "South-Cadbyri standeth Camallate, sumtyme a famose toun or castelle." It was located on a hill and was fortified (the location is an ancient hill-fort, with several ditches girthing a flat, grassy summit); the locals, Leland added, couldn't say much about the place other than that King Arthur much resorted to it.

Locally, the fortified hill was referred to as Arthur's Palace, and legend had it that he and his faithful Knights were sleeping in the hollow hill awaiting their call sometime in the future to come to Britain's aid again, as they had before.

Historians tentatively, or perhaps grudgingly, attribute the South Cadbury Castle location to a presumed fifth century A.D. British King Arthur; grudgingly, in the sense that even this figure has only sketchy historicity and seems to conventional thinking much closer to a myth than an historical actuality. Archeologists have uncovered sufficient physical evidence to support the statement that some kind of significant fortification once existed at Cadbury.

Among the activities cited by the various medieval writers of the Arthurian mythos were jousting, questing for the Holy Grail, defending Britain against the invading Saxons and other enemies of the peace, and assembling annually at Pentecost at the famous Round Table, a gift to Arthur from Queen Guinevere's father, King Leodegrance, King of the Summer Country. At that time, the Knights would discuss their years' worth of questing activities, and sometimes witness the epiphany of the Holy Grail brought there by angels.

Although the Round Table was inherently an egalitarian structure, and no Knight was "better" or better positioned than another, membership in the Round Table fellowship was difficult to achieve, rather rare, and highly esteemed.

Camalate, as portrayed by the medieval writers, such as Chretien de Troyes, Sir Thomas Malory, and Wace and Layamon, was also the pinnacle of chivalry, as the defense and honoring of femininity as a social ideal.

Explanation: Camalate was an esoteric initiation and training center in the geomantic Mysteries of the Earth and human consciousness. There was not just one Camalate; there have been 26 so far in the history of the Earth, situated in different cultures, such as Persia, Tibet-Mongolia, Ireland, and Celtic England.

On 15 occasions, the Camalate has been directly associated with a King Arthur, on eleven occasions without one. King Arthur, the Solar Logos and chief of the Great White Brotherhood in the constellation Ursa Major, has permeated 15 humans in the life of humanity on Earth, inspiring them to be a King Arthur exemplifier. The other key figures have similarly been overshadowed, if not permeated, by the spiritual essence of other celestial figures central to the Arthurian mythos, such as Merlin, Morgan le Fay, the Lady of the Lake, Guinevere, and others.

The exemplification of the Arthurian mythos, an archetypal myth that embodies fundamental energies and relationships of the cosmos, happens in accordance with Arthur waves, moments of convergence among celestial, solar, planetary, and social interests, needs, and fluidity in which the mythos will have especial appeal and relevance to a given culture so as to benefit Earth.

In Ireland, for example, the King Arthur exemplifier was called Fionn MacCumhaill, and his band of warrior colleagues were the Fianna. In Persia, King Arthur was known as Rustam; in Tibet and Mongolia, as Gesar of Ling.

In each instance, the King Arthur exemplifier established a Camalate, Round Table, and cadre of highly trained Knights of the Holy Grail. Their goals were basically the same and archetypal: the fine-tuning of the Earth, human, galaxy relationship as expressed in Earth's visionary geography and as experienced in consciousness and executed in cooperation with the elemental (Nature spirits), angelic, and hierarchical kingdoms (the strata of the Great White Brotherhood; see Einherjar).

In all 26 expressions of Camalate—I call them Camalate Centers—men and women were trained rigorously in spiritual and psychic development in the context of deepening their relationship with Earth and its sacred sites. Knights (see Grail Knight) learned to interact collegially and constructively with Nature spirits, notably the gnomes (see Royal Hall of the King of the Dovrë Trolls); landscape angels, including the Earth Spirit, Gaia; angelic orders, notably the Ofanim (see Garuda, Simurgh, and Ganesh); and at least 14 representatives of the Great White Brotherhood known as Ray Masters (see Seven Rishis).

The totality of the relationship between a Grail Knight and all this was known as the Quest for the Holy Grail. It was a process that simultaneously awakened the individual to the cosmos within themselves and the Earth and the protocols of a constructive and illuminating relationship. The Grail Knight discovered that the same cosmic, archetypal pattern exists within oneself and the planet, and thus the activation of this pattern at either end benefits the other. Questing for self-illumination in the context of Earth's sacred sites simultaneously helped illuminate the Earth and improve its galactic links.

The medieval images of mail-clad knights on horseback knocking each other off their mounts with long lances is mostly a metaphor for an inner event. At some Camalates, notably South Cadbury Castle, the landscape was preequipped with a geomantic feature called a Round Table: The standard division of the horoscope into 12 zodiacal signs was templated on a large stretch of landscape, usually a few miles in diameter, and the Knights "jousted" with—encountered, mastered, and assimilated—various birth chart dynamics—aspects of themselves.

Each of the 26 sites of former Camalates still carries a spiritual charge from the activities and relationships developed there. Each Camalate, for example, opened up the connection between Earth and the Great White Brotherhood and, in effect, grounded the Brotherhood for a time at that location. South Cadbury Castle was called Arthur's Palace because it was *copresent* with the assemblage of enlightened adepts and celestial sages of the Great White Brotherhood.

That means the geomantic features at that physical location made it possible for the Brotherhood, although in Ursa Major, to be also interactively present at Cadbury. Functionally, the "Castle" at South Cadbury was not so much the physical living or training structure as it was the Brotherhood's assembly hall.

Respect for femininity was of course honored at the Camalates, but the medieval description of chivalry tends to sentimentalize the occult reality. Many people came to Camalate, some to be knights, for the purposes of realization of light, understanding humility, truth, love, sincerity, spirituality, integrity, compassion, and other qualities. The goal was to harmonize the energies of consciousness and take it through the process of individuation, or wholeness of the Self.

The name Camalate itself is a sacred word with a gematrial matrix and numerological correspondences that create patterns of light around it. The name is capable of drawing certain individuals to it by resonance and, as a divinely created name held in the heart, it can become a focus for them for the coming together of conscious aspects for the purposes of awareness, truth, light, and love.

The Camalate Center, in whatever era it is expressed, is a gathering of like-minded men and women who are working toward individuation, that is, the unification of the opposites in themselves into a single whole Self, in the context of a group that itself, when fully formed, will also be an individuated whole.

See also: Da Derga's Hostel, Einherjar, Fionn MacCumhaill, Gaia, Ganesh, Grail Knight, Hollow Hill, Indra, King Arthur, Royal Hall of the King of the Dovrë Trolls, Seven Rishis, Simurgh, Trolls.

CANDLEMAS

An infusion of Earth's visionary geography with light every year on the evening of February 1 by the assembled angelic hosts—a mass of Light for the Earth and a lighting up of all its sacred sites and their connections.

Also known as Chandeleur, Festival of Saint Bride, Gwyl Ffair y Canhwyllau, Gwyl Ffraia, Hypante, Imbolc, Imbolq, Oimelc, Oimele, Purification of the Virgin Mary, Saint Bridget's Day.

Description: Candlemas, or Imbolc or Oimele, is one of the eight traditional Celtic turning days (two solstices, two equinoxes, Candlemas, Beltane, Lugnasad, and Samhain), a pivotal day in the yearly cycle when a new phase begins. This day is celebrated on February 2 every year, although the late evening of February 1, like Christmas Eve, is usually considered the crucial moment for ceremonies.

In Celtic cultures, Candlemas marked the first day of spring and corresponds with the British folklore observance of Groundhog Day, when prognostications for the end or continuation of winter are taken. Forty days after Christmas, on Candlemas, candles and torches were lit from the Yule log, then carried in procession. It was a feast of purification and spring-cleaning in which Christmas decorations were finally taken down from the tree and burned.

In Ireland, the day was called Oimelc or Oimele (meaning "ewes' milk" or "butter bag") and later Imbolc (meaning "in the belly") and marked the visibly perceptive lengthening of the days and thus the imminence of spring and the eventual bounty of summer. The day also traditionally marked the time ewes came into their milk in preparation for lambing. It was the time of year when life and light first begin to stir again in the winter-dark womb of Earth and Nature.

Oimelc or Imbolc was also clearly associated with the Irish Fire goddess Brigit who was later Christianized as Saint Brigit (or Brigid, Bridget, Bride, and other variations) of Kildare, the patroness of sheep. The classical Irish name for the day was *La 'il Bride;* the Gaelic, *La Feill Bhr'de;* and the modern Celtic name is *Oiche Fheil Bhrighide.* It is a time of optimism and new beginnings.

Brigit (the Irish name means "the Exalted One") originally was the "pagan" goddess of fire, smithing, fertility, cattle, crops, and poetry. She was the daughter of the Dagda, the chief of the Irish gods, the Tuatha de Danann. Later she metamorphosed, thanks to Christian hagiographers, into Saint Bride of Kildare (450–525 A.D.), and with Saint Patrick and Saint Colum, was one of Ireland's three patron saints as well as the tutelary goddess of Leinster County.

In 1184, the historian Giraldus Cambrensis reported that a flame in honor of Saint Brigid (sometimes called Mary of the Gael) had been burning continuously for 500 years; the "unextinguishable flame" had been faithfully tended by many generations of nuns at Kildare. Over the centuries, her fame spread throughout the British Isles, with 19 churches dedicated to her, and she was regarded as the mother of all virgins and the midwife of the Virgin Mary.

The Irish Saint Bridget (Bride) was associated with Candlemas, so much so that the event was often called the Festival of Saint Bride or Saint Bridget's Day. Corn dollies (called *brideo'g*) were dressed and Bride Cakes prepared; the day was considered a fertility festival and a sheath of corn or oats was dressed in women's clothes and set into a basket or straw cradle called Bride's Bed, surrounded by burning candles. Saint Bride was then invited to visit the homes and enter these beds as a blessing. In Ireland, feasts were held in honor of Saint Bridget on this day in preparation for the favorable planting of crops and propagation of livestock.

Further, Bridgit's Crosses were constructed of rushes and set on homes, stables, and other dwellings to deflect evil powers. Similarly, people wore Bridgit's Girdles, made of woven straw, to protect against baleful influences.

The Welsh called this special day *Gwyl Ffair y Canhwyllau,* the Virgin's Feast of the Candles, and among them it was regarded as a convergence of the Christian and earlier Irish Brigit festivals. All over Wales, until about the eighteenth century, carols were sung and candles lit in homes or placed in window sills in observance.

Christianity abolished this ritual in the sixth century, renamed and refocused it as the Purification of the Virgin Mary, and, by papal order, Catholics offered up burning candles to the Virgin Mary. In the medieval liturgical calendar, Candlemas was observed in the churches with the candle signifying the Christ; each parishioner brought a candle as an offering to the church and walked with it in procession. Other candles were blessed then taken home by the parishioners to be used as spiritual protection against thunderstorms, sickness, demons, and other negative influences, or placed by the beds of the dying.

In general, Candlemas in its Christian formulation meant the purification or churching of the Virgin Mary 40 days after the birth of Jesus. Earlier, the Romans had on this day honored Juno Februata, a goddess known to be the virgin mother of Mars, or Februus, a male god considered the deity of purification. All of February was sacred to Februus and, as the last month in the Roman calendar year, it was the yearly time for cleansing Rome by sacrifices to the dead, a ritual known as Februalia and in which Februus personified these rituals.

The Eastern Orthodox Church called the day Hypante and stated that, on this day, Simeon and Anna met Christ in the Temple and knew him as the Light of the World. The day, which marks the formal end of the Christmas cycle, was also called Presentation of the Christ in the Temple. Processing at night with candles represented the entry of Jesus as the Light into the Temple. Traditionally, a large congregation of people would walk around the altar singing prophetic verses.

The midwinter festival day is also observed among the pagan-Wiccan community as an important Sabbat day, suitable for initiation, the rebirth of goals, dedications, and aspirations, planning and preparing one's life for the coming year, reaffirming vows or creating new ones, and ritualizing new beginnings.

Explanation: Like other important spiritual days, such as Christmas and Michaelmas, a loss of understanding of the significance has been accompanied by a distortion of the correct spelling. In all three cases, the original meaning was a *Mass,* with the focus being Christ, the Archangel Michael, or the Light.

Candlemas is one of a series within an annual geomantic liturgical calendar in which angelic and hierarchical hosts interface with the Earth and humanity. Other events in this cycle include the Wild Hunt (December 20), Epiphany (January 6), and Michaelmas (September 29—see entries for each).

Candlemas is a global mass for the Light presented by the assembled angelic hosts on behalf of humanity and the planet. It happens in real time, every February 1 evening. It has little to do with the Virgin Mary in any doctrinaire, Catholic sense. It is orchestrated by the actual celestial being who is Brigit, and the ancient Irish appellation of Oimelc as "ewe's milk" is apt in an extended sense, for Earth's spiritual body or visionary geography is inundated with celestial Light and benevolent regard on this first day of the year's renewal.

In ancient initiatory parlance, Light was often equated with milk, or the terms were used interchangeably, as in the Hindu concept of "Ocean of Milk" as a fount of original light.

Brigit, the Exalted One, is one of a cadre of 14 special Ascended Masters, members of the Great White Brotherhood (see Einherjar) and known as the Ray Masters of Ursa Major (see Seven Rishis). The Ray Masters are former humans who have ascended into a higher order of existence and responsibility (see Philosopher's Stone, Holy Grail) and who work with the angelic hosts for the benefit of Earth.

The Ray Masters occasionally have human incarnations or create personae in the form of godly figures to accomplish important tasks in Earth culture; among Brigit's have been Aphrodite, Hathor, Mary Magdalene, and Joan of Arc, but as Master of the Pink Ray she is often called Lady Nada ("Sound"). She has also been part, along with three other Masters, of the Virgin Mary apparitions.

On Candlemas Eve, vast numbers of the angelic hosts, notably among the orders called Ofanim (see Ganesh, Garuda), Seraphim, Elohim (see Cyclops Polyphemus), and Nefilim (see Giants), assemble at geomantically charged nodes on the planet. Specifically, these are star points within a geomantic feature called landscape zodiacs, of which Earth has 432 (see White Cow, White Sow). These are interactive holograms of varying sizes of the galaxy and its stars.

The intent of the assemblage is to "light the Grid," meaning the entirety of Earth's visionary geography or subtle bodies, nine layers in all. We commonly know this terrain as the realm of sacred sites and their subtle, spiritual aspects.

Here is one way this might be pictured: Innumerable angels are congregated on sacred sites across the planet; with them are many benevolent spirits, Ancestors, and benign watcher beings and benefactors to Earth. All hold burning candles or small lit torches as offerings. Small numbers of embodied humans are also participating in this event. In earlier days, far more did so. Into the flames one puts one's aspirations, wishes, desires, and plans for the next year.

Down to this vast plain of spirits, humans, and angels come the four great archangels, Michael, Gabriel, Uriel, and Raphael, from out of the four directions. They collect the individual flames as if on an offering plate and add them to their own brilliantly burning torches; with these fiery torches, they set flame to Earth's Light body, the totality of its spiritual or auric fields, a kind of Earth-enveloping placenta, and they burn it (without consuming it) with spiritual fire.

The Earth for a time seems to be encased in layers of sheet lightning, the congealed essence and force of the celestial light transmitted from the angelic hosts into Earth's Light Body. The thousands of star points within the 432 landscape zodiacs are "lit" with angelic light, and the entire Earth receives its first spark of pure new Light for the year from these millions of angelic candles.

Then Ray Master Nada gives the assemblage and the Earth a blessing with her pink light. This energy has the quality of unconditional Mother's love and is congruent with some aspects of the conventional Catholic portrayal of Mary. The pink light swaddles Earth's Light body in a nourishing maternal regard as well as all of humanity, even if this is registered only in people's higher selves. To a large extent, Candlemas, for humanity, is an event mostly of the Higher Self.

In earlier times, though it is still viable today, men and women engaged in the long-term spiritual initiation process called the Quest for the Holy Grail (and thus known as Grail Knights) were active participants every year in Candlemas.

For those embodied humans participating in this grand mass for the Earth, Ray Master Nada—the Irish Bride—does in fact bless one's house, visiting it room by room in spirit form, confirming the efficacy of the Irish Bride's Beds. In a sense, the presentation of a Bride's Bed in a home signified the occupant's willingness to be visited and blessed by the spiritual being they knew as Brigit. Such a blessing from on high, whether at the level of home, sacred site, or the entire planet, is certainly a powerful act of cleansing and purification.

One of the benefits of Candlemas is that the illumination of the planet's Light body, the sparking of Earth's visionary geography with this fresh infusion of celestial Light, and the swaddling of it all with Ray Master Nada's pink light is to burn off a little of the Antichrist's dark grid, the energy that supports atheism, materialism, control, lies, and ignorance.

See also: Antichrist, Cyclops Polyphemus, Einherjar, Epiphany, Ganesh, Garuda, Giants, Grail Knight, Hollow Hill, Holy Grail, Hurqalya, Michaelmas, Ocean of Milk, Philosopher's Stone, Seven Rishis, Tuatha de Danann, White Cow, White Sow, Wild Hunt.

CATTLE OF THE SUN

A symbol for the consumable, experiencable time units, each lasting 864 billion years, in the vast time duration of the Sun.

Also known as Agni's Fire Bricks, Cows of the Dawn, Day of Brahma, Kalpa, Rays of the Dawn, Shining Herds.

Description: The classic description of the Cattle of the Sun is Homer's Book 12 of the *Odyssey.* Odysseus and his men have landed on Thrinacia (today's Sicily) and have been warned to avoid and certainly not eat Helios the Sun god's cattle who graze on the slopes of the massive volcano, Mount Etna. The cattle are herded by Helios's daughters, Phaëthousa and Lampetie, and if any harm comes to the flock of 350 cattle, Odysseus's ship and men would be destroyed.

The words of warning came from Circe, also a daughter of Helios, widely regarded in Odysseus's days as a dangerous enchantress or witch and who had detained him for a year to be her lover on the island of Aeaea. Of course his crew disobeyed him and feasted on the entire flock. Helios, an awesome master who, says Homer, sees and hears all, demanded retribution from Zeus. When Odysseus's ship was well at sea, Zeus blasted it with lightning and drowned all hands save Odysseus who alone among them had not touched Helios's cattle. The Cattle of the Sun were said to be milk-white animals with gold horns.

Explanation: The Cattle of the Sun is an ancient symbol to express the 360 units of solar time in the vast life of the Sun. They are part of every Sun Temple, a geomantic feature templated in 144 locations around the Earth.

Picture a roaring flame that needs to be contained so it doesn't burn out of control and destroy everything around it. Bound it with a circle of 360 degrees. The powerful flames can then be corralled into units of one degree each. The roaring flame is primordial cosmic fire called Agni, the Fire god in Hinduism. The container with 360 segments or degrees is Surya (the Greek Helios), the Sun god as a controlled, time-released expression of the unbounded Agni.

Agni will burn forever, but the Sun god will burn for only One Year, that is, one divine year in the Vedic time reckoning, or 311 trillion human years.

The Sun god's burn time, or life duration, is measured in 360 units, mythically symbolized as the 360 Cattle of the Sun who graze at the periphery of his flames, but more precisely and in congruence with the Vedic time model, it is quantified as 360 *kalpas* or Days of Brahma, the Creator god, the ultimate reference and container for the Vedic time model. Appropriately, the Egyptian Sun god Ra's solar barque is sometimes called the Boat of Millions of Years.

Each kalpa lasts 8.64 billion human years and consists of a Day and Night. There are many subdivisions of this vast duration, but the key point is that the Sun's life is divided into 360 equal parts, and these parts total One Year. Each part (kalpa, Day) is an experienceable and thus consumable (eatable) portion of time. That is why Odysseus's men *ate* the Cattle of the Sun. They consumed the cattle's time.

Similarly, in Hindu esoteric thought, the cow is the symbolic container of consciousness (Light) in the form of knowledge; to eat the Cattle of the Sun is to consume and assimilate the divine knowledge and higher consciousness it contains. The question is this: Can you digest it? Odysseus's men could not.

Vedic symbolism also suggested the Cows were

equivalent to the Sun's rays, and that the Shining Herds of the Sun were Surya's thousand Rays of Light. Surya was an aspect of the Sun in the sense of higher knowledge and revelation. The higher truths of the Sun (similar in nuance to the Dawn) were his Cows. Surya's illuminations of divine consciousness were symbolized as the Herds.

In human, planetary terms, this is only meaningful, if not comprehensible, when understood in the context of Earth's visionary geography. Each of Earth's 144 Sun Temples (see Hitching Post of the Sun) provides an experienceable holographic microcosm of this vast time extent of the Sun. In geomantic terms, Odysseus's men were experiencing *(consuming)* units of the Sun Temple; the elegance of the myth is to say they *ate* the Cattle of the Sun, for in a way they did.

The Cattle of the Sun—360 is the correct number, not Homer's 350—are consumable units of solar time that contain, define, and limit the flames of Agni. As such, by containing and creating the circular boundary, divided into 360 units, the Cattle *create* the Sun because they limit Agni's otherwise unlimited extent.

Although the Sun myth encompasses at one level our solar system's Sun, the reference is more to the archetype of all Suns as containers of cosmic time, and the Great Central Sun.

How big is that Sun? That is the same as asking how long it will endure. It will last One Year of Brahma, or 311,040,000,000,000 human years. The Sun is thus a time container divided into 360 equal and consumable units (Cattle, kalpas, Days), for we consume time by living through it, as do all the planets and organic life.

Sun gods in most myths are given chariots pulled by horses. Picture the solar chariot with one wheel at the center of the flaming circle, the other at its perimeter. This outer wheel moves slowly through the 360 time units, or Cattle, taking 864 billion years to consume each of the Cattle, until the circuit is done.

At an abstract level, the Sun exists by sacrificing its substance—time—a fact registered in the astrophysical value called the solar constant. That is the amount of our Sun's physical energy (time substance) it loses (gives off) each day.

Odysseus encountered Helios's Cattle of the Sun at Mount Etna because that site is one of the 144 Sun Temples. The cattle grazing on the slopes of the volcano are a simple way of indicating the spatial relationship between the perimeter of the Sun Temple and its central fiery forge. Appropriately in Vedic thought, Agni's fire altar consists of 10,800 bricks laid in five layers and bordered by 360 extra fire bricks. These are the Cattle of the Sun, one degree of Agni each.

This interpretation is congruent with the tauroctony, or bull-slaying, of classical Mithraism. In the original Mysteries, no physical bulls were slain for this was beside the point: The bull-slaying was a symbolic expression of the sacrificial "bleeding" into our world or solar system or even galaxy of the "blood" or life force (time duration) of one of the Cattle of the Sun.

It is assumed that "Cattle" refers specifically to bulls, as cows in myth (as in physical life) yield milk and nourishment and have a different geomantic and spiritual decoding (see White Cow). That said, the Cattle of the Sun, if bulls, are still different in nuance from the classical White Bull (see White Bull).

The 360 Cattle of the Sun may be experienced at any Sun Temple and may be found at the perimeter of the geomantic template. In practical terms, at the Santa Fe, New Mexico, Sun Temple, which occupies the Plaza downtown, the Cattle of the Sun may be found at about a half-mile radius out from the Plaza.

Each of the Cattle of the Sun (or kalpa, or Day of Brahma) lasts or contains 864 billion human years. Astronomers tell us that the diameter of our solar system's Sun is 864,000 miles and that one day consists of 86,400 seconds. This suggests that the *time diameter* of the Sun is defined by 864 and that 864 in its various expansions and contractions by zeros is a fundamental measurement. It also implies that our Sun is but one of 360 Cattle of a much greater, older Sun.

See also: Beast of the Apocalypse, Fountain of Youth, Hitching Post of the Sun, White Bull, White Cow.

CHAKRAVARTIN

The watcher angel or egregor assigned to India at the inception of the Earth who, as Bharata, spiritually prepared the land for habitation and continues to guard its borders and the spiritual integrity of India's people.

Also known as Guardian, Guardian Angel of the Nation, Heavenly Minister, Logos of a Nation, Name of God, National Angelic Regent, National Deva, Prince of the Nation, Watcher, the Word in the landscape.

Description: The term *Chakravartin* comes from ancient India and denotes a great spiritual prodigy capable of wielding the *chakravarta,* a heavenly wheel. The Chakravartin can turn and cause to revolve the sacred wheel and thereby establish a world-pacifying monarchy in accord with celestial mandates. The Chakravartin for India was known as Bharata, the original name for that country.

One of India's oldest and most venerated epics (and certainly the longest) is the *Mahabharata,* which relates the latter-day affairs of the clans of Great (Maha) Bharata. The theme of this epic (18 books, 2,109 chapters) is the fight between two lines of princes in the original dynasty of the emperor Bharata.

The Chakravarta is described in ancient Vedic texts as a world wheel or discus of irresistible force and potency, and the Chakravartin is the owner of the chakravarta and is thereby the hub of the universe. The Chakravartin is a universal ruler whose dominions are sometimes said to be the entire Earth, the one who moves and turns the wheel (much like a chariot's wheel, but here with Sun connotations) of truth (Dharma) over a territory with unimpeded movement.

Essentially, the Chakravartin uses this celestial device to prepare, pacify, and unify the land for which he is responsible so that it will be a spiritually suitable living place for a people, in this case, Bharata's descendants in Bharatavarsa, Land of the Bharatas (India). As a mark of his potency, the Chakravartin possesses Seven Treasures and bears 32 auspicious bodily marks.

Vedic legend says Bharata was a partial incarnation of Mahavishnu (an exalted aspect of Vishnu) and that he ruled his land benevolently for 27,000 years, having first destroyed all the wicked when he pacified the territory.

The wheel (chakra) is also called the Sudarsana, the Discus of Vishnu, who is one of India's three primary gods, known as the Preserver, and akin to the Western esoteric description of the Logos (the Word) and Christ. The Sudarsana ("Fair to See") is Vishnu's celestial wheel or discus (Chakra) and symbolizes this deity's unlimited mental power and speed of thought. With the Discus, Vishnu creates, sustains, and destroys worlds, as required.

Explanation: Bharata is the name for the original angelic watcher or egregor assigned at the inception of the Earth to oversee the landmass of India.

In the original plan of the Earth, nine continents were allocated; each would have a presiding watching angel or egregor responsible for it. Then for the 72 primary landmass subdivisions, such as Ireland, another 72 egregors were assigned. Each would supervise the inherent geomantic features of the landscape and the relationship of its people to those subtle landscape features.

The national egregor would also oversee the unfoldment of the inherent soul qualities of the people occupying that land—what makes them Indian, Norse, or Irish, for example. Some esotericists call these folk-soul archangels.

Deuteronomy hints at this where Moses says, "When the Lord divided the nations, he set their borders according to the number of the angels of God." That number, in terms of angels that protect the borders of nations and spiritually lead their people, is 72, and Bharata is one of these.

Judaic lore also says that at the beginning of Creation, God assigned 70 Guardian Angels to watch over and rule the 70 Nations descended from Adam.

In Judaic angelologies, the egregors are called the Tutelary Princes of the Nations or Regents of the Nations. Qabala speaks of the 72 Names of God, or *Shemhamforesh,* and, to a large extent, the totality of the 72 egregors are these. Each folk soul or national character tied to its landmass and egregor expresses a Name. Thus Bharata in his angelic essence embodies one of the Names of God and, in his original pacifying of the land, he inculcated that Name into India's soil.

In the Indian elaboration of a Chakravartin we see how an egregor permeates the landmass, the geomantic features, and the spirit of a landmass, and through this the people, or folk soul, who occupy it and are meant to evolve in it. Those who live in the land of Bharata, in effect, live within the angel Bharata, hence the subcontinent's original name, *Bharatavarsa.*

The chakra or Sudarsana that Bharata wields is on loan to him from Vishnu, as it is to each of the 72 Chakravartins or national egregors. In geomantic language, the Sudarsana is the Mobile Shambhallic Focus, a movable aspect of the planet's primary sixth chakra, the brow or so-called Third Eye center between the eyes and the means for psychic perception and picture formation. Shambhala is an esoteric center for the Great White Brotherhood on Earth—the celestial government and the true "shadow" government behind all seeming governments.

The national egregor for a landmass, in this case, Bharata, uses the divine Name of God entrusted to him in conjunction with the focused beam of Vishnu (here it might be easier to use the Western term Christ or Logos) to prepare a land spiritually. This is a form of primordial terraforming, not so much in a physical, geological sense, but a geomantic and spiritual one: inundating the preexisting geomantic features in a landscape with pure spiritual light.

Ireland's egregor is called Eriu, and it's interesting to note that the ancient Irish stories described her as decked in circlets or rings and said her name means "round." Quite likely, Eriu's rings, circlets, and roundness are a vague perception of her possession of the Chakravarta, a round Sun-like discus or moveable eye.

One of the Seven Treasures Bharata possesses is called the *cintamani* ("Thought-Jewel"), or Magic Jewel, a wishing stone that fulfills every desire. The cintamani is a stone also known as the Emerald.

Judaic lore states that Lucifer, Lord of Light and Light-Bringer, is the chief of all the Princes of the Nations. That means all 72 Chakravartins report to him and he oversees their localized work and is their egregor and watcher angel.

Lucifer gave the 72 egregors an Emerald to hold in trust for him. These Emeralds (a projected expression of the heart within the heart chakra, better understood through Greek myth as the narthex tube in which Prometheus put the gods' fire—self-aware consciousness—he stole to give humanity) are supervised by each national egregor on behalf of its people, and they are usually grounded at a specific site—in Ireland as the Lia Fail at the Hill of Tara. In the case of Bharata, it is one of his Seven Treasures required for him to accomplish his work.

The egregors for India and Ireland are among the two most clearly delineated among the 72 original nations (see also Srin-mo Demoness, Tibet's egregor). But traces of national egregors can be found in other myth systems:

The original founder of mainland Greece is known as either Hellas or Hellen, and the descendants as Hellenes. Hellen was said to be a son or brother of Deucalion, the Greek equivalent of Noah who survived the world Deluge by riding it out in an ark. The Peloponnesus of Greece is named after Pelops ("Pelops's Island"); Pelops is the son of Tantalus, son of Zeus. England, including Wales and Scotland, was anciently called the Island of Prydein, after Prydein, son of the Great

Aedd, who first conquered it. Armenia was originally called Hayastan after its founder, Hayk, possibly a name for that country's egregor.

See also: Emerald, Eriu, House of Atreus, Huitzilopochtli, Lucifer, Navel of the World, Shambhala, Srin-mo Demoness, Vishnu's Discus.

CONNLA'S WELL

The Irish perception of the Grail Castle, Holy Grail, and Rich Fisher King, source for all themes of consciousness for our age.

Also known as the Waters of Mnemosyne, Well of Coelrind, Well of Nechtan, Well of Segais.

Description: In Irish mythology, Connla's Well is known as a source of inspiration and divine knowledge, yet a dangerous well for most mortals and even gods. The actual location of Connla's Well is only vaguely sketched in the old stories, though some suggest it lies somewhere near Tipperary. All are prohibited from visiting the well except for Nechtan and his three cup-bearers.

Nechtan is sometimes said to be the husband of the goddess Boannd, who became the River Boyne. For a while they lived together in the *Brugh na Boinne,* the Hostel on the River Boyne (Newgrange, a large stone tumulus), but earlier Nechtan lived at a small hill-fort called *Sidhe Nechtain,* "the fairy mound of Nechtain," believed to be at the place where the River Boyne arose.

Over the well grow nine hazel trees whose nuts contain cosmic wisdom, knowledge, and inspiration. When the nuts drop into the well, a salmon swimming in the water eats them and then embodies the knowledge. Thereafter it is known as the Salmon of Wisdom, sometimes called Fintan (Fionntan). His name meant "the white ancient," but he was also called "the one-eyed one of the red waterfall" and swam in the well nibbling the hazelnuts. Fintan was a one-eyed ancient bard who through many lives gained all possible wisdom; Irish myth goes back and forth as to whether he is an ancient human or a wise salmon. Confusingly, Nechtan is also said by some to be the Salmon of Wisdom.

Occasionally, a mortal human gains access to this wisdom by touching the salmon. Fionn MacCumhaill, the great Irish hero, once tasted a drop of it when it was being roasted over a fire and its juices splattered on his thumb. He stuck the thumb in his mouth to stop the pain, but instead tasted the wisdom and entered a visionary state in which he could foresee the future. The wisdom may also be had by eating the nuts or drinking from the well (when the nuts strike the water, they produce bubbles of mystic inspiration), as the goddess Boannd learned.

Boannd was originally a goddess whose name meant "white wisdom," "woman of white cows," and "shining cow." Yet she was also known as *Sruth Segsa,* "River of Segais," because she drank from the forbidden Well of Segais (another name, it seems, for Connla's Well). She sought wisdom at the well, but at her approach, its waters rose up suddenly and drowned her and her body became the River Boyne and she merged with not only the river but its ultimate source.

The same story is told of the origin of the River Shannon, Ireland's largest. As a goddess, Sinann ignored a prohibition about approaching the magical well and went to the well in search of wisdom, but the well suddenly overflowed and flooded the land, drowning her. This floodwater became the River Sinann (Shannon), and she became its inhabiting spirit, known thereafter as the goddess of the river and all the land it irrigated.

Explanation: Connla's Well is a profound image with many parts. First, one must understand that the goddesses who become rivers after being drowned by the overflowing well are the terrestrial counterparts of the Oceanids (see River God). These are the 3,000 daughters of Oceanus, the ocean or sea of consciousness that encircles the cosmos known as the Earth to the Greeks. Each Oceanid embodies one theme of the totality of consciousness; the rivers on Earth through their resident deities, the River gods or goddesses, transmit those themes to Earth through the physical body and energetic field of the rivers.

Boannd, Sinann, and the other river deities go to Connla's Well to receive the theme of consciousness they are to impart to the Earth. They then dissolve their spirit into the physical waters of the river and remain resident as the landscape angel or deva who maintains the integrity of the energy-consciousness field that works through the physical river and its watershed.

The Salmon of Wisdom, Fintan, Nechtan, and Connla's Well itself are all the same—the same deep reality seen from different perspectives. The clue, though surprising, is that Fintan is also the name of the most ancient of the Irish, the one who survived the Flood and restarted civilization. He hid in the Hill of Tounthinna (*Tulach Tuindi* or *Tul Tuinne*) overlooking the River Shannon and near Portroe in County Tipperary. From here, with his consort, Cesair, he is credited for repopulating Ireland. Other accounts say he landed at the Dingle Peninsula in County Kerry and lived there for 5,500 years, mostly as a salmon.

Culture heroes like Fintan (the Greek Deucalion, the biblical Noah, Babylonian Utnapishtim, the Vedic Manu) who survived the Deluge to refound civilization are each expressions of the Rich Fisher King of the Grail legends.

The Flood survivor and refounder of world culture is the same figure as the Rich Fisher King. Both preserve all the knowledge of and for the species. Similarly, the Boat of the Vedas, Noah's Ark, and the rest are the Grail Castle.

In possibly the earliest expression of this myth, Vishnu, one of Hinduism's trinity of gods, known as the Preserver and Pervader and the equivalent of the Western Christ and Logos (the Word), assumes the form of a vast fish called Matsya and tows the Boat of the Vedas (identical to Noah's Ark) that contains all the teachings of the Vedas (the vast store of cosmic knowledge), the holy sages from Ursa Major called *rishis,* and Manu, the surviving human, across the Deluge waters until they retreat. Manu then refounds civilization.

Manu was not just an ordinary mortal human. He was *Manu Satyavrata,* a spiritual lawgiver and child of the thousand-rayed Sun. When the Flood subsided, Manu would restart world culture; but this was outside of human history—rather, it would be the start of history, a new aeon, or in Vedic reckoning, a new cycle of cosmic time and life that would last 306 million years.

Manu, as the first spiritual king of the new epoch of existence, was an expression of Vishnu, or the Christ, the embodiment of total cosmic knowledge. Just as the Irish Fintan is both an ancient one-eyed bard and the Salmon of Wisdom, so was Manu both a divine child of the Sun god and *Matsya-avatara,* the incarnation of Vishnu as an eight-million-mile-long divine fish. Echoes of this are found in the Judaic description of Leviathan, the vast whale, and the Waters of Mnemosyne, or deep cosmic memory and the source of the arts in the Greek myths.

The Grail legends, which are far older (and in fact archetypal) than the medieval Europe that most recently encoded them, demonstrate the union: The King is both fish and human, and is rich in cosmic memory and life because of it. The Irish Nechtain and Fintan are both expressions of the Rich Fisher King.

The European Grail myths usually portray the travails and epiphanies of humans seeking the source of wisdom, inspiration, and knowledge in their quest to find and enter the Grail Castle. This is equivalent to Connla's Well. But the Irish perception sets the story back even further into primordial time. Here we see the Oceanids in their planetary guise getting their initial information and programming for their long life on Earth of transmitting aspects of awareness.

Picture the cosmos as an ocean (Oceanus) with 3,000 streams (Oceanids) all flowing to the center and out away from the center, too—this is Connla's Well.

Here the nine hazel trees and their Nuts of Wisdom are central. Fintan, the Salmon of

Wisdom, constantly nibbles on these nuts as they fall into the well. The key to understanding this is the number nine. It is the prime number for Earth's visionary geography and the varying quantities of its light temples; mathematically, in about 75 percent of the 100+ different geomantic features, the number of their expressions or other numbers central to their definition reduces to nine (e.g., 144 Grail Castles, 1+4+4=9; 1,746 domes, 1+7+4+6=18, 1+8=9; see Orpheus's Lyre).

The nine hazelnuts Fintan feeds on are a metaphysical filter or flavoring for the 3,000 streams of consciousness (Boannd, Sinann, and the rest). The number nine is the prime number of the Earth grid because it is the signature number of the Great White Brotherhood (see Einherjar) and the Pleiadian Council of Light; these are both conclaves of exalted beings that oversee the unfolding of consciousness at many levels throughout the galaxy and on Earth.

The prime importance of the number nine is expressed in the Norse formulation of the nine worlds of the Odinic Mysteries and the Egyptian Ennead as a company of nine deities *(neteru)* who represent fundamental governing principles of the cosmos. Nine is the unsurpassable limit, beyond which, starting with the number ten, numbers start repeating and recombining.

Another more abstract form for the filter produced by the nine hazelnuts is the enneagram, a geometic figure with nine parts; it is a growth diagram embodying recurring numbers produced and used as a teaching tool by the Great White Brotherhood and, as mentioned, embodied in the mathematics of Earth's visionary geography. Thus eating the hazelnuts or tasting of the flesh of the Salmon of Wisdom introduces one to this vast field of arcane knowledge.

See also: Einherjar, Fionn MacCumhaill, Fisher King, Grail Castle, Leviathan, Orpheus's Lyre, River God, Salmon of Wisdom.

COSMIC EGG

An undifferentiated condition in which Heaven and Earth exist together but from which the Primal Man (Golden Child) is coagulated.

Also known as Auric Egg, Brahmananda, Egg of Brahma, Egg of Light, Egg of the Serpent, Golden Embryo, Golden Germ, Golden Womb, Hidden Egg of the Great Cackler, Hiranyagarbha, Philosopher's Egg, Shi'ur Komah, Universal Egg.

Description: Many world mythologies postulate that the world and its Creator god first emerged from a massive egg the size of the universe.

First there was primordial chaos, then a first organizing Creator emerged. In the Chinese myth of P'an-Ku, before there was anything discrete, there was only Chaos, a dark, swirling, unformed, gelatinous mass of confusion. Gradually, a coherent sentient being, P'an-Ku, coagulated out of this, though he slept for 18,000 years. When he finally awoke, he perceived the chaos around him, waved his arms, shouted, and broke free of it, and thereby separated Heaven from Earth.

In the Hindu tradition, the Chandogya Upanishad says that in the beginning the world was only nonbeing, then turned itself into an egg, lay dormant for a year, then split asunder. The top half of the eggshell was gold and became the Upper World, Heaven, the bottom half silver, and became the Lower World, Earth.

The Hindu prime Creator god, Brahma, gestated inside this Cosmic Egg as the Hiranyagarbha, the golden germ, embryo, or womb. Sometimes this primal egg is called Brahmananda, Egg *(anda)* of Brahma. The first cosmic being born from the Egg of Brahma is Bala Brahma, Child Brahma, a radiant child with four heads and four arms, as resplendent as the young Sun and King of the Immortals.

Out of the body of P'an-Ku or Brahma subsequently came all of Creation. The Norse mythic perception was of Ymir, the original cosmogonic Man; though he was not said to be inside an egg, he coagulated out of fire-mist and sacrificed his body to create all the features and species of the physical world.

The Cosmic Egg, containing the entirety of potential Creation and its creator but still in its undifferentiated state, is also what the Jewish mystics call the *Shi'ur Komah,* the extent and mystical shape of the Godhead. How big is God? God's universal body expressed as the Primal Man (e.g., P'an-Ku, Ymir) is 7,008,000,000 miles high, according to the Qabalistic model of the Shi'ur Komah.

The Druids called the Cosmic Egg the Egg of the Serpent, perhaps following the Egyptian depiction of Kneph the Serpent producing the Cosmic Egg from his mouth, thus symbolizing the Logos. The medieval alchemists applied similar thinking in their designation of it as the Philosopher's Egg, out of which came the white flower (silver, feminine) and red flower (gold, masculine).

The Egyptians said a Mundane Egg came from the mouth of the unmade and eternal deity Kneph (or Amun) and was the emblem of generative power. Ancient Egyptian myths also say the first god was born from an egg that lay for a long time in a marsh thicket, and old texts refer to the "hidden egg of the great cackler," probably in reference to Amun, who abides in all things as the soul. The Great Cackler is a primordial bird, although sometimes Amun is meant by it.

The Great Cackler is also interpreted to be Geb, a primordial form of Earth, understood as cosmic space and matter, not the planet. In his form of a divine goose, Geb lays the primeval egg from which the cosmos will hatch.

According to Egyptian legend, at one time the primordial egg was taken to Hermopolis along the Nile and preserved as a relic of the origin of all life. The Egyptians also say that Thoth, understood here as the universal creator, hatched the world egg at Hermopolis by which the world emerged as an organized cosmos.

In fact, at Hermopolis there was once a sacred lake called the Lake of the Two Knives, and in the middle of that was an island called the Isle of Flames. Here the Cosmic Egg was first hatched, allowing the gods and world to manifest. The Egyptians also claimed that Osiris arose out of the "egg in the hidden land."

The Cosmic Egg connotes that condition of unity *before* the separation, when all the stars and planets, the Sun and Moon, were inside the Earth, and the Earth was still in Heaven. The Greeks said the Cosmic Egg resided in the Stream of Oceanos, the primal River god that flowed in a circle from the outermost edge of the Earth (all of cosmic space), back upon himself in a circular flux.

In early Gnostic thought, the Egg of Life was brought forth from the boundless Mother Substance; the divine spirit (Father Ether) was inside the egg, sometimes called Phanes. When he shone forth, the entire universe similarly shone forth by the light of his divine fire. The egg was the first and last of all things, primordial matter, Mother substance, energized by the Supreme Spirit.

In esoteric models, such as Theosophy, the Egg of Brahma concept is used to describe the birth and subsequent boundaries of solar systems and aggregates of solar systems and all the interacting planes and worlds of existence. The Egg of Brahma is the boundary of manifestation; all components of existence come from it, planets, worlds, gods, demons, humans, continents, seas, mountains, Nature.

Correspondingly, psychics describe the totality of the human energy field or aura as like an egg with the physical body inside it—hence the term Auric Egg.

Explanation: In practical, experiential terms, the utility of the Cosmic Egg is that the Earth offers 48 replicas within its visionary geography.

Selected locations include Hermopolis, Egypt; Uffington Castle, Dragon Hill, Wiltshire, England; Worley Hill, Kingweston, Somerset, England; Mount Sinai, Egypt; Mount Demavand, Iran; the Idaean Cave, Mount Ida, Crete.

The geomantic Cosmic Egg resembles a massive ball of light, perhaps several hundred feet tall, usually co-occupying the space where a mountain is. In other words, you can potentially see through the physical mountain to the egg. Usually, there will be a geomantic replica of the Great Stream of Oceanos present. In some cases, the egg will be positioned at the root chakra of a landscape zodiac (see White Cow, White Sow), which is a miniature holographic star map.

In general terms, the Cosmic Egg suggests the way in which Heaven and Earth primordially were a single, unseparated form, but this is not entirely accurate. Sometimes they are called Orphic Eggs instead, after Orpheus, the Greek master musician, son of Apollo, and God of the Underworld, said to be egg-born. Probably the reason Orpheus got attached to the egg description is that in the Orphic cults, founded in Orpheus's honor, it was taught that God formed the original unshapen chaotic mass into the shape of an egg from which all derived.

In this light, their geomantic function is to contain a seed that is related at an elemental level to the Earth, pertaining either to landscape or Earth grid activations or the amplification of Earth energy configurations. When the seed is hatched, through human interaction with the egg, then its functions may unfold. That Earth has only 48 Cosmic Eggs attests to their specialized function.

One can tune into the seed formation of a landscape temple (its light or astral components), its chakra hierarchy, and energy relationships at a Cosmic Egg.

In some cases, astounding revelations, often the major content of religions, derive from an experience of a Cosmic Egg, such as the sight of the Shi'ur Komah, the extent and mystical shape of the Godhead as revealed to Moses. God opened the seven heavens on Mount Sinai and revealed Himself, in all His beauty, glory, and shape, as well as His crown and as seated upon the Throne of His glory. Mount Sinai has a Cosmic Egg, as does Mount Moriah in Jerusalem from whence Mohammed had his Night Journey through the seven heavens to God's Throne.

The Cosmic Egg has an initiatory function with people, however. When you locate the geomantic expression of Oceanos at a Cosmic Egg site and spend some time there in meditation, you may collect a seed of light from it.

With further concentration, and the seed placed in your heart chakra, this energy may be perceived as the forward rushing of the Great Stream; the seed will burst into white flames or appear to be enveloped in flames. This is the inner experience of what the Egyptians meant by the Isle of Flames. The landscape Cosmic Egg is enveloped in huge white flames like the Sun's corona.

Taking your burning white seed to the geomantic Cosmic Egg, you may experience it being activated by spiritual beings within the larger Egg, sometimes by a perceived sword stroke straight through the egg and your heart chakra. Some time later (usually a few months), the seed will split in two and a Golden Child will emerge. This is what the Hindus meant by Bala Brahma, the Golden Child.

Thus, through a geomantically facilitated process, you have experienced the separation of Heaven and Earth and the precipitation of the Golden Seed or Embryo (the *Hiranyagarbha*) into the organized form of the first Creator, Brahma. You have birthed your Higher Self as a child from out of your own Auric Egg. You have coagulated a miniature interior form of Ymir, P'an-Ku, the Primal Man.

You may also experience the differentiation of the primal gold and silver elements by way of two more types of geomantic eggs templated across the Earth (see Black Eye of Horus [Silver Egg] and White Eye of Horus [Golden Egg]).

This newborn radiant Golden Child of the egg is Bala Brahma, which means son of Brahma, and, in the Egyptian vocabulary, Horus, both the Elder and Younger. Horus is the Egyptian perception of the Christ; thus you have birthed the Christ child within you using the outer geomantic structures as a guidepost.

See also: Black Eye of Horus, Purusha, White Cow, White Eye of Horus, White Sow, Ymir.

CYCLOPS POLYPHEMUS

An Elohim angel perceived in temporary human giant form as he executes his celestial tasks having to do with the solar energies.

Description: The Cyclops Polyphemus is best known for his encounter with the wily Greek adventurer Odysseus, who bests him in his Sicilian cave.

Polyphemus is a son of Poseidon, the Greek Lord of the Sea, and like the other Cyclopes ("Round-Eyed") has but one large eye in the center of his forehead. He lives in a mountain cave near Mount Etna on Sicily and is, according to Homer, a lawless, ignorant, uncouth, savage lout. He is a towering brute, a wild man, uncivil, a giant who knows only power and cannibalism and cares nothing for Zeus and his will or guidance or rabble of gods.

Odysseus and his men get trapped in Polyphemus's cave, and the Cyclops brutally eats several of Odysseus's companions. Odysseus blinds the giant with a spear, then tricks him by riding out of the cave strapped to the underbelly of a ram. As a final insult to Polyphemus, Odysseus says his own name is Nobody, so when Polyphemus complains to his fellow Cyclopes he says that Nobody did it.

Earlier in Greek myths, three Cyclopes—Brontes, Steropes, and Arges—are credited by Hesiod with having aided Zeus, chief of the Olympian gods, as divine craftsmen in making his thunderbolts. Virgil portrayed three Cyclopes as working with the smith god Hephaistos at his forge inside volcanic Mount Etna.

In the *Aeneid,* Virgil says 100 Cyclopes live in the caves of Mount Etna; they were a tribe, the brotherhood of Etna, lumpish but terrifying and each with his awful single eye as they raged and towered heavenward outside their caves.

Explanation: Odysseus's triumphant encounter with Polyphemus on Sicily was part of his multistaged Mystery initiation tour of the many geomantic temples of the Mediterranean, all part of Earth's visionary geography.

In most cases, myths that recount single-eyed barbarously mannered giants living in caves and liking manflesh are distorted memories of the Elohim. This is an angelic order charged with creating humanity and installing much of Earth's geomantic temple array. For a time, more than 20 million years ago, they inhabited human bodies that stood 18 feet tall—they were Earth's first giants. Three more angelic orders temporarily incarnated as giants on assignment by the Supreme Being to accomplish certain tasks among humanity and for the Earth.

Odysseus's trial with Polyphemus was the test of a human initiate to encounter, withstand, and assimilate the celestial energies transmitted by the Elohim. A variant of this spiritual combat is the David and Goliath tale, wherein David, a human, overcomes and defeats Goliath the giant and takes his sword.

This part was omitted from the Greek version, which highlighted Odysseus as the indefatigable human hero, but the sword is central to the encounter. It is the Word-Sword and represents the protocols of light, sound, magic (reality generation), and creativity as taught by the Elohim, the masters of the primal creative energy, to selected humans (see Dolorous Stroke).

Odysseus's blinding of Polyphemus can be read in two ways: Through initiation he assimilated some aspects of the divine vision represented by the single eye and, true to mythic memory, this dynamic got distorted as blinding Polyphemus; or he "killed" Polyphemus as the bearer of Elohimic revelation in the sense that, because he could not assimilate or transcend this level of reality, he put to death, spiritually, what from his lower level appeared to be in his way.

The single, baleful eye is the somewhat fearful human perception of the Elohim's unremitting divine vision. The single eye connotes unitive vision, their unseverable connection with God, and the mastery of His energies. Technically, the single round eye is a caricature or exaggeration of the human sixth chakra, or Third Eye, the mechanism of clairvoyant sight and perception.

The Elohim, as with the other three angelic orders who took form as giants, had nodes or meeting places for humans in Earth's visionary geography. The caves on the slopes of Mount Etna would be the physical apertures to their more subtle domain for, in Odysseus's time, his encounter with them would have been in the spiritual world accessed through Polyphemus's "cave."

An equivalent to Polyphemus, the Irish Balor of the Evil Eye, lived in a crystal tower on Tory Island off the northwest coast of Ireland. The crystal tower is occult code to indicate the realm of light, dimensionally removed from matter.

The pejorative image of Polyphemus and generally of the Cyclopes is a function of the distance in time in Greek cultural understanding from their actual time on Earth. A lot got distorted in the interval, sometimes to make a better tale.

The reason for the abundance of Cyclopes on Sicily pertains to the geomantic function of Mount Etna in the Earth grid. It is a Sun temple or Mithraeum, one of 144 such installations around the Earth. Here the Solar Logos (an expression of the Christ at the level of the Sun) works through Hephaistos, the smith-fire god of the Olympians, at his forge; the forge "flames" are the solar stream and life force, and his helpers, the three Cyclopes, are Elohim, who focus the Christ through the Sun and, in this case, into numerous objects, such as shields, thrones, palaces, breastplates, and other godly ornaments and devices.

Although myths of other cultures do not always remember this setup in the same vivid detail as the Greeks, at any of the other 143 Sun temples essentially the same function and tableau would be observed. The temple allows solar energy and consciousness to enter the Earth grid at 144 places, and it affords humans, equipped with psychic sensitivity, to witness and interact with this.

The image of three Elohim with Hephaistos at his forge inside Mount Etna also refers to the working relationship between the Solar Logos and the planets. For a time, three Elohim manifested as the 14 planetary logoi, two per planet, in our solar system. A Planetary Logos is a celestial being who embodies and transmits the intelligence of that planet and its cosmic purpose and destiny.

This is reflected in the Greek myths of the Titans, such as Rhea and Kronos, who preceded the Olympian gods such as Zeus and Hera. The Titans were the Elohim acting as the 14 planetary logoi in our solar system. But it's more than the physical planets: "Planets" here also refers to the seven planetary spheres (known in Qabala as seven of the ten Sefiroth) or dimensions of reality and consciousness; these are the archetypes of the seven human chakras.

Thus the Elohim's work with Hephaistos through the 144 Sun temples in the Earth grid uniformly affects all living creatures and all organic planetary life.

See also: Balor of the Evil Eye, Dolorous Stroke, Giants, Hitching Post of the Sun.

DA DERGA'S HOSTEL

An aspect of the inner heart chakra expressed outwardly as a geomantic feature, a celestial residence of spiritual adepts participating in the bliss and perpetual presence of the Christ Consciousness.

Also known as *Ananda-kanda* chakra, Elysian Fields, Elysium, Jeweled Altar, Valhalla.

Description: Irish myth recounts several inns (*bruiden*), residences, banqueting halls, and sumptuous residences, possibly otherworldly in nature, called hostels. A well-known bruiden is the *Brugh na Boinne*, Boand's Hostel, or the Inn on the River Boyne, near Dublin, known today as Newgrange. An Irish tale called *The Destruction of Da Derga's Hostel* describes the awesome guests at Da Derga's inn on the River Dodder in Leinster just before it is ruined by invading pirates. Da Derga is the "Chief Hospitall" in all of Eriu, Ireland's ancient, original name.

Conaire Mor, King of Ireland at the Hill of Tara, a ruler who brought peace and plenty to

Ireland, travels with his retinue to Da Derga's Hostel to collect a debt of hospitality owed the King for an earlier favor. The hostel is an enormous building: It has seven doorways with seven rooms built between every two doorways; 17 of Conaire's chariots stand at every door, and if you're outside looking in, you can see the hearth fires through the chariot wheels.

The company assembled at Da Derga's Hostel is formidable: nine immortal pipers from *Sidhe Bregia* (an otherworldly fortress); Mac Cecht, Conaire's champion whose sword stands 30 feet high and whose eyes are like two large lakes next to a mountain (his nose); the Fomorians, ancient giants with three heads and 300 teeth apiece; Tulchinne the Juggler, who carries nine swords in his hand, nine silver shields, and nine golden apples; the three chief champions, each of whose limbs is as thick as a man's waist and whose lances will kill nine men at one throw; and Da Derga himself, red-haired with a green cloak, who has been constantly boiling food for the men of Eriu in a cauldron that has never been taken from the fire since he opened his inn.

Explanation: Irish myth is describing the psychic perception of an assemblage of the Great White Brotherhood in another dimension, though accessible to ours through openings in Earth's visionary geography.

Norse myth calls this feature a Valhalla, Odin's Hall of the Slain. In Norse myth, 432,000 Einherjar, warriors slain in battle and selected by the Valkyries at Odin's request, are brought to Valhalla for endless feasting and drinking. The Einherjar are "lone fighters," spiritual adepts who have mastered themselves, their body, matter, and consciousness, and have been elected into the Great White Brotherhood; this is a vast conclave of enlightened sages, spiritual adepts, angels, and benign intelligences from other star systems that supervise human evolution, as well as larger affairs of the solar system, galaxy, and universe.

The Einherjar, or, in Irish language, the guests of Da Derga's Hostel, are indeed prodigies of battle, but the battle is against unconsciousness and ignorance. Some, like the three-headed Fomorians, are angels in metaphoric disguise; others, like the various shield-bearers, cup-bearers, harpers, pipers, swordsmen, are Great White Brotherhood members of various specialties.

Da Derga's Hostel is the chief Hospitaller in all Eriu and his hearth fire has never ceased to boil food in his cauldron because it is the Christ Consciousness that is served at his inn. More precisely, the champions feasting in Da Derga's Hostel partake of the inexhaustible Boar of Christ Consciousness; it is a kind of *agape* or Eucharistic celebration of spiritual peers in service to the highest good. In Norse myth, the boar whose flesh is perpetually consumed and renewed is called Saehrimnir, and it is a vivid metaphor for the Christ Consciousness.

Da Derga's Hostel is both an excellent metaphoric description of a geomantic feature in Earth's visionary geography and a specific example of it. Irish myth gives the name of five Hostels, including Da Derga's, and the topographic location of these is more or less known today by archeologists. These five Hostels are otherwordly or astral in nature, however, though they may be accessed in a visionary sense at the specific landscape sites given for them.

There are 360 Hostels, or Valhallas, found across the Earth's surface where one may witness and even partake in, to a degree, the endless feasting of the spiritual champions. Some locations include Monticello in Charlottesville, Virginia; Rondvassbhu, Rondane Mountains, in Norway; Ivy Thorn Hill, Glastonbury, England; Saint Paul's Cathedral, Ludgate Hill, London, England.

Da Derga's Hostel may appear to clairvoyant perception as a vast sports stadium filled with 432,000 enlightened sages resembling thousands of sparkling, sun-drenched jewels. This geomantic feature is an inherent part of the inner heart chakra, called *Ananda-kanda,* expressed in both the human and planet. One of the esoteric features of this chakra is a jeweled altar, which is a precise visual metaphor for the sports stadium of 432,000 sparkling, differently hued adepts.

You can access this arcane aspect of your own inner heart chakra through visionary expeditions into the outer, projected form of the same at the 360 locations on Earth and thereby participate in the unending bliss (feasting) and perpetual presence of the Christ Consciousness enjoyed by the Einherjar.

See also: Einherjar, Eriu, Glass Mountain, Saehrimnir, Seven Rishis, Valhalla.

DJINN

The repudiated early version of humanity, now inhabiting a lower astral realm close to physical reality, awaiting redemption along with Iblis, their fallen, repudiated chief; one of two prototypes for humanity.

Also known as Afrits, Antigods, Asura, Genies, Kings of Edom, Raksasas, Shaytans.

Description: A class of supernatural beings as described by the Islamic tradition, the Djinn are said to have been created before humanity by Allah from the Saharan wind called the simoon or from smokeless fire; existing somewhere between the angels and humans, as a group they rebelled against the divine order and set out to perpetrate violence and evil against the rest of creation.

Iblis (also called Azazel, a fallen angel) is their leader and Lord of the Djinn; in Morocco, he's known as Chaarmarouch. Iblis is also called the king of the Shaytans (Satans), another name for the Djinn in their capacity of leading embodied humans into sin and temptation. The Djinn lived for 25,000 years on Earth but increasingly flaunted the divine laws. Islamic lore says the Djinn now live in an intermediate, immaterial subtle realm *(alam al-malakut)*.

Typically they are humanlike in appearance, but they are said to be shape-shifters as well, appearing either beautiful or deformed or in whatever illusory disguise they choose. The Djinn can be either friendly or hostile to humans, but, generally, they are believed to be malevolent toward humanity in most cases, inhabiting isolated or ruined places, such as the desert.

The Djinn were also known as Shaytans, a race of evil spirits resembling humans who once possessed the Earth until they disobeyed and flaunted the divine laws and were destroyed by an army of angels. They are dangerous because they are strong, unpredictable, and well versed in black magic.

Judaic legend says once King Solomon summoned the Djinn to appear before him to see what they looked like. They appeared in great numbers in the form of bizarre hybrid animals with two heads or that breathed fire. Mastering the Djinn, King Solomon had them perform many useful tasks, such as building, mining, diving for pearls, collecting jewels, and crafting metals. Islamic lore says there are Djinn still alive today in the subtle world who were alive in the time of the Prophet Muhammad; he converted a party of Djinn in the desert and exacted an oath of allegiance from them at the spot called Mosque of the Djinn in Mecca.

Explanation: The Djinn were created before humans as we know ourselves today, as the Supreme Being's first attempt to create humanity. The Djinn were one of two prototypes (see Yeti) created before humanity was perfected. Lilith, Adam's rebellious first wife, was a Djinn, but here Adam must be understood as the spiritual template of the incarnate human and Lilith, and the Djinn as the first attempt to fill this template with a free-will consciousness. Essentially, the Supreme Being tried to make conscious, self-aware beings in material form, didn't quite get it right, and had to abandon the first issue.

Due to their violent, world-damaging excesses from a free will unchecked by morality or limits compounded by vast psychic abilities through mastery of the seven chakras and their occult powers (called *siddhis*), the Supreme Being aborted His first creation and banished the Djinn to a lower astral realm (or trapped them between this world and the next), there to await their eventual release and redemption by a tamer, more controlled second humanity.

The Djinn are still imprisoned or bound into the Earth at 3,496 geomantic sites called Lucifer Binding Sites, Lucifer being another name for Iblis. Examples of such sites are Tiahuanaco, Bolivia; Dome of the Rock, Jerusalem, Israel; Mount Damavand, Iran; and Lincoln Cathedral, Lincoln, England.

As Lucifer is gradually unbound at these sites by humans, a contingent of Djinn is also simultaneously unbound and redeemed (forgiven) at the same site. Their length of imprisonment is determined by the rate at which humanity can forgive and release them. The forgiveness is required because the Djinn's excesses led to a significant reduction in human psychic freedom and cognitive access as a way of preventing the Djinn excesses from happening again in us.

A portion of Lucifer (1/3496th) and a number of Djinn were bound at each of the 3,496 sites as a way of containing, limiting, and even eclipsing their influence on humanity; thus both Iblis (Lucifer) and the Djinn entered the unacknowledged Shadow of the Earth and humanity.

If the Djinn pose any present danger to humans it is a psychic one—their siren call from the lower astral world is to replicate their physical indulgences. This is the meaning of the reference to Iblis as king of the Shaytans who seek to lead humanity into sin and temptation; they can project enticing visions of the pleasures or excesses of the flesh and psychic power into human minds, entreating us to follow the old lifestyle of the Djinn on their behalf.

See also: Adam, Asura, Fall of Man, Kings of Edom, Lucifer, Raksasas, Tower of Babel.

DOLOROUS STROKE

A momentous transition from first to second generation humanity, occasioning a deep wounding in the ability to remember divine origins and purpose, and have easy access to cosmic consciousness.

Also known as Pandora's Box, Expulsion from Paradise, Fall of Man, Loss of the Divine Name, Wasteland.

Description: The term "Dolorous Stroke" comes from the medieval European legends of the Holy Grail and the Knights of the Round Table. The variously named Fisher King or Grail King (Varlan, Brulen, Pellam, Anfortas) grievously wounds himself with the Sword of David due to a lack of knowledge of its proper use. The Sword of David came from the giant Goliath whom David overcame; it was handed down through generations to the Fisher King.

Explanation: The giant Goliath is a coded sign for the Elohim, an angelic family temporarily in human, though giant, form and charged with tutoring early humanity in divine knowledge and practices. David did not overcome and slay Goliath; rather, he mastered the teachings offered him by the Elohim and thus earned the right to wield the sword because he could do so responsibly.

The sword here stands for the array of psychic powers and magical abilities *(siddhis)* that come with the awakening of kundalini (the gods' fire, in Greek myth) illuminating the chakras in an embodied human with free will. It is sometimes called the Word Sword, suggesting spoken incantations or the power of speech to shape reality. Without expert and strict tutoring, it's only a matter of time before this power gets abused and people start getting hurt. The Stroke is also insight used for oneself in a separatist sense, rather than insight used for the good of many with the interests of the individual self secondary.

The wounding of the once Rich Fisher King, who now becomes the Wounded Fisher King, is actually a punishment and limitation, not an injury. The excesses perpetrated on the world and humanity by the undisciplined use of the Sword of Goliath (i.e., divine knowledge of the Elohim) led to the curtailment of the possibility of its use. The injury (the Fisher King wounds himself in the upper thigh or groin, i.e., the root chakra) means consciousness cannot complete the intended circuit of root chakra to crown chakra and the corresponding flow of the gods' fire (kundalini) through it, illuminating all.

The Dolorous Stroke symbolizes this ontological change of status. In a sense, it was the last stroke permitted humanity with this sword of the gods. Equally, the Supreme Being wounded humanity in the root chakra, which is to say, diminished the potency of the kundalini circuit, or simply toned it down.

The consequence of the Dolorous Stroke was the emergence of the Wasteland. Outwardly, a once fertile, Edenic land became barren and fruitless; inwardly, a once unsundered unity with God and the spiritual worlds was broken, and consciousness dried up, aware of only the physical world. The consequences are dolorous because humans can no longer remember their divine origin and thus live in an existential wasteland devoid of purpose.

The Dolorous Stroke and the inception of the Wasteland inaugurated the quest for the Holy Grail and the emergence of the perfected, Christed Grail Knight who could use the Grail to heal the Wounded Fisher King and restore the land to vibrancy. The story marks the transition from open-ended consciousness of the first generation of humanity to the limitations and requirements for spiritual practice in the next.

An allegorical way of interpreting the Dolorous Stroke is through the Masonic and Judiac accounts of the loss of the Builder's Word or Divine Name. Qabalists say that, since the Jewish Exile, the correct pronunciation of the Divine Name or Omnific Word has been lost. Once the high priests knew how to pronounce the consonants and vowel points in *YHVH*, but now they know only the consonants, which are like the outer shell of the great Mystery of the Name.

The importance of knowing how to pronounce the Name in full is that it has a mighty creative power, it is a Word Sword that generates or changes reality. Presently the divine Word Sword is broken; it was fragmented by the Dolorous Stroke, a misuse of its powers, and then a gradual forgetting of the pronunciation.

Various façade words are used instead, such as *Jehovah* or *Tetragrammaton*, but when, someday, humankind recovers the correct pronunciation, we will once again know the secret of our eternal essence, be one with God's power, and competently and responsibly command the divine forces latent in us.

The story of the Dolorous Stroke is akin to the Greek tale of Pandora's Box and the biblical account of the expulsion from the Garden of Eden and the Fall. It is equivalent also to the Egyptian myth of the dismemberment of Osiris into 14 pieces scattered across Egypt; this is also the fragmented Word Sword.

See also: Antichrist, Fall of Man, Fisher King, Garden of Eden, Grail Castle, Grail Knight, Holy Grail, Klingsor, Pandora's Box, Tower of Babel, Wasteland.

DRAGON

A celestial being who acts as a reservoir for prime creative force and the Waters of Life, with multiple geomantic expressions on Earth.

Also known as drake, knucker, serpent, walm, worm, wyvern.

Description: Many of the major myth systems of the world, such as Greek, Celtic, Teutonic, Norse, and Chinese, have tales of dragons and dragon-slayers.

Norse myth says a single massive dragon called Midgardsormr, or Midgard Serpent, lies coiled around the planet, its tail in its vast gaping mouth. Greek myth once said Ophion, the world serpent, lay coiled seven times around the world egg laid by the goddess Eurynome as the precursor for planet Earth.

Various culture heroes made their reputations or secured boons or safety for humanity by slaying dragons. The Greek Olympian god Apollo slew Delphyne or Pytho at Delphi, making the site fit to be his oracular shrine. Cadmus killed a dragon at Thebes; Herakles killed Ladon who was guarding the golden apples in the Gardens of the Hesperides, possibly in Libya. Siegfried (Sigurd) killed Fafnir, who guarded one of the world's jewel treasures. The Russian *bogatyr* Dobrynya dispatched Goryshche who was threatening to destroy Kiev. England's patron saint Saint George killed numerous dragons as did Saint Michael (and his archangelic mentor), often dedicating sacred sites as the result.

The Aztec brothers-heroes Quetzalcoatl and Tezcatlipoca, at the beginning of time and creation, subdued the Earth Monster Tlaltecuhtli, who had gaping mouths on her face, knees, elbows, and other joints. They tore her in half: One half they hurled upward to become the sky; the other became the Earth's surface and out of it came all of Earth's natural features, such as mountains, rivers, springs, and the entire plant kingdom.

Usually the dragon threatens public safety, killing and sometimes eating the unfortunate who approach their dens, or sometimes demanding virgins as sacrifices to keep them from destroying on a greater level. Typically the dragon lives in a cave, or sometimes in a dark pool or lake, and he sits on a great treasure, most often jewels, gold, and precious objects made from them.

Some areas seem to have a preponderance of dragon legends, such as England, which has, by some estimates, 80 dragon legends specific to localities, such as the Lambton Worm, the Dragon of Wantley, the Knucker of Lyminster, Linton Worm, Mordiford Wyvern, Longwitton Dragon, and many more. Often the local landscape names reflect the dragon legends, such as Walmsgate, Worm's Den, Wormhill, Knucker Hole, Wormstall, and Serpent Mound (Ohio).

Certain municipalities and even the seats of royalty or kingship have been established where a dragon has been slain. For example, the ancient royal family of Maui in Hawaii established its seat at Lahaina, home of the dragon Kihawahine; Babylon was founded seemingly on the back of a dragon called Mushussu, slain by the local god Marduk, but whose mammoth coiled body remained under Babylon's Ishtar Gate; Wawel Hill in Cracow, Poland, is the former den of the dragon Smok Wawelski.

One early epithet for Thebes, founded by Cadmus, was City of the Dragon. This dragon was considered the offspring of Ares, the Olympian war god, and he guarded the Spring of Ares. He had a golden crest, his eyes flashed fire, he was filled with poison, his tongue had three forks, and he was as large as the dragon (Draco) lying between the two Bears in the sky, that is, Ursa Major and Ursa Minor.

Dragons specific to a landscape are not always named, but in the Norse legends about Yggdrasil, or World Tree, eight dragons are named—Ogoncho, Graback, Goin, Svafnir, Grafvolluth, Ofnir, Moin, Grafvitnir—and said to lie coiled about the base of this massive, towering tree of the high god, Odin.

On the cosmic level, dragons are implicated in the creation of the world and in hindering the flow of necessary water into it. In the Hindu myths, Sesa-Ananta is the thousand-headed dragon who is older than Creation; in between vast cycles of Creation called Pralaya (in the West, Flood or Deluge), Vishnu (the Hindu version of Christ) dreams atop Sesa-Ananta who floats on the cosmic sea. Later in the unfoldment of the world, Indra, king of the Hindu gods, slays Vrtra, another form of the cosmic dragon who is withholding the Waters of Life.

Not only gods and culture heroes are credited with slaying dragons, but in Christian lore at least 40 saints are praised for having killed formidable dragons.

The English word dragon is derived from the Greek *drakon* or *draconta* and the Latin *draco*. The general sense of these words is "to watch or look at," probably a way of depicting the dragon as ever wakefully guarding something. Probably the ultimate dragon expression in the West is the constellation Draco, which asymmetrically coils about the celestial North Pole. The Olympian goddess

Athena reportedly first hurled Draco from Earth to Heaven where he continued his life as a constellation.

Depending on where you live in the world, dragons are either dangerous, destructive, immoral, and evil (the West), or benevolent, morally upstanding protector beings (the East). Revelation characterizes the "great red dragon" of the Apocalypse as having seven heads and seven horns. Typically, dragons are described as resembling immensely large winged lizards rather than snakes; they are scaly, almost entirely impregnable to swords; they have two horns, massive wings, and forked tails; they exhale spumes of fire.

They prefer the dark and dank, such as caves or pools, yet oddly, they often communicate intelligently with their slayers. When Siegfried slew Fafnir and tasted a mere drop of his blood, he became suddenly able to understand the speech of the birds. Curiously, Fafnir was once a giant who assumed dragon form to protect a vast treasure horde at Gnita-heid. Similarly, Sesa-Ananta was once a celestial being of seeming human stature who was asked by Brahma the Creator to be the dragon upon which he would place the entire world as the prime support.

Explanation: The biggest and truest statement one can make about dragons is that they are real and are legitimate, mandated aspects of Earth's energy body. Dragons exist within Earth's visionary geography at four levels and total 1,067.

First, the Midgard Serpent (equivalent to the Aztec Earth Monster) encircles the planet just as the myths tell; one Norse name for it is revealing: *Jormungrundr,* which means "huge monster," yet the same word also refers to the Earth as "mighty ground." The Midgard Serpent is wrapped around the planet in a single massive coil; its head sits approximately at the South Pacific Ocean around Polynesia. Its face appears like a generic human one, though exaggerated and puffed out; it has a huge nose and mouth. Its eyes are jewels, its body golden, and it is both benevolent and scary to behold.

On the second tier of dragons are 13 major or primary ones. Selected locations include Uluru (Ayer's Rock; see Rainbow Serpent) near Alice Springs, Australia; the Tor, Glastonbury, Somerset, England; Silbury Hill, Wiltshire, England; the Serpent Mound at Locust Grove in Ohio, Grand Canyon in Arizona, and Fajada Butte at Chaco Canyon in New Mexico, all in the United States; and Delphi, Greece.

Each of these 13 dragons produces up to 81 progeny by way of eggs. Some of these secondary dragons are hatched and active, others not. Those dragon eggs among the 1,053 secondary dragons that have been hatched also have been "slain," for the two expressions are equivalent even if initially different.

Selected locations include the sites mentioned here in relation to dragon-slaying, as well as some surprises: Tintagel in Cornwall, England; three at the Lake Tahoe area in California, including one at the Lake (north end), one at Spooner Valley, another at D. L. Bliss State Park; Bell Rock, near Sedona, Arizona; Dinas Emrys (Snowdonia), Wales; Uturoa, Raiatea in French Polynesia; Mount Pilatus, Wilser, Switzerland; and Mont-Saint-Michel, Brittany, France.

The fourth level of dragon is mostly one of potential in the form of dragon eggs intended for humans and other sentient life forms on Earth, such as dolphins and whales, and even some "species" not in recognizable form. These eggs were laid by the 1,067 dragons in the earliest days of the Earth and total 49×49^7, or more than 33 trillion, presumably enough for every soul who will ever inhabit Earth.

The overseer of the four dragon realms is the original cosmic dragon, known by many names. The constellation Draco is its outer form and expression. Some of its guises have been recorded in the myths about Leviathan, Sesa-Ananta, Tiamat, Vrtra, and others.

Dragons do many things for the Earth. The Midgard Serpent is a reservoir of cosmic energy (the withheld "waters" that Vrtra released) also known as kundalini. The 13 major dragons also hold and release vital cosmic life force for Earth. These two tiers of dragons are interacted with solely by the 14 Ray Masters of the Great Bear, known in Hindu myth, for example, as the Seven Rishis. The Ray Masters (see Seven Rishis) ground their celestial energies and Rays through the dragons and help them release their energies ("waters") into the Earth grid.

A clear example of this from British folk legend is that Saint George killed a dragon at Dragon Hill, just below Uffington Castle on the Ridgeway in Oxfordshire, England. The dragon's venomous blood soaked the land so that no grass grows there and his carcass is buried under the hill. Saint George is a culturally shaped description of one of the 14 Ray Masters, all "dragon-slayers." (The Dragon Hill dragon, incidentally, is one of the planet's 13 primary dragons.)

One way to visualize this is to think of the Rainbow Serpent, one of the Australian Aborigines' names for the dragon at Uluru. The Rainbow Serpent is an excellent metaphor for the electromagnetic field spectrum of light, another nuance to the Waters of Life that Vrtra and all "slain" dragons release into the world.

Dragons guard temples and geomantic features such as Golden Apples, as well as specialized geomantic installations such as the Golden Fleece at Colchis near the Black Sea (in today's Republic of Georgia). They protect the national watcher angels (known as egregors; see Marduk) for countries or continents and their landscapes; 81 dragons are devoted to this assignment.

They are associated with spirallic energy lines (sometimes called ley lines) coming out of domes (see Holy Mountain), etheric energy canopies over mountains that comprise a major part of the Earth's geomantic equipment.

Usually, any of the 1,053 secondary dragons are found at the larger dome caps, which are subsidiary dome-like energy centers arrayed in orderly fashion like flower petals out from the central, very bright "blossom" of the dome.

Dragons are not slain; they are encountered and assimilated by trained geomantic experts, remembered in myth as dragon-slayers. When you can master the dragon within you (the lower self; the kundalini in the root chakra and the primordial personality and drives based on this), and you do this at a landscape dragon site (at one of the 1,053 secondary dragons), then this activates the geomantic dragon and allows the celestial light from the dome to flow through the spirallic dome lines to the dragon, illuminating him in place.

This, in turn, illuminates the local physical landscape, all of Nature, and human consciousness and culture. The dragon is no longer a subliminal threat to psychic and social stability, but a benevolent illuminator of life and culture.

Similarly of benefit to the local landscape and of considerable spiritual benefit to the humans undertaking this is to hatch one's own dragon egg. It is an operation that takes time, months or years, and will put you in front of a representation of the human dragon, that is, the chakra system of seven major energy-consciousness centers and their seven subaspects each, totaling 49.

These 49 and the totality of the system make 50, a mystical threshold in many wisdom teachings, called, for example, the 50 Gates of Wisdom (or Binah). Anciently, initiates having passed a certain level of training were called Dragons. Drinking the dragon's blood is another way of saying one has mastered the 50 Gates; Siegfried understanding the "speech of the birds" means he became clairvoyant and understood the communications among the angelic orders.

As for the treasure the dragon guards in his cave, experientially, one finds the treasure hoard is actually inside the dragon itself, and he offers a little of it voluntarily as a gift for good-faith geomantic interactions with him by humans.

The Judaic tradition both disparages the cosmic dragon and gives it a prime role in the times after Judgment Day. Called Lotan, Leviathan, and Rahab, the primordial dragon of the deep cosmic sea, even though a tyrant with seven heads during Creation and human time on Earth, in the future will be the divine flesh served at the feast of the righteous in Heaven. This is another way of saying one day our limited human consciousness will be reunited with the full panoply, or we will eat continuously, joyously of full cosmic awareness (Leviathan's flesh).

This is consistent with the Hindu explanation of Sesa-Ananta as the "Remainder," the residue of consciousness from the previous cycle of creation. He embodies undying consciousness, the rich flesh or waters of immortality, and the *prima materia* from which our universe and everything in it were created.

The most probable reason for the general level of disappreciation and pejoratives thrown at dragons in the West is due to a cultural and religious unwillingness to undertake the awakening of kundalini, or even to acknowledge its existence or potential in humans. That energy was presumably judged dangerous to culture.

See also: Dreamtime, Golden Apple, Golden Fleece, Flood, Holy Mountain, Hurqalya, Leviathan, Marduk, Pele, Quetzalcoatl, Rainbow Serpent, Seven Rishis, Tezcatlipoca, Zep Tepi.

DREAMTIME

The mystical, geomythic, primordial realm in which all the planet's features and its visionary geography were first templated by the gods.

Also known as Akngantentye, Altjeringa, Altyerre, Creation Time, Dome Presence, Faëry, Fairyland, First Occasion, First Time, Golden Age, Ngarranggarni, Panaleri Time, Satya-yuga, Tjukurrpa, Yemurraki, Zep Tepi.

Description: Dreamtime is a Western scholars' interpretation of a variety of different tribal names from the Australian Aborigines for a primordial creative time on Earth when all species, features of the landscape, and humanity were emerging from the thoughts, or dreams, or the gods, and may still be accessed. It is an identical concept to the classical Egyptian First Occasion, or Zep Tepi.

Sample Aboriginal names for the Dreamtime include *Yemurraki,* which means the distant past, Dreamtime legend; *Ngarranggarni,* the "long ago"; *Altyerre,* the time of the Dreaming or creation of the world and its things; *Akngantentye,* the dreaming associated with a particular thing, such as rain. Other names include *Altjeringa, Tjukurrpa,* Creation Time, or *Panaleri* Time.

The Dreamtime, as Western interpreters explain it, refers to the mystical or dreamlike moment outside of normal mundane time in which all the features of the Earth, its species, terrain, and humanity, were created. It is the time when the primeval ancestors, or the gods, did their Dreaming of things into being, dropping them like eggs or infants or seeds through the Dreaming spots in the landscape from their realm into the human, material one.

The Aborigines call this original "seed power" deposited in the landscape *jiva* or *guruwari.* Similarly, they say every feature of the landscape is a symbolic physical footprint left by the metaphysical ancestors as a result of their creative actions. The spiritual power of a landscape site is correlated with the memory it maintains of its own origin, its Dreaming, which, in turn, is a guide to ritual.

In Western terms, the Dreaming of a place, or its innate memory of its own origin, is equivalent to the myth in the landscape, as in a god did this here then. The Dreamtime is a landscape of deep memory where every site has a geomyth.

Such places were afterward known as Kangaroo Dreaming, Wombat Dreaming, Thorny Devil Dreaming, among many others. For example, Wagyal is the great ancestral being of the Nyungar people of Australia. The Wagyal is a primordial snake deity who created everything in the Nyungar domain in the Dreamtime and who can be contacted any time through appropriate ritual.

The Wandjina are the spirit ancestors of the Kimberley region, who walked the world long ago in human form, their heads encircled by thunder and lightning, their bodies enclothed in rain, creating everything, naming plants and animals, and leaving their images on the walls of caves and other sites. Such places are *wunggud*, places of concentrated Earth potency and life force.

During the Dreamtime, the variety of ancestors roamed the virginal land, forming the landscape's features, creating the plants and animals out of the original archetypes. Where the ancestors traveled became Dreaming tracks, or songlines. These are both sacred tracks across the primordial landscape and sound currents left by the creative ancestors; the sacrality of the Dreamtime landscape can be reinvoked by using these sounds in ceremonies, legend says.

Where the ancestors camped, they often left little bundles of stones called *Churinga* containing a residual of their immortal souls. Their campsites became known as *Knanikilla*, or totem centers, later vital for ritual. The Aborigines regarded the Churinga as numinous reminders of the ever-present ancestors from the Dreamtime; in fact, the entire landscape was a vast Churinga—in Western terms, a nonstop theophany, or revelation of the gods.

The gods taught the first humans the rules of life, that is, the protocols of maintaining harmony between Heaven and Earth. The ancient Egyptians called this divine order, rightness, and justice *maat*, and they personified it as well as a beautiful winged goddess, Maat (see Zep Tepi).

The concept of Dreamtime implies the recognition of a preexistent interconnected web among all created things, creatures, and landscapes. Another name the Aborigines use for the fundamental creative energy of the Dreamtime is *djang* (also *malagi*). They understand it to be the spiritual power that sustains, even organizes, life and consciousness and they invoke and recharge it in rituals and dances originally taught by the ancestors.

Sacred places are sites with strong djang, presanctified and energized by the ancestors; djang is the stored-up primal spiritual power, left latent in certain locations by the creative ancestors for their descendants to access through rituals. This concept is similar to the Egyptian description of Pay Lands or Blessed Islands created in the Beginning by the sounds of the gods and still accessible through ceremonies performed in human-made temples erected at the sites.

A site with strong djang is likened to a powerful battery that constantly emits energy to keep species flourishing and the landscape vital and healthy. These sites, called *Thalu* places (or *Tala* places), must be maintained by humans through regular ritual for the benefit of all living creatures around them; the term Walkabout refers to deliberate, regular pilgrimages made by Aborigines to their totemically assigned Dreaming places to conduct revivifying ceremonies.

Explanation: Dreamtime refers to the totality of the design and the purity of the original template of Earth's visionary geography, known to most Westerners, at best sketchily, as the array of sacred sites and power points. It is both the gods' state of mind in which they laid down the sacred sites terrain and the arresting geomythic reality of that realm to contemporary human experience. It refers to the planet's Light body, a placental, multidimensional web of light and sound that encases and nourishes the physical planet.

The Dreamtime is the geomythic moment outside time (like the time between the completion of a newly built house and the arrival of its occupants) when all the planet's sacred sites are pristine, fully functional, open for business. It is also the complete, experienceable map (and rationality) of the original planetary design and the methods and goals of the terraforming of its body.

The totemic tales of the Wagyal, Wandjina, and the numerous Dreaming places and ancestor camps in the landscape are accounts of terraforming, equivalent to other reports from, for example, the Irish mythic canon when the primordial gods, Tuatha de Danann, created and shaped the Irish landscape.

Originally, the Earth's visionary geography, an array of 100+ different geomantic features, with multiple copies of each, was an organizing template laid down for physical reality and human consciousness by the Earth's designers. The geography was installed to work in flexible, interactive alignment and harmony with the galaxy, but it required regular human intervention, through ritual or focused acts of consciousness, to keep it healthy and vital.

In practical Western terms, the Dreamtime is the master blueprint for the workings, mechanics, and interrelationships of what's variously called Earth's interactive energy body, grid, terrain of sacred sites, or visionary geography. Equivalently, it is the Earth Spirit's, or Gaia's, lucid dream of her own body.

In Western European lore, entering the Dreamtime was known, if only sketchily, as entering Faëry or Fairyland, a dreamlike place of supernaturals.

The various Aboriginal terms, such as *djang, wunggud, Churinga, Knanikilla, malagi,* Dreaming places, and songlines, all attest to the primordial purity, potency, and rationality of this galaxy-Earth matrix. When the ancestors taught the First People (a self-referential term used by the Aborigines), implicit in that teaching was the perception that the system was orderly and purposeful.

The time period indicated by the Dreamtime was about 27 million years. That is about how long it took to get all the conditions correct and ready for life on Earth, such as installing and regulating the 100+ different geomantic features.

During this period, the Holy Mountains were being prepared by way of their activation by extraterrestrial devices overlaid on them called domes. Domes were etheric energy canopies brought to Earth from elsewhere in the galaxy, distributed around the planet in accordance with star patterns as a way of creating and nourishing the Earth's etheric structure. The domes shaped the Earth's etheric web by imposing on it a conscious matrix—the overall distribution pattern—that would enable conscious-being evolution.

The domes, devices in between matter and light, came three times to the Earth to reaffirm and energize the intended distribution pattern. Each visit was called a Dome Presence: During the first, there was no human life on Earth; during the second, there was primitive human life; during the third, some humans were able to see the domes and interact with their occupants.

The Dreamtime encompasses all three Dome Presences, the time when the visionary geography was templated, nourished, activated, and made ready.

See also: Atlas, Brigit's Mantle, Gaia, Ghost Dance, Hollow Hill, Holy Mountain, Hurqalya, Hyperboreans, Land of Milk and Honey, Ley Lines, Monster-Slayer, Rainbow Serpent, Tuatha de Danann, White Mount, Zep Tepi.

EARTH CHANGES

Profound shifts in the parameters of physical and psychological reality with the goal of realigning humanity with the planet.

Also known as Apocalypse, Armageddon, End Times, Judgment Day, Ragnarok, Second Advent.

Description: Since the prophecies of Edgar Cayce in the 1930s and 1940s, many psychics have predicted or "foreseen" radical physical changes in the landscape of Earth. Geological upsets, increased volcanism, major weather and climate shifts, continental upheavals and breakups, fires, natural disasters, floods, the sinking of islands, the encroachment of the oceans upon the coasts—such are the types of Earth changes forecast by a variety of intuitives in recent years.

The psychics also forecast that these massive and seemingly apocalyptic physical Earth Changes are the outer material aspect of significant transformations in consciousness sweeping through a certain portion of the population as part of a planetary movement toward a time of enlightenment.

So pervasive has the belief in or expectation of Earth Changes become among some segments of modern society that the term itself has become a myth.

Astrologers tend to correlate Earth Changes with the imminence of the 2,150-year period in which our Sun, and thus planetary conditions, are under the influence of the constellation and zodiacal house of Aquarius. New Age followers tend to associate Earth Changes with the end of the Mayan Calendar in 2012.

Explanation: The concept of Earth Changes has become a grim though strangely popular scenario or future mock-up among white, educated Westerners. Increasingly, the forecasts for Earth Changes have been taken literally and as immutable, almost as if many people want this kind of drastic disruption to physical reality. The fact that most psychic predictions of Earth Changes leave out is that they are negotiable. Apocalyptic forecasts are only pictures of a possible future.

For the most part, global humanity has fallen out of congruence with the Spirit of the Earth known popularly as Gaia. Gaia is the ultimate landscape angel for our planet, charged by the spiritual world with maintaining a certain level of consciousness across the planet, maintaining organic life, and helping the various species living upon Her, primarily humans, to reach certain evolutionary levels.

In the past, radical Earth Changes have happened on the planet; the geological record and residual evidence are fairly incontrovertible. Whether they will happen again in the twenty-first century to that same extent is uncertain. It is a question of whether such drastic measures are *necessary* to shock humanity into reestablishing and maintaining spiritual and material congruence with Gaia.

One fact should always be borne in mind regarding Earth Changes: They are *purposeful,* designed events, planned in advance and executed with caution and compassion by Gaia in conjunction with her myriad landscape angels (see Nymph), the Great White Brotherhood (see Einherjar), and the angelic hierarchies and in agreement at a soul level with the humans who will perish.

Redefining landmass boundaries is not the purpose of Earth Changes nor their likely or necessary result, though some landmass changes will occur. The more important focus is to shake humanity into a more wakeful attitude to the planet, divesting many people of some of their complacent atheist materialism.

The risk of overemphasizing major physical trauma to the planet is that one can easily miss observing the radical Earth Changes already under way. The spiritual or energetic parameters of physical reality and human self-identity have been shifting, in fact, molting and morphing, in the past four decades.

One emphasis of the purposeful Earth Changes is to undo the Wasteland, a mythic term to describe a condition of spiritual entropy and ignorance of the true parameters of life as a human on Earth. Similarly, Earth Changes seek to unfasten the bonds of the Antichrist, whose energy is wrapped around the planet in a dark grid of threads, ropes, and anchor points. Third, Earth Changes seek to realign humanity with the Spirit of the Earth, Gaia, the ultimate landscape angel for the planet, and Her host of subsidiary devas.

The ancient Norse predictions for a future apocalypse called Ragnarok, or the Twilight or Final End of the Gods, is a useful metaphor: We are already living in Ragnarok, but it is in slow motion, easy to miss because the changes are incremental, though inexorable. As more light incarnates on the Earth, time speeds up, lives go faster, changes come quicker, and reality accelerates. Already many people have experienced the fourth dimension and all its causal paradoxes. The Shadow, both individual and collective—all the nasty, suppressed bits about oneself or a nation—confronts people today whether they want it or not.

The approach of the long-term astrological influence of Aquarius is important, but equally so is a profound change in the geometrical energy field encasing the Earth. It is morphing from one classically defined shape (a geometric figure comprising the five Platonic Solids, unique regular polyhedra) to another (one of the 13 Archimedean Solids, more complex polyhedra). This restructuring of the Earth's subtle geometric nest is affecting everything in physical reality.

The world event called the Harmonic Convergence, in which an estimated several million people assembled for days in August 1987 at sacred sites around the planet, marked an "opening shot" in the realignment of humanity with the Earth. It is an excellent example of a voluntary, proactive approach to Earth Changes.

See also: Antichrist, Candlemas, Gaia, Ghost Dance, Grail Knight, Harmonic Convergence, Klingsor, Michaelmas, Ragnarok, Wasteland, Wild Hunt.

EINHERJAR

Spiritual adepts and post-humans who have mastered and slain the lower self and touched a God aspect within themselves to become members of the Great White Brotherhood, the world's spiritual government.

Also known as the Ascended Host, Ascended Masters, Brotherhood of the Grail, Brotherhood of Light, Grail Guardians, Great Ones, Great White Brotherhood, Legion of Light, Lords of the Flame, Lords of Light, Mahantas, Occult Hierarchy, Perfected Beings, Perfected Ones, Rishis, Siddhas, Solar Fathers (Pitris).

Description: The word "Einherjar" is from Old Norse and means "those who fight alone" and refers to those slain in battle and brought to Valhalla, the high god Odin's Hall of the Slain in Norse myth. Valhalla (Old Norse: *Valholl,* "Hall of the Slain") is a warrior's paradise in which the Einherjar spend their days redoing battles then, hale and unharmed again in the evenings, feasting on meat from the divine boar Saehrimnir and mead from the divine goat Heidrun, served to them by the Valkyries.

The key fact about the Einherjar is that at Ragnarok, the Norse conception of the Twilight of the Gods or the Christian Last Judgment Day, they will go into battle with the gods of Asgard against the Fenriswolf and the other enemies. Valhalla has 540 gates through each of which 800 Einherjar can march at once, thus providing Odin with 432,000 slain warriors when he needs them at Ragnarok.

Explanation: The Einherjar are those humans touched by a God aspect within themselves to the point of self-realization and awakening. In the Norse context, they are touched by Odin, chief of the gods of Valhalla and Asgard.

The Einherjar are formerly embodied humans who excelled as spiritual warriors in the solitary battle against themselves—hence they are the lone fighters, those who fight alone. But the "fight" is more a matter of recognizing, assimilating, and integrating all aspects of themselves—past lives, the Shadow, the mastery of kundalini, and the controlled illumination of the 81 bodily chakras.

They are "slain" in the sense that they have succeeded in transmuting their ego and body-based identity, fully waking up, remembering and claiming their divinity, embodying it, and definitively passing out of the human incarnational cycle. They have slain themselves and the cognitive limitations of body-based self-definition, and they have birthed the divine within—touched the God aspect in themselves—in the form of the golden Christ Child, the Higher Self in the form of the Golden Child or newborn Christ Consciousness. This is symbolized by Saehrimnir, the divine boar whose meat is inexhaustible.

Think of the Einherjar as graduates from humanity, the ascended. Some traditions call them the Great White Brotherhood or Great White Lodge, as well as the Occult Hierarchy, Ascended Host, or Lords of the Flame. This is a large conclave of spiritual adepts, from this planet and others, all coordinated through the seven stars of the

Big Dipper in Ursa Major, the seat of the Great White Brotherhood. They do not merely wait for Ragnarok to aid Odin; all the time they work with Odin to preserve consciousness at all levels against entropy.

The total of Einherjar given in Norse myth corresponds to the 432,000 years said in Hindu time reckoning to comprise the Kali Yuga, the darkest of four ages or cycles of existence and conscious unfoldment and the one in which we currently exist. It's as if there is one Einherjar for each year of the Kali Yuga, one spiritual adept to counterbalance each unit of the darkening, entropic trend. The Einherjar (6,000 each) also transmit the 72 Names of God into the Six Worlds, as described in Buddhism and including these realms of existence: humans, animals, gods, Hungry Ghosts (the Dead), Asuras (the antigods), and denizens of Hell.

The reality of the Einherjar in Valhalla is available to interested humans by way of 360 geomantic copies of Odin's great hall found throughout the planet's visionary geography. Some locations include Monticello in Charlottesville, Virginia; Rondvassbhu, Rondane Mountains, Norway; Ivy Thorn Hill, Glastonbury, England; Saint Paul's Cathedral, Ludgate Hill, London, England.

A Valhalla to psychic perception may appear as it's described in Norse myth (in Irish myth too: see Da Derga's Hostel), as a great feasting hall. But it may also appear as a vast sports stadium filled with 432,000 enlightened sages like thousands of sparkling, sun-drenched jewels. This is perhaps why Valhalla is coded in Hindu iconography as a jeweled altar within the *Ananda-kanda* chakra, the inner heart chakra of eight petals that hangs below the *Anahata,* the 12-petaled main heart chakra in proximity to the human chest. The jeweled altar is a condensed way of describing the celestial sports stadium filled with Einherjar.

Human entry into Valhalla requires a sword—a "visitor's pass," so to speak—that is, a focused mind and penetrating psychic insight, just as for entry into Shambhala, another conclave of the Great White Brotherhood. In the King Arthur legend, the young Arthur removes the Sword from the Stone and becomes rightful King of England. The actual meaning of this famous though poorly understood scene is that he can use the sword of his sixth chakra to penetrate the Stone (in effect, put the Sword into the Stone), which is the jeweled altar of Valhalla. He can see into that realm and interact with the Einherjar.

Some members of the Einherjar collectively have been remembered in myth as the Anunnaki of Sumeria and the Tuatha de Danann of Ireland. In both cases, the Einherjar were involved in the early unfoldment of humanity.

See also: Anunnaki, Da Derga's Hostel, Floating Bridge of Heaven, Glass Mountain, Saehrimnir, Seven Rishis, Sword in the Stone, Tuatha de Danann, Valhalla, Valkyries, Wild Hunt.

EMERALD

A secret chakra between the outer and inner heart chakra given to humanity and the Earth by Lucifer, the Light-Bringer, as a gift of freedom and providing full access to cosmic consciousness and illumination.

Also known as Cintamani, Cube of Space, Even ha-Shetiyyah ("Foundation Stone"), Eternal Light, Green Stone, Heart, Jerusalem, Kaustubha, *lapis exillis, lapsit exillis,* Lia Fail, Magic Jewel, narthex tube, Ner Tamid, New Jerusalem, Stone of Destiny, Thought-Jewel, Tzohar, Wishing Stone.

Description: In itself, the Emerald is not discussed openly in Western literature, other than in veiled symbols or obscure references. Wolfram von Eschenbach, in his twelfth-century *Parzival,* refers to a "green stone" (called *lapis exillis* or *lapsit exillis*) brought from Heaven to Earth by the angels, and he implies it is the Holy Grail.

Irish myth tells of the *Lia Fail,* or Stone of Destiny, brought to Ireland long ago by the Tuatha de Danann, that country's primordial gods, from a Celestial City. Similarly, in Anthroposophic writings by or inspired by Rudolf Steiner, mention is made of a stone or jewel from the crown of Lucifer being brought to the Earth.

In Eastern thought, the Emerald is referred to by the Indian sage Ramana Maharshi as the Heart, the ultimate doorway into and out of human incarnation and for consciousness entering or leaving the body, a place of total light.

Earlier, in Vedic myth, the Emerald is called the Kaustubha, the jewel treasure from the Ocean of Milk, which the gods churned at the beginning of time. The god Vishnu (the Pervader, the Hindu Christ) wears the Kaustubha jewel shining like a brilliant gem on his chest. The name means "born from the waters that surround the Earth" *(Sabdacintamani)* and is condensed to the term "Treasure of the Ocean." The jewel represents consciousness as manifested through all things that shine (e.g., Sun, Moon, fire, speech). This total consciousness that is the jewel is the unsullied Soul of the World.

In Tibetan Buddhism, the Emerald is called the *cintamani* stone or the wish-fulfilling jewel, and is often equated with the Philosopher's Stone of Western alchemy. The pre-Islamic mysticism of Iran refers to "Earth of the Emerald Cities" situated at Mount Qaf, a cosmic mountain made entirely of emerald situated in Hurqalya, described as a higher dimension of consciousness.

In Judaic myth, when God was creating the World, He took an emerald stone engraved with the Mysteries of sacred speech and the alphabet and threw it into the primal waters. Then He established the entire world upon it, calling it the *Even ha-Shetiyyah,* Foundation Stone. Later King David dug deep into the Earth to find it, some 1500 cubits down, and saw the immense stone of darkest emerald, the very foundation of the world, as a lid on the waters of chaos *(tehom).*

Another Judiac teaching has it that God took a little of the primordial Light from the inception of creation and put it inside a glowing stone or jewel called the *Tzohar.* He had the angel Raziel give it to Adam after he left the Garden of Eden as a token of how the world had once been filled from end to end with that Light.

This precious jewel was passed down through many generations of Hebrew prophets (it was carried on Noah's Ark) until Moses hung it in the Tabernacle and called it *Ner Tamid,* the Eternal Light, and even today that same Eternal Light symbolically burns over every Ark of the Torah in synagogues.

Explanation: The Emerald, at the human level, is an electromagnetic doorway two inches long and one inch wide that starts at the third rib on the right side of the sternum. It is the Heart within the heart, that is, an esoteric in-between, doorway aspect of the outer (called *Anahata*) and inner heart *(Ananda-kanda)* chakras. It looks like a six-sided, emerald-green, double-terminated crystal.

This is a holographic miniaturization of one of 12 or 13 jewels on the crown of Lucifer, the Lord of Light and Light-Bearer who gave each member of humanity an Emerald at the time of the creation of the second round of humanity, or after what is mistakenly known as "the Fall." The first round of humanity, variously remembered as the Asura, Djinn, Raksasas, and Kings of Edom, did not have an Emerald to contain and structure total consciousness for them. The Emerald, by containing the Absolute Light, structured the approach to it so that consciousness would expand safely, in stages, and in a balanced way.

In Lucifer's Greek guise as the Titan Prometheus, he places the fire of the gods—total consciousness and access to Absolute Light—in the narthex tube (or fennel stalk). This is a veiled reference to the Emerald as the Light container.

Lucifer also gave the Earth one, which he installed in what is now the churchyard of El Templo del Santa Maria near Oaxaca, Mexico, still marked by the 2,000-year-old El Tule tree. This was the epicenter of the Harmonic Convergence of August 1987, the first mass initiation inside the Emerald since Lucifer first gave it to humanity, millions of years ago.

The Emerald is the *Even ha-Shetiyyah,* the "Foundation Stone," in Judaic belief, said to reside even today at the base of the Dome of the Rock on Mount Moriah in the city of Jerusalem in Israel. As an occult symbol, the Emerald is also Jerusalem, not as the documented physical Temple of Solomon, erected twice, but as the archetype of Luciferian consciousness. One of the meanings of "Jerusalem" is "Foundation of Lucifer" because of the word's implied reference to the Morning and Evening Star (Sahar and Salem, known as the planet Venus).

Lucifer, as Guardian of All Nations (per his Judaic reference), gave an Emerald to each of the 72 Regents of the Nations, known as national egregors or angelic princes for a people and landscape, such as Ireland, Germany, France, and many others; each of these 72 Emeralds has a specific landscape location, such as the Hill of Tara, Ireland, and the Hill Cumorah, New York, in the United States. These 72 Emeralds, and the planet's singular one, are consciousness aspects in the chakra system of a distributed geomantic being called Albion, on a regional and planetary scale.

The Emerald is an expression of the Cube of Space, a model of the structure of the universe proposed by Qabala. This theory states that in the beginning, the Supreme Being carved out space in the form of a cube; a certain portion of ultimate cosmic Light is inside the cube, the rest forms its walls. The Cube of Space contains absolute Light; to open it as the Emerald within us is enlightenment on an inconceivable scale. It's the Light that Lucifer brought to humanity, and it's his gift of total freedom in consciousness.

The Lia Fail called out when the rightful King of Ireland stepped upon it. This means he who can open the Emerald, be transmuted by its absolute Light, and ascend from a material body into one of Light is qualified to be King.

The Emerald contains the Holy Grail, which is the receptacle for this vast Light. The Emerald is also the esoteric reference meant in the terms "Jerusalem" and "New Jerusalem" when understood as divinely appointed domains.

The Emerald can only be approached and opened slowly and in stages. Each of the six sides pertains to a fundamental disposition of soul that, in turn, determines how one approaches opening the Emerald. These qualities are understanding, knowledge, compassion, intuition, peace, and bliss. Each quality is an aspect of the truth of oneself, and all six need to be balanced; as you approach the Emerald from one aspect, it starts to remove the Emerald's green outer layer and reveal a little of the Light within.

Although every human has an Emerald, it is likely that not more than 144,000 humans will awaken their Emeralds at roughly the same time; this is considered a minimum, threshold level of activated Emeralds to change Earth reality.

See also: Albion, Asura, Chakravartin, Djinn, Eriu, Holy Grail, Hurqalya, Kings of Edom, Lucifer, Ocean of Milk, Peacock Angel, Prometheus, Raksasas.

EPIPHANY

An annual spiritual event since 4000 B.C. in which the Christ focuses upon a sacred site to infuse the Earth with Christ Consciousness.

Also known as Theophania, Twelfth Night.

Description: January 6 is the day known as Epiphany, the true birth of the Christ on Earth and thus the authentic date for Christmas, a time still recognized by the Eastern Orthodox Church and Anthroposophical circles inspired by Austrian clairvoyant Rudolf Steiner. The word comes from the Greek *epiphaneia,* meaning "manifestation," as of light, the Light being that of Jesus the Christ.

In conventional Christian dogma, Epiphany commemorated four appearances of the Christ: his manifestation to the shepherds; his appearance to the three Magi or kings en route to Bethlehem; his baptism in the River Jordan; and his first miracle at the wedding in Cana in Galilee. The Eastern Church celebrated Epiphany, according to documentation, as early as the third century A.D.; the Roman Catholic Church adopted this observance in the fourth century.

Ample evidence exists that the Feast of the Epiphany was among the three principal Eastern Church festivals; the other two were Easter and Pentecost. The Eastern Church emphasized Epiphany's correlation with Jesus' baptism, thus one of its liturgical aspects was the solemn blessing of the baptismal water. Later, the feast became associated with the manifestation of Christ to the Gentiles (as the three Magi) and gained the alternate name Theophania (manifestation of God).

In essence, Epiphany means the time when the Christ showed forth—manifested His Light—to the three Magi and was present on the Earth.

Epiphany is 12 days after the conventional Christmas date of December 25 and is known as Twelfth Night, a time of revelry and festivities. Twelfth Night marked the official end of the Christmas holiday, a so-called pagan observance later ratified by the Council of Tours in 567 A.D., which stated that the 12 days from Nativity to Epiphany constituted one continuous religious festival.

Explanation: Epiphany is one of a series within an annual geomantic liturgical calendar in which angelic and hierarchical hosts interface with the Earth and humanity. Other events in this cycle include the Wild Hunt on December 20, Candlemas on February 1, and Michaelmas on September 29 (see entries for each). Epiphany specifically deals with Christ and the Earth.

The remarkable fact about the Epiphany is that it was not a single event. It has been repeated every January 6 since about 4000 B.C., in other words, from 4,000 years before Christ officially showed forth, and for more than 2,000 years since. As of 2005 A.D., for example, the Epiphany has happened 6,005 times on Earth, but even more significantly, it has been focused at 6,005 *different* places.

Epiphany, in geomantic terms, is the showing forth of the Christ in planetary reality by his focusing the Christ Consciousness like a laser beam to one dedicated sacred site, different each year, to receive, ground, and transmit the Christ energy across the world through the planet's network of energy lines. Places that have received the Christ focus on Epiphany remain spiritually charged, seemingly indefinitely, so that pilgrimages to previous locations, a geomantic feature called an Epiphany Focus, is still beneficial. One may contact the residual Christ Consciousness previously focused through such places.

Examples of previous sites of an Epiphany Focus since 1989 include Mount Shasta, California; Sedona, Arizona; Bimini Island, near Miami, Florida; Santa Fe, New Mexico; Mount Temehani, Raiatea, French Polynesia; Teotihuacan, Mexico; Rondane Mountains, Norway; and, in 2005, Medellin, Colombia.

Echoes of this awareness may be found in mythology. Spiritual lore of the Indian city of Banaras states that once Vishnu (the Hindu version of Christ) set foot, literally, at a place now called Keshava on the city's northern boundary where the Ganges meets the Varana River. Later he bathed and washed his feet there and, ever after, that site was sanctified and called *Padodaka,* "Foot-Water." Vishnu placing a foot on the Earth at Banaras means the Epiphany Focus one year was concentrated there, and the Foot-Water is its still potent spiritual residue.

The annual infusion of the Earth by the Christ Consciousness focused through a single geomantic node provides an excellent opportunity for initiation. Although it is difficult to know much in advance each year where the site for the Epiphany Focus will be, one can always visit previous known sites. The Focus actually spans a week, like a parabola, with a three-day buildup, the peak on January 6, then a three-day falloff. Thus a week's meditation at an Epiphany Focus can be spiritually rewarding in terms of experiencing the Christ energy.

See also: Black Eye of Horus, Candlemas, Michaelmas, Saehrimnir, White Eye of Horus, Wild Hunt.

ERIU

One of the 72 egregors or watcher angels assigned to the original subdivision of the Earth's landmasses, situated at Ireland's geomantic center.

Also known as Chakravartin, Eire, Eireann, Erin, Erinn, Guardian Angel of the Nation, Heavenly Minister, Logos of a Nation, National Angelic Regent, National Deva, Watcher, the Word in the landscape.

Description: Eriu is the Irish goddess after whom Ireland was anciently named. She was a member of the Tuatha de Danann, Ireland's original gods.

The story is told in Ireland that Eriu was one of three sisters who each petitioned the Milesians, the new race of humans arriving (invading, some say) on Ireland's shore, that they name the land after her. Eriu made her request, however, while standing at the center of Ireland, the country's omphalos, known as the Hill of Uisneach. Here she greeted the Milesians and won her case, first praising them, then promising them great prosperity: The land was thenceforth called Eriu. As a demonstration of her control over the Irish seas and land, Eriu drowned a Milesian who insulted her.

Eriu is usually described as decked in circlets or rings, and her name itself means "round." Often she was seen as a massive woman or in bird form as a long-beaked gray crow. She presided over Ireland as the goddess of the country's center at Uisneach. As such, she embodied the land's sovereignty and ceremonially married each new king in an inauguration ritual called the *banais righe,* which married secular authority with the spirit or goddess of the entire island.

Eriu also established the Oenach, a ritual assembly and seasonal fire festival at Uisneach each year held at Beltane, May 1, one of the eight sacred quarterly turning days in the Celtic calendar and the start of spring. The Oenach assembly was held at important sacred sites in Ireland, such as Uisneach, its topographic center, to reunite the tribes and honor natural cycles. Eriu's sacred Beltane fire at Uisneach was the first to be lit in Ireland each season.

Eriu's grave at Uisneach is still marked by the Stone of Divisions, a large glacial boulder that allegedly presents a map of Ireland on its surface.

Explanation: Eriu clearly illustrates the ancient relationship of an assigned angelic watcher called an egregor to a landmass and its people. In fact, in most cases, Ireland is an excellent textbook in the dynamics of Earth's visionary geography because the correspondence between place-name and geomantic function is as clear today as it was millennia ago when instituted.

In the original plan of the Earth, nine continents were allocated; each would have a presiding, watching angel or egregor responsible for it. Then for the 72 primary landmass subdivisions, such as Ireland, another 72 egregors were assigned. Each would supervise the inherent geomantic features of the landscape and the relationship of its people to those subtle landscape features.

The national egregor would also oversee the unfoldment of the inherent soul qualities of the people occupying that land—what makes them Irish, Norse, or German, for example. Some esotericists call these folk-soul archangels. The egregor preserves the integrity and accommodates the evolution of the "genius of the people," or the geomantic, energy, and consciousness aspects of nationhood.

There is a hint of this in Deuteronomy when Moses says, "When the Lord divided the nations, he set their borders according to the number of the angels of God." That number, originally, in terms of angels that protect the borders of nations and spiritually lead their people, is 72; there are more now, as there are more countries with different soul groups of humans.

Judaic lore also says that at the beginning of Creation, God assigned 70 Guardian Angels to watch over and rule the 70 Nations descended from Adam.

In Judaic angelologies, the egregors are called

the Tutelary Princes of the Nations or Regents of the Nations, but they're also known as the Principalities. Qabala speaks of the 72 Names of God, or *Shemhamforesh,* and to a large extent, the totality of the 72 egregors are these. Each folk-soul or national-soul character tied to its land-mass and egregor expresses a Name.

Thus Eriu in her angelic essence embodies one of the Names of God, and that essence is grounded in the Irish landscape at its geographic center, Uisneach.

The story of Eriu demonstrates the ancients' knowledge of geomantic protocol: Make friends with the angelic watcher who maintains your land and enter into a collegial, cooperative relationship with her, such as through festivals.

It is a topographic fact that Uisneach is at the center of Ireland, but it serves a geomantic function not readily obvious. It is one of the Earth's 72 Energy Focusing Nodes. Each of the 72 land-masses with an egregor has one. This feature is a major nodal point that focuses and concentrates cosmic and geomantic energy for that region, in this case, Ireland as a self-contained island.

Using different language, each Node is one of the 72 minor chakras in the planet, complementing the nine major ones. These minor chakras are part of the geomantic body of Albion, a cosmogonic figure expressed upon the Earth. In the human, minor chakras are located at the armpits, elbows, knees, and ankles, while the major ones are arrayed vertically along the spine, from groin to head.

Judaic lore further states that Lucifer, Lord of Light and Light-Bringer, is the chief of all the Princes of the Nations. This is appropriate because Lucifer gave each of the nine and the 72 egregors an Emerald to hold in trust for him. These Emeralds (a projected expression of the heart within the heart chakra, better understood through Greek myth as the narthex tube in which Prometheus put the gods' fire—self-aware consciousness—that he stole to give humanity) are supervised by each national egregor on behalf of its people, and they are usually grounded at a specific site—in Ireland as the Lia Fail at the Hill of Tara.

Thus Eriu at the Hill of Uisneach maintains the geomantic integrity of the island of Ireland and contributes to the global-cosmogonic body of Albion.

Often an egregor will assume a negotiated shape in cooperation with the psychics or folklorists of a country. Eriu, for example, is a long-beaked gray crow; England's egregor is Grand Britannia, the image of a queenly matron (sometimes known as Matrona or Modron, both meaning "Mother"); America's egregor is the eagle; France's is a rooster or cock; and Norway's is the moose.

Even the egregor for smaller agregates of land such as states can, if desired, assume a bird or animal form as a way of symbolizing the essential energy aspects of the land: California's egregor is a great gray owl; New Mexico's a stallion.

India is another landmass in which the geomantic reality is still apparent in place-names and site lore. Its original name was Bharata, after a primordial spiritual hero (its egregor) called a Chakravartin, who prepared the land (geomantically terraformed it) with the Sudarsana, the Discus of Vishnu. England's egregor is called Britannia, usually pictured as a regal matron and believed to derived from Prydein, an early Welsh name for the island.

See also: Albion, Chakravartin, Emerald, House of Atreus, Huitzilopochtli, Lucifer, Navel of the World, Nymph, Sengen-Sama, Srin-mo Demoness, Tower of Babel, Tuatha de Danann.

EUROPA

One of the Supreme Being's 12 god forms, expressed as a marriage with the spirit of a large landscape area, in this case, called Europa.

Also known as the continent of Europe, Zeus Face.

Description: Greek myth relates how a beautiful mortal female named Europa (from the

Greek, *Europe,* "Wide Eyes") gamboling by the seashore somewhere in Greece (Tyre and Sidon are cited sometimes as the location, making her a Phoenician) caught the fancy of the amorous Zeus. He donned his form of a gentle bull of dazzling whiteness with jeweled crescent horns so as to seduce the maiden. She was beguiled, adorned the mild bull and its horns with fresh flowers, and stroked him affectionately, as if he were a pet dog.

He lay down before her as a gesture of submissiveness, and when she climbed on his big broad white back, he stood up and swiftly carried Europa on his back into the sea to Crete where he coupled with her and produced three sons, Minos (King of Crete), Rhadamanthys, and Sarpedon; these three later became the Judges of the Dead in the Greek Underworld. Zeus gave Europa four gifts, most prominent among them being Talos, a giant man of bronze who would perpetually guard Crete by running the perimeter of the island three times daily.

The exact place of Zeus's coupling with Europa is sometimes given as the Dictaean Cave on Crete where he was born and nurtured or a spring at Gortyna.

Explanation: The tale of Zeus and Europa is an elegant geomyth about a key feature of Earth's energy body or visionary geography. Zeus, like his Hindu counterpart, Shiva, sometimes expressed an aspect of his essence as a dazzlingly white bull; Shiva's bull form was Nandi ("Joyful"). In Celtic England, the white bull was known as Taranus, the Thunder-god, expressing divine strength in manifestation, the roaring, invincible power of the Heavens.

Zeus's seduction and coupling with Europa should not be understood, as it often is, as a rape of a female. It is the ancient Greek way of describing the penetration of a large landscape (Europa) with God-essence (the white bull) and his complete immanence in this landmass, its sacred sites, and consciousness.

The large landscape is most of Europe, from Greece to Germany and the Low Countries, but not Spain, Portugal, Scandinavia, or western France. This region, specified by the mythic term "Europa," involves roughly one-twelfth of the planet's surface area and is known as an Albion Plate. In each of the Albion Plates (a geometric overlay, pentagonal-shaped), the Supreme Being has a symbolic expression or god form; in central Europe, it is as a White Bull; in the British Isles, as a boar called Twrch Trwyth.

These symbolic features are called Zeus Faces; each is a large-scale geomantic feature by which the Supreme Being grounds His presence on Earth.

Here is one way to picture it: Visualize 12 panes of glass, each in the shape of a pentagon (a five-sided geometric figure). Each glass pane has an animal form etched in light across part of its surface: a boar, white bull, swan (another Zeus form as recounted in Greek myth). These are Zeus Faces, metaphors for an aspect of God. Inside each animal form many lights twinkle, bright like stars. These are the holy sites within the geomantic landscape of the Face seen in their spiritual guise, as centers of numinosity.

The animal shapes have metaphoric accuracy, each expressing a sublime aspect of the Supreme Being immanent in our world; they help to ground for human awareness something that far transcends our concepts and understanding.

In geomantic terms, Europa is Zeus as the White Bull; the landscape is feminized to suggest receptivity to the God-immanence, but the geomantic overlay is a bull form so Europe could just as well be called Land of the White Bull. This is reflected and somewhat validated in the former prevalence of the Mithraic Mysteries, based on a cosmic bull-slaying myth, and numerous temples called Mithraea, in the Slavic countries, Italy, Germany, and Switzerland.

Numerous holy sites throughout this region, including the famous Cretan labyrinth (a geomantic feature) at Mount Ida in Crete (see Minotaur), are energy-consciousness centers (major and minor chakras, 81 in total) in the White Bull.

The tale of Zeus's coupling with Europa at the Dictaean Cave, his alleged birthplace on Earth, suggests this site on Crete is a prime point for geomantic interaction with the entire White Bull form. It is where the God-essence first infiltrates the physical landmass of central Europe and its geomantic "wiring."

See also: Albion, Minotaur, White Bull.

EXCALIBUR

An occult sword of psychic insight, penetration, protection, and defense derived from the Tree of Life and Qabalistic formulations used in the Arthurian mythos and acquired by individuals after training.

Also known as Caladbolg, Caladbou, Caladfwlch, Caladhcholg, Caliburnus, Sword of Nuada.

Description: King Arthur, early in his days of kingship, has two named swords. The first is the Sword in the Stone, which he withdraws from the stone as a test of his unique qualifications for kingship; this sword was arranged by Merlin, Arthur's mentor and magus. The second is Excalibur, a gift from the Lady of the Lake, a mystical female who rises from the lake of Avalon to award Arthur his second sword, Excalibur, along with a precious jeweled scabbard. It was precious because it protected its user from all wounds in battle; at one point, Arthur's sister, Morgan le Fay, usually portrayed as an ill-minded witch, steals the scabbard.

Throughout his reign as high king over Celtic England, Arthur's possession of Excalibur is the unimpeachable symbol of his right to be king. When he is dying of a mortal wound and about to be taken to Avalon by Morgan le Fay, he returns Excalibur to the Lady of the Lake; in the stories, either he or his lifelong companion, Bedivere, tosses the adamant blade over the Lake for the Lady to get. She will keep it in trust for the future time when King Arthur returns.

In the earlier Welsh account of King Arthur (the standard Excalibur description comes from Sir Thomas Malory's late fifteenth-century compendium), the king sword is called *Caladfwlch* (in the Welsh tale, *Culhwch and Olwen*).

It is also linked to the sword of the Irish heroes as *Caladbou* ("hard fighter") for Fergus mac Roich, and as *Caladbolg* ("hard lightning") for CuChulainn; another pre-Malory British name for the king sword is Caliburn or Caliburnus. Myths tell us that when Fergus used Caladbolg to lop off the tops of hills, it created rainbows. Yet another Irish hero named Fergus mac Leti had a kingly sword called Caladhcholg, with similar potency as Caladbolg.

Explanation: Excalibur is the name of a sword that symbolizes insight and penetration. It is acquired by one at the point at which one's insight is able to perceive the angelic realms. Although the myths say the Lady of the Lake gave Arthur this sword, it was actually Merlin, Arthur's magus and Camalate's wizard.

In this light, Excalibur was the condensation into a symbol of a spiritual practice of psychic insight maintained for many generations as part of an esoteric Mystery tradition of which Merlin was the chief adept and Arthur a prime member. The Arthurian mythos, including its characters, objects, places, and plots, is the scheme of an archetypal initiation program involving actual humans overshadowed by spiritual beings such as angels and enlightened sages and enacted in many cultures, not just the Celtic or Irish (see King Arthur).

Excalibur is surrounded by a pale lilac flame, known as the Pendragon. It can be developed or acquired by an individual through initiation in the Arthurian Mysteries, after which it can protect the individual and group when required from unfavorable or negative astral influences; indeed, its use can be expanded to protect large landmasses, even, in Arthur's historical times, the nation. Its origin from this perspective as an active force for the Light is the Qabala in its earliest forms, dating back to Atlantis and even earlier times.

The proper use of Excalibur can open the

gateway from our physical realm to the exalted domain of Shambhala, seat of the world's true spiritual government.

As a visualization, one sword points down through the top of the head to the base of the spine, its hilt at the neck; this is the means of self-defense and protection with Excalibur. This sword is inside a jeweled scabbard that runs parallel to the spinal column. A second sword rises from the Earth through the base of the spine, parallel with the first, and just behind it, its point coming out over the head; its hilt is at the pelvis and it has no scabbard. This sword embodies the activating force. Both swords are enveloped in the pale lilac flame.

The two together are one aspect of Excalibur, one of many swords the candidate for Arthurhood and the Grail Knight in the Arthurian Mysteries gains.

The sword contained in the scabbard may be withdrawn through psychic vision and used to penetrate things, as an extension of the brow chakra's psychic ability to see through matter into the pictures, symbols, and energies behind them. The insight gained with Excalibur is grounded with the syllable *HUMG*, spoken aloud several times. *Excalibur* itself is an old Gnostic mantric sound.

The Lady of the Lake and Morgan le Fay both figure in Arthur's attainment of Excalibur by way of Qabala's Tree of Life. The mystical-esoteric aspect of Judaism describes reality in the form of Four Worlds, from material to ultrasubtle, diagrammed as four successive Trees of Life, one atop the next. Each Tree (consisting of three vertical pillars) contains ten spheres of Light or expressions of consciousness in a total hierarchy of manifestation.

The Tree of Life next to our physical world and its Tree is called *Yetzirah* and means "Formation." It is akin to descriptions of the astral plane, known in esoteric code as the Lake, as in the sea of stars or lake of light. The Lady of the Lake is the guardian and authority figure for the entire astral plane and its ten spheres of Light, and Morgan le Fay is one of her three expressions. Both women are individual spiritual adepts, yet both also fill generic cosmic positions.

The Lady of the Lake gave Arthur Excalibur in the sense that it is her body of wisdom and consciousness (Yetzirah's ten spheres of Light) that forms the sword. The scabbard too is made from this Tree's ten Lights; the scabbard at this level of description is a condensation of the matrix or infrastructure of the Tree. Morgan le Fay did not steal the scabbard; rather, she is the guardian and embodiment of its essence and the energies that hold the Tree (sword) together.

Arthur was able to have and wield Excalibur because he was spiritually adept at handling the tenfold energies of Yetzirah and its embodiments. The Lady of the Lake was his lifelong helper and Morgan le Fay his opponent because this sword could not be had without a collegial relationship with these higher adepts.

See also: Fionn MacCumhaill, Grail Knight, King Arthur, Lady of the Lake, Morgan le Fay, Shambhala, Sword in the Stone, Valhalla.

FAIRY QUEEN

The master supervising and ensouling deva for the fairy kingdom, the realm of Nature spirits that facilitate the blossoming of plants.

Also known as Lady of the Raths, Queen Mab (Medb or Maeve), Titania.

Description: Throughout the world's rich treasury of fairy lore, a Fairy Queen is usually described as the ruler of that realm. In Shakespeare's *A Midsummer Night's Dream,* she is Titania, consort to Oberon; in Celtic and Irish fairy lore, she is Queen Mab (Medb or Maeve). Shakespeare, in his *Romeo and Juliet,* called Queen Mab the fairies' midwife who gives birth to dreams and whose coach is pulled by insects. For Irish poet William Butler Yeats, Maeve is the proud, tall Lady of the Raths (a term for Fairyland Doors or dwellings).

Yeats reported a vision of Queen Maeve by a sensitive woman of Mayo. Maeve was the most beautiful woman imaginable, dressed all in white, with her arms and lower legs bare; she bore a dagger in one hand and a sword at her side. She looked to be about thirty years old, slender, fierce and strong but benevolent.

In Irish lore, Queen Maeve's identity is blurred, occupying the uncertain boundary between demigod, human warrior queen, and Fairy Queen. Her tomb in Sligo is an enormous cairn of 50,000 tons of rock atop Mount Knocknarea.

Yeats's term "Lady of the Raths" suggests that the Fairy Queen may be found within the fairy rath, one of many terms that indicate a portal into Fairyland. Yeats himself referred to a "door into Faeryland" atop Ben Bulben, a green, loaf-shaped mountain near Sligo, Yeats's home in western Ireland; he said a small white square on a rock on top of Ben Bulben swings open at night, offering intrepid humans access to Fairyland.

Other Fairyland Doors have been remembered in Celtic folklore such as at Schiehallion, the Faëry Hill of Caledonia (Scotland); the Sidhe (fairy hill) of Ardtalnaig, south of Loch Tay (Scotland); the Fairy Knowe of the Sith Bruach in Aberfoyle (Scotland); the Fairy Gump near Saint Just and the Fairy Dwelling on Selena Moor, both in Cornwall, England; the Fairy Dell near Langport in Somerset, England; and in Ireland, at Gortdonaghy Forth, the *Poul-duve* or Black Hole of Knockfierna in Kilmallock, and the Fairy's Wood in Sligo, among others.

Other names for these portals include dell, knoll, sithein, brugh, mound, forth, sidhe, and ring. The general report by humans passing these doorways is that of hearing lovely, bewitching music; observing dancing throngs, merry carousing, and troops of fairy horses; and banqueting, until sunrise, when it all vanishes.

Regarding the protocol for approaching the *Daoine Shee,* the Irish Men of Peace, humans are advised not to wear green, to walk around the fairy hill nine times, wait for the door to open, and only then to join the dancing fairy troops.

Explanation: The Fairy Queen is a deva or type of angelic being who maintains the energy and consciousness field in which the fairies flourish. There is a great deal of exaggeration and storytelling license in fairy lore, but at the core is an indisputable kernel of truth and reality.

Fairies are a class of Nature spirits specifically charged with working with plant and tree blossoms. Their job is to translate (and supervise) the astral color (and its qualities of energy and consciousness) into the physical blossoms of the plants. Poetically, we might say they paint the colors onto the plant blossoms. The fairies help plants assimilate energetic nourishment and thus feed the Earth.

The Fairyland Door is ultimately the body of the deva herself. The deva for the fairy kingdom works closely with Gaia, the name of the Earth Spirit or watcher angel for the planet and all of Nature. As with other angels, she can duplicate herself and be in many places at once. Thus this deva—let's call her Queen Mab—can be present at all the Fairyland Doors simultaneously.

In the early days of the planet, especially in the epochs before humanity known as Polaria or Planet Plant, when the plant kingdom predominated, the fairy kingdom and its activity on Earth were at their peak, as was the number of active Fairyland Doors, reckoned in the hundreds of millions. As receptor sites for delicate astral energies (ultimately food for plants), the Fairyland Doors and the locales they serviced (usually about a 15- to 20-mile radius), when seen from above the planet, looked like clusters of waving fronds and receptive flower stalks.

Today, there are drastically fewer Doors still open or viable, counted in the mere thousands. Gaia is working with interested humans around the planet who are willing to interact with Queen Mab to recreate the Fairyland Doors, often in new locations, through geomantic rituals. Gaia is trying to create a blue-purple ribbon of new

Fairyland Doors around the planet to ground these vital, life-sustaining energies back into the fabric of etheric and physical matter.

At Ben Bulben, for example, the deva for the fairy kingdom stands atop the mountain. She may be so diaphanous as to be mistaken for sunlight; she may appear to be surrounded by veils and mists, by swirls of pale blue, green, and lavender. She may even resemble a dynamic fountain of light, vigorously cycling energies in many colors through her from above and out into the landscape.

The fairies fly out of her body like swarming bees out of a hive or like gossamer butterflies out of an open sack. The Door, specifically, is like a slit or aperture in the deva's body of light. You pass through it in your astral body into another dimension, that of the fairies. The fairy kingdom is actually inside the deva's body, or scope of consciousness, and inside that are archives on how to get color into plants, how to make plants blossom.

As the copious fairy lore indicates, it is an enchanting, intoxicating, seductive realm. If you're not careful, you may not want to return to the human realm; you may eat the fairy food and marry a fairy, so the tales say. The reality is that the Fairyland is a timeless, very happy place, full of delight and joy.

If you enter this realm psychically unprepared, it is possible you will become ungrounded, disoriented, unmoored from your human self-identity and sense of continuous linear time. Eating the fairy food offered is a metaphoric way of describing this experience of seduction and disorientation; it reflects the deepening of the immersion in Fairyland and its ontological framework.

Many of the Fairyland Doors were closed down by Queen Mab due to lack of human participation in the protocols of fairy-human interaction and the introduction of energetically injurious technologies, such as coal mining. This energy, with its lead and steel machines, emits a jarring vibration that drives fairies away from a region. Due to the restriction on fairy activities by human civilization, the planet has become anemic with respect to this type of energy.

Where the Fairyland Doors have been abandoned, closed, or rendered dysfunctional, other opportunistic astral beings have moved in. These are beings of a less hospitable, happy disposition; they are more like astral vampires or black, oily, and psychotic Nature spirits who suck the life energy out of areas and disrupt human relations with the wholesome Nature spirits.

Fairy lore calls these beings the Unseelie Court and describes them as malignant, ugly spirits who seek to interfere with humans at every opportunity. The Seelie Court, in contrast, consists of the benevolent fairies who work with Queen Mab on behalf of the Earth's plant kingdom and thus all of humanity.

See also: Gaia, Kokopelli, Menehune, Nymph, Pan.

FALL OF MAN

The rebooting of humanity on Earth through a second generation under reduced freedom and certain limitations in consciousness.

Also known as the Expulsion from Paradise, Original Sin, Precession.

Description: The story line is simple: Original humanity, Adam and Eve, living in paradisal conditions in the Garden of Eden disobeyed a divine command not to eat the fruit of the Tree of the Knowledge of Good and Evil. They did anyway and were immediately expelled from Eden. Christianity later used this expulsion as proof and explanation of Original Sin, saying that all subsequently born humans participated in this primal disobedience and sin.

Explanation: Like the Garden of Eden, this is one of the most misunderstood and theologically distorted "myths" of humanity's ancient past.

The Fall of Man refers to the termination of the first round of humanity and the creation of a second humanity, like rebooting a computer with a new operating system. It was not so much "sin" as excess and abuse of powers that caused this, and it was less a Fall and more of a restructuring of consciousness.

First humanity, variously remembered as the Djinn, Asuras, Kings of Edom, and Raksasas, was endowed with vast physical and psychic freedom; these humans were prodigies of matter and spirit, but they abused the divine gift and nearly destroyed themselves and the planet. These powers are classically described in yoga as *siddhis,* magical abilities associated with activation of the seven chakras.

God removed them from the world and exiled them to the astral plane, where they are still accessible (often as executors for magical acts) and bound with Lucifer, the Lord of Light commissioned to supervise humanity on Earth.

At least six major events took place to prepare Earth for second humanity. First, Earth's visionary geography or energy grid was installed. This both provided immediate alignment in consciousness with the galaxy, the spiritual worlds, and the archetypes of divine consciousness and it limited the instant access to the prodigious powers of spirit and matter that first humanity had.

Second, what we now call the Precession of the Equinoxes was established by tilting the planet 23 degrees off its axis. This created a retrograde motion to the planet through the starfields, introduced asymmetry into solar time reckoning (from 360 to 365 days), switched humanity's experience of time from cyclic to sequential, and allowed "evil" (Tezcatlipoca, Ahriman, and the other darker sides of the polarized Lucifer, Lord of Light and free choice) to influence humanity.

Third, Lucifer, though he had not erred or disobeyed God, was forced to limit and fragment his essence as expressed on the Earth by being bound in 3,496 locations (called Lucifer Binding Sites) along with the Djinn (first humanity souls) until such time as second humanity could forgive and release them through both humans' own acts of responsible freedom and spiritual attainment.

The first three events were part of the Saturnian imposition of controls on and limits to human freedom, yet they also structured our gradual reclamation of it. Before there had been continuous co-identity with the gods; after the Fall of Man, there was the Grail Quest, a long-term process of regaining that unity.

Fourth, the Tower of Babel was installed at Babylon in what is now south-central Iraq, along the Euphrates River. The Tower of Babel (it is still there and operational) is a spiritual device operating in the sixth dimension of planetary reality to broadcast the 72 different soul types and languages to Earth. Myth remembers this as the confusion of tongues delivered to humanity as a punishment from God (or at least, from Yahweh), but that is a distorted perception.

The Tower of Babel is a living copy of the *Shemhamforesh,* a term from Judaic mysticism that means the 72 Names of God. Each Name became the mantric foundation for an ethnic people, such as Irish, German, French, Italian, and it came with a special class of angels called watchers or egregors, each assigned to a specific landmass, such as Ireland, Germany, France, or Italy, to maintain the geomantic and spiritual integrity of the people and their land.

Fifth, the 26 expressions of the Garden of Eden, which were actual geomantic templates on the Earth, were closed down, or their vibrations were limited. These 26 (excepting 12 lost when Atlantis and Lemuria sank beneath the sea) are still accessible today, though they operate at a reduced frequency. They had been templated on the Earth to provide a model of the balanced male-female.

Second humanity is not responsible for the "sins" of first humanity, though we live in comparatively reduced conditions of consciousness because of their excesses. Second humanity, ultimately, can have the same freedom as the first, but it is not a given: We must attain it through spiritual striving and insight. The panoply of Earth's visionary geographic features is the scaffolding we climb to gain again the delights of existence immediately enjoyed by first humanity.

Sixth, the Emerald was dropped in second humanity's biophysical base. The Emerald is the Heart within the heart chakra in the chest, an arcane though accessible energy field that affords reimmersion into full, absolute Light. The Emerald belongs to Lucifer, and approaching and eventually entering it, though a long process, is how second humanity can attain the fullness of reality.

This segues to a subtler nuance of the term "Fall of Man." The phylogenetically first round of soul incarnation into human physical form has been interpreted as a fall—let's call it a dimensional "fall" in the sense of shifting from a faster frequency of light to a slower one (physical matter), from bodies of light to bodies of clay, the mud and water (and divine spark) of primal Adam.

Similarly, Lucifer's first step toward matter, executed on humanity's behalf, has been esoterically interpreted as a Fall. Exoterically, Christianity blames Lucifer for causing the Fall of Man, but that is a mistaken perception. Lucifer, as the archangelic spokesman for a spiritually and psychically free humanity flourishing in material bodies, had to provide surety for the gamble, and that surety was his own essence as expressed in this realm.

See also: Adam, Atlas, Dolorous Stroke, Dreamtime, Emerald, Flood, Garden of Eden, Hollow Hill, Lucifer, Tower of Babel, Zep Tepi.

FIONN MACCUMHAILL

One of the 15 human exemplars of King Arthur, the Solar Logos and chief of the Great White Brotherhood.

Also known as Demne Máel, Finn MacCool, Finn MacCumhal.

Description: Fionn MacCumhaill is one of Ireland's two major heroes, the other being the prodigious warrior CuChulainn (Hound of Culann) of Ulster. Fionn was based in Leinster at the hill-fort called Hill of Allen, formerly the residence of Almu, one of Ireland's ancient gods, the Tuatha de Danann.

The hill-fort was personified as Almu ("All-White") and was once the sacred capital of Leinster province, the site of an entrance to the Underworld, and the birthplace of Fionn, whose royal chair (a mound) sat upon the citadel.

His name means "the Fair Boy" (Fionn), son of Cumhall. As a child, Fionn acquired all the world's wisdom and became a formidable, highly skilled fighter. He studied with the Druidic hermit Finneces, from whom he acquired the name *Demne Máel* ("Druid's Tonsure"). He accidentally tasted a droplet of juice from the Salmon of Wisdom while it was roasting and from this gained all its wisdom and the ability to have visions of the past and present and make prophecies of the future.

His primary accomplishment was to assemble a band of warriors to defend Leinster province. These were called the Fianna. Fionn's wife was Grainne, a beautiful young woman who ultimately preferred Diarmait, a younger Fianna.

Ireland has never forgotten Fionn; his name and deeds have permeated Irish literature and are known as the Fenian Cycle. The Finn who will come again in James Joyce's *Finnegans Wake* (1939) is Fionn MacCumhaill, sleeping with his Fianna in the Hollow Hills until his country summons him to awaken.

Explanation: Many scholars have commented on the similarities of the Fionn story with that of the British King Arthur and his Knights of the Round Table, his adulterous wife, Guinevere, and betraying first knight, Lancelot.

Fionn MacCumhaill is one of the 15 different cultural guises the archetypal King Arthur, a celestial being, has taken in Earth's history. Others have included Gesar of Ling (Mongolia), Rustam (Persia), and Siegfried (Germany). It is a case of the same archetypes being enacted on Earth by a group of humans dedicated to exemplifying the story's dynamics and relationships.

King Arthur is the Solar Logos, an expression of the Christ (Logos) at the level of the suns (stars) of the galaxy. He is the leader of the Great Bear (the constellation Ursa Major), galactic seat of the Great White Brotherhood, a conclave of enlightened masters and adepts who comprise the world's spiritual government. As such, King Arthur is equivalent to Hinduism's Indra, chief of the gods, but "gods" here means members of the Great White Brotherhood; the members are also referred to in present times as Ascended Masters, but in earlier days as the Irish Tuatha de Danann and the Anunnaki of Sumer (today's Iraq).

Fionn's defense of Leinster province may have had physical aspects, but largely it was a spiritual and occult defense of all of Ireland, just as the British King Arthur defended Britain against the "barbarians," that is, entropic, negative forces.

Fionn was "born" at the Hill of Allen just as Arthur was born at Tintagel in Cornwall, England. This means that, as the Solar Logos, his energy and celestial presence are always available at these sites for humans interested in interaction. Fionn and the Fianna are sleeping in the Hollow Hills just as Arthur and his Knights to signify that when this archetypal myth is needed to manifest again in the world, it will be reactivated and reenacted, though in a new cultural form.

Each Arthurian exemplifier establishes a Mystery center known esoterically as Camalate. There men and women are trained in the Mysteries of Earth's visionary geography, advancement in consciousness, and the attainment of Christ Consciousness. The postulated sixth-century British King Arthur's Camalate was at South Cadbury Castle in Somerset, England, about 12 miles from well-known Glastonbury. Fionn's center at Almu (Hill of Allen) was another Camalate.

Here is the geomantic setup: Originally, Irish myth tells us, Almu was the residence of Nuada of the Silver Hand, one of the Tuatha de Danann, but sometimes he is called the leader of these gods. He kept his great Sword of Nuada at Almu; it came from the mystical city of Finias and was one of the four celestial treasures the Tuatha brought to Earth (also: a Cauldron, Spear, and Stone).

Esoterically, this means Almu was the portal into Nuada's Retreat; as an Ascended Master, he is able to establish Retreats or Sanctuaries around the planet for interaction with both his colleagues and embodied human initiates. For ease of conceptualization, let's picture the Retreat as an extensive otherworldly palace, far larger than the physical confines of the Almu hill-fort.

Into this center comes the Solar Logos (Fionn as an expression of Arthur). It is like a golden vertical spindle, a rotating cylinder of golden light, that comes straight down into Almu. This is the Solar Logos being resident at this site. The Solar Logos is geomantically resident at a particular place for a brief period, then can be relocated to another site, per a schedule of planetary site activations. This is Fionn being born and taking his "chair" or seat at Almu, Leinster's capital.

Nuada's Retreat also functions as a regional headquarters for members of the Great White Brotherhood; such places are called Council Chambers. Periodically, Nuada's members for Ireland (they oversee Ireland's development) assemble for meetings and perhaps "ride out" into the Irish countryside, which is to say, they extend their spiritual benediction out across the land and, at times, visit various sacred sites in Ireland and interact with selected initiates.

Nuada's colleagues can be understood as the Fianna, yet the Fianna also were embodied, living human men and women initiates at various levels of training and accomplishment under the auspices of the Ascended Masters. The setup ran *parallel:* in the "Otherworld," Nuada and his Fianna, the Ascended Masters; in the outer physical world, the human Fionn and his human Fianna.

As for the Sword of Nuada, this is an expression of Excalibur, King Arthur's great sword, but there is a more occult side to it. At one level,

Excalibur, or the Sword of Nuada, is a magical defense mechanism created out of the energies depicted in Qabala's Tree of Life model, capable of defending groups of people, such as the Fianna, and an entire landscape, the island of Ireland.

Metaphysically, Fionn had the use of Nuada's Sword (the knowledge to create and wield it) and "brandished" or focused it from his citadel at Almu. This is another aspect to a fully developed Camalate: use of Nuada's Sword.

Fionn also had touched a God-aspect in himself, represented by the Salmon of Wisdom. This refers to the Rich Fisher King and the Higher Self. Access to this level of being gives one clairvoyance that encompasses time.

During Fionn MacCumhaill's time, Ireland was blessed by the radiant, celestial presence of the Ascended Masters overshadowing their human protégés. All of Ireland's sacred sites (portals into Earth's visionary geography) were nourished with Light, and by extension, the Earth was fed through this island.

See also: Anunnaki, Bifrost, Camalate, Excalibur, Gesar of Ling, Glass Mountain, Guinevere, Hollow Hill, Indra, King Arthur, Rustam, Salmon of Wisdom, Seven Rishis, Sword in the Stone, Tuatha de Danann, Wild Hunt.

FISHER KING

The regent of the processes of the Holy Grail, namely, deep, total cosmic memory and knowledge of the soul's evolutionary purposes.

Also known as Anfortas, Atra-hasis, Cosmic Christ, Deucalion, Ea the Sublime Fish, God-Self, Great Master Within, Higher Self, King of Suffering, Magic Presence, Manu Satyavrata, *Matsya-avatara,* Méhaigne King, Mighty "I AM" Presence, Noah, Oannes the Man-Fish, Pelles, Perfect Self, Real Self, Rich Fisher King, Salmon of Wisdom, Sinner King, Utnapishtim, Wounded Fisher King.

Description: In the medieval Grail stories, the Fisher King is the lord of the Grail Castle, the protector of the Holy Grail, and the high priest of the Grail Mysteries. He has various names, though Anfortas or Pelles is usually used.

Though he presides over the Grail and its rituals, he himself is grievously wounded and cannot be healed by it. Most versions place his wound in the top of the thigh and attribute it to the misuse of a divine sword by which he maimed himself, an accident thereafter called the Dolorous Stroke. The Stroke wounded the Fisher King who was afterward known as the Wounded Fisher King. It also precipitated a blight on the natural environment of his kingdom; crops failed, drought persisted, Nature, life itself, weakened. Thereafter, his kingdom was called the Wasteland.

The Wounded Fisher King languishes dolorously in the Grail Castle, attended by Grail Maidens, in daily view of the Holy Grail, recipient of the latest medicaments by well-meaning attendants, but nothing can heal him. Only the ministrations of the true, Christed Grail Knight who can wield the sword (or spear) that wounded him can produce healing where before there was injury.

In Richard Wagner's 1882 version of the story, the opera *Parsifal,* Klingsor, formerly a member of the Grail Brotherhood who turned to black magic when he was spurned and humiliated, has stolen the holy spear so Anfortas cannot be healed. Eventually, Parsifal, a Grail Knight, retrieves the lance and heals him.

Explanation: The Fisher King is a mythic figure who has figured in the myths of Lemuria, Atlantis, Mycenae, and Arthurian times. He pertains to that aspect of consciousness that lies at the deepest level: the ability to remember one's divine origins and the descent and history of one's soul since that origin.

The Fisher King is maimed because he cannot remember. The thigh wound is a euphemism for an injury to the root chakra, the first of seven major energy-consciousness centers arrayed along the spine from groin to head. The root chakra, in the groin, cannot connect with the crown chakra atop the head, and the requisite energy circuit needed to provide deep, full cosmic recall is blocked. The Fisher King is thus wounded because he cannot remember himself.

His environment, both his body and the landscape he superintends, is similarly wounded, a Wasteland, due to his inability to obtain the memories.

The Fisher King rules over the deep past and deep memories of the soul; he pertains to the different doorways in the soul and its relation to the deep past, to a time vastly long ago, before the Flood, that is, the time of dissolution between cycles of creation and reckoned in the billions of human years.

The Fisher King is the conduit for deep recall both for the individual (for which he is the Higher Self) and collectively, as a reflection of humanity's status.

The energy is released through passage through the doorways in the soul for the development of soul life. Injury (pain, ill health, unexpiated karma) has closed down access to this root chakra energy that would reveal the soul's purpose and nature, its level of development, and our present ability as individuals to penetrate that veil, understand the situation of our soul, and make good on our life's mission.

Another name for this energy is kundalini, coiled in the root chakra, and also known as Shakti, the goddess who seeks reunion with Shiva in the crown. The possibility of this blending of energies and the radical remembering it provokes is the compensation for the limitation in consciousness imposed on second generation humanity as part of the Fall of Man.

The time before the Flood is symbolized in Hindu myth by Vishnu (the Hindu Christ) dreaming atop the massive coils of Sesa-Ananta, the cosmic dragon, who floats on top of the primeval waters, all of manifest creation withdrawn. All that survived the dissolution of creation (the Flood) is the Christ Consciousness, which is eternal, and contact with that is what the Fisher King desperately needs to heal himself and the land.

The Fisher King vacillates between Rich and Wounded. In relatively recent times, he has been wounded, that is, his memory circuits rendered inoperative. The Fisher King, though an actual celestial being, is also an archetype of the human. As human beings, each of us has a Fisher King within our soul constitution. "He" will be rich or maimed depending on our individual state of knowing and remembering.

There was a time when the Fisher King was rich. He knew, he remembered, he did not suffer, he was the epitome of total cosmic recall. That was his richness—a surfeit of consciousness and knowledge of the soul's continuity. The fish part is a reference to the Salmon of Wisdom, a Celtic contribution to the overall perception of this figure. The fish swims in the deep waters; it is the content of awareness, the fruits of memory, the information of the soul's recall. The Rich Fisher King is the Salmon of Wisdom—the Fish itself.

The fish is also an incarnation of the Christ undertaken long ago. In the Hindu description, Vishnu has ten major incarnations; the first was as *Matsya-avatara*. At first a small fish, he grows to be eight million miles long and tows the Boat of the Vedas (the Vedic equivalent of Noah's Ark) with Manu-satyavrata, the Vedas, and various important celestial beings all present, floating atop the Flood.

When the Flood subsides and the Boat of the Vedas (Ark, or Grail Castle) rests upon the highest landmass to appear above water, the next cycle of Creation begins. Manu-satyavrata is the lord and benefactor of that new epoch because he is rich (he remembers what came before) and he has the fish (Christ Consciousness—in Greek, Christ was called Ichthys, Fish). Other expressions of the same are Oannes the Man-Fish and Ea the Sublime Fish of Mesopotamia.

The Manu sets the spiritual tone and evolutionary parameters for a span of 306,720,000 years, which is called a *manvantara,* his duration as Rich Fisher King. He will be succeeded by 13 more Manus in a Day of Brahma.

Outwardly, he is regent of the Grail Castle and its processes; and he exists microcosmically in each human as the soul enjoying full memory. Other names for this include Real Self, God-Self, Perfect Self, Higher Self, and Mighty "I AM" Presence. In his pure state, the Fisher King has achieved ascension, that is, his physical body has been transmuted into a Light-body; or, he demonstrates the condition of ascension. In this state, he is *rich* because he has unlimited access to the storehouse of universal substance (the Ocean of Milk) and can precipitate (create) anything he wishes; clothes, jewels, food, buildings, a body, as needed. His riches are light.

If conditions of human consciousness remain good and flourishing with recall, the Manu will be called Rich; if psychic oblivion prevails, he is Maimed.

See also: Fall of Man, Flood, Grail Castle, Grail Knight, Grail Maiden, Holy Grail, Klingsor, Manu, Ocean of Milk, Salmon of Wisdom, Wasteland.

FLOATING BRIDGE OF HEAVEN

A higher dimensional platform for terraforming the Earth, creating landmasses, and assigning protector angels.

Also known as Tir-na-Moe.

Description: Japanese myth recounts that in the days soon after the separation of Heaven and Earth, which had been like a chaotic egglike mass with germs of life in it, two primary Creator gods stood on a bridge. They were Izanagi ("Male Who Invites") and Izanami ("Female Who Invites"). They stood on the Floating Bridge of Heaven, which overlooked the still unformed abyss of Earth.

This Bridge (a rainbow arc of light) existed midway between Heaven and Earth. They had been assigned by the Lord of Heaven, who was the creator of Takamagahara, the High Plain of Heaven, to create the eight Japanese islands.

The two Creator gods were uncertain whether far, far below there might already be a landmass or if everything was still in an uncongealed state, like a jellyfish, one said. Below them was like a sea of filmy fragrant fog, like oil floating on the surface of water. The fog was so thick they could see nothing through it.

To find out what was there, they inserted a jeweled spear called *Ama-no-Nuboko* into the ocean. They stirred the tip in the brine. Then examining the tip of the spear, once they withdrew it, the two gods found water droplets on it with a little clot of mud. Those droplets and clot fell, congealed, and formed the island of Onogoro-jima ("Spontaneously Congealed Island"), Japan's first island, now known as Onokoro. The two gods descended to this island.

Even though they were already sister and brother, the two decided to marry. They established a pillar called the *Amanomihashira,* or August Pillar of Heaven, on this first of the Japanese islands, and each walked around it, though in opposite directions. Izanagi and Izanami also built the *Yashirodono,* Hall of Eight Fathoms, a magnificent palace at the base of the pillar, and there they dwelled.

They found pleasure, even amusement, in encountering each other at certain points around the pillar and, in doing so, they mated and produced the first generation of humans. They also created numerous beings, including the Sea Spirit, Mountain Spirit, and numerous spirits of trees, rivers, and fields. (Japanese myth says it was the great round of Heaven they constantly circumambulated, surprised when they met each other, and that from their circling and mating came the islands of Japan and all their features.)

They gave birth to seven more islands in the same manner, and to seas, rivers, mountains, plants and trees, to everything that now constituted *Oyashi-ma-kuni,* the Great Eight Island Country, as Japan was afterward known. Izanami filled everything they created with *kami* spirit, or divine-cosmic life force.

In Shintoism, Izanagi is usually interpreted as the bright, heavenly Sky god, while Izanami is the terrestrial, gloomy Earth Mother, Underworld ruler. In some versions, they are accompanied in their work by up to eight other gods.

Explanation: This is an ancient terraforming memory in which the "gods" shaped landmasses out of the molten clay of a virginal, freshly made Earth. It refers specifically to the creation of the Japanese islands, but also to the process of landshaping globally. The Floating Bridge of Heaven is the poetic way of referring to *where* the Earth-Shapers did this from or in fact come from or reside—a higher dimensional platform, somewhere starting at the fifth dimension or level of reality, and possibly more subtle than that.

In an almost equivalent Irish myth (see Brigit's Mantle), the gods did their terraforming from an otherworldy place called *Tir-na-Moe.* The key element in both myths is not so much the Bridge or the celestial dimension they acted from, but that in both cases they used a divine or godly spear. In the Irish version, it was Lugh's Spear of Victory from the "flame-bright" Celestial City of Gorias, and in the Japanese, it is the jeweled spear *Ama-no-Nuboko.*

Earth is a designer planet, created on demand by the "gods," a consortium of angels, extraterrestrials, and enlightened sages under commission of the Supreme Being. It has a complex array of sacred sites that comprise its visionary geography, and all of its 100+ features (with multiple copies of each) keep the Earth and human consciousness in living alignment with the galaxy.

This geography was installed, activated, regulated, and primed over a 27-million-year period, a primordial time in which the gods were present on Earth and the archetypes underlying all myths were living realities. Egyptian myth recalls this as Zep Tepi, the First Occasion, and, among the Australian Aborigines, this is the Dreamtime. The terraforming with the jeweled spear happened in the earliest phases of the 27 million years of the Dreamtime, earlier, in fact, than the installation of most of the visionary geographic features.

The spear as a symbol is the archetype of fire, but in the case of Earth's earliest days, the spear was not symbolic but actual in the form of a coherent light, like a focused red laser beam sent down to Earth from dozens of extraterrestrial ships in high orbit. The intent was to catalyze the raw, molten, seething primal matter of the planet into coherent, predesigned landmass shapes.

The Japanese (and Irish) myth says the two Creator gods stirred the brine with their jeweled spear. Brine does not actually refer to the oceanic waters of the Earth, but rather to matter in a seething, almost chaotic condition before it is shaped and ordered into livable landmasses, such as islands and continents. The spear—that is, the laser beam—sparked the matter into the desired shapes.

The brine was like prima materia, the original unformed black substance of matter, dissolved like a colloid in the quasi-physical, semi-etheric mass of a newborn Earth. The laser beam, the coherent fire of the gods, precipitated the semi-dissolved solids into specific land shapes and masses, large and small.

Analogically, it was like stirring the cheese brine to coagulate it into curds. To adapt a familiar image from science fiction, it was like the last stage of teleportation, whereby a person or object is dematerialized, transported as a light beam, then reassembled at the desired location. In this case, the information and pattern for the desired shape of the landmass is carried in the laser beam from the ships in high orbit. As the beam strikes the "brine," the information in it organizes the inchoate matter into the intended shape, such as Japan's islands.

Thus the Spear of Victory or *Ama-no-Nuboko* carries the desired landmass pattern as information with its light, or fire, then imparts it to the raw matter. With dozens of ships in orbit, operating with this sophisticated level of terraforming technology, the Earth's original land formation, known to geologists as Pangaia, a single supercontinent, was created relatively quickly, though it may have taken time to congeal and stabilize.

Izanagi and Izanami are two aspects of the angelic watcher or egregor assigned to the landmass and people of Japan. The various spirits they created belong to the hierarchy of subsidiary landscape angels that maintained the various natural features of Japan under the auspices of its premier tutelary prince of the nation, Izanagi-Izanami, one of 72 egregors originally assigned to specific landmasses on the Earth.

The *Amanomihashira,* or August Pillar of Heaven, they established on Onokoro, so as to remain close to the High Plain of Heaven, is the navel of Japan. This is a geomantic feature, also called an Energy Focusing Node (72 on Earth), that justifies a country saying such a place (e.g., the Yashirodono shrine and its shining pillar) is the navel of the world and the center of creation. For that self-contained landmass, it is. Those in Japan wishing to commune with the angelic being who maintains the geomantic and spiritual integrity of Japan and the folk-soul quality of being Japanese can visit this site on Onokoro.

The Yashirodono shrine and the *Amanomihashira* on Onokoro are also one of the 72 minor chakras, or energy-consciousness centers, in a globally distributed being called Albion, a vast cosmological human form with many energy centers.

See also: Albion, Brigit's Mantle, Dreamtime, Hurqalya, Monster-Slayer, Navel of the World, Zep Tepi.

FLOOD

The period of quiescence in between cycles of cosmic creation and dissolution as well as a global memory of the destruction of the first humans.

Also known as Ginnunga-gap, Night of Brahma, Pralaya, Waters of Nun.

Description: Many cultures around the world have a myth about a world-destroying Flood, said to last 40 days and 40 nights and drowning almost all living things on Earth; an ark that preserved a small portion of humanity, plants, and animals; and a prime Flood survivor, or couple, who repopulated the world and founded a lineage when their ark landed on a high land and the waters subsided.

Most familiar in Western culture is Noah's Ark, which allegedly landed on Mount Ararat in Armenia. Deucalion's ark landed on Mount Parnassus in Greece; Fionntan landed on the Dingle Peninsula in Ireland; the Sumerian Ziusudra-Utnapishtim landed his *elippu* (ark, but the size of a ziggurat, or stepped pyramid) at Mount Nimus (or Nisir), possibly in southeast Turkey; the Hawaiian Kahuna Nu'u landed his boat, the *Kai-akinali'i,* on Mauna Kea; Kamalapukwia, First Woman of Hopi myth, landed her ark on San Francisco Mountain in Arizona; the Navajo Flood survivor landed on Blanca Peak, in Colorado; and the Persian solar hero Yima landed his *var* on Mount Damavand.

Most Western scholars have sought to pin down an historical date for the Flood so widely remembered in world myth, and many have settled on approximately 11,000 B.C., with the Flood possibly being coincident, for those who even credit the idea, with the sinking of the continent of Atlantis. The Theosophical tradition, however, posits a date of 18,618,846 years ago, not so much for the Flood, but for the peopling of the Earth under the tutelage of their equivalent of the generational scion, Noah, a figure called Vaivasvata-Manvantara.

Explanation: While there may have been a significant flood on the Earth around the date archeologists and scholars postulate, it is not the same Flood as recounted consistently and almost identically in many different myths.

The Flood is a regular period of quiescence between vast cycles of time in the cosmos, and thus Earth, during which the prime Creator god, such as the Hindu Brahma (for whom the time explanation is most thoroughly worked out), goes into a retreat from existence, a phase known as the Night of Brahma.

Hinduism has an elaborate time reckoning

for cosmic existence based on Days and Years of Brahma. Brahma's size is measured in time, and all aspects, events, and the duration of cosmic, galactic, solar, planetary, and ultimately human biological time are calculated as portions of Brahma's vast extent.

One Day of Brahma (called a *kalpa*) is 4.32 billion human years and consists of 1,000 four-age periods, each lasting 4.32 million years. Creation exists during the Day of Brahma, then all the worlds dissolve during the Night of Brahma. During this Night, all the enlightened sages, the Seven Rishis, the Manus (world regents for one-fourteenth of a Day of Brahma), minor gods, and Brahma, Vishnu, and Shiva (the major gods) all ascend to a higher sphere to preserve cosmic life and wait for the dawn of the next Day of Brahma.

When the Day of Brahma begins again, all the gods return to the lower spheres to resume their cosmic activities, though usually under new names for the new epoch. The Manu, otherwise known as the Flood survivor (e.g., Noah, Deucalion, Fionntan, Yima) who piloted the Boat of the Vedas to safety, regarded by humans as the mythical progenitor of the world, becomes regent of the world for a *manvantara,* or 306,720,000 years. The reigns of 14 Manu fill the time space of one Day of Brahma.

One Year of Brahma consists of 360 Days and Nights of Brahma, or 155,520,000,000 years, and Brahma's entire life span is 100 such years, or 311,040,000,000,000 years. This is how old Brahma is. His 36,000 divine Days are called a *Mahakalpa,* and the Flood that comes at the end of it is a *Mahapralaya* (Great Dissolution). The Nights that come at the end of each Day are called *Pralaya.*

Pralaya, which means destruction or dissolution, is of several kinds, each affecting larger scopes of Creation and occurring at larger time intervals. The Brahmapralaya, after the end of a Day of Brahma (4.32 billion years), involves the destruction of the universe, through drought and intense solar heat. The one Sun will become seven suns and burn all the worlds, both physical and subtle, and all the worlds will resemble globes of fire.

The Hindu description is similar to the Norse concept of Ragnarok, or Twilight of the Gods, in which Surtr (the Sun) similarly burns up all creation and destroys most of the gods in an apocalypse of uncreation. Their term for Pralaya is *Ginnunga-gap,* which means "Yawning Gap," an empty space.

The Flood, or Pralaya, is the ending of the world by inundation and fire and the time of cosmic sleep (Night of Brahma) before the next Day of Brahma. It is a time when the prime creative force floods the space in which creation happened. The Judaic mystical tradition calls this the Vacated Space. When the Supreme Being decided to start Creation, He had to remove Himself from a certain amount of reality so existence could proceed; otherwise, God would still be everywhere, filling everything, and there would be no room for creation.

God retreated from a sphere, leaving it empty of Himself; this was the Vacated Space. Then, so His creation would not be bereft of God, He reinserted Himself by the *Kav,* a thin line of Light that went halfway into the Space. During the Flood, however, God again filled in the Vacated Space with Himself.

The attribution of 40 days and 40 nights to the Flood may be explained in terms of Judaism's Tree of Life. This is a model of reality in terms of four interlinked Trees, each containing ten spheres of Light and consciousness. All have been emanated by God (Brahma) as the act of Creation. During a Pralaya, all 40 spheres (called Sefiroth) are flooded with God; each of them is a miniature Vacated Space, and each is deluged with the return of God to fill the Space. Only the Supreme Being (Brahma) remains above the Flood waters (the four Trees).

Hindu myth says Brahma retreats back into the navel of Vishnu (the Hindu version of Christ, the one who permeates and pervades all space).

Vishnu sleeps and dreams atop Sesa-Ananta, the cosmic dragon, who floats on the Sea. When the Night of Brahma (the Flood) is finished, Vishnu extrudes Brahma once again from his navel and the Creator God awakens on his white lotus and creates.

The Flood commonly remembered in myth pertains to the interval between cycles of Creation and Manus when the first round of humanity (see Asura, Djinn, Kings of Edom, Raksasas) was removed from the Earth by God's order. A second generation of humanity was seeded in its place and its spiritual progenitor, mentor, and benefactor was the next Manu (e.g., Noah, Deucalion, Ziusudra-Utnapishtim, Yima, and the rest).

Egyptian mythology remembers this landing peak a little differently, as the Primeval Hill or White Mound. This is the first land that emerged from the primeval waters, the watery chaos called Nun, and upon which the Creator god Atum (or Ptah) rested. In Memphis, this Hill was called *Ta-tjenen* ("the Elevated Land"), while in Heliopolis (anciently, Annu, now Cairo) it was equated with the *Ben-ben* stone (an omphalos stone); further south along the Nile, Thebes claimed possession of the "glorious hill of the primeval beginning."

The Hill was also called White Mount, the First Place, Ptah's Mound, and God's Mountain, and was the seat of the White House and White Throne. Here the White House with its White Throne equals the throne of the Rich Fisher King in the Grail Castle (Boat of the Vedas, Ark, elippu, var), which settled on the highest peak rising above the Flood waters or arose out of the waters to be the first landmass (and thus the highest peak) above the inundation. It's the same story.

The Flood survivors are not only Manus, world regents and primogenitors of humanity, they are also all different expressions for the Rich Fisher King, Lord of the Grail Castle. The Rich Fisher King is the world benefactor who remembers the Day of Brahma before the Flood (Night of Brahma); he is the one who in consciousness can go back all the way to the Pralaya where it was just Vishnu (Christ) on the cosmic dragon floating on the universal Flood waters.

In Norse myth, the place where humanity is regenerated is called the Plain of Idavöll ("Splendor-Plain"), which is equivalent to the high place or mountain peak above the Flood waters on which the Ark lands.

This is Christ Consciousness, the absolute memory and continuity of awareness that straddles Days and Nights of Brahma, that survives Pralaya. The Quest of the Holy Grail is the reattaining of that vast cosmic memory, preserved by the Rich Fisher King (Manu). In most cases, the named mountain peak where a Flood survivor landed (e.g., Mounts Parnassus, Ararat, Mauna Kea) is the site of a geomantically templated Grail Castle, provided for humans to remember. The Earth has 144 Grail Castles, almost always above mountains or peaks, although there is not always a Flood or Manu myth attributed to all such sites.

See also: Ancient of Days, Fisher King, Grail Castle, Holy Grail, Manu, Ragnarok, Salmon of Wisdom, White Mount.

FOREST OF BLISS

An illuminated, highly numinous array of the 50 aspects of the human chakras templated on a landscape and of variable size.

Also known as Anandavana, Chakra Template, 50 Gates of Binah.

Description: The term Forest of Bliss, or *Anandavana,* is applied to the holy city Banaras in India. The forest refers to the multitude of lingas of Shiva, one of Hinduism's three primary gods, and known as the Destroyer. An old text says the lingas, which resemble erect phalluses made of stone and extend several feet high from their base, arose like little sprouts out of sheer bliss.

Banaras, mystics say, is a thick forest of Shiva lingas, or brilliant light columns, that produce the bliss *(ananda)* of liberation in the presence of the god. It is said that Banaras has 100,000 Shiva lingas, that six million stand in the Ganges River, and all of them bestow yogic achievement and release from the confines of matter and matter-based consciousness. In an old text, Shiva tells his consort, Parvati, that there are "uncounted lingas" in the Forest of Bliss; another time he says he once counted a hundred billion of them, and presumably hadn't finished.

The vast amount of Shiva lingas in Banares is given as the reason for its high, exalted state of consciousness. In fact, Banaras as a whole is called the Luminous City of Light, Shiva's Linga. Each linga can bestow liberation (enlightenment or illumination) and thus freedom from material ignorance. In Banaras, you encounter a linga with every step you take, and there is not a place even as big as a sesame seed that doesn't sprout a linga there, local legend says.

Shiva is said to dwell in Banaras with such intensity (certainly aided by his phalanx of lingas) that everything is composed of his god substance. Many come to Banaras to die, certain that the holy city is a portal for the liberation of the soul.

Explanation: Despite the well-known Indian tendency to exaggerate and embellish, Shiva's attributed statement about there being a hundred billion lingas and legend's claim that every inch of Banaras, down to a sesame seed-sized locale, sprouts a Shiva linga, are actually mostly true and have an authentic geomantic correlate.

The geomantic feature is called a Chakra Template. It can range in size from no larger than a molecule to inches to miles long laid out over the land. The planet has a total of 260 septillion Chakra Templates or Shiva lingas of all sizes. Each contains the seven major energy-consciousness centers, just as they are found in the human; each of the seven major chakras has seven or eight subsidiary expressions, giving a hierarchical array of 50 vibratory stages. In Judaic mystical lore, this is called the 50 Gates of Binah, considered a prime initiatory threshold into the Great Cosmic Mother (Parvati) and her wisdom.

With a Chakra Template, these 50 Gates or chakras can be preactivated, illuminated, and filled to the brim with divine light, Shiva's presence—the goal of yogic practice in which matter (Shakti) merges with spirit (Shiva) in the crown. Geomantic entropy and the lack of maintenance over the eons has led, however, to many of the Templates being in less than perfect condition and they may require some tuning up and detoxification for best effects on consciousness.

An activated Chakra Template or Shiva linga in a landscape radiates immense spiritual light, wakefulness, and bliss, and creates a favorable environment (a highly numinous one) for spiritual advancement.

Judaic mystical tradition calls the Shiva linga a *Kav.* When God decided to start Creation, He designated a spherical space, removed His presence from it, then came back into it by way of a little line of light, the Kav, only halfway into what was now called the Vacated Space. Inside the Kav are all the spheres and hierarchical dimensions of Light, called *Sefiroth;* the Light flows like a waterfall through them, ten stages.

These spheres of Light and consciousness are the archetypes of the chakras, the planetary spheres (of which the physical planets are an approximate echo), and the Tree of Life, both a cosmic reality and an abstract model of reality.

Banaras is accurately called a Forest of Bliss because it could well have 100,000 or 100 billion Chakra Templates of all sizes creating an intensely spiritual environment. Other locales, often cities, have Chakra Templates, which may appear as horizontal walkable templates several hundred yards to miles long.

Since there are 1,080 Chakra Template generators on Earth (called domes), conspicuous, marked Templates may have hundreds of subsidiary Templates. Any location with a prolific array of Chakra Templates of various sizes can rightfully be called a Forest of Bliss in honor of the prime exemplar, Banaras.

The Scottish island of Iona, three miles long, has a Chakra Template that starts at one end and concludes at the other, affording people an interactive experience with their own chakras in the context of a landscape template. Appropriately, Iona was once known as Heredom in the Masonic tradition, which was a mystical mountain, or Mount of Initiation. It was also known as *Innis nan Druidhneah,* Isle of the Druids. Both references are fitting in light of Iona's Chakra Template, an excellent landscape device for initiation.

See also: Argonauts, Golden Fleece, Holy Mountain, Yggdrasill.

FOUNTAIN OF YOUTH

The source of unbroken, uninterrupted, continuously wakeful consciousness from before Creation assuring immortality of awareness, and templated across Earth in 144 Soma or Moon Temples.

Also known as ambrosia, amrita, Celestial City of Kantimati, Haoma, Lake of Sperm, manna, mead, Moon Temple, nectar of the gods, Soma, Soma temple, Water of Kane, Water of Life, Well of Living Water.

Description: The term "Fountain of Youth" entered popular awareness in the early 1500s when Spanish explorer Juan Ponce de Leon (1460–1521), fellow traveler with Christopher Columbus and governor of Puerto Rico, sought a river, spring, or fountain said to possess such potent curative powers that youth and health could instantly be restored by drinking its waters.

Natives of Hispaniola, Puerto Rico, and Cuba told Ponce de Leon the spring of perpetual youth was located on the island of Bimini (easily reached from the southeast coast of Florida), but he was unable to find it. Ponce de Leon knew that others had sought the fabled Fountain of Youth; even the redoubtable conqueror Alexander the Great had sought it in eastern Asia.

Ponce de Leon may not have known that the Fountain of Youth figured significantly in Polynesian and Hawaiian myth and was known as the Water of Kane, after the god who protected it. Access to this miraculous water affords the fortunate ones an infusion of Kane's godly curative powers. The sick become healthy and the dead restored to life after consuming just a few drops.

Kane is the god of healing, rebirth, resurrection, procreation, and life; his waters can restore all life, make a wasteland bloom, and give the lucky hero everlasting life. He was the creator of the three worlds of Earth, sky (lower Heaven), and upper Heaven, the ancestor of all humans, and God of the Sea. Polynesians said he lived in human form on a magical island near Hawaii called *Kane-huna-moku,* "Hidden Land of Kane." Here, if blessed by the gods' favor, one may find *Ka-wai-ola-a-Kane,* the Spring of the Water of Life-Kane.

Explanation: To understand the geomantic reality of the Fountain of Youth we must be careful not to see this feature in materialistic, physical terms. What is referred to is a geomantic feature called a Soma Temple or Moon Temple, of which there are 144 copies in Earth's visionary geography.

Like the Sun Temple (see Hitching Post of the Sun), the Moon Temple represents a primordial state of reality and consciousness and an early step in the sequence of steps in Creation that at long last produced humanity and the Earth.

The Fountain of Youth is most easily understood through the Hindu myth of King Soma. He is the divine embodiment of the substance of undying consciousness, of perpetual wakefulness, of the first wakefulness, of the eye that never sleeps, the unbroken continuity of awareness—immortality. It is immortality not in a physical, bodily sense, but in an ultimate Self sense. It refers to the inextinguishable spark of awareness that cannot die and truly lives forever.

When the gods stirred the Ocean of Milk (the primal Sea of Light), they sought to uncover Soma, the substance of immortal awareness, and they did. Although Hindu culture and liturgy often describes Soma in terms of a palpable plant, the physical plant is actually symbolic of the celestial immaterial Soma.

King Soma, or the Moon god, is the deity

who is always awake, the first among the gods to awaken, and stay awake, and he is an edible substance even if he is also almost unfathomably elusive, as the unpalpable flow of consciousness.

The Moon in myth is not the diminutive satellite of planet Earth, but rather a fundamental condition of the early cosmogony, older even than the Sun. The Sun is the archetype of fire and time, but the Moon is the archetype of wakeful space. King Soma had 27 wives called the *naksatras,* and he visited each for 27 days.

As the naksatras represent the Vedic division of cosmic space (similar to the Western 12 zodiacal signs, only more than double), this myth says immortal, unbrokenly continuous consciousness is distributed uniformly throughout all the divisions of cosmic space and it permeates all the celestial beings (stars) in it. All of universal space is filled with and nourished by Soma.

Similarly, as the microcosm of this, the cells, molecules, and atoms of the human body, all its organic space, are permeated with Soma, unbroken awareness.

The gods continuously desire and consume Soma because it restores to them their state of unified existence, which is the way they were before they were differentiated into stars. Hindu myth says Soma is the substance consumed by Fire, and here we can usefully construe primordial Fire as the differentiated consciousness of stars.

The Star gods, made of Fire and forged in the Sun Temple (they are what the ancient Chaldeans called the great Star-Angels, or Spirits of the stars), perpetually want to eat that which is older than them—Soma, substance of the Moon.

Soma is a profounder state of consciousness than the awareness of discrete stars. Soma is the original uninterrupted state of consciousness, the Uncreate Light or the Plenum before Creation, the source of Light, the Ocean of Milk.

Here is one way a Soma Temple may appear psychically: Picture a domed ceiling with thousands of apricot-colored crystalline squares; in each is a face. This is the Hive of the Immortals, the eternal Star gods, and they are gazing raptly down upon a vat at the center of the floor of a rotunda to which they form the roof. This vat is filled with Soma, the immortal white substance they crave.

Humans visiting a Soma Temple have the opportunity to partake in this unbroken consciousness by sampling the Soma in the vat. It will afford you entry into the Hive of the Immortals and their realm of differentiated awareness. Selected locations of Soma Temples include Barbury Castle on the Ridgeway in Wiltshire and Warden Hill, Bag Enderby, Lincolnshire, both in England; Afrasiab in Samarkand, Uzbekistan; Ekisnugal at Ur, today's Iraq; and Bimini.

In an elegant cosmomyth about Soma, Vedic thought says Rudra (the star Sirius and an early form of Shiva) long ago tried to kill Prajapati, Father of all creatures (equated with the constellation Orion, seen as an antelope), but the arrow hit his testicles. Some of his seed leaked down into the lower worlds, pooling as the Lake of Sperm or Vastu. Rudra had been trying to stop the possibility of Soma leaking out of Prajapati from the Uncreate into the Created worlds, but failing in his attempt to kill him, some dribbled down. (The Uncreate is also known as Aditi, the goddess of infinite being, infinite light, and indivisible consciousness, the undivided unity of the infinite.)

The Vastu, or cosmos, became the House of Stars, with Rudra (Sirius) as the guardian of its Lake of Sperm (also called Lake of Prajapati's Seed and Lake of Fire)—essentially the supercreative essence of continuous consciousness and the quality of unruptured, self-contained, preconscious totality before Creation.

At Bimini, off the east coast of Florida, you have the opportunity to experience this myth, for there is a small landscape zodiac (a miniature holographic star map—see White Cow, White Sow) and a Soma Temple in its center. You can experience the Star gods, the embodiment of cosmic Fire, feeding from the always-full Soma vat.

See also: Hitching Post of the Sun, Ocean of Milk, White Cow, White Sow.

GAIA

The ultimate landscape angel and protector spirit for the planet who oversees all organic life, conscious-being evolution, the interconnected web of visionary geography, and Earth's role and position in the solar system.

Also known as Bhudevi, Bhumidevi, Chthon, Earth Spirit, Earth Woman, First Mother, Gaea, Ge, Geb, Kunapipi, Mother Earth, Tellus, Terra Mater.

Description: In Greek myth, and now, to an extent, in Western popular culture, Gaia is the name for the goddess of the Earth, for the Earth Spirit. The term was popularized in the late 1970s by British atmospheric scientist James Lovelock in his Gaia Hypothesis in which he proposed that the planet was a self-regulating, homeostatic mechanism; Lovelock did not accord Gaia sentience.

The ancient Greeks wrote that Gaia was born of Chaos as the first goddess, then herself as a virgin mother birthed numerous beings fundamental to the cosmogony, such as the Titans, Oceanus, and Typhon, the sky, sea, and mountains. As some of her creatures were monsters and disturbed the gods and humanity, Gaia was seen as ambivalent, sometimes deceitful, even threatening.

Yet she was also nurturing, the focus of many cult centers such as Athens' sanctuary of Ge Kourotrophos. Some accounts said Gaia was the original owner of the renowned oracle at Delphi and had installed the giant snake-dragon Python there to defend her property.

Gaia was the goddess of the Earth, and the Earth itself in the Greek imagination. To the later Romans, she was Tellus, an Earth goddess who personified the planet's productive power, and also *Tellus Mater* ("Tellus Mother"). The Romans dedicated a temple to her in 286 B.C. and celebrated a festival of Tellus on December 13; Gaia as Tellus was also honored in Rome in the Sementivae festival in January and the Fordicidia in April. Another name she was known by in Roman times was *Terra Mater* ("Earth Mother").

In classical India, Gaia was Bhudevi, "the Goddess Who Is the Earth." Once she complained to Vishnu (the Hindu version of Christ) that she was being overrun and victimized by demons, and he came down to rid her of them.

Most Native American tribes had a myth about the Earth as a Primal Woman. The Okanaga of Washington State, for example, told of how the Old One made Earth from a woman who was to be everyone's mother. Once she was a human, but was transformed into a round planet so we cannot see her human form anymore. The elements of the planet, such as the soil, trees, rocks, and wind, are, respectively, her flesh, hair, bones, and breath. All of us live on her extended body.

In Egyptian myth, the surface of the Earth, and sometimes all of Earth, was called Geb, portrayed as the male counterpart and brother-husband to Nut, the Sky goddess with whom he was once in inseparable union. Geb is shown with a goose on his crown, for which he is known as "The Great Cackler" *(Kenkenwer)* because he laid the original Cosmic Egg from which the world arose.

Similarly, the Australian Aborigines of Arnhem Land speak of Kunapipi, the First Mother. She established the songlines in the Dreamtime, that is, the primordial tracks across the landscape along which all life was created. She taught the ancestors how to see the songlines, follow and honor them in their rituals to find the sacred places, such as caves, across and in her planetary body.

Explanation: The nature of Gaia has confused Western thinking for centuries because the ancient Greeks used the name to refer to two different things. Gaia, as part of the original duality of Heaven and Earth (Ge), referred to the totality of cosmic matter, everything that was outside the Pleroma (the fullness of being). Earth, in this sense, encompassed galaxies and innumerable solar systems and planets. It would be parochial to interpret this reference to mean our planet Earth.

But Gaia also referred to the feminine angelic protector spirit of the planet, as the Okanaga and Aboriginal myths clearly suggest. Each planet has a single angelic spirit who presides over the entirety of the planet's life and processes. These beings are sometimes called egregors ("Watchers") or landscape angels. The egregor for Jupiter, for example, is called Brihaspati by the Hindus.

Landscape angels, or egregors, maintain the geomantic integrity of a given landmass, from small scale, such as a garden or valley, to larger, such as a mountain, state, or nation (see Eriu). There are millions of landscape angels, also called Nature devas, servicing the Earth. At the level of nations, they are called Guardian Angels of the Nations, National Angelic Regents, or Tutelary Princes of the Nations. They are a specialized order of angels assigned to the Earth and, along with the landscape angels, work with Gaia, who functions as their overseer.

As the Okanaga and Aboriginal perceptions of Gaia show, she can be seen as a feminine angel whose body is the planet and all its organic life. She was the original owner of Delphi, and in fact its once and future owner, because that geomantic node and its dragon are a part of her global visionary geography. She established the songlines and knows their routes and numinous nodes intimately because they are aspects of her planetary body, pores on her skin, as it were.

Gaia holds the master blueprint for the evolutionary parameters of the Earth, its species-diversification capacity, its possibilities for human conscious evolution, and Earth's function and evolutionary agenda as a planetary body in the solar system. She works closely with Pan to maintain the vitality and integrity of Earth's plant and animal kingdoms, and she works with the angelic hierarchy to support the well-being and awareness of humans.

Gaia is not the physical Earth, any more than the human soul is the physicalized human, but she indwells the materiality of the planet as its soul. As for her appearance, Gaia can assume any guise she chooses for the purposes of psychic perception by and interaction with humans. A Welsh perception of her was as Blodeuwedd, a beautiful young woman whose face or perhaps entire body was made of nine different wildflowers in bloom.

The Aborigines understood their task was to follow the songlines into the sacred spaces within the Earth Mother's planetary body and that their rituals would help keep their landscape whole and healthy. Similarly, any wholesome, respectful human interaction with the Earth's array of sacred sites (Gaia's visionary geography) benefits the planet and is like saying hello to Gaia herself.

Here is one possible guise: Picture the Earth as the familiar blue-white planet suspended in space, close enough so you can see the continents. A single, motherly face is wrapped benevolently around the globe so that wherever you look, you see her full on, and her eyes are full of compassion and tolerance. Within her planet-wide face are millions of angelic handmaidens—the landscape angels and egregors of the nations, all expressing her many aspects. Yet Gaia too is a handmaiden, in her case to the Divine Mother, the female aspect of God.

Just as, according to the Okanaga perception, Gaia was once a woman who became a planet, so some cultures see her body cut up into numerous pieces and distributed across landscapes. The Hindus talk of the 18 (or 51 or 108) body parts of the goddess Sati (or Shakti), each commemorated by a *Shakti Pitha* (shrine), and the Tibetans speak of the Srin-mo Demoness, her body tied down by temples.

See also: Agharta, Candlemas, Eriu, Fairy Queen, Grail Knight, Kokopelli, Michaelmas, Nymph, Pan, Srin-mo Demoness, Tower of Babel, Wasteland, Yeti.

GANESH

A cultural perception of the angelic order called Ofanim connoting their aspect of pure mind through the merry elephant-god form.

Also known as Airavana, Airavata, Ganapati, Ganesa, Ganesha, Iravata, Vinayaka.

Description: Ganesh is the jolly elephant god of Hinduism, son of Shiva and Parvati.

Ganesh is also called Ganapati, for he is chief or leader of the *Ganas* (attendants, troops, hosts, or demigods, although the term is also translated as dwarf-demons). Another name for that position is Vinayaka, whose name means "Remover of Obstacles." Vinayaka was appointed by Shiva and Brahma (the Creator god of Hinduism) to remove obstacles from the paths of humans.

The Ganas were nine groups of minor deities in service to Shiva and Parvati; their task was to punish word-breakers and evil-doers. Vedic lore says the Ganas once were humans who now live in a paradisal realm called Bhogya and love music and dancing. Twelve groups of seven Ganas are said to live with the Sun during parts of each year.

Ganesh is pictured as an elephant standing on his hind legs, or sometimes seated, human-style, as if in meditation or like a teacher discoursing. He is also portrayed as a human with an elephant's head, and he has an elephant's appetite. He has a long trunk and a pronounced potbelly, and is one of India's most popular gods. Among his other names are *Heramba* ("Five-Headed"), *Lambakarna* ("Long-Eared"), *Lambodara* ("Hang-Bellied"), *Gajanana* ("Elephant-Faced"), and *Vighnesvara* ("Remover of Obstacles").

He is regarded as the benevolent, merry remover of obstacles, the god of all good enterprises, such as the start of a journey or the launch of a business. Just as the elephant through its sheer physical size easily pushes through all obstacles and thickets in the jungle, so Ganesh pushes aside obstacles for the faithful. His festival, Ganesha-Chaturthi, between mid-August and early September, is highly popular.

Ganesh is the god of practical wisdom, sciences, and skills, and especially the god of scribes and writing, invoked by writers at the start of a writing project. He is credited with writing the vast Hindu epic and trove of mythic lore, the *Mahabharata,* or having dictated it to the sage Vyasa, though some say Vyasa dictated it to him over the course of three years of steady work.

His encyclopedic knowledge won Ganesh the favor of two wives. In a wager with his brother, Kartikeya, whoever raced around the world could marry two girls. Ganesh did not bother to run because when Kartikeya returned Ganesh described the entire world in exact detail, having learned it all from books.

Devout Hindus often pray to Ganesh to intercede favorably for them with the more austere Shiva. Ganesh's iconographic symbolism is rich. He has four arms, which stand for his immense power to help people. He carries a noose and a goad; these represent his grace and all-pervasiveness. He holds a broken elephant tusk in his right hand to indicate he is the refuge for all. His belly is round, even huge, to denote his tolerance and the fact that he contains all things. The *modaka* (a rice confection) in his hand is *jnana,* conferring bliss and joy.

His round, pendent belly *(Lambodara)* is emphasized, highlighting Ganesh's vastness; devotees even claim that all galaxies and universes, and the spaces between them, are easily contained within his prodigious stomach.

Ganesh devotees have articulated 32 distinctly different images for the elephant god. As Bala Ganapati, Ganesh is a childlike god of golden hue. As Vira Ganapati, he is the valiant warrior in a fierce pose with 16 arms holding every variety of weapon. As Heramba Ganapati, he is the protector of the weak; as Kshipra Ganapati, the red-hued, quick-acting bestower of boons; as Srishti Ganapati, the friendly lord of happy manifestation; and as Dvimukha Ganapati, his two faces remind us that Ganesh sees in all directions at all times.

Ganesh is also called the Gatekeeper because he is depicted as sitting with a watchman's bell on the four petals of the *Muladhara,* or root chakra, at the base of the spine. In this position, he rules over memory and knowledge and guards the gate to the seven psychic centers (chakras) and all their spiritual qualities. To progress in spiritual development beyond the instinctive realms associated with the *Muladhara,* we must have Ganesh's blessings and support, Hindus believe.

Explanation: If you have ever wondered where the angels show up in myths, Ganesh is your answer. The jolly elephant god is one of the prominent cultural expressions that the angelic family called Ofanim have taken over time.

Technically, the Ofanim, always a plurality, can generate up to 40.3 million simultaneous manifestations of their presence anywhere, though their default position or minimum manifestation package is six, and an even more concentrated expression is as a single tiny point of brilliant light, a blazing star.

Other of the Ofanim's familiar though not recognized cultural manifestations have been as Garuda, the celestial bird-mount of Vishnu (the Hindu version of Christ); as Airavata ("Arisen from the Ocean"), a white, four-tusked elephant who emerged when the Ocean of Milk was churned by the gods and became Indra's mount; as Simurgh, the magical bird of Persian lore; as the Ziz, the primordial bird of awesome size in Judaic lore; as the Eagle, black-feathered and enigmatic, as described in Toltec shamanism and by Carlos Castaneda; as the Thunderbird, the Native American perception of the Ofanim in huge bird form; and as the Judaic Behemoth, the elephant with a massive belly created at the beginning of time.

The Ofanim have a paradoxical role with humanity. They are universally accessible to all interested people (contacted through meditation on a point of brilliant light just above the navel), yet are almost universally unknown as angels among humans. Only a very few interact with them knowingly, though the Ofanim influence many subconsciously, even to the extent, today, of inspiring movies *(Stigmata)* and television shows *(Highway to Heaven).*

A prime aspect of Ganesh's ability to push aside obstacles is his parentage of Shiva and Parvati. While the Ofanim do not actually have Shiva as a parent, the meaning is that at times they use Shiva's energy to accomplish their work. Shiva is the Lord of Destruction (a more apocalyptic version of the Greek Hades) who destroys all illusory states of consciousness—certainly, these are obstacles.

As for the *Mahabharata,* the Ofanim state that they dictated the text to Vyasa in a manner we tend to describe today as channeling. The intent was to describe the workings of the inner worlds that were reflective of the outer, human world and state of consciousness at the time it was transmitted to Vyasa. In other words, the *Mahabharata* largely describes situations and conditions in the spiritual worlds.

The Dvimukha Ganapati attribution of two faces that see all directions at one is apt. Religious texts say Opanniel *YHVH,* the Prince of the Ofanim, has 16 faces, four on each side of his neck, 100 wings on each side of his body, and 8,466 eyes. This means they can see what's going on, the Ofanim say. It means they see things from many different perspectives at the same time, like examining a flower from 8,000 different points of view. All aspects of an issue are covered.

Not only do they see all matters from a multitude of perspectives, they are responsible for a multitude of worlds, some 18 billion galaxies and all the sentient, self-aware, and evolving consciousness forms living in them.

As for the elephant attribution in general, the Ofanim state that as the Ofanim are literally a reflection of pure mind, so Ganesh as described in Hinduism is the symbol for the mind and its characteristics. The long trunk symbolizes that the Ofanim stick their trunk in everywhere, in everyone's business—that they are abundantly available in every instant of awareness.

The hugeness of the planetary elephant also

connotes the brightness of the Ofanim in their primary star manifestation. They state that their brightness exceeds that of the brightest star in any galaxy. Angelology texts say the Ofanim's light is so bright it illuminates *Arabot*, the Seventh Heaven and God's resting place.

Another key attribute is motion. Ofanim comes from the Hebrew *ofan*, which means "wheels." The Ofanim are the Wheels of the Merkabah, or God's mystical Chariot. They are the agents through which the Supreme Being moves through existence and are called Galgallim in recognition of this task.

Still another attribute relevant to the elephant is that of memory associated with longevity. Elephants are said to have long memories. The Ofanim were among the first angelic orders, out of 40, to be created, so they are among the oldest. Their age is approximately 60,480,000,000 human years, equal to one Week of Brahma (one Day of Brahma is 4.32 billion years [Day] + 4.32 billion years [Night] = 8.64 billion years), sufficient time to gain the wisdom attributed to them in their Ganesh form.

From the human point of view, their wisdom pertains to the energy aspects of Earth's visionary geography and array of sacred sites, its planning, installation, maintenance, evolution, and protocols of human interaction with it. They were foremost among the Dreamtime ancestors when the Earth was first created, as the Australian Aborigines would put it, or among the primordial gods of the First Time (Zep Tepi) as remembered in classical Egyptian myth.

The Ofanim are not the progeny of Shiva and Parvati, but they have a working relationship with this celestial being of male-female aspects. Ganesh is often pictured at the feet of Shiva, called Lord of the Dance, as he does his cosmic dance called *Ananda Tandava*, symbolizing the constant movement, permutation, death, and rebirth of all elements of existence. All the gods witness this wild dance of creation and the illusion of manifestation. Brahma tings the cymbals, Vishnu strikes a drum, and the Gandharvas play flutes.

The Ofanim explain that one aspect of their being is in the ecstasy of the dance of Lord Shiva, meaning they participate in this ontological revelation.

Contemporary people who have worked with the Ofanim or at least experienced their energy have reported dreams of dancing elephants.

The Ofanim have a central grounding (dancing) place for their energy on Earth and a meeting place for humans. This is Avebury, a 28.5-acre stone circle in Wiltshire, England. There, at the inception of the planet and its visionary geography, they installed a copy of the same blazing star found in all humans. Meditating on your own star at the navel while in proximity to the Earth's copy will amplify your attention on it and its attention on you. The Blazing Star is also the master key to the entirety of the visionary geography of Earth.

See also: Behemoth, Dreamtime, Garuda, Hanuman, Holy Mountain, Hurqalya, Ocean of Milk, Phoenix, Simurgh, Thunderbird, Vocub Caquix, Zep Tepi, Ziz.

GARDEN OF EDEN

The original psychic and physical conditions for a balanced, unified humanity, geomatically placed in multiple locations around the planet.

Also known as Field of Souls, Gan Eden, Land of Dilmun, Olam ha-Ba ("the World to Come"), Paradise.

Description: As described in Genesis, the Garden of Eden was said to be the place where Man, as Adam and Eve, the first male and female humans, were created under paradisal conditions. For a while, they lived in this ideal garden of delight, naked, in bliss, and in perpetual communication with God.

Genesis recounts that the Serpent tempted Eve with an apple (the "forbidden fruit") from the Tree of the Knowledge of Good and Evil, she ate it, and God expelled the couple from Eden for disobedience (the "expulsion from paradise," or "the Fall").

In Judaic rabbinic lore, Eden or Paradise is called the Field of Souls, in which the trees and grasses themselves are holy souls untainted by mortal life. It is very difficult to return to the Field of Souls once you leave, for one leaves naked (without the holy garments of light) as the soul enters spiritual exile. Judaic lore also equates the Garden of Eden with the *Olam ha-Ba,* "the World to Come."

Explanation: This is probably the most misinterpreted story ever, with highly unfortunate consequences to culture, spirituality, human identity, and even the Earth.

The Garden of Eden was a place on Earth, with multiple copies, created by the Supreme Being as an empty space for the Creation to unfold. It was a primary patterning for the potential for unified existence, with the male and female aspects of the human living as one in unitive harmony. Adam and Eve in this sense were the seeds of the perfected man and woman, in potential. The apple was self-consciousness, or the gift of self-aware individuality. The serpent was kundalini, the awesome life force that courses through the chakras, facilitating total awareness and, potentially, considerable psychic abilities and powers called *siddhis*.

The Garden of Eden and Adam and Eve story pertains to the first generation of humanity, vaguely remembered as the Asura, Raksasas, Djinn, and Kings of Edom. The Garden of Eden was placed on the physical Earth in the earliest days of the first round of humanity, but these humans engaged in extreme excesses and abused the freedom and psychic powers accorded them, so were dangerous to the Creation and Earth.

The first generation of humans, given self-aware consciousness and individual, sense-based, sex-differentiated bodies, treated Eden like an unending party, a wild, lost weekend with no cessation, until all of reality became unstabilized. This first generation of humanity was aborted and removed from physical reality and the Supreme Being decommissioned the Garden of Eden, or at least toned it down.

The primary patterning for Eden was located around Rondablikk in the Rondane Mountains of central Norway and is remembered in (or obscured by) Norse myth as Hvergelmir, one of three springs at the base of the Tree of Life.

Worldwide, Eden had 26 parts. Four parts, including this central one, were placed in the Rondanes, which meant that the emanation of the unified field from all four was amplified. Each of the 26 Edens emanated a unified field of consciousness, a unitive state, and Eden itself is an analogy for the potential of what the Mother-Father God (the ultimate archetypes of Adam and Eve) seeded on Earth.

A significant reason for the Norway placement is that the Rondane Mountains are the site for the planetary *Ananda-kanda,* inner heart chakra, and spiritually, or energetically, in terms of chakras, you can reach Eden through the inner heart chakra, like a secret garden behind a lovely park. Geomantically, the Earth's inner heart chakra is a root to the Garden of Eden. Further, the biblical Tree of Life at the center of Paradise or the Garden of Eden is the same as the Norse World Tree Yggdrasil, and this is found in the central Rondane Eden.

Three parts of Eden were in Saudi Arabia, two in Jordan, one in Turkey (Konya), one in China (near the Yangtze River), and one near Papeete, Tahiti; the others were situated in the now vanished continents of Lemuria and Atlantis. One of the five in Saudi Arabia and Jordan was the fabled Land of Dilmun, remembered in Sumerian myth as a holy, virgin, and pure land.

The 12 copies of the Garden of Eden are still on the planet and to some extent geomantically viable and visitable, if operating with reduced potency.

Originally, all of the Edens emanated a unified field, the primary patterning for the perfected male and female poles of consciousness in balance. This feature had consequences not only for the Earth, but also the universe, and its presence on a planet is highly rare and, one surmises, privileged. Out of an estimated 18.7 billion galaxies in the universe, only six planets, including Earth, were given or still have this primary patterning of Eden.

See also: Asura, Avalon, Djinn, Dreamtime, Fall of Man, Hurqalya, Kings of Edom, Raksasas, Yggdrasil, Zep Tepi.

GARUDA

An expression of the angelic family called Ofanim emphasizing their role as celestial support of the Christ Consciousness.

Also known as Angka, Bennu, Bialozar, Chamrosh, Eagle, Kreutzet, Phoenix, Pyong, Rukh, Roc, Saena Meregha, Semuru, Senmurv, Senmurw, Simargl, Taraswin, Tarksya, Thunderbird, Vinayaka, Vocub Caquix, Ziz.

Description: In Hindu lore, Garuda (from the Sanskrit *garut* for "wing" or from the Sanskrit *gr,* "to speak") is the King of the Birds and the celestial mount for Vishnu, the equivalent of the Western Christ or Logos. Usually, he is depicted as a golden eagle, though sometimes as a peacock with a long tail or as a figure with a human torso, but an eagle's head, beak, and talons.

When he was born from an egg, he glowed so beautifully he was thought to be an emanation of Agni, the great Fire god of Hinduism. He appeared as a kindled mass of blazing fire and grew instantly to his giant size as the Bright-Shining Lord of the Birds, as the *Mahabharata* tells it. All the gods and seers prostrated themselves before Garuda and sang his praises. His face is white, he has four human arms, his wings are red, and his body is golden (or green or red).

Among his epithets are Beautiful-of-Wing Lord of Knowledge, Lord of the Sky, the White-Faced, He Who Moves Like Quicksilver, and Vishnu's Mount. Garuda's other names include Amritaharana ("Stealer of the Nectar"), Nagantaka ("Destroyer of Serpents"), and Shalmalin ("Taloned").

Garuda is the destroyer of serpents and the enemy of snakes, called Nagas (he is the "Eater of Snakes"); as Garutmatman, he is identified with the Sun's rays; as Vinayaka, he is the remover and destroyer of obstacles, an epithet he shares with Ganesh, the Hindu elephant god; as Tarksya, he is the Sun portrayed as a white horse that pulls the solar chariot across the heavens; and as Taraswin, the Swift One, he is said to fly as fast as thought.

As Wings of Speech, Garuda embodies the mantric utterances of the Vedas (India's ancient, vast body of spiritual knowledge), the magic words that can transport humans instantly into the spiritual realms. The branches of Vedic lore and hymns are construed to be parts of Garuda's form which means Garuda is all the hymns.

Garuda is powerful, strong, courageous, and master of many disguises, capable of assuming whatever shape he pleases whenever it suits him.

Garuda is the *vahana* (divine vehicle or bearer) of Vishnu, and often he is depicted bearing Vishnu and his consort, Sri, Goddess of Beauty, to Heaven. Garuda is Vishnu's most fervent devotee.

Garuda stole the Soma, the precious elixir of immortality, from the gods' residence to secure the release of his mother. Garuda, roaring like terrifying thunder, fierce and great-spirited, and with a golden body that shone like bundled sunbeams, trashed the gods' hall and overcame most of the guardians of the Soma, consuming the elixir with his 8,100 mouths, even vanquishing Indra, king of the gods, and shattering his thunderbolt. Garuda's triumph earned him their enmity and he was known thereafter as Enemy of the Gods.

Garuda married Unnati (Progress, or Queen of Knowledge) and they produced six sons, and from them descended all snake-eating birds, understood to be the possessors of true knowledge who worship Vishnu as their protector.

Explanation: Garuda is a Hindu cultural expression for the angelic family called Ofanim (from the Hebrew *ofan,* for "wheel"). It is an angelic order with the capability of 40.3 million manifestations and a history of having produced numerous forms in different cultures and myths, such as Ganesh, the elephant god, and Simurgh, the Persian mystical Ruler of the Birds (angels). That is why Garuda is called a master of disguises; over time, the Ofanim have assumed most forms as a way of interacting with humans and symbolizing aspects of their function.

The Ofanim, like other angelic orders, can appear in either male or female valences, as appropriate. Garuda, as an expression of the entire Ofanim order, of course, did not "marry" anyone, but the "six sons" is accurate in that the Ofanim's minimum manifestation as angels is as six, and the mathematics of their full extrapolation into 40.3 million forms (their "descendants") is based on squaring the six. Each of the six has 6^6 major manifestations and 144 minor ones.

Garuda is not the enemy of snakes. Snakes, in Hindu myth, refer to the Nagas, a class of celestial beings who embody wisdom and whose form is depicted as snakelike in the sense of undulatory and intertwining. Snakes also refer to human souls in a state of awakening awareness. Garuda swallows awareness (eats snakes) as humans awaken; his function is to eat awareness, and the awakening of that awareness is the Snake.

Another expression of the Snake of Awareness is kundalini, the force of consciousness, moving through the chakras along the spine from groin to head. Kundalini moves through three channels, one straight and two intertwining, on its journey from the root chakra (groin) to crown chakra (head); hence the snake image.

Garuda may "eat awareness" as kundalini moves through the chakras in the moment of awakening, but this is not the same as possessing it. The awakening of awareness enables a human to ride with Garuda just as Vishnu and Sri do. Garuda carries humans who are awakening in awareness into the Christ Consciousness.

An expression of this in the Judeo-Christian tradition is the Star of Bethlehem, which guided the three Magi to the Christ Child in Bethlehem. This is true in both outer and inner aspects. In the outer aspects, the Ofanim manifested briefly as an anomalous point of light in the night sky; in the inner aspects, the Ofanim manifest in every human as a tiny point of brilliant light two inches above the navel and two inches inside. Meditation on this Blazing Star is the start of an initiation process that inducts one into the Christ Consciousness.

Garuda (the Ofanim) is the enemy of the gods in the sense that the Ofanim's energy, or quality of consciousness, can be experienced as ruthless to any status quo, human or celestial. It is ruthless in its adamant adherence to pure truth.

In Judaic mystical lore (Qabala), the Ofanim are attributed in the Tree of Life model (ten spheres of Light called *Sefiroth*) to the second Sefira called *Chokmah*. One of its cosmic functions is to be the source of the Autiot, the 22-lettered Hebrew alphabet conceived of as a sequence of cosmic creation tools. This is equivalent to the Hindu perception of Garuda's body being the Vedas.

The Ofanim's age is approximately 60,480,000,000 human years, equal to one Week of Brahma (one Day of Brahma is 4.32 billion years [Day] + 4.32 billion years [Night] = 8.64 billion years x 7 Days), sufficient time to gain the wisdom attributed to them in their Garuda form.

Garuda (the Ofanim) has a geomantic grounding point on the Earth at the 28.5-acre stone circle called Avebury in Wiltshire, England.

See also: Behemoth, Ganesh, Hanuman, Nagas, Phoenix, Simurgh, Thunderbird, Vocub Caquix, Ziz.

GESAR OF LING

The Tibetan-Mongolian expression of King Arthur, who is the Solar Logos and leader of the Great White Brotherhood, overshadowing a human initiate and his band of heroes in defense of land, people, and consciousness.

Also known as Bukhe Beligte, Fionn MacCumhaill, Geser, Gesar-Khan, Indra, King Arthur, Rustam, Thubpa Gawa.

Description: Gesar (from the Tibetan meaning "Lotus Temple") is the name of the Asian hero based in the Tibetan kingdom of Ling (or Kham) who inspired a great eleventh-century classic of Tibetan Buddhism that was transmitted by bards, singers, and priests throughout western Asia.

There is no single definitive version of Gesar's life, and for generations it existed only in the oral form; throughout the Himalayas and Asia today, the diversity of Gesar material, were it all collected, reputedly could fill 37 volumes. Among the Buryats of Mongolia, Geser is known as Bukhe Beligte (his name when he was a sky spirit), and bards speak or perform the epic over nine days with a horse-head fiddle.

Tibetan Nyingmapa lamas consider Gesar an incarnation of their founder, Padmasambhava, the Indian saint who brought Buddhism to Tibet.

Gesar's exploits pertained to the overthrow of Tibet's original inhabitants, the magician-shamans called Bon, viewed as evil from the colonizing perspective of Buddhism seeking to claim Tibet. King Gesar was a warrior god who won back his kingdom in a horse race; he was a subduer of demonic powers, a purifier of the land, an establisher of order and truth, a defender of the national religion (Buddhism) and moral law, defeating barbarians in countries as distant as Mongolia and Persia, and a future bringer of salvation.

Gesar is revered today in Tibet as a *dgra lha,* a war god and personal protective deity, and he is often referred to as *ma sangs,* the name of an important pre-Buddhist class of deities. He is also regarded as a protector of the Dharma. He is seen more as a lama than a king, and his victories turned more on the use of magical power than physical strength, as his enemies were most often demon-kings and evil Tantric magicians. He exemplified the proper use of shamanic power in a time in which witchcraft, black magic, and malevolent power ruled.

Even today, Mongolians believe that their great hero Gesar-Khan survives with his warrior retinue in an underground kingdom waiting to be born in Shambhala (the sublime city of spiritual adepts and the true world government), from whence he will one day ride forth triumphantly on a white steed to free the world from barbarians in the final Battle of Shambhala (see Shambhala). Tibetans also believe that Gesar, sleeping in the hills of the North, will once again ride forth to rid Tibet, as well as the entire world, of its demonic horde (barbarians).

After Tibet becomes overrun by demons and barbarians, Padmasambhava, the great Indian culture hero who first brought Buddhism to Tibet, organizes to find a suitable mother to birth Gesar, so that one day he may overrun the demons and accomplish his plans to purify the land and extirpate those who oppose the reign of justice. He persuades the bodhisattva (high spiritual adept) Thubpa Gawa to incarnate in Ling as a human called Gesar to oppose the dark powers.

Gesar's mother becomes a servant to the King of Ling; after Gesar's birth, he and his mother are exiled after a failed political intrigue against them both. He wins back his rightful kingdom of Ling in a horse race in which his steed runs twice as fast as all other horses and seems to fly rather than gallop over the land.

In the Mongolian version, Gesar's father, living in a higher plane, awards him a magical horse called Beligen ("Gift") while he meditates on a mountain. This is a horse from heaven, from the gods: Its hooves strike sparks on the rocks when it runs, lightning glitters in its eyes, and its hooves never slip.

Later, Gesar acquires a great treasure of weapons, armaments, and spiritual devices and talismans, under guard by the 12 goddesses of the Earth, when he enters an otherworldly cave under Padmasambhava's guidance. He marries Brugmo (also called Brugguma), the daughter of the former King of Ling; she is captured by the King of Hor, who is later defeated by Gesar and Brugmo returned. In the Buryat Mongolian version, he marries Alma Mergen, a Valkyrie-like figure, daughter of Uha Loson, chief of the Nature spirits.

Explanation: Gesar of Ling is the Tibetan-Mongolian expression of King Arthur. It is one of 15 reenactments in human culture thus far by embodied humans of the Arthurian mythos, an archetypal myth that describes the relationship between an esoteric group and Earth's visionary geography, the spiritual worlds, and humanity. Other reenactments have taken place in Persia (as Rustam), Ireland (Fionn MacCumhaill with his retinue called the Fianna), and, the most familiar, King Arthur of Camalate at South Cadbury Castle in Somerset, England.

The Tibetan-Mongolian version of King Arthur as Gesar of Ling preserves, even emphasizes, much of the original spiritual adeptship aspects of the story, in contrast, for example, to the British and Irish versions that emphasize the outer warriorship and physical combat nature of the figure.

As with the other cultural manifestations of the archetype, the central figure, Gesar of Ling (Arthur) is a blur between an actual historical figure and a timeless figure from myth. The historicity of this figure has always been difficult to pin down and, in the end, the Arthur figure does not so much die as fade away.

That is because the reality runs on parallel tracks: Above, King Arthur is the Solar Logos, the Word (Christ) expressed at the level of suns, or stars. Arthur is the leader of the Great White Brotherhood (a conclave of spiritual adepts, celestial beings, and angels) based in the constellation Ursa Major (Great Bear). Below, on Earth, King Arthur is embodied through a human (as are all the other key figures in the Arthurian mythos, including Guinevere, Arthur's wife and Queen—Gesar's wife Brugmo) acting in historical time in a specific culture.

It is the confluence of both streams, the above (celestial overshadowing) and below (actual incarnation of the archetype), that makes the story timeless and subject to endless permutations and why Gesar (and the Celtic King Arthur) is said to await in an underground kingdom his time on the world stage again. When the world (human culture and the Earth itself) need the Arthurian mythos again to restore order and truth (the Dharma), Arthur will return in a new form. The confluence explains why Gesar is portrayed as man and god, because he is both.

When the Gesar poets say he defeated the numerous demon-kings and overcame the evil barbarians, the actual reference here is to psychic warfare. Periodically, the numerous doorways in Earth's visionary geography get polluted with human negativity and unwholesome astral forms and beings. Gesar and his psychic-shamanic warriors cleanse the doorways of these noxious influences, making it possible for a more exalted state of consciousness to prevail.

Padmasambhava is one of the many potent human incarnations of the unique celestial being and Earth-mentor called Merlin (King Arthur's magus). In the Celtic version, he arranges for Arthur's birth and tutelage and helps him claim the kingship of England; he does the same in the Tibetan Gesar version.

Gesar's magnificent, supernaturally fast flying horse is matched in the Persian version where Rustam has Rakhsh, a unique steed with magical powers. The horse is an expression of the archetypal White Horse from Hindu lore (Uccaihsravas—see White Horse). This means as part of his self-mastery and the attainment of kingship, Gesar has the assistance of the Christ Consciousness; he can move as swiftly and widely as thought. This is apt because as Solar Logos he is the expression of the Christ at the level of the stars and within the warrior class.

See also: Camalate, Dragon, Einherjar, Fionn MacCumhaill, Guinevere, Indra, King Arthur, Merlin, Rustam, Shambhala, White Horse.

GHOST DANCE

An unfulfilled Native American prophetic vision that may still come to pass in a reacknowledged, reenergized American geomantic landscape maintained and regularly interacted with by resident Americans of all ethnic origins.

Also known as Bole-Maru Cult, Dreamer Cult, Earth Lodge Cult, Round Dance, Southwest Wind Dance, Wanagi-wachipi.

Description: The Ghost Dance prophetic and millennialist vision for a resurrected, Edenic, precontact Indian America surfaced twice in the 1800s.

The first occurred in 1869 when a Paviotso man named Wodziwob (Gray Hair of the Northern Paiutes in the Great Basin, or Midwest) experienced a trance in which he understood that a benign ruler was coming to the land accompanied by the spirits of Indian dead. This ruler would transform America into a paradise, erase distinctions among the tribes and races, and restore Indian America to its precontact status (before the Spanish and later Europeans).

The Indian tribes could hasten his arrival and the return of the dead by dancing and singing for days on end following specific protocols (such as five nights in a row, with joined hands, dancers in a circle, stepping sideways to the left, and performed at least 20 times per year), after decorating their bodies in red, black, and white paint, and sometimes wearing special Ghost shirts. The movement spread west rapidly, acquired different names and nuances, and flourished among many tribes for several decades as a promise of a world without whites, with the return of all that had been golden among the Native Americans.

Then on January 1, 1890, another Northern Paiute visionary named Wovoka, living among the Paviotso at Pyramid Lake in Nevada, had a powerful revelation during a solar eclipse that revived the Ghost Dance movement. Wovoka reported that he entered Heaven, saw his ancestors, and beheld the Christian God who told him about the End Times and instructed him in the Ghost Dance. Reportedly, Wovoka saw Christ singing as the Indians danced and understood that the whites and all the Indians should be as one people on the land.

Among the Paiute, where the Ghost Dance began, it was known as *Nänigükwa,* "dance in a circle." The Shoshoni called it *Tänä räyün,* which means "everybody dragging"; the Comanche called it *A'p-aneka'ra,* meaning "the Father's Dance" or "the Dance with Joined Hands." As with early Christianity, the original version was interpreted and expanded in many different ways.

The Sioux, however, put a different interpretation on this vision of the change in the world. To them, when the Indian dead returned to the land, the intruding whites would be forever removed from America, and the tribes would return to their harmonious, nativist, and pure old ways of living on the land. Merely performing the Ghost Dance with zeal and faith would drive the whites out of America and restore the Indian dead (the "ghosts") to their families.

Among the Sioux in the Great Basin, the Ghost Dance was called *Wanagi-wachipi,* and they spoke in terms of a new dance traveling in on the wind. The Sioux reported the growing legend that a holy man would cause the Earth to roll up like a blanket, rolling up all that was objectionable with the whites and their technologies, and underneath would be revealed the original, still vibrant Indian Earth and all the ancestors who once lived harmoniously upon it. The purpose of the Ghost Dance was to facilitate this rolling up of decadent white America so that the new-old world could arrive. Even the vast buffalo herds would return.

This time the Ghost Dance revitalization movement spread eastward into the Plain states, especially South Dakota. It ended disastrously for the Native Americans on December 29, 1890, when about 260 Ghost Dancers were massacred at Wounded Knee by the U.S. Army, which regarded them as a threat; this effectively ended the Ghost Dance and its millennialist expectations.

Explanation: The Ghost Dance is a potentially benevolent picture of apocalypse or End of the World changes to physical reality, and perhaps preferable because less damaging than the Norse Ragnarok or Christian Armageddon.

As with most powerful psychic visionary experiences, the time frame for events is open to interpretation. It is quite possible the Ghost Dance prophets were correct about the rolling up of the white American blanket, and were only wrong about when it would happen.

Obviously, the whites are not going to leave the American continent and the Indian dead will not resurrect from their graves, but there may be another, surprising, and more peaceful way the Ghost Dance vision still can come to pass.

The European whites who took over the American landscape did so without ever learning from the native inhabitants how to maintain its visionary geography, or terrain of sacred sites. For the most part, the Native Americans departed the scene without ever sharing the rituals and protocols for this. White European culture put its Christianity-technology overlay on the land, or what the Sioux metaphorically referred to as a blanket of "bad white man's stuff."

Although America today has only a small residual Native American presence, mainly in the Southwest, the Indian chiefs and medicine men are still caretaking the continent and their former tribal lands from the Spirit world. They have been doing what they can from the astral realm to keep as much of the land's inherent geomantic charge intact and vibrant, and they have been working with the various landscape angels who help maintain the land's energy quality.

Since there has been almost no participation in this vital maintenance from the incarnate side by people now living in America, it has had only minimal beneficial results. One half of the necessary geomantic "circuit" is still missing.

Yet knowledge of the geomantic layout of the American terrain can be resurrected and the land's visionary geography understood and mapped, and non–Native American residents can learn to interact effectively with sites formerly sacred to Indians and their Indian Spirit caretakers in such a way that it helps purify and revitalize the sites and provides revelation and spiritual growth.

In this way, the American Earth can roll up like an old blanket and reveal the pristine original geomantic terrain, as the Indians knew it, and the "ghosts" or ancestors of the Indians can return to the land in the form of being recognized as its caretakers and valuable Spirit colleagues today. The vast technology of the whites will not go away, but the mechanistic, materialistic, and atheist paradigm and disrespect, even oblivion, for physical matter, body, and land it imparts will dissolve and be replaced with a strong appreciation of a respiritualized Earth.

Although the Ghost Dance mythology was never couched in these terms, within this model of a future regenerated Earth, the white presence on the American continent can be likened to the dark grid or Antichrist energies that compete with the original Light body or visionary geography of the planet.

See also: Antichrist, Earth Changes, Harmonic Convergence, Ragnarok.

GIANTS

The physical manifestation on Earth of any of four different angelic orders by commission of the Supreme Being to aid Earth and humanity.

Also known as Cyclopes, Fallen Angels, Fomorians.

Description: Many myths of different cultures retain a memory of a time when giants walked the Earth. They were giants because they were huge, though essentially human in shape, and usually their time on Earth preceded humanity.

Geoffrey of Monmouth in his twelfth-century *History of the Kings of Britain* said the island of Britain was once occupied by giants, including, in its latter days, a repulsive 12-foot-tall one named Gogmagog based in Cornwall.

Typically, giants are portrayed as mostly male, of low intelligence, slothful, dangerous, and exhibiting a tendency toward human cannibalism. They are also credited, however, with having created many of the Earth's massive megalithic structures, even large or anomalous hills and many mountains.

For example, Saint Michael's Mount in Cornwall, England, and Mont-Saint-Michel in Brittany, France, two low-level rocky peaks on the English Channel, were said to have been created when two giants threw large rocks at each other. Ggantija ("Giant's Grotto") on the island of Gozo (near Malta) was said to have been built in a single night by a giantess named Sunsuna. Tiahuanaco in Bolivia, a 400-acre temple complex, which includes a pyramidal, artificial hill, was said to have been built at the beginning of time by the founder god Viracocha and his followers; they moved the stones through the air to the sound of a trumpet.

Often, heroes have to confront wayward giants and overcome them, such as Odysseus with Polyphemus, a Cyclops ("Round-Eyed"), and David with Goliath. The fifth-century Celtic King Arthur had to overcome a "great giant" at Saint Michael's Mount in Cornwall. This fierce giant had been devouring many of the people and generally ravaging the land. Another giant, named Gargantua, lived at Mont-Saint-Michel in Brittany, a similar peak at sea's edge in northwestern France across the English Channel. Virgil, in the *Aeneid,* writes of the big family of Cyclopes who dwelled in the caves of Mount Etna on Sicily.

When the Spanish were colonizing Ecuador, they heard a legend that a race of giants had once landed near Puerto Viejo at the point of Santa Helena in Peru. These giants looked human but were enormous; their eyes were the size of saucers and one giant ate the meat of 50 people. They bored a dwelling deep in the rocks but later resorted to sodomy and degenerate behaviors, killing the Indian women and children, and were eventually destroyed by the gods.

Archeologists and ethnologists have tried to match skeletal remains of very tall humans with the descriptions of giants from myth, but mostly they have failed to make a persuasive case that giants were merely long-limbed people.

Explanation: The giants of myth are any of four angelic orders temporarily taking large human form to accomplish certain tasks on Earth. The myths of giants are very old, as early as Hyperborea, some 20,000,000+ years ago.

The ancient giants on Earth are variously remembered as the Fomorians of Ireland, that country's first inhabitants, and, mistakenly, as Fallen Angels, and among the Greeks as the Cyclopes, one-eyed cave-dwelling giants.

The first incarnation of angels as very tall humans, or giants, were the Elohim, an executive order of angels charged with installing much of Earth's visionary geography, notably its megalithic features, and genetically engineering humanity. The Elohim were 18 feet tall when embodied, and the extreme height was taken for the purposes of protection against certain hostile animal species present on the Earth in its earliest days, so they wouldn't have to kill them.

Many of the large stone structures still extant around the Earth, such as the aptly named cyclopean stoneworks of Baalbek in Lebanon, Sacsaywayman in Peru, Mycenae and Tiryns in Greece, were created by the Elohim through effortless thought levitation—to most humans, magic—of the stones into the desired places. The Elohim also designed and constructed many of the massive city-size temple complexes such as Teotihuacan near Mexico City in Mexico, or the 28.5-acre stone circle in Wiltshire called Avebury, whose stones the Elohim created.

In fact, in the original design of Earth's visionary geography, the Elohim created 6,300 Cyclopean Cities, or massive megalithic enclosures and temple sites. A few remain as evidence of their handiwork, such as the ruins of Great Zimbabwe in the Republic of Zimbabwe, Baalbek in Lebanon, and Tiahuanaco in Bolivia.

Many of the myths of human contact with solitary one-eyed giants, notably the Cyclopes of Sicily and the Irish Balor of the Evil Eye, involved Elohim. The Elohim had numerous nodes in the Earth grid that functioned as meeting places for humans with them, such as Tory Island in Ireland, Burrowbridge Mump near Glastonbury in England, and Mount Etna and environs on Sicily.

Sometimes you can glimpse the Elohim's celestial function on Earth through some of the Greek myths, such as reported by Homer and Virgil. The Greek fire-smith god and Olympian named Hephaistos worked his forge with three Cyclopes as assistants within the volcano Mount Etna. Geomantically, this means Hephaistos, a celestial creator being (see Seven Rishis), worked with three Elohim within a Sun temple to put solar energy and consciousness into matter.

Simultaneous with the Elohim's physical presence on Earth was another angelic order called the Gibborim in giant human form. Myth and religious history recall this family as "fallen angels," but they were fallen only in the sense that they did not want to incarnate on Earth as giants so they were pushed out of Heaven onto Earth to complete their commission from the Supreme Being to facilitate memory in the early humans of their ancestry.

When the Elohim's initial work was done, they departed the physical plane, as did the Gibborim. They were still available for human interaction, as the myths of human encounters with solitary giants or Cyclopes remember, though the Elohim and Gibborim were in the spiritual realms, not the physical.

Their time period on Earth was Hyperborea, long before the epochs of Lemuria and Atlantis, and tentatively placed at 20,000,000+ years ago.

The next group was the Nefilim. Many mistaken attributions have been accorded this angelic order, and they too have been called fallen angels. They were commissioned to enter giant human form; the Greek god Orpheus, who tried to lead the human woman Eurydice out of the Underworld to join him in Heaven and who charmed everyone with his lyre and beautiful songs, was a Nefilim.

The Nefilim lived for a time on Earth mostly on the continent of MU, prior to Lemuria, or just after the Hyperborean epoch. The continent of MU refers to the presumed single large landmass that existed in the Pacific Ocean before it sank, leaving a few physical remnants such as the Polynesian and Hawaiian islands. The advent of Lemurian culture on the MU continent is sometimes estimated by esotericists such as Theosophist H. P. Blavatsky to be about 18,000,000 years ago.

The Nefilim were commissioned by the Supreme Being to bring a cellular modification of humanity (through genetic engineering) to inspire more potential for higher consciousness states in physically embodied humans on MU. The Polynesian peoples carry that angelically created potential even today. Not all the Nefilim who lived on Earth physically left; some did not finish their work—some became bound to form for various reasons. The biblical story of the fallen angels finding human women attractive is true: Those were the Nefilim.

The fourth group of angels taking giant human form were the Eninim, a subgroup of the order called Enim. These worked in the central Mexican plateau, the Yucatan, and parts of South America, as remembered in the Ecuadorian myth of giants dwelling in the rocks (or caves) at Santa Elena.

See also: Balor of the Evil Eye, Cyclops Polyphemus.

GLASS MOUNTAIN

A perception of the City of Light, one of eight Celestial Cities imprinted in Earth's visionary geography, the headquarters for the 14 Ray Masters of Ursa Major, seat of the Great White Brotherhood.

Also known as Asgard, Cedar Forest, City of Light, City of the Ray Masters, Crystal City, Crystal Palace, E-Kur, Empire of Light, Golden Etheric City of Light, Indra's Svarga, Isle of Glass, Mount Olympus, Pine Mountain, Roïyat, Ynys Gutrin, Ynys Witrin.

Description: The Glass Mountain, or *Ynys Witrin* ("Glass Island"), is a Welsh mythic description of an otherwordly locale that cannot be seen with the physical eyes and that consists of or is bounded by sheer, unclimbable glass walls. Sometimes it was said to be a woman's domain inhabited by nine maidens.

The motif of a mountain made of pure glass located at the end or edge of the world is found in Celtic, European, and Scandinavian myths. Often it is understood to mean a land of the dead, or a magical place of safety into which a threatened princess is placed by her father for safety, or into which the male hero, typically as suitor or dragon-slayer, must gain access to win the princess.

In its nuance as a fortress of glass girded by water, the Glass Mountain became attributed to the anomalous and numinous Tor of Glastonbury in Somerset, England. This is a presumably artificially made earthen hillock somewhat resembling a pyramid, with a great deal of mythic attributions.

Glastonbury is set in the Somerset Levels, which is an English term for a land barely, if at all, above sea level and thus subject to significant spring floods. In earlier centuries, local information says that during flood times only the high places in Glastonbury, such as the Tor, remained above the waters, so that hillocks more accurately could be called islands. Celtic legend said the Tor was a Glass Mountain or fortress of glass bounded by water and thus difficult to access.

Among the Tor's mythic attributions was that it was the palace of the king of the fairies called Gwynn ap Nudd. Once an ill-mannered Christian saint named Saint Collen was invited into Gwyn's sumptuous palace inside the Tor for a grand feast and entertainment; but when he encountered Gywnn in his golden chair, surrounded by handsome, merry feasters, he threw holy water at it, judging it a shameless pagan apparition, and immediately it vanished.

The fairy kin attribution for Gwynn is probably a latter-day adulteration, for his name suggests a more exalted ontological status. Gwynn is son *(ap)* of Nudd, the Celtic Lord of Annwn, the Hades-like Otherworld. Gwynn's name means "The White One, son of the Dark." Gwynn was also leader of the Wild Hunt led by a pack of white-furred hellish dogs (the *Cwyn Annwn*) with red ears that collected the souls of the newly dead (or even the living) among humanity.

Russian myth also tells of a Glass Mountain. This mountain was the home of a ferocious dragon. The longer he lived there, the bigger grew the mountain. First it was a hillock, then as the dragon fed on people, the hillock became a huge glass mountain that dominated the entire kingdom, somewhere in the Ukraine. It was, in fact, steadily growing so that by the time Ivan the dragon-slayer arrived, the Glass Mountain physically occupied three-quarters of the kingdom.

Somehow by inserting a blade of wheat grass under the glass, Ivan managed to melt and drain off the liquid that constituted the glass and the mountain dissolved. Ironically, this great wall of rushing water drowned the dragon.

Explanation: The Glass Mountain is a psychic perception of a Celestial City variously known as Indra's Svarga, Mount Olympus, Asgard, and E-kur. It is a City of Light that is the residence of many of the prime gods, or higher celestial beings, involved in the government and evolution of Earth and humanity.

It is a Glass Mountain because it is crystalline in appearance, at least initially to clairvoyant viewing, and to signify you cannot climb its sheer, glassy sides but must penetrate them with clairvoyant insight and enter them through vision.

One's initial impression of the Glass Mountain can be of a futuristic city under glass in which all structures, roads, and buildings are crystalline and vibrating noticeably, seeming both fluid and solid, like partially frozen pure white light and emitting a blue-white aura. When I first saw this celestial residence I called it a Crystal City as a convenient visual reference. Another explorer of my acquaintance called it Roïyat and said it existed in the far future; others have described it as a Golden Etheric City of Light situated above certain landscapes.

The Glass Mountain or Crystal City exists in

our future, around 3000 A.D., and is an outpost of Shambhala, seat of Earth's spiritual government. It represents a level of consciousness that humanity collectively will grow into by that date but which selectively some humans by grace can access today. The Crystal City facilitates movement of consciousness across dimensions and time.

To say it exists in our future means that by about 3000 A.D. it will have entered human reality, or human perception on average will have matured sufficiently to be able to apprehend the place and interact with its residents.

Inside the Glass Mountain, you find the seat of a selection of the Great White Brotherhood (see Da Derga's Hostel and Einherjar), a conclave of enlightened sages, spiritual adepts, and celestial beings of various descriptions.

Essentially, these are the 14 Ray Masters and all their affiliate Ray adepts (Ascended Masters aligned with a particular Ray and its Master). The Crystal City is the place of embodiment within consciousness where these realized beings, organized by Ray affiliation, gather and support living, embodied humans interested in developing their consciousness through Mystery initiations.

This conclave is sometimes called Asgard (the House of the Aesir, in Norse myth), the Anunnaki (in Sumerian lore), and Mount Olympus (in Greek myth), residence of the Olympian gods who rule and oversee the human world. Asgard is not the home of the full panoply of gods, however, but rather of a crucial selection of them in accordance with the 14 Rays of the Great Bear.

The constellation Ursa Major (Great Bear) is the galactic home of the Great White Brotherhood, and the Big Dipper (the seven bright stars in the sacrum and tail of the Bear) is the home of the 14 Ray Masters, also called the Seven Rishis (each of whom has a partner), Seven Elders, and Teachers of the Great Bear. Some of these Ray Masters' names are familiar from myth such as Apollo, Aphrodite, and Athena, or Theosophy's El Morya, Saint Germain, and Kuthumi.

The Ray Masters (see Seven Rishis) have an administrative headquarters (with 108 portals to it) in Earth's visionary geography. The Glass Mountain, Light City, and Crystal City are mythic names that refer to that place.

In Sumerian geomantic lore, the high god Enlil (equivalent to Zeus, Thor, and Indra) is called "Great Mountain" and presides in *E-Kur* ("Mountain House"), the residence of the chief gods (Anunnaki) at Nippur in today's Iraq. Here the chief god, as the summation of the consciousness of all the assembled affiliate gods, is himself (as well as his hall) equated with a mountain. E-kur was made of lapis-lazuli, a lofty, pure dwelling place, beautiful within, from which Enlil, the Great Mountain, could survey all the lands and people of Sumer.

In Judaic myth, Enoch reported seeing a Crystal Palace in Heaven; it was a structure made of crystals with tongues of living fire burning between them and rivers of living fire (or light) encircling the entire structure. Numerous angels came and went, and even the Ancient of Days was seen entering the place. This is the Crystal City.

While the Russian myth cited above is not site-specific, the dragon association is apt, for there is an astral dragon wrapped around the Glass Mountain at Glastonbury. This is not always so, however, only in some cases.

In Norse myth, Asgard is guarded by a formidable, towering watchman named Heimdall, known as the White *As* (Old Norse for "a god"). In Greek myth, Heimdall's equivalent is Pelops who similarly guards the entrance to the Glass Mountain at Mycenae on the Peloponnesus. In Celtic lore, he is Gwynn ap Nudd ("The White One") supervising entry into the Glass Mountain or Ray Master Celestial City at Glastonbury Tor.

All three figures are identical with the Archangel Gabriel (see Heimdall).

His role at the Glass Mountain is supervisory, mentoring, collegial, and psychopompic and pertains to the flow of cosmic wisdom from the celestial realm into the human and the gradual activation of Mystery centers of the eternal Christ, that is, the Christ Consciousness outside and before Time (see Black Eye of Horus). This is a different aspect of the Christ from that part born into the world through humans as the divine Christ Child (see White Eye of Horus).

Other locations of the Glass Mountain include Uluru at Alice Springs, Australia; Cathedral Rock in Sedona, Arizona; and Mount Shasta, California.

See also: Anunnaki, Bifrost, Black Eye of Horus, Da Derga's Hostel, Dragon, Einherjar, Heimdall, Indra, King Arthur, Mount Meru, Seven Rishis, Shambhala, Tuatha de Danann, White Eye of Horus, Wild Hunt.

GOLDEN APPLE

A container for implicit wisdom and spiritual insight that is synonymous with Avalon, the Isle of Apples, the place where the apples grow.

Also known as the Forbidden Fruit, Peaches of Immortality.

Description: The golden apple is found throughout Western myths, especially the Celtic, Norse, and Greek, where it is typically in the possession of the gods and used by one of them as a lure to mortal humans to visit their realm.

A mysterious woman appears one day before the Irish hero Bran mac Febail bearing a silver branch with white blossoms and golden apples. She bids him accompany her to Emain Ablach ("Fortress of Apples"), a Celtic paradise. At the Hill of Tara, Ireland's ancient seat of the high kings, Cormac mac Airt is greeted on the ramparts one day by a warrior carrying a branch with three golden apples. These emit a marvelous seductive music that lulls him to sleep.

When King Arthur dies on the battlefield, he is ferried across the lake to Avalon, a Celtic fairyland whose name is usually translated as "Appleland." King Arthur's magus-mentor, Merlin, luxuriates under 81 golden apple trees but realizes that the abundance of these intoxicating fruits might be a distraction for him.

In Norse myth, the gods of Asgard are subject to sudden decline if they stop consuming golden apples every day, provided to them by Idun ("the Rejuvenating One") who guards the orchard of golden apple trees. In Greek myth, of course, there is the well-known eleventh labor of Herakles: He must collect a golden apple from the Gardens of the Hesperides, guarded by the dragon Ladon. A golden apple was allegedly the cause of the ten-year Trojan War. The Goddess Eris tossed a golden apple into the midst of three competing goddesses and asked a mortal, Paris, to judge which was the most beautiful and worthy of the fruit.

In Genesis, Eve is tempted by the Serpent to take a fruit, presumed to be a golden apple, from the Tree of the Knowledge of Good and Evil. This act was prohibited by God, Genesis says, and for infracting this rule, Adam and Eve are expelled from the Garden of Eden and thus precipitate the Fall of Man.

In a contemporary mystical account, a man having a visionary tour of the sacred sites of Glastonbury, England, is offered a golden apple, but told if he eats it, his perceptions will radically shift and he will see the astral side of his environment with the full clairvoyant sight of the dragon's dimension. Eating the golden apple was to be a preliminary sacrament before he entered the City of Revelation said to be at the top of Glastonbury Tor, an anomalous sacred hill.

Explanation: The golden apple is a profound symbol with applications at many levels of understanding. The fruits of spiritual practice in certain cultures are traditionally called apples of insight, usually gained at an inner astral plane. Each apple is a stroke of wisdom. When Herakles collected the golden apple, this was him realizing and accepting his innate wisdom, which was pure and golden. It is not necessary to remove the golden apple from the tree to have this realization.

For the Chinese version of the same story, see Peaches of Immortality.

As part of the esoteric side of the Grail Quest, collecting golden apples and "melting" them down (digesting their contents) in the Grail chalice is a way of assimilating already acquired wisdom from one's life (and past-life) experience.

On a larger scale, the apple is the perfect symbol of how the Earth appears as an energy field and light receptor to the angelic realm, and it also approximates the guise or essence structure of the Archangel Sandalphon, who is a guardian angel to Gaia, the Spirit of the Earth. Part of Sandalphon's responsibility for the planet is to adjust continually its spin, rotation, and axis.

The golden apple has a geomantic expression by way of 47 copies placed around the Earth inside another geomantic feature called an Avalon (144 copies). In effect, the golden apple is synonymous with Avalon, the Isle of Apples.

Even though, to visionary sight, an Avalon consists in part of lush apple orchards that are both blooming with lovely white blossoms and rich with golden fruit, two-thirds (97) have illusory golden apples, and only 47 have the authentic ones. Glastonbury, for example, has a genuine golden apple, and it is the same apple, referred to in Genesis, from the Tree of the Knowledge of Good and Evil.

The actual geomantic location of this biblically referenced tree is at Glastonbury in Somerset, England, as it is the planet's primary outer heart chakra, or *Anahata,* the site of this tree of duality, free will, and choice. Eating the golden apple produces self-consciousness; the first humans became aware of themselves as separate, individualized points of consciousness in bodies. Their cognition expanded radically, but in a different, novel direction—into the dragon's dimension; but the dragon (or Serpent) is understood here as kundalini, the basic life force energy that awakens the subtle energy centers (called chakras) and progressively expands consciousness up to the level of the gods' perception.

Appropriately, coiled about the base of this tree and in the same space as Glastonbury Tor is one of the Earth's 13 primary dragons. Similarly, the Norse dragon Nidhoggr lies coiled about the Tree of Life (Yggdrasil) in the Garden of Eden in central Norway where this seemingly mythic or allegorical tree has actual geomantic reality. And in the Garden of the Hesperides, Herakles must first encounter and overcome the dragon Ladon guarding the golden apples.

As with many myths, however, to get the correct meaning, you have to invert the story. Herakles obtains the golden apple from *inside* the dragon. That's why the mystic said, though it seemed counterintuitive, that the golden apple was a sacrament that induced your cognition into the dragon's dimension. Here you reverse humanity's phylogenetic steps from the oneness expressed as the Tree of Life into the awareness of individuality and divine origin—self-awareness—of the golden apple, and then you step through the kundalini reality of the dragon.

As embodied humans, we reverse this route and pass through the dragon of kundalini into the golden apple, which is a state of implicit wisdom. It is not so much a matter of stated or perceived content, as embodied, implicit awareness.

As with Herakles, it is not necessary to remove the golden apple from the tree in Avalon to enjoy the illumination and insight it offers. Experientially, "eating" a golden apple is more accurately described as entering one. The apple is like a living, radiant sun in apple form; you assimilate its contents by entering its information field, for the fruit, after all, is knowledge, cosmic intelligence.

Once I encountered a large golden head inside the Glastonbury golden apple, hollow, like a hot air balloon seen from underneath in the wicker bucket. I stood on a small golden circle on a pedestal at the base of this head and the golden head settled down over my head like a corona and emitted golden pulsations. Soon my head felt full to bursting with downloaded information. It is probably more accurate to say the golden apple eats you, because when you enter this expanded field of cognition that is the golden apple, its reality consumes yours.

With the golden apple of Glastonbury, you get several layers of its reality. First, you may experience the essential reality of a golden apple, one of 47, and this experience, and your approach to it, will depend on your primary soul patterning. Second, you may experience *the* apple of Eden, the forbidden fruit, which is also present at Glastonbury Tor; this is a deeper aspect of the apple.

Here you pass through the dragon into the golden apple, then you experience the implicit axis of the core of the apple. This is the Tree of the Knowledge of Good and Evil and it is inside the golden apple inside the dragon.

It is a tree symbolically because a tree is vertical and can produce fruit, but axis is a more accurate description of its function, for your experience in this fundamental golden apple is one of duality, splitting, separation, division into two: life and death, male and female, stasis and movement, eternity and evolution, good and evil. You are cut in two, like an apple sliced in half, and the tree is both the slicer and the now polarized soul that experiences the sundering of one into two and seeks to reconcile, balance, and reunite them (see Albion).

See also: Albion, Avalon, Garden of Eden, Peaches of Immortality, Rhinegold, Tree of the Knowledge of Good and Evil, Yggdrasil.

GOLDEN FLEECE

A means by which one is translocated into the council chamber of the Time Lords, Kronos, and the Hundred Handed Ones; also an expression of the Time Line in the form of a mathematical matrix.

Description: In Greek myth, the Golden Fleece came from a flying, talking ram, progeny of Poseidon, the Sea Lord, and the mortal Theophane. This magical ram saved Phrixus and Helle from the clutches of their evil stepmother and imminent death by sacrifice by flying them to Aeaea, the capital of Colchis on the eastern edge of the Black Sea in today's Republic of Georgia.

En route, Helle fell off the ram, and where she landed thereafter was called the Hellespont (Helle's Sea), today the dividing point between Europe and Asia known as the Dardanelles. Phrixus made it safely to Colchis where he sacrificed the ram to Zeus and gave its fleece, made of lustrous spun gold, to Aeetes, the king of Aeaea who was a son of Helios the Sun-god and monarch of this reputedly fabulous Sun kingdom to the north of Greece.

It is unclear what the golden fleece does, but it is described much like a golden cloak one could wear. The wool shimmered, cast a fiery glow on Aeetes' cheeks, and illuminated the ground around him with a bright gold luster. It was as dazzling as Zeus's lightning. Slung over his shoulders, the fleece reached his feet.

Aeetes hung the fleece on an oak tree in a grove of Ares (the Olympian war god) and set an unsleeping dragon, progeny of Ares, to guard it against all intruders.

The quest to obtain the Golden Fleece later became the object of Jason and the Argonauts and their epochal voyage through the Mediterranean and up to Colchis as celebrated in Apollonius's *Argonautica.* Aeetes sets Jason several seemingly impossible tasks to complete before he will hand over the fleece, but through the aid of Aeetes' daughter, Medea, Jason stole the fleece.

Greek myth does not record what Jason did with the Golden Fleece, if anything, once he returned home, and it seems the quest for it was paramount, not its use.

Explanation: To penetrate this myth, which conceals an important occult fact, one must disregard the beginning and end of the story, namely, the made-up fable of Phrixus and Helle riding the magical ram to Colchis, and Jason's stealing the Golden Fleece and departing with it. Neither part is relevant or authentic. Jason did not take the fleece anywhere; he used it, and it is still in Colchis.

The key to the story is what the Golden Fleece does. It is a dimensional translocation device that puts one in the throne room of the Time Lords.

It is fitting that a Dragon of Ares guards the Golden Fleece, for the Earth's 1,066 geomantic dragons often guard important sites or geomantic features, such as the dragon Pytho who guards Apollo's oracular shrine at Delphi in Greece. This dragon has a similar function as the Egyptian Apophis and the Beast (Sorath) who guard the Time Line. The Time Line, or the Magical Square of the Sun, is the Golden Fleece.

The initial psychic impression of the Golden Fleece at Colchis is that it is a square sheet of gold, perhaps 50 feet square, standing up vertically like a full-blown sail behind, or more correctly *within*, the dragon's energy enclosure. It is divided into numerous equal-sized squares, each of which contains lettering. The script appears to be Sumerian, consisting of lines and dashes.

Jason journeyed to Colchis not to acquire or steal the Golden Fleece but to read it, like reading the occult script of the Akasha Chronicles, and to use it. By touching certain of the letters in certain blocks, you activate the device. It ushers you into the morphogenetic field of a given time period, say the Age of Aries, a 2,160-year span in which past, present, and future events are fluid and unfixed.

The numerous squares with letters are a kind of time calculator for experimental meditations on different combinations of time periods and events.

At one level, the Golden Fleece was a fourth-dimensional time matrix repository in which you could observe and study all the events in a given time frame and understand the complexities of cause and effect relationships. At another level, you wrapped yourself in it like a cloak and went somewhere.

That somewhere is the golden halls of Kronos in Ogygia, as alluded to in classical sources such as Homer. It is also Aeetes' Sun kingdom of Aeaea as well as the Egyptian Sun god Ra's Boat of Millions of Years. There is a vast circular hall in which everything is golden; dozens of golden thrones sit on the inside periphery of the huge circle, and golden beings sit in the thrones. These are the 104 Time Lords (see Cattle of the Sun) who rule and protect Time. Aeetes and the other progeny of Helios the Sun god are among these Time Lords.

This vast circular golden chamber is the council room for the Time Lords. It is somewhere in the fourth dimension, or perhaps in an even subtler realm. The Golden Fleece, in part, is a translocation device that gets one there.

Occupying three positions on the periphery of the hall are three massive beings, each with 100 arms and hands and 50 heads. These were known to Hesiod in his *Theogony* as the Hundred-Handed Ones, Briareos, Cottus, and Gyges, brothers to the Cyclopes (the one-eyed giants). They were charged by Zeus, chief of the Olympian gods, to hold Kronos fast in his hall. Kronos here means Saturn or the Lord of Time, chief of all the Time Lords.

In the center of the hall, and spreading out as if under the 104 golden thrones of the Time Lords on the periphery of the great circular hall, is Kronos. Greek myth says that Kronos was imprisoned with the unruly Titans in Tartarus after Zeus and the gods overthrew him, but it also says Kronos was benevolently exiled to the golden halls of Ogygia, the domain of the Homeric nymph Kalypso.

Imprisonment and exile are both misleading terms. Kronos, as Lord of Time and, in a sense, a great Time organism himself, was grounded and stabilized for the Earth realm in this dimension outside of time, mythically called Aeaea. The 104 golden thrones on the hall's periphery function like stopcocks or release valves, regulating the flow of Kronos's time essence into the realms of actual time.

They administer and look after the Golden Fleece, which is both the translocator device into the Halls of Ogygia for Jason and other initiates and, from inside the Halls, the Time Line of the galaxy expressed as a mathematical matrix.

Thus Jason and Odysseus, who spent time with Kalypso (another Time Lord), both accessed the Time Lords' council chamber as part of their initiations.

See also: Ancient of Days, Argonauts, Beast of the Apocalypse, Cattle of the Sun, Cyclops Polyphemus, Dragon, Hitching Post of the Sun, Orpheus's Lyre.

GRAIL CASTLE

An experiential workshop, templated geomantically across the Earth, for achieving deep recall of the time before consciousness ever entered form, using the Holy Grail for remembering and healing of the soul.

Also known as Boat of the Vedas, Caer Belli, Caer Sidi, Castle Carbonek (Corbenic), Castle of Eden, Castle of Joy, Castle of King Pelles, Castle of Souls, Castle of Wonders, Chateau Marveil, Grail Mountain, Holy House, Holy Place, House of the Rich Fisher King, Lanka, Munsalvaesche, Noah's Ark, Palace Adventurous, Revolving or Spinning Castle.

Description: In the medieval legends of the Holy Grail, the Grail Castle is the sanctified residence, usually a palace, that contains the Grail and its guardians.

Nearly every chronicler of the Grail saga has a different description of the Grail castle, but one text attributes its construction to Titurel, the first King of the Grail, who received the construction plans from the spiritual worlds.

In a thirteenth-century account called *Der Jungere Titurel,* Parzival's grandfather is Titurel. (Parzival is one of the select few Grail Knights who achieve the Quest.) Under angelic guidance, and starting at age 50, he builds the Grail Castle as a hallows for the Grail, located in the Forest of Salvation upon a solitary mountain, *Munsalvaesche* (Mount of Salvation) in the land of Salvatierre. Often it is called Castle Carbonek.

Previously, the Grail had not had an Earthly home, but was continuously upheld by angelic hands over the future site of the Grail Castle.

Titurel's Castle is high, round, and topped with a grand cupola, surrounded by 22 chapels. At every second chapel stands a bell tower topped by a white crystal cross and a golden eagle. The towers form a circle about the main domed area, which is lacquered in red, gold, and blue enamel. The walls are emerald green; there are numerous arches like green-gold bows.

Inside the central dome of the Castle, the Sun and Moon are depicted against a blue enameled sky of stars; underneath this is a small replica of the Grail Castle, and inside this is the Holy Grail itself. The floor of the Holy Place is pure onyx, at the summit of the tower is a ruby, and on top of that a crystalline cross. At the meeting point of the arches between the chapels glitter carbuncles; the inside roof is of sapphire amidst the depicted stars.

Generally, the Grail Castle was hard to find and difficult to approach or enter. Some said it was bewitched long ago, so only the lucky, invited, or worthy would ever find it. The road leading to it was often full of hazards and obstacles; many in quest of it got lost, distracted, waylaid, injured, or killed, or gave it up.

Usually, most sources say it was situated at the far end of a great valley, encircled by water, sometimes by three rivers difficult to cross. Seen from afar, the Grail Castle was a rich and seemly building, possibly even of vast extent, guarded by lions, and flanked by numerous high-rising turrets; closer up, one saw it was reached by crossing three bridges, each of which offered horrors and dreadful physical risks. Sometimes the Castle itself seemed to spin like a wheel.

Once past the bridges, there was a sculpted gate, a flight of steps, great doors opening into a spacious hall offering one a glimpse of splendor and wealth, sumptuous couches, cushions, carpets, marble hearths, and great blazing lights. Possibly one would see also a silver table on which stood the Holy Grail, draped in samite, or the Wounded Fisher King, languishing on his throne.

For those intrepid few Grail Knights who ever made it into the variously named Grail Castle, it was often a bewildering, extremely hazardous, and unpredictable place. Doors would spin, swords and arrows fly out from walls, beds revolve furiously, trapdoors open suddenly before them, unexpected attacks launched at them from every quarter, surly hosts, duplicitous staff, and if they made one wrong move, said the wrong thing, they were thrown out instantly and the Grail Castle would disappear summarily as if it had never been there.

Lancelot, one of King Arthur's Knights of the Holy Grail, after a long journey and much misdirection, came upon the Grail Castle at night by sea. Its gates opened seaward and were guarded by two fierce lions. He was about to fight the lions when a flaming hand plunged downward at him, knocking him over. Then he came upon a room whose door was closed tight, yet he heard inside it lovely, sweet music, as if sung by angels.

After praying, Lancelot found the door open and a great light flowing out of it. A voice told him he was not allowed to enter, but he might observe from the doorway. He saw the Holy Grail set on a silver table; it was covered by a red samite cloth, and all round it stood angels, some swinging silver censers, some holding lit candles or crosses, and an aged human conducted a service or Mass.

In Celtic traditions preceding the advent of the medieval Grail legends, the Grail Castle was known as Caer Sidi or Caer Belli, one of the names for Annwn, the Celtic Otherworld, the residence of a divine cauldron. In ancient Irish myth, the cauldron of the Dagda was one of four celestial treasures brought to Earth from the Otherworld; the cauldron came from the mystic City of Murias. In another Irish myth CuRoi is a giant who lives in a rotating Otherworld fortress, which contains a magical cauldron so big it holds 30 oxen.

Explanation: The Grail Castle is an actual, experienceable, other-dimensional place accessed through Earth's visionary geography. There are 144 copies of this Castle of the Grail, or 144 gateways to the one Grail Castle. It is one of the eight Celestial Cities about Mount Meru, the World Mountain, as described in Vedic and Hindu texts. Technically, of these 144 copies, none is the original, for that does not exist anywhere on Earth or in its subtle environment.

The original Grail Castle is from elsewhere, as the Irish say, from the gods' City of Murias, most likely somewhere in the Andromeda Galaxy. The Grail Castles present on Earth are etheric copies, brought here and established as subtle buildings or structured Light spaces for the purposes of beholding the Grail.

In the past, particularly in the time of the medieval Grail sagas, access to the Grail Castles was exceedingly difficult. It required a highly refined clairvoyance; at the same time, the general world conditions for clairvoyance were limited, so only a very few Grail Knights (usually just three) ever made it into the Castle and to the adytum or Holy Place where the Grail was displayed.

The unusual physical descriptions of the Castle, as spinning, disappearing, threatening, are commentaries on the psychic difficulties of keeping one's clairvoyance focused on this highly subtle, elusive, other-dimensional energy. As one grew distracted in psychic focus or tired from the exertion, the Castle would spin in one's perception and the image would falter, weaken, and go away.

Until present time, only a very small number of people had access to the level of consciousness needed to perceive the Grail Castle; that's why many Grail Knights in the medieval texts confessed they could not find it. Access was through the etheric Castles on Earth (the 144 replicas) to the actuality of the Castle in another dimension, but this has not occurred since Atlantean times.

The planetary location of the Grail Castles was most often above a mountain or prominence that already had a reputation for numinosity. For example, there is a Grail Castle above Montsegur, a craggy peak in the French Pyrenees; above Alcatraz Island in the San Francisco Bay; above Castle Peak in the Sierra Nevadas at Truckee, California; above Mount Hood, near Portland, Oregon; above Mount Parnassus, Greece; and above Heliopolis (Cairo), Egypt.

In some cases, such as at Heliopolis, the Grail Mountain was the first landmass to arise out of the primeval waters and was known as the White Mount. As such, Grail Mountain, as the foundation or support for the Grail, is another way of referring to the Grail Castle, and it teases out another key nuance.

Other names and attributions for the White Mount include Mount Hetep, the Mount of Heaven, Mount of Glory, White Mountain, Exalted Earth, God's Mountain, the Staircase of the God Osiris, the First Place, First Land, Primordial Hill, the High Hill, High Dune, and Ptah's Mound at Annu. It was also known as *Djeba,* Plain of Ildavöll, the Primeval Hill, and *Tatjenen* ("Elevated Land").

In the Egyptian perception, the Grail Castle as White Mount was the first landmass to arise out of the Flood waters. In other myths, the Grail Mountain was the highest peak above the Flood waters on which the variously named Ark landed. Noah's Ark, and the Vedic version of it, Boat of the Vedas, are references to the Grail Castle. Noah's Ark reputedly landed at Mount Ararat in Armenia; Deucalion's Greek Ark landed on Mount Parnassus: Both have Grail Castles.

How is the Ark a Grail Castle? The Grail Castle is the temple for retrieving deep, vast, and antique memory, of times and conditions of consciousness from before the Flood. Flood refers mostly to previous cycles of human and planetary existence, even to previous Days of Brahma reckoned in billions of human years. The Grail Castle is the place of deep remembering. You potentially remember things saved from the Flood (the dissolution of previous cycles of existence), things that transcend the cycles of creation and dissolution.

The Holy Grail itself, usually pictured as a chalice or cauldron, is the inner temple within the Grail Castle in which you do this deep remembering.

This quality is aptly symbolized in the Hindu myth of Vishnu (the Hindu Christ) dreaming upon the vast coiled flanks of Sesa-Ananta, the cosmic dragon, who floats atop the Flood waters, in between cycles of creation. Vishnu's undying awareness—Christ Consciousness, Logos awareness, the Word—is what you retrieve in the Grail Castle, floating like an Ark at the top of the Flood, which is to say, the Sea of Consciousness and the etheric realm, often shown as water.

Yet there above all Creation, the Grail Castle is also a hologram of the human body, including the chakras and auric layers. That's the meaning of Carbonek: It means carbonic acid cycle, carbon, the human, carbon-based body, the container for human consciousness on Earth. The Castle Carbonek was the individual Grail Knight's exploration of his own inner carbon-body temple.

See also: Fisher King, Flood, Grail Knight, Hanuman, Holy Grail, Manu, Salmon of Wisdom, White Mount.

GRAIL KNIGHT

A man or woman of any culture or time who can bridge the realms of the elemental (Nature spirits) and angelic with the human in the context and for the benefit of Earth's visionary geography as part of a long-term process of deep remembering called the Quest for the Holy Grail.

Also known as Fianna, Grid engineer.

Description: In the Arthurian mythos, King Arthur assembles a group of specialized colleagues called the Knights of Camalate. They sit with him at the Round Table at Camalate, his headquarters, and deliberate matters of state. Sometimes they ride out to defend England against the invading Saxons. They also resolve to find the Holy Grail, for which they are known as Knights of the Holy Grail. They spend most of the year out in the wilds of Celtic England questing for the Grail, having adventures, both physical and mystical, then reassemble at Camalate on Pentecost to share their experiences.

Many of the knights, throughout the medieval corpus of Arthurian sagas, are named, and some stand out for their deeds or misfortunes: Gawain, a bit rash, hotheaded, but ever-faithful; Lancelot du Lac, expert swordsman who had an affair with Queen Guinevere, Arthur's wife; Bedivere, Arthur's lifelong companion, who returned Excalibur, Arthur's king sword, to the Lady of the Lake when he was dying; Galahad, Lancelot's son, who heals the Wounded Fisher King; Bors, a married man, who achieves the Grail; Parsifal, who also achieves the Grail and becomes king of Sarras, the mystical Grail kingdom.

In the years after King Arthur was mortally wounded by his illegitimate son, Mordred, and returned to Avalon, with Camalate torn asunder and ruined by the adultery of Lancelot and Guinevere, the Grail Knights were said to be sleeping in the hollow hills (equivalent to the Irish *sidhe,* into which the Tuatha de Dannan, the Irish high gods, had retreated) with Arthur, waiting for a trumpet call that would announce their return to the world in answer to its need.

It is said of South Cadbury Castle in Somerset, England, the presumed Camalate of the fifth-century Arthur, that, on occasion, the Knights are seen at midnight riding across Arthur's Causeway into Somerset to attend to some matter.

Explanation: Originally and outwardly, the term "knight" was used to indicate a young person, presumably male, who could sit his horse competently. Grail Knight, however, is actually a term indicating a stage of initiation, applies equally to men and women, and has little to do with physical horses and more to do with being able to sit calmly and neutrally within the body (the horse) and its emotions and make excursions in consciousness into the subtle landscape.

Although the Arthurian mythos seems clearly tied to a single quasi-historical epoch, fifth-century Celtic England, it is actually an archetypal myth that has had cultural expression around the world 15 times to date. Other flowerings of this initiatory mythos have been in Wales, Ireland, Tibet, and Iran. In Ireland, for example, the Grail Knights were called the Fianna (Fenians), loyal followers of Fionn MacCumhaill, the Irish King Arthur from an earlier time.

In one's training, a Grail Knight works with the angelic realm and the Nature spirits, notably the gnomes, the elementals who handle the earth element. The Knight works with certain metaphysical tools, such as swords, the Grail chalice, visualizations for the aura (the energy field around the body), and a Gnome Egg (also known as the Royal Hall of the King of the Dovrë Trolls).

A Gnome Egg is a regional headquarters for gnomes (also known in myths as dwarves and trolls); the Grail Knight interacts with the Gnome Egg over a period of months and gains familiarity with the elemental kingdom. Similarly, one interacts with the angelic and hierarchical realms (specific members of the Great White Brotherhood) in a long progressive series of initiations and visionary events.

The goal of the Grail Knight's training is to be an effective intermediary between celestial and terrestrial energies and consciousness. The Grail Knight works with the angelic and elemental kingdoms on behalf of the planet, both its spirit, known as Gaia, its ecosystem, and its resident humanity. The Grail Knight is expert in grounding celestial consciousness into Earth's visionary geography through interacting with both at the planet's many holy sites.

The Grail Knight, through the acquisition of a focused, competent clairvoyance, is also trained in detoxifying the Earth's geomantic nodes of accumulated negativities, unwholesome, entropic energies, and stagnation. In this role, one may be called a Grid engineer, as Earth's visionary geography, though a living matrix, is also describable as a consciousness grid, and the Grail Knight, in one's capacity as an intermediary, functions like a field engineer.

Grail Knights often congregate again while incarnated and throughout their lifetimes because they are part of a Soul Group dedicated to the goals of Camalate.

The work of the Grail benefits the planet, by facilitating the infusion of celestial consciousness and its blending with elemental energies, and it benefits the Grail Knight, because every interaction with Earth's visionary terrain is at the same time a reclamation of another part of one's deep cosmic memory, the transcendental wisdom of the soul, and the healing of the Wounded Fisher King, who is an aspect of both the individual and human collective consciousness.

Typically, Grail Knights, by whatever name they are known in a given culture, participate with the angelic, elemental, and hierarchical kingdoms on spiritually and geomantically important days in the yearly cycle, including Candlemas, Michaelmas, and the Wild Hunt (see entries for each). They also assist Gaia, Pan, the Nature spirits (see Nymph), and the Great White Brotherhood (see Einherjar) in repudiating the Antichrist's hold on Earth and in ameliorating the potentially disastrous effects of Earth Changes.

See also: Antichrist, Camalate, Candlemas, Earth Changes, Einherjar, Fionn MacCumhaill, Fisher King, Gaia, Grail Castle, Grail Maiden, Hanuman, Holy Grail, King Arthur, Kokopelli, Menehune, Michaelmas, Nymph, Pan, Round Table, Royal Hall of the King of the Dovrë Trolls, Trolls, Wild Hunt.

GRAIL MAIDEN

Ultimately an expression of Lucifer, the Light-Bearer and Lord of Light, presenting the Light, or Christ Consciousness, to the Fisher King (Keeper of the Holy Grail), the Higher Self behind every human.

Also known as Bride of God, Kundry, Maiden of the Grail, Repanse de Schoye, Sabbath Queen, Shekinah, Sita, Sri, *Xvarnah*.

Description: In the medieval Grail sagas, the Grail Maiden is one or several "damsels" who carry and accompany the Holy Grail through the Grail Castle as part of the daily Grail Procession on behalf of the Fisher King.

In the medieval Grail text called *Lancelot,* the Maiden of the Grail carries the Precious Vessel, as the Grail was called, through the Grail Castle. She emerges from what the text calls the Hidden Chamber accompanied by lights and thuribles, then after a time, she returns with it to the Secret Chamber. In *Parzival,* 21 Maidens accompany the Grail Procession, one carrying the chalice.

In Wagner's operatic rendition of the Grail saga, *Parsifal* (1882), the Grail Maiden is represented by Kundry, an ambivalent, tortured soul whose loyalties are in conflict, torn between the Fisher King and his enemy, Klingsor.

Explanation: The Grail saga is a complex and sublime mystical drama about the acquiring of Christ Consciousness, total recall of the soul's cosmic history, and full, panoptic understanding of the whys and wheretos of Creation.

The Fisher King (Higher Self) is the repository of this cosmic memory, wisdom, and knowledge, the fruits of Sophia, goddess of wisdom. He is the *Rich* Fisher King if he has Christ Consciousness, but the *Wounded* or *Maimed* if he does not have it. He resides in the Grail Castle and is the Keeper of the Grail, a chalice for Light. Kundry, as the distorted, ambivalent, even malevolent Grail Maiden, reflects humanity's current spiritual condition whereby the intuition is not valued and has been marginalized.

At one level, the Grail Maiden is the feminine aspect of consciousness, the intuitive or clairvoyant faculty, that helps retrieve deep cosmic memory for the Fisher King who pertains to that aspect of consciousness that lies at the deepest level: the ability to remember one's divine origins and the descent and history of one's soul since that origin. The Grail is the process of remembering, and the Grail Maiden supports that process, as signified by her bearing the Holy Grail.

At a deeper level, the Grail Maiden is another name for the Shekinah, in Judaic lore, the feminine aspect of God, although it's also said she is the mother, sister, daughter, and bride of God as well, His divine presence in the world.

Other versions of the same thing are Sophia, the Gnostic goddess of wisdom; Sri, the beautiful primordial female who emerged from the Ocean of Milk; Sita, Rama's divine consort (Rama is a guise of Vishnu, the Hindu Christ); the *Xvarnah,* in Persian mysticism the divine glory enhaloing rightful kings; and characters from myth and legend such as Guinevere ("The White One"), King Arthur's wife, and the egg-born Helen of Troy, wife to King Menelaus of Sparta.

The Shekinah's original home was the Garden of Eden, where her splendor radiated from one end of Creation to the other, and she outshone the Sun by far. Only she knows where God hid all His heavenly treasures (all the paths to wisdom). Later David designed and Solomon built the Temple of Jerusalem as a permanent dwelling place for the Shekinah, a mystical event found also in the Hindu *Ramayana* where Sita dwells in the golden city of Lanka.

Both Solomon's Temple of Jerusalem (designed by David, built by Solomon) and Lanka (designed and built by the cosmic architect Visvakarma) are expressions of the Grail Castle, and that itself is an expression of the heart chakra. The Hidden or Secret Chamber in the Grail Castle out of which the Grail Maiden emerges with the Grail is the same as the Holy of Holies in Solomon's Temple where the Shekinah was invited to dwell as her permanent home.

Sri, the Divine Glory or *Xvarnah,* is a representation of the human soul in all its original beauty, fortune, glory, and splendor, its wisdom permeating the king (the human self). It is the original celestial light of the virginal soul and the illumination of its wisdom, expressed as a feminine quality.

Sri, as Beauty and Fortune, is the exalted expression of Lucifer, Lord of Light and the God-appointed Light-Bearer, present in every embodied human. Lucifer, in his original pure form, is the beautiful individualized light, expressed as a celestial-human-like form, the first self-aware container or chalice for the Light of universal awareness (the Christ Consciousness).

Austrian clairvoyant Rudolf Steiner once said Lucifer *bears* the Light, Christ *is* the Light. Lucifer, ultimately, is the Grail Maiden, along with Sri, Sita, Sophia, Shekinah, and all other expressions of the feminine consort to the Christ. Sri bears (embodies, carries) the Light as a beautiful first form for the soul. The Light itself is her consort (Rama, Christ), that which fills the Holy Grail. The Grail Maiden serves the Light (cosmic consciousness) to the Fisher King.

Just as Sri is always Vishnu's consort during his incarnations, so Lucifer (as the archetype for Sri) *bears* the glory and beauty of the divine Light of the soul while Christ (Vishnu) *is* the Light. Lucifer (as Sri, Guinevere, and the rest) is the beautiful form Light (self-awareness) takes, but whose essence is the Christ.

In more austere terms, Sri as the Grail Maiden is the Light-Bearer, the Grail itself is the container for the Light, and the Light she bears like a garment is the Christ, the cosmic consciousness that pervades all interstices of spacetime. Sri, as both form and light, is thus the food of deep memory for the Fisher King.

See also: Fisher King, Grail Castle, Guinevere, Hanuman, Holy Grail, Klingsor, Lucifer, Ocean of Milk.

GREEN KNIGHT

A Celtic perception of the ever-renewing Lord of the Land of the Dead, also known as Yama, King in the Celestial City of Samyamani.

Also known as Afrasiab, Donn, Hades, Khentamentiu, Lord of Death, Mictlantecuhtli, Milu, Yama.

Description: The Green Knight is the fearsome warrior described in the medieval Arthurian poem called *Sir Gawain and the Green Knight* (circa 1500). One day he strides into King Arthur's Camalate and challenges the knights to trade blows. Gawain accepts and strikes off the Green Knight's head in a single sweep; then nonchalantly cradling his severed head in one arm, the Green Knight demands Gawain to come forth to his castle in a year to lose his head.

The Green Knight lives in the Green Chapel, which the medieval poet describes as a classic earthen-topped barrow. Gawain's adventures en route to his appointment reflect the rigors of initiation and the ease of being distracted. Gawain says the Green Chapel is the most evil place he has ever seen. The Green Knight strikes Gawain's neck three times, but leaves only a knick.

Essentially, the Green Knight is a towering giant, an awesome fiend to behold, grim, fierce, and entirely clad in rich accoutrements of glittering green. His hair is heavy, his beard bushy, and he is foremost among the world's horsemen. His axe is huge and monstrous, a single blow dealing instant death. Laughing, he calls himself the Knight of the Green Chapel, but as to what world or dimension he hails from (is it Fairyland? Gawain wonders), he does not say.

Explanation: The Green Knight is a Celtic perception of the Lord of Death, known in other traditions as Donn (Irish), Yama (Hindu), Milu (Polynesian), Hades (Greek), Hun Came or Vukub Came (Mayan), Osiris (Egyptian), Afrasiab the Alive King of the Dead (Uzbekistan), and Mictlantecuhtli (Aztec), among others.

Each of these figures presides over the Land of the Dead, or Underworld, as described in their respective cultures: Tech Duinn (House of Donn), the Celestial City of Samyamani (Yama), Lua-o-Milu (Pit or Cave of Milu), Mictlan (Aztec), Xibalba (Mayan), or Amenti (Egypt).

Typically, the Underworld is accessed by crossing a river and going through a special door or a cave that leads one down into the murky interior of the Earth.

In terms of a spiritual topography, however, the Underworld is *above* our human, material world, accessed properly through the crown chakra on the head. It is an *Under*world only from the viewpoint of the eternal gods: It lies under their realm, that is, in a slower vibratory level of reality but one still faster than ours.

The Lord of the Dead is usually described in fearsome terms, yet the figure bears paradoxes. The Green Knight is clad in glittering green, the quintessential color of fresh, vigorous new growth. That is because he is undying. The Green Knight allows his head to be chopped off, then laughs as he holds it: See, I am still alive, not dead, his gesture signifies—still green, eternally alive. The alteration to his physical form had no effect on the continuity of his consciousness; it remains continuous, unbroken, fresh, vibrant, alive, *green.*

Another paradox is that Hades, grim ruler over the land named after him, has epithets such as Pluto and Dis that mean "Rich One." How can the Lord of Death, into which human souls come bereft of all their possessions, be rich?

The Hindu Yama reveals more of the nature of this seemingly dark deity. Yama is a red god dressed all in green, or he has a dark green complexion and dresses in red. He's another version of the Green Knight, and he sits on the *Vicarabhu,* the Throne of Deliberation in the Halls of the Dead. His domain, Samyamani, means "City of Bondage" and is one of the eight Celestial Cities of the gods that surround the cosmic axis, Mount Meru (see Mount Meru).

In Yama's earliest formulations, he presides over a blissful afterlife for human souls. He earned that right by being the first human to die, being the pathfinder for souls to the realm of the Fathers (Pitris) or Ancestors. He explored the hidden regions of the spiritual world and discovered the road known as the Path of the Fathers, the route that led human souls to heaven. Thus Yama was the King of the Dead, and later this assumed a judgment aspect.

In the Tibetan depiction of the Wheel of Life, showing the Six Realms of dependent creation (including ours), Yama's face glowers over the top. These realms include most of the created, finite, and thus mortal world: gods, humans, animals, *pretas* ("Hungry Ghosts": departed human souls in purgatory, still hungering for rebirth and physical pleasures), Asuras (see Asura: a former race of humans banished to the astral world), and the Hell realm (souls in torment, still Earthbound, self-absorbed). These are the six domains of unenlightened existence, or *samsara,* whose residents are subject to endless rounds of rebirths.

Yama's frightening face glowers over the top of this vast wheel. It is his domain, his responsibility. His teeth are sharpened, he has three glaring eyes, and he has skulls in his hair. He rides a black buffalo, carries a mace, a noose to seize victims, and travels with two ferocious, four-eyed dogs and a Bird of Doom. Yama's Wheel of Life, if anywhere, is set over and above Earth.

From the Tibetan viewpoint, Yama is an Enlightened One who embodies transcendental consciousness, that is, a state of awareness above the six realms and their cycling mental states that keep all residents snared within them. Yama's gaze into the Wheel (as well as over it: transcendent awareness) is a Ray of hope for all souls enmeshed in the illusion of separate selfhood in the Six Realms, from the deepest astral "Hells" to the most sublime of heavenly realms. Yama (as the Green Knight) chopping off his own head displays life beyond this selfhood.

The Tibetans even say that Yama, Judge of the Dead and King of the Law, is an emanation of the exalted Dhyanibuddha Amitabha taking the form of the compassionate thousand-armed Bodhisattva, Avalokitesvara. As Judge of the Dead, Yama (and the other Judges of the Dead figures) does not judge anyone, but merely holds up the mirror to souls so they may observe their own life actions. This is equivalent to the widely reported near-death experience of reviewing one's life actions as if watching an interactive movie as a purgative experience.

Yama (as Hades) is the Rich One because, as the compassionate Avalokitesvara, he offers the Mirror of Knowledge to residents in all Six Realms. Into each realm, Yama brings understanding, a cleansing fire, and spiritual gifts.

In Egyptian myth, distinctions blur somewhat between Anubis and Osiris as to which is the "official" Lord of the Dead and supervisor of Amenti. (Another Egyptian name for this realm was *Neter-khertet,* "Divine Subterranean Place.") Although many of Osiris's described qualities and functions seem to place him as the equivalent to Yama, he is, ontologically, a bigger being than that. Similarly, Anubis is associated with Underworld functions but is also another version of Shiva, Rudra, and the galaxy's brightest star, Sirius (the Dog Star in Canis Major).

However, Osiris was called *Khentamentiu* ("Foremost among the Westerners"), as Amenti was situated, in terms of Egyptian sacred cosmography, in the West, and in physical terms, burial grounds were west of the River Nile. Khentamentiu was the Lord of the Dead and king of the Egyptian necropolis.

Ra, the Sun god, in his daily journey across the sky enters the Duat through Amenti. Amenti (Hades, Green Chapel, Samyamani, and the others) is like a peach pit embedded in the far vaster Duat, or the full Underworld. Just as Yama's Samyamani is but one of eight Celestial Cities, so is Amenti *in* the Duat.

Ironically, Amenti, or the Halls of Hades, is the one Celestial City of the eight every human is guaranteed to visit, although probably only after physical death; visiting the others is optional, in life (through sacred sites) or after life. In Gawain's case, he met the Lord of Death while alive as an initiation rather than as an obligation after he was dead. Meeting him during life makes the afterlife passage through the Halls of Hades a bit easier, metaphysical experts advise.

The probable reason for the confusion or blurring of distinctions between the figure who is Lord of the Duat and Lord of the Dead is that Amenti, as the eighth Celestial City, overlaps the entry and exit place of the entire Duat. In human terms, this is the top of the head (crown chakra); in galactic terms, it is at Sirius within Canis Major, site of the protector god of all the stars, Anubis. Thus you have the rightful Lord of the Dead at the same place, seemingly, as the Lord of the Duat. In a sense, Yama both peers over the Duat and is looking within it, too.

Similarly, Hades' domain was confused by the Greeks, who saw him both as the Lord of the Underworld (one-third of the created universe, the Realm of Fire) and as Lord of the Dead (the death-land called Hades, hence one of his nicknames: Polydegmon, "Receiver of Many Guests"). Technically, the Greeks should have distinguished two Hades, one for each function, though if we accord Cerberus equal stature with Hades, we get the two Hades that way.

Hades' three-headed dog, Cerberus, is the same as Anubis, and both guard the entire Underworld at Sirius (see Trickster). The truth of this myth, however, is the opposite: The Dog is the guardian of the Underworld (the entire galaxy), and Hades, as Lord of the Dead, is a subsidiary deity with a function secondary to the Dog.

See also: Anubis, Mount Meru, Ocean of Milk, Round Table, Trickster, Underworld.

GRIFFIN

An ancient Pleiadian astral being charged with protecting the living wisdom ("gold") of the Earth's visionary geography.

Also known as Griffen, Griffeth, Griffon, Griphon, Gryffon, Lion-Dragon.

Description: A fabulous (and thus disbelieved-in) creature from Greek mythology, the griffin was a composite of several animal and bird forms: a lion's tawny body; an eagle's head, torso, and legs; large ears and large red eyes—this hybrid monster, as it was regarded, also had either blue or white wings. In brief, the griffin looked like a large winged lion with an eagle's head and beak.

The griffin, the awful spawn of a lion and eagle, was considered malicious, greedy, generally terrifying to behold, and liable to attack any trespassers into its realm, taking them in its massive talons up to its mountain retreat.

The name griffin derives from the Greek *gryps*, but also from the Latin *gryphus*. Its ancestry predates both cultures, however, and is traceable to at least 3300 B.C.; its image was used in Mesopotamian and Egyptian cultures of that time period.

In Mesopotamia, the griffin was called Lion-Dragon or Lion-Griffin, and was depicted as such on temple walls, one example being at Ninurta's temple at Kalhu (modern Nimrud in Iraq). The Ninurta temple griffin was also thought of as a Griffin-Demon, who was an ancient sage in bird disguise.

As for the griffin's purpose, the Greeks said it pulled the gods' chariots, especially those of Apollo, Jupiter, and Nemesis. Griffins were also credited with guarding the treasure hoards stored in the mountains or guarding gold mines in India and the eastern Mediterranean lands. Aeschylus, in *Prometheus Bound*, called griffins the sharp-toothed hounds of Zeus who have no bark.

In his *Histories*, Herodotus remarks, though he admitted he did not know what the reference meant, that the griffins guard the gold of the Hyperboreans. The Greeks also understood that the griffins lived in the far North, near where the Hyperboreans once resided. Griffins were sacred to Apollo, who among the Greek Olympians was the god most associated with the fabled Hyperboreans.

Greek myth also tells us Dionysus relied on griffins to guard his ever-flowing wine bowl and that Alexander the Great enticed eight griffins with food placed on a spear to come to him, then harnessed them to a basket and commanded them to fly him to Heaven or at least to the edge of the visible sky.

In medieval times, griffins entered the realm of heraldry, art, and bestiaries of fantastic and therefore unreal creatures. A fourteenth-century travel account *(Travels of Sir John Mandeville)* of apparent exaggeration, if not fabrication, reported encountering griffins in the "Land of Bactry" whose bodies were eight times larger than grown lions, their heads topped with vast horns.

Dante Alighieri said the griffin symbolized the copresence of the mortal and divine in the Christ, and, in the nineteenth century, Lewis Carroll's *Alice's Adventures in Wonderland* has the child encounter a griffin after her trip down the rabbit hole.

Explanation: When Herodotus refers to Hyperborea as the land of the gold-guarding griffins we should take him at his word. Griffins exist, and they do guard the gold.

Hyperborea has two primary references. First, it refers to a world culture very early in the history of the Earth and humanity's residence on it, and can be approximately dated as occurring long before the Atlantis and Lemurian times. Its epicenter was the British Isles, but its core area also involved Greenland, Iceland, part of Scandinavia, and the Arctic (which was not always icebound).

Second, Hyperborea refers to a group of quasi-humans resident on Earth long ago for a special purpose to do with Earth's visionary geography, their presence commissioned by the Supreme Being. The Hyperboreans were in fact Pleiadians, present on Earth in Light bodies and perhaps bodies a little more substantial than that but far less materialized than human bodies today.

The Pleiadians were part of a contingent of representatives from approximately 36 different star families (beings originating from planets associated with specific stars or constellations) whose task was to birth and nurture Earth's visionary geography, what we recognize today as its array of sacred sites, as well as humanity itself and its (then) emerging self-aware consciousness.

The Hyperboreans were of a much more advanced stage of spiritual evolution and possessed a much greater range of higher consciousness states than ordinary humans. One of the ways they implanted their wisdom as a kind of "plant food" for the Earth and its humanity was through a feature later described as gold, and they placed specialized astral guardians (what legend later called griffins) to guard it.

As for their gold deposits, we must be careful to understand this subtlety; the Hyperborean gold does not refer to tangible gold such as we know it today. Rather, the gold refers to accessible deposits of accumulated Pleiadian wisdom potentially available to and assimilable by humanity, even today (see Rhinegold).

There are 47 locations of Hyperborean gold on the planet (called Griffin Gold Reserves), and some of these locations include the Treasury of Atreus at Mycenae, Greece; the Tor at Glastonbury, England; and the Sanctuary, a megalithic site near Avebury stone circle in Wiltshire, England. Each of these 47 sites has a griffin guarding the gold, which means at least 47 griffins are still present on Earth.

The griffin may assume many different forms as a guardian, but the conventional depiction of this astral protector as part lion, part eagle is apt. Its size may vary, but usually it appears to be about 20 feet tall and mostly golden in color. On some occasions, it may be seen outside the Griffin Gold Reserve; I once saw a very tall griffin proudly leading a procession of angels, spirit beings, Pleiadians, and humans in spirit form at Avebury stone circle.

Typically, the Griffin Gold Reserve is approached by way of an inward-winding, counterclockwise spiral walkway; in current times, you "walk" this spiraling corridor in a visionary state, though perhaps once it was more tangible.

At the core of the spiral corridor stands the griffin before a glittering heap of unshaped but somehow living, liquid or molten gold. The griffin may offer you a small mound of this gold for you to shape into a pendant, shield, helmet, or other form, as you wish. Of course, if the griffin does not wish you to enter the winding corridor, you will never get past the front gate; probably you will not even see it.

It may appear to you, however, that, rather than a heap of gold, it is a fount of molten gold with gold flames rising above it, so the gold is both liquid and burning, yet its quantity is never exhausted by the flames, only made more lustrous. The gold burns in a bronze basin about 30 feet across set inside a space that resembles a Native American *kiva,* with seats along the curving wall.

Humans would come to this site to gain the

Pleiadian wisdom by sticking their head into the gold flames—that is, by immersing their consciousness in the gold or extending their clairvoyance into the energy field of the gold and flames.

Here you are exposed to arcane Pleiadian information, pictures, faces, scenes, spirits, and, potentially, contact with the great Star-Angels who are the Pleiades (the actual suns of the Pleiades) including Alcyone, the brightest and the Logos of the estimated 300 stars of the Pleiades and said to be the Great Central Sun of the Milky Way Galaxy itself. In effect, the Hyperborean gold is a condensation of the entire archives of galactic experience held at Alcyone; even more, the living gold is the Alcyone level of consciousness and information itself.

So clairvoyant immersion in the gold offers humans a taste of universal consciousness and access to the Pleiadian archives of knowledge and wisdom. Through accessing this galactic wisdom stream, you can potentially see all the Pleiadian threads and points of influence to other planets with sentient life.

The griffin's guardian task is to supervise access to these valuable stellar archives and to allow access to them in the first place only to those of pure intent. It is invigorating to contemplate the fact that, if and when you perceive a griffin in Earth's visionary geography, you are seeing a spirit of the Pleiades.

During Hyperborean times, the griffins were designated guardians not only of the 47 Gold Reserves, but also of the wisdom of Earth's Light grid itself as well as numerous temple structures across the land. As for Alexander the Great's reported griffin-facilitated trip to Heaven, this is actually possible. A griffin once gave me a visionary journey to a pale gray-green world on the edge of a starfield; I later understood this was one of the inhabited worlds of the Pleiades star system.

The need for the griffin protection of the Gold Reserves was vividly portrayed by J. R. R. Tolkien in *The Lord of the Rings,* in which Sauron created a world-controlling ring of power out of the living Hyperborean gold.

See also: Golden Apple, House of Atreus, Hyperboreans, Rhinegold.

GUINEVERE

A Celtic expression of the beauty, fortune, and original illuminating light and wisdom of the glorious and virginal human soul.

Also known as Divine Glory, Farr, Grail Maiden, Gwenhwyfar, Helen, Kingly Fortune, Laksmi, Shekinah, Sita, Sophia, Sri, *Xvarnah.*

Description: In the Celtic myths, Guinevere is King Arthur's wife and queen. Her father is Leodegrance, King of the Summer Country (or Cameliard), understood in the stories to be approximately Somerset in southwestern England. Arthur found Guinevere, much younger than he, to be an irresistibly beautiful woman, exceeding all other women in beauty, grace, and fairness. Her father consented to the marriage and awarded Arthur the Round Table as a dowry.

King Arthur sent his chief knight, Sir Lancelot, to collect Guinevere and bring her to Camalate, Arthur's headquarters for the knights. Lancelot and Guinevere fell secretly in love, and their liaison eventually overturned Camalate.

In the Welsh version of the Arthurian tales, Guinevere is called Gwenhwyfar, which means "white, fair, smooth, yielding," or simply "The White One." In the Irish version of the Arthurian tales, she is called Grainne ("she who inspired terror") and is the wife of Fionn MacCumhaill, the Irish King Arthur; the Irish Lancelot is known as Diarmait Ua Duibne.

In the British King Arthur tales, Queen Guinevere is abducted by Meleagaunt (also called Meleagaunce or Melwas) of the Summer Country and taken captive for a time until she is rescued by Sir Lancelot. He defeats Meleagaunt but spares his life, vowing to battle him once every year.

Explanation: The character of Guinevere is a Celtic variation on an ancient and profound symbol of the radiance of the human soul and the beauty of its form in light.

Some of the other versions of Meleagaunt

abducting Guinevere include: Azhi Dahaka (a three-headed monster) steals King Yima's Divine Glory (also called Kingly Fortune and *Xvarnah*) in Persian mythology; in the Hindu *Ramayana,* Ravana (a ten-headed monster) abducts Sita, Rama's consort; and in Homer's *Iliad,* Paris abducts Helen, the immortal wife of King Menelaus.

There is no abduction, however, but rather a bestowal. Meleagaunt, Ravana, Paris, and Azhi Dahaka are all expressions of Lucifer, Lord of Light and Light-Bringer, as the God-appointed bestower of the Divine Glory—the knowledge-rich soul in all its beauty and the essence of Beauty itself. The Divine Glory or *Xvarnah* is an abstract expression of this while Guinevere, Sita, and Helen are feminized, human forms of the same glorious soul radiance.

Three other expressions of the same include the Gnostic Sophia, Goddess of Wisdom; the Judaic Shekinah, the feminine aspect of God, but also said to be the daughter, mother, sister, and bride of God; and the Hindu Sri or Laksmi, primordial goddess of beauty who emerged from the Ocean of Milk.

The Shekinah's original home was the Garden of Eden where her splendor radiated from one end of Creation to the other, and she outshone the Sun by far. Only she knows where God hid all His heavenly treasures (all the paths to wisdom). Later David designed and Solomon built the Temple of Jerusalem as a permanent dwelling place for the Shekinah, a mystical event found also in the Hindu *Ramayana* in Sita dwelling in the golden city of Lanka.

When the gods churned the Ocean of Milk in search of Soma, the elixir of immortality, 14 divine objects and persons emerged from the Sea of Light. One was the goddess Sri of vibrant beauty who appeared standing on a white lotus blossom with a lotus in her hand. Sri is also known as Beauty, Lotus-Lady, and Fortune, or Laksmi, goddess of beauty and fortune with a hundred thousand forms, dressed in white robes, resplendent and shining.

Laksmi-Sri is the wife of the solar principle Aditya, but she is also the perpetual consort of Vishnu, the all-pervading Preserver of reality (the Hindu name for Christ), appearing with him in all his incarnations or descents (10 major, 22 minor) into the world. Sri-Laksmi is the power of multiplicity, the ability to project into thousands of forms, the King's (Vishnu-Christ) fortune and glory. Sri is all that is known as female, and Vishnu (also called Hri) all that is male.

More abstractly, Hindu thought understands Sri as the female form of reality enthroned on the pure lotus of knowledge as consort to the male form that includes Brahma (Immense-Being, an expression of God as Creator) and Dhata (Support). Some of Sri's divine attributes in Hindu thought are Mother of the World, speech, conduct, insight, virtuous action, contentment, wish, desire, the shore, great seer, host of gods, bride, starry night, the sky, power, light, and prosperity.

The god who possesses Sri, as prosperity and fortune, is Lord of Wealth. This is why the Persians called the Divine Glory the Kingly Fortune. In Persian myth, the Divine Glory (Sri) sits on the righteous king as authentication of his legitimacy; when he errs from this path, the Divine Glory is removed. The stories usually describe this in terms of its theft by Azhi Dahaka.

Sri is the constant beauty of the Moon in contrast to the fiery radiance of the King's Sun; she is the Queen needed by the King for his completion.

Sri, the Divine Glory or *Xvarnah*, is a representation of the human soul in all its beauty and fortune, its wisdom overshadowing and permeating the king. It is not stolen, but awarded to the king by Lucifer. It is the glorious, beautiful, original celestial light of the virginal soul and the illumination of its wisdom, expressed as a feminine quality, like the Moon, to the King's Sun.

This is both an inner and outer allegory: The authentic God-mandated solar King of people in the world needs the light and wisdom of the soul to be complete, just as in inner, alchemical terms, rational consciousness needs the illumination of the intuition and Moon aspect of the soul. Lucifer, seen in his true guise and function, awards the Divine Glory to kings, men, and women alike.

Sri, as Beauty and Fortune, is the exalted expression of Lucifer in humanity, present in every embodied human, male or female. It is the beauty of form, embodiment, flesh, thought, image, imagination, the ascending creative thought, the beautiful phrase or picture—anything that partakes of beauty and light and enjoys its riches. Lucifer brings beauty to humanity through the soul. Lucifer places the mantle of Sri, Beauty and Fortune, on human shoulders. Lucifer, the Light-Bringer, brings the beautiful soul light of Sri to all humans.

Just as Sri is always Vishnu's consort during his incarnations, so Lucifer (as the archetype for Sri) *bears* the glory and beauty of the divine Light of the soul, whereas Christ (Vishnu) *is* the Light. Lucifer (as Sri, Guinevere, and the rest) is the beautiful form that Light (self-awareness) takes, but whose essence is the Christ.

Guinevere is also a character or position in a Soul Group that periodically incarnates on Earth in a specific culture (15 so far) to act out the Arthurian mythos to help regenerate world culture. In that position, she is the consort to the one overshadowed by King Arthur (also a celestial being embodying the Solar Logos; see King Arthur). As mentioned, she was Grainne in the Irish expression and Gwenhwyfar in the Welsh. In each version, her character exemplifies the ravishing beauty of the light, the Divine Glory and form of the soul as consort to the King, the representative of the Christ (Vishnu).

See also: Azhi Dahaka, Fionn MacCumhaill, Grail Maiden, Hanuman, King Arthur, Lucifer, Ocean of Milk.

HANUMAN

A popular cultural form assumed by the angelic order called the Ofanim to demonstrate their service to the Christ in all his guises.

Also known as Anili, Anjaneya, Hanumat, Lankadahi, Yogachara.

Description: One of India's most popular gods, Hanuman is usually depicted as a strong human of red skin with a monkey's face and protruding fangs.

Also known as Hanumat, his name means "heavy-jawed," while his other names or epithets include Maruti, Anili, Anjaneya, Lankadahi ("Burner of Lanka"), and Yogachara ("Master of Yoga"). His mother is the Apsara Anjana (one of a family of celestial dancing maidens) and the Lord of the Wind, Vayu.

Other Indian traditions, however, say that his real father is Shiva, the august destroyer god of Hinduism's primordial trinity of deities, and his mother is Parvati, Shiva's divine consort. One day, while disguised as monkeys and playing in the forest, Shiva impregnated Parvati and Hanuman was the result. Shiva transferred the fetus first to Vayu to gestate and then to Anjana, the Monkey-woman, to deliver and nurture. Her husband was Kesari, a monkey.

Except Anjana was not always a monkey: Originally, she was a human (a maidservant called Punjikasthala) who was cursed by her master, Brihaspati (a god associated with the planet Jupiter), and had to assume monkey form for a time, until Hanuman was born. Then she could return to Heaven.

Hanuman is usually depicted carrying either a huge club or an uprooted tree and is portrayed trampling a demonic figure. He was born with ornaments of five metals (gold, copper, iron, tin, and zinc) in his ears. His physical powers are prodigious: He can fly, carry entire mountains across continents, leap 800 miles in one bound. His fur is yellow, his fangs white, his mane like *asoka* flowers, his tail many miles long and resembling Indra's banner, his roar as loud as thunder. He can inflate himself to the size of a mountain when necessary. Once he expanded himself to 40 miles across, then shrunk to thumb-size.

He boasted he could leap to the outer limits of the universe with ease. Flying mightily across the sky, he looks like a comet with a fiery tail or like a winged mountain; his face shines like the Sun; his eyes blaze like sacrificial fires; and his long tail streams behind him like Indra's glorious flag. His body is as hard as a diamond and he is adored and respected by all the gods.

He got his name Hanuman as an infant prodigy when he tried to leap up to the Sun and eat it. When he tried to eat Airavata, Indra's celestial elephant, Indra used his thunderbolt (the *vajrayudha*) to knock Hanuman out of the sky and wounded his chin, leaving a scar on his jawbone *(hanu)*—hence Hanuman. After this incident, the gods awarded him invulnerability and very long life. No other being would equal Hanuman in speed or strength; he would have more speed even than Garuda, Vishnu's celestial mount, and Vayu, the Wind god himself.

He is also a faithful devotee and ally of Rama, one of the incarnations of Vishnu, one of Hinduism's three primary gods (equivalent to the Christ). In fact, he regarded Rama as his eternal master, worthy of his unflagging service.

Hanuman was granted perpetual life by Brahma, Hinduism's Creator god, and was promised to live one million years. Hanuman, though belonging in essence to the animal kingdom, is erudite, powerful, and philosophic, unique among the characters and folk heroes of world myths. He learned the entire Vedas in a mere 60 hours from Surya, the Sun god, who in return asked Hanuman to be the constant companion to his son, Sugriva.

In the *Ramayana,* one of India's two main epic poems, Hanuman fights with Rama as leader of the vast horde of monkey warriors of Sugriva's kingdom. Rama's consort, Sita, has been abducted by Ravana, a ten-headed power-hungry celestial being and Lord of the Raksasas (an equally numerous army of demons), and taken captive to the golden city of Lanka atop Trikuta Mountain.

The story is similar to Homer's *Iliad:* One army (Rama's) besieges the other (Ravana's) holed up in their fortified citadel with their hostage, Sita (Helen).

Explanation: Hanuman is one of many powerful and vivid cultural expressions assumed for a time by the angelic order the Ofanim. Others have included Ganesh, the Hindu elephant god (and Airvata, another elephant god); Garuda, the celestial bird who carries Vishnu across the Heavens; the Simurgh, the Persian version of the same; and the Thunderbird, the Native American version.

Typically, when the Ofanim have taken an unforgettable form, such as Hanuman, its qualities are unique, yet there are some consistencies across the spectrum of guises. The Ofanim manifest the qualities of wisdom, erudition, power, strength, helpfulness, unswerving loyalty to the cosmic Christ, and a certain unclassifiable iconoclasm and independence, almost a wayward kind.

When their parentage is given as Shiva and Parvati, this means the Ofanim are using Shiva's energy in the given manifestation. That means a ruthless adherence to the cosmic truth, which tends to destroy all illusions obscuring it.

Consistent throughout their various mythic guises is the Ofanim's faithfulness to the Christ energy and consciousness, expressed variously as Vishnu or Rama, one of his "descents" or incarnations. Experientially, this means the Ofanim guide humans to the Christ Consciousness, just as the Star of Bethlehem (one of their rare incursions into material visibility) guided the Magi to the Christ Child—an outer expression of the inner initiatory truth.

The essential tableau portrayed in the *Ramayana*—two armies fighting over the female hostage, Sita, held in the golden city of Lanka—is not what it seems. It has, for example, nothing to do with the country called Sri Lanka. It did not take place in our physical world. Rather, it is a sublime picture of the dynamics of the spiritual condition of humanity, both celestial and incarnate. It is a mystical portrait of the Heart (the essence of the heart chakra) made into a story.

The presence of Vayu as a parent or foster parent of Hanuman is one of the signifiers of the heart chakra, for that is the home of Vayu's Air element. Lanka is a structural metaphor for the inner essence of the heart chakra and is an early and pure portrayal of the Grail Castle, residence of the Holy Grail.

Partially, Sita is an expression of the Grail Maiden, the feminine consciousness that serves the Holy Grail to the Rich Fisher King, lord of the Grail Castle. But Sita is even more sublime than that: She is another guise of Sri, the beautiful female form who arose from the Ocean of Milk when the gods churned it at the beginning of time; she was one of 14 precious divine objects retrieved from stirring and precipitating the cosmic Sea of primordial Light.

Other names for Sri include the Shekinah, the female aspect of God in Judaic mysticism; King Arthur's wife, Guinevere, "The White One"; Sophia, Gnostic goddess of wisdom; and *Xvarnah*, the Persian mantle of kingship. Sri is the holy Light and form of the soul, the Divine Glory and form of the soul as consort to the King, in this case, Rama, the representative of the Christ (Vishnu).

She is also Laksmi, the primordial goddess of beauty and fortune. Sri is the beautiful, original celestial light of the virginal soul and the illumination of its wisdom, expressed as a feminine quality, like the Moon, to the King's Sun.

The *Ramayana,* when we freeze-frame its essential action, is a picture of the Heart. The virginal beauty and light of the soul are presented to humanity through the golden city of Lanka. Sita was not abducted and taken there; she belongs there. That is how she enters human life, for Lanka exists in every human.

Humanity has been generated twice on Earth. The first round of humanity (remembered variously and pejoratively as Djinn, Asuras, and Raksasas) had enormous freedoms and prodigious psychic abilities, and were mentored by Lucifer, the Lord of Light and Light-Bearer under commission by the Supreme Being.

This first generation of humanity was given Lanka (as the Heart) and its precious, divine occupant, Sita. Ultimately, Lanka is a Celestial City occupied by the gods, but a copy (or hologram) of this was made for humanity and installed as a structured energy field within the heart chakra. Then Sita was placed inside it.

Rama (Christ) and Hanuman (the Ofanim) and his monkey-warriors (the millions of manifestations the Ofanim can create of themselves) encircle Lanka, which means they come to infuse the heart chakra with Christ Consciousness. (Fittingly, the *Ramayana* says that the gods working with Vishnu [who would assume the guise of Rama] agreed to take incarnations as huge monkeys for the purpose of assisting Vishnu in overturning Ravana's rule.)

In the outer story, it seems that Ravana (Lucifer) and his Raksasas (first humanity) resist this and will not surrender Sri to the Christ Consciousness. But the truth is that it is not so much resistance and fighting as the natural dichotomy of the heart chakra that is depicted in this powerful image of the siege of Lanka.

The outer heart chakra is called *Anahata* in Hindu yogic lore and has 12 petals, and the inner is called the *Ananda-kanda* with eight petals. The function or agenda of the outer part of the heart chakra is individuation: The experience of the primordial 12 aspects of the Self (astrology's horoscope). This is Ravana with his ten heads and his puissant but rebellious Raksasas.

The agenda of the inner heart chakra is unitive consciousness, a return to the bliss of undivided, undifferentiated, unfallen Light and consciousness. The eight petals surrounding this heart center represent the various wisdom paths that will accomplish this reunification of the fallen, divided Self. This is Rama (Christ) and Hanuman with his monkey warriors (the Ofanim).

The middle position between the two hearts is the Heart, or golden Lanka, and its divinely pure, virginal, and gloriously beautiful occupant,

Sita (Sri). In effect, both "armies" encircle Lanka to express their adoration of Sita.

First generation humanity fell away from Christ Consciousness and into the stupendous magical powers *(siddhis)* afforded by awakened kundalini. They represent what happened to Sri when she was given to humanity. From the gods' viewpoint, Sri was unacceptably "abducted" and held hostage by first humanity.

Rama and Hanuman come to remind them of the higher realities and obligations because the fate of the soul, Sri (humanity's spiritual essence), is at stake. Rama and Hanuman come to reboot the collective human heart chakra. The divinely mandated "struggle" or challenge for humanity is to balance through and on behalf of Sri both poles of consciousness, the individuative and unitive, both freedom (Ravana and his Raksasas) and responsibility (Hanuman and his horde).

Paradoxically, Sri is also Ravana. Sri is the pure original dispensation of the soul, the beautiful Light-Bearer, an expression of the "unfallen" Lucifer in everyone. Ravana is what happened to Sri when placed in individualized humans, that is, in separate bodies, but with the celestial panoply of powers.

See also: Behemoth, Emerald, Fall of Man, Fisher King, Ganesh, Garuda, Grail Castle, Grail Knight, Grail Maiden, Guinevere, Holy Grail, Lucifer, Ocean of Milk, Phoenix, Raksasas, Ravana, Simurgh, Thunderbird, Vocub Caquix.

HARMONIC CONVERGENCE

A global initiation of humanity in the Emerald, or the esoteric aspect of the heart chakra, by Lucifer, Lord of Light, in his first return to the Earth in millennia and to the very spot where he first placed his Emerald.

Description: In 1971, Tony Shearer published *Lord of the Dawn,* a book recounting legends of the Zapotec Indians of Oaxaca Valley in southern Mexico. Zapotec prophecy said that Quetzalcoatl, Lord of the Dawn, would return to his buried heart on Earth on August 17, 1987; bright blue lightning would illuminate the Valley of Oaxaca and Quetzalcoatl's heart would burst into millions of pieces and be distributed around the world to all humans as a spiritual blessing. In the late 1980s, visionary Jose Arguelles picked up this theme and popularized the idea of gathering at sacred sites around the Earth during the third week of August.

Considerable New Age, metaphysical, and millennialist expectation was overlaid on this event, including the expectation of UFO arrivals, the descent of the gods, the fulfillment of a prediction from the Mayan Calendar, and more. Despite the expected mainstream ridicule, an estimated several million men and women did gather at recognized holy sites for a week of meditation, illumination, and a kind of informal global *agape* and New Age party.

Explanation: The Harmonic Convergence did not quite play out the way most people expected it to, but it was a fantastic success in terms of its intent.

Quetzalcoatl (Lucifer) did in fact return to the tree under which he had buried his heart, and it did burst into millions of pieces, but this metaphor must be decoded. The heart he returned to is the one Emerald he gave to the Earth and planted at the El Tule tree at the inception of the second generation of humanity.

Regardless of where the attention of participants seemed to be, everyone met inside the Emerald in a space that looked like a vast Gothic cathedral's interior. The cathedral was a flash of the illumination brought into the individual temples (the Emerald in each human) by Lord Lucifer's arrival in the Earth plane. The illumination was gradual, like a dimmer switch lightening a dark room; the celestial event unfolded like a parabola: It began on August 14, peaked on the 17th, and ended on the 24th. The worldwide event was focused through its ground-zero point, at Lucifer's Emerald at the El Tule tree.

The tree at El Tule has specific properties for grounding energy and was preserved for this purpose. It is not an ordinary tree, but a sacred tree with very complex amplification and resonance devices built into its etheric structure. This 2,000-year-old tree formed the link between the etheric, astral, and physical realms, and grounded the Luciferic initiation of the Emerald for the planet. The tree is a massive, stout cedar, 131 feet tall and 138 feet in girth; at the time of the Convergence, it dominated the small churchyard of El Templo del Santa Maria, ten miles east of Oaxaca in Mexico.

The intent of the event, from the viewpoint of the spiritual hierarchy, was to open receptive areas on the material plane to a new source of cosmic energy. Lucifer as Lord of the Light, in full commission by the Supreme Being, illumined the astral sphere around the Earth and fed into those humans who were receptive (at an astral or higher mental level) specific types of illumination. At the same time, this converged with the opening of geomantic nodes or energy doorways on the Earth that could activate the planet's visionary geography in a new way and thereby bring much needed ecological balance.

Another focus of the event was the start of a protracted, painful acknowledgment of the individual and collective Shadow, that vast stuffed, shut, and locked closet of the repressed unconscious that we have, as a final measure, demonized with the seal of the Devil to be sure we never go near it. Lucifer illuminating the hearts of all humans inaugurated that inevitable rapprochement with the repudiated parts of ourselves—the long feast of the Shadow—and with Lucifer as our projected archdevil perpetrator of our discomfort.

The Harmonic Convergence was one of the key events in recent decades in which a mass of humanity attempted consciously to slough off a layer of the dark grid or Antichrist from the Earth's Light-filled visionary geography.

See also: Antichrist, Asura, Djinn, Earth Changes, Emerald, Ghost Dance, Kings of Edom, Lucifer, Prometheus, Quetzalcoatl, Ragnarok, Raksasas, Tree of the Knowledge of Good and Evil.

HEIMDALL

A guise of the Archangel Gabriel, mentor and supervisor of the Mysteries of the eternal Christ through the gods' Celestial City.

Also known as Archangel Gabriel, Gwynn ap Nudd, Heimdallr, He Who Illuminates the World, Humbaba, the White *As,* Wind-Shield, World Brightener.

Description: Heimdall is a singular, enigmatic being from Norse mythology. His name from Old Norse means approximately "He who illuminates the world" and also "World Brightener."

His principal task is to guard the bridge Bifrost, which is the entrance to Asgard, the heavenly residence of the high gods, the Aesir. He guards Bifrost and Asgard against the entrance of the Frost Giants of Niflheim, described in Norse myth as malevolent giants destined one day (on Ragnarok, or Twilight of the Gods, the end of the world) to overrun Asgard and fight the gods. Heimdall's hearing is so acute he can hear the grass grow, and he can see for a hundred miles in any direction, night or day.

Bifrost means "quivering road" or "swaying road to Heaven" (from the Old Norse *bifa,* which means "shake, sway") and is described as a rainbow bridge (*Bifrost* is also translated as "the fleetingly glimpsed rainbow" or "the multicolored way"), and sometimes as *Asbru,* "Aesir-Bridge," the privileged bridge into Asgard. Bifrost rises from the Earth and terminates in the sky at Heimdall's dwelling called *Himinbjorg* (Old Norse for "Heaven's castle" or "Heaven protection"). To get onto Bifrost, you must pass by or through Himinbjorg.

Heimdall keeps the bridge open for the Aesir who every day ride out of Asgard and across Bifrost to assemble for decisions at *Urdarbrunnr,* Urd's Well, the home of the three Norns (or Fates) who weave humanity's destiny at the base of the World Tree called Yggdrasil.

Heimdall always wears shining white armor, carries a flashing sword called *Hofud* ("Man-Head"), rides a mighty horse called *Gulltopr*

("Golden Mane"), and bears *Gjallarhorn* ("loud-sounding horn" or "yelling horn").

The latter is a magic horn capable of being heard throughout all of Heaven. Gjallarhorn may also be a drinking horn, for some Norse texts say it is the same horn that the wise god Mimir uses to drink wisdom from his own well at the base of Yggdrasil; congruent with this is the possibility that the name means "horn of the River Gjoll," an Underworld wisdom stream. Heimdall will blow it once and definitively at Ragnarok to summon all the gods to assist in Asgard's defense. This is why he is also called Vindhler ("Wind-Shield") for, as a watchman, he is on duty on Bifrost in all types of weather.

He's called the White God or White *As* (*As* means a god, Aesir, the gods; Odin, high chief of all the gods, is sometimes called simply "the *As*") and was born of nine sisters, all giantesses. He was born in ancient days of the race of gods on the edge of the Earth and with the strength of the Earth in him. Heimdall is also known as Gullintanni, the one with remarkable golden teeth.

Norse myth credits him with being not only watchman of the gods, but also the father of all humankind. Classically, the gods and humans alike described themselves in the mythic texts as the greater and lesser kinsmen of Heimdall.

Explanation: The identity of Heimdall has always baffled scholars due to his singular qualities and the difficulty of finding correlates in other myth systems. It's probably because most commentators do not consider the archangels. Heimdall is the Archangel Gabriel as seen by ancient Norse psychics.

Gabriel is one of the 18 archangels, and his name means "God Is My Strength." He is said to be the Guardian of the Sixth Heaven (of the seven in Judaic angelologies), chief among the Guards of Paradise, Trumpeter of the Last Judgment, the Angel of Revelation and Truth (he transmitted the Koran to Mohammed), God's Messenger to humanity, the Divine Herald, the Announcer (the Bible has him telling the Virgin Mary she is pregnant with Jesus), and Archangel of the Holy Sefiroth (spheres of Light and reality dimensions on the Tree of Life, as described in Qabala).

Gabriel is also the Voice of God, symbolized by his trumpet (i.e., Heimdall's Gjallarhorn) and, further, Gabriel's prime colors are silver and white. The coincidence of Gabriel's white color and Heimdall's in itself is not the definitive correlation but the identical nature of their function is, even though described in different terms. Heimdall guards Asgard; Gabriel guards Paradise and the Sixth Heaven. The key is understanding what Asgard is.

Asgard, the House of the Aesir, is another name for the Greek Mount Olympus, residence of the Olympian gods who rule and oversee the human world. Asgard is not, however, the home of the full panoply of gods, known as the Great White Brotherhood (see Da Derga's Hostel and Einherjar), but of a crucial selection of them in accordance with the 14 Rays of the Great Bear.

The constellation Ursa Major (Great Bear) is the galactic home of the Great White Brotherhood, and the Big Dipper (the seven bright stars in the sacrum and tail of the Bear) is the home of the 14 Ray Masters, also called the Seven Rishis (each of whom has a partner). Some of these Ray Masters' names are familiar, such as Apollo, Aphrodite, and Athena or El Morya, Saint Germain, and Kuthumi.

The Ray Masters (see Seven Rishis) have an administrative headquarters (actually 108 copies in total) in Earth's visionary geography. Bifrost, as the quivering Rainbow Bridge from Earth (Mitgard) to Heaven (Asgard), is mythic code for the Ray Masters themselves and their double-rainbow color spectrum.

The Ray Masters, either individually (a human may have one or more as an initiator or Mystery psychopomp) or collectively, are the conduit for consciousness into that domain of the celestial and true Earth government. We could equally accurately construe Bifrost as the double-rainbow emanation from Asgard or as the "fleetingly glimpsed rainbow" Aesir-Bridge. In Asgard, the Ray Masters each have their own subsection, accompanied by their affiliate adepts.

The Archangel Gabriel should be understood as an exalted mentor and colleague from the angelic realm, a different order of being (created perfect by God at the beginning of time) from the gods (extremely evolved post-humans, from previous cycles of existence on Earth and elsewhere).

Gabriel (or Heimdall) is the revealer of the truth in that, among other things, Asgard actually exists 1,000 years in humanity's future, at roughly 3000 A.D. In this guise, it is an aspect of Shambhala still existing ahead of us in time. For certain geomantic activations (such as the hatching of a Silver Egg involved in the Christ Mysteries; see Black Eye of Horus), human initiates must retrieve specific information from the future through Asgard to use in the present time.

Obviously, unauthorized or inappropriate accessing of Asgard's archives would be deleterious to Earth evolution, so Heimdall-Gabriel prevents this. In essence, Heimdall is chief of the Mysteries of the Old Christ (appropriate, as he is the Annunciator) in that the Earth's 1,080 Silver Eggs, each bearing a hologram of the eternal, far-seeing Christ in his Horus (Egyptian falcon god) aspect, can only be activated and seeded into the Earth by information from Gabriel's city.

Put more starkly, the Archangel Gabriel supervises the flow of Christ wisdom from the heavenly world into the human, planetary realm and oversees the general level of human accessibility to the Christ outside Time.

Another way of describing Asgard is to say it is one of eight Celestial Cities surrounding Mount Meru, as described in the Vedic texts. Each of these cities has multiple copies in Earth's visionary geography. Asgard as a Celestial City is the sumptuous and spiritually opulent residence of Indra, chief of the gods. In Celtic myth, this Light City was described as a Glass Mountain or Crystal City.

Gabriel's-Heimdall's revelatory aspect is also encoded in the meaning of his sword's name, *Hofud,* usually translated as "Man-Head" or "Human-Head." In Old Norse, one poetic term for sword is "the head of Heimdall" and another for head is "the sword of Heimdall." Thus Heimdall's *Hofud* signifies the searing penetration of his enlightened archangelic insight and wisdom.

Heimdall has at least two other previously unrecognized or correlated cultural guises. To the ancient Sumerians, he was Humbaba, the God-appointed guardian of the mysterious but sacred Cedar Forest (also called Pine Mountain and Land of the Living). This was the *musab ilani,* the dwelling place of the gods. Humbaba was a giant whose voice was like fire (which was a flood-weapon), who had super-acute hearing and a cloak of seven layers of terrifying celestial radiance.

In Celtic lore of the British Isles, especially at Glastonbury in Somerset, England, Heimdall's equivalent is Gwynn ap Nudd, whose name means "The White One." He is the son of Nudd, king of *Annwn,* the Otherworld. Gwynn ap Nudd has his otherworldly palace atop or inside the Tor, an anomalous, pyramid-shaped hillock in Glastonbury, a town anciently known as *Ynys Witrin,* the Glass Island or Glass Mountain. Gwynn guards entry into the Glass Mountain, which is another, quite valid, way of perceiving the Celestial City.

See also: Bifrost, Black Eye of Horus, Da Derga's Hostel, Einherjar, Glass Mountain, House of Atreus, Hyperboreans, Ragnarok, Seven Rishis, Shambhala, Yggdrasil.

HITCHING POST OF THE SUN

A Sun Temple, or Mithraeum, with 144 copies worldwide, for transmitting solar intelligence to Earth and humanity.

Also known as Boat of Millions of Years, Celestial City of Tejovati, City of the Royal Fire, City of the Sun, Dinsul, Heliopolis, Intiwatana, Mithraeum, Mount of the Sun, Sun Fastener, Sun Temple.

Description: Hitching Post of the Sun is a translation of *Intiwatana,* which also means "Sun Fastener" and refers generally to the mountain complex of Machu Picchu in Peru and specifically to a ritual feature at the western end of the site. The term was coined by Yale University archeologist Hiram Bingham around 1911 after his research at this ancient sacred site in southeastern Peru.

Archeologists explain that during the summer and winter solstices, the Incas, who once lived at Machu Picchu, ceremonially "tied" the Sun to a small upraised stone set into a stone base, thereafter known as an *Intiwatana* stone. Thus *Intiwatana* is the Sun Fastener or "place where the Sun is tied up," Inti being the Incan name for the Sun god.

Another name was *Apu Punchau,* and his head was depicted as a gold disk or ball of gold from which solar Rays and flames extended. In fact, the Incas named themselves after the Sun, as descendants of Inti, or Sons of the Sun. Anyone other than an Inca in full initiatory standing who pronounced the name of the Sun god was summarily put to death for the profanation.

The ceremony of fastening the Sun may have been associated with *Inti Raimi,* the Sun festival or "Solemn Resurrection of the Sun," June 21, the winter solstice in the Southern Hemisphere. The shortest day of the year with the least sunlight, on that day the Inca believed Father Sun was potentially departing them and he must be prevented from retreating even farther from Earth by being tied down.

Machu Picchu once offered at least three other Sun honorings. It was the residence of the Mamacunas, the Chosen Women or Virgins of the Sun, presumably a monastic order of women dedicated to the Sun god. The *Intipunku,* or Sun Gate, was a notch in the southeast ridge of the ruins, and the site also offered a Temple of the Sun, a rock outcropping made into a carved rock altar.

A highly similar myth about tying down the Sun god is attributed to Mount Haleakala, the 10,023-foot-tall volcano on the island of Maui in Hawaii. Maui, a Polynesian demigod and prodigy, much like the Greek Herakles, tied down the Sun god and his 16 legs on this mountain with 16 ropes. The same reason was given as with the Incas: The Sun passed over so quickly that the countryfolk could not even dry their bananas. Maui made the Sun move slower. The mountain was thus named Haleakala, the House of the Sun.

Explanation: The Hitching Post of the Sun at Machu Picchu is one of 144 Sun temples templated throughout Earth's visionary geography. In classical Hinduism, it is known as the Celestial City of Tejovati, one of eight celestial residences, each with its qualities, gods, functions, and type of opulence. These eight Celestial Cities are all copied in varying amounts in the Earth grid and may be accessed through specifically designated sacred sites in each culture.

For example, in ancient Persia (now Iran), one Sun temple was located at Takht-i-Sulaiman, the City of the Royal Fire, one of the prime Fire sites in Zoroastrianism. Another was at Rhodes, the Island of the Sun God Helios; another at Heliopolis, Egypt's City of the Sun and residence of Ra the Sun god; and others at Titikala, the Sacred Rock on the Island of the Sun, Lake Titicaca, Peru; the Plaza at Santa Fe, New Mexico, a locale at the center of town anciently known among Native Americans as the Dancing Ground of the Sun; and Saint Michael's Mount in Cornwall, England, once called *Dinsul,* Mount of the Sun.

To psychic vision, a Sun temple may initially look like a great mound and circle of golden fire, for the Sun refers to the archetype of fire and light (typified, for example, in Hinduism by Agni the Fire god), the Sun at the center of our solar system (as in the Greek Sun god Helios), and the Sun within the Sun (an esoteric designation for the Solar Logos), or the Sun's spiritual intelligence (an aspect of the cosmic Christ at the level of a solar system or galaxy).

In Vedic symbolism, the Sun in this guise is Surya, the illuminer, lord of knowledge, luminous vision, and total truth, whose Rays are illuminations.

Yet the Sun temple may resemble a giant golden bull's head as seen from within, and resemble also a vast golden cave. The bull's head aspect was emphasized in Mithraism in which a solar hero (Mithras) slew a cosmic bull, letting its blood pour out of its neck; the place where this ritual was at least symbolically enacted (or psychically experienced) was called a Mithraeum and, in classical times, central Europe had many hundreds of them.

Symbolically, the bull's blood released in the bull-slaying represents solar time and even universal time released into a solar system as its life force and also as a measure of its expected life span. The bull's cave is also a solar time cave.

One of the clearest mythic portrayals of the geomantic action of a Sun temple is from Greek myth: Hephaistos, the Olympian smith-fire god, works his forges inside volcanic Mount Etna on Sicily aided by three Cyclopes. The forge is the Sun temple, the Cyclopes are three Elohim, an angelic order that works with the Sun's energy and sentience on behalf of the Christ, and Hephaistos is a colleague of the Solar Logos, putting solar consciousness into objects of matter.

Hephaistos and his helpers forge numerous implements, objects, and devices for the gods, which is a way of saying that they put the essence of the Sun's spirituality and life force into devices at various levels of material expression. At a more rarified level, Hephaistos puts the solar intelligence into the Periodic Table of Elements, that is, the primal constituents of matter throughout the solar system, and even more subtly, into the essential forms of the constellations.

More than infusing the solar intelligence into the stars, we could interpret this tableau as the making of the stars and constellations from primordial Fire. The stars and their groupings are celestial intelligences made of cosmic Fire in the smithy's forge; they embody differentiated consciousness, that is, they are distinguished and individualized from the preconscious totality of what was before Creation (called the Moon or Soma), yet ever desiring to consume that continuously wakeful, immortalizing substance (see Fountain of Youth).

As the three Elohim also once served as the Planetary Logoi (spiritual intelligences) for the seven classical planets of our solar system, their work with Hephaistos can be seen as distributing solar intelligence to the planets. At the human level, these seven planets are the archetypes of the seven chakras.

The Sun Temple also puts the fire of life into stars, and this fire, which we might see as the soul of a star, then consumes the eternal edible substance of Soma, or continuously wakeful awareness (see Fountain of Youth). The result is a star—myriad Star gods—made of cosmic fire and immortal consciousness.

Sun temples on Earth allow interested humans the opportunity to interact with this cosmic process, which is also a fundamental aspect of the human being. In Hindu thought, the Sun and Moon are primordial energies, created before much of the rest of reality. The Moon was created first and refers not to the satellite of the planet Earth, but the Moon sphere, typified by Soma, the principle of uninterrupted wakefulness or undying consciousness. The Sun came second, and is Agni, the primal cosmic Fire that consumes the substance of Soma.

See also: Argonauts, Balor of the Evil Eye, Beast of the Apocalypse, Cattle of the Sun, Cyclops Polyphemus, Fountain of Youth, Giants, Golden Fleece, Ocean of Milk.

HOLLOW HILL

An experiential doorway into Earth's visionary geography and its 100+ different features, Light temples, and residences of the gods.

Also known as *locus consecratus,* nemeton, sacred ford, sidhe, tirtha, wahi tapu.

Description: The term Hollow Hill is used in Celtic folklore, principally to refer to the after-death, otherworldly location of King Arthur and his Knights of the Round Table after their time in the world ended. For example, folklore says that Arthur and his Knights sleep inside South Cadbury Castle, an old rounded, bare-topped hill-fort in Somerset, some 12 miles from Glastonbury, England. Yet, clearly, the legend does not mean that the Knights literally sleep inside the physical hill; without specifying exactly, the legend implies there is an extradimensional space somehow in the hill, or at least a forgotten, inaccessible cave.

In Tibetan-Mongolian lore about another King Arthur expression in Buddhist-shamanic culture, the faithful still believe that their great hero Gesar-Khan survives with his warrior retinue in an underground kingdom, awaiting to be born in Shambhala (the sublime city of spiritual adepts and the true world government), from whence he will one day ride forth triumphantly on a white steed to free the world from barbarians in the final Battle of Shambhala (see Shambhala). Underground kingdoms can fairly be equated with Hollow Hills.

Irish lore says many of the old hills and mounds in the countryside are hollow in the sense that they accommodate otherworldly fairy palaces, even the residences of the gods, known as the Tuatha de Danann. The Hollow Hill is a portal through to where the fairies or gods are living. Such residences are visible not to ordinary sight, Irish lore says, but to those with second sight (clairvoyance), as they are situated in the Otherworld (another dimension).

The Tuatha de Danann, Ireland's original gods, once lived aboveground and ruled Ireland benevolently for 3,000 years, legend says; then they retreated into the Hollow Hills, known as the *sidhes* (pronounced *shays*), and reduced their influence on human affairs. Each of the major Tuatha got their own sidhe: Midir the Proud lived at Bri Leith; the Dagda (the Tuatha chief) or his son Aengus Og at Bruigh na Boinne; Una lived at Knockshegowna; Lir's palace was called Sidhe Fionnachaidh; Ogma's was Sidhe Airceltrai; Lugh's was Sidhe Rodrubai.

Another nuance has it that the sidhes mark the places where the Tuatha de Danann left the Earth and disappeared into the underground, or Otherworld. On occasion (and Irish myth is rich in this), a Tuatha would suddenly appear out of the sidhe to intervene in human affairs, play enchanting music, or dally with people. Perhaps out of respect for this possibility, Irish farmers traditionally avoided using the sidhe (or the landscape spot marking one, such as a grass-rich, rounded hill) and even the paths to it for cattle grazing or agriculture.

Sometimes the gods or the fairies (the two, confusingly, got blurred together over the centuries, probably due to lack of human contact with and experience of them) were referred to as "people of the sidhe." Similarly, the sidhes (the physically visible aspects, such as a hill-fort, barrow, tumulus, or hillock) were often called fairy mounds.

The well-known banshee is actually written *bean-sidhe,* meaning "woman of the sidhe." Originally it meant any woman who lived in the Hollow Hills, but later it came to more specifically refer to a death harbinger, an otherworldly spirit who announced by shrieking the imminent death of a human.

Similarly, though using different terms, Tibetan traditions of "sacred geography" record how specific locations in the Tibetan landscape, such as a cliff, cave, or land around a monastery, are the dwelling places of sublime deities. The Tibetans do not say Hollow Hills, but the extra-dimensionality is implied. Caves, rocks, land formations, and other geological features act as Hollow Hills.

In one cave, after meditation, a psychic Buddhist practitioner (traveling through Tibet in the 1850s) was able to see "infinite numbers" of the male and female Glorious Realm Protectors. At another location, those of pure vision (clairvoyance) could see the Palace of the Great

Glorious *Heruka* (a wrathful protector being). A pair of high rocks, specific in Buddhist parlance, were the residences of the Lion-Faced Demon Protectors, Great Terrifier (a Realm Protector), the male spiritual warrior Vajra Light, and the female spiritual warrior Powerful Woman of Lanka, reported this traveler.

Explanation: The terms Hollow Hills or *sidhes* are clues to Earth's vast visionary geography, and refer to the openings into this realm through physical landscape features such as hills, caves, mounds, rock faces, or human-made structures.

Earth's visionary geography consists of 100+ different types of portals, doorways, or openings into the planet's subtle landscape. These different types have multiple copies, so that, for example, a Hollow Hill, sidhe, or landscape portal to the Rich Fisher King of Celtic lore is through any of 144 Grail Castles accessed at sacred or holy sites around the Earth. In all, there are many thousands of gateways into the Otherworld, each accessed through a physical site.

Thus Hollow Hill or sidhe can refer accurately to any of these 100 features.

Often the sidhe or Hollow Hill leading to a Tuatha de Danann is already hallowed and culturally recognized as such, or at least it carries an aura of numinosity. Places known as a god's sidhe or King Arthur's Hollow Hill, or even the fairy mounds, are functional passageways from our physical realm to their numinous one and, as the Tibetan visionary cited previously said, those of "pure vision," what the Celtic lore calls "second sight," may enter and visit with the gods and spirits.

Hindu sacred geographic lore calls such places *tirthas,* or spiritual fords, where one can safely cross the "river" between physical and subtle realms. The ancient Druids used the term *nemeton* (from the Latin *nemus* meaning "Heaven") to indicate a sacred center, sanctuary, or enclosure, such as a grove or woodland clearing, as a place of spiritual exchange between the terrestrial and celestial worlds. Similarly, the Romans spoke of a *locus consecratus,* "consecrated place."

The Maori of New Zealand use the term *wahi tapu,* which literally means "sacred place," but the wider connotation of which is "windows to the past." Such places provide genealogical links to the Maori ancestors, original stories of creation, and events that define individual tribes within their landscapes.

Such a portal site is hollow in the sense that, to psychic perception, the inner aspect (varieties of Light temples or celestial residences) seems to be inside the physical aspect, rendering the latter a hollow quality. Or the inner aspect can be seen as overlapping, enveloping the physical, or even as much larger than it.

Irish lore says that Fionn MacCumhaill, the great hero of Ireland and leader of the Fianna (one of the 15 King Arthurs in Earth history), lives at the Sidhe of Almu, now called Hill of Allen, in County Kildare. Almu ("All-White") is an Irish goddess, but the whiteness also referred to Fionn's royal citadel on the hill. As mentioned, the British King Arthur lived at South Cadbury Castle, later called a Hollow Hill. You may access King Arthur as the Solar Logos and his retinue in Ursa Major through either of these geomantic sites.

The blurring of the Tuatha de Danann in their sidhes with the fairies in their mounds is confusing and inaccurate. While both have their legitimate places of entry through the physical landscape, they are not the same order of beings. Fairies are, as the legends say, small, angel-like beings who tend the plant kingdom, whereas the Tuatha are sages and adepts of the Great White Brotherhood.

See also: Dreamtime, Fairy Queen, Fionn MacCumhaill, Fisher King, Grail Castle, Holy Mountain, Hurqalya, King Arthur, Tuatha de Danann, Zep Tepi.

HOLY GRAIL

The human body and complete energy field made into a golden receptacle for the higher Light and consciousness of the cosmic Christ.

Also known as the Cup of Light, Dagda's Cauldron, Holy Dish, Sangrail, Sangreal.

Description: The Holy Grail is probably the most numinous, mystical, and mysterious spiritual object in the Western metaphysical tradition. In the medieval Grail sagas, the Holy Grail was described essentially as a chalice or cup used at the Last Supper of Christ and his Apostles, in which his blood was collected during the Crucifixion. The Grail was secreted away from Palestine and, some legends say, brought to France, then Glastonbury, England, where it was hidden.

In the Arthurian tales, the Holy Grail was presented to the assembled Grail Knights on Pentecost while they were seated at the Round Table inside Camalate. A golden chalice surrounded by a powerful light, it was borne into the hall by angels; after a while, it would be taken away again.

The Quest for the Holy Grail was to behold the Grail in its own residence, the Grail Castle, located somewhere in the wilderness of Logres, an ancient name for Britain. Many knights sought it, but only three ever achieved the Quest—Bors, Galahad, and Parsifal—after many years, great struggle, and perseverance. Galahad swooned in ecstasy after seeing the Grail, then departed the human world for Sarras, the Celestial City of the Grail, where he became king.

Typically, the Grail is in the safekeeping of the Fisher King, lord of the Grail Castle, sometimes called *Montsalvasche* ("Mount of Salvation"). Every day the Grail is borne before the Fisher king in the Grail Procession, most often by one or many Grail Maidens. The Fisher King is usually called the Maimed or Wounded King because he cannot partake of the Grail's miraculous healing. His inability to heal precipitates the Wasteland, in which the lands around the Grail castle are blighted and environmentally damaged and infertile.

In Wolfram von Eschenbach's thirteenth-century version, *Parzival,* the Grail is a green stone fallen from the crown of Lucifer and brought to Earth by angels. This stone was understood to be the last remaining fragment of a former paradise.

In earlier, pre-Christian traditions, the equivalent of the Grail is the Cauldron of the Dagda, chief of the Tuatha de Danann, Ireland's ancient gods. The Dagda brought the Cauldron from a magical city called Murias. The Dagda's Cauldron could also restore life to those killed in battle or heal the wounded.

The Grail has antecedents in the Horn of Plenty or a variously described numinous dish, platter, salver, ciborium, or chalice that will feed everyone precisely what they wish, in both food and drink, for as long as they desire it.

In the 1980s, public support was given to the hypothesis that the Sangreal, or Holy Blood (another name for the Grail), was an actual genetic bloodline created by Jesus and Mary Magdalene and underlay the true kingship lineage in Europe.

Explanation: The Grail's reality has several nuances. It is a process of remembering the soul's deep history and incarnational lineage as a way of feeding the Higher Self (the Fisher King) with the light and wisdom this generates. It is an alchemical retort used as a progressively expanding visualization for consolidating one's life, lessons, and events to produce the gold of understanding and wisdom. It is a series of meditative images provided humans by the angelic realm for the purposes of transiting Earth's visionary geography (its terrain of linked sacred sites) to expand one's consciousness.

Ultimately, the Quest of the Holy Grail involves making your body and aura the receptacle for the Light and consciousness of Christ (Logos or Word). The body and its energy fields are one aspect of Castle Carbonek, an old name for the Grail Castle, signifying the mortal body of carbon and the carbonic cycle.

Earth's visionary geography is provided with 144 copies (or holograms) of the original Grail Castle with an interactive Holy Grail within it.

Eschenbach, though he mystified most scholars, was correct in saying the Grail is a green stone brought from Heaven. Except for one thing: The Holy Grail is inside the green stone, better known as the Emerald, which is represented both inside and outside the human. Inside, it is an electromagnetic doorway within the heart chakra; outside, it is templated all over the Earth.

Other names from different mystical traditions for the Emerald include Solomon's Temple of Jerusalem, Qabala's Cube of Space, the golden city of Lanka in Hinduism's *Ramayana* epic. The Emerald was given to each incarnating human and to the Earth as well, from the Lord of Light and Light-Bearer, Lucifer, as a gift of total freedom in consciousness at the inception of the planet and humanity.

Sri is probably the most vividly evoked description of this numinous quality. Long ago when the Hindu gods churned the Ocean of Milk (the great Sea of astral Light), they precipitated 14 precious objects and persons, including Sri, a beautiful woman, clothed in white, standing on a white lotus. Later in Hindu legend, she is known as Sita, the consort of Rama, and Radha, Krishna's consort. In the *Ramayana,* Sita is abducted and held hostage in Lanka, a celestial residence.

Sri, the Divine Glory or *Xvarnah,* is a representation of the human soul in all its original beauty, fortune, glory, and splendor, its wisdom permeating, encloaking the king (the human self). It is the original celestial light of the virginal soul and the illumination of its wisdom, expressed as a feminine quality.

Sri, as Beauty and Fortune, is the exalted expression in humanity of Lucifer, Lord of Light and the God-appointed Light-Bearer, in every embodied human. Lucifer, in his original pure form, is the beautiful *individualized* light, expressed as a celestial-human-like form, the first self-aware container or chalice for the Light of universal awareness (the Christ).

Austrian clairvoyant Rudolf Steiner once said that Lucifer *bears* the Light, Christ *is* the Light. Lucifer, ultimately, is the Grail Maiden, Sri, Sita, Sophia, Shekinah, and all other expressions of the feminine consort to the Christ, as well as the Holy Grail itself. That is because Lucifer bears and contains the Light.

The Holy Grail is the Light-Bearer for the Light of Christ Consciousness. You can see this either as Lucifer as the Grail Maiden *bearing* the Grail, which contains the Light, or Lucifer *being* the Grail itself, his body bearing the Light.

The divine Light drama takes place inside the Grail Castle (Solomon's Temple, the Cube of Space, Emerald, Lanka, the inner human heart chakra). Ultimately, the Grail Procession and the filling of the Holy Grail with Light is the same as a human opening the Emerald within the heart chakra (called the Heart or *Hridayam* in the Hindu tradition, the Heart behind the heart chakra).

Opening the Emerald, the angelic realm informs us, is akin to exposing ourselves to a quality and quantity of Light inconceivable in normal terms. The experience knocks one out of the subjective stance as experiencer and into a new place beyond space, time, and identity as we know it. The Emerald (the Grail and its Light) contains the *source* of Love and Light, the Christ Consciousness.

Exposure to this Light transmutes the physical, material body into one of Light, and you enter a new state of being called Ascension. Ascended Masters are called that because they occupy bodies of Light; they have each achieved the Holy Grail. One of the legends of the Grail is that it will feed you with whatever food and drink you desire. Habitation of this Light-body, or what some call the Higher Self, God-Self, Perfect Self, or Mighty "I AM" Presence, enables you to draw from the universal substance to precipitate (create) anything you desire. That is why the Holy Grail was called the cauldron of inexhaustible abundance.

A Judaic teaching has it that God took a little of the primordial Light from the inception of creation and put it inside a glowing stone or jewel called the *Tzohar.* He had the angel Raziel give it to Adam after he left the Garden of Eden as a token of how the world had once been filled from end to end with that Light.

When the Emerald (or Tzohar) is opened, after a long, gradual, and progressive approach, the Grail Castle is flooded with Light. It is the same primordial Light that God first made appear. The Holy Grail overflows with Light. Sri, as the Grail Maiden and Light-Bearer, is reunited with her divine consort, Rama, Vishnu, or Krishna, the Christ or Light. The Light-Bearer merges and is one with the Light; the Grail merges and is one with the Light it contains.

Then Grail Castle, Holy Grail, and the Light merge and become a single blinding blaze of effulgence, all differences in form and function dissolved.

See also: Camalate, Emerald, Fisher King, Grail Castle, Grail Knight, Grail Maiden, Guinevere, Lucifer, Ocean of Milk, Round Table, Wasteland, White Mount.

HOLY MOUNTAIN

Spiritually charged space created by overlaying an etheric energy canopy called a dome, a feature that created, then energized, and still encases the major mountains.

Also known as the Home of the Gods.

Description: Throughout the myths of the world reference is made to mountains as holy, numinous, as the home of the gods, and even created by them.

Among the many examples: Mount Fuji in Japan is the home of *Ko-No-hana-saku-ya-hime,* "The Princess Who Maketh the Blossoms of the Trees to Flowers"; she is also called Sangen, Asama, or *O-ana-mochi* ("Possessor of the Great Hole of Crater") and is the volcano's divine guardian. Adam's Peak in Sri Lanka is the home of Samanala Kanda, one of the country's four guardian deities.

Mount Kilimanjaro in Kenya is the home of Ruwa, the god of the Chagga people. Mount Kenya, a 17,000-foot volcano and Africa's second highest peak, is the residence of Ngai, the god who created humans, including the first Kikuyu tribesman, Gikuyu; the Kikuyu call the peak *Kere Nyaga,* "Mountain of Brightness." In Tanzania, Ol Doinyo Lengai, a 10,000-foot active volcano, is the home of Engai, "the one and only God" for the Masai, as well as a spiritual being called Khambegeu, who once created a golden age of prosperity. The Bantu call this peak *Mogongo jo Mugwe,* meaning "Mountain of God." Gunung Agung ("Great Mountain"), the 10,308-foot sacred peak of Bali, is the home of Mahadewa, Great God of Gunung, and the site of numerous temples and shrines.

The Navajo say that every mountain—especially the sacred cardinal ones that border the Navajo Nation in the American Southwest—has an inner form or holy beings inside it known as *bii'istíín,* "Those That Stand within Them." These gods are the chieftains of the peaks, and the mountains are their hogans, or homes. Examples of bii'istíín are Talking God, Rock Crystal Boy, and Rock Crystal Girl.

Holy mountains are frequently the site of revelation, celestial visitations, inspiration, and encounters with gods, aliens, Nature spirits, and other beings. God reveals Himself on the top of holy mountains (or the gods do) and humans slip more easily into mystic states of exaltation on peaks than on the low lands. Black Elk, the holy man among the Lakotas, began his celestial adventure with the Six Grandfathers at Harney Peak in South Dakota. Moses received the Torah, the Ten Commandments, and the design for the Ark of the Covenant on Mount Sinai in Egypt on a peak called Mountain of Yahweh.

Rip van Winkle underwent his 20-year sleep in the Catskill Mountains after being beguiled by a group of very short old men (gnomes). The Virgin Mary has appeared numerous times since 1981 to visionaries on Mount Podbrdo in Medjugorge, Bosnia, and ten million pilgrims have since visited the site, now called the Hill of Apparitions. Those who spend a night alone on the Chair of Idris (a mountain in Wales called Cader Idris) will end up mad, dead, or full of poetic inspiration, so Welsh legend declares. Those who meditate atop Montsegur, a craggy peak in the French Pyrenees, may enter the Grail Castle.

In 1088, the Chinese mystic Chang Shang-ying had numerous visions atop Wu-T'ai Shan (Five Terrace Mountain) in China: He beheld the great god Manjusri astride a lion, numerous bodhisattvas (celestial saints and saviors), a golden stairway and a golden bridge, spirit beings, orbs of light, and more.

As for holy mountains in general, Persian myth says the world's mountains originally grew from out of the surface of the Earth, which was a flat disc. Alburz, in Persian belief the first mountain, probably equated with Mount Damavand, took 800 years to grow up out of the Earth. Most mountains took only 18 years to grow, but Alburz, from which 2,244 other mountains sprouted, grew up through the star, moon, and sun stations, finally reaching the realm of endless light.

Explanation: Around the world, mountains are holy because they have etheric light and energy canopies haloing them. These canopies are called domes, and the Earth has 1,746 of them, mostly over volcanoes, present and past.

As part of the original design of Earth and its visionary geography, the domes were brought to Earth from the star Capella in the constellation Auriga. They were devices, midway in composition between matter and spirit, that settled over the Earth's surface at prearranged locations and in accordance with star patterns above to energize and prepare the Earth for human habitation.

They were not exactly spaceships, though a materialist interpretation would see them that way, but they were mobile, for a while. Hindu myth reflects this by saying that originally the mountains had wings, but their continuous circling around upset the Earth's stability, so Indra cut off their wings, rendering them *achala* (immovable), and set them at appropriate locations to stabilize the world. Here, obviously, the winged mountains were domes.

The domes came and went three times in the Earth's history, during the mythical times remembered variously as the Dreamtime (Aboriginal) or Zep Tepi (Egyptian). Their imprint of sound and light was so powerful that they are *virtually* still present at the holy mountains they created though, technically, they are gone.

The Persian myth about Alburz is correct: The domes summoned the mountains out of the soft clay of the Earth and, in effect, created them. Due to their star alignments (not by way of azimuthal alignments, but by actual holographic presence), the various Star gods were accessible through them. For example, the dome over Mount Damavand in Iran represents the star *Ras al Hawwa,* which is alpha Ophiuchus Serpentarius; the dome over Tintagel in Cornwall, England (an example of a dome not over a mountain) is the Earth presence or star fall of Megrez in the Big Dipper of Ursa Major (Great Bear).

In addition, each physical mountain that the domes created and then settled over had its own guardian deity, a type of landscape angel, who maintained the integrity of the dome's energy and its relationship to the mountain, its organic life, and any other geomantic features it might have (such as light temples). Guardian deities such as Ngai, Engai, Khambegeu, Mahadewa, Samanala Kanda, Ruwa, and the Navajo holy beings are examples of landscape angels maintaining a mountain's geomantic integrity.

The holy mountains were accurately called the homes of the gods because, during the Third Dome Presence (the third arrival of the domes, when some humans were present on the Earth), the gods who brought the domes were resident for a time. These gods included angelic orders called Elohim and Nephilim, as well as other celestial or spiritual beings. Later, when the domes had left, visionary access was still afforded sensitive humans who meditated at the domes and who sought audiences with the higher dimensional gods.

The Yeti, also known as Sasquatch and the Abominable Snowman, were guardians of the domes and their intricate networks, and still are.

Each dome could generate up to 48 subsidiary energy-consciousness centers called dome caps, and these were connected to the "mother" dome by way of spirallic lines. Domes were connected to one another by straight energy lines. The network of straight and spirallic lines mimics the structure of the Akasha, or ethereal space (the fourth dimension), said by Hindu mystics to consist of straight lines *(dishah)* traveling through the sound currents of space that eventually curve back on themselves, creating an intricate webbing.

The domes, including their array of 48 dome caps, were originally each 33 miles in diameter, but owing to their extreme age as an energy imprint, they have shrunk by 50 to 75 percent in width and height since then. Thus the Alburz reference to one mountain generating 2,244 more mountains is accurate in principle, but not in actuality: The most in this interpretation would be 48 "mountains."

These mountains also get a numinous charge from the presence of a variety of landscape angels and Spirit beings (the Navajo *bii'istíín,* "Those That Stand within Them") who maintain the geomantic integrity of the quality of the energy (i.e., consciousness parameters) set at that site. Holy beings such as the Navajo Talking God, Rock Crystal Boy, and Rock Crystal Girl are landscape angels. Every domed peak will have one major landscape angel and several smaller ones.

See also: Dreamtime, Hollow Hill, Hurqalya, Yeti, Zep Tepi.

HOUSE OF ATREUS

An experimental infusion of Pleiadian higher consciousness into living human bodies eons ago, based at Mycenae, Greece.

Also known as Atreidae or Atridae ("Sons of Atreus").

Description: The history of the House of Atreus based at Mycenae, Greece, is the foundation for a large portion of Greek tragedy and myth. The House of Atreus encompasses a lineage of gods and mortals, from Zeus, the chief of the Olympians, to the well-known Trojan War general Agamemnon.

The House begins with Tantalus, a wealthy son of Zeus and Dione, who was a Pleiad (not one of the named seven Pleiadian sisters, but evidently one in the cluster of about 300 stars in the neck of the Taurus constellation) and daughter of the Titan Atlas, the father of the Pleiades. Tantalus dined with the gods at Olympus, heard all the godly gossip, then later indiscreetly divulged the gods' secrets to his friends. Or he stole some of their ambrosia (the food of the immortals) to share with his friends. Or (several versions of the story exist) he carved up his own son, Pelops, and served him in pieces in a soup as an impertinent way of testing their omniscience. The outrage was discovered only after Pelops's shoulder blade had been consumed; the gods reassembled his body from the soup and gave him an ivory shoulder blade in place of his original.

In any event, Zeus punished Tantalus by condemning him to reside in Tartarus (the Underworld, a hell region) and to stand in a pool of water while deathly thirsty, yet unable to slake his thirst and with ripe fruit beyond his reach to be forever *tantalized* (the origin of this word, presumably) by unappeasable thirst and hunger.

The peninsular landmass now known as the Peloponnesus in Greece was named commemoratively after Pelops—"The Island of Pelops." Later Pelops cheated at a chariot race that had a beautiful woman as the prize and he and his future generations were cursed by the woman's father, King Oenomaus. Thus began a series of bloody feuds, murder, adultery, and betrayal that would span many generations, all based at the ancient seat of government, Mycenae.

Pelops and his wife, Hippodamia (the woman he won in the chariot race), produced two sons, Atreus and Thyestes. Atreus's wife Aerope committed adultery with Thyestes and gave him the golden lamb needed for kingship; then Atreus, King of Mycenae, banished Thyestes from the royal citadel. Later, at a feast of supposed reconciliation, Atreus served Thyestes a feast of his own sons' flesh, showed him the severed heads, then banished him again from Mycenae. Eventually, Atreus was killed by Aegisthus, Thyestes' only surviving son—Oenomaus's curse in action, a saga of implacable, unending family feuds.

Before his death, Atreus and Aerope, who was also celestial in parentage, produced Agamemnon (King of Mycenae; married to Clytemnestra) and his brother, Menelaus (King of Sparta; married to Helen, Clytemnestra's sister).

Agamemnon's offspring included Orestes, Electra, and Iphigenia. Menelaus's Helen was abducted (or taken by elopement) by Paris to Troy, precipitating the ten-year Trojan War to get her back. While Agamemnon was away, Aegisthus committed adultery with Clytemnestra. Orestes later killed them both, then was hunted and hounded by the Furies for his matricide.

A large portion of the plots, characters, and themes of Greek tragedy come from this blighted family. According to its outer story, the House of Atreus is the bearer of a curse that won't go away—a kind of spiritual "genetic" taint. The gods cursed Tantalus; then Hermes cursed Pelops for causing the death of Myrtilus; then Pelops cursed his own offspring for killing their own half-brother; then Thyestes cursed Atreus for killing his sons; then Clytemnestra cursed Agamemnon for sending their daughter Iphigenia to be sacrificed to the gods.

Explanation: The most surprising and obvious fact about the House of Atreus is that it is all second-generation Pleiadian in origin, and this is validated by the exoteric conventional mythic sources and résumés handed on by the Greeks. The amusing side to this is that, almost universally, scholars do not give any credence to this other than as some whimsy or error of the classical Greeks. But the Pleiadian ancestry embedded in plain view in the myth is crucial to understanding the House of Atreus myth, especially in geomantic terms.

The essential core of the story is something like this: Pelops is a landscape angel (see Chakravartin, Eriu, Gaia, Marduk, Srin-mo Demoness) especially commissioned by the Supreme Being to transmit specific celestial energies into the peninsula now known as Peloponnesus, the Island of Pelops. Normally, landscape angels ground and transmit energies specific to a landscape and in reciprocal exchange with the people (and living beings) residing there.

At Mycenae, the landscape angel known as Pelops did that and also transmitted Pleiadian consciousness as a kind of steady stream infusing the land. That landmass, still a large portion of the country of today's Greece, would embody, at the physical and geomantic level, Pelops's energy, a blend of angelic and Pleiadian influence suitable to Earth and its freshly incarnating humanity.

Here is one visual way of considering this: Pelops stands several miles high, his "feet" rooted at Panagitsa Hill, the center of Mycenae. Though an angel, ultimately, for this purpose he looks like a slender cylinder or flower stalk, with flames or petals wrapped around his vertical height. His head pierces the "sky" and emerges into the next dimension, which resembles a yellow sea whose waves are faces. These faces are Pleiadian spirits, some waiting to incarnate into human bodies, and some remaining behind as spirit guides, mentors, project overseers.

Their energy flows down through Pelops like a waterfall, then fountains up into a yellow mist, irradiating the land around Pelops with Pleiadian consciousness. At ground level, Pelops is surrounded by perhaps one thousand Pleiadians in their Light bodies, arrayed in about ten concentric circles. These spirits are also mentors and supervisors of the project. Some of the Pleiadian faces from the yellow sea in the next dimension step out of Pelops in human bodies.

This is the House of Atreus—an experimental infusion of Pleidian soul consciousness into newly "designed" and articulated living human bodies. The goal was to see how much consciousness a human body could hold. Pelops, of course, did not father any progeny, but he was the godfather of an entire lineage.

The House of Atreus was an infusion of Pleiadian elements through the geomantic setup at Mycenae into the emerging structure of human consciousness and its vessel, the organic, mortal human-styled body. This experiment was done *very early* in the life of the planet, so long ago that its time must be reckoned in terms of millions of years before the present, at the start of Hyperborea.

Just as Agamemnon, King of Mycenae and son of Atreus, was a very early example of kingship (with its, to us, secret Pleiadian infusion of spirituality), so the House of Atreus was one of the original foundations for spiritual kingship, the celestial basis for royalty, and the original, pure imprimatur for leadership.

Related experiments in extraterrestrial infusion of consciousness into human forms were conducted at perhaps 11 other sites around the Earth, places that we could characterize as human root centers. Even today, Mycenae, as one of humanity's root centers, carries the potency of that original Light infusion because Pelops is still there grounding the energies. Not just Mycenae, but all of the Peloponnesus still carries this Pleiadian influence. The landscape angel Pelops is still the touchstone for this human root center.

Why was Pelops's shoulder blade or scapula replaced by an ivory one? Because the Island of Pelops, his Earth form, resembles a human scapula, and it would be filled with Light, hence the ivory or pure white reference. The gods giving him an ivory scapula to replace his material one means they would infuse his Earth body, the Island of Pelops, with spiritual Light, like ivory. Tantalos was Pelops's celestial overseer and mentor, supervising the project from Heaven.

The "curse" of the House of Atreus? It is a complicated story, but, in essence, it represents the disequilibrium between different infusions of Pleiadian consciousness into the fresh human forms and their emotional parameters. The lineage of Atreus received one infusion, weighted more toward the spiritual. Atreus represents a lineage with a star over its crown chakra (a steady awareness of its higher origins in the Pleiades); Thyestes' lineage lacked this star.

Both lineages, or Pleiadian infusions, had to work out an integration of higher awareness living within a human mortal body, sex differentiated, and made of the five elements and their emotional expressions, powers, and polarities. Both Atreus and Thyestes, and their descendants, had difficulties along the way; their story, with differences, is reminiscent of the biblical brothers Cain and Abel.

Not only was ancient Mycenae one of humanity's primary root centers, its geomantic features and concentrated angelic presence had planetary effects. It was, and is still today, a major transmission point for spiritual Light for Earth. Threads of golden light emanated from Mycenae, an oasis of Light on the planet, like a capillary network across the Earth that infused other sites with its higher vibration Pleiadian Light and the gold wisdom stream from this root center.

That is why Mycenae is still vitally important to us today: It is about our human roots and where certain threads of human consciousness came from.

Similarly, members of the House of Atreus in human form also left Mycenae to benevolently "colonize" other areas of the Earth, setting examples for humanity, and many people made pilgrimages to Mycenae for inspiration.

The Treasury of Atreus, as archeologists describe one of the extant archeological ruins at Mycenae, was a Griffin Gold Reserve, one of 47 sites on Earth that hold reservoirs of Pleiadian Light and wisdom in the form of living astral gold (see Rhinegold). This is the fabled gold of the Hyperboreans that the Greek historian Herodotus said the griffins guarded (see Griffin, Hyperboreans).

Mycenae also has a copy of one of the eight types of Celestial Cities (see Glass Mountain, Mount Meru, Seven Rishis) known as a Mount Olympus. This is a conclave with associated Light temple of the 14 Ray Masters of the Great Bear, a specialized division within the Great White Brotherhood, our galaxy's (and planet's) inner spiritual government (see Einherjar, Seven Rishis).

See also: Atlas, Chakravartin, Einherjar, Eriu, Gaia, Glass Mountain, Griffin, Hyperboreans, Marduk, Mount Meru, Rhinegold, Seven Rishis, Srin-mo Demoness.

HUITZILOPOCHTLI

The national protector angel for the Aztecs of Mexico grounded at the ancient capital Tenochtitlan, now under Mexico City.

Also known as Hummingbird of the Left, Hummingbird of the South.

Description: Huitzilopochtli is the supreme national tutelary deity of the Aztecs, the "people of Aztlan," also known as the Mexicas, who after a lengthy peregrination across Central America settled at Tenochtitlan, now Mexico City.

Their origin myth has the Aztecs coming from Aztlan, a mythical city known as the "Place of Herons" and, by extension, "Place of Whiteness." Huitzilopochtli's name from the Nahuatl language means "Hummingbird of the Left" from *huitzilin* ("hummingbird") and *opochtli* ("of the left"). He was said to be the son of Coatlicue, a primal Mexican expression of the Mother Goddess.

According to post-Conquest descriptions of Huitzilopochtli, he wore a blue-green hummingbird headdress, a golden tiara, feathers of a white heron, and a smoking obsidian mirror (usually attributed to Tezcatlipoca). His face was striped yellow and blue and he wore a black mask dotted with stars over his eyes. Usually, he was shown carrying his *Xiuhcoatl,* or Fire Serpent.

Apparently, this was both an emblem or device (a great stone disk depicting his slain goddess sister, Coyolxauhqui) and a massive fiery war serpent itself. In one depiction, the Xiuhcoatl was shown penetrating the chest of his sister, with only the serpent's lower torso and tail projecting out of the goddess.

The Aztecs regarded themselves as the chosen ones of their supreme deity. Some scholars say the Aztecs changed their name to Mexicas in honor of their god who was also called Mexi; thus the Mexicas were the Sons of Mexi. Their settlement at Tenochtitlan sits in the middle of Anahuac ("Near the Water"), or the Valley of Mexico, once a series of great lakes, and for a time, Tenochtitlan was called Mexico, as if to represent the entire (future) nation.

Huitzilopochtli led his people out of Aztlan in a southerly migration in search of their next homeland. His people are said to comprise all the inhabitants of Mexico, including the Toltecs, Otomi, and other Nahuatlan peoples (some sources say seven tribes in all, and thus the origins of all Central American peoples), all of whom went their own way after a schism with the Aztecs.

This group, traveling for generations, made numerous stops at mythically significant locales, including Teotihuacan, the city of the gods (site of their birth in the Fifth Sun) and a major megalithic temple site (near today's Mexico City).

Mythic accounts differ as to whether after leaving Atzlan they passed through Chicomoztoc (Seven Caves, their place of emergence) or departed from there originally to travel to Aztlan. Huitzilopochtli foresaw the Aztec's final destination by way of a divine omen: He instructed his people to look for an eagle eating a snake and perched on a cactus tree set on a rock on an island in a lake. Appropriate to this myth,

Tenochtitlan means "Place of the Prickly Pear Cactus," just as Huitzilopochtli described in his prophetic vision.

Aztlan, the Aztecs said, was a mystical island in a lake, so its Earth equivalent would be an island in the middle of Lake Tezcoco. There, under Huitzilopochtli's instruction and influence, they founded their great capital Tenochtitlan on an island in the midst of the huge lake (now almost entirely gone) in what is now called the Valley of Mexico, a high altitude plain framed by tall mountains. The temple complex was linked to the mainland by three causeways and archeologists estimate that, at its height, it reportedly supported a population of 200,000.

Purportedly, Tenochtitlan was founded by the Aztecs in 1325 A.D. It was captured and destroyed in 1521 by the Spanish invader Hernandez Cortez.

Huitzilopochtli received top honors at Tenochtitlan through the *Hueteocalli,* or Great Temple, honoring him alongside Tlaloc the Rain god at the royal city's most prominent site and the very center of the vast temple complex, a double pyramid. The myth says that Tlaloc rose from a spring at the site when Huitzilopochtli and his people arrived to found their royal and sacred city.

The Spanish called the chief god there *Huichilobos,* regarded him as the Devil incarnate, and blamed him for the introduction of the infernal live heart sacrifices. Legend has it that Huitzilopochtli ripped out the heart of his enemy Copil, leader of other residents in the Valley of Mexico who did not welcome the Aztec, and hurled it onto a rock in Lake Tezcoco; from this confluence of rock and god's heart arose the island for the Aztec's Earthly city, Tenochtitlan.

Explanation: This is a marvelous account of how a people (the Aztecs) came to the predetermined navel of their country (Tenochtitlan) under the leadership of their national tutelary landscape angel, or egregor, Huitzilopochtli.

In the original disposition of Earth's landmasses, 72 areas were carved out and to each was assigned an angel to maintain the geomantic integrity of that landscape and its numerous visionary geographic features and to nurture and supervise the evolution of the folk soul or people (in this case, the Aztecs) on it.

While each of the 72 landscape angels (also known as egregors, national tutelary deities, or Princes of the Nations) started out the same, over time they assumed the characteristics of the people they oversaw. That means they differentiated somewhat and took on distinctive qualities, in this case, the hummingbird attributes of Huitzilopochtli.

It's not that Huitzilopochtli metamorphosed into a hummingbird shape, but rather that, over time, the qualities of the hummingbird assumed symbolic significance to the Aztec in terms of how they portrayed (clairvoyantly saw) their mirror image, the national deity, who perpetually reflected their *Mexicanness.*

The national egregor oversees the unfoldment of the inherent soul qualities of the people occupying the land and it preserves the integrity and accommodates the evolution of the "genius of the people," or the geomantic, energy, and consciousness aspects of nationhood (see Navel of the World).

Huitzilopochtli led the Aztecs to Tenochtitlan because, for the country of Mexico, that was the predetermined navel point or center of their world. In geomantic terms, this is one of the Earth's 72 Energy Focusing Nodes. This feature is a major nodal point, an omphalos, that focuses and concentrates cosmic and geomantic energy for that region, in this case, for all of Mexico.

The egregor is grounded (that is, lives) at the Energy Focusing Node of a country, here Tenochtitlan, originally, and now, somewhat paved over, at Mexico City. Further, each of the 72 egregors is protected by a dragon, here called Xiuhcoatl, Huitzilopochtli's Fire Serpent (see Dragon). The dragon lives within the Mexico City limits at Tepeyac Hill, one of the homes of Coatlicue, known as "She of the Serpent Skirt," and, of course, Huitzilopochtli's "mother."

Coatlicue, as a landscape dragon, is not the mother of an egregor, but she certainly protects, nurtures, and supports all his activities on behalf of Mexico.

Each of the 72 Nodes is also a functioning consciousness center within a global geomantic feature, an anthropomorphic being called Albion. Specifically, Tenochtitlan, as the navel of Mexico, is one of the 72 minor chakras within Albion; this planetary figure also has nine major chakras, thus a total of 81 centers. In the human, minor chakras are located at the armpits, elbows, knees, and ankles, while the major ones are arrayed vertically along the spine, from groin to head.

Not only are the 72 Nodes minor chakras within a single planetary geomantic being or overlay, they are also each, according to Judaic lore, a Name of God. All 72 Names of God are called the *Shemhamforesh.* Thus each people expresses, through its soul and landscape qualities, a primary vibration of God.

Just as the one glorious citadel of spiritual and temporal authority at Tenochtitlan has been buried under the weight of modern Mexico City, so has, to an extent, the once fiery soul temperament of the Aztecs been subdued by the Spanish Conquest—from Huitzilopochtli and his formidable Fire Serpent to Octavio Paz's labyrinth of solitude as the soul expression of the modern Mexican.

A number of elements in the Huitzilopochtli myth must be discounted. As a landscape angel for Mexico, he does not have a sister. Coyolxauhqui is an aspect of "his" total being, landscape angels not having gender differentiations.

Similarly, it is unlikely that he "killed" Copil; rather, Copil should be seen as a subsidiary landscape angel, preserving the geomantic integrity of a smaller domain, quite possibly the Lake Tezcoco area; Copil's divinely ordained task is to serve the land and people under the supervision of the land's master angel. The Aztecs may have literalized and thus distorted Huitzilopochtli's gesture toward Copil; the egregor's intention was to salute and validate the landscape angel's "heart" (task) in supervising his ordained section of Mexico.

The date of the founding of Tenochtitlan should not be believed. The saga of Huitzilopochtli and his Aztecs is an old geomantic account of the settling of a land by its intended folk. Certainly, this event happened far earlier than 1325.

See also: Albion, Chakravartin, Dragon, Emerald, Eriu, Lucifer, Marduk, Navel of the World, Srin-mo Demoness, Tower of Babel.

HURQALYA

Earth's energy body, visionary geography, or Light grid perceived as an illuminated hologram of the galaxy and spiritual planes.

Also known as Celestial Earth, Earth grid, Earth of Light, Earth of True Reality, Earth's Light body, Gaia's geomythic body, Kingdom of Heaven, Light grid, sacred geography, terrain of sacred sites, visionary geography.

Description: This is a complex but important term from twelfth-century Iranian Islamic mysticism as interpreted for the West by the twentieth-century French scholar Henri Corbin in his *Spiritual Body and Celestial Earth.*

Hurqalya connotes the Earth in its pure, original, mystical, and imaginal state of reality. It is a way of referring to the planet's energy body or auric field, to the Earth seen as a celestial, illuminated body in which archetypal images and spiritual relationships are highlighted and are as apparent as mountains and lakes.

Hurqalya is what Jesus meant when he said the Kingdom of Heaven is laid out all around people, but they do not see it, and that the Kingdom of Heaven is within you. The only thing to add is that this Kingdom is projected *outward* as an interactive holographic environment to make it easier to see the inner expression.

The Earth of Hurqalya, as Corbin translates it, is a landscape of visions and epiphanies, the subtle planetary state where all psychospiritual events, perceptions, and anomalous events transcending the presumed laws of matter and causality take place. In Hurqalya, you see the true appearance of the Earth, removed from all its empirical, physical, and sense-based details: It is the Earth of Truth where the archetypes live and have absolute reality. It is the soul's vision of the planet in which one perceives Earth's visionary geography.

Hurqalya is a spiritually lit version of the Earth, the Earth of Light, or, in Arabic, *Ard haqiqa,* which translates as "Earth of True Reality" and "Earth of Real Truth." It is an intermediary world, between the physical Earth and the subtle Heaven, a realm apprehended by the imaginal perception, a heightened visionary psychism whose "organ" is the active imagination.

Explanation: Corbin's interpretation of Hurqalya gives us an excellent mystical reference point for approaching the planet's sublime celestial body, which is a body of Light.

In its simplest terms, Hurqalya refers to the planet's array of sacred sites as seen from a spiritual and clairvoyant viewpoint—as a living, interconnected web of points and processes of light just behind the appearances of matter.

It is a visionary geography because the diversity and sheer quantity of sacred sites afford humans a new visionary apprehension of their landscape. Holy mountains are numinous and invite one into shamanic journeys and perceptions of light temples, residences of the gods, portals to other worlds. Images from myth are revealed to be actual astral processes and relationships under way as if right before us, only in the next dimension from the material.

Earth's visionary geography is, in essence, a hologram of the important stars, constellations, processes, and spiritual realms and structures of the galaxy. The Earth is celestial because its subtle body is a hologram of the galaxy on Earth.

Otherwise fantastic descriptions of opulent godly palaces and seemingly unattainable mystic perceptions and epiphanies found in myth are real and available to even a modicum of psychic perception by humans on the Earth.

Through the sacred sites (known in Hinduism as *tirthas,* or fords, across the river between matter and spirit), one can see and interact with the angelic hierarchy of 40 orders, the conclaves of enlightened adepts and spiritual masters and what we think of as extraterrestrial intelligences, the fabulous "beasts" of mythology such as dragons, and the sublimities of myth such as Cosmic Eggs.

The Earth of True Reality is the galactic hologram in which we live though without knowing it. All the sacred sites and their numinous structures and inner temples comprise Earth's marvelous spiritual body, Her soul. Hurqalya connotes the pristine perception of the planet in its earliest days, when the visionary geography was first born on the planet, a time remembered variously as the Dreamtime, Zep Tepi ("First Occasion"), and the time of the Hollow Hills.

Looking at the planet clairvoyantly, you can potentially see the entirety of Heaven laid out before you as the illuminated features underlying matter, what the Christian mystics called the Kingdom of God—that's the Earth of Hurqalya.

See also: Atlas, Dreamtime, Gaia, Hollow Hill, Holy Mountain, Hyperboreans, Land of Milk and Honey, Ley Lines, Zep Tepi.

HYPERBOREANS

Representatives from the Pleiades who assisted other celestial beings in the Earth's earliest days in setting up Earth's visionary geography and its numerous megalithic structures and Light temples.

Also known as House of Atreus, Pleiadians, the Wandering Ones.

Description: A few of the classical Greek and Roman writers, such as Herodotus, Pindar, and Diodorus Siculus, refer elusively to the Hyperboreans. Generally, the Hyperboreans were understood to be a legendary ancient race of Apollo-worshippers who lived in the far north

"Beyond the North Wind"—hence the traditional etymology, as *Boreas* was the name of that wind. Sometimes Boreas, as the icy North Wind, suggests the North Pole.

The land of the Hyperboreans is described as paradisal; they are never sick, live a long time, are very happy, have pleasant weather and no strife, make music and dance a lot, honor Apollo, and have a huge circular temple to Apollo somewhere in their land. Apollo spent his winters among the Hyperboreans, and ordinary mortals were unable to visit there; only the superheroes like Herakles could.

Occasionally, Hyperboreans sent representatives to at least two named Greek locations, namely, Delphi, Apollo's oracular shrine, and Delos, his birthplace. The strong identification of Apollo with Hyperborea was due to the fact that his mother, Leto, was born there, so all the residents were priests of Apollo.

Some of the Hyperboreans are named: Abaris, for example, has a magical arrow on which he travels around the world. Two women, named Hyperoche and Laodice, were once sent as emissaries to Delos, bearing gifts; another two women, Arge and Opis, also journeyed there and were received with honors. The Hyperborean Olen, said the second-century Greek historian and travel writer Pausanias, was the original founder of Apollo's oracle of Delphi and its first oracular prophet. When the Gauls attacked Delphi, the Hyperboreans Hyperochus and Laodocus were there in spirit form to help defend the site.

Explanation: The Hyperboreans were representatives from the Pleiades, a star cluster in the Taurus constellation with intimate, long-standing involvement with Earth, humanity's origins, and the planet's visionary geography. True to the etymology of the Pleiades, from the Greek *plein,* "to wander," the Hyperboreans were spirits from stars in the Pleiades who spent their time wandering from planet to planet, helping out in accordance with the spiritual plans for that place.

The location of Hyperborea was approximately the British Isles, Greenland, Iceland, and the North Pole, much warmer and clement then. The "then" is a vastly long time ago, long before the epochs of Atlantis and Lemuria, the latter sometimes estimated in metaphysical circles to be 18,000,000+ years ago.

Hyperborea is both a location and a planetary epoch. The planet's earliest time period was called Polaria, a time of plants; this was followed by Hyperborea, a time when the complex, multifaceted Earth's visionary geography was installed and rendered operational, but largely before humanity had arrived.

Some Hyperborean astral temples established on the Earth are still perceivable in selected locations, such as Castle Rigg stone circle at Keswick, England, and Mycenae in Greece, home of the House of Atreus, a Pleiadian initiative.

The Hyperboreans assisted the other Earth design team members, which included representatives from other star systems (e.g., Sirius, Arcturus, Great Bear) and members of the angelic hierarchy (i.e., Ofanim [see Ganesh, Garuda] and Elohim [see Balor of the Evil Eye, Giants, Cyclops Polyphemus]), in creating many of the planet's physical and geomantic features, notably the megalithic structures. They also worked collegially with the 14 Ray Masters of the Great Bear (see Seven Rishis), among whom Apollo was Master of the pale blue Ray.

It is not possible that the Greeks of approximately the first or second millennium B.C. had any actual physical contact or even memory of such with the Hyperboreans, for, by this time in planetary history, the Hyperboreans had long left the physical and even spiritual planes of the Earth, their work done.

However, Apollo had not left the Earth nor finished his responsibility for it (nor has he today); as part of his oracular (psychic) facilitation through Delphi and Delos, he would have enabled talented clairvoyants to see some of the glorious aspects of the antique planetary time and work of the Hyperboreans.

See also: Dreamtime, Giants, Griffin, Heimdall, Hollow Hill, House of Atreus, Hurqalya, Rhinegold, Seven Rishis, Zep Tepi.

INDRA

The celestial archetype and the Hindu name for King Arthur, the leader of the Great White Brotherhood in Ursa Major and the origin of all 15 King Arthur expressions in various cultures across the Earth.

Description: In Hindu lore, Indra is the chief of the gods and the Ruler of Heaven, perhaps one step below the Hindu trinity of Vishnu (Preserver), Shiva (Destroyer), and Brahma (Creator). Among his epithets are *Indha,* which means "Kindler," the stimulating force that kindles deeds and thoughts. He is also *Sahasraksha,* "Thousand Eyes," because he can see the entire universe in a single glance.

His primary characteristic, as defined in India's ancient spiritual texts, the Vedas, is power or strength, usually signified by his thunderbolt *(vajra),* somewhat like the mace or hammer of other mythic chiefs of the gods. In this guise, Indra is called *Vajrapani* (Wielder of the vajra) and *Vrtrahan* (destroyer of Vrtra, the demon of drought—a cosmic dragon). Indra is credited with slaying the monstrous primordial dragon who selfishly withheld the waters of creation.

Indra was *Satakratu,* "Lord of a Hundred Powers," but he also represents the power of the thunderbolt *(Stanayitnu)* and the electric energy that pervades space. A principal manifestation of this cosmic power is Indra's ability to bring rain to the Earth. Thus he is the storm-ruler, the rain-dispenser, the deity of space, and the main cause of fertility. He used his thunderbolt to slay Vrtra and release the vast store of cosmic waters within it.

The thunderbolt, shaped like a mace, is Indra's chief weapon, and he used it to cleave entire mountains. Other divine weapons include his sword *Paranajaya* ("Conquest"), the bow *Vijaya* ("Victory"), and the conch *Deva-datta* ("Gift of God"), but his principal, most formidable weapon is magic.

Indra is the power of might, action, and force, the leader of warriors in the defeat of the Antigods (Asuras) and the various savages of Earth, including the demon-magicians who create drought. He drove away the Dasus, the enemies of the Aryans (original Indians), and freed the land of baleful influences.

He is said to be the composite and thus the greatest of all the other gods and celestial warriors, embodying all their qualities. Indra is Leader of the Celestial Host, Riding upon the Clouds, Destroyer of Cities, Lord of the Gods, Weather God, and God of Life. Even his name suggests all this: Indra may derive from *ind,* which means "equipping with great power," or it may come from *indu,* "a drop," as in water, as Indra is the benevolent rain-giver to Earth.

Indra has great generative power and was often likened to a vigorous stallion or the bull. He was the original rider of *Uccaihsravas,* the White Horse, one of 14 celestial treasures that emerged from the Ocean of Milk when the gods churned it, usually referred to as Indra's Mount. He also rode *Airavata,* the celestial white elephant generated by the churning of the Milk Ocean.

Indra's divine consort is the Sky goddess Indrani, also called Aindri and Saci (which means Divine Grace, or Eloquence, or Energy). He chose her among all the other available goddesses for her sensuality and golden skin, and killed her demon father, Paulomi, to be able to ravish her and then elope. Indrani is considered the Indian ideal of the beautiful, devoted wife.

Their celestial residence is called Amaravati, the Immortal City, situated near Meru, the cosmic mountain, in the dimension of heaven called Svarga. Indra's palace is called *Vaijayanta,* Palace of Victory, and it is described by mystic visitors (such as Arjuna) as a garden paradise and a sybaritic haven.

Explanation: Indra is the celestial original of all King Arthur manifestations and localized expressions in different cultures, such as the Irish Fionn MacCumhaill, the Persian Rustam, and the

Tibetan-Mongolian Gesar of Ling. As chief of the gods and Ruler of Heaven, Indra is the leader of the Great White Brotherhood (in mythic language, the Celestial Host) based in Ursa Major.

This is a vast conclave of enlightened adepts and spiritual masters, rishis, angels, celestial beings, and intelligences from other planets and star systems (see Einherjar) charged with maintaining truth, divine order, and evolution throughout the galaxy and universe. Hindu lore, for example, says there are 48,000 rishis present (rishi, or *rsi*, derives from the root word for sound in Sanskrit).

This august spiritual assemblage is reflected in all terrestrial exemplars of this archetypal myth in the form of a royal king and his retinue of warriors, as in the Fianna of Fionn MacCumhaill and the Knights of Camalate of King Arthur.

King Arthur has been expressed and embodied by humans 15 times so far in the history of the Earth. It is not correct to say Indra (King Arthur) *incarnates* as such-and-such a living human person, rather, it is that acting as the original model he permeates, overshadows, influences, and inspires the lifetime of one figure. The human King Arthur exemplifier is part of a Soul Group of other humans who similarly express the other key figures in the Arthurian mythos, such as Guinevere, King Arthur's queen and wife (in Indra's case, known as Saci).

During the time of overlighting, the human Soul Group plays out all the dynamics of the Arthurian mythos as, on a parallel track, the originals (the celestial beings among the Great White Brotherhood) stimulate the same patterns.

The intent is to reestablish the human, Earth, angelic, hierarchical, cosmos link by interacting constructively and therapeutically with the planet's vast array of sacred sites that comprise its visionary geography for the benefit of humanity, Nature, and the Earth and the evolution of consciousness in matter.

Indra as the celestial archetype does not incarnate; he remains in Amaravati, that is, the Great Bear constellation. King Arthur, who is the same being, though given a Celtic name, also does not incarnate. Yet at least two of the human Indra-Arthurian exemplifiers were remembered in myth as King Arthur.

While Indra (and the original King Arthur) has his Amaravati, a grand Celestial City, on Earth the Arthurian knights with Arthur have their Camalate. This is usually an esoteric Mystery center for training, initiation, and outreach.

Indra, or King Arthur, is the Solar Logos, which means the Logos (Word, or Christ) at the level of all the suns (stars) of the galaxy. Indra is the dynamic energy of growth and change, the Christ force operating through the Sun to quicken life and consciousness throughout its sphere. Although interacting with the Earth's energy body can increase the likelihood of physical rain, in large measure the "rain" attributed to Indra is higher consciousness from above.

During a lifetime in which the Arthurian mythos is active in an Earth culture, it will rain a great deal in the sense that cosmic consciousness will more easily permeate human awareness (through Earth's visionary geography) and quicken human thoughts, insights, and deeds. Accumulations of dark, heavy, negative energies, thoughts, and beings can be expunged from Earth during such times, reflected in the terrestrial myths as driving out the Dasus (Indra), Saxons (King Arthur in Celtic England), barbarians (Persia's Rustam), or, in modern times, the Antichrist and its legions.

Typically, the myths of the human King Arthur exemplifiers entail a dragon-slaying (e.g., the Celtic King Arthur, the Persian Rustam), the driving from the land of inimical peoples (Fionn MacCumhaill) and energies (Gesar).

Indra's elephant mount, Airavata, the primordial white elephant, is mythic code for the angelic family called Ofanim who always work with the celestial Arthur (Indra) and the Great White Brotherhood on behalf of the Earth. In other Arthurian guises, the Ofanim appear as

Garuda (Vishnu's Mount) or the Simurgh (a mystical, elusive divine bird) as they assist the solar hero and his retinue.

See also: Antichrist, Camalate, Einherjar, Fionn MacCumhaill, Ganesh, Garuda, Gesar of Ling, Glass Mountain, Guinevere, King Arthur, Rustam, Simurgh, White Horse, Wild Hunt.

KING ARTHUR

Solar Logos, chief of the Great White Brotherhood in Ursa Major, once the expression of the Christ for the warrior class, now the embodiment of the perfected 12 signs of the zodiac as Soul aspects.

Also known as Fionn MacCumhaill, Gesar of Ling, Indra, Ra (Re), Rustam.

Description: Arthur is the Celtic "once and future king," as remembered in Western myth, probably the subject of more retellings from different perspectives in books and movies than any other Western mythic character.

King Arthur's historicity is vague and not definitively established or rooted to a specific time period, though historians generally credit the British King Arthur with having flourished in the sixth century A.D. in Somerset. Welsh mythology recounts an earlier Arthur with the same retinue and plotlines.

Arthur's birth is arranged by his magus and mentor, Merlin, who secures Arthur's training and apprenticeship in seclusion until the time is ripe for him to claim the throne, as he is the rightful son of King Uther Pendragon. Arthur demonstrates his unique worthiness to be king by being the only person able to withdraw the Sword from the Stone; later the Lady of the Lake, another lifelong mentor, awards him the magical king sword called Excalibur and its scabbard.

Arthur founds Camalate as a headquarters for his Knights of the Round Table. These elite knights, with Arthur, maintain order and well-being in the land, drive out the barbarians (usually called the Saxons), and seek the Holy Grail. Arthur marries Guinevere, the young daughter of King Leodegrance; his chief knight, Lancelot, has an adulterous affair with her, leading to their banishment and the eventual downfall of Camalate as a bastion of morality.

Arthur's aunt, Morgause, seduces Arthur just when he becomes king; 20 years or so later, the bastard child of the liaison, Mordred, challenges Arthur at Camalate with disastrous consequences. Arthur kills Mordred, but is himself mortally wounded and is ferried by mystical barge to Avalon by his sister, Morgan le Fay, and two other women, to be healed for his next incarnation. Myths ever afterward speak of Arthur and his knights sleeping in the Hollow Hills awaiting the trumpet call to summon them back to the land of England.

Explanation: The essential fact about the Arthurian mythos is that it exists on two levels. The first is cosmic: Arthur is the Solar Logos, the Word or Logos (Christ) unfiltered through human language at the level of all suns (stars). Arthur (his Hindu name is Indra, chief of the gods and leader of the Celestial Host) is chief of all the gods, that is, the Great White Brotherhood, based in the constellation Ursa Major (Great Bear). This is a vast conclave of enlightened adepts, spiritual masters, angels, and rishis (Hindu lore says there are 48,000).

The second level of Arthur is terrestrial. Thus far in planetary history there have been 15 King Arthur exemplifiers in different cultures including Celtic (both English and Welsh), Irish, Persian, and Tibetan-Mongolian. The Arthur exemplifier is a human who is deeply permeated by the cosmic Arthur. He is part of a Soul Group whose members incarnate at the same time and place to exemplify the other key roles in the Arthurian mythos.

The Arthurian Soul Group, while incarnate in human bodies under the auspices of a specific culture (Celtic, Buddhist, Persian), acts out the particularities of the Arthurian myth, which is an archetypal model of existence. The work generally involves creating and maintaining spiritual interfaces between humanity, Earth's visionary geography, and the angelic and hierarchical aspects of the cosmos, especially the Great White Brotherhood.

King Arthur, as a celestial being in Ursa Major, does not incarnate as a human; rather, he deeply overlights, influences, and inspires the exemplifier. Thus characters such as Fionn MacCumhaill of Ireland, Gesar of Ling of Tibet and Mongolia, and Rustam of classical Persia were individual mortal humans, yet so deeply did Arthur permeate them that for a time the two levels were one.

Originally—for the Arthurian mythos spans the life of humanity on Earth—King Arthur was the physical manifestation of the Christ impulse, the collective image of something transcendent, between the Christ (Logos or Word) and the warrior class.

Arthur represented the beginnings of the upright path (the collegial ideals of Camalate), the path of those who know, rather than know *about*, of those who are prepared to stand up for what they believe in. Arthur, with Merlin, was the sponsor and patron of the Grail Quest, the quest for Christ Consciousness.

As humanity evolved in consciousness, King Arthur came to stand for the goal of the metamorphosis of the psyche toward a balancing of the 12 fundamental Soul or Self aspects (indicated by the 12 zodiacal signs) from the 14 major Rays (themes of consciousness) originating in the Great Bear. King Arthur represents the developed 12 Soul aspects as portrayed by the Round Table, itself a condensation of the horoscope of the zodiacal signs. As Solar Logos, Arthur has no seat around the Round Table; he occupies the center.

Each Arthurian exemplifier establishes a Mystery center known esoterically as Camalate and sometimes by another name outwardly. There men and women are trained in the Mysteries of Earth's visionary geography, advancement in consciousness, and the attainment of Christ Consciousness. The postulated sixth-century British King Arthur's Camalate was at South Cadbury Castle in Somerset, England, 12 miles from Glastonbury.

Sites of former Camalates still carry a potent geomantic charge and offer many interactive visionary geographic features to visitors even today. For example, at South Cadbury Castle, a traditional Celtic hill-fort, one may psychically visit Arthur's Palace, an inner meeting place for the Great White Brotherhood.

Similarly, one may stimulate the birthing of Arthur consciousness by visiting his Celtic birthplace, Tintagel, on the far edge of Cornwall in southwestern England. Tintagel—originally and correctly, *tints of angels*—is geomantically the precious scabbard (comprising the Great White Brotherhood) for Arthur's king sword, which is another expression of himself as Solar Logos.

As Solar Logos, the actual name "Arthur" is a mantra or sound vibration for that energy. The full pronunciation of the Solar Logos in human speech is *Ar-Thur-Humg!* This is the solar energy of growth and change (the Light and Logos, in action), grounded in material reality or the body by the syllable *Humg! Ar* is the Sun or solar aspect, *Thur* is the Word or Logos aspect, and *Humg!* grounds both.

The Solar Logos has been grounded at various geomantic locations around Earth over its life, such as at the 15 previous Camalates around the Earth, yet it is also mobile, carried from site to site in a lifetime (as it were) by humans who have been initiated in the Arthurian Mysteries.

One way the Solar Logos may appear to psychic vision is as a golden spindle or corkscrew turning dynamically, even furiously, within a vertical container like a grain silo. As the spindle turns, it sends out solar sparks like a pinwheel in all directions; it also continuously sounds *Ar-Thur-Humg!*, quickening all life and reality everywhere. If you penetrate the spindle in your awareness, you may experience the spinning.

King Arthur, whose name spiritually means Sun-Star, has a seat at the Round Table of the Cosmic Logos, the Logos expressed at the level of galaxies. There he occupies the Heart chakra position among the 12 august seats.

See also: Camalate, Einherjar, Excalibur, Fionn MacCumhaill, Gesar of Ling, Glass Mountain, Guinevere, Holy Grail, Indra, Lady of the Lake, Merlin, Round Table, Rustam, Sword in the Stone, Wild Hunt.

KINGS OF EDOM

The first and aborted race of humans who were an attempt to create a viable humanity possessing free will and self-aware consciousness in material bodies.

Also known as Afrits, Antigods, Asura, Djinn, Genies, Kings of Ancient Time, Raksasas.

Description: Judaic lore (Old Testament) tells us eight kings reigned over the land of Edom before the Israelites under King David established their presence and rule in that area. The Edomites descended from Edom, or Esau, who sold his birthright for pottage and gained his second name, Edom; he is described in Genesis as being red in color, his entire body like a hairy mantle. He is also described as Jacob's older brother; Jacob is the grand patriarch of Israel and the creator of the Twelve Tribes. Genesis says the Kings of Edom reigned before the monarchs of Israel.

Also known as the Land of Seir or Mount Seir, the Edomite land was about 40 miles wide by 100 miles long, between the Dead Sea and Gulf of Aqabah. The Kings were known as Bela, Jobab, Husham, Hadad, Samlab, Saul, Baal-hanan, and Hadar; in some accounts, Hadar was the king over the seven Primordial Kings. David conquered the eight kings of Edom and put his own garrisons throughout their land, but after the Temple of Jerusalem was destroyed in 586 B.C. by the Babylonians, the Edomites rejoiced and began reclaiming Palestine.

Explanation: The term "Kings" does not bear a gender reference; it refers, rather, to the mastery or focus of a dimension of energy known in Qabala as a *Sefira,* a vessel to contain a portion of the divine and ultimate light. The Kings abstractly represent the spectrum of eight containers of celestial Light. Edom here means the Earth as it was originally populated by the Kings of Edom, and Kings here is Qabalistic code for the first and aborted race of human beings. Esau, as the first Edomite, is appropriately Jacob's older brother, older in this sense meaning earlier, primordial, as in the first race of humanity.

The Qabalistic allegory puts the matter in more abstract, energy terms. The term "Kings of Edom," who reigned before there was a king over Israel, according to Qabala, refers to a time of unbalanced forces and psychic instability. The term Israel allegorizes the world once it attained equilibrium after the Kings had been removed from physical existence. Similarly, Jacob represents the second, more balanced generation of humans, occupying Israel, not Edom.

In brief, the mythic code is decoded like this: The first generation of humanity is the Kings of Edom; the second generation is the Monarchs of Israel. Edom is the world of unbalanced forces, destabilized spheres of Light; Israel is the succeeding world of balanced forces and spheres of Light in equilibrium. (The word "Israel" here does not refer to the present-day political or geographic entity called Israel.)

"The Kings" also refers to the instability of the Sefiroth, or divine containers of Light, considered in Qabala to be as a group the original template for creation and the energy foundation for human form and consciousness. These containers got overwhelmed when the Supreme Being first flowed the Light through them, one by one; consequently, the embodied first humans, the Edomites, were similarly overwhelmed by the Light and became unbalanced and dangerous. Equivalently, the seven containers or Primordial Kings are the seven chakras, or major psychic energy centers along the spine; each King embodies a chakra at the archetypal level.

The physical characteristics of the alleged founder of the Edomite line, Esau, are appropriate: He was red in color (indicating life force, will, passion, and anger), and hairy all over (indicating his feral, quasi-animalistic, primitive nature). One of the Edomite Kings (using the term generically) was Lilith, the so-called demonic, rebellious first wife of Adam. The legend has it that she demanded equal power and stature with Adam, who refused; she left the Garden of Eden and refused to return even after God sent three angels to persuade her.

The Kings of Edom, here meaning the entire remaining first spawn of humanity, were removed from physical creation and bound and imprisoned in a lower astral realm tied into specific geomantic nodes around the planet. These are called Lucifer Binding Sites, of which the Earth has 3,496; one of these is at the Dome of the Rock in Jerusalem, Israel. At each site, a portion of Lucifer and a certain number of Edomites are bound between the worlds, awaiting release.

Lucifer is bound up with the Edomite transgressions and removal because part of his essence sacrificially went into the Kings of Edom (the spirit and possibility of total psychic freedom). The Kings of Edom, and Lucifer, may be unbound, one site at a time, by humans willing to forgive the Kings for their excesses, which led to a diminution of human psychic freedom and cognitive access as an attempt to balance consciousness in second generation humanity.

See also: Asura, Djinn, Emerald, Fall of Man, Lucifer, Prometheus, Raksasas.

KLINGSOR

A composite figure, generated by each individual and the human collective unconscious, who embodies the Shadow, all the pain, misery, trauma, and uncompleted karma from all one's lives past and present. Ignored, Klingsor stands in the way of one's spiritual development and healing, and that of the Earth's.

Description: Largely the imaginative contribution to the Grail legend by Richard Wagner in his 1882 opera, *Parsifal,* Klingsor is the enemy of the Fisher King and the Grail Brotherhood. He is a black magician and evil wizard who stole the holy lance or spear from Anfortas, the Fisher King. The lance, wielded by the properly trained Grail Knight (Parsifal), is the only thing that will heal Anfortas, who languishes on a couch from a grievous thigh wound in daily sight of the Holy Grail, but unable to partake of its marvelous healing abilities.

In Wagner's rendition, the holy lance is the Spear of Destiny that lanced Christ on the cross and drew his blood. In older Grail versions, the agent of the wounding of the Fisher King is usually a massive divine sword, misused, that rendered the Dolorous Stroke that maimed the King and created the Wasteland (a blighted landscape).

Wagner explains Klingsor's fall into the black arts as due to his failure to master his own inner demons and to "slay the sins" within him. Anfortas spurned him, and Klingsor, furiously insulted, turned to black magic for revenge. He created a pleasure garden of lovely flowers and flower maidens to lure unsuspecting, naïve Grail Knights away from their quest. His goal was to ruin as many Grail Knights as possible, since he couldn't be one.

Klingsor employs Kundry, a distorted version of the Grail Maiden, to attend to him and his castle and garden. She also is an intermediary, though duplicitous and at best ambivalent, between him and Anfortas at the Grail Castle. In her own way, Kundry suffers as much as the wounded Anfortas.

Explanation: Klingsor is less an actual celestial or human figure than a symbol of an obstacle one encounters on the Grail Quest. He is the reason Anfortas is wounded, and he is also Anfortas's own discarded dark side, or Shadow.

Anfortas is the Wounded Fisher King because his root chakra (euphemistically referred to as a thigh wound) does not have the sufficient lifeforce energy to complete the energy circuit with the crown chakra to precipitate deep and total recall of his soul's origin, nature, purpose, and history to date. Anfortas cannot complete this energy circuit because he has spurned Klingsor.

Klingsor is an excellently descriptive image for the cast off parts of ourselves, the parts thrown into unconsciousness (the Shadow), the parts repudiated, the parts never validated, admitted, loved, or acted upon. He is the unexpiated karma, the untransmuted pain, suffering, abuse, and misery of past lives and conditions, a lot of which remain burdensome to us until we wakefully deal with them.

The cumulative pain of living through many lifetimes that Klingsor represents keeps Anfortas, his daytime self, from remembering his life purpose. Klingsor has already abandoned such quests, and even the questions that prompted them. He has turned instead to malice, tangible results, and black magic. Since he feels invalidated, he will invalidate everyone else. Since he cannot have the Grail, or be a Grail Knight, then neither shall anyone else.

Often, people in an intensely negative state such as Klingsor's will have many spirit beings around them to support and enhance that state of mind. Kundry is one such: She is supposed to be a Grail Maiden, a feminine support for the soul retrieving its vast store of memories and understandings; instead, she has been perverted into a duplicitous, troubled servitor to a black magician.

Every Grail Knight (a man or woman on the path to experiencing the Grail in the context of Earth's visionary geography) has to confront his or her own Klingsor.

Just as the Fisher King is both an outer celestial figure and an expression of our individual status in remembering our soul's origin and purpose, so Klingsor is a figure who embodies everything we have individually not dealt with. If you could clairvoyantly see the side of yourself you never routinely see or acknowledge, the cumulative pain, trauma, misery, hate, unfinished karma, embodied as a human figure, you would see Klingsor—your version of him.

Klingsor is also present in the outer world as a composite creation of the collective unconscious of humanity over time on the Earth—the embodiment of the Shadow of all the world's cultures, religions, belief systems, and politics.

Klingsor is the bridge linking an individual with the Antichrist, also known as the dark grid encasing the Earth and its original Light body grid like a black cancer. For the human shadow, or Klingsor, to remain unexpiated (unresolved, even unaddressed) means one has unrepudiated (unconscious) connections to the Antichrist and its energy web around the planet.

For Earth to be whole and its visionary geography restored to prime working condition, in routine and vigorous dialogue with the galaxy and spiritual worlds, the planetary Klingsor must be healed by Christed Grail Knights, just as in the healing of the Maimed Fisher King, it is the Christed Parsifal or Galahad who heal his wounds and restore him to full memory of his soul's life.

The meeting with Klingsor can also be seen as a stage in spiritual development. This was recognized as such in Freemasonry and a version of it was called Black Masonry. This occupies the initiate from 19 degrees to 30 degrees (out of 33 degrees), which are stages of initiation and mastery. In Black Masonry, you study, through clairvoyance, the working out of karma and observe the evil, darkness, and horror that sometimes accompany it, both on the personal and collective level, and gain the understanding of this karma as divine justice and retribution.

See also: Antichrist, Dolorous Stroke, Earth Changes, Fisher King, Ghost Dance, Grail Castle, Grail Knight, Grail Maiden, Holy Grail, Manu, Ragnarok, Salmon of Wisdom, Wasteland.

KOKOPELLI

The Native American perception of Pan, the chief of all Nature spirits, who enlivens and informs all of Nature, both physical and subtle.

Also known as Chu'lu'laneh, Ek Chuah, Ghanaskidi, Humpbacked Flute Player, Kokopele, Kokopelmana, Kokopeltiyo, Kokopilau, Ololowishkya, Owiwi, Paiyatamu.

Description: In the American Southwest, the

figure of Kokopelli is very popular and widespread. Kokopelli is depicted as a prehistoric male deity: He is humpbacked, plays a flute, has a series of curving horns on his head, and usually has an erection, a condition scholars prefer to call ithyphallic. Archeologists have documented at least 400 rock carvings of Kokopelli throughout the Southwest. The figure also appears copiously as a design motif in pottery, blankets, jewelry, and other regional folk art, as well as in Native American lore and legend.

Kokopelli's primary area of manifestation is the Four Corners region, which includes large portions of New Mexico, Arizona, Utah, and Colorado, especially in ancient settlements once inhabited by the Anasazi ("The Old or Ancient Ones"). Native Americans generally say Kokopelli is a fertility symbol, but with qualities of the trickster, a roving minstrel, a rain priest, seducer of young women, a hunting magician—and on the whole, a likable though mysterious spirit being.

His nature whimsical, his deeds usually charitable, and his spirit vital, Kokopelli stands for fertility, mischief, replenishment, music, and dance. Most often he is shown in a dancing posture, one leg kicked up, head down to his flute. With his flute, he warmed the Earth in springtime, quickening it for new life. During the summer, he roamed the cornfields at night, playing his flute; in the morning, the little cornstalks would have grown to an astonishing four feet high.

Among the Navajo, Kokopelli is known as Ghanaskidi, who is a supernatural spirit being, or *ye'i*, representing harvest, abundance, and mist. This figure wears horns, holds a staff, has a humpback from which feathers radiate; the hump is said to be made of the rainbow and contains numerous seeds and mist.

A Zuni name for this figure is Chu'lu'laneh, which, curiously, is also their name for the specific form of flute used by rain priests. They also have three other names for a figure probably identical with Kokopelli: Paiyatamu, who is a flute-playing culture hero (lacking a hump) associated with rain and fertility; Ololowishkya, a phallic kachina (a stylized representation of a benevolent spirit, deity, or ancestor) central to a Zuni flute-playing and corn-grinding ceremony; and Owiwi, humpbacked and carrying a pack of fetishes on his back.

Kokopelli may be a more recent perception of the ancient Mayan deity called *Ek Chuah* who wears a backpack, holds a staff, and is the patron of hunters.

The Hopis describe Kokopelli as a kachina ("Respected Spirit"), one of their hundreds of benevolent spirit beings or ancestors who maintain the world for them and serve as intermediaries between the people and the high gods. Their version of Kokopelli has a hump and long snout (no flute), and is associated with rain and fertility and thus phallic. The name may come from the Zuni and Hopi languages, meaning perhaps "Kachina hump" or "wooden-backed"; or from the Hopi *Kokopilau,* in which *koko* means "wood" and *pilau* means "hump."

A very early Hopi legend says that when this people first emerged from inside the Earth (see Agharta), they were met by two *mahus,* insect-like creatures who carried the power of the Earth's heat. The two mahus, encountering the newly emerged Hopi, started playing beautiful, healing melodies on their flutes and scattered seeds for fruits and vegetables onto the barren land for the Hopi.

In many cases, rock art depictions of Kokopelli are found at the mouths of canyons, on mesa tops, in the vicinity of former inhabited sites, and near water. In whatever guise he takes, Kokopelli is credited widely with bringing fertility, through seeds, moisture, rain, and abundance to plants, animals, and people.

Explanation: Kokopelli is the Southwest version of the European Nature god, Pan.

Pan was the Greek god of Nature and shepherds and the Shepherd of the flocks. Usually he is depicted as half-man, half-goat, with a goat's head and man's torso, though sometimes as a bearded, hirsute, feral primitive-looking man with little stubby goat horns and sometimes a horse's torso as in the centaur image or goat's legs and feet, for which he was known as the Goat-Foot God. Pan was a lusty god of the pastures and countryside, seeing to the fertility of the flocks and herds; he was often portrayed with an erect phallus for his penchant for chasing alluring nymphs, and he was invoked by people when fertility was required.

You can see Kokopelli's essential characteristics present in Pan: the lusty nature, the flute or syrinx, and the spirit of natural fertility. Kokopelli's humpbacked feature is largely symbolic: He carries the symbols and energy signatures for all the categories of Nature spirits on his back, but even that is still symbolic. His knowledge of the diversity of Nature spirits over whom he has charge is implicit within his being; he doesn't need a sack to carry them.

Kokopelli-Pan is the protector spirit of the plant and animal kingdoms on Earth. He works under commission by a deva or angelic being at the cosmic level; his task is to incarnate in appropriate forms, through different expressions of Pan (different according to conscious perception) on different planets that have plants and animals, though not necessarily like on Earth. There can be as many different guises of Pan as there are planets with flora and fauna.

This figure is the carrier of spiritual life force running through organic life. His priapic images are metaphors for how Pan injects the spirit of focused consciousness into matter. The fertility aspect refers to how Pan continuously contributes life-force energy to plant and animal species, as if from a vast reservoir of biological vitality, enabling them to flourish, propagate, spread, and evolve. The flute (or for Pan, the syrinx) signifies his ability to communicate with all levels of Nature, to awaken, enliven, inform, and summon all the Nature spirits.

A primary reason why Kokopelli left such a strong residual impression in the Southwest is that once, very long ago, the Four Corners area was a paradise. Humans, animals, plants, minerals, and all the Nature spirits associated with these lived together in harmony, close collegiality, familiarity, even joy.

Although this region today is largely arid high desert, in approximately the Lemurian epoch (circa 18,000,000 years ago), it was a teeming green oasis, a spiritual and geomantic high point on the continent. It was like an ancient version of our modern-day Findhorn in Scotland where, in the 1970s, acknowledgment of Pan and his hosts led to the conversion of seeming wasteland in northern Scotland into an agricultural breadbasket.

So thoroughly was Kokopelli-Pan acknowledged and welcomed into native human life in the Four Corners region that he virtually lived there full time. Pan, of course, can be present in many locales simultaneously and in many guises, but his presence was regular and sustained in this paradisal zone. He was seen frequently by sensitives; heard daily by the clairaudient as he summoned and instructed his hosts of joyous Nature spirits and elementals to maintain the land; and honored ceremonially in rituals, invocations, dances, and festivals.

Kokopelli-Pan threaded his way throughout the region, his constant flute-playing knitting the land, its geomantic features, and life forms into a healthy web of light and sound created by his movements, thoughts, and gestures. All the resident geomantic features (the land's allotment of the 100 + types of visionary geographic Light temples) were switched "on," allowing a regular commerce of angelic and celestial energies to mix with the terrestrial and human energies.

Kokopelli would then circulate through this living matrix, fine-tuning the Southwest songlines, as the Australian Aborigines would say. The Native Americans present in this region were entirely in accord with this and contributed their human share of the maintenance required to keep the geomantic system, literally, humming with life and light. As they kept saying "hello" to Kokopelli, honoring his work, happy in his presence, so he remained.

"I was here among them all the time," you can almost hear Kokopelli say of those halcyon days when he was constantly on call in the Southwest.

See also: Agharta, Fairy Queen, Gaia, Menehune, Nymph, Pan, River God, Royal Hall of the King of the Dovrë Trolls, Trolls, Wasteland.

LADY OF THE LAKE

The guardian of the entire astral plane, symbolized as a Lake, and administrator of its nine spheres of consciousness.

Also known as Mnemosyne, Nimuë, Nineve, Viviane, Vivienne.

Description: A somewhat imprecisely defined female figure from the Arthurian mythos, the Lady of the Lake arises out of a lake to award the young Arthur his second sword called Excalibur soon after his kingship was secured by claiming the Sword in the Stone, his first sword, an act facilitated by the magus Merlin.

She is variously called Nimuë, Nineve, Viviane, Vivienne, or simply the Lady of the Lake; her lake is magical, numinous, and otherworldly; and she lives in it surrounded by her maiden servants, or she lives in a palace on an Island of Women somewhere in the misty middle of the Lake, or she lives in a fair, richly furnished place inside a rock in the center of the Lake.

King Arthur's knight, Sir Lancelot du Lac (Lancelot of the Lake) is said to be the Lady's son, lover, or protector. King Arthur's magus, Merlin, late in life is seduced by the Lady of the Lake, who first entices him to divulge his magical secrets, then traps him in an inescapable crystal cave, which will break open only when King Arthur, now sleeping in the Hollow Hills, returns.

During King Arthur's tenure as king at Camalate and leader of the Knights of the Round Table, the Lady of the Lake remains his mentor, protector, and sponsor. At the end of his reign, King Arthur (or Bedivere, one of his closest Knight colleagues) returns Excalibur to the Lake, tossing it over the Lake as a hand "clothed in white samite," as Sir Thomas Malory wrote, rises out of the water to grab it and take it into the Lake again. It was the same hand that first rose to award Arthur the sword and the scabbard.

Explanation: The Lady of the Lake is the guardian of the astral realms, which were symbolized anciently as a Lake, as in a lake or sea of light. She is a figure of authority for the astral realms, from the highest to lowest. She is an expression of Sophia, the great Gnostic goddess of wisdom, expressed at an astral level.

The Lady of the Lake has three main aspects, all described in the Arthurian mythos: Nimuë (Merlin's enchantress), Morgan le Fay, (a witch, and Arthur's sister or half-sister), and Morgause (Arthur's perfidious aunt). While these women are individual adepts, they also occupy basic roles or cosmic positions.

In the stories, each of the three is presented as treacherous: Nimuë seduces a doting Merlin to divulge his magical lore, then traps him in a crystal cave; Morgan steals the scabbard for Excalibur, Arthur's king sword; and Morgause seduces Arthur, producing a bastard named Mordred who, as an adult, will ruin Camalate. But none of these characterizations is ultimately accurate; they only show the potency of the energies represented and guarded by each.

The Lady of the Lake in her three guises is actually akin to: the Irish Morrigan, a trio of dangerous war goddesses (Babd, Nemain, and Macha); their Norse equivalent, the nine Valkyries, led by Brynnhildr; and their Greek equivalent, the Nine Muses led by the Sun god Apollo.

Qabala, the esoteric side of Judaism, developed an abstract model to diagram the flow, hierarchy, and relationships of energy and consciousness in what it calls the Four Worlds. It uses a diagram called the Tree of Life, one for each world; each Tree has ten spheres of Light. The first Tree corresponds to energy relationships in our material world. The second one pertains to the astral world, the Lake, and is called *Yetzirah,* the "Place of Formation." The astral world is often described as a seedbed for the physical.

The Lady of the Lake is in charge of the entire Yetzirah Tree, the astral Lake, and her three guises each supervise a polarity within it. The Tree of Life diagram is usually drawn with three vertical pillars and lines connecting the ten spheres. Nimuë, Morgan, and Morgause each embody and transmit a pillar.

The Greek equivalent is Mnemosyne, goddess of memory and mother of the Nine Muses, the same as Morgan and her eight sisters of Avalon and the nine spheres on the Yetzirah Tree of Life.

In the Arthurian scheme of esoteric initiation, the Lady of the Lake in any of her guises would supervise the initiations of the candidates. Earth's visionary geography is provided with a portal into her realm, the Lake, known as a Pointer's Ball because in earlier days and, to an extent, even today, you can look through it into other planes of existence and, if you're game, pass through the Ball into the Lake and its ten realms. (The Earth has 174,060 Pointer's Balls.)

Selected locations include Ponter's Ball [sic] in Glastonbury, England; Ashlawn, Charlottesville, Virginia; Acropolis, Athens, Greece; Kerkado tumulus, Carnac, France; and Calendar I Site, South Royalton, Vermont.

Arthur's sword, Excalibur, given to him by the Lady of the Lake, is actually the condensation of insight represented by the ten spheres in Yetzirah. The scabbard, said to be stolen by Morgan, is actually the three guises of the Lady of the Lake: Nimuë, Morgan, and Morgause and the levels of awareness they represent. The Lady of the Lake's gift of Excalibur is a dynamic expression of the Yetzirah Tree of Life, the sword from the Lake.

When King Arthur is mortally wounded on the battlefield by Mordred, the Lady of the Lake in her three guises carries him on the mystic barge to Avalon where he can heal or pass on to higher realms. Similarly, Norse myth says the Valkyries select the best of those slain on the battlefield to join Odin and the other Einherjar ("lone fighters") in the great Hall of the Slain, known as Valhalla, for endless feasting and drinking. It's the same story.

The meaning is this: Arthur, and the Norse warriors, are "slain" only in the sense that they, in their lone fights, have defeated themselves—that is, their lower, dragon aspects. They have mastered their kundalini and its effect on the chakras. They are capable of penetrating the Lake, seeing into the Yetzirah Tree, wielding the sword forged from that tenfold realm, as well as entering the Lake at will.

See also: Avalon, Excalibur, King Arthur, Morgan le Fay, Sword in the Stone, Valkyries.

LAND OF MILK AND HONEY

An operational description of the planet's array of instant portals to other stars and constellations, called stargates.

Also known as the stargate network.

Description: The phrase "the land of milk and honey" is a biblical reference to a paradisal landscape whose physical conditions are perfect for human life. In Exodus, for example, the land we now know as Israel was called "a land flowing with milk and honey." Yahweh addresses Moses out of the Burning Bush and says, He will lead Israel out of Egypt "unto a land flowing with milk and honey," presumably Palestine, the land earlier promised to Abraham and Jacob.

In Welsh lore, the second of three ancient names for the Island of Britain is *Y Vel Ynys,* the Island of Honey.

Most scholars have taken the term "Land of Milk and Honey" to mean either a landscape capable of producing a lush lifestyle and ample well-being or, even more literally, as the outlines for a healthful, longevity diet. The phrase is also used loosely to refer to places where the living conditions seem opulent and the means to enjoy them are at hand.

Explanation: Is this meant as an image of agricultural bounty? No, not originally or geomantically. It's a picture of the stargate network turned on.

In Earth's visionary geography, stargates are fifth-dimensionally placed geomantic devices for actual physical transportation of people and goods from points on Earth to points on other planets. There are 2,200,000 stargates that terminate in constellations, and 1,080 that terminate at specific stars (actually, on planets within their systems).

The average stargate diameter is 30 yards, though the range is three feet to 40 miles. Earth's largest stargate is in the Gobi Desert of Mongolia.

Although stargates are almost entirely unknown today, other than in science fiction, they are a prime component of Earth's original energy-geomantic design and were once, very long ago, used widely and frequently. The Bermuda Triangle, for example, and all its mysterious, baffling phenomena are caused by two overlapping stargates that are malfunctioning due to lack of use and maintenance.

The applicability of the phrase "Land of Milk and Honey" to stargates comes into play as an accurate description when you observe their operation.

The activation and use of the stargates involves the coordinated participation of the Archangel Michael and the Supreme Being. Archangel Michael uses his sword to make the connection between the individual stargate and the Throne of the Supreme Being. When this connection is made, it seems as if a golden yellow light of a high, subtle quality rains or flows down upon the stargate, seen as an effulgent globular beacon in the landscape. This rain of golden-yellow light on the white globe has the consistency of honey.

As a metaphor, honey is sweet and an almost perfect food, so it works well as a symbol for the sweetness of divine consciousness perpetually flowing down upon Earth as nourishment for all sentient life—the honey of God's attention.

The milk quality pertains to celestial light and its influx on Earth when the stargates are turned on and the network flourishing in a locality. The milk also refers to the intense light of the individual stargates and their galactic nexus.

To live in a land flowing with milk and honey is to participate in the stargate network under the auspices of the Archangel Michael and the Supreme Being. The *land* is the fifth dimension where the stargates on Earth are found; the *flowing* is the rain of golden-yellow light from Above when the stargate is turned on; the *milk* is the brightness of the stargate; and the *honey* is the golden-yellow rain from Above. Spiritually *and* physically, one is connected to the galaxy and capable of bodily moving across vast spatial distances in an eye blink.

The phrase evokes an Edenic time when Earth's geomantic array was operational and full of light and the focus of continual human interaction. The Land of Milk and Honey refers to the Earth's original dispensation by its celestial designers to be in regular, fluid exchange with the major stars of the galaxy. It refers to a land geomantically prepared, activated, and maintained, into which celestial light (milk) and the sweetness (honey) of divine consciousness perpetually flow for the well-being and spiritual evolution of all life forms.

Britain was anciently called the Island of Honey because its stargate network was fully operational and luminous. The land was continually bathed in divine nectar as the conduits between Earth and various stars flourished.

Similarly, the landscape of Palestine was once enriched by its operational stargate array. The term *Israel* is often used as initiate's code to refer not so much to a specific ethnic people in a specific landscape as to any humans of elevated consciousness and accomplishment. As the stargate network exists in the fifth dimension, highly acute psychic abilities are required to interact with it. Yahweh, in effect, was saying He will interact with the spiritually developed ones collectively, symbolically called Israel, in a landscape (Palestine) rich with operational stargates.

Selected locations of stargates include: Devil's Tower, Wyoming; Tetford, England; Vinstra, Norway; Mount Orohena, Tahiti, French Polynesia; Tetford, Lincolnshire, England.

See also: Dreamtime, Garden of Eden, Holy Mountain, Hurqalya, Lucifer, Rising Rock, Zep Tepi.

LEVIATHAN

A perception of the primordial cosmic dragon, source of God's primal creative potency and still unmanifested divine consciousness.

Also known as Angel of the Sea, Draco, Dragon, Livjatan, Lotan, Nun, Prince of the Sea, Rahab, Sesa-Ananta, Tiamat, Vrtra, World Dragon.

Description: In Judaic lore, Leviathan was one of the great sea monsters *(Tanninim Gedolim)* created on the Fifth Day of Creation. Other names for this creature included *tannin* (dragon), *rahav* (expanse), and *yam* (sea). The Hebrew name, *Livyatan,* may mean "to coil," while Isaiah described this creature as a "twisting serpent" and others say it means "crooked or piercing serpent."

Leviathan, King of the Sea and all marine creatures, is generally assumed to be a monstrous whale, though sometimes he is depicted with seven heads, more like a dragon.

Leviathan has iridescent skin, a repulsive smell (although it might be simply the salt smell), a voracious appetite, and boiling breath. His fiery breath, when exhaled, makes the ocean waters seething hot. From his nostrils comes steam as from a boiling cauldron. To him, iron is like straw, brass like rotten wood. Flung stones are turned into stubble by him, and he laughs at spears.

Leviathan is a gigantic being, vaguely construed to be female (although referred to as male) but without a mate of the same species and thus a singular creation. To quench his thirst, every day he has to drink all the water that flows from the River Jordan into the sea.

He is said to be 900 miles long, have seven heads, and 300 eyes. Leviathan was invulnerable to attack and originally encircled the entire world in the great abyss or the depths of the cosmic ocean (primordial Sea, equated with Chaos). He was blamed for devouring all the dragons in Creation.

Despite his size and seeming ferocity, Leviathan is portrayed as a favorite of God. His fins radiate such an intensity of light that they obscure the Sun; his eyes emit such splendor that they illuminate the sea as in a sudden flash of light. God is said to sport with Leviathan in the last three hours of a 12-hour day.

At the time of the Day of Judgment, God will summon the angels to enter combat with Leviathan, but they will flee the field of battle in fear, so fierce is a single glance from his baleful eyes. God will then incite Leviathan to fight his land equivalent and mate, Behemoth (a huge bloated elephant). Leviathan will kill Behemoth with a slash of his fins, and Leviathan will die from a lash of Behemoth's tail. Before Leviathan is consumed, he will be a delectable sight to the assembled pious souls, as was planned by God at the start of Creation.

The righteous will then feast on the delicious flesh of both primordial creatures at the Messianic or eschatological banquet in Heaven, Jewish lore says. A tent will be made for the pious at their tables out of the stretched skin of Leviathan; in fact, it will canopy all of Jerusalem and the rich light that streams out of it will illuminate the entire world.

Judaic lore further says that the original clothes (garments of light) of Adam and Eve, humanity's first couple, were made of the effulgent hide of Leviathan.

Some rabbinical texts equate Leviathan with Tiamat, the primordial cosmic dragon as portrayed in Babylonian mythology. Behemoth, Leviathan's land consort (though they never are together), is equated with Kingu, Tiamat's mate. When Marduk killed Kingu, humanity was generated from his blood.

Tiamat, in Babylonian myth, is a female dragon, with a vast, serpentine body, impenetrable scaly skin, horns on her head, an immense tail, and two forelegs. Tiamat created the Heavens, Earth (cosmic space), and all the gods. When she was finally slain, reputedly by Marduk, her body was cut into many pieces and from it came the Milky Way and Earth, and Earth's rivers from her blood.

Leviathan's portrayal also parallels that of the earlier Ugaritic *Lotan* (or *Litanu:* both mean "the twisted one"), a monstrous, seven-headed, snake-like sea creature of primordial Chaos who continuously threatens all of Creation.

Explanation: Leviathan is a perception of the cosmic dragon, known around the world under many names, including the ones given here. Perhaps its most thorough description and résumé is that of Sesa-Ananta.

In the Hindu myths, Sesa-Ananta is the thousand-headed dragon who is older than Creation; in between vast cycles of Creation called *Pralaya* (in the West, "Flood" or "Deluge"), Vishnu (the Hindu version of Christ) dreams atop Sesa-Ananta who floats on the cosmic sea. Brahma, the Creator, commissions Sesa-Ananta, whose name means both "Remainder" and "Endless or Infinite One," to support the world by encircling it with his endless, twisting coils.

Earth here must be understood as more than the planet; rather, it is the entirety of cosmic space. Not only will Sesa-Ananta encircle it, but, though it seems contradictory, he will also bear Goddess Earth stably upon his thousand heads.

Appropriately, the *Mahabharata,* a great trove of Hindu myth, states that Brahma gave Sesa-Ananta a helper in this task: the fair-winged bird Garuda. Garuda is one of the many guises of the angelic order called the Ofanim, and it's relevant here because Behemoth, Leviathan's land mate and future rival, is a filtered perception of the Ofanim who in Hindu perception were Ganesh, the benevolent, merry elephant god. Thus the Ofanim (as Behemoth) work collegially with Leviathan and have done so since the beginning of Creation.

Sesa-Ananta is called the Remainder because he bears the residues of consciousness achieved and saved from the previous round of existence, such as another universe or multiverse or complete cycle of creation and dissolution (see Flood). He also carries the remainder of Brahma's unmanifested divine power, the part still not used in Creation and withheld for later days or perhaps a paradisal afterlife.

He is the endless and infinite reservoir of the Supreme Being's (Brahma's) prime creative power and light, of the complete electromagnetic field spectrum; he is the cosmic equivalent of the Goddess Kundalini, said to be coiled at the base of the human root chakra, appropriately called *Muladhara,* "Root Support."

Brahma begins creation with Sesa-Ananta, the cosmic root chakra, the first that God works with and the vast reservoir of kundalini, or primordial creative force.

Later in the unfoldment of the world, Indra, king of the Hindu gods, slays Vrtra, another form of the cosmic dragon who withholds the Waters of Life. Here "Waters of Life" is used in place of "kundalini," but they indicate the same thing.

Leviathan devours all the dragons of Creation because his consciousness subsumes them all. He is the master dragon, the first and original one, the mother of all dragons expressed at subsequent levels of creation, such as the 1,067 on planet Earth and the constellation Draco, the outer form of a celestial being in dragon form. Leviathan devours the dragons because his essence *includes* them all; generated from his flesh, they respond instantly and always to his call.

Leviathan will be the meat at the Messianic banquet and his hide illuminates the world and the oceans because he is primordial consciousness. To say his divine flesh will be served at the feast of the righteous in Heaven means one day our limited human consciousness will be reunited with the full panoply of light and awareness; we will eat continuously and joyously of full cosmic awareness, surfeiting ourselves with Leviathan's godly flesh.

To participate in this banquet is to return to a state of unity with God not experienced since humanity's primordial separation into a phylogenetic species. It is akin to Adam and Eve returning their garments of light (clothes) to God.

This is consistent with the Hindu explanation of Sesa-Ananta as the "Remainder," the residue of consciousness from the previous cycle of creation. He embodies undying consciousness, the rich flesh or waters of immortality, and the *prima materia* from which our universe and everything in it were created.

One does not have to wait for the End of Days and the achievement of unquestionable piety and righteousness to feast on Leviathan. Access to kundalini is a God-given gift to every human, should one wish to develop it. Every embodied human has a miniature Leviathan coiled in the root chakra at the base of the spine. We must remember: God started creation with this root center with its dragon.

See also: Behemoth, Dragon, Ganesh, Garuda, Marduk, Rainbow Serpent.

LEY LINES

Energy tracks at multiple levels crisscrossing the planet's surface, creating a matrix of light and consciousness that feeds the Earth.

Also known as ceques, dragon paths, fairy paths, Holy Trails, landscape lines, light pathways, lines of the Earth current, lung-mei, Old Straight Tracks, sacred paths, songlines, trackways, traders' tracks.

Description: The term "ley lines" entered the Western archeological vocabulary in 1921, when Alfred Watkins, a 66-year-old English businessman who liked the rural countryside, discovered that many of the visible landmarks in the landscape, such as churches and old roads, were positioned along straight lines that ran for miles. When he first discerned the pattern on a summer's day in Herefordshire, it was like experiencing "a flood of ancestral memory," he later wrote in the first of four books on the subject.

He dubbed these straight-running lines across the landscape the Old Straight Tracks, but he also called them leys. The word is old, and may derive from *lea,* which means a tract of open ground, but it may more deeply come from the Latin *lucus,* meaning "grove," itself derived from *lucere,* "to shine." *Leye* is an obsolete word that means "flame or fire." Watkins thought "ley" was a sufficiently evocative term, with all its associated nuances, to signify what he had found.

Watkins postulated that the ley system was created by Neolithic humanity with an uncanny precision, as if done by professional surveyors. Numerous megalithic features, such as stones, mounds, stone circles, and barrows as well as old churches, were found to be situated on these straight tracks across the land.

Later in the twentieth century, Earth mysteries researchers extended Watkins' initial discovery by plotting many more ley alignments and, in some cases, postulating that some kind of magnetic or Earth current must run along the leys. Dowsers reported anomalous but detectable energies associated with some leys.

Leys were noted not only in England, but also, for example, in Peru, in the form of radiating lines or Rays called *ceques* originating in the sacred city of Cusco or streaking across the barren high plains near Nazca and resembling landing strips. In Peru, the numinous holy places called *huacas* were laid out like holy stopping places or pilgrimage destinations along the straight lines (ceques: or *siq'i,* a Peruvian Aymara Indian term meaning lines of things, straight rows of holy places).

The ancient Chinese called ley lines *lung-mei,* the paths of the dragon current or *qi,* and charted their courses across mountains and through valleys. To them, the lung-mei never flowed in a straight path, but always in a curve.

Navajo myth of the American Southwest hints at ley lines. Some stories describe how

Navajo heroes long ago ascended a mountain quickly by way of a Holy Trail *(etin digini)*, a miraculous path. The understanding was that the gods and selected Navajos could use these Holy Trails for easy, rapid journeys; Holy Trails could include journeys on rainbows, sunbeams, and lightning streaks.

Usually, the ley lines were implied by the placement of the sites in a row, but, in some cases, the straight track was physically visible in the landscape, as if etched out of earth and stone, such as a 20-mile straight-running line at 13,000 feet in the Western Cordillera of the Andes in Bolivia.

In 1989, English dowsers proposed an even longer ley line they called the Saint Michael Line, which runs from the southwestern tip of Cornwall to the far eastern tip of East Anglia in southern Britain. Along its 300-mile track, it passes through many noted megalithic or old Christian sites, including Saint Michael's Mount (a rocky hill-island), Glastonbury, Avebury (a stone circle), and numerous churches. Along this corridor or landscape route, with a tolerance of 1,500 feet allowed on either side of the line, lie 63 churches in total, 10 dedicated to Saint Michael or Saint George (a dragon-slaying saint) and 23 to Saint Mary.

Public acceptance of the theory of ley lines has run the gamut from universal dismissal by mainstream archeology to New Age speculation.

Explanation: The reality of ley lines is complex and easily subject to misinterpretation because it is a physically observed phenomenon that actually straddles several different aspects of Earth's visionary geography. Watkins' essential intuition was correct: There are straight-running alignments and deliberate placements of holy sites across the landscape, but not all map-plotted alignments have geomantic reality; some are artifacts of one's expectations.

Further, it is very difficult to make accurate inductions to the larger picture from microscale dowsing results; again, misinterpretation is often the case because the bigger geomantic picture is far more complex and multidimensional than dowsing or map-plotted data can possibly suggest.

The geomantic explanation for observed ley lines can be accounted for by at least six different visionary geography features, out of a possible 100+.

First, across the surface of the Earth are 1,746 etheric energy canopies many miles wide and high called domes; most are situated over mountains or volcanoes (see Holy Mountain). The domes are all connected by straight-running energy lines. The English shire of Somerset, for example, has 22 domes.

Picture standing on a hill (Somerset has few mountains) that has a dome over it; everywhere you can clairvoyantly see another dome, the dome under you has a straight energy line going to it. Thus the nexus of 22 domes is interlinked with these leys or, better termed, dome lines, typically ranging in distance from about 10–20 miles to 100 miles. The various domes emit particular (different) patterns of energy to neighboring domes, and the dome lines are pulsating energy lines that oscillate in intensity at various times during the year.

In earlier times, when the system was functioning with more life force and was used regularly by people, initiates could travel rapidly from one dome to the next on the ley line connecting them. It acted like a rapid transport escalator and may correspond to one aspect of the Holy Trails of Navajo legend.

Second, the domes each potentially generate 48 subsidiary energy centers, called dome caps, and these are connected with the "mother" dome by spirallic dome lines arrayed according to the Golden Mean, a principle of geometry, extending for a typical radius of up to 16 miles from the dome center.

Obviously, you will not get straight alignments on curving lines, but you can have a series of aligned sites placed on adjacent spirallic lines and misconstrue these as existing on a single straight-running ley line.

Third, 15 larger ley lines called Oroboros Lines completely encircle the Earth. They are spaced at regular intervals and cross one another in 62 places. Each is the approximate length of Earth's circumference. The Saint Michael's Line is one of these although it completely goes around the planet (its promoters say it only spans England).

This line originates at Avebury in Wiltshire and carries half of the primary umbilical energies entering the planet at its navel, Avebury, from the stars Sirius and Canopus. Obviously, many sacred sites can be arrayed along an Oroboros Line, which typically is four feet to several hundred yards wide. Multiply this by 14 and you begin to see how many sites globally can be made numinous by placement on an Oroboros Line. Paradoxically, these ley lines are both straight (a conceit of short-distance sighting of course) and circular.

Fourth, the Earth has a geomantic feature called an energy funnel, of which there are 2,864,000,224 on the planet. These are straight energy tracks, a bit like an invisible wind tunnel with high walls along which energy flows. Anciently, energy funnels were marked by parallel rows of trees or stones; a typical average distance would be about 500 yards. Some megalithic features, and later, Christian churches, were placed on these energy funnel tracks (part of Earth's original geomantic template), which could accurately be called ley lines.

Fifth, originally, all the Earth's stone circles (1,746) had a double row of stones leading up to them, like a corridor or avenue. Many of the stone rows (originally 1,746) are now gone, as are many of the stone circles, but their original energy tracks and any subsequent megalithic alignments along them remain. So again, these vanished stone rows leading to stone circles can be called ley lines.

Sixth, Earth's entire energy body (the totality of its visionary geography) has a geometrical aspect. All five of the classically defined Platonic Solids (five unique regular polyhedra) are expressed on a global scale. Picture the physical Earth sitting inside a nest of five interpenetrating geometric figures. These figures have 90 edges that cut across the planet's surface. Each of these edges (e.g., the five straight edges of a dodecahedron) can be seen as a ley line.

Overall, these six variations on ley lines create a planetary matrix of light and interconnection. Energies and consciousness flow along them, congruent with Watkins' intuition about the etymology of leys involving light and fire.

The classical Chinese said *qi* or subtle life-force energy (or *prana*) flows along the lung-mei. This life force is vitalizing to physical health and uplifting to consciousness, so walking along a reliable ley line can be beneficial. The Australian Aborigines call such tracks songlines and periodically go Walkabout along particular lines to refresh both the lines and their affiliation with them.

See also: Dreamtime, Holy Mountain, Hurqalya, Zep Tepi.

LUCIFER

A unique angelic being commissioned by the Supreme Being to give humans physical individuality, free will, and full psychic access; he sacrificially allowed himself to "fall" into matter to supervise and be responsible for his commission.

Also known as Azhi Dahaka, Epimetheus, Eros, Fenrir (Fenris) the Wolf, Heosphoros, Iblis, Light-Bearer, Light-Bringer, Loki, Maasauu, Malak Tawus ("Peacock Angel"), Midir, Morning Star, Phanes, Phosphoros, Prometheus, Protogonos, Quetzalcoatl, Raksasas, Ravana, Tezcatlipoca.

Description: According to Jewish tradition, Lucifer was originally God's chief archangel and cherub; on the third day of Creation, he "walked in Eden amid blazing jewels, his body a-fire" with the light of precious stones, all set in pure gold. These jewels included carnelian, topaz, diamond, beryl, onyx, jasper, sapphire, carbuncle, and emerald. God had made Lucifer Guardian of All Nations. He was *Lucem ferre,* from the Latin for "bringer or bearer of light."

Ezekiel says he was the "seal of perfection, full of wisdom and flawless in beauty," and resided as God's highest archangel on God's own mountain.

Similarly, the Greeks knew him as Phosphoros, "he who brings light," or Heosphoros, and saw him as the god of the Morning Star, Venus, depicting him as a naked, winged youth hurrying ahead of his mother, Eos, the Dawn, with a torch.

The biblical account has it that Lucifer's pride got the better of him. He wanted to enthrone himself on Mount Saphon, the Mountain of the North, also called Mount of Assembly or Mount of God, and thereby be God's equal. God wanted Lucifer to serve the newly created humanity, but instead, he organized a revolt of the angels against God's intentions.

Biblical legend says God curtailed Lucifer's ambitions and cast him out of Heaven to the Bottomless Pit of Sheol, along with his fellow rebellious angels. As he fell from grace, he was said to shine like lightning, but was reduced to ashes on impact; only his spirit flutters blindly and ceaselessly in the deep gloom of Sheol. "How art thou fallen from heaven, O Lucifer, son of the morning," wrote Isaiah (14:12).

Explanation: Lucifer is often confused with Satan, as the chief of the demonic, negative hierarchy; equated with Iblis, as king of the fallen Djinn; and identified as Mephistopheles, the sly guru-mentor of the European scholar-mystic Faust. Lucifer's wrongful demonization has obscured our understanding his function.

Humanity has been created twice. For the first creation, known in retrospect, variously, as the Kings of Edom, Djinn, Asura, and Raksasas, Lucifer proposed to the Supreme Being that these souls be given visibility, tangibility, individuality, freedom of will, full psychic access, and the Light, in the form of the Emerald. Hence Lucifer's name as Light-Bringer: He gave humanity the Light, which means full cosmic awareness, celestial consciousness, and self-aware consciousness set in a living, organic body—the fire of wakefulness.

The first attempt to create viable humans with self-aware consciousness and free will ended disastrously and they were removed from the physical world. This removal is known, inaccurately, as the Fall of Man. The humans were placed in between this and the next world where they remain still bound at any of 3,496 geomantic nodes called Lucifer Binding Sites.

The first round of humanity thus entered the Shadow of second-round humanity and was remembered, at best, as troublesome, intimidating, or tempting demons. To some extent, their imprecisely understood presence on the fringes of waking reality contributed largely to the creation of the model of a negative demonic hierarchy.

For the second creation, Lucifer had to pledge himself as surety against possible future excesses like the Djinn had committed. Metaphorically, he had to post a bond, take a lien against his cosmic freedom, and cosign the loan for the second humanity. Part of his essence would be bound into Earth at these sites in conjunction with the already bound Djinn, or first humans created.

Lucifer's gift of freedom to the first humans had led to the excess, destruction, and their withdrawal from physical reality. Limitations were imposed on second humanity's access to the Light, and corresponding limits were installed in the Earth as its energy grid or visionary geography. The Emerald was given to humanity to contain the Light (as a secret, inner aspect of the heart chakra), copies were placed around the Earth; the entire Earth was put inside an Emerald as well and this became part of Lucifer's responsibility.

Just as there were two generations of humanity, there were two Lucifers. The first lives in cultural memory as the demonized scapegoat, the tempter responsible for humanity's fall from grace. But the blame is a wrongful displacement. Various names for the first, demonized Lucifer include Iblis (the Islamic King of the Djinn, a fallen angel who taught humanity the gods' secrets); Epimetheus (the inept brother of Prometheus, responsible for being seduced by Pandora who opened the Box, releasing evil and misery into the world); Tezcatlipoca ("Lord of the Smoking Mirror," evil brother of Quetzalcoatl); and Ravana (ten-headed demon of ancient India who occupied the Celestial City Lanka and who had to be overcome by Rama himself [an incarnation of Vishnu]).

The second Lucifer offers more of his cultural benefactor aspects, though he is punished, in many myths, for defying the gods to help people. Here we see him as Lucifer, the Light-Bringer; Prometheus, the Titan with forethought; Loki and Fenrir the Wolf, Norse trickster father and son, dangerous to the world; and Quetzalcoatl, divinely appointed messenger and helper to humanity.

The combination of both Lucifers is the Tree of the Knowledge of Good and Evil; his profound gift to humanity was to demonstrate this polarity.

Humanity could eventually reclaim the cosmic freedom enjoyed by its forefathers by opening the Emerald, but it will require some time and effort.

The transition from first humanity to second is remembered as the exile from the Garden of Eden. The Garden of Eden represented the original template for an embodied humanity on Earth; the exile from the Garden of Eden represents the condition of the second humanity entering life with limitations. The temptation (symbolized by the Serpent in the Garden) was the life-force energy, or kundalini, and the vast psychic powers it awakened in the chakras. This was confused with Lucifer (and vilified as a duplicitous serpent) because psychic freedom and free will were his gifts to a brand-new physical humanity.

Lucifer embodied and demonstrated the Tree of the Knowledge of Good and Evil. He showed how it is possible to exercise free will to choose good or evil in the context of having self-aware consciousness in a material human form.

Lucifer, originally considered the most glorious appearing and beautiful angel of God's presence, is involved in anything in human life to do with beauty; creative, ascendant thoughts or images; and the illumination of consciousness by the soul with all its wisdom and light (see Guinevere). Lucifer is the beautiful form that the Light (self-awareness) takes, while Christ *is* the Light.

The freedom Lucifer offered to humanity was so awesome and, in retrospect, dangerous, that only small amounts could be made available to humans at a time. As humans interact spiritually with a Lucifer Binding Site, then a little of Lucifer's full ontological essence is released onto the planet and a small amount of humanity's collective Shadow (the Djinn) is redeemed. We are still paying for (and forgiving) the sins (excesses) of our forefathers (the Djinn).

On a subtle level, the entire Earth is within Lucifer's Emerald and thus under his direct oversight even if, paradoxically, he is bound at 3,496 sites. Across the planet, at any given moment, Lucifer is perpetually arriving in glory (see Quetzalcoatl), being bound (as described here), or being unbound (see Prometheus).

The reinvigoration of Earth and humanity through activating the planet's visionary geography will and can only happen simultaneously with the unbinding of Lucifer from the Earth grid and the redemption of humanity's Shadow.

In Judaic lore, Lucifer is the Prince of All the Nations, of which there are 72. These Princes are actually egregors or watcher angels set to guard an entire landmass and its people, such as Eriu for Ireland and Bharata for India. Each of these 72 egregors bears one of the 72 Names of God, known as the *Shemhamforesh,* and inculcates it into the land and its people as a kind of spiritual mark. As Prince of All the Nations, then, Lucifer embodies the *Shemhamforesh* and is the watcher, guardian angel, for the 72 national angels and the Names they hold in trust for him.

Lucifer is also the prime context and container for the Earth's stargate array, which consists of 1,080 portals to stars and 2,200,000 to constellations. When the stargate array was fully operational, it created an exalted, enriched planetary condition remembered in myth as the Land of Milk and Honey.

See also: Azhi Dahaka, Chakravartin, Emerald, Eriu, Fall of Man, Garden of Eden, Grail Maiden, Guinevere, Hanuman, Harmonic Convergence, Land of Milk and Honey, Mephistopheles, Pandora's Box, Peacock Angel, Prometheus, Quetzalcoatl, Ravana, Tree of the Knowledge of Good and Evil.

MANU

A world regent administering for a 360-million-year time span, embodying the Christ as a spiritual progenitor and overseer for a new epoch, known in the Western Mystery Grail tradition as the Rich Fisher King.

Also known as Amen, Ceridwen's Cauldron, Christ Consciousness, Connla's Well, Deucalion, Fintan (Fionntan), Fisher King, Leviathan, *Matsya-avatara*, Nechtan, Noah, Salmon of Wisdom, Taliessin, Ta-tjenen, Well of Coelrind, Well of Nechtan, Well of Segais, Yima, Ziusudra-Utnapishtim.

Description: *Manu* is the Sanskrit name for a succession of divine beings who oversee vast stretches of cosmic and human time. It derives from the Sanskrit root *man*, which means "to think," and is associated with *manas*, the quality of thought in humans, or "the mind." The first of many Manus was Swayambhu ("the self-existent"), who is considered the progenitor of humankind.

Hindu mythology says that the first of Vishnu's ten major incarnations was as a great fish called *Matsya-avatara*. (Vishnu is the Hindu version of the Christ.) This fish warned Manu that a great flood was coming to deluge the world and that he should build the Boat of the Vedas to carry all the teachings of the Vedas, as well as plants, animals, the enlightened sages and rishis, and all seeds of life. The Boat also carried the Sun, Moon, Lokapalas (celestial guardians), the gods Brahma and Vishnu, the holy river Narmada, and other august personages. The fish told Manu that he should expect to remain in the Boat of the Vedas for an entire Night of Brahma.

The great fish towed the Boat of the Vedas across the Flood waters, and to accomplish this task it increased its size so it was finally eight million miles long. The Boat docked at what became known as Manu's Descent, and from there Manu recreated and repopulated the world from the treasures carried in the Boat. Manu Satyavrata became the lord, mentor, and protector of the next round of life.

Manu Satyavrata would reign for one-fourteenth of a Day of Brahma or a *manvantara*, part of a complex time-reckoning system devised by Hinduism, lasting 306,720,000 human years. The reign of 14 Manus would be one Day of Brahma, which lasts 4,320,000,000 human years. Hindu mystics calculated the age of the universe as time units within the vast age or time size of the prime creator, Brahma (the Judaic Ancient of Days; the Christian God).

One Day of Brahma is 4.32 billion years and a Night is the same length, totaling 8.64 billion years for both. One Year of Brahma consists of 360 Days and Nights of Brahma, or 3,110,400,000,000 years. Brahma's entire life span, a *Mahakalpa*, is 100 Years of Brahma, or 311,040,000,000,000 years. Thus the Manu is a time regent for a small segment of Brahma's time size or cosmic life span; in the entire life of Brahma there are 50,400 successive Manus.

Explanation: Manu Satyavrata is a survivor of the Flood and the progenitor of the new world. Various other myths remember this same august figure either simply as Noah, Deucalion, Yima, or Ziusudra-Utnapishtim, or grandly as the Salmon of Wisdom or Rich Fisher King, Lord of the Grail

Castle. Manu, as the regent of a manvantara, is the spiritual "godfather" of an epoch.

The Boat of the Vedas is the Noah's Ark and all the other boats and arks in which the same figure, differently named in different cultures, preserved the spiritual seeds—the cosmic wisdom, knowledge, and techniques of the Vedas, that is, the original teachings of the gods on reality—for the next round of existence.

The seeds of life and the Vedic wisdom teachings are themselves a myth referring to the Christ Consciousness. This consciousness is the profound awareness that encompasses the universe, that pervades (like Vishnu) all of time and space and knows what is happening, when it started, where it's going, and why. In the context of an individual human, what Christ Consciousness is and what the Boat of the Vedas contain is the entire vast sweep of information and wisdom gained by one's soul through all its lifetimes anywhere in the universe.

One name for this repository of vast knowledge of one's soul life is the Grail Castle, and the Rich Fisher King is the awakened soul who remembers. In essence, Manu Satyavrata, as the Vedic Noah, is identical with *Matsya-avatara*, Vishnu (Christ) as the benefactor and eight-million-mile-long fish. During Manu's reign (his manvantara, or his duration as Rich Fisher King), he is one with the fish. You go to him for a taste of the Salmon of Wisdom, as the Irish myths say, and afterward you are ecstatically inspired and poetically visionary.

The Manu sets the tone for an epoch of life and human conscious evolution. He oversees the processes whereby deep memory, that is, immersion in the Christ consciousness, or a taste of the Salmon of Wisdom, will occur. He is Lord of the Grail Castle (helmsman of the Boat of the Vedas) because he supervises—is the fulfillment of—the Quest of the Holy Grail, which is the long-term process of remembering deeply to reassemble all the soul's wisdom across time.

The Manu is extremely long-lived, as reflected in his various names: Utnapishtim means "He Found Life" and Ziusudra means "Long Life."

The Manu exists outwardly as an august spiritual overseer of a manvantara; he exists spiritually and in myth as Lord of the Grail Castle; and he exists microcosmically in each human as the soul in possesion of full memory. The Manu is the seat of deep cosmic memory that straddles the periods of the Flood, known in Hinduism as *Pralaya,* or time of great dissolution, a Night of Brahma.

Creation exists during the Day of Brahma, then all the worlds dissolve during the Night of Brahma. During this Night, all the enlightened sages, the Seven Rishis, the Manus, the minor gods, and Brahma, Vishnu, and Shiva (the major gods), all ascend to a higher sphere to preserve cosmic life and wait for the dawn of the next Day of Brahma. There is also a Deluge after 100 Years of Brahma.

During the time of dissolution between Days and lifetimes of Brahma, the great god temporarily perishes and is subsumed back into the body of Vishnu. The great pervader and preserver, Vishnu, sleeps and dreams atop the cosmic dragon Sesa-Ananta, atop the Deluge waters until the next round of Creation shall start and Brahma is extruded again from his navel to begin another 100 Years of Brahma. Since Vishnu is the Christ Consciousness, however, full immersion in the Grail (the Salmon of Wisdom) and identification with the Manu put one potentially entirely outside of time and creation—a Flood survivor.

See also: Ancient of Days, Bran the Blessed, Fisher King, Flood, Grail Castle, Holy Grail, Salmon of Wisdom, White Mount.

MARDUK

The national egregor for Iraq, but in that nation's ancient formative days of city-states, the tutelary god of Babylon, the umbilicus for the landmass of that country.

Also known as Bel, Merodach.

Description: Originally, Marduk was the

patron and city-god of Babylon in Mesopotamia, the region between the Tigris and Euphrates Rivers in today's Iraq. His name, from the Sumerian *Amar-utuk* or *amar.UD*) seems to mean "bull calf of the Sun," and sometimes he was called simply *Bel,* which meant "Lord." Later in his biography, his stature rose so that his followers claimed for him his descent from the high god Enki.

His primary shrine was the *E-sagil* temple and the *E-temenanki* ziggurat, both at Babylon where he was worshipped amidst wealth and splendor with his wife, Sarpanitu. He was often depicted with his *marru,* a triangular-headed spade or hoe and accompanied by a snake-dragon named *Mushussu.*

In the later inflation of his legend, Marduk was credited with slaying the cosmic dragon Tiamat and precipitating the cosmogony. In honor of his accomplishments, Mesopotamian myth says, the Tower of Babel, the great work of the gods, was awarded to Marduk as his temple and residence in Babylon.

When the city-state Babylon expanded its domain into an empire in the First Dynasty of Babylon under King Hammurabi, Marduk was its national god. Along with Samas, the Sun god, and Ea, Lord of the Sea, Marduk was frequently solicited through incantations by those wishing to avert evil influences.

By the time of the Second Dynasty of Babylon under Isin, Marduk was formally recognized as the "Lord of the Gods," and his influence spread north even into the realm of Assyria where he was greatly honored. The famous Babylonian Creation myth, *Enuma elis,* celebrates Marduk's ascension by listing his 50 names and divine functions as the inimitable subduer of cosmic chaos.

Explanation: The account of Marduk is an excellent example of how a city-god can grow in stature and attributions as the city itself expands its hegemony. Anciently, city-states, like Babylon, had a type of angelic watcher or egregor who presided over their region. This angelic being would be in service to even larger egregors who presided over entire nations, such as the country of Iraq, though at that time it did not formally exist, but did exist energetically (geomantically).

How the local city-god appeared was a negotiation between that angelic being and the various psychics who saw it, or the political or religious leaders who found it advantageous to dress the egregor up with certain potent symbolic expressions. As the city-state of Babylon expanded its region of control, they similarly expanded the hegemony of their tutelary god and correspondingly inflated his image and résumé to cosmic (though inaccurate) proportions.

Marduk, as Babylon's egregor, did not slay the cosmic Tiamat, but he did have an energetic-geomantic relationship with the dragon present at Babylon. One of the original massive gates to the city of Babylon, the Ishtar, was said to have been placed over the slain body of a dragon destroyed by Marduk (Mushussu).

The geomantic reality is that one of the Earth's 1,053 second-level dragons is present at Babylon and the original city founders were sufficiently audacious to establish Babylon right where the dragon dwells. Marduk did not slay the dragon; rather the relationship is that the dragon guards the egregor of the nation, Marduk.

Marduk is also the angelic watcher for all of Iraq, though, as said, it did not then formally recognize itself as a coherent national landmass. However, the clue is the etymology of the word "Babylon": Gateway of the Gods. It derives from the Akkadian *Babilum* and the Sumerian *Bab-ilim* or *Bab-Ilu,* which means "Gate of the Deity" or "Gate of God," from *bab* which means "gate" or "door."

The gate referred to has several legitimate references (see Tower of Babel), but one of them is that Babylon—even though a ruin today—is the Energy Focusing Node or national omphalos for Iraq. Earth has 72 of these world navels in which a specific geomantic node, in conjunction with the country's angelic egregor, grounds the geomantic and spiritual energy for that landmass and its people and has a global energy function as well. This grounding took place, and still does, at the *E-sagil* temple and *E-temenanki* ziggurat in the heart of Babylon.

While it is not too likely that an angelic watcher could be seduced or forced into support for territorial expansion and warfare on behalf of a city-state, it is known that, in ancient times, astute war leaders seeking to conquer new city-states or territories would have their magicians enlist the aid of or simply try to control the egregors or local city-gods who were, in effect, the area's *genius loci.*

The Babylonian leaders instead used the name of their city-god, Marduk, as a rallying cry, banner, and aggressive logo signature of their expansionary goals. In other circumstances, occultists would enlist the aid of demonic servitors to help accomplish their territorial goals or to impede the targeted local egregors.

At a time when nations as we know them today did not yet exist except in energetic outline and preexisting geomantic template, many city-gods were well known: Zababa of Kis in northern Babylonia, honored at the temple *E-mete-ursag;* Sara, local god of the Sumerian city Umma, whose temple was *E-mah;* Assur, tutelary god of Assur, later expanded to encompass all of Assyria; Baal-Addir of Byblos; Baal-Biq'ah of Baalbek in today's Lebanon; and Elagabal of Emesa in Syria.

See also: Dragon, Eriu, Floating Bridge of Heaven, Huitzilopochtli, Navel of the World, Tower of Babel.

MEDUSA

An expression of the crown chakra at the galactic level, whose millions of light currents or "beautiful hair" thread through the Stone of space.

Also known as Gorgo, Gorgon.

Description: In Greek myth, Medusa was one of the three Gorgons (the other two were Stheno, meaning "Strength," and Euryale, meaning "Wide-Leaping") who were daughters of Phorcys and Ceto. Of the three, Medusa ("Ruler" or "Queen") was mortal. Phorcys was an ancient Sea god, son of Gaia (the Earth) and Pontus (the Sea itself); Ceto was his sister, and her name was generic for any kind of large sea-monster. Medusa was believed to have been the lover of Poseidon, the Lord of the Sea and brother to Zeus, the High God.

The Gorgons lived in the far West of the world, beyond human habitation, even beyond Oceanus, the cosmic river that encircled the world, or perhaps on the shore of Oceanus's stream. They were fearsome because of their awesome ugliness: Their heads were entwined with snakes rather than hair; their necks were adorned with dragon scales; out of their faces protruded huge boarlike tusks; their grins were huge and gaping; their hands were bronze, their noses snub, their faces bearded, and they had mare's hindquarters and golden wings.

Their most dangerous, even lethal, aspect, however, was their gaze: The merest glance turned people permanently to stone.

Medusa was a terror to the Greek world, until finally the immortal hero Perseus managed to slay her. Two Olympian gods, Athena and Hermes, aided Perseus: He was equipped with a shoulder bag called a *kibisis;* Hades' Helmet, which rendered him invisible; winged sandals; and the *harpe,* an invincible sickle.

Perseus accosted Medusa while she was asleep. He hovered in the air above her (thanks to his winged sandals) while Athena held up a shield of polished bronze that acted like a mirror to ward off Medusa's deadly gaze. Perseus looked at Medusa only through her mirror reflection and was safe. Then Perseus decapitated the monster. From her neck sprang Pegasus, the winged horse, and a giant named Chrysaor. Perseus put the severed head in his kibisis, and Hades' Helmet protected him from reprisals from the other two angry Gorgons.

Later, Athena affixed Medusa's head to her

shield, enabling her to turn her enemies instantly to stone. This became known as the Gorgoneion, and was later copied by numerous mortal Greek soldiers to terrify their opponents. But the Greeks also said Athena buried Medusa's head under Athen's marketplace.

As for Perseus, he learned that Medusa's blood had magical properties. That which flowed from the left vein of her head was poisonous, but the blood from the right could restore the dead to life. A single lock of Medusa's hair (the mythographers are not clear if this means a single snake or actually hair) held up before an attacking army could deflect their onslaught.

Originally, the Gorgons, and especially Medusa, who tended to represent the group and is best remembered in Greek myth, were seen as pre-Olympian monsters. Later, Medusa's story metamorphosed and she was said to have once been a beautiful girl who compared her beauty (especially her lustrous hair) with that of the Olympian goddess Pallas Athena. Piqued and jealous, Athena transformed Medusa's locks into a nest of snarling snakes and made her ugly.

Explanation: Comprehending the reality of Medusa (or even a portion of it) is a Mystery initiation sponsored and supervised by Pallas Athena, one of the 14 Ray Masters of Ursa Major (see Seven Rishis), a specialized group of highly evolved celestial beings within the Great White Brotherhood. Perseus, in the story, is the representative human initiate undergoing the Medusa revelation.

It is a complicated myth that must be explicated in layers. Gaia refers here not to the Spirit of Earth (our planet) but to all of cosmic space as part of the original dichotomy of creation, namely, Heaven (Ouranos) and Earth (Ge, Gaia). Specifically, Gaia means the space bounded by the Milky Way Galaxy, but before it was filled with its billions of stars. (It also means all of universal space, filled with galaxies, but that is too big a frame of reference for this explication.)

Poseidon, Phorcys, Pontus, and Oceanus are all aspects of the same level of reality, namely, the Sea of Consciousness encompassing and enveloping all of created space (Gaia), filling it, metaphorically, like a cosmic sea of awareness.

The Gorgons are not three separate beings, but rather one cosmic spirit with three faces or gazes—two are focused on and in the Absolute, that state before and beyond the created realm; one is focused inside the mortal world. Medusa is described as shockingly ugly and scary as a stay-away defense for the unprepared. Often, initiates, in conjunction with their initiators (such as Pallas Athena, of the Great White Brotherhood), deliberately distorted the reality of an experience so as to keep away the dilettantes for the latters' own cognitive safety.

In truth, Gorgon Medusa is not ugly, deformed, or monstrous. As the alternate Greek version of her suggested, she was (and is) beautiful and her hair is her most conspicuous feature. Her hair is not a mass of snarling snakes, yet as a metaphor that is apt. Medusa's hair is a complex array of streaming currents.

Perhaps the easiest way to approach this Mystery is to say that Medusa is an outer, cosmic picture of the human crown chakra, the *Sahasraha,* said to have a thousand petals, or interlacing vibratory fields, much like a thousand flickering flames or writhing snakes. The movement suggested refers to the fluidity of consciousness at its higher level of expression, that closest to the Supreme Being.

To clairvoyant perception, the human crown chakra (on top of the head) looks like a bright mound of living molten gold that is also a furnace at high heat. This ever-burning mound of gold brightens the thousand petals around it. As the crown chakra is the point of human connection with God, when there is communication from God, it—the message, the "hello," or sound—comes down to the crown through a kind of hollow tube or golden axle and diffracts into a thousand echoes that form (and enliven) the crown's petals, flames, or spikes.

On the galactic level, Medusa is a crown chakra within the galaxy's hierarchy of energy and consciousness. This function is grounded at the galactic level through the star Algol (Beta Perseus) within the Perseus constellation. The ancient star mythographers depicted Algol as Medusa's severed head in Perseus's extended hand. Algol is also known as the Demon Star, Blinking Demon, and *Ra's al Ghul*, the "Demon's Head," as well as *Gorgonea prima, Gorgoneum Caput, Caput Larvae* ("Spectre's Head"), *Rosh ha Satan* ("Satan's Head"), and Medusa's Head.

Within the ecology of consciousness of the galaxy, individual stars typically have global effects, affecting all the other stars and the entire galaxy. Medusa's head is a crown chakra at the center or core of the galaxy that radiates out millions of golden streamers or rivulets (or writhing serpents or beautiful strands of hair) through the galactic interior, touching all of space in this way.

On a galactic level, Perseus introduces the flaming, light-irradiating head of Medusa to the vast starfields and all the great Star-Angels. Medusa's head, at another level, is an expression of the severed head of the Supreme Being, memorialized in at least six different myths around the world, as, for example, Brahma's fifth head, cut off by Shiva and planted at Banaras, India. The radiant severed head is a potent expression of the Supreme Being's gaze into the galaxy.

Medusa's gaze does not turn living creatures into stone. Rather, her rivulets or streamers form a vast capillary network through the Stone of Space. This is an old term to denote the density, though it's subtle, of etheric space. All of galactic space, originally, before the stars appeared in it, was a dense Stone, that is, its content, though seemingly empty, was slightly denser than pure Light. The Stone of Space means *prima materia*, the original raw matter of creation, the inchoate Stone that would one day become the Philosopher's Stone, a Light Body.

It sounds foreign to common sense today to think of the etheric realm as a stone, but ancient Polynesian belief, for example, held that before the Earth and Sky were fully separated, the "sky of blue rock" pressed down close to Earth and humanity and it was covered in sharp nobbles like a rough stone. *Haehae* is the gateway in the hard blue rock of the sky through which the Sun emerges.

Medusa's hair threads the galaxy like veins of a precious metal vein a stone. Picture a million strands of hair, some in parallel rows of a dozen strands, rippling through galactic space like fronds, crisscrossing, interweaving space. Her beautiful hair or light and sound currents thread through all of the galaxy.

Similarly, the currents or hair threads of the human crown chakra infiltrate the seven layers of the human aura or energy field (sometimes called an egg), the 81 chakras (72 minor and 9 major, with the heart having three), and the body.

Medusa's snakey hair infiltrates all of the galaxy's Stone of Space like a million *nadis*, the subtle quasi-nerve networks of the human energy system. Nothing is turned to stone; rather, the stone is irradiated, nurtured, enriched, with the celestial light and communication of the Supreme Being as received through the galactic crown chakra at Medusa-Algol. Just as the human crown chakra can be in constant communication with the Supreme Being for the edification of the human and the health of its spirit and body, so can the galaxy, through its crown chakra at Medusa-Algol, be in constant interchange with God.

The Mystery revelation that Pallas Athena offers humans (and which Perseus, as a representative, underwent) is to experience this alignment of human and galactic crown chakras. Even more sublime is *whose* crown chakra it is on the galactic level. Judaic lore calls this galactic composite being Adam Kadmon, and they say it is God's perfect idea of existence expressed as a cosmic Human form. Various myths describe this being as Ymir, Purusha, and Gayomart, among others.

There is a third level to this alignment: all the

expressions in Earth's visionary geography that correspond to a crown chakra function. All Light temple structures have a hierarchy of energy, that is, a series of seven energy-consciousness levels, or chakras, and thus a crown chakra. Landscape zodiacs (see White Cow, White Sow) have crown chakras through their composite expression called Albion (see Albion, Purusha, Ymir), who is the hologram of Adam Kadmon expressed on a planetary level. The planetary body itself has a series of Earth chakras within the singular expression of Albion, and 12 more subsidiary ones (still in addition to the ones in landscape zodiacs—see Forest of Bliss).

Thus everywhere on Earth where you touch upon the crown chakra level of a geomantic system, holographically, you are holding Medusa's head.

See also: Albion, Forest of Bliss, Philosopher's Stone, Purusha, Seven Rishis, White Cow, White Sow, Ymir.

MENEHUNE

The Polynesian perception of earth elementals, Nature spirits known in European folklore as gnomes and charged with maintaining the interplay between Earth's electromagnetic field and its geomantic terrain.

Also known as Patu-pai-arehe.

Description: In Polynesian myth, the Menehune are the Little Folk of the land, much like the gnomes of European folklore. Typically, they stand two to three feet tall and are sometimes called pygmies; they are thickset, strong, stocky, sometimes bowlegged, with deep voices, said to have ugly red faces and markedly distended abdomens. They prefer living in caves, and their ancient trails along the cliffs of Kauai are still visible; playful and mischievous, they enjoy cooked taro leaves and squash, music, revelry, and various amusing sports.

The Menehune are divided into different tribes, each with kings, and they are known to aid humans when approached correctly. This includes feeding them or rewarding them properly for tasks performed. They are regaled as master craftsmen and expert builders, and their services were once always in demand.

Some of these tasks include building waterways, dams, canoes, fishponds, sacred stone temple structures called *heiau,* and other stonework, and these massive jobs are often completed in a single night. In fact, they are known to work only during the night, often unseen by humans, dispersing to their own subtle realm at the first trace of morning sunlight.

The Menehune are described as forest dwellers who are like little human men and women, though much stronger than people. One contemporary traveler (specifically to the rain forest surrounding volcanic Mount Kilauea on Hawaii) said they look like miniature Hawaiians in native dress; in his experience, they were friendly and frolicking, but would not leave the lush vegetation to cross the open lava floor of the Kilauea crater.

Polynesians are not certain about the origin of the Menehune, and sometimes they suggest that the Little People were the first *kama'aina,* or native-born, of the land, that they were the original or former inhabitants of the Polynesian islands. Many Hawaiian families at one time proudly counted the Menehune as their ancestral spirits and helpers and looked on the Menehune as benevolent godparents to their families. The father of all Menehune is called Lua-nu'u.

Polynesian legends hint at the regular migrations of the Menehune. Once they were on *Ka-aina-i-ka-houpo-a-Kane* ("Fat Land of Kane," the Polynesian high god), understood to be the original Pacific continent that once connected all the island groups before it was inundated—the fabled, sunken land of Lemuria. Legends speak of the Menehune coming to Oahu in Hawaii, led by Ku-leo-nui ("Ku Loud Voice"), whose voice was so loud it was heard all over Oahu summoning the Menehune to start working.

Another tale has them migrating to New

Zealand under the leadership of Maoli-ku-laiakea. Later they migrate to Kauai to work as builders and craftsmen. At one time, their population was estimated at half a million; over time, their numbers dwindled as they went into hiding or otherwise disappeared or migrated to the more remote Hawaiian islands Nihau and Necker. Hawaiian lore says they lived in the Lanihuli valley for some time, then were forced to migrate because the male Menehune were intermarrying with the human Hawaiians.

Most of the Hawaiian islands have heiau said to have been built by the Menehune. They built a sacred stone enclosure on a cliff on Molokai that no human has ever been able to reach and another heiau at Pakui dedicated to Hina; on Maui, the Menehune built the Pihana heiau at Wailuku in a single night; also on Maui, the Hale-o-kane and Pu'u-kini heiau are credited to the Menehune. On Kauai, they are credited with building the Alekoko Fishpond (for raising mullet) near Nawiliwili Harbor outside Lihue for a Kauai prince.

Scholars say the Menehune are equivalent to the *Patu-pai-arehe,* a wild race of mountain spirits, according to Maori legend in New Zealand. They have reddish skin with a golden tinge to their hair, and black or blue eyes. Typically, they work only during the night, can sometimes be seen early in the morning, wear white, are very numerous, peaceful, merry, and cheerful, sing like crickets, and play bone flutes. They are guardians of the Maori sacred sites called *wahi tapu.*

Folklorists remain unsure as to the identity of the Menehune. Some say they were a once short-stature human slave race of the Tahitians; others say they are the Polynesian version of the Irish leprechauns or European gnomes.

Explanation: The Menehune are a combination of what European fairy lore calls gnomes and brownies. The gnomes are the Nature spirits or elementals who maintain the integrity of the earth element on the planet; the brownies assist them. Typically, European gnomes are three to four feet tall, stocky, bearded, and jovial, and the brownies are similar, though about half the height. As Nature spirits, they have no ultimate or true form, but copy the prevailing forms of the land.

In the case of the Menehune, their negotiated form derives from millions of years ago when Ka-aina-i-ka-houpo-a-Kane (Lemuria) flourished, at which time the Menehune were much more visible than in later millennia. They were not physical or palpable in our modern sense, but their material composition was easier to see effortlessly because, in general, the Lemurians were far more naturally psychic than people today or even Europeans several centuries ago to whom the perception of Nature spirits and fairies was possible.

With the demise of Lemuria, the Menehune were dispatched to the remaining land fragments (the hundreds of islands from Polynesia to Hawaii), some of which, through volcanism, were still forming and settling. The Menehune did not build the stone temples and other works credited to them. Rather, through their knowledge of the microlandscape and its diversely flowing magnetic currents, wells, and troughs, they instructed the human builders as to the best locations and most durable architectural forms to use for those places.

They were, strictly speaking, the first kama'aina (native-born) in all of Polynesia (and all other Earth landmasses too) because it was their job to create the land bridges connecting the landscape to the energy fields informing it. They would work closely with the sensitives among the Polynesians, pointing out suitable locations for heiau, fishponds, waterways, and the rest, and preparing the spaces energetically from their side of the physical-etheric worlds divide.

Their function is to maintain the earth element on the planet, all things to do with solidity, density, minerals, crystals, rocks, and, generally, Earth's interior. They also maintain the differential (they call it "the splice") between Earth's electromagnetic field and its gradients and the visionary geography.

The Menehune were not forced to migrate and did not come to dislike the Hawaiians, as the legends suggest. Rather, with the global densification of human consciousness in recent millennia, they stopped being recognized or acknowledged by human society and stopped being included in human plans.

Conversely, the meaning of feeding the Menehune as a reward for good work refers to the God-mandated responsibility of humans to transduce and channel celestial and angelic energies and consciousness into the world of all Nature spirits. This is a form of high nourishment for the Menehune and others. Celestial and angelic energies are too strong for the Menehune, indigestible, and must be filtered through focused human attention into an assimilable form.

The reinstitution of these human-Menehune "feeding" rituals would bring their reality and presence back into human perception and interaction. This is of more than folklore curiosity: The regular exchange of energies between humans and the Menehune (all Nature spirits) is essential to planetary health.

The Menehune do prefer the rain forests and mountains over the volcanoes if these are still active or only recently dormant. Lava floors of volcanic craters, such as at Mount Kilauea, are still too unsettled, uncongealed, and unstable for the Menehune to feel comfortable. Lava straddles the domain of two groups of Nature spirits: the salamanders, or fire elementals, and gnomes, earth elementals, and here "earth" should be understood to mean solidity, density, hard rocks.

On Mount Temehani, for example, a sacred mountain on the sacred island of Raiatea, said to be the holiest of the Tahitian group, you may see even today many hundreds of Menehune teeming about the slopes, coming and going from a geomantic feature called a Gnome Egg (see Royal Hall of the King of the Dovrë Trolls) situated halfway up the rain-forested slope. The Gnome Egg is a regional headquarters for the Menehune, with access into the etheric depths of the Earth.

See also: Gaia, Holy Mountain, Kokopelli, Nymph, Pan, Royal Hall of the King of the Dovrë Trolls, Trolls.

MEPHISTOPHELES

A slow-motion expression of the Antichrist who seduces humans for their knowledge (soul) and cognitive-psychic freedom.

Also known as the Devil, guru-being.

Description: Mephistopheles is a relatively modern expression of the Western conception of the Devil, having arisen as a folk myth in the sixteenth century.

The story is told by many, including Christopher Marlowe (1564–1593), Shakespeare's contemporary, in *The Tragical History of the Life and Death of Doctor Faustus* (1588), and, most famously, by Johann Wolfgang Goethe (1749–1832), in his celebrated *Faust* (1808). Even Thomas Mann (1875–1955) tried his hand at the legend in his *Doctor Faustus* (1947).

The plot is simple and archetypal: Faust, a frustrated scholar, sells his soul to the Devil in exchange for wisdom, illumination, power, and access to the Mysteries. In some versions, he abandons philosophy or religion as unproductive dead ends and deliberately takes up magic and its protocols to get his answers, invoking infernal spirits, sometimes by name, such as Beelzebub. Goethe's Faust gets Mephistopheles in response to his petitions.

The etymology of Mephistopheles is uncertain, but if it comes from the Greek then its elements are revealing, for *me* means "not," *phos* or *photos* means "light," and *philos,* "lover." Thus the name means "The lover of not light," or "He who is not a lover of light"—in effect, a parodic opposite of Lucifer, "Light-Bearer," to whom Mephistopheles is sometimes compared or equated. Other derivations are suggestive: The Latin *mephitis* means "pungent, sulfurous, stinking," and the Hebrew *tophel* means "liar," hence "the stinking liar."

Faust's weakness is pride; he wants knowledge without effort or grace. Mephistopheles, in

Marlowe's version, uses flattery, false promises, and threats to gain the upper hand in the bargaining before Faust realizes his spiritual peril.

In Goethe's version, Mephistopheles is ambivalent, elusive in nature; sometimes he seems to be Satan himself, other times a mere minion of the Devil; a few times, he is a black poodle, a traditional guise of the Western Devil. Faust despairs that he will ever crack the occult mysteries. Mephistopheles offers him a lift up into the occult in exchange for his allegiance (his soul).

This is the deal and contract: If Faust will take Mephistopheles as his mate, pledge himself to his command, go through his life with him, and, after death, stand up for him in the beyond, then Mephistopheles will be his steadfast comrade and slave during this life. Mephistopheles, of course, is duplicitous, for, intent on the scholar's destruction, he lures Faust further into matter rather than the occult, specifically into lust, fornication, and the dark side of sensuality. This leads to the ruin and death of an innocent young woman, and Faust's guilt.

Faust does not understand he has summoned the Devil or, at least, he doesn't appreciate the spiritual danger in which he has put himself. Mephistopheles is sly and urbane, knowledgeable and cynical, helpful and devious, subtle and treacherous; he says that, while he is not all-knowing, much is known to him.

In Goethe's version, Faust is redeemed from the Devil's clutches and the soul contract voided because he learns love. At the end of *Faust, Part Two,* which Goethe completed shortly before his death, angels bear Faust to Heaven.

Explanation: Mephistopheles is a cleverly disguised spirit being, conveniently mistaken for the Devil for many centuries in the West. He is far smarter and subtler than the common ranks of devils (astral demonic beings), and because very few in the West have discerned his true nature or spoken about it openly, he (and his colleagues) have continued to flourish in the world, seducing then collecting human souls by contract, just as the legends and plays show.

The category of spirit being that is Mephistopheles is called a guru-being. Clairvoyants trained in the systematic protocols of cleansing pollution, residue, and obstacles from a person's auric layers, chakras, and karmic bodies attest that such beings are fairly commonly found attached to human men and women.

In conventional understanding, a guru (from Indian culture) is an illumined human who, as a teacher, dispels the darkness of ignorance among people. To have a guru, in Indian culture, is traditionally considered a necessity and a blessing in the spiritual path to enlightenment and release from suffering.

Much of that benevolent assumption about gurus was translated successfully to the West, notably the United States, in the late nineteenth century with the arrival of the "swans" (gurus) from the East. During the twentieth century, many gurus came to the West and gained followers, sometimes numbering in the millions.

Here is where selling your soul to the Devil comes in: The guru, a physically embodied man or woman with a numinous aura, promises to take away your pain, despair, misery, suffering, or ignorance if you join his or her cult, movement, church, or ashram, and take an initiation into that spiritual fold.

What is never told the aspiring, trusting student (traditionally called the *chela*) is that the guru inserts a cord of dark light into the student's crown chakra, sinks it all the way through the chakra column to the root center in the groin, and allows it to branch out throughout the body's energy field to anchor into points. Any possibility of developing independent clairvoyance (through the sixth and seventh consciousness centers, or chakras) is gone until the contract is voided.

After death and in one's next life, the contract remains in place, still there, in the new body and its energy field, and it will remain so—and does, often for centuries and many lives—until removed by canceling the contract. The saying "selling your soul to the Devil" means that the soul, which survives physical death, bears the consequences of that contract into its future lives.

Goethe hinted that such contracts can be undone (through love); according to trained clairvoyants, the soul is freed by canceling a series of agreements one has made in past lives with the guru-being and accepting the unresolved pain that led to the making of the contracts and the signing of the agreements initially. Even if the decision to cancel the contract is made 500 years later, the agreements are still viable with the original cording guru-being from 500 years ago, regardless of how many subsequent incarnations (if any) that human guru may have had.

Human embodied teachers presenting themselves as gurus are themselves corded similarly by much larger astral beings. The Earth-based gurus act as scouts or recruiters for the vaster, more ambitious astral beings so that potentially millions of human souls are corded (pledged) to a single astral guru-being.

Periodically, perhaps every 300 years or so, the information and knowledge gained by the human souls pledged to a guru are collected by the guru-being, leaving the humans in their current lives like an empty husk. While it seemed the guru would provide riches of knowledge, the reverse is true and he really is the "stinking liar" that the name Mephistopheles suggests: The guru sucks out all the human-retrieved knowledge for himself. In return, the human gets the sensation of being loved, looked after, and protected, like passive sheep or young children.

Many people want and love their attachments to guru-beings. In many respects, it is a natural part of the long-term, multi-lifetime spiritual maturation process all humans go through. But it does have a fine-print clause, which is never referred to when the soul contract is being negotiated; almost nowhere in Western metaphysical traditions is any reliable information about this available, especially since the mechanism in our cultural framework is cleverly disguised as working with the Devil.

You think you are immune to demonic influences because you don't dabble in magic or consort with the Devil in any conscious way, yet the great con is that the guru-beings and their agents or scouts usually work through spirituality to make their contracts with people. It's usually the last place a person would expect to be manipulated.

From the viewpoint of human spiritual and cognitive freedom, the full and free use of the higher psychic faculties, and the ability to know on your own, the Mephistophelean contract with the guru-being pledges you to a slow-motion version of the Antichrist. It makes it harder for people to participate in birthing the Christ Child (the second birth: Christ Consciousness, by definition, is antithetical and yet transcendent to guru-consciousness) and contributing to the healing of the Earth, which requires unfettered, freely willed clairvoyance.

Guru-being attachment also makes it difficult for a person to establish a direct, clear link with the Supreme Being through the crown chakra, especially as the guru-beings, at the astral and, to us, subliminal, level, prefer one to regard them as gods, or even in competition with God, even though they are false gods.

Guru-being attachment has ramifications in Earth's visionary geography as well. In some geomantically charged places, such as Sedona, Arizona, the guru-beings can create (and have) an artificial energy overlay (or obstructive filter) on the natural geomantic features. These may appear to clairvoyant vision as guru-heads, statuesque godlike images sprouting like large, cranium-topped mushrooms in the psychic landscape.

This array interferes with the mandated circulation of authentic spiritual consciousness through the geomantic terrain and, like pathogenic bacteria in the intestines, creates favorable conditions for unwholesome opportunistic beings to gain a foothold in that terrain and amplify the general level of psychic distortion.

Ironically, guru-being attachment actually supports the Antichrist. Although on the personality level, it seems a guru is a useful spiritual guide, on a soul level, a guru suppresses one's authentic cognitive freedom (use of the crown chakra) and thus the ability to know on one's own, to have Christ Consciousness.

See also: Antichrist, Grail Knight, Klingsor, Lucifer.

MERLIN

A shape-shifting celestial benefactor, angelic colleague, and high magus who has aided Earth and humanity many times in different guises.

Also known as Cuchulainn, Enchanter of Britain, Herakles, John the Evangelist, Lailoken, Llallogan, Maui, Merlinus, Monster-Slayer, Myrddin, Myrddin Wyllt, Padmasambhava, Saint Columba (ColumCille), Suibhne Geilt, Zal.

Description: Merlin is best known for his role in the Celtic Arthurian saga as the young King Arthur's mentor in the formation of Camalate. He is portrayed as an enigmatic wizard and magus, much older than Arthur, perpetually involved in arcane plots and stratagems on behalf of all of Britain in a time of chaos and political instability. Merlin orchestrates Arthur's accession to the throne of England through the Sword in the Stone kingship test.

Merlin's parentage is both murky and bizarre: His father was the Devil or an incubus (a malevolent male spirit), so the folk legends say, and his wife a mortal woman, possibly a nun. He was a child prodigy, at a very early age advising kings on the placement of castles and the existence of interfering dragons. As an adult, he orchestrated the conception, birth, and training of the young Arthur. He is credited with devising or procuring the fabled Round Table, which, he explained, was an image of the cosmos; he is further credited, by some, with having moved Stonehenge from Ireland to Salisbury Plain, England.

Peculiar things were said of Merlin: He was caretaker of the 13 Treasures of Britain; he lived in a glass house on the Welsh island of Bardsey; he would frequently disappear up a tree or vanish suddenly and magically through his *eplumoir* (as the medieval French chroniclers called it, a term suggesting a molting cage or perch); he was the Enchanter of Britain, the chief magus of the land; in Welsh legend, the first of three ancient names for the Island of Britain was *Clas Merdin,* "Myrddin's Precinct," signifying that, for a time, the entirety of Britain was named after him.

In Merlin's Welsh version, as Myrddin Wyllt, and his Scottish, as Suibhne Geillt, he is a prophet who goes mad after witnessing a disastrous military defeat and, deranged, retreats to the wild forests where he avoids human contact and converses with the animals.

The legend says Merlin was seduced in his old age by a young priestess named Viviane (also called Vivienne or Nimuë, an apprentice to the Lady of the Lake). She took his occult knowledge, then sealed him almost permanently in a cave, oak tree, or stone chamber. The spell holding him fast could only be broken by the future, prophesied return of King Arthur. The legend also says Merlin periodically met with his mentor and "master," a man named Blaise, who wrote down the adventures of King Arthur's Round Table at Merlin's dictation.

Explanation: Merlin is a unique being who periodically takes embodiment in the human evolutionary stream to assist at crucial moments. The angelic hierarchy refers to him as a Grand Square Master, a highly accomplished adept, and one family particularly, the Ofanim, reports they have worked with Merlin in his various guises throughout his cultural incarnations.

Among Merlin's noteworthy guises: Maui, the demigod of Polynesia, after whom the island in Hawaii was named; Cuchulainn, the Hound of Culann, a warrior-prodigy of ancient Ulster County in Ireland; Padmasambhava, the Indian sage who brought Buddhism to Tibet and prepared that land to receive it; John the Evangelist, who wrote

Revelation on Patmos (exhibiting Merlin's prophetic [clairvoyant] qualities, as alluded to in his Welsh and Scottish guises); Herakles (Hercules), the archetypal Greek hero of the 12 Labors fame; Saint Columba, the medieval saint of the holy island of Iona in western Scotland; and the Navajo Earth-Shaper, Monster-Slayer, who rid the American Southwest of "monsters."

Merlin's parentage, half-human, half-demonic, is a distorted clue to his identity. He is a celestial being who enters the human stream on occasion, requiring a human mother; the demonic father reference is typical of Christian pejoratives in which undesirable celestial energies and beings were demonized.

Britain, before it was inhabited by humans, was called Myrddin's Precinct because from Atlantis, the lost continent in the Atlantic Ocean, he energized Britain and its geomantic Light temples. In fact, in several of his cultural guises, Merlin is shown taming, working, or preparing large landmasses, in some cases fishing up islands from under the ocean (as Maui), driving out the autochthonous "devils" from Tibet to cleanse it for Buddhism, or overcoming awesome obstacles, creatures, and monsters in his 12 Labors as Herakles at Mycenae.

In his prodigious terraforming work, Merlin was also instrumental in binding Lucifer to the Lucifer Binding Sites, yet also selectively unbinding him. You can see this in his guise of Herakles who unchained Prometheus (Lucifer).

The claim that he moved Stonehenge from Ireland to Britain, though laughed at by historians, is actually correct, though he had the transportation assistance of the Ofanim.

The 13 Treasures of Britain that he cared for were actually manifestations of his adeptship, what we would conventionally call magical powers, like external representations of his consciousness. The *eplumoir* he disappeared through is a geomantic feature called a Shambhala Doorway, a portal through the Earth's visionary geography to the etheric City of Light in Mongolia.

His dalliance and disastrous seduction by young Nimuë is a distortion. Nimuë is another name for the Lady of the Lake, guardian of the astral world and its nine spheres of Light. Merlin, as an adept, was a regular visitor in that realm; on occasion, he spent time in certain astral paradises as a kind of adept's vacation.

Merlin's relationship with his master, Blaise, is revealing. Blaise is not a single man, but rather an entire angelic order called the Ofanim intimately and perpetually involved in Earth's visionary geography. In one of the Ofanim's more conspicuous cultural manifestations, as the Hindu elephant god and scribe Ganesh, they were credited with having written the vast epic the *Mahabharata*.

Related to this is the fact that Merlin helped to create the Qabala as we know it today, long before it came into the custodianship of the Judaic tradition; as such, Merlin was very familiar with the different spheres of light, energy, and consciousness that system describes and its alluring paradisal realms.

It was not only Arthur whose birth Merlin orchestrated. He was known as the Star Worker, for he planned the astrological configurations of numerous Grail Knights and candidates for adeptship through his "Arthurian" incarnations.

Insofar as there have been 15 embodied King Arthurs thus far in Earth history, though under different names (see Fionn MacCumhaill, Gesar of Ling, Rustam) and cultures (Irish, Mongolian, Persian), in each there was also a Merlin figure. For Rustam, it was his father, Zal; for Gesar of Ling, Padmasambhava.

Merlin has a special relationship with the heavenly hierarchy, which is discernible in his Greek name, Herakles, which means "Glory of Hera." Hera is the consort of Zeus, king of the Olympian gods; he is the executive aspect of the Supreme Being, so Hera in effect is Mrs. God, the Supreme Being's female aspect, also known as the Great Mother of the World or the Divine Mother.

His Celtic name also encodes this relationship, though less obviously. Merlin is actually the

Mer-Line, the line of consciousness from Earth to Her. Merlin is the line to the sea *(Mer)* of consciousness, the love of the Great Mother. That sea is the unconscious or the greater consciousness available to humans. Merlin is the umbilicus for all to the Great Mother and Her love and caring.

See also: Camalate, Fionn MacCumhaill, Ganesh, Gesar of Ling, King Arthur, Lady of the Lake, Land of Milk and Honey, Lucifer, Monster-Slayer, Round Table, Rustam, Shambhala, Sword in the Stone.

MICHAELMAS

An annual festival of cleansing and a mass for Earth conducted by the Archangel Michael through Earth's many sacred sites.

Also known as Autumn Festival, Feast of Saint Michael and All Angels, Michael Festival.

Description: Michaelmas is a spiritual festival day dedicated to the Archangel Michael and, in Christian observance, to Saint Michael, on September 29. It is barely known in the United States, outside of Waldorf Schools, though it is still remembered and sometimes celebrated in Europe, especially in Anthroposophical circles inspired by the Austrian clairvoyant Rudolf Steiner.

In medieval times, the celebration of Michaelmas was widespread throughout Europe, though increasingly it gained a secular connotation. For a time it was a great religious feast day commemorating Archangel Michael (or his contraction by the Catholic Church into a postulated human Saint Michael), then later a popular festival day coinciding with the fall harvests in most countries.

In England, it was customary to eat a roast goose on Michaelmas to protect one against financial need for the next year. Also in England, Michaelmas was one of the year's Quarter Days (in the year's fourfold division) and the time for rent payments and the start or closing of contracts and hiring engagements. In Ireland, if you found a ring in your Michaelmas pie, you would soon get married; special cakes called *struan Micheil* were baked from all the cereals grown on the farms.

The Archangel Michael, whose name means "He Who Is Like unto God," was often depicted as the leader of the angelic hosts and as slaying dragons with his mighty sword. Numerous churches were dedicated to him in Europe, often based on reports by individuals of having witnessed the Archangel at that spot. Michael has also been portrayed as the Prince of Light and Captain of the Heavenly Hosts, leading the angelic legions against the demonic realm (often signified by the dragon or serpent) and their continual assault on the human soul.

Explanation: As with Candlemas and Christmas, this word's correct spelling or pronunciation is not observed and hence its spiritual significance is distorted. The correct spelling as *Michaelmass* indicates its meaning, as a Mass consecrated by the Archangel Michael in conjunction with the angelic orders and participating humanity on behalf of Earth, its Spirit, Gaia, and its sacred sites.

Michaelmas is one of a series within an annual geomantic liturgical calendar in which angelic and hierarchical hosts interface with Earth and humanity. Other events in this cycle include the Wild Hunt on December 20, Epiphany on January 6, and Candlemas on February 1 (see entries for each).

In the case of Michaelmas, it is a mass for the Earth consecrated by Archangel Michael and it is also a mass for Michael presented by the angelic hosts. The date was chosen by the Archangel Michael and it pertains to the Moon. On this date, the Moon is farthest from the Earth in the yearly cycle. The energy of all living organic matter, including humans, responds to this change and alters its nature at this point. The energy matrix of Earth (the Earth grid or Light body) also changes its polarity due to this phenomenon around this time.

On September 29, throughout the day, but

peaking at noon, the Archangel Michael blesses Earth with his sword to cleanse and shift planetary energy. He connects his sword with the major ley lines around the Earth (see Ley Lines) and flushes them like a plumbing network with light to remove negativities and blockages (the demonic host, as folklore has it) that have accumulated in the preceding 12 months. In earlier times, men and women would congregate at sacred sites (portals into the Earth's Light body or grid) and participate in Michael's planetary cleansing event.

It is important to note that since 1879, the Archangel Michael has been the chief of all 18 archangels, in a regency that will last 268 years. Under normal circumstances, when Michael is not regent, he has 9,400 manifestations, but during his regency, his manifestations are infinite. Thus he can be present with equal reality on Michaelmas at innumerable locations around the Earth while simultaneously fulfilling a manifold of galactic and cosmic responsibilities.

The Archangel Michael is the harbinger of the Holy Spirit moving through Earth's visionary geography and he brings the Supramundane Light to all the subtle being bodies of Gaia, the planet's Spirit, and the physical Earth as well. Michael is also in charge of the development of human consciousness on Earth and supports all activities leading to the unfoldment of spiritual freedom. Thus his energy infusion of the Earth grid on Michaelmas also supports all those people working toward the unfolding of awareness in conditions of freedom.

Michaelmas is an excellent day for group meditative work and ritual, especially when coordinated with a physical presence at a sacred site. While any sacred site will suffice, the Archangel Michael has 24,441 dedicated etheric sanctuaries (called Jewels of Michael) accessed at and above physical sacred sites; one's Michaelmas participation at such sites will enhance the effects. Selected locations include Mont-Saint-Michel, France; Snoqualmie Falls, Seattle, Washington; the Tor, Glastonbury, England; Wu-Ta'i Shan Mountain, China.

On Michaelmas, for example, the Archangel Michael may be observed activating and stimulating—not slaying—the Earth's array of 1,067 dragons, enabling them to discharge vital life force and "electrical" potency into the Earth grid. In mythic terms, this is remembered as the dragonslayer (Michael, Indra, and others) "slaying" the cosmic dragon (such as Vrtra) to make it release its nourishing waters (life-force energy) desperately needed by a parched Earth.

Similarly, on Michaelmas, the Archangel Michael has been observed cleansing, detoxifying, reenergizing, and rededicating the Earth's numerous star wheels (a geomantic feature called landscape zodiacs, holograms of the galaxy; see White Cow, White Sow), assisted by numerous angelic hosts. Into the hub of each star wheel (the zodiacal center, geomantically) Michael inserts his sword of light and channels an infusion of archangelic consciousness.

Traditionally, Knights of the Holy Grail under the auspices of King Arthur (see Grail Knight, Holy Grail, King Arthur—all terms signifying an esoteric cabal of clairvoyant men and women in service to the planet) would assemble at selected nodes in the Earth's visionary geography. There they would participate in the Michaelmas infusion and help ground the celestial energies in a human context, channeling them through their awareness into the Earth. In this manner, they cooperated with the angelic realm in cleansing the planet this day.

See also: Antichrist, Candlemas, Dragon, Epiphany, Gaia, Grail Knight, Hollow Hill, Holy Grail, Hurqalya, King Arthur, Leviathan, Ley Lines, Seven Rishis, White Cow, White Sow, Wild Hunt.

MINOTAUR

The Supreme Being (the Greek Zeus) in his White Bull form infiltrating human awareness with God-consciousness at the heart of one of the planet's 108 geomantic features constructed of Light and called a labyrinth.

Also known as Asterion, Asterius, Bull of Minos.

Description: In Greek myth, the fearsome Minotaur, a bull's head on a human's torso, lives at the center of the Cretan Labyrinth. This was commissioned by King Minos of Crete and designed and built by Daedalus, the gods' architect, to house it. Every year seven young men and seven young women were sacrificed to the Minotaur as tribute from Athens. Eventually, Theseus, Athens' founder, successfully threaded the labyrinth, slew the Minotaur, and walked out alive.

King Minos's time was in extreme antiquity, three generations before the Trojan War, itself of only sketchy historicity. His father was Zeus, chief of the Olympian gods, and his mother, Europa, one of Zeus's consorts and his granddaughter. Minos's wife, Pasiphae, was a daughter of the Sun god Helios and Perseis, an Oceanid. In brief, they were immortals, offspring of the high gods.

Pasiphae mated with a divine bull sent to Minos by Poseidon, Lord of the Sea (Zeus's brother), and this mating produced Asterius (or Asterion), the Minotaur, or Bull of Minos.

Earlier, Minos asserted his claim to rulership of Crete over his two brothers and asked Poseidon to yield a sacrificial bull from the sea as validation. He got the bull, but refused to sacrifice, so taken was he by the bull's majesty. Poseidon took his revenge for the reneged deal by making the bull mad. Later Paisphae fell in love with this bull (aided by spells from Poseidon, and possibly also Aphrodite, the Greek Love goddess) and the Minotaur resulted from their union.

Daedalus built the labyrinth in the vicinity of Knossos, Crete's capital at that time, as a vast palace of interconnecting rooms or as a complex, unfathomable maze, and imprisoned the Minotaur in its heart, essentially to protect the world from it. But it is also said that Daedalus constructed the labyrinth in such a way as to conceal the Minotaur and to prevent any humans threading it from escaping the beast.

Explanation: The Minotaur is not a biological aberration of a coupling outside of Nature, with a predilection for consuming young virgins. It is, rather, an expression of the Supreme Being in His White Bull aspect. Both Zeus and the Hindu Shiva have a formidable White Bull manifestation.

Shiva's is called Nandi ("Joyful") and it is as white as Himalayan snow, the myths say. Zeus's white bull form is not named, but he appeared as a beautiful bull, mild and gentle, with jeweled horns and snow-white flanks, to seduce Europa whom he fancied; he then carried her on his broad back into the sea.

The Minotaur is the merging of human awareness with God-awareness so that the initiate wears Zeus's head like Asterius, a process facilitated by a geomantic feature called a labyrinth.

One of the planet's 100 + geomantic features, the labyrinth exists in nine different forms with 12 copies of each, totaling 108. The Cretan Labyrinth is one of these nine types, and possibly one of the largest. It was not a palace or even a maze, nor is it, strictly, at Knossus, though it is nearby.

This type of labyrinth is created by the intersection of spiraling energy lines from eight somewhat overlapping dome caps generated by the dome over Mount Ida on Crete. Domes are large etheric canopies over mountains, often many miles wide, and dome caps are subsidiary smaller canopies connected to them by spirallic lines (see Holy Mountain). Geomantically, they are what makes mountains holy and terrains numinous, capable of elevating human awareness.

Originally, the Mount Ida dome was 33 miles wide (since installation, they all have "shrunk" somewhat), which means the maximum width of the Cretan labyrinth was 33 miles. The dome cap lines naturally spiral in opposite directions, in accordance with the Golden Mean (phi), and intersect regularly.

Daedalus was originally a member of the

angelic family called Nephilim and was present on Earth long ago (when Earth's visionary geography was being implemented) to install the labyrinth and other geomantic features. He adjusted the spiral lines matrix to produce a labyrinth shape in light.

The goal of walking the labyrinth, which is a visionary event, is not to slay the Minotaur, but to become one with it for a time. The Minotaur is any human who has penetrated, assimilated, and mastered the higher Mind aspects of Zeus (the Bull of Minos); at the level of spiritual initiation, it is accurate to say the Minotaur slays all humans who approach it. God-consciousness is always and necessarily transcendent to human awareness.

The diameter of the Cretan labyrinth today is approximately 5 to 10 miles. Seen from above, the labyrinth resembles a figure of eight points of brilliant light (the dome caps) symmetrically arrayed around a central bright point (the Minotaur). Numerous spiral lines of light unfold to the left and right in all directions. The labyrinth has seven veils or layers, each with guardians and initiatory content. The center of the labyrinth, where you will find the Minotaur, is Mount Ida, said to be the birthplace of Zeus, where his mother, Rhea, hid him from Kronos, his father.

The Cretan labyrinth performs a function relative to a large surface area of the Earth described in terms of Albion Plates. For central and southern Europe, this larger area was anthropomorphized as the beautiful mortal female Europa. The labyrinth is the mental body or Mind for this large landscape figure. Each of Earth's 12 Albions has one "Cretan" labyrinth; other locations include Addis Ababa in Ethiopia and the Plantation in Fiji in the South Pacific.

The Cretan labyrinth is one of nine keys given to humanity and Earth to open the Mind, both human and deific, in the context of an Albion Plate. Interacting with a Cretan labyrinth is illuminating both with respect to the mind in human terms and to the larger living geomythic body and mind of an Albion.

Theseus slaying the Minotaur must be inverted. The son of Poseidon, the Lord of the Sea and one of Zeus's two brothers (Hades is the other), Theseus threads the labyrinth and survives the God-infusion of the Minotaur. Ostensibly, he went in lieu of one of the required virgins so that the annual tribute Crete exacted from Athens for an earlier offense could be ended. Geomantically, Theseus, as the representative of Athens (in fact, its founder and leader) grounds the God-essence in Athens and links its Mind center at Mount Ida with the capital city.

It is quite likely that Theseus, as a semidivine initiate, threaded the Cretan labyrinth to purify and help reactivate it, perhaps after long nonuse. (All geomantic features need regular maintenance and cannot be expected to maintain their original pristine quality, as in Daedalus's antique time.)

See also: Albion, Ancient of Days, Bran the Blessed, Europa, Holy Mountain, White Bull.

MONSTER-SLAYER

The Navajo perception of Merlin, Earth's primary culture hero and Earth-Shaper, who prepares the land for the *Diné* ("The People," or Navajo) to live in.

Also known as Nayenezgani ("Slayer of the Alien Gods").

Description: In this Navajo myth of the American Southwest, two culture heroes and brothers named Monster-Slayer and Born for Water make the land safe for human habitation by overcoming and slaying a variety of primeval monsters.

Monster-Slayer and his younger brother, Born for Water, are among the 14 *yeii,* or principal Navajo gods, created after the Navajo Emergence into the world.

Changing Woman, or Estsanatlehi, is magically impregnated by the Sun who merely shines on her one day as she reclines atop Gobernador Knob (*Ntl'iz Dziil,* "Hard Goods Mountain," in Rio Arriba County, New Mexico; it is one of the Navajo's sacred mountains) where she was "born," from a piece of turquoise. Estsanatlehi's sister, Yolkai Estsan (White Shell Woman), is also impregnated by the Sun. The Navajo describe them as divine sisters; both give birth to sons, Estsanatlehi to Monster-Slayer and Yolkai Estsan to Born for Water.

Neither sister told her child that his father was the Sun, but one day both boys decide to journey to the Sun for a meeting and for help in overcoming monsters. Tsohanoai's ("Bearer of the Sun"; also written as *Jóhonaa'éí*) house is a square pueblo made of turquoise set on the shore of a great water. Tests are involved in getting to his house and, after they arrive, to prove their mettle, but eventually the Sun awards their perseverance with counsel and magical weapons including shirts, leggings, and moccasins, all made from iron, and also various celestial arrows and knives.

The basic problem is that the Navajo land is beset by numerous *anaye,* demons and monsters who devour the people and make life dangerous or unlivable. Monster-Slayer and Born for Water are determined to get rid of them. Before the boys leave Tsohanoai, he takes them to *Yagahoka,* the "sky-hole," in the center of the sky; through this they see their tribal lands and sacred peaks below.

Then they descend to the Earth and land on *Tsotsil* (Mount Taylor, also called *Dootl'izhii Dziil,* "Turquoise Mountain" or "Blue Bead Mountain" in New Mexico), the Navajo's sacred mountain of the South. It is also the home of the first anaye to be slain: *Ye'iitsoh La'í Naaghaíí* ("Giant Ye'ii," "One Walking Giant," or Yeitso, for short), the giant chief of the enemy gods. They succeed in killing the giant, and his blood flows to fill a large valley near Grants, New Mexico, later coagulating into the Malpais lava flows. In fact, there is so much blood it is like a flood, and the brothers dam it in the valley.

As a result of this first triumph, the younger brother, formerly known as *Tobadzistsini* ("Child of the Water" or "Child Born of Water") is renamed *Naidikisi* ("He Who Cuts Around"), and the elder brother (Monster-Slayer), whose original name is not recorded, becomes *Nayenezgani* ("Slayer of the Alien Gods").

Among the other monsters dispatched by the brothers (although often only Monster-Slayer's deeds are recorded and perhaps he is the sole or principal hero), in addition to Big Monster or Big Giant (Yeitso) at Mount Taylor, are Bird Monster (called *Tse Nináhálééh,* meaning "It Puts People Down on a Rock") at Shiprock Pinnacle (*Tsebitai,* "Winged Rock," near Farmington, New Mexico); Monster That Kicked People Off the Cliff (*Tse'ta'-ho-tsil-tali,* located at *Naatsis'aan,* Navajo Mountain on the Utah-Arizona border); *Sasnalkahi* ("Bear That Pursues"), who lives at *Tse'bahastsit* ("Rock That Frightens"); Monster That Killed with [Lightning in] His Eyes at *Tse'ahalzini* ("Rock with Black Hole," modern location uncertain); *Teelget* (the Giant Elk); and Horned Monster.

In all, six major (and some minor) anaye were killed by Monster-Slayer.

The brothers allowed five less malevolent anaye to live: Hunger, Poverty, Sleep, Lice Man, and Old Age. When they were finished cleansing the land, they revisited the four sacred mountains bounding Navajo country in the cardinal directions to be sure no more monsters required removal from the world. They also collected all the body parts of the slain anaye and buried them with Yeitso. Then the brothers retired to *Toyetli,* where two rivers join in the San Juan Valley in New Mexico.

Explanation: The tale of Monster-Slayer is about the earliest days of preparing a coherent, spiritualized, safe landscape for the *Diné* ("The People," or Navajo) just after they emerged on Earth's surface from inside the planet.

This area is known today as Navajo Nation, an area of 25,000 square miles that straddles the corners of four adjacent states of the Southwest (Utah, Arizona, Colorado, and New Mexico, which has the bulk of it). The land, *Diné Bikéyah,* is bounded and defined by the Rio Grande,

Colorado, and Little Colorado Rivers, as well as the four sacred peaks in the cardinal directions plus two other mountains.

This area, bounded by three rivers and the four cardinal mountains, is encased in a massive zodiac dome that is about 500 miles across. It encloses a huge interactive hologram of the galaxy called a landscape zodiac (see White Cow, White Sow) including the major constellations and bright stars. The zodiac dome, which rises many dozens of miles high above the ground, creates and defines the archetypal, geomantic, tribal boundaries for Diné Bikéyah.

The Navajo emerge into a ritually numinous landscape with many special geomantic features (star energies in the land) not found everywhere else, as Earth has only 432 such zodiacs and most of them are much smaller than this. From the viewpoint of early humanity, however, these star energies thriving in the landscape of Diné Bikéyah are raw, rough, dangerous, almost unassimilable.

The star energies templated across this vast landscape are sentient, just like the Spirits living in the holy mountains. They are holograms of the great Star-Angels, the Spirits behind or within the major stars, and these are formidable, scary beings, especially encountered on a pristine Earth so long ago. They are "alien gods" in that they are not yet digestible by human consciousness.

Metaphorically, they are like a congeries of wild beasts that need taming and tying before presentation to the public in the zoo, which is amusingly apt as zodiac comes from the Greek word *zoon* for a "circle of animals." Monster-Slayer is the "lion tamer" who will make their energies safe and assimilable.

The Navajo myth speaks of two brothers, each named; however, in the majority of the encounters with the anaye, it is only the Elder Brother, Monster-Slayer, who is involved in overcoming them. It is likely that the Navajo expanded Monster-Slayer into two fraternal figures for storytelling purposes.

The identity of Monster-Slayer is surprising yet apt: It is Merlin, known in Celtic myth as the magus to King Arthur. His résumé encompasses, however, numerous incarnations in different cultures where he works as an Earth-Shaper, preparing landscapes for human habitation. In Polynesia, he was Maui, who dredged some of the Hawaiian islands out of the Pacific; in Tibet, he was Padmasambhava, Indian missionary of Buddhism who drove all the demons out of Tibet; and in ancient Ireland, he was Cuchulainn (Hound of Culann), defending a major landscape zodiac in the Murtheimne Plain against entropy and darkness.

In Celtic myth, Merlin was caretaker of the 13 Treasures of the Island of Britain. These were specific magical devices and protocols of his; in Navajo legend, he is equipped by his father, Sun Bearer, with magical arrows, clothing and armor made of iron, and knives. These are the same as the 13 magic Treasures.

In his Greek guise as Herakles, the prodigious hero of the 12 Labors, Merlin's name meant "Glory of Hera," and Hera was a reference to the Great Mother, Mother Goddess, Queen of Heaven, or the female aspect of the Supreme Being. Merlin's energy and consciousness was the "line" to the *Mer* or *Mere* (Mother), and thus he was able to ground Her energy into the Earth at various sacred sites. In effect, Herakles was Hera's agent on the Earth. Similarly, Changing Woman (an image of the Great Mother) is his Navajo mother and his mentor-sponsor.

Incidentally, Herakles also had a brother, named Iphicles, born of the same mother, Alcmene, impregnated by Zeus, the high god. Even as a child, Herakles was the one with divine power, and Iphicles the fearful mortal; however, Iphicles was a loyal warrior who accompanied Herakles on his Labors. It's relevant to note that most of Herakles' Labors involved subduing monsters.

Similarly, in Merlin's life as Padmasambhava, the Buddhist missionary to Tibet, he primarily subdued monsters and baleful spirits in the land, including the Srin-mo Demoness whose demonic body sprawled across Tibet, preparing the terrain for the grounding of the new religious impulse called Buddhism.

Did Monster-Slayer actually kill the various anaye in the land? No. The time period implied in the myth is vastly ancient, reckoned in millions of years ago at a time when Earth in its various geomantic oases was being prepared for human habitation. The raw, autochthonous, and celestial energies had to be transduced a bit to make them survivable by a young humanity. Their ontological rawness and bigness can easily make them seem like threatening monsters.

These various powerful landscape angels, protector beings, and Spirit forms initially seemed scary, strange, foreign, and alien to the early Navajo. They had to be "domesticated," instructed in the protocols of exchange and interaction with the newly arrived Navajo, freshly "born" to this new "Glittering World."

The Navajo say that every mountain has an inner form and holy beings inside it—*bii'istíín,* "Those That Stand within Them." These gods are the chieftains of the peaks, and the mountains are their hogans, or homes. Monster-Slayer helped the bii'istíín of the mountains release their spiritual charge and numinosity into the landscape and to thoroughly infiltrate it, like flowing blood.

Merlin as Monster-Slayer did what he does best: He subdued the energies. That means he grounded them, metaphorically tied them down to their geomantic "hogans," put "timers" on their activity, put in "plumbing" so that their energy could flow in a controlled manner into human geomantic and psychological reality rather than disastrously flood it. He pacified the raw star forces as necessary, but in other cases energized and activated them—turned them on. He *domesticated* them, making them safe and assimilable to a fresh humanity, adjusting them and fine-tuning them to Earth's conditions of matter and consciousness.

The Navajo legend specifies that all the anaye are, despite their seeming opposition to the Diné, progeny of the Sun Bearer, just like Monster-Slayer.

Monster-Slayer did not kill Yeitso at Mount Taylor. Yeitso is the towering, sword-brandishing, fiercely miened temple protector being, similar, in fact, to Talos, the giant bronze man in Greek myth said to guard Crete from invaders, throwing rocks at intruders. Greek myth says the Argonauts killed Talos, but they did not, just as Monster-Slayer did not slay Yeitso. Giant Yeii's "blood" fills the valley (or lava field) around Mount Taylor, which means his unfaltering *attention permeates* the area surrounding the secret temple he protects. Talos was "killed" when a plug was pulled out of his ankle, allowing his precious blood (called *ichor,* "god's blood") to drain out of him and into the landscape.

Monster-Slayer's work also involved creating *congruence* and harmony between the inner spirit form of a landscape feature, its bii'istíín, and the outer, physical aspect, such as a mountain, hill, valley, river. Just as the Navajo were freshly emerged on Earth's surface, so were the numerous Spirit beings newly incarnate in the physical landscape forms for which they were now responsible.

Thus Monster-Slayer has to match the Spirit beings with their new landscape bodies and the Navajo people with their new landscape holy beings. His Earth-shaping duties meant arranging the harmonious *conjunction* of the outer form with its inner life essence or soul—"The One Who Lies within It."

As Padmasambhava, Merlin "converted" the landscape Spirit beings of Tibet to a vibration and consciousness level that would sustain Buddhism. Similarly, in his activities as Monster-Slayer, Merlin converted the spirits within this huge zodiac dome to be amenable, compatible with, and supportive of the emerging Diné and their evolutionary-consciousness parameters and agenda.

See also: Agharta, Hitching Post of the Sun, Holy Mountain, Merlin, Srin-mo Demoness, White Cow, White Sow.

MORGAN LE FAY

A spiritual adept from the astral realm also known as the Lake who embodies the ninefold levels of consciousness of that realm and facilitates the human mastery of those energies by way of a sword and scabbard.

Also known as the Valkyrie Brynnhildr.

Description: In the Arthurian stories, Morgan le Fay is King Arthur's sister or half-sister and generally his opponent throughout his career as king. The Celtic imagination paints her as a witch up to no good, while the "Fay" suffix denotes her presumed origin among the supernatural, unsettling world of faëry.

The Celtic stories describe Morgan as a wayward enchantress, beguiling, seducing, or generally obstructing various heroes of Arthur's court. She creates the Perilous Valley as a punishment for unfaithful knights; they would become trapped in their own self-created illusions within the valley. Morgan stole the scabbard for Arthur's sword Excalibur; the scabbard, said Merlin, Arthur's magus, is more valuable than the sword because it protects him in battle.

Accounts earlier than the Arthurian material say Morgan was one of nine beautiful sisters, their chief, or oldest, living on the Fortunate Isle, or in Avalon, a land of awesome fertility, beauty, and Golden Apple trees. Certain medieval scholars, such as Geoffrey of Monmouth in his *Vita Merlini,* placed Morgan's realm at Glastonbury, in Somerset, England. For him, Morgan was less an ambivalent witch-enchantress and more a mistress of a paradise.

Outwardly, Morgan seemed to oppose King Arthur's reign at every step, yet when he was mortally wounded in the Battle of Camlann, she brought him on the mystic barge back to Avalon, or the Otherworld, to be healed or to ascend to a higher realm. She was accompanied on the barge by two other women, one of them identified in the stories as Nimuë, an aspect of the Lady of the Lake.

Explanation: Morgan is not so much Arthur's sister as his colleague. She is the master and representative of the nine spheres of consciousness of the Lake. The Lake is an old symbol for the astral plane, the sea of Light, the ocean of stars. In Qabalistic terms, it is the second of four Trees of Life, each representing a fundamental World or level of creation. Morgan's Tree is called *Yetzirah* and means "Formation"; it is equivalent to the Lake or astral realm. Morgan and her eight sisters are separate expressions of the energies and her sisters are aspects of herself.

A tamer, almost urbane version of the same is found in the Greek description of the Nine Muses, nine females who inspire the arts. A more feral and ontologically raw version is the Norse Valkyries, nine war goddesses and death maidens assigned by the high god, Odin, to select the best of the slain warriors to feast and drink with him in his Hall of the Slain, Valhalla. Morgan, in her Nordic guise, is Brynnhildr, who championed Siegfried (Sigurd), the Norse equivalent of King Arthur. As Brynnhildr, she is presented as sleeping under a godly enchantment (by her father, Odin) on a pyre surrounded by a fire ring.

The circle of towering flames around the unconscious Brynnhildr symbolizes the cognitive threshold one must cross to enter her astral domain. In the Norse version, Siegfried rescues Brynnhildr, waking her up to his physical world, while in the Arthurian, in the end, Morgan rescues Arthur, transporting him out of his material realm into her Light-filled, astral domain. Both show her as psychopomp to the solar hero, Arthur or Siegfried, conducting him across the threshold into her astral, ninefold tree of Life.

Morgan is also an aspect of the Lady of the Lake, the ultimate authority and guardian of the entire astral realm. Two other aspects of this Lady are Nimuë and Morgause, Arthur's aunt. The three women represent the three pillars or primary valences of consciousness in the Yetzirah tree. Qabalists model the Trees as having three vertical pillars with ten spheres of light arrayed on them.

Yet Morgan, Nimuë, and Morgause are also solidly individualized adepts who move in and out of human incarnation and history. Just as in Catholicism there is a set number of cardinals in the College of Cardinals and one pope, though the specific individuals occupying these positions change, similarly, Morgan, Nimuë, and Morgause, as Valkyries, Muses, or fays of Avalon, occupy certain metaphysically generic positions within the astral realm.

As Morgan of the Avalon fays or Brynnhildr of the Valkyries, she does not steal King Arthur's scabbard, but rather, as the ninefold adept, she *is* the scabbard. Excalibur's precious, jeweled scabbard is the nine Avalon fays, Valkyries, and Muses—the nine spheres of Light in the Yetzirah Tree of Life.

The myth says the Lady of the Lake gave Arthur Excalibur and the scabbard. The clairvoyant reality is that Arthur was able to concentrate his insight into the nine spheres of the Lake or astral realm into a mental focus expressed classically in the Mysteries as a sword. Excalibur is a dynamic expression of Arthur's ability to extract, condense, embody, and wield the ninefold energies of the Lady of the Lake's world in his own material world.

The Lady of the Lake remained his lifelong mentor in the guise of her three agents, Morgan, Nimuë, and Morgause, each of whom transmitted an aspect of the total. These three necessarily remained vitally connected with Arthur and Excalibur in the material world as its scabbard because they were the embodiments of the metaphysical matrix that created the sword in the first place.

See also: Avalon, Excalibur, King Arthur, Lady of the Lake, Valkyries.

MOUNT MERU

A profound cosmographic model and cosmic mechanism that has geomantic reality on the Earth at two levels.

Also known as Axial Mountain, Center of the World, Cosmic Axis, Cosmic Mountain, Devaparvata (Mountain of the Gods), Haraberezaiti (Mount Alburz), Hemadri (Golden Mountain), Himingbjörg, Karnikacala (Lotus Mountain), Land of Bliss, Mahameru, Mount Analogue, Mount of the Lands, Ratnasanu (Jewel Peak), Seven-Story Mountain, Sumeru, World Axis, World Mountain.

Description: Mount Meru in Vedic and Hindu lore is the archetypal Cosmic Mountain and ultimate abode of all the gods. A golden mountain, it is located at the center of the universe, directly at or under the cosmic North Pole.

Notable among the gods resident at Meru is Shiva, one of Hinduism's trinity (with Vishnu and Brahma) and known as the destroyer of illusion. In fact, Mount Meru, regarded as King of all Mountains, is usually said to be the prime abode of Shiva and his consort, Himavan ("Owner of Snow"). Her sister is Ganga, the River Ganges.

Mount Meru is brighter than the sun in its dazzling golden radiance, like a flame without smoke, and it keeps Heaven in its correct place by supporting it. The Pole Star hangs directly above it and all the stars are attached to it by ropes of wind or aerial cords (see Atlas), making Meru the axis of the world. It's called a shining mountain; an immeasurable mountain; a mass of energy with blazing golden peaks, and glittering, gold-adorned slopes. It is said that only Brahma in his square golden city there comprehends the spiritual enormity of Mount Meru.

The Sun, Moon, and Wind (Vayu, Lord of the Air) circle Mount Meru every day. Numerous spiritual beings known as *Devas* (Shining Ones, or angels), *Apsaras* (dancing nymphs), *Kinnaris* (celestial singing girls), and *Gandharvas* (celestial musicians) live upon it. In fact, all the known gods (including Vishnu and Brahma) live on the mountain, all 33 crores (330 million) of Vedic gods.

A total of 20 named mountains surround Mount Meru; mystics say Mount Meru shines like a resplendent sun in the center of these mountains.

Mount Meru is surrounded concentrically by six circular lands or continents, rising out of the center of the seventh *(Jambudvipa)* like the calyx of a lotus. The lotus's flower is the Earth and Mount Meru is wider at the top than bottom.

On top of Mount Meru are nine Celestial Cities of the gods: In the center is Brahma's *Manovati* or *Brahmapuri,* and occupying the eight cardinal directions (such as south and southeast, north and northeast) are the residences of the eight major deities called *Lokapalas,* Lords or Guardians of the Directions (*Lokas,* meaning "Heavens" or "Spheres"); they are also known as Lords of the Eight Worlds.

Countless celestial songbirds keep the air rich with song; precious stones and jewels adorn the mountain's flanks; celestial healing herbs flourish on its slopes; a vast number of magic wishing trees grow on its slopes.

The celestial river called Ganges or Ganga falls on the summit of Mount Meru before it flows anywhere else; striking Mount Meru, the Ganges divides into four spiritual streams, each flowing out to a cardinal direction. Vedic tradition says that the celestial Ganges flows directly down into Brahma's city on Meru, but it also says it flows down through the matted hair of Shiva on Meru.

Vedic myth says Mount Meru is staggeringly tall: It rises 84,000 *yojanas* (672,000 miles; one *yojana* = 8 miles) above Earth and penetrates Earth to a depth of 16,000 yojanas. The diameter of the summit is 32,000 yojanas, and its base, 16,000 yojanas. Due to its enormous size and its situation at the umbilicus of the universe, Mount Meru was called the Seed-Cup or Lotus of the Earth.

Underneath Mount Meru are seven nether or demonic worlds called Potala, and at the bottom resides Vasuki, a giant snake-dragon (a variation on the cosmic dragon Sesa-Ananta; see Dragon) who supports Mount Meru and all its subsidiary mountains and Celestial Cities on his sevenfold hood. When he yawns, Earth experiences tremors; sometime in the far future, Vasuki will uncoil his gigantic length and consume all of Creation with his fiery breath.

The holy mountain is inaccessible to those humans who abound in *adharma* (lack of Dharma, the rightful way, or spiritual purity: "sinners"). In 1952, French metaphysical writer René Daumal wrote about Mount Meru under the allegorical name Mount Analogue, calling it the ultimate symbolic mountain because, even though it must exist geographically, it is completely inaccessible to living humans; it exists, but invisibly, and is impossible to find and enter.

Explanation: Mount Meru is a profound cosmographic model and cosmic mechanism that has geomantic reality on the Earth at two levels.

On the galactic level, which is a hologram of the same organization at the higher, cosmic level, Mount Meru is a grounding point (a spiritual mass) upraised to meet the incoming purity of the celestial Ganges River. At this level, the Ganges refers to a steady stream of exalted consciousness coming from the Pole Star, known in the West as Polaris (despite Precessional changes that technically put other stars for a time in that role) and as Dhruva in Vedic astronomy.

Dhruva, described as a celestial spiritual being, is, of all the star gods or what the Chaldeans called the great Star-Angels, the most revered devotee of Vishnu (the Hindu Christ). Vishnu appointed Dhruva to be the *grahadhara,* the pivot of the stars, as a reward for his steadfast spiritual devotion to him (see Atlas).

The chariots of all the planets (heavenly spheres or dimensions) and all the constellations and stars are attached to Dhruva by "aerial cords." This keeps them in their proper and allotted orbits, revolving around Dhruva. For "aerial cords," we can usefully substitute "threads" or "beams of light" from Polaris.

Vishnu refers to the cosmic Christ, the great Sun within the Sun or Great Central Sun and, in terms of the galaxy's stars, the Logos, the divine rationality that pervades and coheres the galaxy's great star fields. Dhruva is the portal for the Logos to enter and permeate the galaxy and its star beings. Its first point of entry is Mount Meru, and it enters as the celestial river Ganges as a "food" for the 330 million gods assembled in glory on its radiant slopes and peaks.

This pattern is copied on Earth through its hologram of Mount Meru. This copy receives the equivalent of the Ganges River or Polaris stream and grounds it for all of Earth. This stream enters Earth, then spreads out in two opposite directions, encircling the planet. This is called an Oroboros Line, and it is one of 15 primary energy tracks (or very large ley lines) that significantly help create and sustain physical reality, Earth's ecosystems, and consciousness.

Technically, the Ganges divides into only two spiritual streams, and even those two are actually the same single oroboric current encircling Earth.

This copy, though physically real and not an astral apparition, is, for the most part, inaccessible to humans trying to reach it while in the body because it is phase-shifted from our physical reality. As René Daumal said, it is invisible, though geographically present. Meru's planetary location is roughly off the east coast of New Zealand's South Island. If you were to sail up to it, you would be diverted around it without ever seeing it or even knowing your course had been deflected.

A Maori myth, however, hints at the presence of this mystical mountain. In the earliest days, Taane-mahuta (the Maori equivalent of the Greek Titan Atlas) traveled to the end of the world and complete darkness until he reached *Maunganui,* the Great Mountain, home of the Shining Ones, children of Uru. It is plausible that the Maori would know of Mount Meru in some manner since it lies, shielded, in the Pacific Ocean not that far from their homeland.

This motif of inaccessible presence was intuited by J. R. R. Tolkien in his descriptions of Valinor or Aman, the immortal land of the gods in the West. Once the way to the Blessed Isles was straight, then it became bent and unavailable.

Those with Dharma, that is, a very high level of adeptship, may enter Mount Meru, presumably on a physical level. Others may, with grace, receive an invitation from the angelic realm and be awarded a brief reconnaissance visit.

During such a visit, two colleagues and I saw, from above, an island in the middle of the sea, with a very tall mountain on it, surrounded by many tall hills. At the harbor were numerous ocean transport vehicles of all sorts, from primitive coracles to futuristic bubbles, possibly symbolizing different stages of spiritual development of the visitors, the boats signifying their spiritual process.

Our host, the Ofanim, an angelic order (see Ganesh, Garuda, Hanuman) deeply involved in maintenance and educational aspects of Earth's visionary geography, stood in their angelic form as tall as Mount Meru itself. Numerous people stood about on the beach; emeralds blazed in the sand. Inland a short distance was a healing temple, a golden dome surmounting a building made of seven large globes, each a different color, stacked vertically one upon the other. You enter one of these color globes and get a thorough aura cleanse in that color.

The Mount Meru paradigm is repeated on Earth 12 more times in essence, though without the complex array of residences of the 330 million gods. One aspect of Earth's visionary geography is a twelvefold division of the planet's surface into adjacent pentagons (five-sided polygons). Over each is a massive dome or etheric energy canopy called a Universe Dome, hundreds of miles wide and high (see Holy Mountain).

Into the top of each Universe Dome flows the same Polaris stream or Ganges River (the Greeks called it Atlas), and it is grounded below on the land somewhere at a Dhruva Anchor Point, a miniature, streamlined Mount Meru.

This model is replicated in the subtle anatomy of the human chakra system. Seven major centers of energy, force, and consciousness, called chakras, are arrayed from the groin to the top of the head. Energy called kundalini ideally flows upward through these centers through two intertwining channels called *ida* and *pingala*, corresponding to Moon and Sun, negative and positive valences.

Yet a third channel, the *sushumna*, neutral in valence, flows directly up through them like an arrow; it is also called the *Merudanda*, the miniature Mount Meru within the human organization. The Polaris stream from Dhruva, or the Logos, flows into the crown of the head where Shiva sits on Mount Meru.

The eight residences of the Lokapalas are replicated many times (3,546 for the eight types) across Earth and are known, geomantically, as Celestial Cities, under such names as the Grail Castle, Mithraeum (see Hitching Post of the Sun), Shambhala, Soma Temple (see Fountain of Youth), Mount Olympus (see Glass Mountain, House of Atreus, and Seven Rishis), and the Underworld.

The Mount Meru complex with its affiliate mountains and celestial gods' residences is thus geomantically distributed across the planet. The one Mount Meru is situated in the South Pacific, but the eight *Lokapala* cities are spread out in multiple holographic copies across the Earth's surface. This means our entire Earth is threaded and permeated by the 330 million gods.

See also: Atlas, Avalon, Dragon, Fountain of Youth, Glass Mountain, Grail Castle, Hitching Post of the Sun, Holy Mountain, House of Atreus, Seven Rishis, Shambhala, Underworld.

NAGAS

Awakened spiritual beings and masters of wisdom and the dragon energies residing in their opulent Celestial City called Nagaloka.

Also known as Dragon Demons, Dragon Kings, Dragon Spirits, Nats, Serpent Gods, Serpents, Serpents of Wisdom, Snakes, the Ever-Moving.

Description: Nagas are a class of semidivine spiritual beings described in Hinduism and said to look like serpents, or cobras, sometimes with multiple heads, or like humans from the neck up with a serpentine torso. Typically, Nagas are depicted as attractive, richly adorned, bejeweled men and women with a snake's lower body; over their heads rear three, five, seven, or ten expanded cobra hoods, while on their heads are jeweled crowns and large earrings.

They live luxuriously and in sensual delight in splendid palaces. Nagas are said to guard the treasures of the Earth (minerals, gemstones, and other riches), in fact, to reside deep inside the Earth in a nine-leveled realm called Patala; they also live in inaccessible mountain caves. Patala is an immense region with numerous palaces, houses, towers, and pleasure gardens. Another name for their realm is Nagaloka, "the Realm of the Nagas," a division of the Underworld, whose capital is Bhogavati, residence of the three Naga kings: Vasuki, Taksaka, and Sesa-Ananta (this one lies under the Earth supporting its entire weight).

Legend says there is a pond in Nagaloka, and if one drinks of it, the water gives you the strength of a thousand elephants. Legend also says Patala is thousands of miles away from Earth, it is surrounded by jewel-encrusted forts, the steps at its entrance are decorated with gems and gold, and its outer doors are 100 yojanas long (about 800 miles; one *yojana* = 8 miles) and five yojanas high (40 miles) and its interior exceeds 1,000 yojanas (about 8,000 square miles).

Yet Nagas are also associated with water, living in subaquatic abodes, serving as protectors of rivers, lakes, reservoirs, and seas, and controlling rainfall and fertility. In this capacity, they are called *Nagarajas*, or Dragon Kings, the guardian spirits of lakes and rivers. In Kashmir, India, 527 Nagas have been named and worshipped there for centuries, according to an ancient text. Originally, the Kashmir Valley was a vast lake populated by Nagas, the region's guardians; after the lake drained, the Nagas remained to protect the land.

Analogically, as snakes slough their skins, so the Nagas are immortal, surviving the shedding of cycles of cosmic time and of creation-dissolution.

Among their epithets are: Serpents *(Sarpa);* the Ever-Moving; Creeping Creatures *(Pannaga);* Those Creeping on Their Chests *(Uraga);* Those Creeping on Their Shoulders *(Bhujanga);* and Goat-Eaters *(Ajagara).* Nagas are well respected for their spiritual wisdom, prodigious powers, beauty, skill, and great courage, but sometimes feared for their violence and quick tempers.

In Buddhism, they are credited with safeguarding key spiritual texts, including the valuable *Prajnaparamita Sutra.* The philosopher Nagarjuna ("the Great Naga," or spiritual adept) rediscovered this text in a special visit he made to Naga Land, then Gautama Buddha asked the Nagas to keep it safe until humanity was ready to receive it. Buddhist tradition says that Nagas washed Gautama at his birth, protected him during his life, and guarded his bodily relics after his death.

The primordial cosmic dragon known in Hinduism as Sesa-Ananta, one of the very first creatures manifested by Brahma at the start of Creation, is a Naga, who serves as a rest for Vishnu (the Hindu Christ) during *Pralaya* (the "Night of Brahma," after Creation is dissolved). The great cosmic snake or dragon Vasuki is also a Naga; he was used as a rope in the gods' Churning of the Ocean of Milk.

Hindu folklore says the Nagas originated from *Surabhi* ("Fragrant"), the celestial Cow and daughter of the ancient sage or rishi Kashyapa ("Vision"); or from Kashyapa and Kadru ("Chalice of Immortality"), a daughter of the rishi Daksa ("Ritual Skill"). The Nagas are said to be the implacable enemy of Vishnu's celestial bird-mount, Garuda, called Destroyer of Serpents.

Somewhat confusingly, the Nagas are also said to be the progeny of Airavata, a primordial elephant god that emerged from the Ocean of Milk. Nagasa are sometimes called elephants, possibly through association with the long trunk. Airavata is the Naga lord, the King of Snakes, says the *Mahabharata,* an ancient Indian text, which adds that the Nagas number in the tens of millions.

Explanation: In understanding Nagas, it is vital not to take their physical descriptions as literal: Nagas are *not* snakes or serpents. Their spiritual form is serpentine or snakelike, but only as a metaphor for their true nature. Naga worship based on veneration of actual snakes is a misplaced concreteness.

It is also crucial to appreciate that the cosmic dragon and its affiliate Nagaloka pertain to the archetype of the root chakra, the *Muladhara,* which means "root support." From the standpoint of Creation, it is the first created center. In the human, the root chakra is found in the groin, but in the cosmos it is right under God's nose, so to speak, the foundation for the entire *cosmic* Earth. "Earth" in this sense means all space created to hold matter. God started with the root.

The equivalent of Sesa-Ananta in the human root chakra is called kundalini. Hindu yogis describe it as like a serpent coiled three and a half times around the base of the "Shiva linga," another name for the *sushumna,* a central energy conduit that passes through the seven chakras from groin to brow. Interestingly, Hindu iconography for the root chakra depicts the elephant Airavata amidst the four broad petals or vibratory fields associated with this energy-consciousness center.

The variously described Naga realm—Bhogavati, Nagaloka, Patala—is an expression of this archetype of the root chakra and it is found in Earth's visionary geography in 144 places. The Naga realm is one of eight Celestial Cities arrayed about the cosmic peak Mount Meru, as described in Hindu lore (see Mount Meru). Implicitly, this realm is closely associated with the original cosmic dragon Sesa-Ananta and all its subsidiary expressions across Earth's visionary geography (the Earth has 1,067 dragons in all; see Dragon).

In some cases, the Naga realm is located on Earth at the site of a dragon; in others, not. The prime Naga realm is situated with respect to Earth's prime dragon, described in Norse myth, for example, as the Midgard Serpent, wrapped entirely around the Earth. This is geomantically true, and its head is in the South Pacific. So is the primary Naga realm. The others, which are like holograms of this original one, are located elsewhere, for example, at Croagh Patrick in Ireland, Lake Tahoe in California-Nevada, and Lake Manasarovar near Mount Kailash, Tibet.

The Hindu "mythic" descriptions of the Nagas and their realms are largely accurate and may be verified by clairvoyant viewing of both. The Nagas are living expressions of awakened kundalini: Their serpentine torsos represent the activated, undulatory, interweaving energy circuit (like a sentient caduceus); and their illumined, radiant, and effulgent golden heads, with the earrings, jewelry, crown, and the rest, represent the brilliant "fruit" of that total awakening.

Although Hindu lore says the Nagas are the enemies of Garuda, they are not; actually, they are cousins. Garuda's mother, Vinata, is the sister of Kadru, the Nagas's mother, and Garuda is the same being in different guise as Airavata (see Ganesh). Both are among the many expressions of the angelic order called the Ofanim who say they "eat awareness," but it is not the Naga's awareness.

Snakes or Nagas also refer to human souls in a state of awakening awareness. Garuda swallows awareness (eats snakes) as humans awaken; his function is to eat awareness, and the awakening of that awareness is the Snake. But "eat" refers more to coparticipation in and support for the process. As celestial "cousins," Garuda and the Nagas are colleagues in the same grand task, the Nagas of Nagaloka being perhaps the prototypes for this embodied awakening. Garuda works closely with the Nagas, emissaries of this first created realm.

Nagas are not water spirits; if anything, they pertain to the archetype of the earth element, just as the *Muladhara* chakra does. In some cases, their residences are situated in vast physical valleys that started out dry then became lakes: the Kashmir Valley in India and Lake Tahoe on the California-Nevada border are two examples of this. Their association with water is metaphoric: In the spiritual world, water is consciousness, so we could say the Nagas occupy (or are) vast lakes of awareness.

The Naga palace is experientially much as it is described classically: opulent, majestic, enormous, jewel-encrusted, a lake of brilliant light. The hall is very long and wide, the ceiling domed; at the far end sits the Naga King, Vasuki. Along the promenade through the hall to the throne are numerous beings, mostly human, presumably in spiritual form, and thousands of resplendent Nagas.

A Naga may offer you a jewel, as a condensation of a potential wisdom experience. The jewel, perhaps a lapis lazuli the size of your fist, acts as a portal for you to enter a dimension or experiential place where a revelation awaits.

See also: Dragon, Ganesh, Garuda, Mount Meru, Ocean of Milk.

NAVEL OF THE WORLD

One of 72 Energy Focusing Nodes for planetary landmass subdivisions that feed the land with celestial energies.

Also known as Earth Navel, Energy Focusing Node, minor Albion chakra, Name of God, omphalos.

Description: Many cultures claim a particular mountain, hill, town, or landscape feature to be the navel of the world, the omphalic place of primordial creation, or at least the center of a given landmass, such as a nation. Notable on this list are Ireland, Greece, Peru, Easter Island, and even the United States.

The Hill of Uisneach is claimed to be Ireland's navel and the residence of Eriu, an ancient Irish goddess after whom the island was first named (Eriu's Island, or Eire). She presided over Ireland as the goddess of the country's center at Uisneach. As such, she embodied the land's sovereignty and ceremonially married each new king in an inauguration ritual called the *banais righe,* which married secular authority with the spirit or goddess of the entire island.

Delphi, on the slopes of Mount Parnassus in Greece, was classically called the omphalos of that country and even originally had a conical egglike stone a few feet high to mark the exact navel. It was a famous and much-visited oracular site said to be founded over the slain carcass of Python, an immense Earth dragon killed by the Sun god Apollo. Greek myth says that Zeus, the high god of the Olympians, once dispatched two ravens (or eagles) from the ends of the Earth to find the planet's center; their flights converged at Delphi.

The ancient Incan city of Cusco in southeastern Peru is also called the navel of the world, indicated in its original name and its spelling, *qosqo,* "Earth's navel," in the local Quechua language. Long ago, the legend says, a culture hero (or god) named Manco Capac plunged a golden staff into the ground there, establishing Cusco as the Earth's omphalos. The exact foundation site for Cusco was later called *cuzco cara urumi,* or "uncovered navel stone."

The original name of Easter Island, a remote island all of 63 square miles and 2,200 miles west of Chile, was *Te-Pito-o-Te-Henua,* "The Center of Navel of the World." Another old name was *Mata-Ki-Re-Rani,* "Eyes Looking at Heaven."

The nineteenth-century Native American Lakota visionary Black Elk implied that Harney Peak in the Black Hills of South Dakota was the center of the world. His foundational vision of standing on the world's highest mountain and beholding the "hoop of the world" and numerous smaller hoops with a massive flowering tree in the center took place while he was meditating on that peak.

Mexican myth says that Lake Texcoco (now drained and the site of Mexico City), the ancient site of two important cities, Tenochtitlan and Teotihuacan, was the navel of the world. In classical Rome, there once stood a column next to the Arch of Severus, called *umbilicus urbis romae.* This is usually translated as "the navel of the city of Rome," but it could also mean "the navel of the world" as in "the world of the Roman Empire."

The Bons, Tibet's original pre-Buddhist and shamanic inhabitants, claimed that Mount Kailas, a 22,028-foot peak 800 miles northwest of Lhasa, was the world's navel. They said it was the Nine-Story Swastika Mountain rising into Heaven and the Soul Mountain for the entire geographic region.

The Balinese regard their sacred mountain Gunung Agung in Besakih, a 10,308-foot volcano and multiple temple site, as the navel of the world. Biblical tradition calls Mount Girizim in Palestine the navel of the Earth.

Explanation: How can so many sites claim to be the world's navel? The answer is that there are at least 72 sites that can accurately make this claim.

Within Earth's visionary geography are 72 Energy Focusing Nodes. Each is placed somewhere (not necessarily the geographic center) in one of the 72 original landmass subdivisions of the Earth. Originally, the Earth had nine major landmasses, to each of which was assigned a major angelic protector; within these landmasses, 72 subdivisions were recognized, to each of which was assigned a subsidiary angelic protector (called an egregor; see Chakravartin and Eriu) and a people. The landmass and the angelic protector would nurture the particularities and folk-soul characteristics of the people placed there, ensuring the purity of their distinguishing essence as Irish, Peruvian, Greek, and the rest.

Each of these 72 landmass subdivisions, such as Ireland, Peru, and Greece, has a location that focuses and concentrates incoming cosmic and upwelling geomantic energies for that region, just like a biological umbilicus. Such locations (Delphi, Cusco, the Hill of Uisneach) are truly navels of the world in the sense that they feed their predefined, integrated geomantic territory just like a body, or more precisely, a fetus inside the mother's womb.

In many cases, the national angelic protector is present at the navel point, as in Eriu at the Hill of Uisneach, which is also the exact geographic center of Ireland, or Izanagi-Izanami at the otherworldly Yashirodono shrine on the island of Onokoro, Japan, where stands the August Pillar of Heaven, the *Amanomihashira.*

It was not ignorance of world geography that led the ancients to term such locations "world navels," but rather a sophisticated knowledge of the geomantic integrity of a given landmass subdivision and its centermost energy point.

The 72 Energy Focusing Nodes also perform a function in a larger geomantic territory or body. Each is a minor chakra in the global body of an anthropomorphic yet cosmogonic figure called Albion (see Albion). Also, each expresses one of the 72 Names of God (*Shemhamforesh,* in Judaic mysticism).

In the case of Delphi, the actual navel-stone that once stood there served an additional function. It marked the grounding point of a line of energy and consciousness from the constellation Ursa Major. The story of the two birds flying around the Earth and meeting precisely at Delphi is a geomantic code for the grounding of an Oroboros Line, one of Earth's 15 primary energy tracks.

With the Easter Island omphalos, the designation was originally in reference to a much larger landmass, part of the postulated sunken former continent called Lemuria, which included the Hawaiian islands.

The actual navel for the entire world (the planet) is at Avebury stone circle, a 28.5-acre megalithic enclosure in Wiltshire, England. Here, Earth itself plugs into the galaxy and receives its celestial-cosmic nourishment.

See also: Albion, Chakravartin, Eriu, Floating Bridge of Heaven, Huitzilopochtli, Ley Lines, Marduk, Tower of Babel.

NYMPH

An umbrella term designating several classes of Nature spirits, including elementals, devas, and landscape angels, ensouling different features of the environment and bridging physical and celestial energies for their areas.

Also known as Awki, deva, elemental, Gazriinezen, *genius loci,* gramadevata, kami, Landscape Angel, manitou, Nature spirit, Nome gods, Numen, numina, village gods.

Description: The term "nymph" comes from the Greek *nymphe,* which means "young girl or bride." While widely recognized, the word, and the being it describes, is actually poorly and only vaguely understood. The general understanding, taking our cue from Ovid's *Metamorphoses,* is that it is the soul of a former human, usually a youth, and most often a female, who, to avoid danger or to escape misery, changed appearance to enter a form in nature, such as a tree, spring, well, grotto, river, or mountain, or a human-occupied place, such as a city.

For example, Rhode is the nymph of the island of Rhodes; Peirene, nymph of the spring of the same name at Corinth; Thebe, nymph and daughter of a River god whose name was given to Thebes; Cyane, a nymph after whom a spring was named near Syracuse in Sicily; Castalia, nymph of a spring at Delphi; and Aetna, nymph of Mount Etna on Sicily. Ovid recounts how the five Echinades islands were once five nymphs and how Lichas, once a mortal, turned himself into flinty rock on the Euboea coast, the rock shelf still (several thousand years ago) exhibiting traces of his former human shape.

Thus nymphs are said to be primarily beautiful female and amorous spirits dwelling in particular natural environments or features. They wear diaphanous, flowing garments, have golden bands in their hair, play instruments, educate infant gods, offer prophecies, and, though mortal, live for thousands of years.

Homer called the nymphs "daughters of Zeus," and the Greeks described several types according to where they lived. Oreads were mountain nymphs; Alseids lived in groves; Naiads in water, such as lakes, springs, or streams, or, for

Nereids, the ocean. Dryads were tree nymphs, originally of oaks specifically; Hamadryads spent their entire existence associated with a single tree, dying with its death; and Meliads were nymphs of the ash trees.

In Roman times, the word *Numen* referred to a minor deity or Nature spirit that made a location numinous or divine, that raised its vibration. The classical Romans and even the Greeks before them commonly thought certain places in the landscape were inhabited by spirits or *numina*, whose presence enlivened a site. These *numina* are the same as nymphs.

Nymphs were once honored by the Greeks and Romans in such forms as a *nymphaeum*, a special shrine for the nymphs, usually a fountain or grotto, but later a decorative wall or façade with columns, statues, and flowing water; a fountain house dedicated to them in the Agora of Athens; or a temple dedicated to the nymphs in the Campus Martius of Rome. In classical Rome, nymphs were honored on August 23 each year as part of the Volcanalia festival, and often in conjunction with Silvanus, the Roman version of Pan.

Nymphs were often associated with Pan, said to dance with him in the hills; they would hunt with Artemis; revel and rout with Dionysus; even help raise the children of the gods, such as Aeneas, Aphrodite's son, on Mount Ida in Crete. They were frequently either the lovers or mothers of the gods, heroes, and satyrs, and certain locales were recognized as sacred and dedicated to them.

Examples included a cave at Lera, sacred to Pan and the nymphs; the grotto on Mount Hymettus, sacred to Pan, Apollo, and the nymphs; and the Cave of the Nymphs (or Marmarospilia Cave) at Vathy on Ithaca, a cult center dedicated to the Naiads and used by both gods and mortals, especially Odysseus, says Homer. Odysseus also maintained an altar to the nymphs near a waterfall near his home.

Certain nymphs were credited with cofounding ancient citadels, usually in conjunction with the local River god. Troy's beginnings are attributed to a union between the River god Scamander and Idaea, the nymph of nearby Mount Ida (in today's western Turkey). Ovid writes how barefoot river nymphs attended Achelous the River god in his sumptuous abode under the river.

Explanation: Nymph is a multipurpose term that actually refers to several different classes of Nature spirits, including elementals, devas, and landscape angels. To call them all "nymph" is both accurate and confusing.

The Greek picture of nymphs offers us a wonderful image of the ensouling of every aspect of nature with celestial intelligence. When Ovid writes of humans metamorphosing into trees, streams, springs, and the rest, he is recounting the *process* long ago whereby the spirits entered all natural forms. Most of the account, however, is fanciful window dressing to explain how spirits enter plants, minerals, and water forms in the environment—how the soul gets in there.

Nymphs can be said to be beautiful, diaphanous female spirits, but only if we treat this image casually and poetically. Clairvoyants "reading" Nature spirits have reported various classes of Nature spirits along these lines, yet they emphasize that their "bodies" are dynamic, alive, responsive, and protean, primarily engaged in the cycling of higher energies into the auras and physical matter of their charges, be it plants, mountains, rivers, streams, or lakes.

In the case of nymphs of individual trees, groves, rocks, or springs, these are typically either elementals (the Nature spirits who manage the different classes of matter, including earth, air, fire, and water, and known, respectively, as gnomes, sylphs, salamanders, and undines) or devas, a branch of angels charged with ensouling and enspiriting different classes of Nature. On the larger scale of lakes, rivers, valleys, canyons, and mountains, we are dealing with landscape angels, again a class of devas, but executing more responsibility over a larger area.

In general the term *genius loci* is applicable here. From the Roman usage, it means the spirit of a place, the focal point that gives an area a particular ambiance. What gives a grove or grotto a special vibration is its *genius loci*—the nymphs.

In India, this class of being is called *gramadevatas,* the village gods. These are gods who preside over the life and welfare of villages as well as animal and plant fertility, but they can express their displeasure through drought or floods. In more general terms, the Hindus use the term *Deva* to indicate a spirit being of Light (angel) inhabiting or ensouling a landscape and its features.

In ancient Egypt, the land was divided into 42 small provinces, or nomes, each presided over by a Nome god and its subsidiary hierarchy of assistants. The Nome god was the local god—a regional nymph, landscape angel, or egregor.

Native American psychic perception speaks of *manitou,* which are spirits that inhabit all aspects of Nature, including the wind, thunder, species, minerals, and lakes. They animate all physical objects in the natural world; manitou may appear in dreams to award special protection or power; or they may be encountered in natural settings as guardians such as Water gods or land features. Similarly, Japan's Shintoism speaks of *kami,* an undifferentiated class of spirits who animate all aspects of nature, such as stars, mountains, rivers, fields, and the wind. In Peru, *Awki* are the protectors of caves, springs, rocks, lakes, and trees. In Mongolian shamanism, the *Gazriinezen* are the spirits of mountains, rocks, trees, bodies of water, settlements, and even countries.

In Dryads, Hamadryads, and Meliads, nymphs of particular types of trees, and presumably allocated one per tree, we have a devic form highly open to human interaction. J. R. R. Tolkien's Ents in *The Lord of the Rings* is a highly useful image for how this might work. The older tree spirits, especially those ensouling the longer-lived trees (such as beech and redwood), have a deep memory of events that have happened around them over the years and centuries, which they will share with interested humans who "talk" with them.

At the level of valleys, canyons, lakes, and mountains, the landscape angel oversees the vibration for a large area and all its subsidiary Nature spirits. The nymph Aetna, for example, will oversee the activity of all the fire elementals in the volcano as well as the diversity of devas and Nature spirits for miles around.

In the case of cities or islands named after the resident nymph, such as Rhodes for the nymph Rhode and Thebes for the nymph Thebe, here the devas maintain the integrity of energy, ambiance, and consciousness for that region. You could say the nymph or landscape angel Rhode ensouls the entire island and that, energetically, the island, its physical and etheric matter, all its human, plant, animal, and mineral life, is enspirited by her and in fact dwells within her field.

Modern culture may no longer have formal *nymphaea* for honoring the nymphs, but we can include them in any outdoor geomantic rituals we perform. For example, if you bring down celestial and angelic light and consciousness to a sacred site, you can dedicate some of it as spiritual food for the local nymphs.

See also: Eriu, Fairy Queen, Gaia, Kokopelli, Marduk, Menehune, Pan, River God, Royal Hall of the King of the Dovrë Trolls.

OCEAN OF MILK

The primordial, pre-Creation state of unified, undifferentiated, self-contained consciousness, or Light, before any life, the stars, constellations, cosmoses, or galaxies were manifested—God's total awareness.

Also known as Aditi, Heaven, Ksirasagara, Ocean of Sweet Milk, Pleroma, Samudramanthana, Uncreate Light, Unmanifest.

Description: The ancient Hindu epic the *Mahabharata* tells how long ago the gods decided to churn the Ocean of Milk to extract the ambrosial substance of immortality called Soma. It was a divine substance they could not live without.

They used Mount Mandara as the churning-stick and the serpent-dragon Vasuki as the cord, and churned the Ocean of Milk as if making clarified butter. They got the Soma and immortality, and 13 other divine substances, objects, and deities, but the gods did not want Svarbhanu, the cosmic dragon, to have any of it. They cut him in half, rendering him into Rahu and Ketu, the head and tail. Thereafter in Vedic astrology, the two parts of Svarbhanu became known as the North and South Nodes, and Rahu and Ketu always tried to eat the passing Sun.

Another Vedic account of the Ocean of Milk has it that Brahma, the Creator god, once drank too much amrita or Soma and vomited it out. This formed the celestial cow Surabhi, and Surabhi's milk or Soma flowed out of her and collected into a sea called the Milk-Sea (Ocean of Milk), or *Ksirasagara.* But Vedic myth also says Surabhi was formed from the *Humkara,* or the mantric sound of *Hum,* from Brahma. As the cow matured, milk dripped out of her udder and formed the Ocean of Milk and she was afterward called the Cow of the Devas.

The dripping or dribbling motif in connection with the Ocean of Milk is emphasized in a third Vedic tale. An elegant cosmomyth about Soma says that long ago Rudra (the star Sirius and an early form of Shiva) shot an arrow at Prajapati, Father of all creatures (equated with the constellation Orion, seen as an antelope) and hit his testicles. Some of his seed leaked down into the lower worlds, pooling as the Lake of Sperm or *vastu* (or Lake of Prajapati's Seed and Lake of Fire).

Explanation: The Ocean of Milk is a profound image to connote the state before Creation in which all consciousness was homogeneous, undifferentiated, and unified. The Ocean was the repository of all potentialities, but for these to manifest, and especially for key gods and precious divine objects to be expressed, it had to be churned, a process of subcreation called *Samudramanthana.*

The Gnostics called the Ocean the Pleroma and, esoterically, it is Heaven (the realm of absolute, unruptured Light) in the primordial duality of Heaven and Earth (all cosmic matter, subtle and gross, including all the stars and planets).

Pleroma means "Fullness," but the Ocean of Milk is also a Void, a space of emptiness *(Sunyata),* completely free of matter, and the boundless Infinite. Other names include Chaos, the unfathomable Abyss, Womb of Being, Great Sea of Space, Endless Deep, Boundless Spirit, Unknown Darkness, Bythos, the Deep.

The Uncreate is also known as Aditi, the goddess of infinite being, infinite light, and indivisible consciousness, the undivided unity of the infinite. One essential quality of this infinite state is bliss *(Ananda).* The Ocean of Milk is the ocean of eternal, infinite existence permeated by absolute sweetness, or bliss.

It's also been described as the one eternal element, a great universal sea of "Blazing White Essence"; from this, God created all forms, beings, and creatures. The Ocean of Milk is the storehouse of universal substance, a sea of what one authority called obedient electrons (an Electronic Sea), from which a being in the ascended state (occupying a Light-body; see Fisher King, Salmon of Wisdom) may precipitate (create) anything desired, without limitation.

Rudra was trying to stop Soma from leaking from the Uncreate into the Created worlds, but failed, as some dribbled down. Soma is the quality of unbroken awareness; King Soma is the god who is truly and always awake; Soma is primordial wakefulness distributed throughout space as a precondition or fabric in which to place the stars that always desire to partake of it to secure their immortality. It doesn't make them immortal; it is the substance of their predifferentiated state when, by definition, they were immortal because they had not been individualized into star gods whose bodies (the physical stars) would die.

Soma is also the pure, absolute, and original bliss *(Ananda)* of existence.

As star gods made of cosmic fire, the stars consumed Soma, an edible substance affording immortality—a taste of or even a return to their original state of uninterrupted, unified wakefulness and the bliss of continuous consciousness.

The *vastu,* or cosmos, became the House of Stars with Rudra (Sirius) as its guardian. The myth should be inverted: Rudra (Shiva, Sirius) is the guardian of the flow of Light from Heaven to Earth, of Uncreate Light to the *vastu* or cosmos.

This flow has been memorialized in myth, though with an overly physical emphasis, as the Fountain of Youth, the Waters of Life that give immortality, a little bit of the supercreative essence of continuous consciousness and the quality of unruptured, self-contained, preconscious totality *before* Creation dribbles down from Heaven or its intermediary, Surabhi, Brahma's vomit cow.

The myth about the gods preventing Svarbhanu from drinking the Soma must also be turned around. Soma is the exudate of the cosmic dragon, known also as Sesa-Ananta in Vedic myth. This thousand-headed dragon is the remainder of the previous universe or round of Brahma and contains the residues of its consciousness. It contains what survived the end of Creation, called *Pralaya,* which is to say, that which precedes or transcends all manifestation—Soma.

Svarbhanu does not need to drink Soma; the substance of immortal consciousness, unbroken, continuous wakefulness, comes from him, is him.

Hindu myth says that in between cycles of creation when Brahma is quiescent, Vishnu the Preserver (the Hindu Christ or Logos) lies upon Sesa-Ananta and dreams as the vast coiled dragon floats atop the primordial Sea. It is equivalent and just as descriptively accurate to say Sesa-Ananta is the Ocean of Milk, or it is his substance and exudate, just as the milk dribbles from Surabhi. Both are containers bearing pure unified consciousness before Creation, that is, before the myriad stars and constellations are formed in the vastu.

The gods stirring the Ocean of Milk to yield its Soma is equivalent to the Soma dribbling out of an overfull udder of Surabhi to form the Ksirasagara or Prajapati's seed dripping down into the created world and pooling as the Lake of Sperm. The dribbling, dripping, or flowing of the Milk (absolute Light, unbroken wakefulness, or Soma) is also the fabled Fountain of Youth in its original though rarified expression, and the Lake of Sperm or Ksirasagara is a Soma Temple. This is an interactive geomantic template found in 144 locations around the Earth.

Hindu esoteric yoga says that the microcosmic version of the Ocean of Milk is called the Soma chakra (or energy-consciousness center) located just below the cranium and considered a subset of the seventh or crown chakra. Known as the City of Freedom, here dwells the Unmanifest, the nectar of Light.

See also: Cattle of the Sun, Cosmic Egg, Fisher King, Fountain of Youth, Hitching Post of the Sun, Salmon of Wisdom, White Horse.

ORANYAN'S STAFF

The umbilical link connecting the Yoruba and their original homeland in Nigeria with the celestial realms, and nourishing both.

Also known as Obatala's Gold Chain, Obatala's opasoro.

Description: Oranyan's Staff is a myth from the Yoruba people of Nigeria and set in their holy city, Ile-Ife (pronounced ee-lay ee-fay), the place where the Yoruban people were first created and possibly where all life began long ago.

The high creator god Olodumare (also called Olorun, "Owner of the Sky") commissioned Obatala (also called Oduduwa) to create dry land for living creatures on a flooded Earth. He equipped himself with a gold chain long enough to reach from Heaven to the wet Earth, a snail's shell filled with sand, a white hen, a black cat, and a palm nut, all of which he carried in a bag.

Obatala's name means "the King of the White Cloth" and all of his images and objects, such as his cloth, lace, beads, flowers, and cowries, are pure white. His name comes from *Oba,* which means "king" and *tala* or *ala,* which means "undyed fabric," as in a blank canvas.

Obatala hung the gold chain from the sky and descended. Some distance above the flooded Earth, he dribbled some sand down and let the chicken spread it around to form dry land. The larger sand piles became hills, the smaller piles valleys, and the seven sacred hills surrounding Ile-Ife were formed. Obatala jumped down to the newly formed land and called it Ile-Ife, House of Ife (which means "Old Home" or "Wide House"); he planted the palm nut, which quickly grew into a palm tree. Then he created all 16 tribes of the Yoruba people.

Afterward, the other gods, whom the Yoruba call Orishas (whose number is given as 16, 401, or 601), descended the gold chain to visit with Obatala and observe his creations, both land and people. Thus all Yoruban life and culture began at Ile-Ife, as well as the institution and validation of all Yoruban kingship, since Obatala's world-creating descent. In fact, Obatala became the first Yoruban king with his royal seat at Ile-Ife. Sometimes his staff of kingship is called *opasoro,* which he used to create 200 civilizing customs for the Yoruba.

Among his epithets, Obatala is known as *Alamo Re Re,* "The One Who Turns Blood into Children"; *Alabalashe,* "The Wielder of the Scepter of Life"; and *Obatala gbingbiniki,* "The Enormous Obatala." He is styled as the Protector of the Town Gates, represented as mounted on a horse and armed with a spear.

He fathered 16 sons who spread out across Yoruban land to start their own kingdoms. But another version of the legend says Olodumare created seven princes and sent them down to Ile-Ife, equipping them with special items including cowrie shells, a chicken, 20 iron bars, beads, and a mysterious substance wrapped in cloth. Six of the princes failed Oludumare's test, which was to choose the objects most essential to creating life and justifying kingship.

The seventh prince, named Oranyan (or Oranmiyan), took the chicken, iron bars, and cloth-wrapped substance. This was a black powder. Oranyan, perched in a great palm tree that Oludumare created for him to sit on just above the flooded expanse below, sprinkled the black powder, and the chicken distributed it far and wide, thus creating dry land. Oranyan changed the iron bars into weapons and established himself as the first Yoruban king at Ile-Ife.

A third myth blends elements of the previous two. Here Oduduwa, the founder of Ile-Ife, leaves rulership of the holy city to Oranyan, his son. Oranyan was a brave warrior and wise ruler, and as long as he lived, Ile-Ife was safe. When death finally approached him in his old age, Oranyan instructed his priests in the secret words that would summon him even after his departure if the city needed him. He planted his wooden staff of office in the center of Ile-Ife and at once it turned into a stone column, still present today, called Oranyan's Staff.

Once, years after, the people of Ile-Ife had great need of his protection, called on him, and Oranyan emerged with a thunderclap out of the ground at Ile-Ife. He was fully armed, his weapons flashing, and he defended the city against its enemies. Afterward, he returned to the Earth, which closed up over him.

His status after this rescue of the holy city is contradictory. One legend says Oranyan lives still, sleeping inside the Earth or in a recessed grove at Ile-Ife, waiting for the next great trouble the Yorubans encounter, when he will rise up to defend them. Another legend says he was once called out of confusion during a time of revelry and mistakenly killed the Yorubans since he saw no other enemies, and he has not been seen at Ile-Ife ever since.

Only his mighty staff remains, or the remains of it. Yoruba legend says broken stone remains of the petrified staff were later dug up and fitted together to create a 20-foot pillar studded with iron nails.

Explanation: The Yoruban myth of Oranyan's Staff is a description of the Energy Focusing Node for the Yoruba original homeland present at Ile-Ife.

An Energy Focusing Node is a geomantic feature otherwise known in myth as the Navel of the World or the omphalos for a country. It is the essential grounding point for celestial incoming energies for a specific landmass; it focuses and concentrates cosmic and geomantic energy for that region, and it functions just the way an umbilical cord does to connect a fetus to its mother. The mother here is Heaven or the spiritual worlds, for the Yoruba, Olodumare.

Often myths attribute a specific tree to a primary holy site; in Ile-Ife's case, it is the palm. The palm tree at Ile-Ife is another reference to the omphalos. The umbilical link and Tree of Life connecting Heaven and Earth are the same.

As for Obatala sprinkling celestial sand and a chicken spreading it to produce dry land for Ile-Ife, this is a geomantic metaphor for the grounding of the Energy Focusing Node. Since the Node concentrates and focuses essential energy for the Yoruban landscape, it is reasonable to picture this as a congealing or drying of land (solidity, a center, the grounding point) from out of the fluidic, less formally defined "waters" of the Earth's Light body (see Dreamtime).

The Yoruba myth gives us two views of the umbilical link. First, as Obatala's gold chain whereby he descends from Heaven to Earth, and second, as Oranyan's Staff, mark of his pledge to forever protect his sacred city, Ile-Ife. The gold chain and the staff are identical, although the two named gods are different. Obatala is the creator god, but Oranyan is the Yoruban national landscape angel.

Peruvian myth offers a similar story: Viracocha, the great creator god, creates humanity in the vicinity of Lake Titicaca in Bolivia, then sends his son Manco Capac with a long golden staff to found a city at what is now Cusco. Alternatively, Peruvian lore says Manco Capac was a Child of the Sun god. After testing a number of locales, Manco plunges his staff into the ground at a place known thereafter as Cusco (later, Cuzco), which means "navel of the Earth."

Manco Capac and Oranyan are national guardian angels, two of the Earth's original 72 assigned to discretely defined landmasses at the inception of Earth. Other names for this type of spiritual being are egregor, Watcher, Tutelary Prince of the Nation, or Regent of the Nation. Originally, they were angels, 72 manifestations from the same family, assigned to different landmasses and cultures. In this way, each was the King of the White Cloth in the sense of an undyed fabric—that is, without the content of lived cultural experience that would accrue to them in watching over land and people over the millennia.

Each such egregor supervises the inherent geomantic features of the landscape and the relationship of its people to those subtle landscape features. In the case of Oranyan, his brief is to oversee the original Yoruban homeland, occupied by the 16 tribes at the inception of this differentiated people. With the frequent political boundary divisions in Africa in the last two centuries, Oranyan's territory may not completely coincide with Nigeria's national borders.

The national egregor oversees the unfoldment of the inherent soul qualities of the people occupying that land—what makes them Yoruban. The egregor preserves the integrity and accommodates the evolution of the "genius of the people," or the geomantic, energy, and consciousness aspects of nationhood.

Judaic Qabala speaks of the 72 Names of God, or *Shemhamforesh,* and, to a large extent, the totality of the 72 egregors are these. Each folk soul (egregor or national soul character) tied to its landmass expresses a Name of God. This is why, in part, Oranyan is the son of Obatala or sometimes of Oludumare. Oranyan in his angelic essence embodies one of the Names, and that essence is grounded in the Yorubans and the Nigerian landscape at its geomantic center, Ile-Ife.

Were the Yorubans actually first created at Ile-Ife? Yes, in two ways. First, clairvoyant investigation of the omphalic grounding point reveals a picture of full-grown adult Yoruban men and women in great vitality and vigor emerging from Obatala's gold chain as if walking into the Earth world from another realm.

Presumably this was the first, pristine generation of Yorubans, the living seed of this people. Ile-Ife is the place where one of the Earth's 72 original peoples was first manifested, grounded, and received orientation to Earth life.

Second, Ile-Ife is where the soul essence of the Yoruban people is known, held, and nourished by that people's national Guardian Angel, Oranyan. As egregor, he maintains the integrity and soul virtue of both landscape and people. Ile-Ife is the Yoruban omphalos because it is the energy archives for the Yoruban people—the place that perpetually nourishes its folk essence and soul qualities.

As for the occasional visitation of Obatala's Orisha colleagues, that possibility was institutionalized, geomantically speaking, by way of the presence of one of the eight Celestial Cities found in multiple copies on Earth. The one at Ile-Ife pertains to the Lords of the Seven Rays or Seven Rishis of esoteric and Hindu myth, respectively. These are the 14 Ray Masters from Ursa Major, the seat of the Great White Brotherhood for the galaxy. This Brotherhood (see Einherjar, Glass Mountain, Seven Rishis) is the galaxy's spiritual government.

See also: Dreamtime, Einherjar, Eriu, Glass Mountain, Huitzilopochtli, Marduk, Navel of the World, Sengen-Sama, Seven Rishis, Srin-mo Demoness.

ORPHEUS'S LYRE

A vibratory and sound method of harmonizing the human's seven chakras and their aspects, totaling 49, to induce a God realization.

Description: In Greek myth, Orpheus is the consummate singer-harpist. He is the son of the Olympian god Apollo and one of the Nine Muses, all of whom Apollo directed. This particular muse's name was Calliope, which means "Lovely Voice." Orpheus's father is also given as Oeager, the son of the Olympian war god Ares, or as Oiagros, a Thracian River god.

He is principally known for three accomplishments: He was the founder and teacher of the Orphic Mysteries; the lover of the human female Eurydice, whom he was unable to rescue from the Underworld, even with his musical gifts; and a prime member of the 50 immortals and gods known as Jason's Argonauts who sought and found the Golden Fleece in the distant, magic-ridden land of Colchis (in today's Republic of Georgia).

On that expedition, he was officially the *Keleustes,* the one who sang shanties to set the pace for the rowers, but he was also in charge of all religious matters, having been initiated in many of the ancient Mystery centers like Samothrace.

Orpheus is probably best known for his skill on the lyre, a nine-stringed harp created by Apollo then given to him. His beautiful and seductive songs and music, which encompassed epic poetry, incantations, oracles, and initiation rites, beguiled and enchanted all listeners. Throughout the voyage of the Argonauts, Orpheus frequently calmed his distraught companions, entertained them with song, or coaxed them into mystical, contemplative states with his lyrics. He lulled the tempestuous waves and outsung with sweetness the alluring Sirens.

It's also told that Hermes, not Apollo, made the lyre from an empty tortoise shell he found by the banks of the river Nile. He attached strings to the already resonant concave shell, and the resulting instrument produced subtle, delicious sounds some say were audible only to the gods. While visiting Olympus, Hermes traded his lyre for Apollo's caduceus; Hermes taught Apollo how to play the lyre, then departed the gods' hall. Apollo gave it to Orpheus.

Orpheus is credited with increasing the number of strings on the lyre from seven to nine because that is the number of the Muses, his aunts.

Orpheus was torn to pieces by the Maenads of Thrace (today's northern Turkey or southern Bulgaria). All of Nature wept for him. His head was thrown into the river Hebrus and floated downstream, still singing, to the island of Lesbos, where it was buried with reverence. The Muses gathered up his body fragments and buried them in Pieria; afterward, the nightingale there was said to sing more sweetly over Orpheus's grave than anywhere else in all of Greece.

Finally, Zeus set his lyre in the Heavens as a constellation known as Lyra, or Orpheus's Lyre, which contains our galaxy's fourth brightest star, Vega.

Explanation: Orpheus was a member of the angelic order called Nefilim, one of three angelic families to take temporary human incarnation in giant form. Orpheus's commission from the Supreme Being was to instill higher levels of consciousness in humanity (which he largely accomplished in the creation of the Polynesian "race" or genetic strain of humanity) and to teach the Mysteries, systematic forms of initiation into the higher truths and realities of existence.

He was not the son of Apollo, but rather a colleague. Apollo is one of the 14 Ray Masters from the Great Bear (see Seven Rishis), and some of Orpheus's work involved the Ray (theme of consciousness and light) and its themes and initiates that Apollo administers.

The central fact about Orpheus's Lyre is its number of strings: nine.

Mathematically, nine represents the number of limits and extension. It is the seventh of the Pythagorean numbers (starting with three) and the last original number before the numbers become endless permutations of themselves. Nine is the limit that the generative principles of numbers can reach; it is the number of completion, balance, and perfection, and, to the Greeks, it was the horizon, the limit that could not be surpassed, the ultimate extension, edge of reality and boundary.

In terms of Earth's visionary geography, nine is a central number. The majority of its 100+ geomantic features, in terms of the quantities of their copies, have digits that reduce to nine. This number is also the prime signature and design logo of the Great White Brotherhood and the Pleiadian Council of Light (see Connla's Well).

Orpheus was able to induct human consciousness into the sonic reality of the star being we normally think of as the constellation Lyra. Pythagoras would later show the effect of sound and music on human awareness and the chakras, but Orpheus already knew this and applied it wisely with his songs and music.

His playing for the Argonauts was, esoterically, a way of harmonizing the seven major chakras (energy-consciousness centers) and their seven aspects each, or 49. He was the fiftieth Argonaut, located in the pineal gland of the sixth chakra, the one whose lyre harmonized the 49 different and potentially disparate tones.

His harmonizing the 49 chakra aspects enabled the Argonauts (the chakras) to bypass a dragon and acquire the Golden Fleece, the object of their journey. The Lyre harmonizes the 49 energy-consciousness components of this system at any level of expression, from a molecular Chakra Template (see Forest of Bliss) to one at the level of a solar system comprising the seven classical planets and their seven aspects.

Orpheus's skill was to induce his listeners—initiates—into the celestial reality of the star being Lyra and its functions in the galaxy. When you observe a star or constellation executing its mandated function, it appears to be at the center of the galaxy. With Lyra, nine sound tubes divide the spherical galactic space into nine segments, each 11.111111 degrees, with a little left over. Galloping on solar chariots through these sound tubes are nine celestial star gods or perhaps the Muses. Each emits a different sound, or harmonic sound pattern, like a string.

Another way to see the harp or lyre with nine strings (sound tubes) is as a torus, which looks like a smoke ring or doughnut with the center taken out. The torus is a mathematically defined shape whose beauty is that it is in continuous motion, yet does not expand; this gives you infinite motion within finite limits.

Picture the ring as divided into numerous ribbed sections; these continually flow into the hollow center, go through it, and come back up the torus's outside. Here is a mathematical way to depict it: Plot the square roots of nine up to the 24th square root (e.g., $\sqrt{9} = 3$, $\sqrt{3} = 1.7320508$). The 24th square root totals one. Orpheus's Lyre is a number matrix based on the 24 square roots of nine.

The Lyre produces imploding infinity. This is the 24 square roots of nine reducing to one at the 24th calculation. This is the ribbed edges of the torus cycling into the open nothingness of the torus's center and entering a new place.

With each successive square root of nine, as you approach the number one, you get ever closer to the Source, to the hollow center of the torus, to God.

That is the beauty, seduction, and mystical revelation of Orpheus's Lyre: the ability to conduct you through sound attunements into an alternate reality. The Lyre will conduct you in 24 stages down to one, to *The One.*

Greek myth says that after Orpheus's descent into the Underworld (or Hades) to rescue his beloved human lover, Eurydice, he brought back for the gods esoteric information about how to reach the even more exalted land of the Blessed Ones. The soul of Orpheus, said to be garmented in a long white robe, continued to sing in Elysian Fields with seductive beauty for the immortal gods.

The gods did not need to learn how to reach the Blessed Land. They were already there. But mortal humans wanted to learn this and Orpheus taught them.

Qabalists teach that God has three arcane Heads, or dimensional expressions. Each is more mysterious and harder to reach than the one before, yet each is a truer revelation of what the Supreme Being looks like and is. When the cycling torus of Orpheus's Lyre implodes into infinity, this moves you into the next Head, into a deeper revelation of the Supreme Being's ontological status.

The Lyre is a way out of the galactic labyrinth by going inward to the center (both topologically and mathematically). It is a way of expanding into a new dimension of reality and being within the proscribed boundaries by contracting into the center. Just follow the 24 square roots of nine into the center.

Perhaps it is easier to think of the 24 square roots as harmonics of the nine. They are implicit in the Lyre's nine strings, but need to be played to be made explicit. As the nine strings are plucked, the harmonics are teased out and you cycle through the center of the torus (the matrix of 24 square roots) into infinity.

See also: Argonauts, Beast of the Apocalypse, Connla's Well, Forest of Bliss, Giants, Golden Fleece, Hitching Post of the Sun, Seven Rishis.

PAN

A devic being commissioned to work on Earth to inject life force energy, vitality, fertility, and consciousness into the plant and animal kingdoms.

Also known as Ba-Neb-Djet, Cernunnos, Faunus, Green Man, Innus, Kokopelli, Lupercus, Silenus, Silvanus.

Description: The Greek god of Nature and shepherds, and the Shepherd of the flocks, Pan's home was rural Arcadia, his birthplace, Mount Lycaeum.

His name might derive from the Greek root *pa(s),* which means "guardian of the flocks" or "shepherd," though it may also mean "feeder," derived from *Paon* or "to pasture" from *paein.* His name was sometimes associated with the identical word *pan,* though with a different meaning, as it means "all." In the *Homeric Hymn to Pan,* all the immortals of Olympus take delight in the unusual young boy-god and call him Pan ("All") because he delighted all their hearts.

Usually, he is depicted as half-man, half-goat, with a goat's head and man's torso, though sometimes as a bearded, hirsute, feral, primitive-looking man with little stubby goat horns and sometimes a horse's torso, as in the centaur image, or goat's legs and feet, for which he was known as the Goat-Foot God. His parentage is heavenly though vague and variable, but often his father is Hermes, the Olympian messenger, and his mother, probably, the nymph Dryopes.

Pan always carries his favorite reed pipes, the syrinx or, simply, Pan-pipes, which he invented. The nymphs and satyrs would dance wildly to his tunes and Pan was known to beguile or startle humans—creating a sudden panic in them with the pipes. Pan's presence could also produce *panolepsia,* a savage, even violent, state of possession and loss of one's human center of identity. Pan was a lusty god of the pastures and countryside, seeing to the fertility of the flocks and herds; he was often portrayed with an erect phallus for his penchant for chasing alluring nymphs and he was invoked by people when fertility was required.

Pan was also perceived as the wildlife deity Silenus, the half-man, half-animal patron of the Sileni, which the Greeks depicted as older satyrs.

A special shrine was dedicated to Pan on the Acropolis in classical Athens, and yearly festivities involving torch races were held in his honor. The historian Plutarch presented the now well-known though enigmatic story that one day a mysterious voice announced as if out of a clear blue sky, "The great Pan is dead." This was around the time of the early rise of Christianity, which, later, in the medieval period, used Pan's goat-human appearance as an image of Satan.

In Roman times, Pan was described as Faunus, a pastoral god, primarily of the forests, who could speak eloquently, made strange noises in the woods, and revealed the future in dreams and spectral voices heard in groves. Faunus had a human torso and head, carried a drinking horn and hefty club, wore a panther skin, and sported a crown. Faunalia, a festival of Faunus, was held December 5 and consisted of a rural feast with animal sacrifices, eating, and much drinking.

Faunus was not officially depicted as having Pan's goat characteristics, yet Fauns, presumably the source of the Faunus image, were. These were deities who were half-human, half-goat, with horns and cloven goat hooves. They were eventually equated with the Greek satyrs and understood to be woodland spirits; numerous rural temples to Faunus were erected, though there was one in Rome on Tiber Island.

Another Roman guise for Pan was Silvanus, the god of uncultivated lands and woods, agriculture, hunting, and boundaries. He was the subject of at least 1,100 documented Roman inscriptions from 39 B.C. to 339 A.D. He was often depicted as a full-grown, robust, and bearded man with a sickle, a cornucopia of harvested plants and killed animals, and with exposed human male genitals.

Still another Roman guise for Pan was Innus ("He who makes fruitful"), a god of fertility and possibly sexual intercourse, possibly from the word *inire,* which means "to copulate." He was the god originally worshipped at the Lupercalia, a fertility rite celebrated on February 15 in honor of Lupercus, a pastoral god in charge of fertility of fields and flocks—still another Pan guise.

The Greeks identified the Egyptian *Ba-Neb-Djet,* the sacred ram of Mendes (his city of worship), as the same as their Pan. He was a ram with flat branching horns topped by a uraeus, and sometimes given four heads. He was considered a figure of male sexual power and fertility, even an aspect of Ra.

Except for a brief resurgence of interest in Pan in the 1970s through the New Age Findhorn Community of Scotland, Pan has left public awareness.

Explanation: Pan is the protector spirit of the

plant and animal kingdoms on Earth. He works under commission by a deva or angelic being at the cosmic level; Pan's task is to incarnate in appropriate forms and different expressions (different according to conscious perception), on different planets that have plants and animals, though not necessarily like on Earth. There can be as many different guises of Pan as there are planets with flora and fauna.

Pan is the carrier of spiritual life force running through organic life. His priapic images (including the lusty goat form and his progeny, the satyrs) are metaphors for how Pan injects the spirit of focused consciousness into matter. The fertility aspect refers to how Pan continuously contributes life-force energy to plant and animal species as if from a vast reservoir of biological vitality, enabling them to flourish, propagate, spread, and evolve as part of the planet.

To psychic perception, Pan's face may appear to teem with representatives of all the Earth's animal species, like living, moving tattoos, while his limbs and torso are foliated with the planet's flora, trees, bushes, leaves, and flowers.

He is a subcreator and shape-shifter, allowed to generate thousands of different guises in the form of Nature spirits (fauns, satyrs, gnomes, fairies, centaurs, and many others) as his agents to work in appropriate ecological niches. Just as God generated numerous angelic orders to be messengers, so Pan created numerous Nature spirit groups to send his message and life force into Nature.

The Pan-pipes, or syrinx, is a metaphor for how Pan summons the flora and fauna into attention and the awareness that they exist in a living web. Humans, hearing the unworldly pipes, get into a "panic" in the sense that Pan injects the force of spiritual awareness into the physical body, into matter itself, and that can be alarming, even frightening, to a cerebral, atheistic humanity largely alienated from matter and its primal, instinct-driven impulses.

Pan works with Gaia, the Earth Spirit, to help her achieve the set parameters for conscious evolution in matter on this planet. His blueprints specify the planet's maximum carrying load for species diversification. He stands as a white god-human inside the Earth, his head touching the North Pole, his feet at the South Pole, inserting thousands of fingers of light through the Earth's surface into various ecological domains to fortify and nourish the flora and fauna.

As the force of consciousness in matter, as expressed through plants and animals, Pan was depicted by the Celtic folk soul as Cernunnos, the Horned One, who represents the force of abundance and prosperity, and as the Green Man, a human face made of leaves and greenery, as the masculine power of abundance.

Theosophists speak of the totality of the elemental kingdom and their different energies as a planetary elemental. Pan is the master of that elemental.

Pan, in constantly giving of his energy essence to the plant and animal kingdom of Earth, participates in the Christ Consciousness and is functionally an expression of the Holy Ghost and Christ in Nature. Pan is the unquenchable force of awareness that permeates supposedly dense matter (plants and animals) and forms the bodily context and food for higher human consciousness.

As a devic being, he sacrificially incarnated in Earth matter to be the guardian of the planet's flora, fauna, and the Nature spirits he generated to maintain these kingdoms energetically. His substance is continuously consumed, like a Eucharist, yet in recent centuries, human neglect and now oblivion of Pan has led to his energetic diminution because humans no longer take part in the great chain of reciprocal maintenance that is supposed to knit humanity with Earth, Nature, nature spirits, and the angelic orders.

Where once Pan was celebrated annually at festivals like the Faunalia and Lupercalia, today he is left to fend for himself and has grown anemic, having been forced to abandon certain flora and fauna species to maintain his energy reserves.

See also: Fairy Queen, Gaia, Kokopelli, Menehune, Nymph, River God, Royal Hall of the King of the Dovrë Trolls, Trolls.

PANDORA'S BOX

A myth referring to the first generation of humanity and the long-term karmic consequences of its excessive use of free will, remembered metaphorically as the expulsion from the Garden of Eden and the Fall of Man.

Also known as the Dolorous Stroke, Expulsion from Paradise, the Fall.

Description: Greek myth recounts that Epimetheus ("After-thought"), the brother of the Titan Prometheus, was warned by his brother never to accept a gift from Zeus, chief of the Olympian gods (the Supreme Being). He did anyway when he accepted Pandora ("All Gifts"), the first woman ever created, made from earth and water (clay) in the likeness of the immortal goddesses.

Epimetheus desired to possess such loveliness as the beautiful Pandora embodied, and married her. Soon after, against all advice, she opened a great jar, later called Pandora's Box, and released all the sorrows, miseries, and evils it contained into the world of humanity. Both Epimetheus and Pandora are generally blamed by Western humankind for condemning humanity to suffering.

Explanation: This is a story about the first Lucifer and the first generation of humanity. Pandora is a metaphor for all men and women in this first, open-ended creation of a humanity with free will, the gods' fire (kundalini), and all the psychic and physical powers these gifts entail. Pandora refers to humanity in the transition from the Garden of Eden to their expulsion from Paradise for disobeying the injunction against tasting the fruit from the Tree of the Knowledge of Good and Evil. What happens when Pandora opens the box is a taste of the knowledge of good and evil—the excruciating freedom to choose one.

Epimetheus, as the first Lucifer and brother of Prometheus, the second Lucifer, could not foresee how humanity would use the gifts of the gods, from free will to individualized bodies with self-aware consciousness. Only his brother could foresee this. Epimetheus could see, and thus comprehend, the complications of the gift of the gods' fire to the first humanity only afterward—hence his afterthought.

The miseries, sorrows, diseases, and evils released from Pandora's Box are metaphors for the consequences of the use of free will in the physical world. The box's contents are humanity's karma, or accrued spiritual debt for the uses and abuses of their great gift of consciousness while physically incarnate. The box (or jar) itself is the chakra system interthreaded with the three subtle channels for kundalini; the seven layers of the aura or energy field around the human; the body itself and its abilities, free will, and extensive consciousness; and the lower astral plane surrounding Earth, now filled with new, inharmonious content.

The metaphoric story is akin to the Grail saga of the Dolorous Stroke, whereby the Fisher King wounds himself grievously in the groin (root chakra) from misuse (unprepared, uninitiated, inept, unstructured use) of the sword of the gods. The Pandora tale also refers to the transition from the Rich Fisher King to the Wounded Fisher King, as recounted in Western Grail myths. In Judeo-Christian culture, this is called the expulsion from Paradise, or the Fall of Man.

Pandora was All Gifts, the fresh, virginal humanity, free-willing, self-aware consciousness inhabiting karma-free bodies and with access to total cosmic consciousness—rich indeed—who misused this godly gift and karmically wounded itself, that is, all of subsequent humanity. No longer will humans have immediate access to the riches of deep cosmic memory symbolized by the Grail Castle. The second generation of humans will start incarnation under the guise of the Wounded Fisher King, unable to connect easily the consciousness circuit of the chakras to facilitate total awareness, deep cosmic memory, and the unitive state.

See also: Asura, Djinn, Dolorous Stroke, Fall of Man, Fisher King, Garden of Eden, Kings of Edom, Lucifer, Prometheus, Raksasas, Ravana, Tree of the Knowledge of Good and Evil.

PEACHES OF IMMORTALITY

A container for implicit wisdom and achieved spiritual insight as seen through Chinese culture and equivalent to the Celtic Golden Apples of the otherworldly Avalon, the Isle of Apples.

Also known as Forbidden Fruit, Golden Apples.

Description: In Chinese myth, Xi Wang Mu, the Queen Mother of the West (or *Hsi-mu,* "West Mother"), lives in a marvelous golden palace atop the K'un-lun Mountains in western China. This snowcapped range extends almost 7,500 miles across western China, from the Tibetan Plateau in the south to the Taklamakan Desert in the north, with a typical elevation of 16,500 to 18,000 feet.

Chinese myth, however, indicates that one peak among the K'un-lun is foremost. The specific peak is called Jade Mountain or, sometimes, Mount Flamingfire. Here Xi Wang Mu lives, but sometimes she is said to be the consort of the Pure August Jade Emperor (*Yu Huang Shang Ti,* or *Tien Kung*) who also lives here in his Jade Castle of Abstraction high above Earth and the heavens.

The Chinese regarded her residence (some accounts say it is of jade, not gold), which overlooks Jewel Lake, as the core of the Western Paradise, and Western interpreters generally depict it as vast, ringed by a golden wall 330 miles (or 1,000 miles) long and topped with precious stones. The Mountain Paradise is guarded by serpents, dragons, birds of prey (a six-headed hawk), wild cats, the *Shi-Rou* ("Lookflesh"), and K'aiming and Hsiang Liu, both nine-headed. K'aiming is sometimes referred to as the ferocious Openbright, a feline beast with human faces on its nine heads. Yet benevolent beings are present as well, such as three Birds of Paradise, and all who dwell there lead lives of unending delight and the purest pleasures of body and spirit.

A beautiful woman, Xi Wang Mu lives there with a celestial entourage that includes the five Jade Fairy Maids as well as numerous male and female Immortals distributed throughout her residence in accordance with the color of their garments. In the palace, she sits on her leopard throne; when she leaves, she flies on a white crane; when she sends messages, she dispatches them with magical bluebirds.

The chief feature of Xi Wang Mu's residence is the Peaches of Immortality. Precious fruits, it takes them 3,000 years to grow, and 3,000 to ripen. Eating a Peach keeps the immortals in their undying condition. Chinese legend says that a few of China's earliest human rulers received a Peach of Immortality. Twelve other heavenly trees with marvelous virtues are found there, such as the Never-die Tree, Jade Tree, Wise Man tree, and Sweet Water tree.

Thus her K'un-lun Mountain residence was also, potentially, a paradise for human mortals who had been favored with her gift of immortality and the regular communion with the gods that that achievement brought. Xi Wang Mu is often depicted holding a staff, scepter, or wand in her left hand and a basket of the Peaches of Immortality in her right. The Peaches are linked with another Chinese myth, that of a giant cosmic peach tree that is a sky-ladder for the gods to ascend and descend from Heaven to Earth and said to be 3,000 leagues across.

When a Peach ripened, the Queen Mother served it to her guests, the Immortals, as the centerpiece of a magnificent feast called *P'an-t'ao Hui,* "the Feast of Peaches" set at her fountain made of precious stones near the Lake of Gems (*Yao Ch'ih,* also called Jewel Lake). The feast's offerings also included monkey's lip, dragon's liver, and phoenix marrow. During the feast, guests were entertained by lovely music and song, reportedly by invisible performers.

Explanation: In the opulent, detailed description of Xi Wang Mu's Feast of Peaches, her court, and heavenly trees, we have a Chinese perception of one of the eight Celestial Cities of the gods, better known in Celtic myth as Avalon.

It certainly is city-size. With a perimeter of 330 miles, Xi Wang Mu's Mountain Paradise occupies 6,806 square miles with square sides of 82.5 miles. As this realm is an astral place accessed through the physical, this size is not to be taken literally in either realm, but as a statement about its opulence.

In Avalon, a term sometimes translated as "Apple-Land," Morgan le Fay and her eight immortal sisters tend the undying land and its apple trees. The Fortunate Isle (Avalon) is a land of awesome fertility and beauty, with trees bearing Golden Apples. The medieval writer Geoffrey of Monmouth, in his *Vita Merlini,* identified Morgan's realm as at Glastonbury, in Somerset, England.

An equivalent Norse version has the goddess Idun ("Rejuvenator") custodian of the Golden Apples of immortality. Every day the Aesir (high gods) eat a Golden Apple and by this maintain their youthful appearance and longevity.

Xi Wang Mu of course is the Chinese perception of Morgan and Idun, and her five Jade Fairies an approximation of Morgan's eight Avalonian sisters. Xi Wang Mu's consort-husband, the Jade Emperor, finds a parallel in the Celtic myth in which Morgan and her sisters live with their father, Avallach, King of the Summer Country (Avalon). Avallach may be considered the lord of this Celestial City, though the Jade Emperor may be an even more exalted being.

The Chinese description of the features of K'un-lun generally and Jade Mountain specifically points to many geomantic features. This is not surprising, as Glastonbury's Avalon is surrounded by more than a dozen other features. The one pertinent to the Peaches of Immortality is that the place has an Avalon portal.

Without going into all the particulars of the beasts guarding the palace, we can say with certainty that one of the named creatures is a dragon whose rightful task is to guard the Golden Apples of Avalon. We see this more clearly in the Greek account of Ladon, the dragon coiled at the base of the Golden Apple trees of the Gardens of the Hesperides in the far West.

As for the Peaches of Immortality, though the type of fruit differs in the Chinese version, the function is consistent and even acknowledged in the title. In whatever form they are perceived, the fruits of the Tree of Life in Paradise (or the Garden of Eden in its original celestial model) bestow immortality. As the biblical injunction testifies, normally these fruits are forbidden to humanity. Mortality is the fate (or gift) awarded humanity, so tasting the fruit (knowledge, being) of the Tree of Life (eternity, immortality, nondeath) is proscribed.

Humanity, in seeking incarnation with free will and choice, and thus mortality and consequences (karma, "sin"), surrendered its right to the Tree of Life (see Yggdrasil) and its unbroken eternal oneness in consciousness for the experience of duality, fruit of the Tree of the Knowledge of Good and Evil.

Yet the Golden Apple has other benefits to those who encounter one.

The fruits of spiritual practice in certain cultures are traditionally called apples of insight, usually gained at an inner astral plane. Each apple is a stroke of wisdom. When the Greek Herakles obtained the Golden Apple from the Garden of the Hesperides as part of his Twelve Labors, the accomplishment marked his realizing and accepting his innate wisdom, which was pure and golden. It was not necessary to remove the Golden Apple from the tree to have this realization. But you may have to be patient: It could take a few lifetimes (perhaps the 6,000 years in the story) to ripen spiritually to a sufficient level to claim an apple or peach of insight.

It was necessary, though, for Herakles to be able to discern the genuine from the illusory.

Some Golden Apples are fakes. There are 47 authentic Golden Apples, one per Avalon, even though myths speak of multiple orchards and apples; and there are 97 illusory Golden Apples, found in 97 of the Avalons. Of the Peaches that ripen in Xi Wang Mu's orchards, only one is the real thing yet, paradoxically, everyone throughout time may feast on it without it diminishing.

There are 144 Avalons in total, or perhaps more accurately, there are 144 *portals* into the one Avalon, known by many different names, such as Jade Mountain or the Queen Mother of the West's Mountain Paradise.

Experientially, "eating" a Golden Apple is more accurately described as entering one. The apple is like a living, radiant sun in apple form; you assimilate its contents by entering its information field, for the fruit, after all, is knowledge and cosmic intelligence.

Herakles, by visiting the Avalon known as the Gardens of the Hesperides, gets an authentic Golden Apple and all its insight and wisdom, just as did the reputed ancient human rulers of China visiting the K'un-lun Mountain Paradise.

Since the gods, by definition, are already and forever immortal, then they do not need to eat the Golden Apples or Peaches of Immortality for that benefit. Rather, they perpetually consume—they have as the *essence* of their being—the riches of spiritual wisdom these fruits represent. In the myths, their regular access to these celestial fruits serves to inspire humans to emulate them.

See also: Avalon, Dragon, Garden of Eden, Golden Apples, Morgan le Fay, Mount Meru, Tree of the Knowledge of Good and Evil, Yggdrasil.

PEACOCK ANGEL

A profound perception of Lucifer, Lord of Light and humanity's maligned, ambivalent benefactor, as already pardoned by God.

Also known as King Peacock, Lucifer, Malak Tawus, Melek Tawwat, Mighty King.

Description: The Yezidi formulation of the Peacock Angel, also known as Malak Tawus, is marvelous among myths of the world in that it forthrightly identifies the spiritual personage meant by its mythic portrayal: Lucifer.

The Yezidis are an Iraqi sect, representing five percent of the Kurdish population of Syria, Turkey, Georgia, Armenia, and the city of Mosul in Iraq where they are known as devil-propitiators and the chosen people of a rebellious archangel. Not surprisingly, they have been persecuted over the centuries by Christians and Muslims, the latter referring to them as *Muraddun,* "Infidels."

Even so, the name Yezidi derives from the Iranic *yazata* or *yezad,* which means "angels," thus making the Yezidis Angelicans. Scholars regard them as an unusual Gnostic offshoot of the Nestorian Church whose members believe that Lucifer, the Devil, has *already* been forgiven and pardoned by God and reinstated as Chief Angel supervising the running of the world's affairs.

Yezidi tradition says the Peacock Angel appeared majestically before a shepherd. Heralding Malak Tawus's epiphany, the sky was torn asunder by a lightning flash and Earth rocked under the impact of a roar of thunder. The shepherd saw an angel standing in the middle of the heavens with a huge spear in his hand. Then the angel hurled something down onto the mountaintop.

The shepherd found that it was a peacock, damaged by the fall. He tended the bird during the night and, by morning, it had recovered and spoke to him. "I am the Spirit of Evil thrown out of Heaven by my twin, the Spirit of Good," it said. It instructed the shepherd to teach his descendents to accept evil as he accepted the bird. "Be compassionate toward evil both in yourselves and in others."

Lucifer is Malak Tawus, the Peacock Angel, the chief of God's archangels, the Yezidis state. Their mythology holds that, before the Beginning, the Supreme Being made a ship for Himself and spent 30,000 years sailing for pleasure on the primordial Sea. Then He created the bird *Anqr* (or *Anzal* or *Anfar*) on whose back He placed the

White Pearl, made of His essence. The Pearl dwelled on Anqr's back for 40,000 years.

Then on a Sunday, the first day of creation, God created His first archangel, Malak Tawus (also called *Azazil* or *Izrail*), the Peacock Angel; He created the Archangel Michael on Wednesday. Thus Malak Tawus existed before all other spiritual beings and creatures, according to the Yezidis.

Yezidi belief, however, seems to merge Malak Tawus and the celestial Anqr, suggesting they are two aspects of the same spiritual being. For example, the prime Yezidi feast days for Malak Tawus are October 6 to 13 at Lalish in Iraq, during which time a sculptured bronze bird called Anzal is ritually revealed and presented to the assembled people, presumably as an icon for Malak Tawus.

So Malak Tawus was the prime avatar of the universal spirit in the First Epoch of Creation, the Yezidis say. The other six archangels were created one per day during that "week" of creation. The identification of Malak Tawus as Anqr is like the Aztec-Mayan view of Quetzalcoatl, the Plumed Serpent.

As for the White Pearl, this contained the germ of all things that would be created and introduced into the world, all of Heaven and Earth (see Cosmic Egg). The Egg broke into four pieces; the Supreme Being put one piece below Earth, another at the door of Heaven, and put the Sun and Moon in both of them.

Out of the scattered fragments of the two other pieces of the Cosmic Egg or White Pearl, Malak Tawus created the stars, which he suspended in the sky for decoration. Then God commissioned Malak Tawus to create and govern the world for 10,000 "years"; 4,000 years of his reign still remain. After Adam and Eve were created, Malak Tawus descended to Lalish in Iraq to live among the people and to instruct them in kingship.

The Yezidis maintain that whatever "evil" Malak Tawus may have committed, God has already pardoned him and reinstated him as chief archangel. The Yezidis' self-appointed task is to keep Lucifer happy in that reinstated role, because they, alone among humankind, never blamed or cursed him in his disgrace.

Explanation: The Yezidi myth of the Peacock Angel is unique among world myths for its unflinching acknowledgment of the bivalent reality of Lucifer, Lord of Light, Light-Bearer, and God-appointed living expression of the ambivalence of the Tree of the Knowledge of Good and Evil—human free will.

In their formulation of the already pardoned Peacock Angel, the Yezidis, an obscure and intensely persecuted sect, set an example highly worth emulating by humanity as it struggles to come to terms with this complexity.

At the beginning of humanity's phylogenetic incarnation, Lucifer posted surety for humanity's extraordinary gift of free will and total consciousness. He embodied and demonstrated this as the Tree of the Knowledge of Good and Evil. Lucifer showed how it is possible to exercise free will to choose good or evil in the context of having self-aware consciousness in a material human form.

One expression of Lucifer in his original, unsullied, divinely appointed glory, from the Aztec-Mayan cultures, is as the Plumed Serpent, Quetzalcoatl. Here his magnificent bird form and glorious plumage are similar to the Yezidi Anqr and the chromatic nuances suggested by Peacock Angel. Malak Tawus comes to Earth plumed in the full array of consciousness states, plumed with the angelic realms.

Lucifer never rebelled against the Supreme Being's directions. Rather, he acted with the full commission of God to bestow free will and self-aware consciousness with, potentially, a full cosmic range of potency among humanity. So while the Yezidi myth pays some allegiance to (mistaken) world consensus on the rebellious aspect of Lucifer, they also are far ahead of that consensus in terms of insight and spiritual maturity in recognizing Lucifer is already forgiven by God. It is humanity's unwillingness to pardon Lucifer that holds everything up.

Even this observation is fraught with irony since, ultimately, Lucifer requires no pardoning by humanity since he acted entirely on our behalf. Yet since a great portion of humanity holds Lucifer to blame for current conditions, though he is blameless, he still needs to be reinstated by those humans.

The Yezidi formulation of the Peacock Angel is prescient from a geomantic, and even theological, viewpoint. That is because Earth and its vast array of visionary geographic features energetically sits inside a special precious gem that originated in Lucifer's crown and is known as the Emerald. The same feature sits in miniature as a hologram within the human heart chakra. This is called the Emerald and is the key to revivifying Earth and humanity.

The entirety of Earth's Light grid, its spiritual or energy body, sits within Lucifer's Emerald, and Lucifer, certainly in Western consciousness, sits in a seemingly unpardonable dungeon of repudiation and punishment. Only the Yezidis have forgiven Lucifer, following God's example, but for Earth to become whole and healthy again, for its visionary geography to flourish, and for humanity to feel happy and fulfilled in material life, everyone must do the same.

The Yezidi identification of Lalish in Iraq as the residence of the Peacock Angel after the birth of Adam and Eve is fitting as it is one of Earth's 3,496 Lucifer Binding Sites. This is a feature at which Lucifer, as the Lord of Light, is arriving in glory, being bound in disgrace, or unbound in pardon. Among the 3,496 sites, the full range of this three-way manifestation is constantly under way.

Malak Tawus creating the stars out of the White Pearl is geomantically apt also. It is a veiled reference to Earth's stargate network (see Land of Milk and Honey, Rising Rock), which is completely interconnected with Lucifer's status.

The stargate network is an array of about two million transportation portals across the Earth linking Earth with hundreds of stars and constellations. Its operation is dependent on a healthy and pardoned Lucifer, as they are expressions of the Light he bears. If the Lord of Light is incapacitated due to humanity's binding of him or nonforgiveness, then the stars that his Light implicitly connects will not be accessible by stargates from the Earth and an important part of our spiritual birthright will continue to be unavailable to us.

Lucifer does not "rule" humanity, yet his tenure may well last 10,000 years—understood of course to be time units far longer than our solar years. What the Yezidi mean is that as long as there is an Earth with a Light grid comprised of visionary geography features and a humanity living and spiritually evolving within that context, Lucifer will remain planet-bound. The 4,000 years remaining to the Peacock Angel's reign may be a metaphor for the estimated time allotted for humanity to reconsider this vital spiritual being.

See also: Cosmic Egg, Emerald, Land of Milk and Honey, Lucifer, Prometheus, Quetzalcoatl, Rising Rock, Tree of the Knowledge of Good and Evil.

PELE

A landscape angel of high order and responsibility charged by Gaia, the Earth Spirit, to supervise and monitor all the planet's volcanic activity.

Also known as Ai-laau, Ka-ula-o-ke-ahi, Pele-ai-honua, Pele-honua-mea, Pere.

Description: In Polynesian myth, Pele is the impetuous, passionate Fire and Volcano Goddess, specifically attributed to Mount Kilauea, a still potentially active volcano on the big island of Hawaii. Pele is believed to inhabit Kilauea with a family of Fire gods, including five brothers and eight sisters, whose activities include overseeing thunderstorms, volcanic activities, and cloud forms. With them, she governs all the activities of lava flow from this volcano.

Pele is not originally from Hawaii. In fact, Kilauea is only her most recent stopping place. In the beginning, Pele was born to Haumea (or Papa, the personification of Mother Earth, or Gaia) and

Moe-moea-au-lii, a chief, far away in the Pacific in a land called Honua-mea in Kahiki. She migrated eastward continuously in search of a suitable place to dig a fire pit deep enough for her family of 13 fire deities and to enable them to exhibit their flame spirit forms as well as enact their volcanic, weather, and cloud activities.

Before settling at the crater Moku-a-weoweo ("Land of Burning") at Kilauea, Pele and her entourage had formerly inhabited many volcanoes in the Pacific Ocean including on Nihau, Kauai, Oahu, and Maui in the Hawaiian Islands. She traveled in a canoe provided by her older brother, Ka-moho-alii, the king of dragons (also called sharks, and sometimes, as a group, the *mo'o*), and carried her special digging spade, the *Pa-oa,* to create the fire pits in her new locations. Each of her fire pits soon got washed away by the ocean until she dug one on Kilauea, which proved to be a mighty and enduring palace of fire, legends say.

When Pele stamped the floor of her fire pit in anger, the result was an earthquake. Her voice when angry was explosive like gunshots and called *pu.* Flames breaking through cracks in a lava crust were understood to be the fire-spears of the *au-makuas,* the ghost-gods of Pele's household. If Pele grew impatient with her sisters or brothers, or anyone else, such as humans, she would send burning lava into their valleys to destroy their homes and eat up their land.

Hawaiian myth speaks of her taking the form of a beautiful woman when it suited her, having love affairs with human mortals, such as Lohiau, the Prince of Kauai, and of being elemental in her passions and impetuous in her actions.

Earlier in her migrations, she was known in Tahiti as *Pere* ("Conceiving Heat"), produced by the heat of the Earth. Thus Pere was the goddess of fire and spontaneous burning in the Earth, and fire was understood to be the physical agent of the gods' power. Her residence down inside the Earth is awe-inspiring, Tahitians say.

Pele has numerous epithets: She is *Pele-ai-honua* ("Eater of Land"); *Ai-laau* ("Wood Eater"), in the sense that Pele supplanted this older named volcano god and took over his fire pits; *Pele-honua-mea* ("Pele of the Sacred Earth"); and *Ka-ula-o-ke-ahi* ("The Redness of the Fire"), the sacred name for her manifestation in her spirit form. (Pele is her name for her physical fire form.)

***Explanation*:** In many respects, Pele is actually one of Earth's oldest deities since her field of responsibility encompasses *all* the planet's volcanoes. She is well known in Polynesian lore because in large measure the Pacific islands from Tahiti to Hawaii represent the most recent area of planetary volcanism. But Pele is implicit in all the planet's volcanic activity, much of which predated the advent of humanity on its surface, so her name in many places is not known.

Mount Kilauea (elevation 4,190 feet), the fire goddess's most recent residence, is the youngest and most active volcano in the world; geologists estimate its first eruption as about 300,000 years ago and say that 90 percent of its surface is covered by congealed lava flow less than 1,100 years old.

Since 1952, Kilauea has erupted 34 times. Since January 1983, eruptive activity along the mountain's east rift zone has been continuous. Flows in 1986 both destroyed homes and created new land. Kilauea's name is appropriate to its high activity volcanism: It means "spewing" or "much spreading."

Pele is a landscape angel of a high order of responsibility who works closely with Gaia, the Spirit of the Earth, or the planet's master landscape angel. Pele may be pictured as a female angel whose body is made of red flames. In terms of Mount Kilauea, she is inside and outside the volcano, and, generally, when she extends herself to full stature, she is many times larger than the mountain and even its three volcano neighbors Mauna Kea, Mauna Loa, and Kohala.

Yet at the same time, Pele sits inside Earth, as it were, tending the vast reservoir of molten lava at Earth's core. She has numerous arms, each able to reach up through an existing volcano (one of the many fire pits she dug) to stimulate or subdue activity as appropriate, which means in concert with Gaia.

The Polynesian image of Pele migrating continuously across the Pacific until she found an enduring location for her fire pit is descriptive of how she allowed some short-term volcanic activity to occur at numerous Pacific islands over a period of probably many hundreds of thousands of years. Each volcano had its time of activity, then quiescence; Mount Kilauea is still in the active phase.

Metaphorically, Pele keeps the lid on the pot until Gaia instructs her to lift it up for a short time and allow some volcanism at her latest residence. It might be a little release at Kilauea in Hawaii and halfway round the world at Mount Etna in Sicily or some stirrings at Mount Saint Helens in the United States. Though Pele is not credited as being a global volcano goddess, in fact she is.

That Pele is given an older brother named Ka-moho-alii who is the king of dragons is highly appropriate in geomantic terms. Norse myth describes the Midgard Serpent, a vast dragon coiled around the planet (see Dragon). This is a correct perception, and the Midgard Serpent's head or focus of consciousness is in the central Pacific Ocean. The several hundreds of islands of Tahiti and Hawaii (and their volcanoes) are like freckles on its massive, fire-exhaling face. Pele works with this singular Earth dragon (her "older brother") to release and distribute the fire element around the Earth as part of terraforming activities.

Pele flies around inside this dragon, bringing up threads of fire to the surface. She uses her pa-oa digging stick to poke through the dragon's skin (Earth's surface) to allow the fire element to burst and spume upward. The result is what we call volcanic eruption and mountain formation. Pele's job was, over time, to pass her "sewing needle" (pa-oa) and fire thread (molten lava and all the expressions of the fire element working through volcanism) up through the dragon's skin so that the fire element within the Earth could enter the outer physical world and create mountains and detoxify the planet as well.

Pele's 13 brothers and sisters (minus the dragon king) and the *au-makuas*, or ghost-gods of her fire household, are subsidiary landscape angels in her charge.

Volcanic activity from a human viewpoint is frightening, dangerous, and often physically disastrous, yet volcanism has planetary purposes. For one, it has been part of Earth's terraforming process, creating new land, changing landscapes, destroying old landforms. Terraforming on this scale was much more significant in Earth's earliest days, but signs of its potency can be glimpsed even today through the actions of the still semiactive volcanoes.

Another purpose of volcanism has to do with planetary detoxification. In most cases, volcanoes are topped by a subtle geomantic feature called a dome (see Holy Mountain), an etheric energy canopy transmitting the energies of a specific star and with an original diameter (when first installed, millions of years ago) of 33 miles, though today the diameter is typically less than half of that due to entropy.

Technically, the domes summoned the volcanoes up out of the Earth to create themselves on the surface as mountains. In terms of the planet's energy economy, volcanoes are like pimples or boils on the skin of the Earth. They are a means by which internal toxins can rise to the planet's surface and be ejected; they break through and ooze or explode, enabling detoxification. Dormant or mostly inactive volcanoes are boils that no longer exude pus.

The toxins are, to a large extent, human-generated, not physical in composition, but products of consciousness, and usually of a low vibration. An image may help to illustrate this: Say one area of the planet is engaged in a brutal war; all the thoughts and emotions associated with this nasty activity, as well as the cumulative death trauma of the killed, will form a toxic black cloud of misery (perceivable to clairvoyants) over the site. At some point, the Earth absorbs this. Over time, the Earth has absorbed too many toxins and must expel them to live.

The accumulation of human-exuded toxins is like a layer of psychic sludge inside Earth, that is, within Gaia's consciousness and Earth's mass.

In concert with Pele, Gaia will determine the most suitable discharge node to eject a layer of cumulative toxicity, and volcanic activity will result. The force of the volcanic eruption will purge the planet of some toxicity and, through the energy released with the volcanic explosion, also cleanse the atmosphere.

This illustration, of course, is not a scientific one, but it sketches the general purpose on a spiritual or geomantic level of volcanic activity and Pele. As with Earth Changes, volcanism is not accidental, but carefully planned, executed, and monitored with care by Pele, Gaia, and representatives from the Great White Brotherhood (see Einherjar) and angelic orders who oversee Earth affairs.

In the human, pimples emerge on the face at crossings of *nadis* (subtle energy meridians) or at acupuncture treatment points and can often be traced back to the organ in dysfunction, discomfort, or toxicity, such as the liver. The purpose of the pimple is to discharge a little of the toxicity through the skin as a kind of bodily safety valve and to send a message to the person that his or her organ system has some imbalances requiring attention.

Similarly, Gaia will select the appropriate geomantic node (a dome-topped volcano) to purge some accumulated toxicity and Pele will execute the action. She will direct her attention to the chosen node and let the lid off the pot for a time. Earlier in Earth's history, when Pele was migrating across the Pacific digging fire pits that kept getting washed away, Gaia was selectively releasing energy through dozens of geomantic nodes, like cleaning the pipes, not intending to keep specific volcanoes permanently active, only temporarily so.

Geologists generally say that Pele's Pacific route matched the geological order in which the various landmasses she visited came into physical being.

See also: Dragon, Earth Changes, Einherjar, Gaia, Holy Mountain.

PHILOSOPHER'S STONE

The ascended state in which the material body has been purified and alchemically raised into a resplendent Light-body.

Also known as Ascension Body, Diamond Body, Diamond Soul, Electronic Body, Elixir of Life, *filius philosophorum,* Miraculous Stone, Glorified Body, Hermetic Stone, Higher Self, *lapis philosophorum,* Mighty "I AM" Presence, Seamless Robe, Soul of the World, Spirit of Truth, Stone of the Wise Man, White-Fire Body, White Stone by the River.

Description: The creation of the Philosopher's Stone was considered the *Magister,* or Great Work of medieval alchemy. Although the popular conception of alchemy was that it was a kind of proto-chemistry that sought to transmute base metals, typically lead, into pure gold, it was actually a symbolic description of initiation conceived as taking place over a long period of time and in stages. The essential goal was to find, release, amplify, and exalt the trapped spiritual light within the human body and soul and to redefine, even recreate, the body with it.

Alchemists regarded the Philosopher's Stone as the *prima materia,* or First Substance, from which everything else was created. Thus, they believed, since all the metals must derive from it, it could be used to transmute base metals into gold, the quintessential expression of spiritual purity. Alchemical language often referred to the mystic Stone as an Elixir of Life or Glorified Body; mention was also made of the Powder of Projection, a name for the one definite substance that would work the miraculous transformation of matter into something better.

Paradoxically, the Philosopher's Stone is both the key ingredient sought to complete the opus of radical transmutation, and an expression of the completion of the opus itself: Seemingly, one uses the Stone to create and become the Stone.

C. G. Jung, who wrote about alchemy and its symbolism, suggested that alchemy's fundamental aim was to create a *corpus subtile,* which he defined as a transfigured and resurrected body, one that was both matter and spirit, and perhaps akin to what Chinese alchemists called the Diamond Body, which guaranteed immortality by transforming the physical body.

Other Western alchemical names for this included *lapis invisibilitatis* (the Stone of Invisibility) and *lapis aethereus* (the Ethereal Stone).

In the most general, though perhaps most profound terms, the alchemist seeks to transmute something lower (matter, or a specific quality of it) to something higher, that is, of a more subtle, or in terms of the electromagnetic field spectrum, a faster vibration (wavelength), closer to white and the speed of light. In human terms, this can mean the transmutation of the human body-based and emotions-founded personality into something more purified and spiritualized.

Explanation: Perhaps the clearest explanation of the Philosopher's Stone can be found in a series of books that never even mentioned this specific term. In the 1930s, an American named Guy Ballard (he later changed his name to Ray Godfre King) began publishing a series of books in which he claimed to have had direct teaching and physical-personal interaction with Saint Germain, an Ascended Master (see Seven Rishis) who came and went from physical form as he wished.

Saint Germain explained that ascension, what defines and makes an Ascended Master, is the raising of the vibratory level of the body's physical atoms into light, thus creating a Light-body, which supplants the material one. The ascension process is identical to what Jesus Christ demonstrated on the Cross. He transformed his physical body into Light and thereby ascended. The physical body no longer exists, but is subsumed, transmuted into the Light body.

Saint Germain, in Ray Godfre King's writings, proposed a number of equivalent, descriptive names for the ascended Light-body: the Electronic Body (made of obedient electrons), the Magic Presence, the Mighty "I AM" Presence, God-Self, Perfect Self, Seamless Robe or Bridal Garment of the Spirit (Jesus' terms), Perfect Electronic Structure, and White-Fire Body, among others.

These terms all refer to a modern term that is widely used though poorly understood or experienced: the Higher Self, our immortal part. We need to remember that in medieval times, the term "philosopher" meant a person sincerely seeking after truth through experience, what today we would call an initiate.

Ascended Masters, or those who create their own incorruptible Light-body, may travel anywhere they wish, through any plane of existence; take on a palpable physical form and dissolve it as needed; precipitate (create) out of the ethers (Saint Germain's term is Universal Substance, a limitless storehouse of protean, obedient light, or electrons; see Ocean of Milk) any object, food, or substance desired, even create entire buildings; and, in effect, live forever.

The Elixir of Life correlation is found in the fact that, according to Saint Germain, the ascended Electronic Body remains eternally youthful and pure. It can function wherever in the universe it desires, free of all limitations, including time, space, and all conditions of existence. This is called a Perfect Condition of Existence and is potentially achievable by any interested human over time. It is also the Rich Fisher King.

The Philosopher's Stone both resides in every human as the Higher Self, or what Saint Germain calls the Mighty "I AM" Presence (the God-Self), and sits from 12 to 50 feet above the physical body as a glorious, radiant presence.

The stone aspect of the Philosopher's Stone

reference is accounted for by the fact that the source of Light that transmutes the physical body is contained in a "stone" inside the body (the auric field) in the form of a small Emerald. This is located on the right side of the sternum at the top of the rib cage and is an electromagnetic doorway and an esoteric aspect of the heart chakra. Medieval esotericists such as Wolfram von Eschenbach wrote (in *Parzival*) that the Holy Grail was a green stone brought to Earth from Heaven.

That green stone is the Emerald, present in every human, containing the Holy Grail, which itself contains (or potentially will contain as the opus proceeds) the intensity of light that will transform the material body and its atomic substance into the immutable Light-body, or Stone of the Philosophers.

Thus when you combine three seemingly unrelated vocabularies—Holy Grail, alchemy, and Ascension—you begin to glimpse the reality of the Philosopher's Stone.

If you care for a preliminary taste of this process, spend some time meditating within the huge stone circle at Avebury in Wiltshire, England. Concentrate your attention, breathing, and warm regard on a tiny point of brilliant light just above the navel and a little inside. It is possible you will see this point of light or blazing star expand in size until it is larger than your body and you are inside it. You may also see yourself, as if from a distance, as having changed form from a human to a block of white stone perhaps 15 feet high and the same across, blazing and burning high with a fierce white fire.

See also: Emerald, Fisher King, Grail Castle, Holy Grail, Ocean of Milk, Saehrimnir, Salmon of Wisdom, Sword in the Stone.

PHOENIX

A manifestation of the angelic order called the Ofanim as celestial mentor and Mystery revealer at ancient Egypt's omphalos point.

Also known as Bennu, Benu, Benu-Bird, Feng Hwang, Fenix, Kerkes, Lwan, Lwan Shui.

Description: The phoenix was a bird with fabulous, otherworldly qualities as described in both Egyptian and Greek myth.

Known to the Egyptians as the Benu, the bird was a composite of a golden hawk with a heron's head and with red and gold (solar or flame-colored) plumage. Or it was a stork or large, white, wading bird with long red legs and two elongated feathers in a crest on the top of its head; or, sometimes, it was a god, a hybrid of a human with a heron head, carrying the ankh, symbol of eternal life.

In essence, the Benu-Phoenix was considered a primeval form of the High God. Out of its throat came the breath of life in the primeval darkness.

It was self-created from fire at the top of the sacred persea tree at Heliopolis (originally called An) in the north of Egypt (subsumed by today's Cairo). The Egyptians believed the Benu symbolized the god Osiris, from whose heart the bird sprang, in a different account, and also the rising and setting Sun. Thus the Benu, which regenerated itself from its ashes, stood for resurrection.

The Greek historian Herodotus said the Benu, or Phoenix (from the Greek word for "purple," as its plumage was also said to be reddish-purple) to the Greeks, reappeared every 500 years at Heliopolis, one of Egypt's most sacrosanct cities. Its plumage was both red and golden, and in form it most resembled an eagle. Reportedly, the Benu-Phoenix came from Arabia carrying the corpse of its former body encased in an egg of myrrh, which the bird deposited at the Temple of the Sun. In Arabia (or India or Ethiopia), it lived on only the purest, finest plant aromas.

The Benu resided on the top of the *benben* stone (an obelisk) at Heliopolis. The benben was both an upthrust sacred stone and an insignia depicting a pyramid and the Sun's Rays and kept in the shrine of Ra at Heliopolis. It represented resurrection and, as an insignia, appeared on numerous important and sacred structures; in fact, the pyramids were considered to be gigantic benbens, vehicles of the Sun god's resurrection.

After residing in Heliopolis for 500 years, the Benu spontaneously combusted and burned to ashes on the Sun temple altar; soon, a new, fully formed Benu emerged from out of the cold ashes at the same place. The ancient world considered the Benu-Phoenix a unique creature, with no peer.

The word *Benu* (or *Bennu*) derives from the Egyptian *weben,* which means "to shine" or "to rise in brilliance." It enjoyed a popular cult at Heliopolis along with Ra, the Egyptian Sun god whose Temple of the Sun was also situated at Heliopolis. The Egyptians regarded the Benu as the *ba,* or subtle aspect (etheric body), of Ra, and later the hieroglyph for the Benu also stood for Ra. Yet the Benu also represented the creator god Atum and was said to have flown over the primordial waters of Nun before Creation; when it came to rest on a rock, its cry pierced the primeval silence and determined what things would be in Creation.

Some scholars interpret this philosophically and suggest the Benu-Phoenix's cry or utterance before Creation is akin to the Logos or Word that mediates between divinity and created things, and that the Benu's call started all the cycles of time, making it the patron of Time's division into units. Its dissolution by fire and regeneration, then, would book-end large time units.

Further, scholars propose that, as a self-created god, the Benu-Phoenix came from the mythical Isle of Fire, a place of everlasting Light and where the gods were born, as a messenger from eternity to those about to live in the finite world. Some authorities suggest that Herodotus did not appreciate the profundity of the symbol of the Benu-Phoenix and rendered its story in "fairy-tale" simplification.

The magical bird was also regaled as the "Lord of Jubilees," an attribution probably associated with its longevity. Benu symbolized life renewed after a fiery death and dissolution to ashes and, as such, was equated with the miracle of the Sun rising again each morning. A later description said the Benu-Phoenix lived on a nest of precious spaces it made itself and sang melodiously to Ra (transfixing all the gods) who filled it with a consuming fire that led to its burning up.

The Phoenix was recognized in its essential features by other cultures, as in the figures of Kerkes (Turkey), Feng Hwang (China; born of fire, it stood nine feet tall and presaged good fortune), and the Lwan and Lwan Shui (China).

Explanation: The Benu-Bird or Phoenix is the Egyptian perception of an angelic order called the Ofanim, which has left impressions of similar giant bird manifestations in other cultures, such as India (Garuda), Persia (Simurgh), Israel (Ziz), Toltec-Mexico (the Eagle), Native North America (Thunderbird), and Mayan Central America (Vocub Caquix).

The Ofanim is one of the first created of the 40 different angelic families and calculates its age, in human terms, as about 60,480,000,000 years. The Ofanim were present with the Supreme Being *before* Creation began; thus the Egyptian image of the Benu-Bird breaking the primeval silence with its Logos-like utterance is apt. The Ofanim do, in fact, have a sound, which is recorded in the Hebrew as *waw,* a letter of fundamental creativity and virility.

The Benu-Bird's affiliation with Ra, as the etheric body, ba, or vital principle of the Sun god, is also apt, for in the Ofanim's guise as Garuda, this magnificent bird is the celestial mount and transport vessel for Vishnu, the Hindu version of the Christ or Logos, just as Ra, to an extent, represented that to Egypt. In later formulations, Horus the falcon god was also the sign of Christ.

To be the mount of Vishnu or the ba of Ra means the Ofanim are the portal for humans to the eternal Christ consciousness. The Ofanim, in their pure angelic form, transport the human soul into the Mysteries and reality of Christ.

The red and gold plumage of the Benu-Phoenix is of course highly suggestive of the Sun. More subtly, it represents the glory of the Christ light.

The Phoenix does not literally burn to ashes,

but this is a very helpful metaphor. The Ofanim originate in eternity, with the Supreme Being (Atum); when they come into perceivable form (even if it's only to clairvoyance), they assume the Benu-Bird or Phoenix form and are reborn from the ashes of its nonpresence. When they leave this form and the world of human subtle perception and Earth reality, this is symbolized by burning up, leaving only ashes as a trace.

The Ofanim, capable of 40.3 million manifestations and with God-commissioned responsibilities in an estimated 18 billion galaxies, are constantly coming and going. Coming to Heliopolis, they become the Benu-Bird; leaving, the Benu-Bird burns up, with only a pile of ashes remaining, and the Ofanim are gone. The Benu-Bird, "burning up" in a conflagration of fire, signified the extreme spiritual Light the Ofanim brought to Egypt in full, magnificent, illuminating display.

Coming to Heliopolis, the red- and gold-feathered celestial bird stood about 200 feet tall. It did not sit on the benben, but rather next to it, or it superimposed its Light body over and above and beyond the benben. Why Heliopolis specifically? Because that was the navel of the world for Egypt, a geomantic feature called an Energy Focusing Node, a country's omphalos, where the essential celestial and angelic energies for that land and people are grounded.

The appearance of the Benu-Phoenix at Heliopolis, Egypt's navel, is fitting because, within the human body and energy field, that order of angels is contacted by way of its actual presence two inches above the navel as a tiny point of light.

When the Benu-Bird was present at Heliopolis, everything was many degrees brighter, both in visible light and in spiritual Light and consciousness. The Benu-Bird raised the level of awareness, bestowed bliss and joy throughout, and filled all of ancient An, Egypt's omphalos, with its high angelic vibration.

Priests with clairvoyant perception could interview the Benu-Phoenix at such times, receiving clarification, instruction, inspiration, revelation, and Light. The Ofanim, in this bird guise, was thus mentor and spiritual guide to all Egypt. That is why the attribution "Lord of Jubilees" was accorded to the Benu-Bird. On special occasions, the Benu-Phoenix would take a few Egyptian sensitives (per their free-will agreement) back to the Isle of Fire or to other mystical venues.

See also: Behemoth, Ganesh, Garuda, Hanuman, Navel of the World, Simurgh, Thunderbird, Vocub Caquix, Zep Tepi, Ziz.

PROMETHEUS

Lucifer, prime angelic benefactor of humanity who voluntarily underwent incarceration in matter as surety for his gift of freedom to humans.

Also known as Albion, Eros, Fenrir the Wolf, Light-Bearer, Light-Bringer, Loki, Lucifer, Malak Tawus ("Peacock Angel"), Midir, Morning Star, Phanes, Phosphorus, Protogonos, Quetzalcoatl.

Description: One of the Titans, the original creator gods in Greek myth, Prometheus's name means "fore-thought" and "he who knows in advance." The essential story of Prometheus is that, in defiance of the will of Zeus, the chief of the Olympian gods, he gave humanity "the unwearying fire." He stole the fire, stuffed it in a hollow fennel stalk or narthex tube, and gave it to humanity.

As punishment for his theft of the gods' fire, Zeus ordered that Prometheus be chained on Mount Caucasus. The Greek smith-god, Hephaistos, prepared the chains and supervised his binding. Each day, Zeus's eagle gnawed at Prometheus's liver, then at night the liver grew back. In Aeschylus's *Prometheus Bound,* Prometheus bewails his cruel fate, the injustice of the younger, arrogant god Zeus, and how he only wanted to help humanity. Eventually, as Prometheus foresaw, Herakles, the prodigious hero of Greek myth, unbinds him.

Explanation: Prometheus is Lucifer seen through a nontheological Greek filter. In the

Judeo-Christian filter, Lucifer rebelled against God and refused to serve humanity; in the Greek filter, he rebelled against God in order to serve humanity. Neither is correct. Prometheus under commission by God (Zeus) awarded the gods' unwearying fire (self-aware consciousness coupled with kundalini) to a freshly created humanity. The hollow fennel stalk or narthex tube is the Emerald, the structured container for Absolute Light of consciousness. The Emerald, within the human form, is an electromagnetic doorway, to the right of the sternum, and the esoteric part of the threefold heart chakra.

The gods' fire is fully dilated and awakened cosmic consciousness. The fire is also kundalini, the primal life-force energy that, when awakened, irradiates and illuminates the seven chakras along the spine and their minor subsidiaries throughout the body, affording divine awareness—reality as the gods' see it. It also, potentially, facilitates the acquisition of godly powers, called *siddhis,* which are akin to magical, psychic powers, such as levitation, clairvoyance, and others.

Prometheus gave the gods' fire (consciousness) to the second generation of humanity in the form of the Emerald, a structured container that allowed gradual release of the Absolute Light into human awareness and the physical body. This was to counterbalance the excesses and imbalance of how the first generation of humanity had handled the gods' fire (especially the kundalini aspect) and free will.

Appropriately, Prometheus's brother, Epimetheus ("after-thought"), was credited with the disastrous creation of the first woman, Pandora, who against all advice opened what's now called Pandora's Box and released evil, illness, and contagion into the world. Pandora here represents the first generation of humanity but the specific gender reference is a red herring; it's the same false pejorative as the biblical blame heaped on Eve. It was all of humanity that did it.

The box is a metaphor for the gamut of possibilities of expression from the use of free will. Through free will, coupled with awakened kundalini (the gods' fire), first humanity destabilized creation and itself created a great deal of trouble (the contents of Pandora's Box, described as sorrows, miseries, and disease, that is, the price or consequences, also called karma, of free will), which entered the world as a kind of subcreation and is still with us today to deal with.

Epimetheus is the Greek name, then, for the variously described supervising god of the first humanity, elsewhere called Iblis and Tezcatlipoca. His name, "after-thought," is apt, for though championing first humanity and its gift of freedom, he could not foresee the disastrous consequences when he took Pandora (first humanity) as his bride, pledging himself as surety.

Only his wiser brother (still himself) Prometheus ("fore-thought"), on this the second time around on the issue of humanity with free will, could foresee the possible problems with this bequest and take suitable precautions: Put the gods' fire (the Light) inside a structured container (the Emerald) that could not be broken open all in one go, as Pandora's Box could, but only over a long period of spiritual work.

Mount Caucasus, as well as being an actual mountain (although its exact location is still uncertain: possibly the Atlas Mountains in Morocco or Mount Damavand in Iran), functions as a Lucifer Binding Site. Across the Earth at 3,496 sites, Prometheus (Lucifer) is bound to the Earth, to the material realm, as surety for the astounding gift of the gods' fire to humanity. Prometheus had to pledge himself against possible misuses of this gift, which included not only the availability of total cosmic consciousness, but free will. A part of his essence, then, had to enter matter as escort to that part of himself given to humanity.

Herakles, the Greek guise for Merlin, a primary benefactor for Earth and humanity and a principal planet builder and activator, has always been essential to the grounding and release of Luciferian energy on Earth. Although it seems paradoxical, Herakles is involved in both the binding and release of Lucifer through the Lucifer Binding Sites. The binding and release (arriving is the third aspect; see Quetzalcoatl) of Lucifer is a fourth-dimensional activity to do with the management of the awesome light and freedom that Lucifer brings.

A site where Prometheus is still being bound (by restrictive human consciousness, stimulated by religion and dogma) is called a Mount Caucasus.

Prometheus could see his eventual release from Mount Caucasus and his unbinding by the hero Herakles. This is still true today: Prometheus, as Lucifer, knows that one day human consciousness will catch up with the magnitude and ramifications of his gift and start to unbind him at a majority of the Binding Sites. For this to happen, humanity (through individuals, one by one) must come to terms with its collective Shadow.

See also: Azhi Dahaka, Emerald, Fall of Man, Harmonic Convergence, Lucifer, Merlin, Pandora's Box, Quetzalcoatl.

PURUSHA

An expression of the cosmogonic totality of Creation in the form of a Cosmic Man, which finds geomantic replication across the Earth in the form of interactive holographic copies of the stars and constellations of the galaxy.

Also known as Adam Kadmon, Albion, Anthropos, Atman, Cosmic Man, Eternal Man, Fallen Man, Gayomart, Grand Man, Humphrey Chimpden Earwicker (HCE), Manzasiri, P'an Ku, Person, Primordial Giant, Primordial Man, Self, Universal Man *(al-insan al-kamil),* Ymir.

Description: Purusha is the prime cosmogonic figure in Hinduism, conceived of as a vast cosmic Man containing all of manifest Creation.

The word *Purusha,* or "Person," is defined in Hindu thought as that which fills all or that which dwells in a bodily container. Purusha, as the Cosmic Man, is also an expression of the Self or Atman. It is the manifestation of the Immensity, the totality of manifestation, and called a Person, with a "male" valence; its "consort," the female aspect, is Nature at the cosmic level and called *Prakriti.* Together these two create the manifest world of action, called *Prapanca.*

In one accounting of the origin of Purusha, Siva, one of Hinduism's three prime gods, considered the fiery destroyer of forms, let fall a drop of his blood into the Flood waters, before Creation began (or resumed), and it became a huge egg. This is usually referred to as the Cosmic Egg.

First born from the egg was Purusha, followed by Prakriti; later, due to Purusha's arrogance, Siva chopped off his head, but vowed always to carry Purusha's severed head in his hand. Siva further took the two halves of the great egg to create the sky *(akasa)* and Earth *(bhumi).* Thus Purusha's dismembered body became the foundations for the sky and Earth—the space for Creation.

The sacrificial dismemberment of Purusha's cosmic body generated the four occupational or functional categories in ancient Vedic society, known as the *brahmana* (from his mouth), the *rajanya* (his arms), *vaisya* (thighs), and *sudra* (feet). Further, from his mind came the Moon; from his eyes the Sun; his breath yields the winds; his navel the atmosphere; and from his head or skull came the star-filled heavens. Also from his bodily parts, sacrificially offered up to Creation, came speech, sight, and hearing. Thus Purusha is the original material the World was made from, the Indestructible Person, the cosmological human body.

More vividly, Purusha has one thousand heads, eyes, and feet; he is both immanent and transcendent; he surrounds the Earth (all of reality that is created as a space for life: the cosmos); he is its past, present, and future; and one-fourth of him is all created beings, three-fourths the immortals in Heaven. The 14 worlds, which came from Purusha, were called the limbs of the Great Man.

Explanation: Purusha finds expression on the Earth in the form of its 445 Albions. An

Albion is the anthropomorphic fulfillment of a landscape zodiac.

Across the planet are 432 interactive miniature holograms of the galaxy's major stars and constellations relevant to the composition of humanity in bodies. These holograms are called landscape zodiacs and can range in diameter from one mile to 200 miles; they consist of two contiguous spheres templated on the land, each containing a portion of the galaxy's pertinent stars. Albion is the totality of all the stars in both halves, exactly what the Vedic texts said of Purusha.

Purusha's original cosmic sacrificial dismemberment is mirrored in Albion's fragmentation into the two halves of a landscape zodiac. In a three-leveled hierarchy, the landscape zodiac Albions are part of 12 larger Albions, each of which overlays one-twelfth of the surface of the Earth; these in turn are subsets of a singular planetary Albion, wrapped around it. The equivalent in Albion to the plethora of created beings inside Purusha are holograms of stars, 81 chakras (subtle consciousness centers), and numerous geomantic features across the landscape in the form of astral or Light temples.

Hindu lore says that if all the parts of Purusha were one day reassembled, the universe and all Creation would end. This means if, on the planetary level, all 445 Albions (Purusha's geomantic expression) were completed and illuminated, then the circuit between Heaven and Earth would be reinvigorated, and the two would be in the same place and thus be the end of the world as we know it.

Even better, humanity would reexperience the unity of the three realms of the angelic, human, and elemental, sundered since the Fall of Man. Originally, Purusha (and his other guises Ymir, Albion, P'an-Ku [or Pan Gu, or Coiled Antiquity], and the rest) embodied the three realms in his form: the angelic hierarchy from the neck up (the higher head chakras), the human from the root to throat chakra, and the elementals (Nature spirits) from the thighs to the feet. All lived in the one body of Purusha, which, in turn, was the template for the archetype of Adam—human beings.

When this primordial unity was sundered to accommodate physical incarnation on Earth based on material bodies with free will and self-aware consciousness, the angels retreated upward, the elementals downward, and the humans remained in the middle in the midst of the five elements. On Earth, then, the elementals became our mobility in the world of Nature, the angels became our awareness in the realm of higher reality.

Sustained human interaction with a landscape zodiac, and generally with Earth's visionary geography, begins the process of reknitting this original unity.

See also: Adam, Albion, Atlas, Cosmic Egg, Tree of the Knowledge of Good and Evil, White Cow, White Sow, Ymir.

QUETZALCOATL

Humanity's prime angelic benefactor and bestower of self-aware consciousness and free will (Lucifer) seen without a negative filter.

Also known as Eros, Fenrir the Wolf, Kucumatz, Kukulkan, Light-Bearer, Light-Bringer, Loki, Lucifer, Malak Tawus ("Peacock Angel"), Midir, Morning Star, Phanes, Phosphorus, Prometheus, Protogonos.

Description: The name *Quetzalcoatl* means "the Plumed Serpent," combining two words from the Nahuatl language of Mesoamerica, *quetzal,* an emerald-plumed bird, and *coatl,* a serpent. Among the Aztecs and Olmecs of ancient Mexico and the Mayans of Central America, Quetzalcoatl was a highly respected, ultra-wise god, one of four sons of the high deity, Ometeotl.

Quetzalcoatl, also called Kukulkan (Maya) and Kucumatz (Quiche), came from Tollan, the Land of the Sun, whose name means "Place of Cattail Reeds" or "Place of Rushes." Tollan was a paradisal realm and source of all high culture in which

Quetzalcoatl was king; many of its buildings were made of green stone. He is often depicted as sitting on the Jaguar Throne, holding the staff of fertility, his garments signifying the aspiration toward the divine, his father, Ometeotl, and conveying authority and a high degree of spiritual awareness.

His mission was to establish communication between Heaven and Earth, to unite humanity with the All-Father, Ometeotl. Quetzalcoatl, in performing this mission, was a culture benefactor, bestowing all the arts upon humanity. He was the Lord of Healing, the Lord of Hope, Father of the Toltecs, Lord of the Breath of Life, and the radiant Lord of the Morning Star (Venus).

He was widely revered throughout sites in Mesoamerica and consistently associated with the planet Venus, both in terms of archeoastronomical alignments at sites dedicated to his worship and in his mythology.

Quetzalcoatl's name also can be interpreted as "Precious Twin," since *quetzal* means both "bird" and "twin." The twin in this case was Tezcatlipoca, God of the First Sun of Earth, Quetzalcoatl's dark brother, whose name means "Lord of the Smoking Mirror." Legend says Quetzalcoatl, God of the Second Sun of Water, was dethroned by machinations of his evil brother, then immolated himself. The ashes, rising heavenward, turned into birds with glorious plumage, while his heart (or spirit) soared back to Venus; afterward he was known as Lord of the Dawn and Lord of the Eastern Light.

Yet Quetzalcoatl's triumphant return to Earth and humanity was prophesied. According to Zapotec (a tribe of Native Americans living in the Oaxaca Valley of southern Mexico) legend, Quetzalcoatl would one day return to his heart, which he had buried under the Tree of Life in the Valley of Oaxaca. When he returned, he would overthrow Tezcatlipoca and end his 900-year rule. Zapotec belief, coupled with New Age millennialism, claimed that the Harmonic Convergence of August 1987 marked the actual return to Earth of Quetzalcoatl.

Explanation: In Quetzalcoatl, we can observe the positive attributes, the culture-benefiting activities of Lucifer, the Light-Bringer, without any theological or moral filter. In Quetzalcoatl, we can see Lucifer in his pure state, without his alleged refusal to serve humanity (Judeo-Christian filter) or defiance of the gods (as Prometheus, through the Greek filter) and his punishment in either case. As Quetzalcoatl, he is at peace with both God (Ometeotl) and humanity.

Sites that registered a high degree of Quetzalcoatl veneration, such as at Teotihuacan and Chichén Itzá in Mexico, are likely to be Lucifer Binding Sites.

This geomantic feature, however, has three valences. Where Lucifer, as the Lord of Light, is arriving in glory, as Quetzalcoatl, the site is called a *Tollan,* in honor of Quetzalcoatl's divine origin. Where he is being bound, as in the Greek guise of Prometheus, it is called a *Mount Caucasus*. Where he is being released, it is a *Jerusalem,* in recognition of the esoteric meaning of this word, "Foundation of Lucifer," based on Venus as Morning and Evening Star and Lucifer's ancient identification with this planet, both known as Phosphorus.

Quetzalcoatl, the Toltec Lucifer, was the benefactor of the second generation of humanity, bestowing upon them the Emerald, a structured container for Absolute Light, known to the Greeks, for example, as the gods' fire. In a sense, he is the Lord of the Heart as befits his Quiche Indian characterization as Kucumatz who is the androgynous "Heart of Heaven."

Quetzalcoatl was called God of the Second Sun of Water in reference to this second generation of humans and his intimate involvement with their destiny. His dark brother, Tezcatlipoca, was called God of the First Sun of Earth, in reference to his oversight of the first generation of humans, later aborted and withdrawn from physical creation and placed in a netherworld.

Quetzalcoatl's Lord of the Dawn and Morning Star attributions are metaphors for his gift of self-aware consciousness and free will to humanity at its dawn. He is the benefactor and supervisor of the dawning of self-awareness in humans individualized in material bodies, a significant change of ontological state from natural union with God and all of Creation to a unity that is voluntarily achieved.

The Zapotec prophecy of the return of Quetzalcoatl to his heart in the Valley of Oaxaca was correct. The Harmonic Convergence of August 1987, a worldwide millennialist event in which estimated millions of people meditated at holy sites around the Earth, marked the return of Lucifer, arriving in glory and plumed with angels, to the physical world, after millennia.

Esoterically, the Harmonic Convergence took place inside Lucifer's own Emerald, and its copy inside every living human—the Emerald is an aspect of the heart chakra—and at the prime copy of the Emerald as placed on Earth, at the churchyard of El Templo del Santa Maria and its 2,000-year-old El Tule tree. Through this mass event, all of humanity, whether aware of it or not, got to experience the presence of the unfallen Lucifer, the brilliantly plumed Quetzalcoatl, arriving in glory, complete freedom, and absolution from his divine home with Ometeotl (the Supreme Being) within the heart temple of humanity.

See also: Asura, Azhi Dahaka, Djinn, Emerald, Fall of Man, Harmonic Convergence, Kings of Edom, Lucifer, Merlin, Prometheus, Raksasas, Tezcatlipoca.

RAGNAROK

The end of a cycle of cosmic creation and life, also known as the Flood and Pralaya, in which all structures and beings are destroyed; in a lesser sense, the tumultuous contemporary planetary transition known as Earth Changes.

Also known as Apocalypse, Armageddon, Battle of Shambhala, End-Time, Flood, Götterdämerung, Last Judgment, Night of Brahma, Pralaya, Twilight of the Gods.

Description: *Ragnarok* comes from Old Norse and is usually translated as "Twilight of the Gods" or "the Final Destiny or Doom of the Gods." It generally means the apocalyptic end of the world, including that of most of the gods and their structures and cities, by fire, floods, and mortal battle.

The Nordic eschatology, or enumeration of the final end of things, involves four major events: the Fimbulwinter (a disastrously long and hard winter); the world fire by which Surtr the Fire-Giant god burns up everything; the sinking of Earth into the oceans churned up by the Midgard Serpent (the primordial dragon wrapped around the planet); and the darkening and consumption of the Sun by the escaped Fenriswolf. Odin, high god of Asgard, will summon the 432,000 Einherjar (slain warriors) of Valhalla to come to his aid.

Ragnarok also is foreseen to entail earthquakes and rock falls, the collapse of Bifrost (the gods' rainbow bridge into Asgard), the shaking of Yggdrasil, the World Tree, the storming of Asgard by the ancient Frost Giants, and a titanic battle of the gods, with almost all of them slaying one another. Yet a new world will arise out of the shattered ruins of the old on the plain called Idavöll, the site of the former, now defunct, Asgard, city of the Norse gods; four surviving minor gods will recreate the world and repopulate humanity from a new Adam and Eve.

Explanation: In the Norse Ragnarok, we have a dramatic, highly detailed, even cinematic elaboration of what the Vedas call the Night of Brahma or the Flood.

In the Vedic-Hindu formulation, cosmic time is calculated as units in the vast time-size of the creator god, Brahma, equivalent to the Norse Odin. His entire life span of 309 trillion years is divided up into a hierarchy of segments including Days, Nights, and Years of Brahma. At the end of each Day of Brahma, which lasts 4.32 billion human years, there is a Night of Brahma (lasting the same), also called *Pralaya,* which means dissolution and destruction. It is a period of cosmic quiescence, in between cycles of Pralaya and new Creation.

It is equivalent to the Flood or World Deluge, as remembered by many different cultures, in which the Earth is inundated and nearly all humanity drowned except for those few who survive in an ark (Noah's Ark), boat (Manu Satyavrata's Boat of the Vedas), or other seaworthy vessel (Yima's *var*). At the end of the Flood (when Ragnarok is completed), the worlds, Earth, and humanity are recreated by the Flood survivor (e.g., Noah, Deucalion, Ziusudra-Utnapishtim).

The Plain of Idavöll ("Splendor-Plain") is equivalent to the high mountain peak on which the ark lands, such as Mounts Ararat (Noah), Parnassus (Deucalion), and Nisir (Ziusudra-Utnapishtim), or slightly differently, the Egyptian White Mount or Primeval Hill that arises out of the Waters of Nun.

This high mountain peak with the ark or Boat of the Vedas on top is the same as the Grail Castle of Western Mysteries. The Flood survivor and progenitor of the next round of humanity is the Rich Fisher King, who lives there.

Ragnarok is similar to the Vedic elaboration of Pralaya, the processes leading up to the end of a Day of Brahma and the start of a Night of Brahma. The world will look famished; there will be a devastating drought; the Sun will dry up (drink) all the waters of the world, then split into seven Suns that will burn up all the worlds, both physical and spiritual, until the Earth resembles the top shell of a tortoise and all the worlds look like globes of fire. Then it will rain incessantly for a hundred years, the worlds will be flooded and drowned, and the only surviving god, Vishnu (the Hindu Christ), will sleep atop the Deluge.

While Ragnarok is usually interpreted as a highly vivid description of an imminent Apocalypse, when seen through the Hindu Pralaya, it relaxes into a metaphoric description of a natural, predictable inhale and exhale of cosmic life.

On a lesser scale, Ragnarok is a useful metaphor for understanding our own tumultuous world changes under way since about 1970 in the form of climatological, geologic, and political upheavals and numerous high-profile natural disasters. I use the phrase *Ragnarok in slow motion* to describe Earth Changes, the protracted effect on physical and human reality of the morphing of Earth's energy fields or aura (also called the visionary geography or Earth grid) from one geometrical shape to the next. Truly, all of reality is shifting and transforming, almost before our eyes (just a little slower than we can perceive).

Since Earth's visionary geography is the matrix for all human life, thought, identity, and consciousness, then Earth Changes can seem like the end of the world, Apocalypse, the Last Judgment, and all the other End-Time scenarios.

The Hindus and Buddhists put forward an apocalyptic prophecy called the Battle of Shambhala. Shambhala is the city of enlightened sages and world government on Earth, but phase-shifted from human physical reality. The prophecies hold that, sometime in the future, Vishnu (the Hindu Christ) will be born in Shambhala as Sri Kalki-avatara, the tenth of his major incarnations. Buddhists postulate the same future, but call the savior the Maitreya Buddha.

He will gather an army of enlightened souls to conquer the barbarians who have infiltrated the world and he will lead the charge on a supernatural white horse. After the battle, the forces of entropy will be overcome and the world returned to the Golden Age, its original pure, high consciousness condition.

Similarly (and this does not contradict the Kalki avatar scenario), the next King of Shambhala, Rudra Cakrin, will be an incarnation of Manjusri, the Buddhist Bodhisattva of Wisdom and Insight (the Hebraic Archangel Michael). When the barbarian hordes are amassed at the very gates of Shambhala, Rudra Cakrin will rise out on a flying blue or white horse and vanquish the hordes.

Mongolian belief holds that at the same time and probably in support of these two scenarios, Gesar of Ling, residing in an underground kingdom with his warriors, will awaken and also ride forth to defend Shambhala.

In this vision, barbarians is a metaphor for widespread adulteration of human consciousness and culture. This is a time when drought, famine, disease, materialism, conflict, atheism, greed, power, and lust will prevail—Hinduism's Kali Yuga. Ragnarok, or the Battle of Shambhala, is the antidote to world entropy.

Buddhist estimates say the Battle of Shambhala is likely to happen in 2327 A.D. when the twenty-fifth Kulika King ascends the Shambhala throne. He will be known as the "Wrathful One with the Wheel" and will defeat the barbarians with the help of the Army of Shambhala, said to include high Tibetan lamas (equivalent to Odin's 432,000 Einherjar or slain, chosen warriors of Valhalla).

Angelic estimates by the Ofanim, however, place the date at around 3000 A.D. The King's wheel might be a wheel of iron or a spinning discus or perhaps the archetype of all wheels (chakras), the Sudarsana of Vishnu, his golden discus. The wielder of this celestial weapon of consciousness is the Chakravartin.

See also: Agharti, Ancient of Days, Antichrist, Bifrost, Chakravartin, Earth Changes, Einherjar, Fisher King, Flood, Gesar of Ling, Ghost Dance, Grail Castle, Holy Grail, Manu, Salmon of Wisdom, Shambhala, Vishnu's Discus, White Mount.

RAINBOW SERPENT

The Australian Aborigines' perception of one of Earth's 13 primary dragons and its functions, this one situated at Uluru.

Also known as Aido-Hwedo, Akurra Serpent, Bobi-Bobi, Da, Degei, Dhakhan, Jarapiri, Julunggul, Kaleru, Kungmanggur, Ngaljod, Oshumare, Rainbow Monster, Rainbow Snake, Wagyal, Wanambi, Warramurrungundji, Waugal, Woggal, Wollunquain, Worombi, Yurlunggul.

Description: The Rainbow Serpent is, to Westerners, probably the most well-known aspect of Australian Aboriginal lore and, to the Aborigines, a central feature of their comprehensive landscape-based mythology (see Dreamtime).

Also known as the Rainbow Snake and Akurra Serpent, it is perhaps the most important of all deities in Aboriginal experience. It is the giver and guardian of all mystical healing rites of shamans, protector of all waterholes and the general food supply, and is associated with the All-Father deity, Biame, and sometimes with the All-Mother, Birrahgnooloo, Biame's consort; as such, the Rainbow Serpent is regarded as the Mother of all created things.

Thus the Rainbow Serpent is generally seen as both male and female, as the ancestor of many deities, as almost a cocreator with Biame and Birrahgnooloo. If disturbed, the Serpent may bring catastrophe upon the people. It is *pulwaiya,* "Father's Father," the primordial Ancestor, both Great Mother and Great Father, and always associated with water. In fact, if it were not for the Rainbow Serpent's water-bestowing presence on Earth, the rains would stop, the Earth would become parched, and all organic life would cease, Aborigines say.

Some tribes say that originally the Rainbow Serpent contained all the creatures, waters, and vegetation of Earth within Her and would not release them. Meanwhile, humanity was starving for lack of nourishment. Finally, a shaman transformed himself into a multicolored kookaburra bird and distracted the Serpent long enough so other shamans could destroy Her and release the waters.

Yet another version says it differently: First, the Ancestors deposited all the seeds or Dreamings for the forms and species of life during their Dreamtime wanderings; then the Rainbow Serpent touched these sites and energized them, allowing the diversity of organic life to arise and enter physical reality.

The Rainbow Serpent is named and described differently among the tribes. The Aboriginal Elders describe the Akurra Serpent as a huge water snake with beard, scales, fangs, and a mane. In the Northern Territory, it was known as Warramurrungundji, the All-Mother in fabulous rainbow snake form; she came out of the sea then traveled across the land, establishing laws and forming the landscape's features; she later turned herself into a rock.

In Arnhem Land, the Rainbow Serpent was called Ngaljod. His first form was a gigantic version of the *ubar,* a long, hollow log used in Aboriginal ceremonies to produce a hypnotic vibration, somewhat like a didgeridoo. The interior of the ubar is often referred to, using Western terms, as the Great Mother's uterus. Ngaljod's body is long and flowing, like an energy current, the Aborigines say.

Some tribes describe the Serpent's body as brilliantly multicolored, or with long red and yellow stripes, or that its skin is entirely celestial blue. The Dalabon Aborigines say that originally Earth was entirely water, a serpent-like expanse colored like the rainbow; all life lay within this Serpent.

The great serpent-god Jarapiri emerged from the Earth at Yuendumu (northwest of Alice Springs, which is the nearest town to Uluru or Ayer's Rock in central Australia); he taught the Walbiri people the laws and customs of living.

The Nyungar call it Wagyal and say this Snake is their primordial creative ancestor, a huge black water snake with a hairy neck and flaplike wings, almost dragon-like. In southwestern Australia in the Flinders Range, traces of Wagyal's movement across the land during the Dreamtime can be seen everywhere. During its writhing passage across ancient Australia, the Wagyal created all the river beds, channels, gullies, and tracks (later known as Dreaming tracks and songlines) that now characterize the continent.

In the area around Roper River, the Rainbow Serpent was called Julunggul. His eyes were all-seeing, and his gigantic snakelike body was looped in a circle around an important waterhole and the human dwellings around it. When he opened his mouth, he instantly swallowed everything around him.

Aboriginal belief also holds that Uluru, the huge red sandstone rock (1.25 miles long and 4.5 miles in circumference) of the Northern Territories, one of the Aborigines' most sacred sites, was originally an Intelligent Snake. This Snake first lived in the cosmos as a great rainbow, then settled on the Earth at Uluru, after shaping the landscape, digging holes, creating lakes, and piling hills.

A myth from northern Australia says that once the Rainbow Serpent flew high in the air and dropped huge white balls onto the Earth, then came down and burrowed into the land. Later Aboriginal Elders dug holes where the balls had fallen and found a worm in each hole; they informed their tribespeople that the Rainbow Serpent had laid eggs, which had then hatched its progeny.

Interestingly, the Rainbow Serpent is mythologized in other cultures, including Central West Africa, Dahomey, Nigeria, and Haiti, and has been accorded some attention in Melanesia, Polynesia, and Papua New Guinea.

Explanation: The Rainbow Serpent is the Aboriginal perception of one of Earth's 13 primary dragons, this one situated at Uluru in Australia. It is also a lucid functional description of the archetype and mother of all dragons, the cosmic dragon, known variously throughout world myth, in Hinduism, for example, as Sesa-Ananta, the Endless Remainder, and in Judaic lore as Leviathan.

Earth has 1,067 dragons on four levels within its complex visionary geography. One entirely circles the planet (the Norse called it the Midgard Serpent) and has 13 primary progeny, very large coiled dragons; one is at Uluru. Each of the 13 can generate up to 81 offspring, smaller dragons generally situated in the vicinity (within a several hundred mile radius).

Dragons, in terms of mythic memory and description, are often confused or equated with snakes. Uluru has a great deal of snake attributions and myths about Dreamtime snake events. Geomantically, this is explained due to the relative proximity of a fair number of the Rainbow Serpent's 81 progeny.

The 13 dragons are capable of laying dragon eggs. Astonishingly, a total of 33 trillion dragon eggs are deposited on Earth, each awaiting fruitful interaction with humans as part of a supervised initiation or shamanic pathway. The Aboriginal memory of the "huge white balls" dropped by the airborne Rainbow Serpent is rare (and highly laudable because accurate) among dragon myths for it is a true and correct perception of the placement of dragon eggs.

Similarly, the Aborigines' term (admittedly, translated) *Rainbow Serpent* is geomantically correct as well for two important reasons. First, the Rainbow Serpent, as one of the 13 primary Earth dragons, embodies and transmits the full radiational range of light known as the electromagnetic field (EMF) spectrum. Its body truly encompasses the complete range of visible light, the rainbow spectrum.

Second, the 13 primary dragons are the geomantic responsibility of 14 Dreamtime Ancestors known in other esoteric traditions as the Lords of the Seven Rays, the Seven Rishis, or, more precisely, as the 14 (Ascended) Ray Masters of Ursa Major, the constellation of the Great Bear. In the Dreamtime (the formative days of Earth's visionary geography), these Masters—like the shaman who shape-shifted into a kookaburra—activated the Earth's dragons ("plugged" them into the Earth grid) and "released their waters" (kundalini) and fertility into the landscape.

The Dreamtime Ancestors (including the 14 Ray Masters) used the dragon energy and its EMF spectrum radiation to prepare the landscape for life and to energize the myriad Dreaming sites we now call sacred sites or power places.

The Aboriginal memory of the Rainbow Serpent refusing to release its fructifying waters and creatures to a starving humanity has an exact equivalent in the Vedic story of the cosmic dragon Vrtra holding back all the waters of life within its mountainlike body; it took the god Indra "slaying" Vrtra to get the waters flowing into the human world. Think of "waters" here as the levels of consciousness necessary for human self-consciousness in bodies, and "slaying" as a cooperative, progressive activation of the dragon to benefit Earth and all life.

At the cosmic level, Vrtra or the Rainbow Serpent finally releasing the waters means the flooding of spacetime (as a container) with the Astral Light, or EMF spectrum.

On the planetary level, and even in the realm of local ecosystems, the Rainbow Serpent, as all the Earth dragons, is intimately related to the water flow. When the energy exchanges among people, dragon, and Nature spirits are in balance and all realms acknowledged, then the rain falls sufficiently because the energy matrix that determines physical reality is in optimal working order.

See also: Dragon, Dreamtime, Flood, Indra, Leviathan, Ocean of Milk, Seven Rishis.

RAKSASAS

The first generation of humans living in bodies on an Edenic Earth under conditions of great freedom and tremendous psychic powers.

Also known as Demons, Rakshasas.

Description: As described in the Indian Vedas, the Raksasas are Night-Wanderers, demonic, ogreish children of darkness who roam at night devouring humans, harassing the pious, and generally afflicting humankind. They can assume any form they wish, but almost always are large, strong, hideous, and scary, although they can seem beautiful when it suits their stratagems, such as deceiving humans. The ten-headed Ravana is their chief at their residence in Lanka, a golden Celestial City atop Mount Trikuta, said in the myths to be south of India.

The Raksasas are ranked as a particular sect of Asuras, or antigods, born from Brahma, the Creator god, when he was angry while reciting the Vedas.

The ancient Hindu epic called the *Ramayana* describes the battle between Rama (an emanation of Vishnu, the Hindu Christ) and his godly colleagues in monkey form against Ravana and his thousands of Raksasas in Lanka. Some of the Raksasas chieftains are formidable warriors in terms of their psychic prowess and magical abilities, fueled by their mastery of kundalini and the attainment of *siddhis* (prodigious physical-psychic powers attained from mastery of the chakras, the multiple subtle energy centers along the spine). One, named Kumbhakarna, Ravana's brother, was colossal, resembling a shining mountain.

Explanation: The image of the Raksasas is a somewhat skewed perception of the first generation of humanity, seen in retrospect, after they had been removed from the physical world and demonized by culture. In other words, the Indian perception of the Raksasas is not of this first race of humans in their original pure state, but rather in their fallen, dangerous, and soon to be defeated condition.

They were truly Night-Wanderers and somewhat demonic *after* they had been removed from physical reality and bound in an in-between realm with Ravana. Then they lurked on the borders (the Night) of physical and astral reality, disturbing incarnate humans who, over time, entirely forgot about them and only experienced them peripherally as upsetting phantasms or specters.

Ironically, the retrospective demonization of first-generation humanity as the Raksasas caused second-generation humanity to misperceive the reality of that first generation and fail to comprehend the astonishing glory of creation that their wild forebears once were and the possibilities and scope of complete freedom in consciousness.

As with the other cultural perceptions of the first humanity (Asura, Djinn, Kings of Edom), the Raksasas possessed formidable psychic and magical abilities through mastery of kundalini and the attainment of *siddhis*. The first generation of humanity was given total freedom of will, self-aware consciousness, and physical individuality and selfhood, with Ravana as their mentor, chief, and supervisor.

Ravana was ten-headed because his consciousness extended throughout the ten dimensions of reality or what's known as the Cube of Space (see Emerald); the Raksasas potentially participated in this same extreme dilation of consciousness. Ravana is an expression of Lucifer, the Lord of Light and initiator of human freedom and embodied selfhood. His headquarters in Lanka were actually a global domain, his influence expressed in the form of a golden crown overlaid on all of Earth; Mount Trikuta was thus the physical planet, or matter.

The *Ramayana* describes the high point of first humanity in the Garden of Eden or Lanka just before the transition to what's known as the Fall of Man. The Raksasas had become such prodigies in their control over matter that they were judged a threat to the planet, the balance of the ten dimensions, and Creation. Rama and his heavenly colleagues came to Earth not to fight Ravana and his horde, but to transmute that raw "anger" of Brahma (passion coupled with free will) that comprised the essence of the Raksasas and infuse some of the Christ essence.

Yet, in this mythic tableau of Rama versus Ravana, we see also the moment when first humanity was put down and taken out of physical reality, bound with Ravana into the Earth in between dimensions at 3,496 Lucifer Binding Sites until such time as the second generation of humanity can absolve them of their excesses that led to a later curtailment of our freedom.

See also: Asura, Djinn, Fall of Man, Garden of Eden, Kings of Edom, Lucifer, Pandora's Box, Prometheus, Ravana.

RAVANA

An expression of Lucifer creating and maintaining a world for the first generation of humanity, the Raksasas, for which he was responsible.

Also known as Azhi Dahaka, Dashakantha, Dashanana, Epimetheus, Iblis, Lucifer, Tezcatlipoca.

Description: Ravana, a ten-headed celestial being who opposed all the gods and sought to control the universe, is the antihero of India's epic narrative, the *Ramayana.* A long period of austerities (10,000 years) earned him a boon from Brahma, the Hindu creator god: Only a human, not any of the gods, could kill him. This inflated his sense of himself, and he started to create havoc in the universe. His body was black and gemlike; he had 20 arms, was robed in jeweled ornaments, and resembled a ten-peaked mountain. He had ten heads and 20 reddish eyes, and his arms could arrest the movements of stars and planets.

His name means "roaring" or "causing to cry," and his epithets include *Dashanana* ("Ten-Faced") and *Dashakantha* ("Ten-Throated"). His ten heads were symbolic of his great learning, and his 20 arms of his great prowess.

Ravana possessed (had stolen) two formidable celestial weapons: the *Brahmastra,* a mystic arrow of Brahma's that could destroy the world; and the *Raksaha-astra,* which filled the air around it with every conceivable weapon. Excessively strong, the most powerful person in the universe, and the Lord of the Raksasas, Ravana was the world tormentor, invulnerable to godly reprisals.

Ravana occupied the golden city of Lanka set on top of Trikuta Mountain, generally believed by scholars today to be somewhere on the island of Sri Lanka. The accounts are inconsistent as to whether Lanka was rightfully his or if he usurped it from his half-brother, Kubera, the Hindu god of wealth and riches, or if he seized it from the gods. Ravana lived in Lanka with thousands of Raksasas, his retainers and fighters. These are generally described as demonic in appearance, though clearly humanlike also: They have large, blackish bodies, fearful faces, pointed ears, fangs for teeth, and masses of red hair on their heads.

In his earlier incarnations, Ravana was appointed by Vishnu (the Hindu Christ) to be a guardian at the gates of Vaikuntha, an exalted celestial realm having to do with Vishnu's knowledge and wisdom aspect. In the lifetime recounted in the *Ramayana,* Ravana was Rama's enemy, on the verge of conquering all the worlds, planets, and dimensions until Rama (an emanation of Vishnu) incarnated as a human named Rama, and his fellow gods embodied themselves as monkeys, led by Hanuman, the Monkey-King. Together they would storm Lanka and remove Ravana from reality. As a further goad to Rama, Ravana abducted his consort (once Rama was incarnated), Sita, and held her as a hostage in Lanka.

Explanation: The *Ramayana* is a sublime metaphoric drama of the status of the first-generation humanity in the Garden of Eden at the point when the spiritual hierarchies, led by the Christ, attempt to balance and spiritualize them.

Ravana is a perception of Lucifer after he has been given permission by the Supreme Being, for the first time, to institute a physically embodied humanity on a material planet under his aegis and supervision. He has ten heads because his consciousness penetrates and fills the ten dimensions of reality; an abstract expression of his "ten heads" is the Qabalistic model of the Cube of Space in which the ten dimensions of existence (called Sefiroth; see Emerald) are mapped in accordance with the edges and vertices of the cube.

Rather than as a humanlike figure with ten separate but adjacent heads, requiring ten necks and all sprouting out of one torso, Ravana's complex form is more easily conceived as a single square block of obsidian out of which ten contiguous faces are carved, with no necks or torso. The form conveys the function of multidirectional awareness, of consciousness, through its 20 eyes, seeing into all realms and dimensions of space-time, that is, fully illuminated consciousness.

Lanka is the foundation of Ravana, an early version of Jerusalem as the archetype of the perfect city, structure, or foundation for consciousness. Lanka is Lucifer's golden crown overlaid on the entire planet; Mount Trikuta is not a single, specific peak, but rather all of physical Earth, and thus has nothing in particular to do with the island called Sri Lanka, or even India, for that matter. The crown, or golden city of Lanka, represents Lucifer's ideal conditions for consciousness abiding in matter, here both the physical body and planet Earth.

Lanka is a heavenly point of reference, Lucifer's conception for the conditions and parameters for the first, bold incarnation of consciousness in human bodies with free will. Lanka is a kind of etheric matrix, template, mold, or collective etheric body holding all the imprints, programming, and information for this pristine generation of first humans—a living engineering diagram.

These conditions can be described as ontological opulence, abundance, illumination, the full expression of the "serpent power," kundalini given to first humanity. It is a time of "dragons," in the sense that the kundalini circuit fully links and activates the energy-consciousness circuit from root to crown chakra in these first, blessed humans; the dragon in this situation is empowered selfhood.

The Raksasas, through Ravana's foundation of Lanka, have access to the Tree of Life and its panoply of perceptions, abilities, and "celestial weapons." They are fortunate, even if, ultimately, they abuse the privilege; for second humanity, the Tree of Life will be fenced off limits, and they (we) will have to pass first through the outer perimeter bounded by the Tree of the Knowledge of Good and Evil, and come to terms with its bequests and requirements before having access to the Tree of Life.

The Raksasas, or first-generation humanity, live under Ravana's aegis in his foundation of Lanka, an expression of the Emerald (a structured container for Absolute Light, also known as the Cube of Space and Jerusalem), but they do not have their own Emeralds, as will second humanity. So they have more freedom, and less structure and in-built discipline or imposed limits on their behavior.

The Raksasas, or the first generation of humanity, all exist within the ten-faced black Ravana who holds space, or structures the incarnational conditions, for them. The Raksasas, many of whom become psychic prodigies, masters of celestial weapons (*siddhis:* the magical powers arising from mastery of the chakras), are each miniatures of their sponsor and quasi-creator, Ravana-Lucifer. They eventually alarmed the spiritual hierarchy with their freedom and formidable abilities. In large measure, the *Ramayana* is the saga of first humanity entering material life under Edenic conditions told from the gods' viewpoint.

The battle recounted in the *Ramayana* of Rama and his monkey army versus Ravana and his Raksasas horde is more subtle than fighting and combat. Rama (an emanation of Vishnu, who is Christ or the Logos seen through a Hindu filter) seeks to balance and spiritualize the Raksasas, who resist. In a sense, Rama wants the Raksasas to integrate Sita (a symbol for the Spirit, a spiritual awareness deeper, older, profounder than the dragon-selfhood reality: see Guinivere) into their being; they have captured her and hold her hostage, but nothing further happens.

In Qabalistic terminology, Sita is the *Aleph,* the first principle and point of consciousness, and the spiritual hierarchy, led by Rama, want to incarnate this in humanity. Qabala expresses this in the interpretation of ADAM, which is not a gender reference to the first male created in Eden, but to a humanity capable of embodying the *Aleph (A)* in the blood *(DAM)* of a material body. Rama and his assistants want to put the *Aleph* (Sita) in the bodies of the Raksasas, but they resist. The Raksasas have captured Sita, but they have not integrated her; Rama does not so much want Sita back as to see her assimilated in this generation of humans.

Sita also represents the mother of the physical world, Nature, primordial power working through matter, the cause of the universe, shining as pale gold. To say Ravana captured her and his Raksasas hold her captive means the first generation of humanity was abusing the physical world and Nature herself. Their *siddhi*-empowered presence and free-wheeling, no-limits lifestyle were destabilizing physical matter and the natural processes of the Earth.

Rama and his monkey colleagues come to tame the dragon, the fierce, kundalini-empowered physical selfhood that the Raksasas embody, and to release Sita (Nature, the physical planet) from their grip; the *Ramayana* describes it as fighting and battle, but it is more a matter of transmutation. The story chronicles, from a sublime, higher dimensional perspective, the final moments of the deeds of the first generation of humanity as they resist spiritualization and balancing—the Christ infusion by Rama—of their wild, unchecked selfhood.

Another way to put this is to say Ravana and his Raksasas are dark or black and described as demonic in appearance because they are un-Christed "clay," earth and water beings possessing prodigious godly powers. Rama, as an emissary of the Christ, comes to Christ, or spiritually illuminate, this first humanity, that is, instill the Christ Consciousness in this first round of embodied humans

See also: Adam, Asura, Azhi Dahaka, Djinn, Emerald, Fall of Man, Garden of Eden, Guinivere, Kings of Edom, Lucifer, Raksasas, Tezcatlipoca.

RHINEGOLD

Explicit wisdom and knowledge of the functioning of Earth's visionary geography left as a gift to humanity by the Pleiadians long ago.

Also known as the Gold of the Hyperboreans, Griffin Gold Reserve, Treasure of the Nibelungs.

Description: The Rhinegold is the focus of one of the most intriguing Teutonic myths about the seduction and corruption of power. It has been the subject of many important literary and musical works, including J. R. R. Tolkien's *The Lord of the Rings* (it is the gold used to make the master control ring of Sauron, who wants to rule the world with it) and Richard Wagner's opera *Das Rheingold*. Possibly the original version of this tale was the *Nibelungenlied* set in the German Rhine River city called Worms.

The Rhine, of course, is the major river that flows from Lake Constance in Switzerland through Germany into the Netherlands and the North Sea. The gold is a treasure hidden deep in its waters by Gunnarr and Guttomr who stole it from Sigurdr (Siegfried). Originally it belonged to the dwarfs. It is often called the Treasure of the Nibelungs, as *Nibelungs* is a Teutonic term for dwarfs.

In a related tale, Andvari, a dwarf king, accidentally kills Itr, a god's son. Loki, the Norse Trickster god, demanded recompense by Andvari in the form of his vast hoard of gold. Andvari obliged, but tried to withhold a special gold ring called Andvaranaut (or later, Andvari's Ring) from Loki. The ring was cursed and later brought misfortune to its owner and ultimately Siegfried's death.

These two versions come together in Wagner's operatic story. Three Rhinemaidens named Woglinde, Wellgunde, and Flosshilde gambol in the Rhine, guarding the Rhinegold, a treasure deposited on a prominent rock. Alberich, prince of the Nibelungs (the dwarfs) first tries to flirt with the Rhinemaidens; when he sees the treasure glowing with a golden light like a globe of fire in the green-blue Rhine waters, he turns his attention to acquiring it at all costs.

What piques his avidity is the report by the Rhinemaidens that should this gold be forged into a ring, its wielder could control the world and be its lord, provided he renounce love forever. Alberich steals the Rhinegold, makes the ring, and forces his master craftsman, Mime, to make out of it a golden helmet, the Tarnhelm, that renders its wearer invisible. Later the gods of Asgard compel Alberich to surrender his entire gold horde as ransom for their goddess Freia. The giants of Jotunnheim end up possessing the gold and the ring, but Alberich, who never got to use it, has cursed it, so all future users will suffer from any contact with this gold.

Explanation: The story of the Rhinegold veils a profound secret about Earth, consciousness, and a gift from our benevolent extraterrestrial mentors.

We start with another name for the Rhinegold: the gold of the Hyperboreans. A few of the classical Greek writers referred enigmatically to griffins guarding the gold of the Hyperboreans, a statement routinely dismissed as an oddity or fantasy of the ancients. It is actually a meaningful code, however.

"Hyperboreans" is a name for the original Pleiadian beings, that is, intelligences from planets in the star system in Taurus called the Pleiades, who participated in the creation and implementation of Earth's visionary geography many eons ago. The griffins were astral protector beings indigenous to the Pleiades placed at various locations around the Earth to guard the Pleiadian gold. The gold is living solar wisdom; to initial psychic perception, it can resemble a large mound of glowing, molten gold.

The Hyperborean gold was a fabulous gift of cosmic wisdom left to us by our "forebears" the Pleiadians when they had finished implementing Earth's visionary geography, sometimes called the Earth grid. There are 47 locations where this Pleiadian gold is lodged; I call such locations Griffin Gold Reserves. Selected locations include the Tor, Glastonbury, Somerset, England; the Sanctuary, near Avebury, Wiltshire, England; Treasury of Atreus, Mycenae, Greece; and somewhere in or near Worms along the Rhine River in Germany.

The Griffin Gold Reserve may seem to resemble a cavern or sculpted chamber inside a hill; it is guarded by a golden griffin, an allegedly mythical being (they're real: I've seen at least five griffins) with a lion's body, an eagle's head and wings, and usually presenting itself standing upright perhaps ten to 20 feet in height. Behind them is a shallow vat or fountain heaped high with shimmering, seemingly molten gold, though it is closer to congealed sunlight than to a semi-hard precious physical metal. If you are fortunate, the griffin will award you a small amount of gold to shape into whatever you wish.

This is still the outer shell of the mystery of the Hyperborean gold. These gold deposits are countermatched by Golden Apples, often guarded by dragons. A Golden Apple is, in part, implicit cosmic wisdom, subtle, and supportive of immortality; Hyperborean gold is explicit wisdom, workable, usable, tangible. Both features are present in the Worms area: a Golden Apple with dragon and a Griffin Gold Reserve. This is the Treasure of the Nibelungs that the Rhinemaidens were protecting and whose loss they so grievously mourned in *Das Rheingold.*

There is no diminution of the gold; it is, rather, a spiritual experience you have, then take away with you. The outer layer of the experience of the gold is the sense that you can shape it into things: a necklace, a crown, a ring. These objects then appear on your astral body and may be used in ceremonies and meditations.

The inner layer is where you enter the glowing gold mass and imbibe its wisdom. This is a clairvoyant immersion; in a sense, you stick your head into the flames. With your awareness expanded into the Pleiadian realm, you have access to the wisdom archives of the Pleiades through its central Logos, the star Alcyone.

Simultaneously present are all 100+ geomantic features (and all their copies) of Earth's visionary geography, all the Light temples, devices, connections, dragons, eggs, domes, and the many other different types of functional features. You see their interconnections, interdependencies, hierarchical relationships; you see the timing of it all, the astrological vectors that influence activation and quiescence of features; you understand what they are, how they work, how they *make reality.* Potentially, you see as Alcyone sees, panoptic galactic awareness.

There is yet another layer. The array of geomantic features are at this next level but are functional symbols for a more sublime reality whose language is geometry and mathematics. Earth's visionary geography is also, or more primarily, a mathematical grid, a formula whose verbs are certain constants of Nature such as phi, pi, e, the fine structure constant, and many others, and whose interrelationships are definable in terms of numbers, formulae, and harmonics.

This is the grammar of the Earth grid's rationality and the key to its functioning—the control panel for this dimensional expression, if you will. It is the mechanism for our planetary reality and its visionary geography, or grid.

Alberich's ring, Andvaranaut, has reality, and its moral valence—is it cursed, or not—depends on one's maturity. It's an initiate's test to use the gold.

You can make a ring, necklace, crown, or other shaped device to act as a miniaturized holographic resonator or projector of this complex reality to keep you continuously in attunement with its profound mechanisms while you go about your business as an embodied human concerned with Earth's well-being. If you approach the proposition from the point of wisdom (the crown chakra), all is well; if you approach it from hunger for power (the solar plexus chakra), then the ring (the Pleiadian explicit knowledge) is cursed for you.

Alberich and the Nibelungs, as dwarfs, were actually gnomes. These are Nature spirits, or Earth elementals, responsible for the element of earth, that is, solidity, hardness, the entire mineral kingdom, the planet's stones and jewels. They are not in a position to exploit the planetary control aspect of the gold; it is far beyond the parameters of their generic level of consciousness, though they can assist humans in shaping the gold into forms, though humans don't need the help.

In the Rhinegold myth, the Rhinemaidens are mostly Wagner's addition and have no functional reality with respect to the gold. The griffins guard the gold, so perhaps the Rhinemaidens are a human-style version of griffins. Similarly, the gods do not covet the Nibelungen gold; they already have wisdom. It is humans who want the cosmic wisdom implicit in the Hyperborean gold.

The Pleiadians-Hyperboreans left their wisdom in 47 deposits around the Earth, sometimes in the same locations as the 47 Golden Apples, as a gift to be used later by discerning humans who wish to plumb the mysteries of Earth, humanity, and the manifold intimate connections of both with the galaxy.

See also: Agharta, Avalon, Dragon, Golden Apple, Griffin, House of Atreus, Hyperboreans.

RISING ROCK

A stargate for physically transporting people or objects almost instantaneously from Earth to a point on another planet in the galaxy.

Also known as Growing Rock, Rock with Wings, stargate, Wings of Rock.

Description: Native American folklore has numerous examples of a rock that inexplicably grows and rises as if overnight or suddenly with a person on it. A person sleeps on a rock or small mound, then, upon waking, finds it has grown high into the air, and he cannot safely get down and needs a supernatural rescue. Such tales, according to folklorists, are favorites among the Indians of the Great Basin, Southwest (Chiricahua Apache), and California. The following are a few examples.

The Washo Indians of the Lake Tahoe area, which straddles the state borders of California and Nevada, have a tale about two sisters looking at the stars. One of them wants to marry a star-man associated with a specific star. They are sitting out in the landscape under a pine tree at a place called Wild Grub Hole near what is now Gardnerville, Nevada, just below Lake Tahoe in the Nevada flatlands near Reno.

They fall asleep. In the morning, one or both find themselves married to a star-man and holding her own newly delivered star-baby. They live in their new camp high in the sky and raise the baby, and every day they visit a hole in the sky and look down on Earth, wishing they could return to their home.

One day, Old Moon, the star-babies' grandfather, comes upon them; as he approaches, the sky trembles and thunders. Then he hurls the girls down through the sky hole where they land on another grandfather who is walking past.

They strike the man and the ground with such force that a deep hole in the Earth is made, almost burying them. The Washo say that hole is still there "over by Gardnerville" and one can always find plenty of "grub" there to eat.

The second example is Devil's Tower, the flattened cone of a mountain in Wyoming that figured centrally in Steven Spielberg's *Close Encounters of the Third Kind* (1979). This is a conical peak held sacred by many Native American tribes, including the Crow, Arapaho, Cheyenne, and Sioux, and once used frequently as a vision quest site.

The term "Devil's Tower" is an American transliteration of an old Indian name that means "The Bad God's Tower." It rises 1,267 feet above the ground to a total elevation of 5,112 feet above sea level. Geologists estimate the tower to be about 60 million years old, made of uprising subterranean molten magma.

Five different Native American myths of the tower have seven young sisters playing in the woods until they are chased by a grizzly bear; they flee into *Mato Tipila* ("Grizzly Bear Lodge"—their name for Devil's Tower), which is, at the time, only a small rock. They ask the rock to rescue them and it obliges, growing into the sky. The bear tries to climb up the expanding rock but fails, though it leaves its claw marks on the tower's flanks. It rises ever more and grows radically upward until it reaches the Pleiades and the women are safe. The Indians imply that these seven human sisters became the seven Pleiades.

A third example with a different nuance is Shiprock in northwestern New Mexico. An 1,800-foot soaring volcanic neck or plug that has been likened to a galleon or fully rigged schooner, Shiprock, which is on the Navajo Reservation, is known by the Navajo as *Tse Bi Dahi*, "the Rock with Wings," or *Tse Bit a'i*, "Winged Rock" or "Wings of Rock." It's also called the Pinnacle or Needle.

Shiprock is visible for many miles from every direction in the high plains country, and the Navajo say it is the rocky remains of a once living gigantic bird called *Tsé Ninával̲éeh* ("It Puts People Down on a Rock—as Eagles Do When Eating Their Prey") that appeared long ago to fly its people to safety. They also say Shiprock is a medicine pouch or bow in a larger landscape configuration.

The story says that long ago when the Navajo were hard-pressed by an enemy, their medicine men prayed to the Great Spirit. The Earth suddenly rose and lifted the Navajos up then moved them overland as if on a mighty wave, then settled down as Shiprock peak. After this, the Navajos lived on Shiprock, only coming down to plant crops. Geologically, Shiprock is said to be about 12 million years old; it was once much larger, possibly an immense mountain; and it was the result of a huge uprising of molten magma (similar to Devil's Tower).

Explanation: The Indian references to rocks that grow and rise to tremendous heights, even to the stars, is a code for a geomantic feature called stargates. To our cognition and experience today, stargates are an arcane aspect of Earth's many visionary geographic features, hardly used any more, and almost entirely forgotten. But once they were widely in use, and they could be again.

The three examples of a rising rock entail miraculous physical transportation from the ground to a place in the stars, or in the case of Shiprock, the arrival of a group of people from elsewhere via a growing rock or magical bird. Stargates do just that: They physically transport people or objects from points on Earth to many destinations on other planets in relationship to specific stars or constellations.

Unbelievably, no doubt, Earth has 2,200,000 stargates; these provide almost instant physical relocation to 264 constellations (with 8,333 copies of each) or 32 stars (with 32 copies of each—a considerable amount of duplication).

In terms of size, stargates range from three feet to 40 miles in diameter, though the average is about 30 yards. In appearance, they seem to resemble white, rounded-edge square containers such as are used to store large quantities of crude oil. Inside they resemble train stations, at least in essence; the actual transportation mechanism looks like a small conical stage with two curved, sliding, overlapping doors. You stand inside this chamber and you are transported elsewhere in body.

At Gardnerville, the stargate sits on a small butte at the eastern end of the flatlands and just before a larger rise of mountains. At Devil's Tower, the stargate is at the top of the peak, but, at Shiprock, it is physically inside the former mountain (which, as geologists suspect, was formerly about ten times larger) and slightly below ground level in a very large open chamber or cave. This site has two adjacent stargates; the ancestors of the Navajo were transported to Shiprock from elsewhere in the galaxy using these two stargates. The two stargates are the Rock with Wings or *Tsé Ninéháléé́h,* the bird that landed them on the big rock.

The Native American perception of a rock that magically grows vertically to take people to the stars is an elegant, nontechnologic image of a stargate. Looking down through a sky hole at one's former habitation on Earth is a way of saying the two points remain connected, Earth's stargate and the destination.

See also: Anunnaki, Atlas, Dreamtime, Holy Mountain, Hurqalya, Land of Milk and Honey, Lucifer, Tower of Babel, Zep Tepi.

RIVER GOD

Landscape angels whose bodies are physical rivers, in correspondence with the 3,000 Oceanids, or themes of cosmic consciousness; each river on Earth embodies and transmits one theme of consciousness.

Also known as Old Man River, River goddesses, River soul.

Description: The Greek and Celtic mythoi are particularly rich in their descriptions of gods or goddesses whose body is an actual physical river.

Theseus, the Greek hero of Cretan labyrinth fame, luxuriated on a couch with the River god Achelous in his underwater residence of pumice, tufa-rock, and conch shell ceiling, and was served lunch by barefoot River nymphs. On another occasion and evidently in a different mood, Heracles fought Achelous, who tried to outwit the hero by changing shape, first into a snake, then a bull. Similarly, Achilles engaged the River god Scamander near Troy in a prodigious battle that took the intervention of Hephaistos the Fire god to quell.

Troy was said to have been founded at the confluence of the residence of the River god Scamander (the main river on the Trojan plain, now in Turkey) and the home of Idaea, the nymph of nearby Mount Ida. In fact, the myths say that Idaea and Scamander produced a son, Teucer, who was the ancestor of the Trojan kings. The River god Cayster in Lydia, now Turkey, was the father of Ephesus, the founder of the sanctuary of Artemis and the holy city called Ephesus. And judging from Virgil's account, Rome may have been founded because of its nearness to the River god Tiber's residence—that place in the landscape where the River god may be visited.

The *Brugh na Boinne,* the Hostel on the River Boyne—today it's called Newgrange—was understood to be the residence of Boannd, the River goddess of the Boyne, a 70-mile waterway fairly near to Dublin in Ireland. It sounds like Newgrange was built there *because* that's where the River goddess lived. The River goddess Sequana, whose body is the River Seine in France, was honored at the source of the river, *Fontes*

Sequanae ("Springs of Sequana") near Dijon; that site was presumed to be her residence and she was depicted in the Roman shrine as a crowned woman with her arms raised aloft standing in a duck-shaped boat.

Verbeia was the River goddess and resident spirit of the River Warfe near Tadcaster, England; legend says she would appear on May 1 morning (Beltaine, an important Celtic festival day) as an apparitional white horse. Life (or sometimes Ana Life) is the goddess of the River Liffey that flows through Dublin, Ireland, as well as of its watershed; James Joyce immortalized her in literature by calling her Anna Livia Plurabelle in his *Finnegans Wake.* Sabrina is the River goddess of the Severn River in southwestern England.

Fial was the resident spirit of the River Feale and its watershed in Ireland; this river empties into the River Shannon (Sinann). Sinann is the granddaughter of the great Lir, the vastly ancient Sea god and Lord of the Sea. As a goddess, Sinann ignored a prohibition against approaching a magical well, variously called the Well of Segais or Connla's Well. She went to the well in search of wisdom, but the well suddenly overflowed and flooded the land, drowning her. This floodwater became the River Sinann, and she became its inhabiting spirit.

The same story is told of Boannd (who became the River Boyne). As a goddess, she sought wisdom at Connla's Well or the Well of Segais, but at her approach, it rose up suddenly and drowned her and her body became the River Boyne. In fact, one of the river's earliest names was *Sruth Segsa,* "River of Segais"; thus Boannd merged not only with the river, but with its ultimate source.

Throughout the numerous Greek and Celtic tales, the god or goddess seems to dissolve their divine power into the river or become one with the flowing waters or to somehow coexist with the river and enrich the land.

Explanation: The Greek myths give us a clue. They say the River gods are the brothers of the River nymphs called Oceanids. Oceanus was the paramount Water god for the Greeks, the personification of an ocean said to encircle Earth at its farthest edge, and he was the father, with Tethys, of 3,000 Oceanids. The story doesn't quite make sense until you adjust its locality.

Earth is usually understood to mean planet Earth, but if we interpret Earth here as the vast cosmos, the space for all matter, gross and subtle, then Oceanus (the great Lir) is a vast stream encircling the cosmos (cosmic Earth) like a ring. In this sense, the whole cosmos, at some level, is an ocean. Mystics talk of the Sea of Consciousness or Ocean of Milk, so Oceanus is a plausible name for that sea and the 3,000 Oceanids are differentiated streams of consciousness within it.

Oceanus is simply too vast to comprehend, so each Oceanid or nymph is a theme in that Sea of Consciousness. Perhaps this is why the Greeks say Zeus would often assemble the Oceanids at Mount Olympus to discuss worldly affairs.

If Oceanids are 3,000 aspects of the totality of consciousness *above,* then their brothers, the River gods (or sisters, River goddesses—the gender fluctuates in the myths) of Earth *below* must be the many physical rivers of the planet. Each river—Scamander, Tiber, Achelous, Boyne, Sinann—is both a physical flowing body of water and the "body" of a River god who embodies and transmits a theme in consciousness to the Earth, who ensouls the river with spiritual life.

In terms of their order of being, River gods are part of the large category called landscape angels or devas, angelic spirits assigned to natural Earth features.

Where River gods live—Scamander at Troy, Boannd at Newgrange, Tiber near the White City, the future Rome, Sequana at Fontes Sequanae—is where you may encounter them and, apparently quite often, where ancient settlements were made, such as Troy and Rome, or important megalithic sites, like Newgrange. Their residence is a geomantic node in Earth's visionary geography and an interactive theater for visionary exchanges.

The River god ensouls a river, permeating its waters and movement with its celestial life. It also oversees the activities of all the Nature spirits in that area, such as the various types of water spirits (undines, "water babies," and others). To an extent, the River god can be experienced as a personality, as reflected in the phrase Old Man River, in reference to the River soul of the Mississippi.

Much of this knowledge has faded, and only a few myth systems remember the spirits of rivers. The River gods of the 3,000 rivers on Earth (that correspond with the 3,000 Oceanids), however, may still be found and interacted with. The River god for the River Truckee, for example, which flows from Lake Tahoe, California, to Pyramid Lake, Nevada, has its residence within one hundred yards of where the river emerges from Lake Tahoe, in Tahoe City.

Similarly, if you find the ancient shrine dedicated to a given River god—for example, the River Achelous had a shrine by the Illissus in Attica, and Tiberinus, god of the River Tiber near Rome, had a temple on an island in the river—there is an excellent chance you may still meet with that River god.

The geomantic and spiritual intent of the Earth's many rivers was to inundate the collective consciousness serially with the 3,000 themes of cosmic consciousness, and to irrigate different watersheds with these selective themes.

What might we expect from an encounter with a River god? The Rhine River god brought gold to the wedding of Poseidon, Lord of the Sea, and Beroe. The Simois River god near Troy made ambrosia spring up for the horses of Hera, Queen of the gods, and Pallas Athena, an Olympian, during the Trojan War. The River god Erasinus acted as a guardian of its people, refusing to abandon the citizens of Argos in Greece to the conquering Spartan king.

Ganga, the goddess of the River Ganges, petitioned Brahma, the Hindu Creator god, to allow her waters to descend from Heaven to Earth to purify the ashes of 60,000 burnt sons of King Sagara so as to allow them to enter Paradise. So strong was Ganga's spiritual current that first it had to flow through Shiva's matted hair before it could safely touch Earth and not drown all of India.

See also: Connla's Well, Gaia, Nymph, Ocean of Milk.

ROUND TABLE

A concentrated image of the *Duat,* or Egyptian conception of the Underworld, through which the Sun god Ra makes his journey through a twelvefold division of primal cosmic space and its guardian beings.

Also known as Amentet, Body of Osiris, Duat (Dwat, Tuat), Hidden Place, Interior of Nut, Jousting Field, Neterkhert, Place of Morning Twilight, Underworld.

Description: In the King Arthur saga, King Leodegrance, King of the "land of Camelerd," or sometimes the Summer Country (Somerset, England), awards Arthur the Round Table as a dowry for his daughter, Guinevere, in marriage. The Round Table, generally understood to be a large wooden circular table, seats 150 Knights equably with no one sitting at the head of the table since it is round and has no head.

This was the standard account, as in Sir Thomas Malory's fifteenth-century compilation *Le Morte d'Arthur,* but in the earlier *Quest of the Holy Grail* (1225), the anonymous author has Merlin, King Arthur's magus, declare that he devised the Round Table to embody a subtle meaning. It mirrors the roundness of the Earth, the concentric spheres of the planets, the elements of the firmament, and all the stars and is thus a "true epitome" of the universe. This is hardly a mere wooden table.

In the stories, only the worthiest of men could be inducted into the fellowship of the Knights of the Round Table. This was a mark of high honor and carried great responsibility, for one had to uphold the ideals of Camalate and participate in the often lifelong Quest for the Holy

Grail, both arduous and dangerous and without any guarantee of ultimate success or peer validation. Arthur's Knights also frequently had to prove themselves in the jousting field.

Explanation: The Round Table is a dynamic image, in concentrated form, of what the Egyptians called the Duat or Underworld, which was conceptualized as the body of Osiris made into a circle.

Osiris, the high god and the male aspect of the Supreme Being (his wife, and God's female aspect in the Egyptian mythos, was Isis), was Lord of the Duat. The Egyptians depicted him in this guise as forming an oroboric circuit, his head biting his toes, making a circle. Inside this was the Duat, an interior space.

A better translation of *Duat* than "Underworld" is "Place of Morning Twilight," a realm in which darkness is yielding to morning light. Another term the Egyptians used is *amentet,* "the Hidden Place," personified by a beautiful goddess, the Lady of the West (Nut) who receives the Sun into the mysterious region within her (Duat). A third is *neterkhert,* "the divine under place."

The Duat was described as being inside the star-filled body of the Sky goddess Nut; she was depicted as a feminine form arched over the Earth, her body filled with stars and all the star gods. The Duat was her interior space.

The term *Duat* is usually translated from the Egyptian as "Underworld," but this is misleading and confusing. It is an Underworld from the point of view of higher levels of creation and unfoldment, such as the Cosmic Egg, and the Black and White Eyes of Horus, the falcon god and Egyptian Christ. From the human view, the Duat is definitely the Upper World, and the inner.

The Duat is a secret world, a place of mystery and initiation. It is the route of Ra, the Egyptian Sun god's nighttime journey through the Underworld. In the Egyptian text called *Book of Gates,* Ra (Re) travels in his solar barque through the 12 gateways of the Duat; on this journey, he is called "Flesh of Re." Each gateway has guardians and foes, but Ra's safe passage through each is assured by his knowledge of the secret passwords, or names of the divinities.

Ra's passage is eventful, full of meetings: jackals and cobra gods guarding the Lake of Life; the 12 barley gods; numerous guardian spirits such as Enveloper, Stinger, Flame-face, Darting of Eye, Earth-tusk, and Effluent One. He is accosted by Apophis, the demonic monster of the Deep; he enters the Hall of Osiris; four baboons announce his imminent arrival at the Eastern Horizon.

Ra's passage through the Duat is an earlier, deeper, subtler form of the zodiac, its Houses, and the numerous constellations as depicted in traditional maps of the Heavens, including those of the Egyptians. The zodiac as such is the outside of Nut, her skin (see White Cow, White Sow), while the Duat is inside her. The concentrated expression of the Duat is what the Celts called the Round Table.

The Duat is the first expression of a twelvefold division of cosmic space and consciousness. On his journey through the Underworld, Ra samples each of the 12 divisions and, as the stories say, survives the perilous encounters.

Yet, as Sun god, he also enlivens and illuminates these 12 archetypal stations. The Duat comprises the first embodiment of the two basic principles of fire and substance: the fire of the Sun (Time) and the substance of the Moon (Soma, Space), understood here not as sun and Earth satellite of our solar system, but as expressions at a more fundamental, original state of cosmic creation. Ra travels through a world in which the archetypes of Time and Space, fire and substance, first come together to create the souls of the stars and constellations.

The Sun, expressive of the Self or Ego, undergoes division into 12 parts as equal divisions of identity and space, making Self-knowledge easier.

The Duat, or Round Table, is expressed geomantically in Earth's visionary geography in the form of 360 landscape Round Tables. These are experiential playing fields, often several miles in diameter, in which the energies of the 12 zodiacal signs, or in Egyptian terms, the 12 gateways and their guardians, are astrally present. One interacts with this template through jousting.

The medieval Arthurian sagas have numerous accounts of armor-clad Knights on armor-clad horses going at each other with long lances, trying to unseat the other. This may have happened physically, but the reality is occult: The landscape Round Table, or terrestrial Duat template, is the jousting field.

You essentially confront conflicted parts of your horoscope and past-life karma by way of visionary jousting. There is a Round Table of this type surrounding King Arthur's fifth-century Camalate at South Cadbury Castle in Somerset, England. Once, during the month of Scorpio (late November), I had a series of visionary encounters (jousts) with dark-clad men on horses. I unseated most of them and extracted a life lesson from each, and a few unseated me. On another occasion, members of the angelic family called the Seraphim jousted with me.

In all cases, I was trying to acknowledge, transmute, and assimilate the energies represented by these nuances of Scorpio. I was Ra, on the human scale, encountering the various threatening guardians of the 12 gateways in the Duat as a way of coming to better know my Self, the twelvefold Sun, or Ego.

The Egyptian texts show Ra in his solar barque moving through each gateway and domain of the Duat as if transiting the perimeter of the circle. But it is equally true to say Ra resides at the center of the Round Table and, like an eye, shines his solar light equally on each of the 12 divisions of the Duat in turn.

Equivalently, King Arthur—The *AR* in his name like a mirror image of *RA*— also sits in the center of the Round Table as the cohering solar principle, the Solar Logos.

Picture yourself at the center of the Round Table. You are Ra, the Sun, or King Arthur, the Sun; both are expressions of the Solar Logos. You see the 12 divisions of the Table (or Duat) as wedges, the narrow ends of which face you. You may also see the 27 divisions of cosmic space into the *Naksatras,* the "wives" of King Soma (wakeful consciousness) interspersed with the 12. At each wedge point, there is a celestial being, a guardian of that wedge of space, time, consciousness, and the innumerable star gods and constellations within it.

As you move your gaze from wedge to wedge, you are Ra transiting the stations of the Duat, Arthur greeting and validating his Round Table Knights. You the Solar Logos, the Word at the level of stars, are immediately surrounded by a circle of 12, 27, or 39 gods, the guardians of the primal divisions of cosmic space.

At the human level, the Round Table is a circle of 12 or 24 men and women (often in pairs) whose level of spiritual development, astrological makeup, and soul constitution matches the stations of the Duat. Standing behind these 12 positions are 12 of the 14 Ray Masters of Ursa Major (known to Hinduism as the Seven Rishis; they each have consorts). They supervise and mentor both the Grail Knights occupying the astrological positions at the Round Table and the original galactic constellations and their energies.

See also: Anubis, Black Eye of Horus, Camalate, Cosmic Egg, Fountain of Youth, Grail Knight, Guinevere, Hitching Post of the Sun, Holy Grail, King Arthur, Underworld, White Cow, White Eye of Horus, White Sow.

ROYAL HALL OF THE KING OF THE DOVRË TROLLS

Regional headquarters for Nature spirits called gnomes who maintain the earth element and work with humans in maintaining the planet's visionary geography.

Also known as Gnome Egg, Hall of the Nibelungs, Megacenter Nature Temple.

Description: This name comes from Henrik Ibsen's *Peer Gynt,* a drama he published in 1867. The story takes place in the Rondane Mountains of south-central Norway in the vicinity of Gudbrandsdalen, since known locally as Peer Gynt country. A cocky young man named Peer Gynt is invited by the alluring daughter of the king to visit the Royal Hall of the King of the Dovrë Trolls. In Scandinavian countries, trolls are considered ill-mannered, ugly, treacherous, and even dangerous otherworldly creatures, best avoided for safety.

Once inside the Hall, Peer Gynt is told that troll-folk are less black than they're painted, less ugly and less fearsome. He witnesses dancing, enjoys harp music, talks with troll-maidens and troll-witches, as Ibsen writes, and is invited to join their revelries. His lack of understanding of their pagan reality and his general poor manners get Peer Gynt thrown out of the hall, which immediately disappears, leaving the man as before, alone in the hills.

Explanation: Peer Gynt has wandered into a Gnome Egg, a regional headquarters for the Nature spirits of the earth element called gnomes. Although Ibsen frequently refers to trolls in his plays, it is unlikely that he realized two important facts: First, trolls are simply large gnomes; and second, his Royal Hall is a Gnome Egg, of which there are 60,660 copies in total across the Earth, including ten in the "Rondë Hills," as Ibsen called the Rondane Mountains.

Gnome Eggs are most often located in remote areas, away from population centers, even villages. They are often deep in the woods or on mountaintops, although sometimes they are located in copses or dells near hamlets.

The essence of what Ibsen wrote in *Peer Gynt* is accurate, however. A Gnome Egg usually appears as a very large translucent sphere, pockmarked like a golf ball, about one hundred feet in diameter and set slightly into the ground. You walk through the egg in a visionary, psychic sense and enter the neighboring realm of the earth elementals. The appearance of gnomes may vary with culture and terrain, as well as with one's psychic clarity, but generally (or approximately) they are short-statured, stocky males about two to three feet tall, sometimes bearded, with caps, jerkins, high boots, and eighteenth-century Northern European or Celtic garb.

Their function is to maintain the earth element on the planet, all things to do with solidity, density, minerals, crystals, rocks, and generally the Earth's interior. They also maintain the differential (they call it "the splice") between Earth's electromagnetic field and its gradients and Earth's etheric or subtle energy matrix.

Their assignment is to work with humans (in this professional capacity, such people are known as Grail Knights or Grid engineers) to ground celestial and angelic energy and distribute it throughout the elemental kingdom (the energy field around all of Nature and its ecosystems) as a kind of high-potency plant food. The gnomes often form long-term working relationships with humans and can be excellent guides to the microlandscape of Earth's visionary terrain. The Gnome Egg is a reliable place to meet with gnomes and to form professional relationships.

As for the Royal Hall aspects, the Gnome Eggs have long tunnels leading deep into the Earth, opening out into what are best described as great halls. There are archival aspects to these halls, and you may observe something like an interactive holographic museum of late and great gnomes and gnome kings.

Gnomes, as the Nature spirits for the element of earth, solidity, and stone, also look after Earth's minerals and precious gems. This is why they are often shown as miners, jewelers, stone craftsmen, or guardians of immense hoards of jewels inside caverns. The Germanic myth of the Hall of the Nibelungs shows this. The hero Siegfried enters this hall, astounded by the outspread treasure. The gnomes work closely with dragons who also guard jewel hoards, and sometimes the two locales get merged in myth and even psychic vision.

In a sense, all the Gnome Eggs lead to the same Hall of the Gnome King, who, despite the seeming fairy-tale-like quality of the concept, has an actual reality. Though "the King of the Dovrë Trolls" is Ibsen's Norwegian name for this figure, he is the head of the gnome order worldwide, much like the Fairy Queen is the chief of the fairies. In a sense, the Gnome King keeps the gnomes somewhat in line, as they tend to be fun-loving, mischievous, and easily distracted—again, qualities captured by Ibsen in his depiction of the trolls' party atmosphere.

Further, the planetary headquarters for the gnomes and the organizing center for all gnome activities worldwide is located at the tip of Scandinavia, where Norway, Sweden, and Finland meet, in the Porsanger-Halvöya area. This is the master Gnome Egg for Earth, where the gnomes assemble the earth element and all that pertains to solidity and density, and maintain it all.

The Gnome Egg has been described from a different perspective as a megacenter Nature temple that appears as a huge sphere just beneath the ground and composed of many facets of different colors. Elementals, including gnomes, come and go from this structure, which services a large portion of the landscape.

See also: Camalate, Fairy Queen, Gaia, Grail Knight, Menehune, Pan, Trolls.

RUSTAM

The Persian expression of King Arthur, Solar Logos and leader of the Great White Brotherhood of Ursa Major, overshadowing a human hero.

Also known as Fionn MacCumhaill, Gesar of Ling, Indra, King Arthur, Rostem.

Description: The life and deeds of Rustam, one of Persia's greatest heroes, a prodigy of physical strength, spiritual goodness, and devotion to his country, are described in Firdowsi's eleventh-century *Shahnameh* ("Book of Kings"). His father, Zal, was raised by the Simurgh in the Alburz Mountains of Persia; the Simurgh is a mystical, celestial bird who lives on top of that holy mountain. Rustam's lineage ruled as kings of Sistan in southeastern Persia near the Gulf.

Rustam performs many heroic deeds and feats of tremendous strength, assisted by his magical horse, Rakhsh. In fact, he completes seven heroic deeds, including overcoming a lion, journeying through a waterless desert, slaying a dragon (240 feet from head to tail), killing a witch, and slaying numerous *divs* (demons), among them the Great White Demon. With his army of other heroes, Rustam restores King Kay Kavus to royal power, as king of all kings in Iran, after which Rustam is regaled as the hero of the world. Rustam served a succession of Persian kings after Kay Kavus.

In a variation of this tale from Afghanistan, Rustam derives his strength from the Sun, called *Yazdan Pak* or *Khur;* he has great and secret knowledge of the Sun, and whatever he asks of the Sun, he is granted. The Sun gave him formidable strength (two thousand warriors could not withstand him) and, one time, invisibility (he walked unseen through a camp of thousands of enemy soldiers). Rustam's strength peaked at noon, as does the Sun's light, and declined in the afternoon.

Rustam's horse, Rakhsh, is a prodigy among horses. Strong as an elephant, tall as a camel, with red spots on its flank like the shining sun, it is worth the entire value of Persia. Rakhsh assists Rustam in his many dangerous exploits.

Rustam marries Tahmineh, the beautiful daughter of a local king, and they produce a child named Sohrab. Years later, Rustam unknowingly fights Sohrab, mistaking him for an enemy soldier, and slays him, only then realizing his identity. In another version, the Simurgh heals Sohrab over the course of a year, using its power of licking a mortal human wound to heal it.

Some accounts say Rustam was killed by treachery in the sixth century B.C., but generally his authenticity as a historical figure is difficult to pin down.

Explanation: Rustam and his band of heroes in defense of the Kings of Persia are one of the 15 expressions of the King Arthur mythos as enacted in a specific culture. Rustam was both a human hero and one overshadowed by the celestial King Arthur and his heroic band, the Great White Brotherhood.

King Arthur is called the "once and future king" because as the centerpiece of an archetypal myth that crops up in numerous cultures over the life of the Earth, his relevance never dies, but it does wax and wane. Among humans, it involves a Soul Group whose members periodically incarnate together in the same culture to reenact the dynamics of the Arthurian mythos on behalf of Earth, its visionary geography, and all the planet's life forms and levels of consciousness. In such a reenactment, celestial law and truth are reestablished.

King Arthur, although packaged in Celtic names and lore, is actually the name of the Solar Logos, the Logos or Word at the level of all Suns. This is the expression of Christ at the level of suns, or stars; as Logos, Christ is the connectivity and rationality binding all the stars and states of consciousness together. In Hinduism, he is known as Vishnu the Preserver and Pervader.

Arthur, whose energy pertains to growth and change, is the leader of the Great White Brotherhood (see Einherjar) based in Ursa Major (the Great Bear). This is an extensive conclave of enlightened adepts, celestial beings, and angels who maintain divine order and the celestial laws and truth throughout the galaxy.

Rustam receives great strength and unusual abilities from the Sun god *Yazdan Pak,* because he is its active expression as Solar Logos in human form and is overshadowed and permeated by the actual Solar Logos in spiritual form.

Similarly, he rides the Christ (the horse Rakhsh) in one of his expressions as a White Horse. This means that, as part of his self-mastery and the attainment of kingship, Rustam has the assistance of the Christ Consciousness; he can move as swiftly and widely as thought. (His Tibetan-Mongolian equivalent, Gesar of Ling, also has a magical helper horse.)

The Arthurian mythos, when it is enacted in an actual time period in a specific culture (other examples have been Gesar of Ling in Mongolia and Fionn MacCumhaill in Ireland), runs on a parallel track. Above, the Great White Brotherhood and King Arthur as Solar Logos work with their human equivalents (e.g., Arthur and his Knights of Camalate; Fionn and his Fianna; Rustam and his heroic band), overshadowing them, infusing them with spiritual potency and direction.

The involvement of the Simurgh in the parentage of Rustam and his father, Zal, is appropriate, for the Persian mystical bird is an expression taken by the angelic family called Ofanim. The Ofanim are always involved in Arthurian reenactments and central to the parentage and exploits of the Arthurian hero.

The Persian Zal is Rustam's father in a spiritual, mentoring sense. Zal is the expression of Merlin, King Arthur's magus who arranged for Arthur's birth by organizing the correct parentage, then saw to Arthur's training as a knight. Merlin, through all his incarnations and folk legends (e.g., the Polynesian Maui, the Greek Herakles, the Buddhist Padmasambhava), always worked closely with the Ofanim (the Simurgh), receiving from them new instructions from the angelic world.

Each Arthurian reenactment follows standard lines of development, missions, and themes, yet has differences in execution. The Persian Tahmineh is the Celtic Guinevere, King Arthur's wife (see Guinevere), but there is no report of an adulterous liaison with Arthur's chief knight, Sir Lancelot. Guinevere stands for the king's soul, the glory and beauty of the Divine Light—the archetype of the human soul as a glorious, radiant being of purity and truth.

In the Celtic version, Mordred is Arthur's bastard and, in a battle, they knowingly mortally wound each other. With Rustam and Sohrab, Sohrab dies (or is healed) through the genuine ignorance of the opponent's true identity. Mordred usually represents the Scorpionic power of radical transformation through a kind of spiritual poisoning to provoke Arthur to evolve further.

The seven heroic deeds of Rustam are appropriate for a human initiate working on behalf of Earth and human culture. King Arthur slays a dragon, as does Rustam, but that is only the outer story; the inner one is that they master the dragon energy, in themselves and in Earth's visionary geography, so that its fructifying light and consciousness may flow beneficially into the land and people. They do not kill the dragon, but activate its life-renewing energies.

The other heroic deeds must be similarly understood in terms of geomantic interaction with Earth and its numerous Light temples. The overall goal of each Arthurian reenactment is to create favorable physical and spiritual conditions, through interacting with Earth's geomancy, for the advancement of human consciousness and culture and the interpenetration of both celestial and elemental (Nature spirits) energies and information.

In some versions of the Arthurian mythos, the Arthur figure is an outer king, as in the Celtic King Arthur, but in others, he serves the existing kingship. Arthur's kingship is more of an inner, alchemical mastery of the self, the marriage of the two fundamental halves (e.g., Sun and Moon, rationality and intuition) reflected in the outer bond of Arthur and Guinevere (Rustam and Tahmineh).

Further, Arthur (Rustam) and his knights work mostly as an esoteric cabal, often behind the scenes through higher states of consciousness and geomantic interfacings. So outer recognition and reward as kingship are often inappropriate.

See also: Dragon, Einherjar, Fionn MacCumhaill, Gesar of Ling, Guinevere, Indra, King Arthur, Merlin, Simurgh.

SAEHRIMNIR

An ancient metaphor for Christ Consciousness to which the spiritual adepts of the Great White Brotherhood have perpetual access.

Also known as Varahi.

Description: The term is from Old Norse and means "sooty sea-animal," although the literal translation does not do the concept justice. Saehrimnir is the magical boar in Valhalla whose flesh is consumed daily, but replenished at night; in other words, Saehrimnir is an inexhaustible meat supply for the feasting gods of Odin, the high god of Asgard in Norse myth. The feasting gods in the Hall of the Slain (Valhalla) are called Einherjar ("lone fighters").

Odin assembled 432,000 slain battlefield warriors (the Einherjar) to sit with him in Valhalla. During the day, the warriors reenact their battle scenes, killing one another seemingly, but in the evening they are all intact again and spend the night feasting on the inexhaustible supply of boar meat—called "the best of meats"—and drinking mead from Odin's magic goat, Heidrun.

Every day, Saehrimnir is cooked in the cauldron Eldrimnir and consumed by the Einherjar, and by the end of every evening, he is whole again. Saehrimnir is the gods' ever-renewed boar. Very few among mortals know the food of the Einherjar, Norse myth says.

The same motif flourishes in Irish myths of the hostels, understood to be inns, centers of hospitality, banqueting halls, and sumptuous residences. The Hostel of Da Derga along the River Dodder in Leinster earned Da Derga the reputation of the Chief Hospitaller in Eriu (Ireland). Numerous prodigies of battles, even one-eyed giants and three-headed Fomorians with three hundred teeth apiece, continually feast on boar meat and rich ale at Da Derga's Hostel.

In Hindu mythology, the third incarnation of Vishnu (the Christ) was as Varahi (also called Varaha or Emusa), a massive boar who saved Earth from the waters of chaos by raising it out of the primeval waters on its great tusks. The waters streaming off his tusks and brow purified the great sages, Hindu myth says—an image equivalent to the warrior prodigies of Valhalla and Da Derga's Hostel feasting on the boar's endlessly renewable meat, or consciousness.

Explanation: Saehrimnir is the Christ Consciousness perpetually available to the Einherjar, who are members of the Great White Brotherhood. It is perpetually renewed because it is inexhaustible and pervades reality.

It is akin, though the animal symbolism differs, to the Celtic Salmon of Wisdom, one taste of whose flesh produces clairvoyance and prophetic-poetic insight. It is also the same as the Rich Fisher King of Western European Grail Mysteries, and *Matsya-avatara*, Vishnu's first incarnation as an eight-million-mile-long fish who tows the Boat of the Vedas (Grail Castle) over the Flood waters. Vishnu, the Vedic version of the Christ, pervades and preserves space.

The Einherjar are "lone fighters" who have "defeated" themselves in the "battle" of spiritual development and the mastery of self, matter, and consciousness. Battle and defeat are better understood in terms of transmutation. One of the prime rewards of this self-mastery is membership in the Great White Brotherhood, a cabal of enlightened sages, spiritual adepts, angels, and accomplished beings from other star systems known as the Einherjar of Valhalla.

Odin's Hall of the Slain and Da Derga's inn of hospitality are assembly places for the Einherjar where, in a kind of cosmic *agape* or Eucharist, they partake of the Christ awareness. The boar, to the ancients, was an appropriate image for a source of unending abundance of meat; it is, however, a metaphor for the Christ.

Even more than a metaphor, the endlessly "meaty" boar signifies access to the universal substance, the protean Christ Light, which is the endlessly abundant source of supply for everything the Einherjar wish to create. Also called the Cosmic Light, it is a limitless storehouse of primal raw material out of which they may create (precipitate) anything required; in fact, all of Creation was originally shaped from this pervasive Light (see Ocean of Milk).

That these ascended adepts have unlimited access to this universal creative substance is indicated by the boar's flesh that is perpetually renewed.

See also: Connla's Well, Da Derga's Hostel, Einherjar, Fisher King, Ocean of Milk, Salmon of Wisdom, Seven Rishis, Valhalla.

SALMON OF WISDOM

The Celtic description of the Rich Fisher King, the guardian and embodiment of total cosmic knowledge, and King of the Grail Castle, the esoteric place where this wisdom may be obtained.

Also known as Amen, Ceridwen's Cauldron, Christ Consciousness, Connla's Well, Cosmic Christ, Fintan (Fionntan), God-Self, Great Master Within, Fisher King, Higher Self, Leviathan, Mighty "I AM" Presence, Nechtan, Perfect Self, Taliessin, Ta-tjenen, Waters of Mnemosyne, Well of Coelrind, Well of Nechtan, Well of Segais.

Description: Irish myth recounts that Fintan (Fionntan) was an ancient bard who over many lifetimes accumulated a vast store of wisdom and remembered what he had learned. This same Fintan is credited with being Ireland's Noah, having survived the Flood, landing at either the Dingle Peninsula in County Kerry or at Hill of Tounthinna (*Tulach Tuindi* or *Tul Tuinne*) overlooking the River Shannon and near Portroe in County Tipperary.

From here, with his consort, Cesair, he is credited with repopulating Ireland and restarting world culture. Fintan often assumes salmon form, and lives in Connla's Well, a well of inspiration, knowledge, and wisdom, superintended by Nechtan and his three cupbearers. Nine hazel trees grow over the well, and Fintan, in his salmon form, often nibbles on them, absorbing their wisdom. All humans and even the gods and goddesses are prohibited from drinking from the well. Even to approach Connla's Well caused it to overflow and drown two goddesses, Boannd and Sinann, who got transformed into rivers of the same name (see River God).

Fintan is called the Salmon of Wisdom, and only a very few of the most select Druids of all Ireland had the requisite permission or standing to taste its flesh. One time the hermit Druid Finneces was turning this salmon on a spit, and Fionn MacCumhaill (later a great Irish hero and leader, but here a youth in training) got splattered on his thumb with some hot juice from the roasting fish. Fionn immediately sucked his thumb to cool the burn and absorbed all of the salmon's wisdom. He had visionary experiences, and from then on, whenever he wanted to foretell the future, he would suck the salmon-splattered thumb.

A similar story, though with a different figure, is told in Wales. As a boy, Gwion Bach had the task of stirring Amen, the cauldron of the goddess Ceridwen ("White, Blessed") who lived at the bottom of Bala Lake *(Llyn Tegid)* in Wales. He was warned not to taste the brew of herbs, which Ceridwen was simmering for a year to make her ugly son Afagddu (or Morfran) wise and poetically gifted.

One day while stirring, Gwion got splattered by the brew, which bubbled out of the cauldron. Three drops touched his thumb and forefinger, which he stuck in his mouth to cool them and immediately absorbed all the goddess's wisdom, insight, knowledge, poetic gifts, and the ability to change shape.

Ceridwen, unhappy with this, chased Gwion all over Wales until he turned himself into numerous different animals (including a salmon) and finally a grain of wheat to hide from her, but Ceridwen, also a shape-shifter, at last turned herself into a hen and ate the grain of wheat. She became pregnant, and when she gave birth, it was to Gwion in his next life and transformation, as Taliessin. This name means "Radiant Brow," "Shining Brow," or "Beautiful Forehead," and he was destined to be a great prophetic poet, both eloquent and psychic. He was able to look through the veil of matter into the Otherworld.

Explanation: The Salmon of Wisdom is the Celtic version of the Vedic *Matsya-avatara,* an eight-million-mile-long fish that towed the Boat of the Vedas, all the esoteric wisdom teachings, the ancient sages, and the Vedic Noah named Manu Satyavrata across the Flood waters and eventually to safety. The enormous fish was an incarnation of the god Vishnu, the Preserver and Pervader of the cosmos, akin to the Western Christ and Logos (the Word). *Matsya-avatara,* as a form of Vishnu, is the cosmic intelligence and universal wisdom that pervade Heaven.

In early Christianity, Christ is called Ichthys, which means "Fish," so Vishnu-Christ in the form of a vast, knowledge-rich fish is the Christ Consciousness, and that is awareness distributed across (pervading) the entire cosmos. One knows everything that is happening, has happened, will happen, and why.

Although the animal symbolism is different, the Christ-Vishnu Fish is akin to the Norse formulation of Christ Consciousness in the form of Saehrimnir, the boar who is perpetually roasted and eaten in Valhalla, yet whose flesh grows back to feed all the slain warriors (Einherjar) the next day. The difference is that the boar is always just a boar and, in this Eucharistic metaphor, the Einherjar perpetually enjoy the Christ Consciousness, whereas with the Salmon of Wisdom, the fish is both the Christ Consciousness and its administrator, the Grail King.

Manu was a spiritual lawgiver and child of the thousand-rayed Sun. When the Flood subsided, Manu would restart world culture; but this was outside of human history—rather, it would be the start of history, a new aeon, or in Vedic reckoning, a new cycle of cosmic time and life that would last over four billion years.

Manu, as the first spiritual king of the new epoch of existence, was an expression of Vishnu, or the Christ, the embodiment of total cosmic knowledge. As such, he was the Vishnu Fish, or Celtic Salmon of Wisdom, and its administrator, guardian, and dispenser—the Rich Fisher King of the Grail Castle. Similarly, the Irish Fintan is both an ancient one-eyed bard and the Salmon of Wisdom, both the wisdom and the disseminator of that wisdom.

Possession of that cosmic wisdom also meant prophetic, clairvoyant insight, which is why Fintan was described as one-eyed and Taliessin means radiant, shining brow. These are references to the brow or *Ajna* chakra between the eyes, the seat of psychic perception, clairvoyance, and divine understanding.

These tremendous gifts are possible through the merest touch of the Salmon of Wisdom because this figure is the guardian of the Holy Grail and its Mysteries. He is the Rich Fisher King—the King who is the rich fish—and master of the Grail Castle. The Grail, among other things, is the process of retrieving deep cosmic memory and past-life information about the soul. The Greeks referred to this as the Waters of Mnemosyne, or deep remembering.

The Rich Fisher King is also what is called the Higher Self, the Mighty "I AM" Presence, the Magic Presence, or the Ascended state, in which matter has been transmuted into Light, and one's body is not flesh anymore, but Light.

The figure of Gwion Bach splits the difference between two Grail characters. He is the Rich Fisher King and Salmon of Wisdom, but he is also the Grail Knight who successfully penetrates the Grail Castle to taste the Salmon. This is Parsifal (the one who pierces the veil between worlds). Parsifal experiences the Grail Castle when he is fairly young, by grace and invitation; then it takes him decades to return on his own psychic merits.

This is mirrored in the transformation (or reincarnation) of Gwion Bach into Taliessin. Gwion Bach accidentally tastes the cosmic wisdom; Taliessin, through his brow chakra or psychic insight, earns the right to feast on it.

The attainment of the Salmon of Wisdom, the transformation into radiant-browed Taliessin, the richness that is the Fisher King's, is not something solely relegated to myth or ultrasophisticated spiritual accomplishment. It is actually a picture of the completed, reawakened human being rectified, reconciled, and unified with his or her soul and all its knowledge and experiences across the aeons.

Nechtan, who guards Connla's Well and its Salmon of Wisdom, has three cupbearers. These are the Grail Maidens of classical Grail sagas. They represent the intuitive aspects of consciousness freely available for penetrating the astral realm to gain the knowledge, experiences, and lessons of the soul across lifetimes.

Why did the Celtic psychic bards specifically choose a salmon among all the fishes? Because it belongs to the oldest layers of Celtic mythology and was believed by them to be the most archaic of all creatures and oldest of the fish. Their assumption was that all subsequent living creatures evolved from mutations of this primordial water creature who lived in Earth's earliest sea. If the salmon was the oldest creature in existence, then it must know all mysteries and secrets of the world and be able to divulge them to humans.

Those interested may interact with the Salmon of Wisdom (Rich Fisher King) at any of the 144 Grail Castles templated in Earth's visionary terrain.

See also: Connla's Well, Fionn MacCumhaill, Fisher King, Grail Castle, Grail Knight, Grail Maiden, Holy Grail, Lady of the Lake, Manu, River God, Saehrimnir, White Mount.

SENGEN-SAMA

The resident Mountain Spirit or landscape angel at Mount Fuji who ensouls and sanctifies the mountain and its environment.

Also known as Konohana Sakuahime.

Description: Sengen-Sama is the prime deity in goddess form worshipped in the Shinto religion through her residence at Mount Fuji, Japan's main sacred mountain. She is also known as *Konohana Sakuahime,* which means "Radiant blooming as the flowers of the trees," "Causing the Blossom to Bloom Brightly," "the Princess Who Makes the Blossoms of the Trees to Flower," or simply "the Goddess of Flowering Trees."

The goddess's beauty is compared to or perhaps equated with the arresting appearance of the cherry and plum blossoms seen against the snow on Mount Fuji's slopes and reflected in its five lakes below. In ancient Japan, Sengen-Sama was said to hover above the mountain in a luminous cloud, attended by numerous though invisible servants.

Mount Fuji (elevation 12,397 feet) is a semi-active volcano and Japan's tallest mountain. Its full name, *Fuji-no-yama* means "the Mountain of Fuji," but it is also respectfully called *O Yama* ("the Honorable Mountain"), and an even older name, attributed to the Ainu, Japan's aboriginal inhabitants, is the word for fire, *Huchi, Huzi,* or *Fuchi,* and refers to the Ainu Fire Goddess at Fuji. Yet the mountain is also *Fuji-san* ("Everlasting Life"), *Fuji-yama* ("Never-Dying Mountain"), and Japan's supreme sacred High Place, the nation's soul itself.

Much of this numinosity is attributed to Sengen-Sama, Fuji's goddess and the name of the peak's central shrine. So highly is Sengen-Sama venerated that after an eight-hour climb to the top, people have flung themselves into the volcanic fires, believing this would give them perpetual companionship with her.

Once a young man named Yosoji sought help to cure his mother of smallpox by collecting some water from a small stream that flowed on Fuji's southwestern flank. The water was said to come from a shrine to the God of Long Breath on Fuji. Yosoji encountered a young woman clad in white, and she directed him to the stream. He collected water for his mother and drank a little himself. He returned five more times, at the woman's request, until his mother was healed. During a later visit, the woman swung a camellia branch in the air and soon a cloud descended from Fuji and carried her away. Yosoji, who had long asked the woman to reveal her identity, now understood that she was the Goddess of Fuji.

Explanation: Sengen-Sama is the resident landscape angel and spirit guardian of Mount Fuji. All mountains on Earth have a primary spiritual being who acts as the conduit for celestial energies to feed into the physical realm.

They are known by various names: in western European lore, as landscape angels or Mountain Spirits; in Peruvian myth, they are *Apus,* the Spirits of the Mountains. The Navajo say that every mountain has an inner form and holy beings inside it called *bii'istíín,* "Those That Stand Within Them." These gods are the chieftains of the peaks, and the mountains are their hogans, or homes.

To the ancient Greeks, a mountain landscape angel was called a nymph, and nymphs often gave their names to the physical landmass they supervise, such as the nymph Aetna to Mount Etna, the massive volcano on Sicily.

In Roman times, the word *numen* referred to a minor deity or Nature spirit that made a location numinous or divine, that raised its vibration. It was commonly thought that certain places in the landscape were inhabited by spirits or *numina,* whose presence enlivened a site. These numina are the same as nymphs.

Sengen-Sama, then, is the devic overseer of Mount Fuji, a nymph or handmaiden of Gaia, as the Greeks would say, whose energy essence appears as a lovely riot of white blossoms, like a Fairy Queen. In many respects, Sengen-Sama's energy—her essence as a devic guardian—is an alluring paradisal realm.

Making a location such as a massive volcanic peak numinous and exuding a divine vibration is part of the landscape angel's task. As a Mountain Spirit, Sengen-Sama ensouls the mountain and region around it for miles, so that all its life—human, animal, plant, mineral—comes under Sengen-Sama's influence and aegis. Although Japanese legend says that Sengen-Sama lives on top of Fuji or in a luminous cloud above it, in functional terms she is many times larger than the mountain and the shadow it would cast in a 360-degree circle if such could be seen.

Clairvoyants who have psychically looked at landscape angels report that their "bodies" are very dynamic, alive, responsive, and protean, primarily engaged in the cycling of higher energies into the auras and physical matter of their charges, be it plants, rivers, streams, lakes, or mountains.

While landscape angels for mountains have certain qualities in common (related to their function), their character, that quality of ensoulment they impart, varies widely in accordance with the culture inhabiting the landscape and the history of that angel's presence at the landmass, in this case, Mount Fuji.

For example, the British clairvoyant Geoffrey Hodson in 1922 viewed the Mountain Spirit of Helvellyn, a peak in England. The spirit appeared to Hodson as a mighty seated figure of enormous proportions; from one vantage point, this mighty being resided inside the mountain, but from another, his head reached high above the peak. His eyes were ablaze with wakened consciousness and glowed like lakes of fire. His auric emanations consisted of tongues of flames radiating out in all directions for about 500 yards, and his aura, or total visible radiating influence, encompassed the entire mountain, or a 40-mile diameter.

Japanese myth says that, one day in around 300 B.C., a woodcutter named Visu was wakened in the night by a deep rumbling in the Earth. Rushing out of his hut, he was astonished to see not the usual broad flat plain, but a massive mountain (Mount Fuji) with flames leaping out of its summit and smoke swirling all around it. Whether or not Mount Fuji arose to its 12,397-foot glory in one apocalyptic night or not, when it appeared on Earth, Sengen-Sama was with it.

It is important to realize that every mountain, not just those recognized as sacred sites, has ensouling resident landscape angels similar to Sengen-Sama. Stories about the Mountain Spirits may or may not be extant: If they are, they are useful guides to that Deva's geomantic qualities and respectful ways to approach it; if they are not, consider it an invitation to start a dialogue with a mountain's landscape angel to find out its qualities and perhaps create some original and accurate new stories.

See also: Chakravartin, Eriu, Fairy Queen, Gaia, Huitzilopochtli, Marduk, Monster-Slayer, Nymph, Pele, Srin-mo Demoness.

SEVEN RISHIS

Seven immortals and their partners, based in Ursa Major, who administer the 14 Rays of consciousness, energy, and soul evolution.

Also known as Ascended Masters, Brothers of Wisdom, Cosmic Master Beings, Elders, Lords of Progeny, Lords of the Seven Rays, Ray Masters, Seven Abdals, Seven Apkallu, Seven Chohans, Seven Ray Lords, Seven Sages.

Description: In classical Hindu thought, the Seven Rishis (from *rsi*) were divine beings and seers, mind-generated by Brahma, the Creator god in the Hindu pantheon, as ones who could recognize, uphold, and teach the divine laws to humans. They were also considered manifestations of Sarasvati, one name for Brahma's consort, in her function as Power-of-Knowledge.

Most often the Seven Rishis were depicted as august celestial seers who would occasionally take human form as teachers and appear in every new cycle of creation whenever a new revelation of cosmic law and divine order was needed. In each new cycle, the Seven Rishis reappear, though under different names.

The immutable laws they uphold were collectively called Dharma, or sometimes *rta* (the correct order), and were revealed in the holy texts called the Vedas; they represent and are the basic energies that create and sustain life. The Seven Rishis see these laws and energies and express them as transmittable knowledge. They are also known as Lords of Progeny, overseers of all created sentient life.

Vedic thought says that the world's stability is due to the fact that the rishis perform their world-preserving rituals (reciting the mantras) three times daily. The word *rsi* derives from the root "R," which means sound, in this case, mantric sound, sound currents, primordial creative syllables. Other sources attribute the word *rsi* to the roots *rs* and *drs*, which mean "to see," so that *rsi-krt* would mean "causing to see" or a singer of sacred songs (mantras).

Usually Seven Rishis are named, but they also have wives or consorts, making the total 14, though sometimes only 12 are credited. As a generic term for enlightened adept, however, the Vedas say there are 48,000 rishis. During the Flood, the rishis preserved the teachings by taking them on the Boat of the Vedas, the Hindu equivalent to Noah's Ark, where they joined the other high gods.

The Seven Rishis reside in the seven stars of the tail of the constellation Ursa Major (the Great Bear), popularly known in the West as the Big Dipper. Each of the Seven Rishis is assigned one of the Bear's primary stars as his residence. The Seven Rishis are also said to soar effortlessly through space to the mysterious initiate's realm called Svetadvipa, a pure, mystical, paradisal land (or island) on the northern side of the Ocean of Milk, 32,000 miles around Mount Meru. There, all the residents are rich in *Jnana* (knowledge) and exude a perpetual fragrance.

The seven male rishis are named as follows: Marici ("Light"), Atri ("Devourer"), Angiras ("Fiery"), Pulaha ("Bridger of Space"), Kratu ("Inspiration"), Pulastya ("Smooth Hair"), and Vasistha ("Owner of Wealth"). Their female consorts are: Sambhuti ("Fitness"), Anasuya ("Without Spite"), Lajja ("Modesty"), Ksama ("Forgiveness"), Sannati ("Humility"), Priti ("Love"), and Arundhati ("Faithfulness").

Mesopotamian myth recognized an equivalent group of celestial adepts known as the Seven *Apkallu* (Sages). Their task was to teach humanity wisdom and to ensure the correct functioning of the plan of Heaven and Earth. In pre-Islamic Iranian mysticism, the rishis were known as the Seven *Abdals* of the Great Bear, but also as the Seven Poles or *Aqtab,* the seven masters of initiation. They are intercessors invisibly apportioned to the human world, seven apertures through which God shows Himself in the world, God's Eyes, as it were. They are the invisible spiritual hierarchy necessary for the continuation of all life.

Between the 1930s and 1950s, the American psychic Alice Bailey published a series of channeled books discussing the Masters of the Seven Rays. Bailey said that the seven rays, subdivisions of one of seven great Rays of the cosmos, are wielded by the Solar Logos as channels through which all consciousness flows; they are seven predominant characteristics of modifications of life.

Examples of Bailey's Rays include the Ray of Love-Wisdom, Ray of Active Creative Intelligence, Ray of Idealism or Devotion, and Ray of Ceremonial Magic. Each Ray is also associated with a profound initiation, which, she says, it might take a given soul many lifetimes to prepare to undergo and master.

Each Ray has a Lord, and each human, through one's soul, is affiliated with a single Ray. This Ray colors the mind, determines the temperament, controls energy distribution, predisposes one to certain strengths and weaknesses, and generally flavors the mode of spiritual development and types of experiences one has. Each Ray is a name for a particular type of force or energy and its exhibited quality, and, for Bailey, the Ray is essentially equivalent to the Ray Lord.

Explanation: The Seven Rishis are a specialized group within the Great White Brotherhood, a large assemblage of enlightened adepts based in Ursa Major. They are known as the Elders or Teachers of the Great Bear. The Rishis are 14 in number and consist of seven pairs of masters matched by Ray color.

The pairing is based not so much on male-female relationships as differentiation of white light into a color spectrum of seven major and seven minor colors—two rainbows, if you will. For example: scarlet and pink; navy blue and sky blue; emerald and pale spring green; rich purple and lilac; light orange and dark orange-gold; deep yellow and pale yellow. A Ray Master (or Ray Lord) administers one of the 14 colors throughout the galaxy.

As Alice Bailey wrote, each Ray represents a basic quality of energy and consciousness, and its

Lord administers the relationship of the specific Ray with the group of humans who, on a soul level, are in affinity with it and its themes. Each Ray represents a theme of consciousness and filter for soul evolution; all 14 represent the spectrum of consciousness, mythically represented by the Egyptian Osiris. His body (of Light) was cut into 14 parts; these are the 14 Rays.

The Ray Masters, as well as the rest of the Great White Brotherhood (what the Vedas called the 48,000 rishis), are under the leadership of King Arthur, the Solar Logos, based in the star Megrez of Ursa Major. They are the archetypes, or originals, of King Arthur's legendary Knights of the Round Table; at the human level, and through Camalate, King Arthur's esoteric training academy for human men and women seeking individuation and wholeness, they supervise the progressive initiations of the knights in accordance with their Ray affinity.

If you construe the Round Table as an expression of the 12 signs of the zodiac, then 12 of the Ray Masters are positioned at the table, each at a sign. Each of these 12 Ray Masters oversees the unfolding of an aspect of the soul, as represented by a zodiacal sign (e.g., Taurus, Gemini, Libra) at the Round Table.

Norse myth describes the Ray Masters in terms of a special bridge called Bifrost. It is the Rainbow Bridge ("Shimmering Path," Asabru, or "Bridge of the Aesir") that leads from Midgard (ordinary human reality) to Asgard (the gods' realm, or the Great White Brotherhood assemblage). The Ray Masters are the bridge, in that they are the advance team of the Brotherhood of Asgard.

The Ray Masters have manifested in human culture and history, sometimes in the guise of gods, but other times as mysterious, seeming humans. Among the gods, the Master of the pale sky blue Ray was Apollo; scarlet was Hephaistos, the smith and craftsman of Olympus; blue-violet, Pallas Athena, Homer's "grey-eyed Athena" and steadfast mentor to Odysseus.

In the human realm, the Lilac Ray Master has manifested as the Comte de Saint Germain, William Shakespeare, and Francis Bacon; the Ray Master of deep yellow as Lao Tzu and Saint Patrick; Ray Master of gold as Benjamin Franklin; Ray Master of pink as Mary Magdalene, Joan of Arc, and Saint Bridget. Four of the Ray Masters in their female valence periodically manifest, singly or as a group, as the Virgin Mary and her other cultural counterparts (the Buddhist-Tibetan Tara; the Chinese Qwan Yin; and the Aztec Coatlaxopueh).

Often the cosmic pairings of Ray Masters are exemplified in their manifestations in human culture. Master Jesus (scarlet) was paired in biblical times with his archetypal consort, Mary Magdalene (pink—Aphrodite and Hathor, the Greek and Egyptian Love goddess).

In H. P. Blavatsky's nineteenth-century Theosophy and its adulation of the secret Himalayan Chiefs and arcane masters, we see a few of the Ray Masters making a cultural appearance, for example, Kuthumi, El Morya, Serapis Bey, and Alice Bailey's celestial mentor for all her books, Djwhal Khul, the "Tibetan Master," was Ray Master of the Emerald-green Ray.

Similarly, in New Age circles and among psychic channels, the term Ascended Master is often used to denote the Ray Masters, notably Saint Germain.

In terms of Earth's visionary geography, one of the Ray Masters' primary tasks is to interface with the planet's 1,067 dragons, sometimes referred to as the Rainbow Serpent. In a sense, each Ray Master owns or is or supervises a color slice of the Rainbow Serpent, here construed as the electromagnetic spectrum of light. The Ray Masters "bleed" these energies (and their consciousness themes) into Earth, culture, and human consciousness.

The Ray Masters have two meeting places for humans on Earth. The first is called a Ray Master Sanctuary, of which there are 1,080 on the planet.

These are interactive sanctuaries for human–Ray Master exchange; each is dedicated to a single Ray Master; for example: the Pink Ray Master has one at Kildare, Ireland, dedicated to her guise as Saint Bridget; she has another one at Lourdes, France, where she was perceived as the Lady in White (Virgin Mary); Apollo has a dedicated temple at Mount Cynthus on Delos, Greece, said to be his birthplace.

Hephaistos has a Sanctuary on Lemnos; Artemis at Ephesus, Turkey; Aphrodite at Paphos on Cyprus and, as the Egyptian Hathor, she maintained a Sanctuary at Dendera. Ray Master Lao Tzu has a Sanctuary at Zephyr Cove, Lake Tahoe, California.

The second meeting place is a Celestial City called Mount Olympus, after the headquarters of the Olympian gods, under Zeus, in Greek myth. There, the various named gods of Olympus, such as Pallas Athena, Apollo, Hephaistos, Artemis, Aphrodite, and others, periodically gathered to take counsel from (or resist or work around) Zeus (the "male" aspect of the Supreme Being) and his queen, consort, and sometime rival, Hera (God's "female" aspect).

In the ancient world, in some cases, the seat of temporal government was situated precisely at the same place where, geomantically, there was an entrance to Mount Olympus. A prime example of this expedient overlap was *E-kur*, Enlil's (equivalent to Zeus) "Mountain House" at Nippur in Sumer (today's Iraq). Elsewhere in myth, the Ray Master's residence is aptly encoded in the mythic descriptions of the Glass Mountain, for it resembles a Crystal City or Light City.

Here, each of the 14 Ray Masters has a subtemple within the larger celestial meeting place. There are 108 Mount Olympuses or, more properly, 108 doorways, each from a given planetary locale into the one and only celestial Mount Olympus holographically present on Earth. Mount Olympus, in all its guises, works through the third chakra in all seven levels of expression (variously also called the Third Heaven, third planetary realm) and is called Manipura, City of Gems.

Selected locations include Uluru, Alice Springs, Australia; Assisi, Italy; the Sphinx at the Great Pyramid, Giza, Egypt; Mount Shasta, California; Pyramid Lake, Nevada; and Brown's Hill, near Monticello, Charlottesville, Virginia.

The Ray Masters also "wire" their energies from Ursa Major into Earth's holy mountains by way of a geomantic feature called domes (see Holy Mountain). Similarly, Grail Knights (humans engaged in the field of interactive visionary geography) working with the Ray Masters may have their auras "wired" to the 14 Rays and imprinted with their double rainbow spectrum.

Each Ray Master has a potential of 1,746,000 manifestations, which means they can be in that many places simultaneously. Collectively, the 14 Ray Masters can simultaneously be present at 24,444,000 different locations in the galaxy.

See also: Bifrost, Camalate, Candlemas, Da Derga's Hostel, Dragon, Einherjar, Floating Bridge of Heaven, Glass Mountain, Grail Knight, Heimdall, Holy Mountain, King Arthur, Mount Meru, Ocean of Milk.

SHAMBHALA

An exalted seat of spiritual government and influence existing on another plane on Earth and reachable through 1,080 doorways.

Also known as Belovodya ("White Waters"), Imperishable Sacred Land, Indestructible Vajra Continent, Land of the Turquoise-Winged Cuckoos, Olmolungring, Sacred Island, Shangri-La, Treasure Continent, Varuna's Shraddhavati, White Island.

Description: In the Buddhist world, Shambhala is the name of a fabled paradisal kingdom of Buddhas, enlightened teachers, and other high adepts. Its actual location is not known for sure, though many suspect it lies somewhere in the Gobi Desert or Kun Lun Mountains of Mongolia. James Hilton's famous 1933 classic, *Lost Horizon*, described Shambhala as a land of the nondying called Shangri-La.

Some refer to Shambhala, said to be an oasis in the Gobi Desert, as the Sacred Island, based on the clairvoyant picture that long ago it was an island in the Central Asian Sea. Theosophical tradition says that the Lord of the World, Sanat Kumara, dwells in Shambhala and administers the spiritual plan for human evolution.

It also claims that Shambhala was first occupied by Sanat Kumara and 29 other august spiritual beings (called the Lords of the Flame, who came from Venus) to be the center of all Earth occult life 6.5 million years ago. Later in planetary history, around 45000 B.C., the great City of the Bridge was built around the shores of the Gobi Sea, the bridge linking it with the sacred White Island in the Sea's middle.

Tibetan Buddhists claim that Shambhala is the source of esoteric teachings called the *Kalachakra* ("Wheel of Time"), taught in current times by His Holiness, the Fourteenth Dalai Lama. They also believe that humanity's future savior or world teacher, the Maitreya Buddha, will come from Shambhala into our world at a time of great need. Legend also says that when the twenty-fifth Kulika King of Shambhala assumes the throne (the twenty-first now occupies it), the connection between Shambhala and our world will become manifest in world events and general consciousness.

The name *Shambhala* is Sanskrit and means "the Source of Happiness." It is generally equated with Sukavati (also Sanskrit: "the Blissful"), one of the most important "Buddha-fields" (a realm dominated by Buddhas, or Awakened Ones). The place is said to be flooded in radiance, filled with exquisite fragrances, wondrous flowers, and trees of jewels, the sound of rushing water is music, and all souls there cleave to the Truth (Dharma) until they reach nirvana. They are taught by Amitabha ("Boundless Light"), an exalted Buddha credited with creating Sukavati out of his own consciousness, and Avalokitesvara, a Bodhisattva.

Shambhala as a Celestial City set somewhere on Earth is said to be shaped like an eight-petaled lotus, with Kalapa, its capital, at the center. The King of Shambhala sits on a golden throne supported by eight carved lions. All ministers and Shambhala residents are vibrantly healthy and immortal.

The Bon, the original inhabitants of Tibet, highly accomplished shamans before the country was converted to Buddhism, call Shambhala *Olmolungring,* their fabulous eternal city, home of the gods, and source of their teachings. Olmolungring is described as a square city with 12 palaces.

Russian metaphysician and explorer Nicholas Roerich wrote of Belovodya, another name for Shambhala, in the Altai Mountains of central Asia, that it is a sacred place in which all truth flourishes. It is the source of supreme knowledge and humanity's future salvation; its name means "White Waters."

In Western esoteric circles, Shambhala is considered the seat of Earth's true spiritual government—the original Shadow government—although it intervenes in humanity's worldly affairs only infrequently and always discreetly. Some claim that the true King of the World is the leader of Shambhala.

Alice Bailey, the author of many metaphysical works credited to a Shambhalan adept named Djwhal Khul, says that Shambhala was founded 18.5 million years ago; it occupies a definite location in space, but is somewhere in the "higher ethers" of the physical plane. It was organized to be a headquarters for the Mystery teachings and to disseminate these gradually into human spiritual culture, as well as subtly direct the evolution of human consciousness.

Explanation: The central fact about Shambhala is that it is a real place, but is not reachable, for the most part, from the physical world in human bodies. It exists out of phase with our physical reality under a huge dome or etheric energy canopy, dozens of miles wide, in the Gobi

Desert of Mongolia. It is accessible to humans in the spirit body or via mystical travel, however.

In fact, 1,080 Shambhala Doorways have been provided for us in Earth's visionary geography. These are immediate access nodes to Shambhala. Some locations include Glastonbury (beside Chalice Well), Aller churchyard, and South Cadbury Castle in Somerset, England; Iao Needle, Iao State Park, Maui; the Cadmeia, Thebes, Greece; Hummellfjell Mountain, Os, Norway; Bardsey Island and Merlin's Hill, Wales; and Mount Kailash, Tibet.

Glastonbury, at the present time, offers the easiest access to Shambhala through a doorway. It appears as a pillar existing between the fourth and fifth dimension; you walk through the pillar, pass through an etheric tunnel, and arrive. The Shambhala Doorway is like a pipe for channeling and transportation.

As a validation that Glastonbury provides prime access to Shambhala today is the little observed link, if not correspondence, between King *Avallach*, Lord of the Summer Country whose domain is Glastonbury Tor, and Avalokitesvara, prime Bodhisattva and assistant to Amitabha in Shambhala. Hidden in plain sight in an old myth about Glastonbury, Avalokitesvara, the prime Bodhisattva of compassion and, literally, the Lord Who Surveys, surveys Glastonbury from Shambhala and through the Tor (an anomalous, pyramid-shaped artificial hill, presumed human-made and the focus of many legends).

Another mark of recognition for Glastonbury's status as the gateway on the physical plane to Shambhala that is most available is another old name: Glastonbury is *Domus Dei,* "The Secret of Our Lord." It is also the recipient of the Mobile Shambhalic Focus (see Vishnu's Discus), a spiritual beam or sustained regard from Shambhala and its enlightened sages resident in a locality for 200 years to influence culture and spiritual growth. The Shambhalic Focus is an aspect of Earth's sixth chakra, seat of psychic perception and authority, broadcast from Shambhala.

Shambhala is an outpost of Mount Meru, the holy cosmic mountain of the 330 million gods. Shambhala is one of eight affiliate residences of the gods, called *Lokapalas* ("Direction Guardians"), that surround the original Mount Meru. It is one of the eight Celestial Cities (imprinted on Earth) known as Varuna's Shraddhavati.

To get to Shambhala on a visionary level, you need a sword, which is an expression of focused psychic insight and a poised mind. When one's insight is refined enough and consciousness has reached the point it can see the pattern behind the apparent, then the sword of insight can open the Shambhala Doorway. Some of the stacked quoits (large stones that seem to form an open fort) in England, such as Zennor in Cornwall, are Shambhala Doorways.

Shambhala, though present on Earth in a phase-shifted sense, is not influenced by human activities though it is symbiotically related to Earth culture and has a degree of intercommunication when necessary. Merlin, the sage-magician of King Arthur's Camalate, would frequently and suddenly disappear from the human realm, reappearing hours or days later. Legend says that he went into his *eplumoir,* but scholars could never figure out what that was. It's a Shambhala Doorway, and Merlin was a prime emissary of Shambhala to Earth culture.

One of the purposes for humans visiting Shambhala is to receive initiation, training, and confirmation by the various spiritual adepts who may be supervising one's spiritual unfoldment over many lifetimes. These adepts may originate in Ursa Major, the Great Bear, the home of the celestial sages, known to Hindu culture as the rishis, to the Norse as the Einherjar (the slain battlefield warriors), and to Western esotericism as the Great White Brotherhood.

See also: Bifrost, Da Derga's Hostel, Einherjar, Merlin, Mount Meru, Seven Rishis, Valhalla, Vishnu's Discus, Wild Hunt.

SIMURGH

One manifestation of many in human perception and spiritual culture by the angelic family called the Ofanim, meant to carry human consciousness into the spiritual realms, to Christ, and to the Supreme Being.

Also known as Angka, Bennu, Bialozar, Chamrosh, Eagle, Garuda, Kreutzet, Phoenix, Pyong, Roc, Rukh, Saena Meregha, Semuru, Senmurv, Senmurw, Simargl, Thunderbird, Vocub Caquix, Ziz.

Description: The immortal phoenix bird from Persian mythology (also known in Kashmir, India), the Simurgh rose from its ashes every year. In Old Persian symbology, this magical and mystical bird was known as *Saena Meregha,* "dragon peacock," a symbol used to represent the Persian king, but Simurgh also was understood as a name for God and an enigmatic, barely glimpsed form of God.

In a classic twelfth-century Persian mystical text, the *Bird's Parliament* (also known as *The Conference of the Birds*), all the birds assemble and set out to find the Simurgh to elect it their king. Some perish, but 30 of the birds finally find the Simurgh and merge with it, becoming part of the divine Simurgh.

The Simurgh was described as a vast, fabulous, beautifully plumed bird who lived in the Alburz Mountains of northern Persia (today's Iran), possibly at Mount Damavand. Yet its home was also given as behind the mountains called Kaf, generally regarded as mystical and not in the physical world. Its feathers had healing properties, while human exposure to the Simurgh induced peace and wisdom. The Simurgh is close to us, yet humans are far from it; once one of its feathers fell in China and filled everyone's soul around the world with its image.

The Simurgh is a hidden, arcane bird whose ways are mysterious; she lives like a queen in the high mountains, but every Sunday goes forth into the human world to visit the Kings of the Earth. Once the Simurgh visited Hirmiz Shah and granted his request to behold Melka d'Anhura, "the King of Light" (also called Melka Ziwa, "the Radiant Lord")—a celestial being of the Sun and of great brilliance.

An earlier name for the heavenly bird was Senmurw, which was said to combine the features of a dog, bird, and musk ox or to appear as a peacock-dragon with a dog's head; another was Senmurv, which referred specifically to a dragon form. In Mesopotamia, the bird was called the Chamrosh, depicted as a winged monster with a dog's body and bird's head; it lived on the ground at the base of the Soma (substance of immortality) tree, at the top of which dwelled the Senmurv. When the Senmurv landed on the tree, it shook loose all the ripened seeds, which the Chamrosh then distributed around the world.

A similar account is given in Slavic folklore in Eastern Europe, but the bird is called Simargl. It is a winged monster that looks like a dragon but has bird attributes. It is the guardian of a tree of the seeds of all the world's trees.

Among the Arabs, the bird was called Angka, with a human face and either a bird's body or a griffin's (lion's torso, eagle's head); it lived in the Kaf Mountains and devoured anything that came across its path. Eventually, it consumed everything, leaving it no food, and thus it died. The Russians knew this bird as Kreutzet (in Poland, as Bialozar), said to resemble a gigantic eagle, much like the Roc or Rukh, as it was known to the Arabs living near the Persian Gulf.

The Roc was an enormous horned eagle with a vast wingspan and talons so large it could seize and carry an elephant. In the tale of Sinbad the Sailor, he was shipwrecked on an island and lived next to a large spherical object. Eventually, he realized this was a bird's egg and he was living in the nest of a giant bird.

Persian lore says that the Simurgh is so old it has seen the world destroyed three times already. It lived for 1,700 years, then immolated itself in a rush of fire, or it died of heartbreak when a mirror was substituted for its actual mate.

Persian lore also associates the Simurgh with the Saena Tree (also called Tree of All Remedies or Tree of All Seeds) that grew on an island in the middle of the Vourukasha Sea (a peaceful lake in Paradise, and the origin of all terrestrial waters). The bird kept a nest in this miraculous "Tree of Medicine" and Mother of All the Trees, which produced a copious supply of precious seeds for all the plants, and when the bird stirred, it scattered the seeds worldwide.

Explanation: The Simurgh in all its cultural variations is a psychic perception implanted into culture of the angelic family called the Ofanim.

The spiritual stature and ontological primacy of the Ofanim in their bird form is best expressed in the Hindu perception of them as Garuda, the celestial mount for Vishnu, one of the three main gods and the Hindu equivalent to Christ. Garuda is the fabulous bird-mount for the Christ Consciousness or, in more practical terms, the guide for the human soul to the Christ Consciousness.

The Ofanim are one of the oldest of 40 angelic families, being at this point about 60 billion years old, hence the attribution that they had witnessed the world destroyed (and renewed) three times. In Hindu time reckoning, they are One Week of Brahma—in human terms, a very long time, predating much of Creation and even some of the gods.

The Persian reference to the expedition and conference of the birds refers to both human souls in quest of the Ofanim and the other angelic families as well. The Ofanim have been described as teachers to the angels ("Birds") and while they have never sought kingship as such, their antiquity and level of insight warrant this.

The Arab allegation that the Angka ate everything in sight until all of Creation was consumed is accurate, though it must be understood mystically. The Ofanim consume awareness—human, angelic, and hierarchical. They do not remove it from existence, but, rather, it is subsumed in their vast body, which comprises 40.3 million individual manifestations—as anything they choose, such as (confusingly to us, amusingly to them) the Senmurv atop the tree and the Chamrosh at the base. Both are manifestations of the Ofanim.

As for the tree, that is the Tree of Life in Paradise (see Yggdrasil).

Thus the Angka (Simurgh) was sought as a fount of wisdom because it contained all the accumulated wisdom up to that point (it had eaten it). In the somewhat paranoid perception of Carlos Castaneda in the Toltec tradition, the Simurgh (Ofanim) is described as the Eagle that must be avoided at all costs.

This Eagle is described by Castaneda as an immeasurable jet-black bird, standing erect with its head in infinity. It governs the destiny of all living things, and it devours awareness, with dead souls ceaselessly swarming into its cavernous mouth like fireflies. The Eagle grants to human seers and initiates, Castaneda says, the right to keep their own flame of awareness as they pass through it at death, if they develop themselves while alive, and gain freedom.

Castaneda's portrayal of the Eagle makes it seem formidable and scary, perhaps akin to the old Persian winged monster nuances. The Eagle-Ofanim work with humans through the vibration of Love from Above and can be accessed in meditation through a point of brilliant light just above the navel, yet their energy can be experienced by humans as ruthless due to its purity of focus.

The immortality-phoenix aspect pertains to the Ofanim's extreme fluidity in terms of manifest form. They may be perceived in their Simurgh form for a while, then dissolve this and relapse into their essence, which is a tiny point of brilliant, absolute light. When they regenerate, they reassume the Simurgh form.

As a tiny point of absolute light, the Ofanim have also manifested themselves as the actual Star of Bethlehem that guided the Magi to the Christ, just as the Star or Simurgh form guides human souls to Christ Consciousness. This relationship is reflected in the story of Mirmiz Shah beholding the King of Light, Radiant Lord whose likeness appears in the Sun. He beholds the Christ.

As for the Simurgh visiting Kings on Sunday, the Judaic tradition says the Ofanim often consult with the Jewish prophets among humans.

All orders of angels, of course, are messengers for God and testaments to God's existence, and the Simurgh, as a form taken by the Ofanim, acts as a transcendental doorway for human experience to step through into the presence of the Supreme Being. The Persian Simurgh is presented as being virtually the same as God, and when the 30 birds are finally in the Great Bird's presence, they experience themselves as all part of the Simurgh and see it as a mirror.

The Simurgh (the Ofanim) has a geomantic grounding point on Earth at the 28.5-acre stone circle called Avebury in Wiltshire, England, but may also be beheld at Earth's sole Tree of Life in the Rondane Mountains of Norway.

See also: Fountain of Youth, Ganesh, Garuda, Phoenix, Thunderbird, Vocub Caquix, Yggdrasil, Ziz.

SRIN-MO DEMONESS

The national protector angel for the Tibetan landscape as pejoratively seen by Buddhists while converting the country from its original shamanic-animistic beliefs to the new religion of Buddhism.

Also known as Frog-head Bloody-Eye, Guardian Angel of the Nation, Heavenly Minister, Logos of a Nation, Name of God, National Angelic Regent, National Deva, Supine Demoness, Watcher, the Word in the landscape.

Description: In early Tibetan animistic belief, the *Srin* are a fierce type of female evil spirit or demon, often affiliated with specific regions of the country. The Srin-mo Demoness is so vast that her supine body occupies the entire landmass of Tibet; one text called her the Frog-head Bloody-Eye.

From the viewpoint of early Buddhists coming from India as religious colonialists to animistic, Bon-dominated Tibet, this countrywide being must be controlled before the Buddha-Dharma could take root in the wild land. The prime Buddhist missionary, Padmasambhava, was credited with binding many of Tibet's Srin to become wrathful Dharma protectors rather than its opposers. Subduing of the Srin-mo Demoness thus became the Buddhist founding myth.

It all started when the Chinese princess Kong-jo, the betrothed of a Tibetan king called Srong Btsan, first perceived the Demoness. She was making geomantic chart calculations to figure out why it was difficult to transport a statue of Sakyamuni Buddha to the Tibetan court. The chariot bearing the statue kept getting stuck in the mud. Then Kong-jo had a vision of the landscape that highlighted its particular configurations and revealed an anthropomorphic aspect.

Kong-jo perceived that Tibet as a whole was like a Srin-mo Demoness lying on her back. The area around Lhasa, Tibet's capital, with the Plain of Milk, as it was known, and the lake in its middle, was the heart's blood of the Srin-mo. The three mountains encircling the Plain of Milk were Srin-mo's two breasts and her lifeline. All of the Plain of Milk was a palace of the King of the *Klu*. Kong-jo understood that the entire shape of the landscape was inauspicious and harmful.

Through her knowledge of geomancy, she perceived ways to erect temples on the Plain of Milk to counteract the landscape's inherent deleterious aspects and to balance out its inauspicious configurations. Places of high concentration of indigenous Tibetan spirits, such as the palace of the Klu, the camp of the *'Dre,* and the bed of the *Ma-mo,* must be transformed, she saw. The image of Sakyamuni must be established in the center of the land to suppress the Klu palace, that is, the unfavorable activities and influence of these spirits.

In fact, Kong-jo realized, the best solution was to build numerous Buddhist shrines and temples at key landscape spots, called *me-btsa,* to bring the Srin-mo Demoness into submission. Unrestrained, the Srin-mo Demoness could be psychically perceived as flailing her arms and legs, but by placing chapels—called "the twelve nails of immobility"—on her land-body, she could physically be pressed down, pinned into the Earth, and effectively immobilized.

A scheme for the placement of 13 Buddhist temples was developed in three concentric squares that encompassed all of Tibet. These would enclose Tibet's center, its borders, and even beyond its borders. Buildings would pin down Srin-mo's two shoulders and two hips, four more would hold down her elbows and knees, and another four would suppress her hands and feet.

The thirteenth would be the Jo-khang temple in Lhasa, placed on her heart. The Jo-khang, built over 1300 years ago by King Songtsen Gampo, is regarded as Tibet's spiritual center. Even today, legend says that a stone lies in or under the Jo-khang foundation, and behind this stone is a passageway to an ancient, underground lake.

This lake (also called the Plain of Milk in the center of the *Srin*-land) is the heart of the Srin-mo Demoness. Some say it is her heart's blood, and that if you place your ear to the floor of the Jo-khang, you might hear a faint heartbeat.

These Buddhist temples in Tibet, Kham, and Bhutan would immobilize Srin-mo's two arms (three sections each, including the hands), two legs (three sections each, with the feet), and heart—13 parts in all. She would be pacified, though not defeated, her life force in the heart repressed by the Jo-khang.

Explanation: The Srin-mo Demoness is the Tibetan perception of the national egregor, or watcher angelic spirit, for the land and its people. It wasn't so much that she had to be impaled on the landscape, for, as her other title, Supine Demoness, suggests, her angelic form was already spread out over Tibet.

It was more a matter of opening up physical portals (the "pegs") into her energetic consciousness as the original soul of the Land of Snows, one of Tibet's early names, and the prime holder and reflector of the Tibetans' soul essence.

In creating a mandala of three concentric squares throughout Tibet, and beyond its borders, the early Tibetans acknowledged the extent of her influence. To say her body is tied down by 13 pegs means she is omnipresent throughout the land to which she was assigned at the beginning of Earth. The Srin-mo mandala, with its heart at Lhasa, Tibet's capital, illustrates the organic unity of the land, organized and kept spiritually and geomantically integral by Srin-mo.

Hindu myth recounts a similar dismemberment of a goddess, named Sati or Shakti, whose 51 body parts are distributed over the Indian subcontinent, each, for millennia, the focus of a pilgrimage and each a venerated sacred site. Similarly, Egyptian myth cites the locations in Egypt of Osiris's 14 body parts and, in ancient Greece, all of the Peloponnesus ("The Island of Pelops") was the landscape body of the god Pelops, an "assistant" to Greece's national angel.

The Plain of Milk with the Srin-mo's heart at its center is an expression of the celestial light she grounds at the site of the Jo-khang for all of Tibet. The other classes of Tibetan-named beings, such as Klu, 'Dre, Ma-mo, and other "demons" are mostly references to subsidiary landscape angels and Nature spirits under the influence of the Bon spiritual practices and namings.

In the original plan of Earth, to each of the 72 primary landmass subdivisions, such as Tibet, an egregor was assigned. Each would supervise the inherent geomantic features of the landscape and the relationship of its people to those subtle landscape features. The national egregor would also oversee the unfoldment of the inherent soul qualities of the people occupying that land—what makes them Tibetan or Irish, for example (see Eriu, Ireland's egregor).

In Judaic angelologies, the egregors are called the Tutelary Princes of the Nations or Regents of the Nations. Qabala speaks of the 72 Names of God, or *Shemhamforesh,* and, to a large extent, the totality of the 72 egregors are these. Each folk soul or national character tied to its landmass and egregor expresses a Name. Thus Srin-mo, in her angelic essence, embodies one of the Names of God, and that essence is grounded into the Tibetan landscape at its geographic center, Lhasa.

The original inhabitants of Tibet were the Bon, a shamanic, animistic, psychic culture—technically what colonizing religious cultures call pagan. To the Bon, the landscape, in fact, all of reality, teemed with beings of all kinds; some were protectors, others opposers, of spiritual life, but in the overall psychic-geomantic ecology of the early Tibetan landscape, the Bon found balance.

One of the founding myths of Tibet was about how Brag-Srin-mo, a rock demoness considered an ancestor of Srin-mo, but more likely the same being seen earlier, seduced the Bodhisattva Avalokitesvara, incarnated as a monkey king called Hilumandju, into coupling with her and thereby producing the first Tibetans. Brag-Srin-mo was sometimes said to be an emanation of the goddess Drolma (Tibetan) or Tara (Buddhist), a compassionate Mother Goddess figure.

The union of the rock ogress and the monkey led to the country being called "Land of the Two Divine Ogres." A Tibetan text later attributed many of the Tibetan people's prime traits (as seen long ago)—physical strength, the love of killing, and courage—to their primordial demonic ancestor. It is more the opposite: The national landscape angel holds, sustains, nurtures, and reflects a people's inherent, God-assigned soul qualities, and their evolution over time.

Then came Buddhism, with its different beliefs, practices, and *beings*—the host of astral Dharma protectors and religious control beings who maintained the integrity and unity of Buddhism as a living astral thought form and cognitive framework. This new energetic matrix had to find roots in the Bon's animistic landscape, and the key agent in this acceptance was the Srin-mo Demoness, Tibet's national egregor who was used to the Bon beings and wary of the new ones.

Thus the introduction of Buddhism to Tibet was less a matter of persuasive missionary work and more one of the confrontation and overcoming of magical forces already present in the landscape as part of its natural soul life.

The Buddhists wanted to change the vibration of the Tibetan landscape to match the vibration of their religion, and to do that they had to change the vibration of the beings that held the animistic vibration in the land. This way, thought forms, landscape, and astral landscape beings would be congruent. (A similar approach with the same magical intention was taken by the newly formed Christianity and the hegemony-seeking Catholic Church that took over numerous megalithic pagan sites in Europe and put up their own churches.) It is not surprising that the Buddhists would demonize the original land deities as a way of accelerating the conversion of the people's beliefs to Buddhism.

The Srin-mo Demoness had to convert her own angelic orientation away from the magical-animistic Bon to the new metaphysicians and their Dharma. Metaphorically, erecting 13 Buddhist temples on the Srin-mo's mobility points (the arms and legs) was a kind of Buddhist blood transfusion into the land. Tibetan Buddhism had a vast host of religious beings associated with it, many of them different from those worked with by the Bon, but some were Bon converts.

Where the country's national egregor is grounded is also a geomantic feature called an Energy Focusing Node; Earth has 72 of these, and they are also minor chakras in a global anthropomorphic geomantic being called Albion. This feature is a major nodal point that focuses and concentrates cosmic and geomantic energy for that region. The Node is also the country's omphalos, sometimes locally called the Navel of the World in terms of a people's myth about their land and its origin.

Thus the Jo-khang temple in Tibet's capital city and the nation's sacred center, Lhasa, the thirteenth Buddhist peg in the distributed landscape body of the Srin-mo Demoness, is Tibet's Energy Focusing Node and egregor home.

See also: Albion, Chakravartin, Eriu, House of Atreus, Huitzilopochtli, Marduk, Navel of the World, Tower of Babel.

SWORD IN THE STONE

An early test of psychic development for candidates for Arthurhood demonstrating an ability to penetrate the etheric world, symbolized by the stone, with psychic perception and understanding.

Also known as Mithra.

Description: In the Arthurian sagas, the young Arthur demonstrated his worthiness to be king by pulling the sword out of the stone, a feat no other petty king or rival for the kingship was able to do. Arthur, though fathered by the previous king, Uther Pendragon, was raised in secrecy and was, in fact, ignorant of his own royalty. This was arranged by his mentor and magus, Merlin.

On the death of Uther, a temporary power vacuum prevailed; Merlin instructed the Archbishop of Canterbury to send for all the lords of the realm to assemble at the greatest church in London (Sir Thomas Malory, writing of this in his classic fifteenth-century compendium, *Le Morte d'Arthur,* did not specify which) for New Year's Day. In preparation for that assemblage, Merlin inserted a sword into a great marble stone set on a steel anvil in the center of the churchyard. Letters inscribed in gold on the sword declared that whoever could pull this sword from the stone was the next rightful king of all England. None could.

The young Arthur, probably a teenager in the story, sought a replacement sword for Sir Kay, his foster brother for whom he was squire. Not knowing anything about the Sword in the Stone test, he saw that sword as suitable for Kay and without reading the inscription or being aware of anything, he easily pulled it out of the otherwise adamant stone. Merlin, having foreseen this, arranged for Arthur to pull it out several more times in front of all the petty kings as proof.

After some squabbling, skepticism, and wrangling among the lords, and further demonstrations by Arthur, he was finally crowned King of England.

Explanation: By this feat, the young Arthur claims the first of several swords in his development; although the Arthurian mythos only mentions the second sword, Excalibur, a gift from the mystical Lady of the Lake, he acquires many swords in his unfolding, each indicating a refinement of psychic ability.

Arthur is not so much a person as a stage of spiritual development in an esoteric training system encapsulated outwardly in the Arthurian mythos. Arthur in himself is the Solar Logos, an aspect of the Christ working through the Sun; within human culture, Arthur may overshadow human individuals who are part of a soul group organized around the Arthurian mythos (see King Arthur) in a particular culture.

The Sword in the Stone episode is about mastering the psychic insight to penetrate the stone of the etheric world, of the angelic realm and its hierarchies. The sword (similar to the unicorn) is a classic symbol for the extension of the sixth chakra, the seat of psychic insight, into the physically invisible realms in the form of a sharp sword; the sword also symbolizes mastery and concentration of the air element, an aspect of the purified mind.

The Stone is the seeming density of the spiritual worlds to ordinary human perception, especially in an earlier stage in the evolution of humanity when psychic abilities were more rare than today and required far more effort to develop. The young Arthur is the only one who can penetrate the stone with the sword (his brow chakra), for the tableau is both backward and dual. Arthur must remove the sword *and* insert it again to prove his worthiness to be King.

The Stone is also the jeweled altar said to reside in the inner heart chakra, the *Anandakanda;* it is a symbol for the assembly of the Great White Brotherhood, a large conclave of enlightened sages and spiritual masters who oversee cosmic, galactic, and solar system developments in consciousness (see Da Derga's Hostel and Valhalla).

Inserting the sword means Arthur can see into this realm of the ascended hierarchies of sages and angels; removing the sword means he can wield this insight and even transmit the consciousness of the Great White Brotherhood in the physical human world.

Inserting and removing the sword—seeing this as a rhythm, like breathing—means Arthur can stay awake in his awareness while he moves between the two worlds, gaining insight and guidance from the Great White Brotherhood (inserting the Sword) and applying it with mastery in the human, physical world (pulling the Sword out of the Stone). Arthur's qualification to be king is his psychic prowess and fluidity: He can wield the psychic sword in both directions.

The Sword in the Stone has meaning in the opposite direction, too. The angelic hierarchy and members of the Great White Brotherhood, as a point of initiation for candidates in Arthurhood, will insert their golden blade into the stone of the human heart chakra. Here the Stone, in addition to its specific reference to the many-jeweled altar of the inner heart chakra, also signifies the darkened cave of the Heart, the unilluminated, materially dense and thick stone of the unenlightened heart.

This aspect of the Sword in the Stone is highlighted in the account of Mithra, the Persian antecedent of the Roman Mithras. Mithra, destined to slay the Bull of Heaven and to watch over all Creation, was born from a stone, sometimes called the Generative Rock. Mithra emerging from a stone (being born from a rock, or the spiritual worlds) is the same act as Arthur withdrawing the Sword from the Stone. Metaphorically, Mithra is the Sword in the Stone.

The elements of the Arthurian mythos are largely representative of stages of initiation, so they are not exclusively owned or demonstrated by single people. Those who can pull the Sword from the Stone will find themselves on occasion part of a vast assembly of other Grail Knights who similarly pulled out the Sword from the Stone.

Merlin arranged for the Sword in the Stone demonstration for Arthur because, generally, he was in charge of the Grail Knights' training and initiations. The achievement of the Sword in the Stone is an early stage (a preliminary encounter with the Stone) in the creation of the Philosopher's Stone.

See also: Da Derga's Hostel, Excalibur, Grail Knight, Indra, King Arthur, Lady of the Lake, Morgan le Fay, Philosopher's Stone, Valhalla.

TEZCATLIPOCA

The dark side of Lucifer, Lord of Light, in his guise as mentor for the first generation of humanity who precipitated the Fall of Man.

Also known as Azhi Dahaka, Iblis, Lucifer, Midir, Ravana.

Description: Tezcatlipoca, among the Toltecs, Aztecs, and Maya of Central America, was the Lord of the Smoking Mirror, an antithesis and prime opponent to the divine culture benefactor, Quetzalcoatl, the Plumed Serpent. His name derives from his emblematic mirror that emanates smoke spirals. As a solar deity, Tezcatlipoca was regarded as the resident Aztec deity of Tezcoco city, the center of Aztec culture, located on the edge of Lake Tezcoco in central Mexico.

Tezcatlipoca was said to have smoking obsidian mirrors for feet and, among his many epithets, notable ones included "night wind," "the enemy," "he whose slaves we are," and "possessor of the sky and Earth." He was Lord of the Surface of the Earth, Lord of the Nine Hells, Black God of the North, ruler of the past world, and god of death and destruction. He was the god of sin and feasting; he sowed dissension and sexual desire and excess; he was the undisputed lord over all material things of the world and the embodiment of their natural life force. Compatible with this was his appellation as the god of fire, because both fire and the natural energy imbued in all matter can support or destroy life.

The Aztec explain the obsidian mirrors on Tezcatlipoca's feet with an account that, before humanity existed, he struggled with Earth Monster Tlaltecuhtli to separate solid matter from the waters. He used one of his feet as bait to lure her up to the surface. She bit off one of his feet in the titanic struggle, but lost her lower jaw and was unable to sink back into the waters. The planet Earth was then created from her body. Thus Tezcatlipoca was a prime terraformer for the planet, providing dry land for humanity.

As the god ruling Earth's surface, Tezcatlipoca has many valences, colors, and attributions. He was considered the spirit of witchcraft and black magic, the patron of war and warriors, the source of material gain and glory for his servants, the Aztec, and, as Titlauacan, "he who is closest to the shoulder," he was believed to whisper suggestions and temptation continually in people's ears.

In the Mexican myth of the Five Suns, or epochs of creation and incarnation, Tezcatlipoca was the god of the First Sun of Earth, while his archenemy, Quetzalcoatl, was God of the Second Sun of Water. The two were perpetually in conflict, with Tezcatlipoca causing discord and stimulating evil among humans; he was a destroyer and source of misfortune, yet he was a boon-bestower, giving humanity the gifts of understanding and intelligence.

According to legend, Tezcatlipoca finally overcame Quetzalcoatl in 999 A.D., and it was prophesied he would reign for 900 years, then be finally overthrown by Quetzalcoatl. According to Zapotec legend, Quetzalcoatl returned to his buried heart and Tree of Life in the Valley of Oaxaca in southern Mexico in August 1987 (88 years late), marked by many around the world as the Harmonic Convergence.

Explanation: Tezcatlipoca is one side of the duality of Lucifer as Lord of Light and mentor to the first generation of humanity. As such, he was the god of the First Sun of Earth, meaning the first round of humans, marked by free will, self-aware consciousness, and unlimited freedom.

Humanity was created and placed on Earth twice. The first time corresponds to the Garden of Eden, a time of unlimited free will and prodigious physical and psychic powers by embodied humans. In his aspect as the Aztec maker of the first fire (the implantation of self-aware consciousness in humanity), Tezcatlipoca was called Mizcoatl ("cloud-snake"). This first generation was later repudiated by the Supreme Being and removed from physical reality; a second issue of humanity was placed on Earth, but with more limitations.

As in his Vedic guise as the ten-headed Ravana whose body is black and gemlike, Tezcatlipoca has obsidian (a black reflective gem) mirrors for feet. The black represents earth, clay, the density, darkness, and resistance of matter to light. When Quetzalcoatl killed Tezcatlipoca, turning him into a jaguar, this marked the end of the first round of humanity and the inception of the second, known as the Second Sun of Water. For this, Lucifer would assume a different cultural guise as the benevolent Quetzalcoatl.

Tezcatlipoca's struggles with Earth Monster Tlaltecuhtli represent this celestial being's early terraforming work on behalf of Earth. The Earth Monster is one of many names for the singular dragon that encircles the planet. For organic and sentient life on Earth to be possible, this dragon's energies must be released into the prepared energy matrix of Earth's visionary geography.

Tezcatlipoca was not killed nor has he left reality; as an expression of Lucifer, the Lord of Light and benefactor of both humanities, Tezcatlipoca was bound to Earth at 3,496 places called Lucifer Binding Sites, along with his first generation of humans, variously called Asura, Djinn, Kings of Edom, and Raksasas. Tezcoco in Mexico is such a site, although the Lucifer Binding Sites have three valences according to the emphasis given to the activity of this being: arriving (Tezcatlipoca is arriving in glory at Tezcoco), being bound, or released.

You can observe the same polarity in this one angelic being, Lucifer, in the dichotomy of Epimetheus ("after-thought") and his brother,

Prometheus ("fore-thought"), in Greek myth. Epimetheus, like Tezcatlipoca (and Ravana) was first humanity's mentor. In the duality of Tezcatlipoca and Quetzalcoatl, we can see the dark and light sides of Lucifer, as long as we realize these are cultural filters. Tezcatlipoca has been demonized only because first-generation humanity, under his tutelage, failed the test of incarnate freedom and caused the Fall of Man.

The experience of both aspects of Lucifer, the first and second Lucifer in all his guises and polarities, is for us tasting the fruit of the Tree of the Knowledge of Good and Evil.

The story of Tezcatlipoca in his struggle with the Earth Monster has a striking parallel in his Irish guise as Midir the Proud. In an ancient tale called "The Earth-Shapers," Midir (the Irish Lucifer) and the Tuatha de Danann, "the Shining Ones" and original creator gods of the Irish pantheon, are preparing Earth for life. First Midir descended into the black writhing abyss of the planet with his Fiery Spear until he subdued the chaos. Then Brigit, the Mother of the Gods, unrolled her mantle over the rough, virginal land like a silver flame.

The foot reference shows up in Tezcatlipoca's guise as the Vedic Ravana, whose protégés, the Raksasas (first humanity), are said to have been born from the foot of Brahma, the prime creator god of Hinduism. In the Aztec formulation, Tezcatlipoca sacrifices a foot to the Earth Monster and wears an obsidian mirror in its place as if it were a prosthetic. His people, the Aztec, directly benefit from this Earth-shaping feat and have life and a place to live because of his foot.

See also: Azhi Dahaka, Djinn, Dragon, Fall of Man, Garden of Eden, Harmonic Convergence, Kings of Edom, Lucifer, Prometheus, Quetzalcoatl, Rainbow Serpent, Raksasas, Ravana, Tree of the Knowledge of Good and Evil.

THUNDERBIRD

A Native American perception of the Ofanim, an angelic order central to the manifestation of consciousness throughout creation.

Also known as Keneun, Osha-Dagea, Skyamsen, Tinmiukpuk, Wakinyan Tanka.

Description: The Thunderbird, a huge eagle-like bird whose movements produce thunder and whose eyes flash lightning, is recognized and described by many Native American tribes, from the northeast to the plains to the Pacific Northwest. The Thunderbird personifies thunder in the form of one large bird or a group.

Native Americans have various names for the Thunderbird, including *Skyamsen* (Tlingit), *Keneun* (Iroquois), and *Osha-Dagea* (Iroquois).

The Brule Sioux of South Dakota call the Thunderbird *Wakinyan Tanka* and say he lives in his tipi on a high mountain (Harney Peak) in the Black Hills, known to them as the sacred *Paha Sapa.* Harney Peak is also famous as the site of Black Elk's epiphany, spirit journey, and Great Hoops vision of 1872.

The term *Wakinyan* comes from the Dakota word *kinyan,* which means "winged." But the word may also be linked to *wakan,* or sacred power, often also attributed to the Native American perception of the Supreme Being.

In many instances, the Thunderbird is described as a great eagle, though visionaries admit they rarely see the bird in its entirety, as it is usually veiled in layers of cloud or smoke. Nobody has ever seen the Thunderbird in full, only parts of him, so his overall image has been pieced together from the fragments of many visionaries. Sioux visionaries say that, inside his tipi, Thunderbird has a nest with an egg full of Thunderbirds, and that egg is bigger than South Dakota.

When he beats his wings, thunder sounds forth; when he moves his eyes, lightning flashes from them; and when he speaks, thunderclaps explode out of his mouth, and the smaller rolling thunders are his progeny, the little Thunderbirds.

The Sioux myths state that there are four Thunderbirds, each a different color. The Great Wakinyan of the West is black, clothed in clouds. His body has no distinct shape, yet he has giant wings with four joints, no feet but huge claws, no head, but a sharp beak and rows of sharpened teeth. The other three are red, yellow, and white for the North, East, and South, respectively.

Although nobody can see the Thunderbird fully, many can sense his presence. Generally, he is a good spirit, intent on helping people. The Thunderbird and all thunder beings are guardians of the truth, and those who lie may be struck by lightning bolts hurled by a displeased Thunderbird. If you dream about the Thunderbird, you may become a *heyoka,* or sacred clown, one for whom the world and all of reality has been turned inside out, upside down. If you dream of a Thunderbird, you get a little of his power and become one of his relatives.

One of Thunderbird's prime tasks was to battle the Unktehi, a giant water monster with a huge horn on her head and whose serpentine body filled all of the Missouri River. Unktehi had disliked humanity since they were put on Earth. Finally, the Thunderbird, after a great battle, defeated and destroyed Unktehi, and the Sioux say that, after its body burned up, its dried bones turned to rock and became the Mako Sicha, known to Americans as the Badlands of North Dakota.

The Algonquins of the northeastern United States refer to Thunderbird and his progeny as "Our Grandfathers" and address prayers to him. Native Americans in the plains and woodland areas attest to Thunderbird's war against horned underwater snakes and the insidious, antihuman powers under the waters. Indians of the northwest say he feeds on monstrous killer whales. Others say Thunderbird exists to challenge White Owl Woman who brings winter storms.

The Crow Indians say the Thunderbird wears an eagle cloak or a cape of eagle feathers over its huge bird form, while in the Yukon, the Thunderbird is a mighty eagle called *Tinmiukpuk,* who carries off reindeer, whales, and humans. The Plains Indians see Thunderbird as both frightening (he brings storms) and as a protector and liberator (he kills the water snakes). The Quillayute of the Olympic Peninsula in Washington State say that Thunderbird's feathers are as long as canoe paddles and he lives in a cave in the Olympic Mountains that everyone avoids.

The Chippewa say the eyes of this supreme bird are fire, its glance is lightning, and its wings in motion fill the air with thunder. Other tribes speak of Thunderbird as a friend to humanity, a willing protector, and a wise teacher.

In many cases, the spirits associated with thunder itself are seen as the same as Thunderbird. The Apaches identify the Creator as Killer-of-Enemies and call him Thunderer; for the Cree, Thunderbird is constantly at war with *Misikinipik,* a great horned snake. Most tribes who discuss Thunderbird say he and his progeny were the first beings to appear in the Creation and have an especially close connection with *Wakan Taka,* the Great Mysterious (God).

Explanation: The Thunderbird is a filtered perception of the angelic family called the Ofanim, which has expressed itself in other cultures in a massive, celestial bird form, such as the Eagle (Toltec), Garuda (Hinduism), Phoenix-Benu (Egyptian), Simurgh (Persian), Vocub Caquix (Mayan), and Ziz (Judaic).

The Ofanim (their name comes from the Hebrew *ofan* for "wheels") are among the oldest of the 40 angelic orders and are about 60 billion years old. They are very close to Wakan Taka because of their age and cosmic assignment. They can express themselves as a single massive bird or as many little Thunderbirds; this is borne out by the fact that they can manifest as a single tiny point of brilliant light, a minimum of six angels and a maximum of 40.3 million.

Much of the Native American description of Thunderbird's qualities and tasks is understood through another cultural expression the Ofanim have taken: as Ganesh, the merry elephant god of Hinduism. Ganesh is the remover of obstacles; the wise teacher; the scribe; the protector of humanity.

As Garuda, the celestial bird-mount of

Vishnu, the Hindu version of the Christ, the Ofanim are known as Eater of Snakes, which corresponds well with Thunderbird's enmity with Unktehi, the various great horned water snakes, and other water monsters. All of these are filtered perceptions of the cosmic dragon, known in classical Vedic perception as Sesa-Ananta, the prime colleague of Vishnu, and in Judaic lore as Leviathan, the vast whale of the Great Sea.

Often myths must be inverted to understand their meaning. The Ofanim do not battle the cosmic dragon; rather, they are its colleagues. This is apparent through the Judaic description of the enmity-collegiality of Behemoth (a giant, malign primordial female elephant) and Leviathan (the primordial whale, male). They are mates who never are together; they will fight each other to the death at the End of Days; their flesh will be consumed by the righteous in Heaven.

Behemoth is another form the Ofanim have taken. Both the Ofanim and the cosmic dragon are firstborn in the Creation. The dragon embodies the residue of consciousness from the previous cycle of creation and the unmanifested divine power ready to be deployed in the next round of creation. The Ofanim are the primary point of consciousness, the first point to form out of the original void.

Hebrew lore says that those few humans who interacted with the Ofanim became prophets, such as Enoch and Ezekiel. In contemporary times, those who have encountered the Ofanim's energy have found their lives turned inside out. They may not have felt like *heyoka* or holy fools, but often, to the outside world, they were seen that way, what Native Americans call an upside-down, hot-cold, forward-backward man—a man turned inside out and living upside down.

That amusing (or appalling) description is ratified by the Ofanim who state that their task with humans, for those who choose to work with them, is to keep them rigorously, ruthlessly in adherence to the "star they are," which means to the true self and point of primal awareness that lives as a divine spark in all people. The Ofanim do not punish liars, evildoers, or those who deny the truth; but for those who work with them, they inspire a straightforward allegiance to truth.

As for the attribution of thunder and lightning, we must be subtle in interpreting this, for it is more symbolic than literal. Behemoth is said to have a roar that echoes (thunders) throughout the cosmos when sounded. The Ofanim are said to be so bright they illuminate *Arabot,* the Seventh Heaven, and they say of themselves that, in their star form, they are brighter than the brightest star.

On a physical level, I have observed that the Ofanim often produce noticeable weather effects, usually through their cooperation with archangels or Nature spirits. These effects include sudden thick clouds, storms, intense short-lived downpours, rainbows, roaring winds. They prefer producing precipitation to accompany interactive events with humans, explaining that to them water is consciousness, so more water precipitated is more consciousness sparked.

As for the claim that nobody has seen the Thunderbird in his entirety, this is correct and affirmed by the Ofanim. They have assumed many forms for human interactions over time, many forgotten, others still not recognized, and they state that their ultimate form is, for the most part, beyond human cognition.

The Ofanim may be accessed by any interested person by meditating on a tiny, brilliant point of light just above the navel, and by visiting Avebury, the 28.5-acre stone circle in Wiltshire, England, their "tipi" and Earth's Blazing Star.

See also: Behemoth, Dragon, Ganesh, Garuda, Hanuman, Leviathan, Phoenix, Simurgh, Vocub Caquix, Ziz.

TOWER OF BABEL

A geomantic device, installed by angels and still operational, that facilitates the differentiation of the human soul through the 72 Names of God, each of which is the root sound and essence of an ethnic group.

Also known as Ka Dingir Ra Ki, 72 Names of God, Shemhamforesh, Tower of Babylon.

Description: *Babel* is the Hebrew word for Babylon, so the expression more correctly is the Tower of Babylon. *Babylon* derives from the Akkadian *Babilum* and the Sumerian cuneiform script *Bab-ilim* or *Bab-ilu,* which means "Gate of the Deity" or "Gate of God," from *bab* which means "gate" or "door."

One of the foremost of ancient cities, Babylon flourished in the second millennium B.C. Its ruins are located on the Euphrates River, not far from Baghdad in south-central Iraq. This area was anciently called Mesopotamia ("Land between Two Rivers," the other being the Tigris), and earlier, the Plain of Shinar in Babylonia.

Shinar was the biblical name for Sumer (or Shumer: "Land of the Ones Who Watch" [i.e., the gods]), widely regarded as the foundation of civilization, older than all others recorded, flourishing as early as the fourth millennium B.C. (circa 3800 B.C.), according to texts and the archeological record. The Sumerian name for *Bab-ilu* was *Ka Dingir Ra Ki.*

The biblical account says that Noah's descendants journeyed to the Plain of Shinar, mastered the art of architecture, and built the Tower of Babel. The Babylonians, under King Nimrod, allegedly wanted to build a powerful city whose consummate expression was a tower with its top in the Heavens; the size and height of the tower was meant to be the Babylonians' war on God Himself, their statement of supremacy and independence from their creator.

Nimrod's tower of bricks was built by 600,000 workers and was so tall it took a year to climb to the top, so the legend says. Some scholars interpret the tower as the ziggurat (a stepped pyramid) of Marduk at Babylon, called *E-temen-an-ki* ("Foundation of Heaven and Earth"), 300 feet square and 270 feet high, rising to that height in seven delineated stages; the top was all blue-grazed brick.

Genesis says this was judged an act of arrogance, presumably by God or at least Yahweh, who then, as punishment, decisively changed human history by dispatching 70 angels to destroy the incomplete tower.

At that time, legend says, all humans spoke the same universal language, and it was a magical tongue, such that if they spoke something, it was manifested.

The angelic visitation shattered the single world language then in use and forever confused the tongues of men, that is, with numerous languages and the peoples using them scattered worldwide. Ancient sources say 70 different languages were created, all humans started fighting since they could not understand one another, and some even devolved into apes and demons.

With all the tribes of humanity suddenly having separate languages, unintelligible to one another, they could no longer communicate, and humanity grew fragmented and alienated through its lack of commonality of language.

The city where this fundamental human change happened was Babylon. Legend still holds that if you walk past where the Tower of Babel once stood, you will lose your memory entirely. Judeo-Christian culture demonized Babylon, labeling it "the Great Whore" and apostle of false religions.

Thus *Bab-ilim,* "Gate of God," got changed to *Balal,* "to confuse or mix," and the Tower of Babel came to represent humanity's sin that led to the confusion of speech and the sundering of a primal unity of consciousness through one tongue. Congruent with this post-Babylon heaping of pejoratives, centuries later, Middle East Muslims regarded Babylon as the fountainhead of black magic.

The Tower of Babel (*Babili,* still another spelling) means "Gateway of the Gods," the gods, in this case, being the legendary Anunnaki. Scholars such as Zecharia Sitchin suggest that the first "Gateway of the Gods" at Babylon was constructed not by Noah's descendants, but by the gods. The structure was called variously *mu, shu-mu, sham,* or *shem,* words usually interpreted to mean "name," but for Sitchin, they mean "sky chamber," the gods' "skyborne vehicle" for ascending to the heavenly realms.

Explanation: To understand the reality behind the myth of the Tower of Babel, you must first erase all Judeo-Christian pejoratives from the picture. Second, you must allow for considerable distortion and confusion in the myth; and third, you must view it clairvoyantly as a geomantic aspect of Earth.

The Tower of Babel is three things: first, a stargate; second, a geomantic device that allows for the diversification of the human soul into 72 types; and third, once, for a time, about 100,000 years ago, an actual physical tower built by the Nefilim, one of three angelic orders who incarnated as human giants.

The Tower of Babel as a gate or door to the deity, God, or the gods, or, in Sitchin's interpretation, as a space-port for extraterrestrial ships, refers to an arcane geomantic feature called a stargate. It is arcane because it is almost entirely forgotten as a planetary reality and is acknowledged only in the context of fantasy or speculation in science fiction and never as an actual geomantic feature.

Earth has 1,080 stargates that connect to stars and 2,200,000 that connect to constellations—more precisely, to inhabited planets relative to either. The stargate transports you bodily and almost instantaneously to the intended destination; stargates range in size from three feet to 40 miles, but the average is 30 yards across; and there is duplication among the destinations: 32 different stars and 264 different constellations are serviced by the stargate network. This network exists at Earth's fifth level (out of nine) of geomantic reality, or, despite the confusion in the term, what we could call the fifth dimension.

Three stargates existed at Babylon, presumably at or in the ziggurat of Marduk. Most likely, the ziggurat was built to house the stargates physically. Humans and gods (i.e., extraterrestrial beings) used the stargates regularly, though most likely, among the humans, it was primarily the priests and initiates.

The Tower of Babel as the "sky chamber" and "skyborne vehicle" of the gods (and *to* the gods) is echoed in Native American myths about rising or growing rocks, which suggest the stargates as a kind of inexplicable elevator. Typically, a person visits or sleeps on a special rock or peak, and finds upon waking that it has grown vertically to an unbelievable height, from which the person can't get down.

Myths along these lines are attributed to Devil's Peak in Wyoming (which has a stargate), the numinous conical peak featured in *Close Encounters of the Third Kind,* Steven Spielberg's 1978 masterpiece about human-alien visitation. The benevolent ETs (the "gods") met humans at the peak and one human left with them—essentially the same scenario as ascribed to the Tower of Babel.

The Tower of Babel is also a geomantic device the angelic orders installed (it's still in place and operational), which grounded the 72 Names of God (called *Shemhamforesh* in Judaic mysticism) on Earth. The installation of the Tower was one of several key geomantic aspects of the biblical Fall of Man.

Humanity has been generated twice on the Earth. The first humanity enjoyed paradisal conditions, both physically and spiritually. They were spiritual prodigies, masters of matter, and participants in unitive consciousness. This is the postulated original single language before the confusion of tongues.

It was a language of light, akin to angelic communication; it was a divine language, a tongue that could create beings, conditions, and events, both beneficial and harmful. It was, from our perspective today, a language of magic, of invocation, of reality generation and immediate wish fulfillment. Mythically, this singular language is vaguely remembered in references to the Word Sword and the Dolorous Stroke, which in the Arthurian mythos created the Wasteland.

In part, its misuse led to the Fall of Man and the introduction of the 72 Names of God as a new parameter with tighter definitions for consciousness. Not surprisingly, second humanity demonized the Tower as a way of placing blame for their reduced conditions, that is, the loss of unitive consciousness (language).

To say that if you walk past the Tower of Babel (or today, where it once stood), you will lose your memory means you will forget your linear, time-based, abstract, nonmagical, and individuated way of thinking; you will lapse back into that universal dreamlike language of unitive consciousness that the Tower enshrined.

Here is a way to picture the Tower of Babel: Visualize a wooden square with 72 square subdivisions, say in 12 rows with six squares per row. This square sits on a post (like a Ping-Pong paddle and its handle) and the post goes into the ground. Each of the 72 squares contains an angel and a Name of God, continuously sounding, like a mantric utterance, or a division of the Word. These are the 70 (the correct number is 72; often religious myths delete the two to hide the occult reality of the original number) angels who came to destroy Babylon.

Now the square gains dimensionality and seems wrapped around a central pillar or tower set into the ground. It is a tall tower, rising hundreds of feet; the same 72 subdivisions are there, each sounding a different Name of God. It is, in a sense, a babble of divine voices, a riot of the sounding of the Names of God; it is the planetary grounding point for a fundamental aspect of second humanity. This is where the Shemhamforesh is grounded on Earth; it was done at Babylon for geomantic reasons, largely having to do with the specific star connections of the stargates.

The Tower of Babel, just described, was installed to differentiate the one language of Light into 72 languages of meaning. It was not exactly a punishment for the "sins" and excesses of first humanity, but more of a compassionate limitation devised by the Supreme Being to keep second humanity from destroying itself.

The 72 angels in the squares each became an egregor or angelic Watcher-Guardian for a specific people on a specific landmass. For example, Eriu is the Name of God and egregor for Ireland, Srinmo Demoness for Tibet, Bharata for India. These egregors were assigned to maintain spiritual and geomantic conditions in a landscape for the evolution in consciousness of the soul aspect inhabiting it, for example, Irish, Tibetan, Indian, each seen as a 1/72nd soul expression.

The Shemhamforesh Tower grounded at Babylon holds the language and thus soul differentiations as a morphogenetic information field and continuously broadcasts them into Earth's visionary geography (or Earth grid) from a higher dimension (a geomantic layer or reality level of Earth). The Tower of Babel is still operational as a global Name of God resonator-broadcaster and as a prime constituent of our geomantically created and delivered Earth reality.

The Tower holds the codings and parameters for each of the 72 different soul types or peoples on Earth. In each of the 72 egregors, you can see the full extent of the plan and the essence of, for example, Irish in Ireland, Indians in India. You have, in effect, a hologram for the full reality of the Irish in Ireland, that is, a people inhabiting a specific landmass geomantically maintained by its egregor.

The Judeo-Christian pejoratives cloud the reality of the Tower's purpose. It was not meant to confuse the tongues, but split the one unitive language of Light into 72 individuative languages of meaning. The purpose was to allow for human soul evolution through the Names (expressed as peoples) toward the goal of individuation, on a personal and global level, in which the 72 Names of God are united in a person as a karmic completion and, geomantically, for Earth.

The Tower of Babel is how the differentiation into 72 languages was grounded on the Earth for the second round of humanity. The first round was removed from the Earth and entered the astral plane, thereafter known variously as Djinn,

Asuras, the Kings of Edom, and Raksasas. The Muslims believed Babylon to be the seat of black magic because the Djinns, which execute black magic spells for practitioners, are accessible through this site, and many others.

One of the many geomantic features of Babylon, still extant, even if the city is long gone, is a Lucifer Binding Site (see Lucifer), hence the black magic attributions and implied Djinn involvement (the "apes and demons"; see Djinn).

An additional factor making it appropriate that the Tower of Babel be established at the Gateway of the Gods is that Babylon was a world navel, one of the Earth's 72 Energy Focusing Nodes. Here one of 72 specifically assigned angelic watchers or egregors grounded and protected the celestial energy for the landmass in their charge (the implicit if future country of Iraq). Thus, at such a site as Babylon, there is the vertical energetic conduit to the spiritual worlds and usually a temple honoring the egregor, in Babylon's case, Marduk, the local god.

Anciently, Marduk was honored at the *E-sagil* temple and *E-temenanki* ziggurat in Babylon, and though these are no longer extant and Babylon merely a ruin, the energy connections and functions are still operational for all of Iraq.

See also: Adam, Chakravartin, Djinn, Dolorous Stroke, Eriu, Fall of Man, Flood, Garden of Eden, Giants, Huitzilopochtli, Land of Milk and Honey, Lucifer, Marduk, Rising Rock, Wasteland.

TREE OF THE KNOWLEDGE OF GOOD AND EVIL

An expression of the gift of free will to a self-aware conscious humanity and embodied by Lucifer, the Lord of Light, demonstrating both poles of choice and their consequences.

Also known as the two aspects of Lucifer, the warring twins Tezcatlipoca and Quetzalcoatl, Epimetheus and Prometheus.

Description: Biblical lore has it that there are two trees in Paradise or the Garden of Eden. The Tree of Life is one: It is so huge that it would take a person 500 years to walk a distance equal to its diameter, and equally vast is the space its branches shade. (The Norse tradition calls this vast world tree Yggdrasil.)

Judaic lore says this tree shades the entire Garden, is canopied by seven clouds of glory, and its fruit has 15,000 different tastes and perfumes. Its ten or 12 fruits are considered forms of the Sun and, by eating one (or drinking the tree's sap), you gain immortality; Chinese myth calls them the Peaches of Immortality. From this Tree drips the Dew of Light (in Judaic lore) by which the dead are resurrected, again suggesting regeneration and immortal life. You can have unitive consciousness, perpetual oneness with God, versus individuative consciousness, a seeming separation from God with the possibility of reuniting.

God rests atop this tree when He visits Paradise. Four rivers flow into the Earth and irrigate it from under this tree—the Ganges, Tigris, Euphrates, and Nile—and these pour out honey, milk, wine, and oil into the world.

The Tree of Life is hedged by the second tree, the Tree of the Knowledge of Good and Evil. This tree is said to be the height of a fir, its leaves like those of a carob tree, and its fruit grows in clusters of a vine. Judaic sources also suggest, however, that both trees formed one tree at the bottom and only branched into two when they attained a certain height. To get to the inner tree, you must first pass through the outer hedge and its dualistic tree. In Genesis, the primal couple, Adam and Eve, are expelled from Eden when Eve disobeys God and eats a fruit from the second, outer tree. The forbidden fruit is said to be a fig, grape, or apple.

Explanation: The Tree of the Knowledge of Good and Evil is Lucifer. Lucifer, the Lord of Light and God-commissioned Light-Bringer to humanity, awarded humanity free will, that is, the free, conscious choice between good and evil. Lucifer took responsibility for this choice by embodying the duality so that humans could observe the rotating polarity in Lucifer's two guises, as satanic and light-filled, as Tezcatlipoca and Quetzalcoatl, Epimetheus and Prometheus—duality.

The two Trees in Paradise offer humanity a choice, seemingly: from the Tree of Life, you may have eternal life, immortality; from the Tree of the Knowledge of Good and Evil, you may have conscious embodied individuality, free will, the choice between good and evil, "sin," karma, illness, and death.

Qabalists in the esoteric side of Judaism interpret this dualistic Tree as a destroying whirlwind. The Good (*Tov,* in Hebrew) does not inherently refer to moral qualities or goodness as such, but the clinging to the continuity of existence, while the Evil *(Raa)* is the energy that upsets static conditions and habits. The life of this Tree, then, is about intense, dynamic movement between these opposites.

In the biblical allegory, the forbidden fruit (an apple—more likely a golden apple) gave Adam and Eve self-aware individual consciousness; the serpent who tempted Eve is kundalini, the awesome life-force energy coiled in the spine at the root chakra and desiring to illuminate all aspects of consciousness by moving through the chakras. There was no temptation by the serpent; access to kundalini was a gift to humans from God. When Adam and Eve became "naked," that means they became aware of themselves as individual points of consciousness, and when they covered their nakedness, that means they assumed a sheath of subtle Light bodies (including the aura).

Both biblically described Trees have a geomantic expression and location on the Earth and together comprise the inner and outer aspects of the heart chakra. The Tree of Life (also called the *Kalpataru,* or Wish-Fulfilling Tree) is situated in Earth's inner heart chakra known as the eight-petaled *Ananda-kanda.* In terms of Earth's visionary geography, this chakra is located at and around Rondablikk, a tiny hamlet in the Rondane Mountains of central Norway; the Norse remembered and described this tree as Yggdrasil.

The Tree of the Knowledge of Good and Evil is located in Earth's outer heart chakra, called *Anahata,* consisting of 12 petals and the foundation of the paired opposites in the scheme of the zodiac. Earth's primary *Anahata* chakra (there are other expressions of this at other levels in the hierarchy of energy of Earth's visionary geography) is at Glastonbury in Somerset, England: That is the location of the Tree of the Knowledge of Good and Evil.

Like the Tree of Life, the branches of this tree shade an extensive area, but the centermost part of the trunk is at Glastonbury Tor, an anomalous, pyramid-shaped artificial hill in the center of the town said to be the residence of numerous deities from different cultures: King Avallach of the Summer Country, Gwynn ap Nudd (King of the Fairies), the Archangel Michael, Melwas (who abducted Guinevere, King Arthur's wife), and Glasteing. The latter was one of 12 brothers, all giants, who followed his pregnant, eight-legged sow across England until it sat down under an apple tree on a hill, and here he founded his village, *Glasteingaburgh.* This is the oldest foundation myth for Glastonbury.

Glastonbury Tor is the site of one of the planet's 47 Golden Apples, a geomantic feature having to do with the acquisition of spiritual knowledge. It is also the entry to an Avalon, a Celestial City marked by abundant, fruit-laden apple trees. Avalon, of course, is also the Celtic paradise (or fairyland). The 47 Golden Apples come from this one Tree, but 46 of them were distributed around the Earth.

I once saw a visionary tableau inside the Tor in which a fabulously handsome man and woman stood on either side of a Tree of Life replete with fruit; they handed me a Golden Apple. Eating the apple, you taste the fruit, the quickening tartness and sweetness of self-aware consciousness; you awaken to your God-given choice in all moments and actions to do good or evil, and you become aware of the consequences of these actions. This eating of the Golden Apple is the birth of "sin," better understood as karma; in modern terms, it's like getting a new credit card with a high allowance and starting to charge things on it.

This Golden Apple, incidentally, is never exhausted; all can eat of it, and it is still always whole and full of juicy golden wisdom. Similarly, its size is relative: You can hold it in your hand to examine or eat, if you wish; you can enter it as if it were a spherical temple; and it can be the size of the Tor itself. The "forbidden" fruit—more accurately, the freely offered by God fruit—is an apple specifically because, according to the angelic realm, this shape most clearly matches the energy field and dynamics of Earth's total visionary geography.

Both spiritually and geomantically, you progress through the heart chakra by starting at the outer part, *Anahata,* at Glastonbury, and tasting the Golden Apple. With this knowledge of duality and its ramifications, you progress inward to the *Ananda-kanda,* to the wish-fulfilling Tree of Life of Eden at Rondablikk in Norway—from Avalon to Eden—and fortified with this divine knowledge of the possibilities and consequences of free action, you make your wishes at the Tree.

Surprisingly, then, the seemingly mythic, or at least allegorical, images in Genesis regarding the Garden of Eden have literal geomantic locations on Earth. You actually can visit both Trees in person, in the body, any time in your life, and replicate the archetypal, timeless choice of our vastly ancient forebears. Inner and outer, this aspect of Genesis is the story of the human heart chakra.

Appropriately for this geomyth, coiled at the base of the Glastonbury Tree and around its Golden Apple is a dragon. It is one of the planet's 13 primordial dragons; another is under the Rondablikk tree; both are very large. The dragon could be interpreted as the "serpent" who tempted Adam and Eve, but it is more accurate to understand it as an expression of awakened, engaged kundalini. Similarly, in Greek myth, the dragon Ladon is coiled under the Golden Apple trees in the Garden of the Hesperides, another version of Avalon's apple-land.

Experientially, if you use this landscape temple for self-initiation, you pass through the dragon coiled around Glastonbury Tor into the Golden Apple which is inside the geomantic expression of kundalini. This is the domain of the "forbidden" fruit, which, of course, was not prohibited but offered to us by God. Inside the apple you find the Tree, which is more of an implicit vertical axis running through the apple, like an imagined line between the stem and underside of the apple.

This axis is called Albion, an expression of the unawakened Lucifer at a lower level, as human awareness experiencing duality. Albion is that part of the human who witnesses, engages in, endures the primary cutting of the apple into two parts and two poles: life and death, male and female, above and below, change and stasis, Heaven and Earth, physical and etheric, conscious and unconscious, eternal and temporal, good and evil, and all the other named dualities of life. Yet Albion, too, is sliced in half, and knows it, reveling and agonizing in the duality.

To say this Tree primarily concerns itself with "good and evil" is too limiting; the experience, rather, is with all polarities and dualities, with fundamentally slicing the apple in two, and experiencing the two halves as dynamically related parts that are inherently, implicitly, one, a unity. The slicing of the Golden Apple and Albion into two halves is the inception of individuative consciousness, awareness that is split in two, polarized, but seeks reunification.

Geomantically, the halved apple is expressed across the Earth in the form of 432 landscape zodiacs (see White Cow, White Sow). These are holographic miniatures of the galaxy of varying sizes (one-half mile to 200 miles in diameter), but structurally, since this reality is too complex and multidimensional to lay out horizontally on the Earth, the apple shape of the galaxy is cut in two and flattened.

The result is a hologram of the galaxy approached as two halves of an apple, each half containing a portion of the stars of the galaxy in accordance with one's location on the planet.

Each landscape zodiac has an Albion as its implicit central axis and culmination.

This template is expressed at Glastonbury in the form of a landscape zodiac that is about 34 miles wide, the diameter of each half being about 17 miles. These two star-filled halves are laid out on either side of Glastonbury Tor as a geomantic expression of the fundamental schism of the Golden Apple and Albion, which is the reality of the Tree of the Knowledge of Good and Evil.

Appropriately, Glastonbury's foundation myth, already mentioned, encapsulates all this: Glasteing is Albion; the apple tree on the hill is the Tree of the Knowledge of Good and Evil at the Tor; and the pregnant sow is an old symbol for a landscape zodiac, which in turn is a symbol for the halved apple.

See also: Albion, Antichrist, Avalon, Dragon, Earth Changes, Fall of Man, Garden of Eden, Golden Apple, Klingsor, Lucifer, Peacock Angel, Prometheus, Tezcatlipoca, Tower of Babel, White Cow, White Sow, Yggdrasil.

TRICKSTER

A perception by native peoples, especially those of North America, of the Hindu god Shiva, destroyer of illusions and false appearances.

Also known as Ananse, Br'er Rabbit, Esu-Elegbara, Glooscap, Great Dikithi, Great Hare, Hermes, Heyoka, Hlakanyana, Iktome, Inkotomi, Koshare, Koyemshi, Legba, Manabozho, Mercurius, Newekwe, Nihansan, Reynard the Fox, Sendeh Old Man, Sitkonski, Spider, Thoth, Wisakedjak (Whiskey Jack).

Description: The Trickster is a complex mythologic figure described by many Native North American tribes as well as the peoples of West Africa where he is known as Spider. He is a prankster, deceiver, lecher, culture hero, creator god, liar, cheat, thief, teacher, rogue, and buffoon. He can be pretentious, stupid, playful, lusty, wily, imitative, a braggart, or incompetent. He's credited with introducing the arts of living to humanity and was the first storyteller.

Trickster spans the gamut from sublime to chthonic. Some tribes call him *Heyoka,* the holy fool or sacred clown, while some scholars say it is he who is depicted in the famous Paleolithic rock painting of the Sorcerer, the trickster-shaman god of the Les Trois Frères cave in France (circa 14,000 B.C.).

With the exception of Africa, Native North America is the most intensely Trickster-oriented landscape in the world. Although the term "Trickster" was introduced to anthropology by a Western scholar in 1885 from a translation by a French researcher of Indian myths in 1878, Trickster's qualities have been consistently and uniformly extolled by numerous different tribes.

He has many guises, mostly drawn from the animal kingdom, including coyote (probably the most popular), raven, mink, blue jay, crow, rabbit, fox, cock, and raccoon among still others. Trickster is a study in contradictions and paradoxes: He is a figure elevated above humans, yet he is grossly erotic and crudely gluttonous. He is the consummate prankster, yet he often pranks himself; he is unquenchably curious and highly unpredictable. He is almost always male, and often his sexuality and sexual parts are exaggerated; he can be very creative, yet perverse, brutal, greedy, ridiculous, and physically deformed.

Trickster is credited (or blamed) with the introduction of physical death, work, and even suffering; some tribes say he came from the Moon, stole the Sun, and made the world dark. Yet as Ananse the Spider (an African version), he persuaded the high god Nyame to give the people rain to soften the harsh sunlight and night to provide a time of rest. Ananse was divine, the people's first king. Among the Hopi of the American Southwest, Trickster as Coyote is credited with having distributed all the galaxy's stars, although he supposedly just tossed them.

Among the tribes of Dahomey, Trickster is known as Legba (or Esu-Elegbara), the youngest son of the Creator, and was understood as the principle of accident. Legba is the god of entrances and crossroads, described as an old man who goes about in tatters, functioning in cult rituals to open the way for other gods to enter into the cultists in a possessive trance-state manner. Legba is a dancer, wearing a mask, who dances the phallic dance of creation and regeneration. Legba is also the penetrator of the dark world of the unknown—a psychopomp; and he is also the source of the Word, of language and communication skills.

As Reynard the Fox, popular in the French medieval period, he is the clever, amoral rebel against all authority, the opposite of *chanson de geste* ideals. As such, the Trickster is the consummate denier of all boundaries, cultural, moral, and physical, which makes him the ideal assistant to the Creator; he works in the human world, yet he is the masterful shape-shifter and protean transformer.

Ultimately, Trickster tricks humans into learning through his bizarre, entirely unconventional behavior and antics, often seemingly at his own expense. He teaches awareness of the element of disorder and how to survive amidst it.

Explanation: The figure from European mythology most often equated with Trickster is the Greek Olympian god Hermes. He is a thief and liar, wily, charming, mischievous, and a cattle-rustler with trickery always brewing in his heart; he guards the crossroads (his name might even come from that: *hermaion,* which means "a pile of stones"); he is associated with sexuality and is often said to be oversexed; and he is the premier psychopomp, the conductor of souls through the Underworld.

Hermes is the gods' herald and messenger to humanity, but he was also the god, guide, and escort of travelers: Statues of Hermes called hermae or herms were set up at crossroads and outside houses for protection. Like Legba, Hermes was the god of boundaries, territorial demarcations, and the transgressions of boundaries; he was the wakeful god, the wayfinder, and the founder of the Mysteries at Eleusis in Greece, the classical world's preeminent Mystery initiation center, where he mediated between the worlds of night and day, spirits and men, gods and humanity.

So Hermes is not only the psychopomp at the temple gates, but he is also the hinge that opens the door, the middle point and socket of the door into the Mystery of death and the alternation of life, death, and rebirth. As the inventor of language, he is *hermeneus,* the interpreter, who creates and brings something lightlike to culture; he is a clarifier, a god of communication, words, and interpretation.

His Roman counterpart was Mercurius (Mercury), and both he and Hermes were depicted as carrying the caduceus, a herald's staff consisting of two intertwined, carved snakes. With this staff, Hermes-Mercurius could wake humans or put them to sleep, as he willed. In medieval alchemy, Mercurius or Quicksilver assumed a more abstract quality: *Hermes Trismegistus,* "Thrice-Greatest Hermes," is the elusive, alien "other" in humans, God, daemon, and Man's innermost secret and energy, a duplex figure and the source of all opposites, capable of being both polarities—the entirety of the unconscious.

Hermes' Egyptian counterpart was Thoth (or Tehuti), Moon god, the god of wisdom, and initiator of humans. He recorded the names of souls entering the *Duat,* or the Egyptian Underworld; he knew the verbal formulae enabling the dead to pass safely through the Underworld; he was in charge of all the sacred texts in the House of Life (wisdom documents); he introduced arithmetic, geometry, and astronomy; and he was "Lord of the Sacred Words" (the hieroglyphs and sacred speech).

Trickster, Hermes, Mercurius, Thoth—a deeper level still awaits us. We get the most profound and comprehensive interpretation of this figure through the Hindu god Shiva, the destroyer of illusions, part of Hinduism's Trinity. Here, Hermes-Thoth, while a separate spiritual being from Shiva, works with and transmits much of the Shiva energy.

Shiva is the blue-throated Moon god, Lord of wisdom, revelation, initiation, yoga, asceticism, truth, self-control, and energy. The following are the matches of his qualities with those attributed to the Trickster and Hermes-Thoth.

Hindu psychic astronomers associated Shiva (in his earlier form as Rudra) with the star Sirius (in Canis Major, the Greater Dog) and called this star *Mrgavyadha.* One of Rudra's prime tasks in the cosmos is to guard the dwelling of the stars; he is the *Vastospati,* Protector of the *Vastu,* the House of Stars. He is the ever-vigilant celestial Dog at the gate of the House of Stars, maintaining its life and integrity.

To say Trickster threw the stars out haphazardly so they sit in the cosmos in disorder is inverted: If anything, Rudra appointed and now protects the lawful distribution of stars, and through the star Sirius, he maintains order among the stars in the galaxy. He is both doorkeeper and guide to the great star House.

The hermae and heaps of stones attributed to Hermes finds their equivalent in Shiva's lingas, phallic-like vertical stones said to represent and contain his vast power. The oversexed emphasis in the Trickster is only an exaggeration (and a mild distortion) of this aspect of divine lust and primordial procreative power.

Legba as the masked dancer of creation and regeneration is Shiva in his Nataraja form, Lord of the Dance. Shiva dances in *Citamparam,* the "Space of Consciousness" at the heart of the universe within a circle of flames. His movements represent the continuous creation, disclosure, and destruction of the world of appearances. He dances away all illusory consciousness and existence. In this guise, he is the Lord of Death, like the Greek Hades, but it is the more profound death of false realities, half-truths, delusions, meretricious conditions.

In the *Ananda Tandava* dance, Shiva's four arms move wildly, expressing cosmic energy in its unfettered, creative, expressive guise, but his head does not move, indicating Shiva as the unperturbed Absolute beyond time and space. He creates, he sustains, he conceals, he reveals, he destroys, he dissolves, over and over, and the entire cosmos and all its gods are Shiva's enraptured audience.

Hermes' caduceus is the *ida-pingala* network of kundalini that rises from groin to head. In esoteric yoga, the human is said to have seven major energy-force and consciousness centers, called chakras, from the groin to the top of the head. Through these pass two intertwining currents, the *ida* (Moon) and *pingala* (Sun) channels, like two serpents, meeting in the sixth, or brow, chakra.

Shiva, the force of awakened consciousness, sits in the crown chakra and awaits the rising of his divine spouse, Shakti, who lives coiled in the root chakra as unawakened kundalini, the divine force of total, transcendent wakefulness. Often Shiva is depicted with his consort Parvati in the physical act of copulation, indicating the penetration of Shiva into every aspect of reality at all levels.

The Trickster as the source of speech and Hermes-Thoth as the revealer of initiatory wisdom, revelation, and sacred utterances are found in Shiva's Garland. The seven chakras each have a number of vibratory petals or fields, and on each, in traditional depictions, is one of Sanskrit's 50 letters. In reality, the letters are said to create and sustain the vibratory patterns of the chakras. The totality is called Shiva's Garland, the basis of hierophantic and creative speech.

Just as Hermes and Thoth are the revealers of esoteric wisdom, so is Shiva *Mahesvara,* the Lord of Knowledge, the true Self behind all forms, the sublime state beyond all differentiations. He brings transcendent God-knowledge. He is the Lord of Yoga because he shows how to silence the mind to reach beyond all sense-based data to the Absolute, the unmanifest source of all manifestations.

The Trickster's propensity to disrespect, even abolish, all boundaries is Shiva's wild dance that shatters the illusion of distinctions, definitions, and the myriad snares of illusion and delusion that fetter and bound human cognition. Shiva perpetually pulls the rug of assumptions and presumptions out from under us, a quality the Native American sensitives interpreted as that of a prankster.

Shiva is Tarot's Joker or Holy Fool at the

heart of every atom of Creation; he is the quantum uncertainty behind every act and thought, the paradox of reconciled opposites, the exacerbation of duality, exhibited, embodied, balanced, shattered, dissolved, and recreated every moment—the Harlequin with equal black and white patches. He demonstrates the ontological freedom from all conditions and boundaries—a death of sorts, but a deep and joyous revelation.

As the Trickster, he shows he doesn't care and it doesn't matter if he is the butt of his own joke, because his energy dissolves the opposites and dualities. He is beyond the boundaries of judgment, interpretation, left-right or up-down. He is the thief of illusion; he deceives to enlighten, to reveal the emptiness of form; he plays both ends against your middle, in a merry cosmic prank of illumination.

Shiva is present on Earth in at least 1,748 geomantic locations. You may encounter him at Avebury, a 28.5-acre stone circle in Wiltshire, England, the planet's umbilicus, or at any of the 1,746 domes (see Holy Mountain), large etheric energy canopies usually over major mountains held to be sacred. Shiva also resides on Mount Meru, the Earth's singular cosmic mountain.

Shiva has 1,008 epithets and numerous guises—the Native Americans saw him essentially as irreverent and funny, the Hindus as deeply serious and exultantly scary; he may appear to psychic perception as a towering blue-skinned humanlike god with a peaked, scaled, or petaled silvery-white crown.

See also: Ganesh, Green Knight, Hanuman, Holy Mountain, Mount Meru, Ocean of Milk, Underworld, White Bull.

TROLLS

Misperceived gnomes, though larger in stature, who work with the earth element and humans in maintaining the planet's visionary geography.

Also known as Fodden Skemaend, gnomes, Hollow Men, Maahiset, Maanalaiset, Sjötroll, trolld, trows, Underground People.

Description: The word "troll" is from Old Norse and means "fiend, monster, giant." Norwegian folklore paints trolls as ugly, hairy, malignant, fearsome, even loathly creatures; often they have three heads, one eye or a single eye shared among several trolls, and a very low, subhuman intelligence. They are usually larger than the average adult human, but highly unpleasant to be around. They are nocturnal and turn to stone if caught in the morning sunlight.

Trolls live in caves, rocks, or the remote reaches of mountains; they are treacherous, ogreish, malicious, and can harm humans, abduct or even eat them, or make them unbalanced, even crazy. Typically, male trolls interact with humans, but live with troll wives, and, surprisingly, their homes are described as delightful palaces full of treasures, jewels, and riches. Trolls are expert metal smiths, herbal healers, and even magicians and can occasionally bestow good fortune on a few select humans.

In the works of Norwegian playwright Henrik Ibsen, trolls are frequently referred to and maligned, and wayward or distracted characters in his dramas are sometimes said to have been taken off by the horrid, miserly, mean trolls or have a troll in them who is making them say things. Even in Norway today, tourist gift shops offer postcards, dolls, and carvings depicting trolls as loathsome, haglike, pathetic creatures, so primitive as to be amusing and seemingly harmless.

On a few occasions, trolls are given a benevolent cast, as in the *Grettis Saga Asmundarsonar* (a fourteenth-century Icelandic saga) in which the troll Thorir and his troll daughters offer hospitality to the outlaw human Grettir Asmundarson. Similarly, Grendel and his mother in the Old English tale *Beowulf* are understood to be trolls somewhat favorable to humans.

Explanation: Trolls are simply large gnomes and the recipients of a great deal of human negative filtering and pejorative description due to fear.

The term "gnome" may derive from the Greek *genomoi*, meaning "earth-dwellers," a meaning reflected in the Finnish equivalent, *Maahiset*, dwarflike beings who live in the Earth, or *Maanalaiset*, "the subterranean ones."

Ironically, Norway as a country that is rich with earth elementals, including gnomes, as well as the ideal natural landscape features that favor their presence, is also, as a culture over time, fearful of these same beings that maintain the ecosystem for them. As a means of taking the frightful edge off the proximity of these Nature spirits, the Norwegians developed an exaggerated, inflated, and ultimately comical-pathetic image of gnomes as demented, ugly, noisome trolls.

I have seen "trolls" in Norway, in the Rondane Mountains, in fact, the very area described by Ibsen in his 1867 drama *Peer Gynt*, in which the hero visits the Royal Hall of the King of the Dovrë Trolls in the Rondë Hills. They can be of human stature, between five and six feet tall, but they are otherwise of the same disposition and charged with the same divine commission as their shorter colleagues, the gnomes or dwarves. They noticeably suffer, however, from centuries of pejoratives and invalidation heaped on them by the Scandinavians.

Their function is the same as that of gnomes: to work with all aspects of the earth element, solidity, density, and the mineral kingdom of the planet; to maintain the interface between Earth's electromagnetic field and its visionary geography; and to coordinate geomantic activities with humans at holy sites.

Trolls and gnomes do not turn to stone when exposed to morning sunlight, despite the popularization of this motif in J. R. R. Tolkien's *The Hobbit*. Rather, they are most at home inside the cathedralic spaces of stones; it is their natural element. Trolls turned to stone symbolizes their immobility and insentience in the human visible, tangible world created and validated by sunlight.

Trolls existed before humans and the advent of the Sun on Earth, so they can only function at night and are somewhat immobilized at dawn. They cannot cognitively cross this threshold and thus cognitively turn to stone at sunlight. Stone also is an old symbol for the etheric realm, the next subtle dimension abutting our physical; trolls turning to stone means they slip back into that place.

See also: Gaia, Grail Knight, Menehune, Pan, Royal Hall of the King of the Dovrë Trolls.

TUATHA DE DANANN

A group of enlightened beings from the Great White Brotherhood who oversaw the terraforming of Ireland and the blossoming of its special spiritual agenda, as both land and people, on behalf of the planet.

Also known as Aes Sidhe, Ever-Living Ones, Fir Dea, Fir Tri nDea, Followers of the Goddess Danu, Lords of the Flame, Lords of Wisdom, Solar Fathers.

Description: According to earliest Irish lore, the Tuatha de Danann were a magical race of gods who invaded and inhabited the land of Ireland long ago. They ruled over Ireland for about 3,000 years and successfully fought against the monstrous Fomorians and the doughty Fir Bolg. Eventually, another invading race, called the Milesians, forced the Tuatha to retreat from the surface of the world and enter the numerous *sidhe* or Otherworld palaces across Ireland. Irish myth then blurred their identity and likened them to the elusive Fairy Folk.

Their name literally means "Followers or People of the Goddess Danu," the Mother goddess from whom they descended. They were also called the *Fir Dea*, meaning "Men of the Goddess," the Ever-Living Ones (because they were immortal), the *Aes Sidhe* ("People of the sidhes"), or *Fir Tri nDea* ("Men of the Three Gods").

Many of the Tuatha are even today well known in Irish lore as among the greatest divinities of that land: Brigit, goddess of healing; Eriu, after whom Ireland was named; Dian Cecht, the physician; Lugh, the god of light with many gifts;

Dagda, the lord of all the Tuatha; Boannd, the white cow goddess of rivers, especially the River Boyne, named after her; Goibhniu, the smith; Ogma, the warrior; Fidach, the musician; Midir the Proud; Aengus Oc, god of music and poetry; Donn, ruler of the dead; Manannan mac Lir, Lord of the Sea. In all, Irish myth names and describes somewhere between 24 and 30 different Tuatha.

After their retreat from the physical world, the Tuatha took up residence in the ten principal Otherworld dwellings, or sidhes, many of which are still extant today, although more than ten residences and their occupants are remembered.

The sidhe, which refers to a barrow, hill, mound, cairn, or other stonework or earthen mass in the landscape, is considered a portal into the Otherworld realm in which the Tuatha reside. That domain is sometimes called *Magh Meall* ("the Delightful Plain"), *Emain Ablach* ("the Fortress of Apples," like the Celtic Avalon), or *Tir na nOg* ("the Land of Youth").

The Tuatha called Una got the sidhe called *Knockshegowna;* Midir got *Bri Leith;* Aengus Oc got *Brugh na Boinne* (known today as Newgrange near Dublin). Many of Ireland's sacred sites are the sidhes of the elusive Tuatha, and the twelfth-century *Acallam na Senorach* ("Tales of the Elders of Ireland") lists the locations and inhabitants of several dozen of the Tuatha sidhes across the country.

Irish myth also recounts how, periodically, the Tuatha, either singly or in groups, would emerge from their sidhes to meet with a few living Irish people or invite them into their Otherworld palaces for a brief look and maybe a gift and to enjoy the lovely music and singing. The Tuatha had the power of *feth fiada,* or invisibility, which enabled them to roam the human world undetected.

When the Tuatha originally came to Ireland, they brought four divine gifts to the land and its people from four celestial or magical cities known as Falias, Findias, Gorias, and Murias whose gifts were, respectively, the Lia Fail, or Stone of Destiny, which heralded the rightful king; the invincible Sword of Nuadu; the Spear of Lugh-Lamfhota, which guarantees victory; and the Cauldron of the Dagda, which feeds and satisfies everyone.

Irish myth also recounts how, in the Earth's earliest days, the Tuatha were instrumental in carving out and animating the specific land features of Ireland.

Explanation: The Tuatha de Danann was a delegation from the Great White Brotherhood, based in the constellation Ursa Major (Great Bear), dispatched along with members of the angelic hierarchy to assist in the terraforming of the land of Ireland and the fulfillment of its spiritual agenda.

They are called, esoterically, Lords of the Flame, Solar Fathers, or Lords of Wisdom because they helped humanity develop *Manas* (mind principle) and discernment in consciousness, represented by the image of fire or a flame.

Other delegations were sent to other Lands of Light, such as Sumer (later called Mesopotamia and, today, part of Iraq; see Anunnaki), with different assignments, specific to that landmass, its visionary geographic allocation, and its intended role to fill in Earth's evolution. In the cases of Ireland and Sumer, the delegations' name refers to its source: the Great Mother Bear.

In Ireland, the Mother aspect of the Supreme Being was reflected by the name Danu or Dana; in Sumer, the Father aspect, as the Great Father of all the gods, as An; and as a third example, as the name of the divine city of An or Annu (Heliopolis) in Egypt, seat of the arrival and establishment of their original gods. In these three examples, the gods were sent under the auspices of the Supreme Being and through the galactic residency of the gods in Ursa Major.

Basically, the Tuatha de Danann consisted of a cadre of enlightened beings, angels, and a few archangels, working together to prepare Ireland for its people. Midir the Proud, for example, was the Irish name for Lucifer who came to establish his Emerald (the Lia Fail) in the Irish landmass; Manannan mac Lir was the Irish version of the Greek Poseidon, Lord of the Sea, which means master of the great etheric realm of sound currents, mantras, and subtle energy streams.

Boannd was (and still is) the River goddess for the River Boyne, the guardian or embodiment of a specific stream and theme of cosmic consciousness. Eriu is the landscape angel or national egregor assigned to Ireland, one of Earth's 72. The Dagda who brought the Cauldron is an expression of the Rich Fisher King (an aspect of the Christ) and the Cauldron is a perception of the Holy Grail.

For a time, the Tuatha walked the earth of Ireland in Light bodies whose glorious, harmonious auras extended for hundreds of feet around them. They fine-tuned the array of visionary geographic features given to Ireland and worked collegially with the Fomorians (who were the angelic Elohim in human-giant guise). Later, they left the physical plane, but remained accessible through the geomantic portals across the landscape, the various sacred sites (sidhes) they had created.

The Tuatha, under commission of the variously named Danu, Dana, or An of Ursa Major, came to Ireland to imprint it with divine consciousness and life. They also supervised Ireland's special dispensation: to cultivate a certain untainted quality from the original Garden of Eden for the rest of the Earth.

Rudolf Steiner explained in 1917 how Ireland had been set aside to preserve what the Garden of Eden was like *before* Lucifer facilitated the gift of free choice and access to the Tree of the Knowledge of Good and Evil—before the Fall of Man. The Tuatha's commission was to oversee the flowering of this. So Ireland, its landforms, people, and sacred sites maintain, unique among all the planet's landmasses, a pristine condition of matter from *before* the Fall of Man.

The Tuatha's task was to act as benevolent Watchers of the unfoldment of Ireland under these conditions and to be on hand to human clairvoyants seeking them out through the various sacred site portals into their ever-living realm.

Unlike Sumer, which was more of a celestial concourse with a great deal of continuous traffic from other stars and planets, Ireland was more of a self-contained, even insular, Land of Light with named and almost avuncular gods dedicated to preserving and evolving terrestrial aspects of the original Paradise.

See also: Anunnaki, Balor of the Evil Eye, Einherjar, Emerald, Eriu, Fall of Man, Fisher King, Giants, Holy Grail, Lucifer, River God, Seven Rishis.

UNDERWORLD

The Milky Way galaxy and all its dimensional levels as seen from the Upper World beyond form, guarded by Hades (the star Sirius).

Also known as Amenti, Cave of Machpelah, Celestial City of Samyamani, Duat, Gehenna, Hades, House of the Stars, Lake of Sperm, Lua-o-Milu (Pit or Cave of Milu), Mictlan, Sheol, Tech Duinn, Vastu, Well of Souls, Xibalba.

Description: In myths throughout the world, consistent mention is made of an Underworld, an infernal, grim realm of the dead usually accessed through a cave, rock, lake, or some kind of portal, and lying inside the Earth.

According to Sophocles, a rocky hill near Colonus in Greece is an Underworld entrance. Apollodorus tells us that Herakles descended to the Underworld through an entrance at Taenarum and that, at Hermione, facing the island of Hydra in Greece, there is a chasm that communicates with the infernal regions. Troezen is an Underworld exit once used by Heracles and Dionysus.

The Underworld in classical Greek and Roman culture was the place to which the culture hero such as Odysseus or Aeneas journeyed to consult with the dead. In classical thought, the Underworld was under the dominion of Lord Hades.

In Irish lore, the newly dead journey to the

Skellig Rocks off the Kelly coast on their way to *Tech Duinn,* the House of Donn, Lord of Death. At Knockfierna, in Ireland, you pass through a cleft in a rock to enter Donn's realm. Hawaiians say that, at Kahakaloa on Maui, there is an entrance to the Pit of Milu, Milu being the Polynesian Lord of Death; another entrance is at the head of the Waipio Valley on the big island of Hawaii, and ghostly processions were once seen marching down the Mahiki Road to enter the *Lua-o-Milu,* or Cave of Milu.

At Point Concepción near Santa Barbara, California, the souls of the Indian dead were said to process over land and into the Underworld *(Shimilaqsha)* through this location, which they called *Humqaq* or *Tolakwe,* the Western Gate; the Chumash, the site's traditional caretakers, considered Humqaq the most sacred site in all of California.

The Well of Souls *(Bir el-Arweh)* under the Dome of the Rock in Jerusalem is a cavern in which you can sometimes hear the voices of the Dead, their cries mingled with the rushing of the rivers of Paradise. At Bag Enderby, a tiny English hamlet in the village next to the birthplace of Sir Alfred, Lord Tennyson, you can stand before the old stone church and see the great closed gates of Hell.

The Biblical equivalent of the Underworld is referred to as the Cave of Machpelah. It is the first of seven portals the newly dead soul must pass through before reaching *Arabot*, the Seventh (highest) Heaven. It is near Paradise and under the supervision of Adam, the first human to die.

Generally, in Christian conceptions, the Underworld is a hellish realm of torture and misery, a place of punishment for "sins" and mortal transgressions. The earlier Judaic concepts of Sheol and Gehenna are similar in dark nuance.

Explanation: The conventional understanding of the Underworld is a confusing blur of two different but overlapping spiritual realms.

With regard to both levels of the Underworld, it is not accessed inside planet Earth. In terms of a spiritual topography, the Underworld is *above* our human, material world, accessed properly through the crown chakra on the head. It is an *Under*world only from the viewpoint of the eternal gods: It lies beneath their realm, in a slower vibratory level of reality—*under* their world, which could be called cosmic Earth (the created space for matter); thus the Underworld is inside the (cosmic) Earth.

In Greek myth, three principal gods were each assigned one-third of created reality: Zeus got the Air, Poseidon the Sea, and Hades got cosmic Fire. The realm of Hades, named after him, was later construed to be a hellish fire realm, but the greater part of Hades' actual responsibility got lost in this easy definition.

Hades is actually in charge of all the light (fire) of the galaxy. This makes more (and quicker) sense by presenting another of his guises: he is also the Hindu god Shiva, one of that religion's Trinity and known as the Destroyer. He is often depicted as dancing four-armed inside a ring of fire, his moving form filling it. That ring of fire is our Milky Way galaxy; in effect, holographically, every galaxy. Shiva can guard the galaxy because he exists outside of form and thus independent of it; that ring of fire is the essence of life within the galaxy, a cornucopia of forms.

In Hindu astronomy, Shiva (in his earlier form as Rudra) is associated with the star Sirius, our galaxy's brightest star in the throat of Canis Major, the Greater Dog. Rudra's task is to guard the Dwelling of the Stars—the entire galaxy. He is called *Vastospati* (Guardian of the *Vastu*) and the Hound of Heaven. Sirius is often called the Dog Star, standing for the entire Dog constellation (Canis Major).

Hades has a dog called Cerberus, and it has three heads, is fierce, and guards the Underworld. Osiris in Egyptian myth has his jackal-headed dog, Anubis. The essential equation is that the Underworld Lord *equals* his Dog. They are equivalent, interchangeable figures just as Shiva *is* the galaxy's Dog-Star guardian.

Shiva (Hades, Anubis, Canis Major, Cerberus, Sirius) guards the galaxy, dancing before its "front gate" at Sirius and within every atom in the galaxy, too. He is the true Lord of the Underworld when it is understood to mean the galaxy (underneath or behind him), and that is comprehended as a vast field of light and sentient beings—the stars. The ring of fire in this analogy is galactic perimeter, the edge of galactic light.

Guarding the galaxy also entails supervising the flow of consciousness from the Upper World, or what Hindu philosophers call the Uncreate (or the goddess Aditi, an expression of unbroken absolute consciousness; see Ocean of Milk) into the Lower World (Underworld), which is the realm of created form, both gross (physical stars) and subtle (the great Star-Angels who are their souls).

In Egyptian myth, Ra the Sun God sails in his solar barque through the Duat and its 12 stations. In Western astrology, we have the 12 signs of the zodiac or wedgelike divisions of galactic space headed by a constellation. Hindu astronomy has its own galactic space division into 27 regions or *Naksatras*. The King Arthur legends have their Round Table, a miniaturized galactic wheel.

These are each equivalent apportionments of the interior of Shiva's ring of fire, the light-filled galaxy—all experiential subdivisions of the Underworld.

Here is the link between the two Underworld nuances: Ra's solar barque enters the Duat (the Underworld or galaxy) at Amenti, the Land of the Dead in the far West, at the end of the sunlit day. This is the conventional understanding of Underworld, as Land of the Dead. But Amenti (or Hades, Cave of Machpelah, Gehenna, Lua-o-Milu [Cave of Milu], Mictlan, Sheol, Tech Duinn, Well of Souls, Xibalba) is also a legitimate and discretely bounded domain *within* the Duat, like a peach pit embedded in the greater mass of peach pith.

The Underworld as the Land of the Dead is, in fact, one of eight Celestial Cities as described in Hindu sacred cosmography arrayed about Mount Meru. Specifically, the Land of the Dead is called the Celestial City of Samyamani under the rulership of Yama (see Green Knight). Within Earth's visionary geography, there are 1,746 Underworld Entrances; these appear as massive, closed gates that open into the outer threshold of the Land of the Dead. All Entrances essentially lead to the same singular holographic Underworld, itself a copy (a hologram) of the galactic original within the astral plane around and above Earth.

Here is one way an Underworld Entrance may appear to psychic sight: Massive gates, hundreds of feet high, connected to equally high and massive circular walls set in a crystal basin in the landscape, occupying, in physical terms, several miles in diameter. Inside is a semicircular hall of mirrors; this is where the soul (or one experiencing a near-death experience) reviews one's life events. The three Judges of the Dead (as described in Greek myth; the Egyptians have more) hold the mirrors in which the soul sees itself spiritually, karmically naked.

Elsewhere in here, you may glimpse the Garden of Eden, the original astral archetype of the earthly Paradise (see Garden of Eden). Past the "front gates" (the Hall of the Three Judges of the Dead, or Halls of Maat in Egypt), you may get a glimpse of the whole place as if you stand at ground level in a gigantic sports stadium or an eighteenth-century European opera house the size of the Grand Canyon. You look up into the astral realm, into the complete Duat, where the star gods dwell along with their physical forms (the burning stars). Yama (Hades) stands in the center of this vast open realm with its many tiers and portals along the perimeter.

This Underworld, as Amenti, or the Land of the Dead, *overlaps* the entrance to the bigger Underworld, or the entire galaxy within Shiva's ring of fire. You enter the Land of the Dead–Underworld through the crown chakra atop the head, either at death or before death in a vision, clairvoyant visit, or near-death experience.

Among the eight Celestial Cities, this one is associated with the crown chakra, which in kundalini yoga is called the thousand-petaled Seat of Shiva—like a miniature, human context version of the Dog-Star Sirius in front of the galaxy. Paradoxically, the human body and all its energy fields and centers (chakras) below the crown chakra are also rightfully considered the Underworld.

From the top of the crown chakra down to the feet and out through the layers of the aura is the miniaturized, mirror-image Underworld that is the human being. From the crown chakra up, you pass into the Land of the Dead aspect of the Underworld and from there into the galactic level of Underworld. Access by the newly dead to these Underworld portals seems to assure a focused and even optimized entrance into the next realm of existence.

Equivalently at the galactic level, this is where Ra and his solar barque (the annual apparent transit of the Sun through the galaxy and its subtle aspects) leave the bright world at the end of his journey to enter the dark Night world.

Thus the Underworld, as the Land of the Dead, or a Celestial City, is the portal into the Underworld as the greater galaxy guarded by Shiva at Sirius.

See also: Anubis, Garden of Eden, Green Knight, Mount Meru, Ocean of Milk, Round Table, Trickster.

VALHALLA

An assemblage point for the Great White Brotherhood, spiritual adepts who "feast" on the Christ Consciousness and defend the world.

Also known as *Ananda-kanda* chakra, Da Derga's Hostel, Elysian Fields, Elysium, Jeweled Altar.

Description: In Norse myth, Valhalla, from the Old Norse *Valholl,* is the hall *(holl)* of those slain on the battlefield *(valr)*—the Hall of the Slain. The slain are called Einherjar ("lone fighters") and are brought to Valhalla, the great hall of Odin, Norse myth's high god of Asgard, by Odin's Valkyries, the female spirits who select those slain on the battlefield for admission to Valhalla.

Valhalla is located in Gladsheimr, a division of Asgard, the celestial realm of the gods, according to Norse myth. The hall is thatched with spears and shields, and a great array of the Einherjar's armor is displayed on the benches. Valhalla has 540 gates through which 800 Einherjar will one day stream at Ragnarok, the end of the world and the Twilight of the Gods, in the far future. Then the 432,000 Einherjar will aid Odin in the last defense of the world.

Meanwhile, the Einherjar spend their days battling one another, then feasting and drinking in the evening, free of all injury and pain. They feast on Saehrimnir, Odin's boar whose flesh is consumed every day then is replenished by the next morning; they drink mead from the udders of Odin's goat, Heidrun.

Essentially, Valhalla is depicted as a Norse paradise for slain warriors who spend their time preparing with Odin for the final apocalyptic battle at Ragnarok.

An equivalent description is found in Irish myth in Da Derga's Hostel, where prodigies of the battlefield feast and drink endlessly and, to a lesser extent, in the Greek description of Elysian Fields, a happy land and Island of the Blessed where a few privileged mortals, such as the war heroes Menelaus, Achilles, Ajax, and others from the Trojan War, may dwell in blissful comfort.

Explanation: Valhalla is not a retirement paradise for dead, militaristic Vikings physically slain in war, but a metaphor for a peer group of spiritual adepts. The Einherjar is a Norse description of the Great White Brotherhood, an assemblage of spiritual adepts, enlightened sages, angels, ascended masters, and benevolent intelligences from other star systems in alignment with God (Odin).

They are slain in battle in the sense that, through many lifetimes of inner work and transmutation, they have mastered all aspects of themselves, the body, matter, consciousness, and the inner dragon (kundalini and its *siddhis*, or magical powers) and have aligned themselves with the Christ Consciousness, symbolized by Saehrimnir, the boar whose flesh is inexhaustible. They continually feast on the boar meat, which means, they continuously enjoy or devour the presence of the Christ Consciousness; even more precisely, they are always one with it, having permanently illuminated that divine aspect of themselves in the "battle."

They defend the world—Earth, solar system, Milky Way galaxy, and the cosmos—against entropy, unconsciousness, ignorance, and retrograde evolution. In practical terms, for the Einherjar, Ragnarok must be resisted every day.

Valhalla is accessible by living, embodied humans through visionary, psychic perception at 360 doors found in Earth's visionary geography. Here one may witness and even partake in, to a degree, the endless feasting of the spiritual champions. Some locations include Monticello in Charlottesville, Virginia; Rondvassbhu, Rondane Mountains, in Norway; Ivy Thorn Hill, Glastonbury, England; Saint Paul's Cathedral, Ludgate Hill, London, England.

Valhalla may appear to clairvoyant perception as a vast sports stadium filled with 432,000 enlightened sages resembling thousands of sparkling, sun-drenched jewels. This geomantic feature is an inherent part of the inner heart chakra, called *Ananda-kanda*, expressed in both the human and the planet. One of the esoteric features of this chakra is a jeweled altar, which is a precise visual metaphor for the sports stadium of 432,000 sparkling, differently hued adepts.

See also: Bifrost, Da Derga's Hostel, Einherjar, Glass Mountain, Saehrimnir, Seven Rishis, Valkyries, Wild Hunt.

VALKYRIES

Guardians of the nine spheres of the astral Tree of Life, led by the Lady of the Lake, and validators of human initiation into this Tree or level of reality.

Also known as the Nine Muses, Morgan le Fay and her sisters, Morrigan, Morrigna, Odin's Girls, Wish Girls.

Description: Known popularly as the female demons of death, the Valkyries are described in Norse myth as fierce female spirits on the battlefield. The name *Valkyrjar* derives from the Old Norse *valr*, for the corpses laying on a battlefield, and *kjosa*, to choose; hence *Valkyrja*, "she who selects the dead." Thus the Valkyries are those who choose warriors slain on the battlefield to live in Valhalla, Odin's great Hall of the Slain in Asgard, the gods' residence.

The Valkyries, who number three, nine, 12, or 13, and are all accorded names, are sometimes called "Odin's Girls" and "Wish Girls" because they are the battle maidens who fulfill his requests. They are beautiful, golden-haired, and have dazzling white arms. They ride great white horses, are attired in shining helmets and armor, and often their sudden appearance among men heralds a coming battle. Those warriors who receive a kiss from a Valkyrie are often next to be killed.

At Valhalla, dressed in long white robes, they serve mead to the Einherjar, the "lone fighters" chosen to sit with Odin at the banqueting tables. They select the most worthy among those slain in battle to journey to Valhalla, but sometimes they intervene in battles so as to assure a place at Valhalla for their favorites.

Similarly, they are capable of falling in love with human mortals, best typified by the romance of Brynnhildr (Brünhilde, meaning "Bright Battle"), chief of the Valkyries, and Siegfried (Sigurd), mortal dragon-slayer. She defied Odin and sacrificed herself to dwell, unconscious (in an "enchanted sleep"), in a flame-encircled hall on a mountain. Siegfried penetrates the wall of fire and spends a night with Brynnhildr, an act which frees Brynnhildr from her pyre-prison so she may marry Siegfried.

Irish myth remembers another, though fiercer form of the Valkyries called Morrigan, or the Three

Morrigan. Morrigan, which might mean "Phantom Queen, Death Queen, or Great Queen," was a goddess of the Tuatha de Danann, Ireland's ancient gods who now live in the *sidhes* (otherwordly dwellings), hill-forts, and megalithic enclosures that provide access to their otherworldly domain. As a war goddess, Morrigan was sometimes joined by (or sometimes associated with) three others: Babd ("scalding crow"), Nemain (she spreads panic), and Macha (speedy horse).

She was a gigantic female who foretold the future of those about to battle; like a bard, she sometimes sang her favorites to victory; she would swoop over the corpse-lined battlefield in a bird form to devour the bodies of the slain; and she had a strong sexual appetite for the leading mortal heroes, such as Cuchulainn, whom she punished with injuries and battlefield obstacles when he declined her favors. She lusted after Cuchulainn, but was equally formidable protecting him.

The Morrigan is an accomplished shapeshifter. She can appear as a beautiful, young woman; an eel; wolf; red heifer; carrion bird; crown; raven; an old woman milking a cow; the war fury; or the Washer at the Ford, a prophetess who foretells the doom of warriors as she washes their armor and weapons.

The story finds echoes in the Arthurian mythos in which King Arthur, mortally wounded at the Battle of Camlann by his illegitimate son, Mordred, is ferried on the mystic barge to Avalon, the Celtic Otherworld, by three spectral females: the Lady of the Lake (sometimes called Nimuë); his mother, Ygraine; and his half-sister, Morgan le Fay (one of nine sisters). King Arthur, the slain and chosen warrior, is escorted on the verge of death to the Celtic Valhalla by the Celtic version of the Valkyries, the three women on the mystic barge.

Explanation: The key to understanding the Valkyries is to perceive them through the Arthurian mythos, which maintains a purer expression of them.

First, some equivalencies: Morgan le Fay is Brynnhildr; Nimuë, one guise of the Lady of the Lake who gave Arthur his first sword, and Morgause, Arthur's aunt, who schemed against him and seduced him to produce his nemesis, Mordred, are two of the Irish Morrigan, Morgan making the third.

Their exact correspondences with the three named figures of Babd, Nemain, and Macha are not clear, as the Arthurian mythos gives them a different valence. With Morgan (and her eight sisters), we have the Arthurian version of the war goddesses, the Morrigan, and it is these three women (Ygraine, Arthur's mother, is an accretion and does not belong in the group) who ferry the dying Arthur to Avalon, the Celtic equivalent of the Norse Valhalla.

As Morgan has eight sisters, and she is the ninth, it is safe to say there are nine Valkyries in three groups, according to their specialty or focus of consciousness, typified by Morgan, the Lady of the Lake, and Morgause.

The actual key to the meaning of the Valkyries and their war-goddess function, or, in the Celtic formation, the three women with Arthur on the Avalon ferry, is to step out of the disorienting militaristic, battlefield guise and penetrate the symbols.

The Lady of the Lake in the Arthurian stories gives Arthur his second sword and remains his mentor throughout his career. This is a calmer version of how the Irish saw the Morrigan constantly trying to seduce Cuchulainn; it is akin to the Teutonic version in which Brynnhildr (Morgan le Fay) is in love with Siegfried (another version of King Arthur). In the Celtic version, Morgause does sexually seduce the young Arthur, with seemingly disastrous consequences.

An important clue to this complex initiatory scheme is the statement in the Arthurian stories that Morgan stole the scabbard for Arthur's first sword. She didn't steal it; rather, Morgan and her eight sisters *are* the scabbard. In a condensed way, they are the mystic barge, too; in fact, the barge is the scabbard.

These three women are the guardians of the nine aspects of the astral world (called *Yetzirah,* or "Formation," one of the Four Worlds or Trees of Life described in Qabala), each embodying one of its nine aspects (or in Qabalistic terms, its nine spheres of light, or *Sefiroth,* on the Yetzirah Tree of Life—the one closest to the physical world). They are the same as the Greeks' Nine Muses.

Qabala traditionally depicts the Tree of Life as ten spheres arrayed upon three parallel pillars. The first sphere is the exalted, transcendental one attributed to Odin; the lower nine are attributed to his Wish Girls, with three in each of the three pillars (with an esoteric eleventh sphere in the central pillar); and Arthur, Siegfried, and the candidate for initiation (the warrior "chosen" and "slain" on the battlefield) being the tenth, bottom sphere, pertaining to embodiment.

Odin, as above the nine spheres of the Lake, is, in effect, Lord of the Waters, making him functionally equivalent to the Greek Poseidon, King of the Sea. Both Odin and Poseidon here are expressions of the Supreme Being in Yetzirah.

The Valkyries, or Morgan and her eight sisters, are the gatekeepers for the Yetzirah or World of Formation (astral) Tree of Life and its mysteries. When humans have sufficiently mastered a level of training, insight, and psychic development, they are invited (ferried, chosen) to join their new spiritual peers in the great feasting Hall of the Slain, Valhalla, or the Celtic Avalon. Technically, these are not the same: Valhalla is a specific division of the astral world, while Avalon is a name that usually encompasses the entirety of the astral plane.

This level of mastery is a kind of death, and it is metaphorically accurate to say they are slain on the battlefield, but it is more a battle of inner transmutation of the Shadow, the personality and its conflicts, kundalini and its magical powers.

The Valkyries are the scabbard or matrix of Light out of which Arthur draws (and creates) his sword of insight, or his level of psychic penetration into the Mysteries. The Lady of the Lake does not give Arthur (Siegfried) this sword; he earns it, and she allows him to have it, or simply confirms his achievement, because he is able to extract this level of wisdom and wield the necessary focused concentration (the sword again) in and out of the astral world she oversees.

The Lady of the Lake is the queen of the entire astral plane, symbolized by the ancients as a vast lake (as in lake of Light) but also as a Tree of Light and a nine-jeweled scabbard from which Arthur draws (or congeals) his sword. Morgause, Morgan, and Nimuë represent three aspects of the Lady of the Lake, whose "Lake" is the World of Yetzirah, the astral seedbed of physical reality.

In the end, to understand the meaning of the Valkyries or Morrigan, you have to invert the story and read it backward or in a mirror. The Irish say one of the guises of the Morrigan is the Washer at the Ford, the crone cleansing the armor of a slain (or soon to be killed) warrior in the stream. Rather, the Morrigan is facilitating the candidate for spiritual adeptship to claim his sword from her. In a sense, she (all the Valkyries as protectors of Yetzirah) allows the sword to be withdrawn from the scabbard, which is the nine Light spheres she guards.

The ramification of the story, interpreted in this way, is that the living hero (Arthur, Siegried, and any human candidate for this level of initiation) is ultimately meant to wield the astral sword in the world of living people. It is, of course, not a fighting weapon, but a means of penetration into the Mysteries and a way of grounding that penetration and the insight gained in the human realm.

Earth's visionary geography has been provided with multiple copies of the entrance into the Lady of the Lake's domain. These portals into the Lake (Yetzirah) are called Pointer's Balls, although in Arthurian myth they were known as Nimuë's Crystal Cave. There are 174,060 of them around the Earth. Selected locations include Ponter's Ball [sic] in Glastonbury, England; Ashlawn, Charlottesville, Virginia; Acropolis, Athens,

Greece; Kerkado tumulus, Carnac, France; and Calendar I Site, South Royalton, Vermont.

See also: Avalon, Einherjar, King Arthur, Lady of the Lake, Morgan le Fay, Valhalla.

VISHNU'S DISCUS

A mobile focus of conscious awareness emanating from Shambhala, under the direction of the Christ, to further human spirituality.

Also known as Ajna chakra, Mobile Shambhalic Focus, Sudarsana.

Description: The Discus or solar wheel is one of Vishnu's possessions, meant to symbolize an aspect of his cosmic puissance. Vishnu is one of the three primary gods of Hinduism, known as the Preserver and Pervader, and equivalent to the Western Christ and Logos (Word).

The word *Sudarsana* means "Beauteous Sight" or "Fair to See," and the Discus is usually described as a wheel with six spokes, much like a six-petaled lotus. In Hindu thought, it represents the universal Mind and Vishnu's limitless power by which he creates and destroys all the realms and forms in the universe, all of which have the quality of revolving (like a wheel).

At the center of the wheel is a sacred syllable *(Hrm)* understood to signify the still, unmoving center, while the rest of the wheel (rim and spokes) represents *maya,* the heavenly power of illusion. In this sense, the Sudarsana is like a controlled hurricane, with the calm eye of the hurricane being the magic syllable and the furiously spinning part the rim and spokes (maya).

In India's sacred literature, the Sudarsana is described as a celestial weapon, one of many different kinds attributed to the gods. It is a fiery wheel, sometimes said to have one thousand spokes, which Vishnu wields in his right hand. The Discus resides in the sky (or celestial heavens), resembles a wheel (called a chakra), and comes back to Vishnu's hand after he throws it.

He uses its razor-sharp circular edge to slice off the heads of demons and agents of spiritual darkness, even if they are the size of mountains; the Discus also emits sparks of fire, beams of light, blasts, and lightning, when needed; it is capable of burning down entire cities, and Vishnu often aims it at enemy cities. In one throw it can fell, cut, and burn thousands in an opposing army. The *Mahabharata* describes the Sudarsana as fearsome, terrible, invincible, supreme. In action against enemies, the Sudarsana shone like a horrifying, roaring fire.

India's spiritual founder, Bharata, after whom the country was originally named, used the Sudarsana to prepare the Indian subcontinent for habitation. His use of the Sudarsana, clearly a mark of spiritual advancement and potency, earned him the title of Chakravartin, which means the universal ruler who wields the revolving wheel for the benefit of the people.

Explanation: Vishnu's Discus is a beam of Vishnu's searing consciousness emanating as a mobile focus from the Celestial City of the gods, Shambhala.

One of the features of Earth's visionary geography and its numerous geomantic aspects is a hierarchy of chakras, or subtle consciousness centers. These are chakras ("spinning wheels") in the geomythic body of Albion, a cosmogonic figure expressed at three levels on Earth. Sudarsana concerns the sixth chakra in a series of nine major and 72 minor, or 81 global chakras in all.

The sixth chakra in the human is located between the two eyes and is known as the brow chakra, Third Eye, or Ajna chakra. Its quality is authority, command, and unlimited power; it is often described as gold in color or as a white circle with two luminescent petals; and its function is psychic perception.

The primary sixth chakra for Earth (the Earth chakras exist in a hierarchy of levels) is located in Shambhala and is known as the Mobile Shambhalic Focus, a kind of slowly moving celestial roving eye or focused beam. Shambhala, its point of origin, is widely regarded in esoteric circles as the true seat of planetary government and authority, occupied by a conclave of spiritual masters, post-humans, angels, and enlightened beings from other stars.

The Focus is resident in a given locality for 100 years, but there is a 50-year buildup and a 50-year decline, making it 200 years that it focuses on one place. Over the vast history of Earth, presumably it has focused on nearly every area of geomantic importance, and in the Hindu tales of the Chakravartin, you see evidence of its benign use to prepare a landscape for human life.

Presently, the Sudarsana is focused on Glastonbury in Somerset, England. In previous epochs, it has focused on Mount Kailash in Tibet and Jerusalem in Israel, among many other locations. The focus of conscious awareness of the sixth chakra of Earth moves periodically to resonate equally through each culture, creed, and religion like a peripatetic living Master.

Although the Indian tales like to dramatize the potency of Vishnu's Discus and its awesome enemy-killing powers, the real enemies are darkness and ignorance, and the real death exacted is the destruction of apathy and atheism.

Imagine sitting in the energy field or emanation of a celestial being of complete enlightenment, wisdom, world-creating power, love, and compassion, of being held in this undeviating benevolent regard for 200 years. Such a Focus will certainly catalyze and facilitate spiritual growth and understanding and eventually destroy by fire all errors of cognition and action (sin or karma).

The Discus or Focus is attributed to Vishnu (Christ) because he is the head of the spiritual hierarchies in Shambhala, but the Focus is also from Shambhala itself and all of its spiritual and celestial energies and beings. Seen over the vast stretch of planetary time, it is accurate to say the Focus is a mobile point, never fixed in one location for long, and continually moving, like an always-open eye in the sky continually traveling over Earth's surface.

See also: Albion, Chakravartin, Eriu, Shambhala.

VOCUB CAQUIX

The Mayan perception of the angelic order called the Ofanim, who often take cultural manifestation as a great celestial bird.

Also known as El Ave de Pico Ancho, Fauces de Cielo, Principal Bird Deity, Seven Macaws.

Description: Vocub Caquix is described as a monstrous, self-inflated bird who presided over the murky twilight after the Flood and before the Sun and Moon came out, says the *Popol Vuh* of the Quiche-Maya of Central America.

The *Popol Vuh* recounts how, in ancient days when only early dawn lit the world, the Mayan Hero Twins Hunahpu and Xbalanque ran toward Vocub Caquix (also called Seven Macaws) who was perching in his fruit tree. They planned to fight him. They criticized Seven Macaws for magnifying his importance, for puffing himself up, for wishing only for unsurpassed greatness.

According to Mayan legend, Seven Macaws claimed that his face reached into the distance and his light illuminated the world so that the Sun and Moon were occluded. His eyes and nest were of metal and lit up the world; his teeth glittered like jewels, and some said they were turquoise, blue sapphires, or emerald. By virtue of his wonderful teeth, he was lord and king, Seven Macaws stated. His plumage was splendid, composed of precious metals and gemstones; his face was framed by jeweled metal plates; his great white beak shone into the far distance like the Moon.

I am the Sun, the light, the genius, and the mouths of all humanity, Seven Macaws said. He was definitely the brightest being in Creation prior to the separation of the Sun and Moon, but the Hero Twins saw him as a false sun before the dawn of time. Seven Macaws even claimed dominion over time.

In addition to his riches, brilliance, gems, metals, jewels, jade, and great light, Seven Macaws had two sons, each a prodigy. Zipacna ("Mountain Maker") built up the great mountains (six are named) of Earth at the dawn of time and in a single night. Cabraca ("Earthquake"), the second son, moved and softened the mountains as needed; he shook the great mountains from time to time. The first son boasted he could move the Earth, the second that he could overturn the sky.

The Hero Twins, meanwhile, wanted to kill Seven Macaws; though the Twins were gods, the first mother and father of humanity could not be born until Seven Macaws' influence was removed. Also, they considered his self-magnification evil and arrogant and thus harmful to the world.

First they fired a blowgun at Seven Macaws and injured his precious turquoise teeth, breaking his mouth. Seven Macaws broke off Hunahpu's arm. Then the Hero Twins tricked the great bird. Accompanied by their grandfather Great White Peccary and grandmother Great White Tapir, they induced Seven Macaws to ask the grandparents to ease the terrible pain in his teeth and cure them. Posing as dentists, they offered to pull them out and replace them with teeth made of ground bone.

They removed the great jeweled teeth and also plucked out Seven Macaws' injured silver eyes, collecting the jewels and metals from both, replacing them with mere white corn. His greatness and splendor having departed him, the Earth giant—and his wife, Chimalamat—died.

Other names for Vocub Caquix included *El Ave de Pico Ancho* ("The Bird with the Broad Beak") and *Fauces de Cielo* ("Jaws of Heaven") of the Zapotecs of Mexico, and Principal Bird Deity, another Mayan classification. In the earliest Mayan representations of this bird, his qualities were more positive, with depictions of him appearing as huge stucco sculptures at the pyramids of Cerros and Nakbe in central Mexico. Certain early Mayan kings used his image (often holding a snake in his mouth) to symbolize their temporal power. In the Mayan Classic Period (circa 300–900 A.D.), the great bird was depicted in stone carvings in a proud posture, its wings stretched out wide, and wearing a large necklace.

In fact, in the earliest known days of Mayan civilization (circa 200–100 B.C.), Vocub Caquix was not a boastful imposter, but possibly the supreme god of the Maya, a position that seemed to alternate between him and Itzamna, god of writing, curing, and divination (like the Greek Hermes). In those early days, Vocub Caquix exerted a powerful and benign influence over the Maya.

Explanation: Vocub Caquix is a filtered perception through Mayan culture of the angelic family called Ofanim. This angelic order, capable of 40.3 million simultaneous manifestations, often shows up as a huge, seemingly ominous bird and has expressed itself this way as the Eagle (Toltec), Garuda (Hinduism), Simurgh (Persian), Thunderbird (Native American), and Ziz (Judaic).

As an angelic order, the Ofanim (from the Hebrew *ofan* for "wheels") is said to be so brilliant that their light illuminates *Arabot,* the Seventh Heaven, in Judaic lore. Their intent has never been to eclipse the Sun and Moon nor to magnify their importance to make people regard them as a false sun; rather, the Mayan description is inverted: The Ofanim's celestial light *precedes* the Sun and Moon and if their brilliance (their face) fills the entire sky, that is how the Supreme Being intended this angelic family to be.

For peculiar cultural reasons, the Ofanim in their giant bird form have tended to inspire a paranoid perception in some areas. Both the Toltec Eagle and the Mayan Vocub Caquix present the Ofanim as an Earth Monster best avoided by shamans (Toltec) or removed from the world due to its flagrant immodesty (Mayan). This is in marked contrast to the almost ecstatic, benevolent portrayal of the Ofanim as Garuda (Hinduism) and Simurgh (Persian) and the respectful awe of their numinosity as the Thunderbird (Native American).

The Mayan description of jeweled teeth and precious metals and gems adorning the face, nest, and wings of Vocub Caquix is matched by Hebrew angelologies, which say the Ofanim's presence is marked by innumerable eyes and wings, each angel wearing 72 sapphires in his robe and four emeralds in his crown. Another tabulation says that the Prince of the Ofanim has 16 faces, 100 wings on each side of his body, and 8,466 eyes. Esoterically, this means the Ofanim can be in many places at once and can *see* every conceivable side to an issue.

Vocub Caquix's claim to have dominion over time because, in fact, the units of time reside in his great body, has actual merit when seen differently. The Ofanim family, among the 40 angelic orders, is one of the oldest and first created. Its age, in human time reckoning, is approximately 60,480,000,000 years and its scope of responsibility some 18 billion galaxies, all with sentient life forms.

It's not that the Ofanim have dominion over time; rather they exist before and after Time, on a planetary, galactic, and cosmic level. They are not bound by time (or the speed of light) and can be before, behind, in, and after every event.

The time of Vocub Caquix is given as just after the Flood, but before the advent of human life and the separation of the Sun and Moon as discrete objects. This is the formative time of the planet's visionary geography, when its numerous geomantic and physical features were being elaborated by the gods, as remembered in various terms such as the Dreamtime (Australian Aborigines), Zep Tepi ("First Occasion," Egyptian), and Hurqalya (Persian).

Like the Monster-Slayer myth from the North American Navajo, in the story of Vocub Caquix, the Hero Twins are encountering the primal forces existent in our world at the start of planetary life. It is not a question of killing or even subduing them, but rather one of assimilating and grounding their energies in the landscape.

The Ofanim have been central to the creation, grounding, and maintenance of Earth's visionary geography and to humanity and the planet itself. The Ofanim as an angelic order do not have a "wife" or "sons," but some of their manifestations may receive particular emphasis and seem to be separate agents.

In their Hindu form as the elephant god Ganesh, for example, they are called Lord of the Hosts, and these Hosts are the *Ganas,* deities in service of Shiva, one of Hinduism's trinity of original gods. The Mayan equivalent of Shiva is Itzamna, and two more familiar forms of the same include Hermes (Greek) and Thoth (Egyptian), described as gods of writing, initiation, and communication. The Ofanim work closely with Shiva in all his forms and often use his energy.

Thus Zipacna and Cabraca are active expressions of the Ofanim, seemingly individualized to express certain key geomantic functions on Earth. Zipacna is the mover of mountains because the Ofanim's light is present at all holy mountains (1,746) by way of a geomantic feature called domes. Cabraca creates earthquakes in the sky the same way Thunderbird's thunder roars through the heavens and across the Earth, trembling all souls with its spiritual potency.

Regarding their presence being an obstacle to the creation of humanity, the Mayan account again has inverted the truth. The Ofanim are vital to the emergence of sentient, self-conscious life forms, including humanity. They were commissioned to put reflexive self-awareness into human souls inhabiting material bodies, and their light (and presence within all humans) would be a seed for the elaboration of higher states of consciousness (celestial awareness).

Obviously, the Hero Twins did not slay, declaw, or detooth Seven Macaws, but they may represent some initial resistance by the gods to the project. In parallel fashion, in their Hindu guise as Garuda, the celestial bird-mount for Vishnu (the Hindu Christ), the Ofanim met a great deal of opposition from the gods when they "stole" the Soma (nectar of immortality) and trashed the gods' heavenly residences.

The true meaning of the account is that, under commission by the Supreme Being, the Ofanim put self-aware consciousness into the human body, an act or upgrade some gods opposed.

The fruit tree that Vocub Caquix lived in, and on whose fruit he subsisted, is the biblical Tree of Life. The Persian Simurgh, a mystical, magical bird who aids kings and heroes, lived at the top of the Haoma (or Soma) Tree, associated with immortality, eternal consciousness, and closeness to God, just as the Norse Eagle perched atop Odin's Yggdrasil tree (see Yggdrasil).

See also: Dreamtime, Ganesh, Garuda, Hurqalya, Monster-Slayer, Phoenix, Simurgh, Thunderbird, Yggdrasil, Zep Tepi, Ziz.

WASTELAND

A condition of spiritual impoverishment in which all of matter, including body, Nature, and planet, suffers due to humanity's cumulative pain and existential amnesia about its own soul origins, purpose, and history.

Also known as Desert, Isfet, Koyaanisqatsi, Logres.

Description: The term was popularized in the early twentieth century in T. S. Eliot's famous poem *The Waste Land* (1922), in which he characterized modern culture as a heap of broken images, a land of stony rubbish, a dead tree that provides no shelter, dry stones, a beating sun, and no trace of water—a desert.

But Eliot got the term from the medieval Grail sagas in which the Wasteland resulted from the misuse of a divine sword by the Fisher King.

That misuse was called the Dolorous Stroke. The variously named Fisher King or Grail King grievously wounds himself with the Sword of David due to a lack of knowledge in its proper use. The Sword of David came from the giant Goliath whom David overcame; it was handed down through many generations to the Fisher King.

The Dolorous Stroke not only wounds the Fisher King, transforming him from the Rich Fisher King to the Maimed Fisher King, it also blights the land. Crops fail, drought prevails, all of Nature loses its life force, and the people of the Fisher King's realm similarly decline in morality, well-being, and spirituality. King, land, and people suffer deeply until the Grail Knight redeems them.

Sometimes the Wasteland is called Logres, also a term for the physical aspects of Britain, to distinguish it from Sarras, the homeland of the Holy Grail.

Explanation: The Dolorous Stroke caused the Wasteland. This mythic equation refers to first generation humanity's misuse of consciousness and the divinely given psychic powers called *siddhis* and symbolized by a great sword. The sword came from Goliath, who was an Elohim (member of an angelic order; see Giants) temporarily in human giant form in the earliest days of the Earth to instruct humanity. The sword represents the protocols for consciousness and how to create and change reality; first-generation humanity used it for self-centered magic.

More acutely, though, the Wasteland refers to the more recent experience of humanity. The Fisher King is an outer and inner figure; as an inner figure, he is that part of every human who potentially has access to the deep memory of the history of one's soul, its origin, nature, purpose, and biography. If one cannot access that memory, then the Fisher King, once rich, is now wounded or maimed. This refers to a compromise in the energy circuit connecting the root with the crown chakra, the necessary connection to precipitate vast memory.

If the majority of humans cannot access their soul's information, then the outer expression of the Fisher King comes to reflect this: He is the Maimed King.

The consequence of not being able to remember one's ultimate origins and purpose leads to a condition of chronic existential ignorance: Why am I here? This question goes unanswered because the necessary ingredients for a satisfying answer cannot be acquired through the higher functions of consciousness. All of matter begins to suffer: The body, the outer environment, the planet, all come under this pall of not-knowing, of this existential amnesia. This spiritual pain and disorientation permeate the world and create the dry and blighted Wasteland.

The general psychic and spiritual conditions of twenty-first-century humanity largely exemplify the qualities of the Wasteland at its most intense. Largely, all expressions of matter, from the body to the kingdoms of Nature, are abused, exploited, polluted, sick, and treated like soulless, throwaway mechanisms.

In classical Egyptian thought, the Wasteland is a condition known as *isfet,* an entropic state in which the original spiritual rationality of Maat has dissipated from the world. Maat, both the personified goddess and the abstract quality of law, justice, and order, was implicit in Earth's visionary geography. It is the expression of the cosmic logic and rationality inherently part of this planetwide layout. Isfet, in contrast, is the condition of this matrix today, after millennia of entropy and inadequate or, increasingly, nonexistent maintenance.

Another metaphor for this condition is the Desert, which, in Hindu esoteric thought, means material existence not watered by bliss or truth.

Though the Hopi of the American Southwest do not speak in terms of the Wasteland, it is implicit in their beliefs and practices. The Hopi say that when they follow the Hopi Life Plan as taught by the ancient ancestors, then the *kachinas,* or "rain power beings" from the San Francisco Peaks near Flagstaff, Arizona, will do their part in bringing sufficient rainfall to their crops. When the Hopi depart from their ways of balance with the land and cease to honor Mother Earth, then the kachinas do not help, drought prevails, and their life suffers. For the Hopi, the inner and outer aspects of the Wasteland mirror each other.

Koyaanisqatsi is a Hopi word meaning "life out of balance" (also the title of a 1982 film), and it is a fitting description from another viewpoint of the Wasteland.

T. S. Eliot's observations are apt, too: Our myths, stories, fables, legends, and dream and psychic lives are largely disregarded, ignored, or viewed with noncomprehension, as an inert heap of outmoded, useless, jejune tales from humanity's infancy rather than as rich, life-sustaining spiritual insights. All the fruits of humanity's psychic past and its deep understanding of the web of life are for many people today at best an unedifying, mute archive of ancient history.

When Eliot said that death had undone so many, one interpretation of this is that due to the unredeemed Dolorous Stroke, much of humanity is dead to the spirit—that is, they are materialists and atheists at heart despite religious affiliations that might persuade them otherwise. Many are spiritually dead, oblivious not only to the spirit, but also to their own unexpiated pain, suffering, and uncompleted karma, all pushed out of consciousness into the Shadow.

This Shadow takes on a life of its own as a kind of alternate individuality known in the Grail myths as Klingsor, enemy of the Grail and the reason the Fisher King cannot be healed. Klingsor is the King of the Wasteland.

Similarly, Earth's visionary geography, the subtle but complex web of energy relationships and geomantic features that support the physical world, is neglected, entropic, and, in many cases, psychically polluted—today a Wasteland.

The antidote or cure for the Wasteland is the Grail Quest: the systematic spiritual process of reacquiring deep soul memory in the context of Earth's numerous sacred sites and their celestial connections, healing humans and planet.

See also: Antichrist, Dolorous Stroke, Earth Changes, Fisher King, Giants, Grail Castle, Grail Knight, Holy Grail, Klingsor, Ragnarok, Zep Tepi.

WHITE BULL

An animal symbol for the strength, might, potency, and awesome activity of the Light emitted by the male aspect of the Supreme Being.

Also known as Apis Bull, Bhrngi, Bull of Heaven, Bull of Israel, Geush Urvun, Goshuurun, Hadhayosh, Merwer, Mnves, Nandi, Nandikesvara, Nandin, Sarsaok, Taranus, Vrishabha.

Description: Several expressions of the high god in different myth systems, such as Zeus in the Greek pantheon and Shiva in Hinduism, take the form of a white bull of dazzling brightness when it suits their goals. In Zeus's case, it is to fulfill amorous desires for mortal but beautiful human females, such as Europa.

Europa was gamboling by the seashore, possibly in Phoenicia near Tyre or Sidon, when Zeus became filled with desire for her. He assumed the form of a white bull of dazzling brightness, with jeweled crescent horns. He seduced Europa with his meekness, lay down before her, allowed her to adorn his horns with wreaths of blossoms, then when she climbed on his back, leaped up, entered the sea, and swam to Crete where he coupled with her in his cave.

Hindu myth describes how Shiva, the Destroyer and Lord of Sleep, one of Hinduism's three major deities, assumes a white bull shape or uses it as his vehicle. This bull is called *Nandi* ("Joyful," "He Who Pleases," or "The Happy One") or *Nandikesvara* ("Lord of Gladness"); it is white as snow, its body huge, its eyes soft brown, its horns as hard as diamonds with sharp red points capable of tearing up the Earth. Nandi wanders around India looking for a mate, sometimes with Shiva riding him. Then he is called *Bhrngi,* "Wanderer."

Nandi is sometimes represented as having a bull's head and human torso, very much like the Greek conception of the Minotaur ("Bull of Minos"). Nandi is also depicted in temples as a white bull lying prostrate before the image of Shiva; worshippers, before entering the temple, touch Nandi's testicles, understanding that they are ultimately the source of the seeds of life.

Similarly, the bull represents the potency of sexual desire and lust, but Shiva riding the bull means mastery of that; it also suggests cosmic order, Dharma, and is sometimes called unfathomable. Nandi also embodies male procreative strength and fertility, considered Shiva's attributes.

The bull's attributes of tireless, even uncontrolled, fertility, ferocious vitality, irresistible might, male impulsiveness, and the powers of protean creation illustrate more aspects of Shiva. Shiva's archaic form, Rudra, is depicted as a savage, bellowing bull, whose sperm flows everywhere, fertilizing all the worlds.

Nandi is guardian of all Shiva's temples, the provider of celestial music for his cosmic dance of bliss, *Ananda Tandava,* and the protector of all animals.

As for the whiteness, Hindu thought says that Shiva is as white as camphor and his limbs shine like jewels. The whiteness is Light, the all-pervading consciousness whose form is knowledge and whose whiteness is the source of all differentiated forms, just as white exists before and after the rainbow spectrum. Shiva is called the White One and wears a shining white garment; all his appurtenances (bull, garland, sacred thread, and banner) are brilliantly white.

The Apis Bull of Egypt was considered an incarnation or god form of Osiris. It was also called Mnves or Merwer and was sacred to Ra, the Sun god, himself called the Bull of Heaven because he daily impregnated the sky goddess, Nut. The Apis Bull's cult center was Memphis, also the cult home of Ptah, so the Apis Bull came to be seen as Ptah's "glorious soul" reappearing on Earth. Later, Ptah merged into Osiris and the bull was the soul incarnation of him instead.

Other ancient mythical White Bull expressions included Yahweh as the "Bull of Israel," emphasizing the god's might; the first letter of the Hebrew alphabet, considered the most sacred and potent of all 26, is *Aleph,* which means "bull or oxen" and suggests, Qabalists say, worldly reality and the lower animal soul that relates instinctively to physical creation.

Teshub, the Hittite-Hurrian Sun god, was shown as a bull or riding one; the Syrian-Phoenician Sun-god Baal, prime deity of fertility for soil and flocks, was symbolized by a bull. In Celtic England, the white bull was known as

Taranus, the Thunder god, expressing divine strength in manifestation, the roaring, invincible power of the Heavens. Hindu lore also speaks of Vrishabha, the cosmic bull, who stands motionless at the hub of the cosmic wheel of the world and sets it turning.

In Persian myth, the world's first animal was the "uniquely created bull," as the ancient texts call it, who was white and as bright as the Moon. This beast was called *Hadhayosh* (in Pahlavi, *Sarsaok*). It lived on the bank of the river Veh Daiti, which flowed east out of the Vourukasha Sea, a paradisal, otherworldly body of water in Persian myth. Persian myth also says that early humans rode upon this ox's broad back as it crossed the Vourukasha Sea in primordial days. In the End Days, an ambrosia will be made from this bull's fat and *haoma* (Soma).

This cosmic bull was also sometimes called *Geush Urvan* (or *Goshuurun*); it was so vast that it held in it all the seeds of every animal and plant species, and it grazed the Earth for 3,000 years.

Zoroastrian tradition says that this primal bull was slain by Angra Mainyu (Ahriman), the Evil Spirit, and its seed transported to the Moon; from there it produced the seeds for all the animals and plants of Earth. In the rites of Mithraism, Mithras, the Sun spirit, is credited with slaying the primordial bull, but here it is considered a life-bestowing, benevolent act on behalf of humanity.

Explanation: The White Bull is a god form for the Supreme Being in one of His executive aspects, as the Greek Zeus and the Hindu Shiva. Through Shiva's bull form, we see the Supreme Being's ability to destroy illusions, to gore the illusion-holder (analogically, the bullfighter, or metaphysical toreador) resisting the astounding revelation of truth and ultimate reality that the White Bull suggests. With Zeus, however, the White Bull has a specific geomantic reference.

In the myth of Zeus assuming his White Bull form so as to seduce and couple with Europa, we have an indication of how the Supreme Being infiltrates a landmass with His reality. Decoding this profound geomyth, the White Bull, of course, is Zeus; Europa is the landmass of most of Europe, from Greece to the Low Countries, but excluding the western part of France and all of Spain, Portugal, and the British Isles.

Overshadowing this area is one of the Earth's 12 Albion Plates, a geometric division of the Earth's surface into 12 contiguous pentagons that resemble large transparent glass panes overlaid on the planet (see Albion). Each of these "glass panes" and the landmass under it have an imprint of the Supreme Being on it, like a manufacturer's watermark on fine paper. These are called Zeus Faces, because each "watermark" is the image of a different god form that Zeus takes.

For Europe, that god form is the White Bull, and its insertion point is at Crete, specifically, where the Cretan Labyrinth overlaps Mount Ida. The labyrinth is a large geomantic feature (5–10 miles wide) and one of 108 labyrinths in nine different groups. This is where Zeus as the White Bull "couples" with Europa; the myth is really saying that here is where the Mind of Zeus infiltrates and impregnates the physical landmass of Europe.

The prime place of insertion and human interaction with this landmass is the Cretan Labyrinth at Mount Ida, a peak said by the Greeks to be Zeus's birthplace on Earth. It's where he grounds his energy for Europe.

When human consciousness merges, even if for a moment, at the center of the labyrinth, then the Minotaur is experienced. The human dons the Bull's head and experiences an aspect of the Mind of God as it inserts itself into a landscape.

The Mithraic picture of bull-slaying does not refer to the Supreme Being in his White Bull god form, but to another, subsequent dimensional expression of the same thing. The human interaction with the White Bull (Zeus) is to don the bull's head and become the Minotaur; with the Cosmic Bull in all its guises, the human interaction is to "slay" it, that is, release its Light into the world.

See also: Albion, Europa, Minotaur.

WHITE COW

An ancient symbol for a geomantic feature on the Earth consisting of an interactive star map said to be the body of the Great Mother.

Also known as Audhumla, Bo Find, Dun Cow, Earth Cow, Fuwch Gyfeilioru, Glas Ghaibhleann, Glas Teanhrach, Io, Kama-Dhenu, Sarasvati, Sata-Rupa, Shabala, White Sow.

Description: Many stories are found in world myths about a meandering white cow who settles at a location where culture heroes then found cities.

In ancient Greece, Cadmus consulted the Oracle at Delphi about his future and life purpose. There Apollo told Cadmus to follow a cow and that where it sat down, he should found Thebes. Everything went according to plan, and Cadmus founded Thebes in Boeotia, "Land of the Cow." Ilus was told to follow a cow and to found a city where it lay down on the ground. That was Troy, now in Turkey, originally called Illium after Ilus, its founder.

Io, the daughter of a Greek River god, was turned into a cow for her own protection by Hera, queen of the Olympians. Io was tethered at Mycenae in Greece and guarded by Argus, a fabulous mythic being with one hundred eyes who never slept, except once later when Hermes lulled him into a deep drowsiness with his stories and Pan-pipes so he could rescue Io.

In England, we find the tale of the Dun Cow of Warwick. This was a gigantic, enchanted cow of the giants who built Staple Hill in Shropshire as her pen (*dun* means "fortified place" or royal residence, sometimes one with magical properties, in Irish and Scottish Gaelic). She gave an inexhaustible supply of fresh milk until a woman took advantage of her, then the Dun Cow turned malevolent and ravaged the countryside; finally, Sir Guy of Warwick killed her on Dunsmore Heath. The Irish, and possibly older, version of this has a cow following Saint Ciaran to Clonmacnoise, a major ecclesiastical center; later, the tale of the cow and journey was written on vellum made from the cow's hide.

Irish myth also recalls the Glas Ghaibhleann, a magical cow who produced prodigious, unending supplies of rich milk capable of feeding multitudes. She was guarded by a smith named Gaivnin Gow in the hills of County Cavan at Druin na Teine. This cow was known to wander throughout Ireland, traveling a minimum of six miles a day. Balor of the Evil Eye, a Fomorian giant with one huge eye, stole the cow and took her to his fortress on nearby Tory Island.

Even earlier than Glas Ghaibhleann was Bo Find, an Irish goddess in the form of a magical white cow who wandered the land with her two sisters, Bo Ruadh (red cow) and Bo Dhu (black cow), before there were any humans there. The cow goddess of abundance was also revered in Ireland at the Mound of the Cow and its two affiliate wells at the Hill of Tara near Dublin. One well was dedicated to the White Cow, *Glas Teanhrach*, the other to her calf.

Explanation: In a manner similar to the symbolism involved in the white sow, anciently a white cow was understood to symbolize the Great Mother in her valence of abundance and as the source of spiritual and physical nourishment.

From a human perspective, most of the cow can be consumed or used, and certainly the regular flow of milk (and the range of foods made from it) led the ancients, who depended on cows for sustenance, to equate it with the Great Mother. The whiteness of the cow, of course, symbolizes pure cosmic Light.

In Greek myth, Hera, the wife of Zeus, the chief of the Olympian gods, once assumed the form of a snow-white cow, and in Norse myth, Audhumla is the primeval cow who feeds and nourishes Ymir, the original Man, with milk. Welsh myth speaks of *Fuwch Gyfeilioru*, a pure white cow giving endless milk (also called *Y Fuwch Laethwen Lefrith*, "the milk-white milch cow"); and Egyptian lore speaks of a white cow from the Nile and Hathor (the equivalent to the Greek love goddess, Aphrodite) as cow-headed or a cow herself, on occasion.

In Hindu culture where cows are sacred animals, the white cow was known as Kama-Dhenu, the Wish Cow, the Cow of Plenty, the Wish-Fulfilling Cow born of the Ocean of Milk. She was a miraculous treasure who fulfilled all desires. Even Earth at one time assumed the form of a white cow to entreat the gods to get humans to stop abusing her (despoiling the environment).

Consistent with this description, the *Ramayana,* one of India's narrative classics, recounts how the sage Vasishtha got his marvelous white cow called Shabala to display her creative power, utter certain mantric sounds, and produce several classes of beings, such as the Pahlavas and Kambojas, bright as the sun.

Also in Hindu myth and religion, the daughter and consort of Brahma, the Creator god, is Sarasvati, the Flowing One. She is the divinity of knowledge and sacred speech; she is a pool of transcendent knowledge, the power of the Immense Being (Brahma), Womb of the Seed, and the Wish Cow *(Kama-Dhenu).*

She was portrayed as a graceful woman, all in white with two or eight arms, and was also known as Sata-Rupa, "She of the Hundred Forms." Brahma looked at her at every opportunity, all day and all night—she was that beautiful, that enchanting. It's said that he grew five heads so he could watch her from every angle of space, every moment of time, without distraction or missing a move.

Sata-Rupa, the daughter of a hundred forms, was the great cosmic matrix of spacetime, full of stars and beings and life and fantastic possibilities of experience. She was Brahma's creation, his first and only, his total creation. She was Brahma's sphere, his spacetime filled with energy, and all he wanted to do was *observe* her because, in observing his "daughter," he would come to know himself. Who am I? Brahma wonders. Why am I in existence?

His daughter, the fabulous milky realm of spacetime, the white cow full of milk and forms, is his answer. By observing material reality, even at this grand cosmic level, Brahma becomes self-aware.

So Brahma's "daughter," a metaphor for spacetime and its net of stars, is a pool of knowledge, the union of power and intelligence. She is the Flowing One, the Wandering One, the original divinity of transcendental knowledge and speech, the container of all the worlds, a graceful woman all in white, made of Light, sitting on a lotus, the Wish Cow feeding all in Brahma's field of dreams.

In Brahma's "daughter," that wonderful white cow, all wishes come true. Everything is possible, all permutations likely, and most things eventually happen. And from the "milk" of that knowledge comes self-awareness. Now I know! declares Brahma, and the Wish Cow has fulfilled her purpose in life.

This celestial drama of self-knowledge through contemplating a white cow in all her shape permutations is expressed on Earth in the form of landscape zodiacs. These are interactive, miniaturized holograms of the galaxy's major stars and constellations overlaid as a flat template on a stretch of landscape; their diameters range from one mile to 200 miles, consisting of two slightly interlocking circles, each containing about one-half of the stars in the galaxy. Humans can use a landscape zodiac (there are 432 on Earth) just as Brahma used his daughter: to become self-aware of one's cosmic origins and self-nature.

In the cases of the white cows of Thebes, Troy, Mycenae, and Hill of Tara, each location has a landscape zodiac; in many cases, the affiliation of a site-specific white cow myth to a location usually indicates a landscape zodiac.

See also: Albion, Golden Apple, Ocean of Milk, Round Table, White Sow, Ymir.

WHITE EYE OF HORUS

The Egyptian depiction of the newly born, farseeing Christ Child as templated across the Earth as 666 Golden Eggs.

Also known as Eye of Isis, Golden Egg, Heru-pa-khart, Hor-sa-iset, Sun Eye.

Description: Horus, the Egyptian falcon god and considered the Face of Heaven, has two Eyes and two guises. As Horus the Younger, he is *Heru-pa-khart,* the Sun (associated with Ra [or Re], the Sun god), the White Eye (his right); as Horus the Elder he is *Heru-ur,* the Black Eye (his left) called *wedjat* (*wadjet* or *udjat*), associated with the Moon and the Wisdom god Thoth.

Horus, in general, is the son of Isis and Osiris. At Heliopolis, he was known as *Harakhtes,* "Horus of the Horizon," while at Edfu he was Horus the *Behdetite,* the celestial falcon god or hawk-winged Sun disk. One of the oldest of Egyptian gods, Horus's name probably derives from *her,* which means "the one on high" or "the distant one," references to the soaring flight typical of a hunting falcon. As an all-seeing falcon, Horus's right eye was the Sun, his left the Moon, giving his long-range sight a celestial cast. Some interpreted his speckled breast feathers as representative of the stars, while his wings in downsweep were the windy sky.

Horus was the god of the rising and setting sun, and thus called *Horakhty,* "Horus of the Two Horizons." As *Hor-em-akhet* or *Harmachis* ("Horus in the Horizon"), Horus was perceived as a Sun god who took the form of a falcon. At Heliopolis, he was so associated with the Sun cult that he became *Re-Horakhty.* Horus was also closely linked with kingship, its legitimacy and rites, and as *Har-mau* or *Harsomptus* ("Horus the Uniter"), he united and ruled over all of Egypt.

He had a strong connection with Nekhen in southern Egypt, which the Greeks called Hierakonpolis, "City of the Hawk," in his honor; and at Edfu, people observed a yearly festival called Coronation of the Sacred Falcon, in which an actual falcon represented Horus as King of Egypt.

As Horus the Younger, he was often depicted as a child seated on the lap of his mother, the great goddess Isis, much like the Christ Child with the Madonna. One of his most popular forms as Horus the Younger was as *Hor-sa-iset* (Greek *Harsiesis*), as a child god who was also known as *Horpakhered (Harpocrates).*

He was sired on Isis by the dead Osiris, hidden during his youth on the island of Chemmis and protected by the goddess Wadjet, protector of Lower Egypt, who took a serpent form to watch over Isis and him and kept him covered by reeds and papyrus so the agents of Seth, his future enemy, could not find him.

Explanation: Horus the Younger is an aspect of the Christ as seen through the Egyptian mythic-psychic perception as the newly born cosmic principle. The falcon imagery is appropriate, for the Christ (or Logos) is the farseeing one; in the Hindu perception, Christ as Vishnu the Pervader, this is even more clear: Vishnu pervades all of spacetime, permeating all of space with his consciousness.

The Sun or White Eye is actually the Eye of Isis (the female aspect of God) seeing through Horus into our world. The *wedjat* (Black Eye) is the Eye of Horus that looks upon the Father and His Mysteries; it is the Eye of Osiris (the male aspect of God) seeing through Horus. Thus Horus's Eyes transmit both aspects of God.

This also means that Horus, with both Eyes, has insight into the Sun and Moon gods and their temples, as templated across the Earth as Sun Temples (see Hitching Post of the Sun) and Moon-Soma Temples (see Fountain of Youth).

Geomantically, Horus's Sun-eye has an expression in the form of 666 Golden Eggs. In the myth of the Cosmic Egg, found in many cultures, when the primal Chaos inside the egg started to separate out, the top half became Heaven and was silver, the bottom half gold and was Earth (all of cosmic space and matter). The silver and gold parts both have geomantic expression on our planet.

Selected locations of a Golden Egg (Horus's White Eye) include Blood Hill, Dornach, Switzerland; Tetford, Lincolnshire, England; Glastonbury Abbey, Glastonbury, Somerset, England; Shrine of Our Lady of Walsingham,

Walsingham, Norfolk, England; Wawel Hill, Cracow, Poland; and Edfu, Egypt.

A Golden Egg contains Horus the Younger or the Christ Child as a contribution to Earth's visionary geography and especially the local aspects. But it must be "hatched" or activated through human-Egg interaction over time.

Typically, the Golden Egg will occupy up to five miles of landscape and have at least three distinct parts described in accordance with the seven chakras.

First, there is an egg cup or saucer that contains the Golden Egg, which rises about one hundred feet from its base on the saucer. The saucer occupies the first two chakras of the Christ Child and serves as a door into the sacralized domain of the Egg itself, which occupies chakras three through six laid out across the land.

From the doorway at the second chakra, the Golden Egg looks like a single radiant golden pea in a long unzipped pea pod resting upon several miles of land. Inside the pea pod (or Egg), you can see the golden Christ Child (or in the Hindu model, Bala Brahma [Child Brahma], or in the Egyptian, Horus the Younger).

At its crown chakra is a geomantic feature called a Maidenwell. It looks like a Madonna or Isis cradling the child to her heart with her long arms sweeping down to enfold the Egg and saucer, all the way to the base and first chakra of it. The Maidenwell is the baptismal font for the divine child's crown chakra.

The benefit to the local landscape to "hatching" a Golden Egg is that it allows a little of the Christ Consciousness, purely born on Earth, to trickle into Earth's visionary geography and its capillary network, hence into physical reality. The benefit to individuals interacting with this feature is that it is a prime opportunity to unfold the Christ Child within us (also called Inner God Self or second birth, or Higher Man) by being in resonance with its outer expression.

Ideally, go to a Cosmic Egg site and immerse yourself in that energy and the processes it sparks in you (see Cosmic Egg), then come to a Golden Egg for the next phase of that unfoldment of the birth of the Christ Child.

See also: Black Eye of Horus, Cosmic Egg, Fountain of Youth, Hitching Post of the Sun.

WHITE HORSE

The mantric sound shape created by the sounding of the Solar Logos expressed as *Ar-Thur-Humg!* as a way of connecting all the galaxy's stars with the Solar Logos (Arthur) in the constellation Ursa Major.

Also known as Beligen, Enbharr, Hayagriva, Hayasiras, Pegasus, Rakhsh, Uccaihsravas.

Description: In Hindu myths, at the beginning of time, the gods churned the Ocean of Milk (a metaphor for the astral Sea of Light or the primordial galaxy or universe) and brought forth 14 treasures including Uccaihsravas, the White Horse. The name means "long-eared" or "neighing aloud," but it also connotes "high," which is why Uccaihsravas was thereafter known as the king of horses. It was Moon-colored, white of flank with a black tail.

The White Horse was also associated with the Sun, said to have been fashioned from it, and was afterward associated with solar gods. Uccaihsravas is the celestial horse that follows swiftly the course of the Sun through the heavens. Indra, king of the gods in Hindu myth, was its first rider, and the White Horse became known in part as Indra's Mount. Yet the White Horse is also associated with Vishnu, one of three prime Hindu gods, the Pervader (equivalent to the Christ).

Vishnu's eighteenth *avatara,* or descent (incarnation), into the world was Hayagriva (also called Hayasiras), a horse-headed god known as Protector of the Scripture. Brahma (the Hindu creator god) asked Hayagriva to dive to the bottom of the ocean to rescue Vedic texts stolen by two Djinn (conventionally, ancient demonic beings).

In the profound and very ancient Asvamedha horse sacrifice ritual, the horse was understood to represent Hayasirsas, Vishnu (Christ) as the cosmic sacrifice. *Asva* is Sanskrit for "horse" and literally means "pervader," the prime epithet for Vishnu as the Christ Consciousness (Logos, Word) that pervades all spacetime existence. The horse is thus a symbol of luminous or solar deities, and in most myths about a Sun god, his chariot is drawn by celestial horses.

Vishnu has ten major and 22 minor incarnations. In his tenth and final major descent, he will be the Kalki Avatar riding a great white horse to redeem the world, bringing peace and salvation to a darkened human world.

The Greek description of the White Horse is as Pegasus, the winged, immortal horse whose parents are Poseidon (Lord of the Sea) and the Gorgon Medusa. When the Greek demigod Perseus (son of Zeus and a mortal woman) cut off Medusa's snake-entwined head, from the blood spurting out of her severed neck sprang Pegasus. He was so named because this event apparently took place near the Springs (*Pegae*) of Ocean, a cosmic locale. The white horse's name is also derived from the Greek *pege*, meaning "a spring of water."

Pegasus carried the thunder and lightning bolts of Zeus, chief of the gods, and was said to have been caught and tamed originally at the fountain of Pirene in Corinth in Greece by the human hero Bellerophon (his parentage is given as Poseidon and Eurynome, both celestial beings), who rode Pegasus to accomplish certain highly difficult tasks. Pegasus was later credited with creating various springs around Greece by the mere stamping of his hooves on the ground.

Bellerophon was the first to bridle Pegasus and he did this with the gods' help. The seer Polyidus told Bellerophon to spend a night sleeping on the Altar of Athena (one of the Olympian gods), presumably in Corinth where he lived. In his dream, Athena presented Bellerophon with a golden bridle to tame the horse and advised him to sacrifice a bull to Poseidon the Tamer (and Pegasus's father). In the morning, the golden bridle manifested and the sacrifice performed, Bellerophon easily bridled a tame Pegasus at the Pirene fountain.

Other cultural expressions of the White Horse include Beligen, the supernatural, fleet-footed mount of Gesar of Ling (Mongolia, Tibet), and Rakhsh, the equally formidable, magical flying horse of the Persian hero Rustam. The chariot of Mithra, the Iranian solar god, was pulled by white horses; the white horse is the vehicle or form for Bato Kwannon, the Japanese version of Avalokitesvara, a Buddhist bodhisattva of mercy and compassion; and the Celtic Epona was the Great Horse deity and goddess-mare, her name meaning horse.

Still another white horse figure is the Irish Enbharr ("Splendid Mane" or "Water Foam"), the steed of the Sea Lord Manannan mac Lir (the Irish version of the Greek Poseidon). Manannan traveled constantly across the sea, faster than the wind, in a copper boat pulled by the enchanted Enbharr whose hair was wave froth. To an extent, his horses were the sea waves themselves, in recognition of which Manannan was often called "rider of the maned sea."

Explanation: The White Horse of the Sun is the sound current of the Solar Logos moving swiftly through space. The Solar Logos is King Arthur (also known as Indra), leader of the Great White Brotherhood in Ursa Major, the constellation of the Great Bear. There, as chief of the gods (enlightened sages, spiritual adepts, celestial beings, angels, intelligences from the stars, and the 48,000 rishis [according to Hindu lore]), King Arthur keeps in perpetual connection with all the suns or points of consciousness within the galaxy.

Arthur is both the leader of the gods (Celestial Host) and the name of the sound current that connects him in Ursa Major to all the suns. Arthur is the energy of growth and change; it is the Word or Logos (the Christ) expressed at the level of the stars (suns), quickening all with celestial life and consciousness.

Arthur, sounded correctly, is a mantra, a shaped sound vibration, the Word (Logos) unfiltered through human speech or language, that creates a sonic shape and container that swirls and "rides" through space, carrying the King. He sends his sound current horse (mantra) out to all the stars simultaneously. Here another meaning of Uccaihsravas, as "Neighing Aloud" and "Loud Neigh," is congruent: The Solar Logos sounds forth loudly, its voice heard throughout the galaxy.

The various heroes with White Horses ride the Arthur sound current throughout etheric space (the Sea with its waves, or sound currents). The horse is the sound of *Arthur* as the Solar Logos, the sea foam, the Logos sea wave.

As the Irish myths about Manannan mac Lir say, it was as if the sea waves themselves were the horses. That is true in the sense that the horses as waves are actually different sound currents traveling through the cosmic ethers. Each horse is a permutation of the Word, a diffraction of the Logos, made cohesive by the Solar Logos. The 48,000 rishis take their name, Hindu lore says, from the root for sound, meaning that each rishi is a sound or transmits a sound current.

Hindu myth also tells us that once the Buffalo demon-king captured all of Indra's treasures, including the "hundred times ten million horses" headed by Uccaihsravas, and kept them in his elegant stables. These one billion horses could be construed as the vast array of Word permutations riding the ethers, organized, led, and kept coherent by the one White Horse, the Solar Logos sound.

See also: Gesar of Ling, Indra, King Arthur, Ocean of Milk, Rustam.

WHITE MOUNT

The higher dimensional Grail mountain above the Flood waters on which the Ark or Boat of the Vedas (Grail Castle) resides and from which a new cycle of creation and humanity was generated; also the place for embodied humans to attain deep cosmic memory and Christ Consciousness.

Also known as Djeba, Exalted Earth, First Land, First Place, God's Mountain, Grail Castle, High Dune, High Hill, Mount Hetep, Mount of Glory, Mount of Heaven, Munsalvaesche ("Mountain of Salvation"), Plain of Ildavöll, Primeval Hill, Primordial Hill, Ptah's Mound at Annu, Staircase of the God Osiris, Ta-tjenen ("Elevated Land"), White Mountain.

Description: Egyptian mythology speaks of a Primeval Hill or White Mount that was the first landmass to arise out of the watery chaos of Nun (primeval waters, like a permanent Flood) at the beginning of creation. Upon this Mount, Atum, Ptah, or Ta-tjenen initiated Creation and precipitated the emergence of the world, the panoply of gods, humanity, and life on Earth.

Generally, the White Mount is situated at Heliopolis, the Greek name for the ancient Greek citadel An or Annu, on the outskirts of present-day Cairo. Memphis also claimed the Mount, calling it *Ta-Tjenen* ("the Elevated Land"), as did Thebes (which claimed it possessed the glorious hill of the beginning), Hermopolis (which said an egg bearing the Sun rested on the primordial mound), and Edfu, where it was guarded by two Companions of the Most Divine Heart.

The White Mount afforded the gods the high perch or seat of creation called the *Djeba,* a reed that split in two when it rose out of Nun to serve as a seat for the creation deity. The Djeba was the perch on which the Creator landed when He emerged from the waters of Nun. On top of the Primeval Hill (the same as the Djeba), one found Annu, the Eternal City, the White House on the Mount, the Eternal City with a White Wall, the Fields of Aaru, and the White Throne.

In Memphis, Ta-tjenen was both the Risen Land (or White Mount) and the deity who rose out of the Earth on it. Ta-tjenen (or Tatenen or Tenen) was described as a bearded male whose crown had two feathers and a solar disk above two ram's horns. He was the Revered One who emerged from the waters of Nun with two great staffs to repel the cosmic serpent from the White Mount. He also had a magical mace called "Great White of the Earth Creator," dedicated to the falcon (symbol of Horus, sometimes called Lord of the Djeba).

Explanation: Egyptian myth is rich, even to the point of confusion, with references to the White Mount. Part of the confusion is that some of the qualities of the White Mount, which is a Grail Castle and its Holy Mountain, are blurred with another mythic feature called a Cosmic Egg, some of which are in the same place. Atum and Ptah pertain to the Cosmic Eggs, but the White Mount is Ta-tjenen's.

The defining distinction of a Grail Castle is that it is a citadel arising above the Flood Waters and from which a god recreates and repopulates Earth. The White Mount is the Egyptian perception of the Grail Castle and its mount for the god, the mount being the Djeba or "Mountain of Salvation" *(Munsalvaesche),* as it was known in the medieval Western Grail Mysteries. The god in this case is the Rich Fisher King.

Nearly all of the myths about a primordial Flood that destroyed almost all of humanity have a man or a couple surviving on an ark or boat, landing on a high peak above the waters, and starting the world and humanity afresh from there. Some of the names for this same figure are Noah, Manu Satyavrata, Fionntan, Deucalion, Yima, Ziusudra-Utnapishtim, and, in Egypt, Ta-tjenen.

The difference with the Egyptian perception is that rather than an ark landing on the White Mount, the primordial hill rises from out of the water to become the world-regenerating god's seat; thus the seat, or Djeba, is Noah's Ark.

The Flood survivor is known, in Hinduism, as a Manu, the world regent for a vast cycle of time lasting 306 million years. After a period of cosmic quiescence, known as *Pralaya,* the Flood, or the Night of Brahma, creation is renewed by the Manu from his seat (Djeba) at the Grail Castle. The Grail Castle connection is that this is the place where humans can remember deeply all the events in the last Day (a vast time) of Brahma and their own soul's participation in them.

Potentially, one could remember all the events in the entire life of Brahma (100 Divine Years, or 311 trillion human years) all the way back to the beginning.

The Manu, or in this case, Ta-tjenen, is the guardian and repository of this deep cosmic memory. The Celts called him the Salmon of Wisdom because one taste of its flesh by a human provoked immediate clairvoyance and prophecy. The connection with the falcon and Horus (Lord of the Djeba) is appropriate because Horus is the Egyptian name for the Christ (the Hindu Vishnu who pervades and preserves space). Christ is the Logos, the Word that pervades all space, and the Grail Castle is where you may experience Christ Consciousness, in this instance, the vast, deep, and pervasive cosmic memory back to the Flood.

The reason the White Mount and the various other expressions of the Grail Mountain are said to be elevated, risen land is that the Djeba above (Grail Castle) exists in a subtler dimension than much of Earth's visionary terrain. You have to climb higher in consciousness (climb the Grail Mountain) to get there. The name of one Grail Castle location in England (Castle Rigg, Keswick, Lake District) reflects this clearly: You climb the rigging up to the Grail Castle.

The Grail Castle, and its variants as the White Mount, is a geomantic feature with 144 copies on the Earth, including several in Egypt (Heliopolis). Elsewhere in the world, Grail Castles exist at Mount Parnassus, Greece; Mount Ararat, Armenia; Montsegur, France; and Chalice Hill, Glastonbury, England.

See also: Black Eye of Horus, Cosmic Egg, Fisher King, Flood, Grail Castle, Holy Grail, Manu, Salmon of Wisdom, White Eye of Horus.

WHITE SOW

An ancient symbol, based on Mother goddess fecundity imagery, for a landscape zodiac, a miniaturized hologram of the galaxy's major constellations overlaid on a landscape for interactive use in the Grail Quest.

Also known as Adamantine Sow, Ceridwen, Diamond, Laurentine Sow, Nut, Phaea, the Shining One, Vajravarahi, White Cow.

Description: There are several almost identical tales found in Western myths involving a sow showing a human where to found a community. The founding myth for Glastonbury, England, has a giant named Glasteing follow his pregnant, eight-legged sow all across England until she sits down on a hill under an apple tree. There she gives birth to 30 piglets, which she immediately suckles. Glasteing takes all this as an omen to found his community there, which he calls *Glasteingaburgh,* "Glasteing's place," a name which later elides into Glastonbury.

Virgil's *Aeneid* recounts a similar story in the founding of Rome. Aeneas has just landed in Italy and is advised by the Tiber River god that nearby he will find a huge white sow (later called the Laurentine Sow) lying on the ground with a newborn litter of 30 white piglets at her udders and that he should take this as a token for a new city that in 30 years his son will found: the White City, Rome.

Less dramatic but equally descriptive of a secret in the landscape is the sculptured frieze on the front of Croyland Abbey depicting a sow and pigs under a tree. The abbey is a Benedictine monastery founded in 716 in Croyland in southeastern Lincolnshire, England. Legend has it that a vision of this sow and piglets led the founder of the monastery to establish it there within the fens.

Similarly, Saint Brannock (circa 500 A.D.) dreamed that he must build a church and monastery at the precise spot where he witnessed a wild sow lying down with her litter. This is now the site of the Saint Brannock's Church in Braunton in Devonshire, England.

Explanation: Anciently, many cultures, from Celtic to Buddhist, symbolized the Great Mother Goddess in all her prosperity and fecundity as a white sow. The Celts knew her as Ceridwen, the Sow Goddess, and "the Old White One," and also as Phaea, "the Shining One," while the Buddhists called her Vajravarahi, the "Diamond Sow" or "Adamantine Sow," the Queen of Heaven. The high god of the Greek pantheon, Zeus, was suckled by a great sow in his infancy.

In Egypt, the Sky goddess was called Nut; she swallowed the sun at dusk and disgorged it at dawn, so she was known as the sow who eats up her piglets. That meant her sky body ultimately included all the celestial bodies (stars).

Decoding the symbol, first, the sow is white because the Great Mother is the effulgence of pure cosmic Light. She is a sow because, in human experience, this animal is perpetually fertile, prolific, and a rich source of food.

The white sow is a symbol for the galaxy of stars, all fed, nourished, and suckled by the Great Mother, the Queen of Heaven (Nut), whose supply of "milk" or total awakened consciousness is inexhaustible and perpetually available. She has 30 suckling piglets because when you divide the planisphere of the stars equally into 12 divisions, each contains 30 degrees, making 360 in total. These 12 divisions, of course, refer to the signs of the zodiac, each occupying a 30-degree slice of the galaxy as seen from Earth. Each division is a piglet with 30 mouths hungrily sucking divine light and life from the sow.

On Earth, this pattern is templated in 432 different locations. Each copy is called a landscape zodiac and comprises a miniaturized hologram of the high-magnitude stars and important constellations of the Milky Way Galaxy. These zodiacs are laid out across a flat stretch of landscape, with diameters that range from one mile to 200 miles. They are interactive and designed for people to use as part of the individuation process known as the Quest for the Holy Grail. Thus the landscape zodiac is the terrestrial version of the sow Sky goddess Nut, whose vast body subsumes (and nourishes) all the stars and planets of the galaxy.

The Glastonbury sow has eight legs because in many wisdom and initiation traditions there are eight ways, devices, objects, methods, or teachings that will get the candidate through the process of spiritual awakening.

In most cases, site-specific myths that relate the wanderings of a white sow and her settling at a place indicate the presence of a viable landscape zodiac.

In the examples cited here, there is a landscape zodiac at each location; at Glastonbury, it is about 34 miles in width; in Rome, it is 96 miles wide. However, in both cases (and this is true of all 432 copies), the zodiac (white sow) is in two parts: Picture a Golden Apple full of the galaxy's stars; cut it in half, flatten both halves, and lay them out upon the landscape. In the Glastonbury zodiac, each half is about 17 miles in diameter, in Rome, 48 miles. Within each half, all the stars (the "piglets") enjoy perpetually suckling the great Mother whose body is full of Light, an Ocean of Milk.

See also: Albion, Golden Apple, Ocean of Milk, River God, Round Table, White Cow.

WILD HUNT

An annual occult event in which enlightened adepts of the Great White Brotherhood inundate humanity with the energies and consciousness of the 14 Rays of Ursa Major through 108 geomantic portals across the Earth.

Also known as Arthur's Hunt, Ascended Host, Asgardreid, Cwyn Mamau (Hounds of the Mothers), Dando and His Dogs, Devil's Dandy Dogs, Fairy Rade, Furious Host, Herlethingus, Herl's Rade, Odin's Hunt, Raging Host, Seven Whistlers, Sky Yelpers, Wild Host, Wish Hounds, Woden's Hunt, Yell Hounds.

Description: The Wild Hunt is a folkloric myth found in the British Isles, German-speaking lands, and Scandinavia, though it has vestiges in other cultures, too. In essence, it involves the spectral ride of fearsome Otherworld horsemen in pursuit of human souls, either recently dead or still living. The folk belief was that the Huntsmen sought unbaptized human souls, damned souls, or imprudent onlookers and would take them mercilessly down with them to Hell.

Various identities were given to the Wild Huntsman or Leader. He was a demonized hero figure, such as King Arthur; chief of the gods, such as Odin; a spirit huntsman (*Le Grand Vaneur* in France); a demonized ordinary human, such as Wild Darrell or Black Vaughan; or the Devil in person. Whoever the Leader is, he blows a chilling hunting horn as he leads the galloping host.

In one of the earliest recorded accounts of the Wild Hunt, in 1127, English monks described the appearance between Lent and Easter of loathsome, huge, black riders mounted on black horses and goats and accompanied by nasty-looking, wide-eyed dogs.

The consensus of folk traditions tends to place the Wild Hunt as beginning on October 31 (the eve of *Samhain* in the Celtic calendar) and ending April 30 (the eve of *Beltaine*), but the height of the ride is placed at the winter solstice, the year's longest night and one acknowledged as the Yule festival (Yuletide), December 21. In Nordic lands, on Yule Eve, children placed socks filled with hay outside house doors to feed Sleipnir (Odin's steed) as he passed by with Odin and the Huntsmen.

In Norse myth, Odin (the German Woden or Wotan), chief of all the gods in Asgard, is the leader of the Wild Hunt, which storms out of the Otherworld into the human realm, snatching people from their homes and physical lives. The Huntsmen were often depicted as riding across the sky at night on storm clouds. Odin rides Sleipnir, his eight-legged steed, and is accompanied by the Valkyries and the dead warriors (Einherjar) who reside with him in Valhalla.

In the Celtic version, Gwynn ap Nudd, chief of Fairyland or king of Annwn, the Otherworld, leads a pack of white-skinned, red-eared dogs called the *Cwyn Annwn,* Hounds of Annwn, which folklorists interpret to mean Dog of Hell. In Scotland, King Arthur was also credited with being the leader of the Wild Hunt.

The Hounds of Annwn motif was extended in the description of the Gabriel Hounds, especially in the northern counties of England. They were also known as Gabriel ratchets, Gabble Rachets, Gabbleracket, Gabble Retchets, gaze hounds, and lyme hounds. In the expression "Gabriel ratchets," Gabriel was understood to be another name for Gwynn ap Nudd, and ratchet referred to a fiercely determined hunting dog.

The Hounds of Annwn were spectral black dogs who would disguise themselves as (shape-shift into) wild geese or other migratory birds and fly overhead, making loud, scary birdcalls. But they were also described as dogs with human heads flying high in the skies on stormy nights; others said they were a group of demons, the souls of the unbaptized, or the restless souls of human sinners sent by the Devil to bring bad luck and disaster to the living.

If they circled a specific house, it meant the occupants would surely die or have a domestic disaster. Generally, it was considered dangerous even to look at the riders, but those who placed a twig of rowan over their front doors might be exempt from abduction and usually could watch the procession with impunity.

Explanation: The Wild Hunt is an occult reality onto which a great deal of folklore, superstition, misunderstanding, and cultural fear has been heaped.

The Wild Hunt is one of a series of events in an annual geomantic liturgical calendar in which angelic and hierarchical hosts interface with Earth and humanity. Other events in this cycle include Epiphany on January 6, Candlemas on February 1, and Michaelmas on September 29 (see entries for each).

To understand the event, we must rely on the earliest accounts or those that involve the high gods rather than demonic or spectral and malevolent beings, for example, the account of Odin and his Einherjar riding forth on Yuletide.

Once a year, on the eve of December 21, the Great White Brotherhood, the galaxy's occult government based in the constellation Ursa Major (Great Bear), in affiliation with the star Sirius (also a seat of celestial spiritual government), inundate Earth's visionary geography with the higher energies and consciousness of their realm, essentially in search of recruits for initiation, but also as a blessing from on high to the planet and all its residents, mainly humans.

The Great White Brotherhood (see Einherjar) has a dedicated outpost on Earth of selected members. These are known as the 14 Ray Masters (see Seven Rishis), who are enlightened former humans each in charge of one major stream of consciousness, color vibration, and evolutionary potential (called a Ray). The Ray Masters are sometimes referred to as Ascended Masters and, more anciently, as the gods. The Ray Masters have numerous adepts and Ascended Masters who work in affiliation with their particular Ray, and together these comprise the Wild Hunt.

The Ray Masters are based in a Celestial City accessible through Earth's visionary geography and known variously as Asgard, the Crystal City, City of Light, or Glass Mountain. This realm exists in another dimension and far into the human future, roughly around 3000 A.D. It represents a state of awareness and possibility that humanity collectively will gradually mature into.

Norse myth says that every day the Aesir, the gods of Asgard, ride forth out of their Celestial City across a Rainbow Bridge (called Bifrost) that connects Asgard with Earth. They ride forth every day to consult with the three Norns (or Fates) at the Well of Urd to decide or review individual human destinies. Another way of putting this is to say they consult with their human protégés, or review their progress through the initiation sequence, or generally say hello.

In geomantic terms, Earth is provided with 108 portals into Asgard, or 108 copies of Asgard imprinted across the planet at various sites. You enter any of these 108 portals and pass into the one Celestial City whose primary reality and place of singular manifestation are based in the Great Bear.

In dynamic terms, the Ray Masters are perpetually riding forth across Bifrost, which means they are always *extending* their Rays and consciousness into the human world, like streams of colored light, each of which encodes a path of consciousness, evolution, initiation, and soul affiliation for humans. Bifrost is the perpetual extension of the Ray Masters into the human world through the portals.

On December 21, however, that process is intensified. On the annual day of the Wild Hunt, the Ray Masters and their retinue of adepts (the Huntsmen) stream out into the human world in much fuller force than at any other time. It can seem like a wild, scary, life-threatening hunt to the death for those who resist it. Cultural resistance over time has demonized this well-intentioned occult festival, similar in operation to the Buddhist esoteric ritual of Wesak in May.

If Bifrost normally transmits ten percent of the impulse of the Ray Masters during the year, at the Wild Hunt, perhaps 50 percent streams forth into our world. The riders "hunt" souls only in the sense that they seek humans who are ready to deepen or even awaken their preexisting soul affiliation with a given Ray. Every soul at the start of its long saga of incarnations begins "life" on one such Ray.

Odin, one name for the chief of the occult hierarchy, sits at the center of Asgard, never moving. But his many riders do, on his behalf, streaming out of the 108 "pipes" or portals that lead from Asgard out to Earth. Each of the 108 sacred sites on Earth that is a portal to the Celestial City of Asgard will experience a temporary flooding of its pipe on December 21, like an arroyo after a rain. The 14 streams of cosmic essence and consciousness rush down the portals into Earth's visionary geography and from there move into the physical human world.

The sensitive among humans will be aware of an extra pressure to be wakeful on this day. Those who know their soul affiliation may feel a deepening of their spiritual life on the day of the Wild Hunt. Atheists and materialists may find themselves discomfited at a deep level of their psyche on that day.

The Hounds of Annwn deliver some of the spiritual impulse that is the star (and star god) Sirius, associated in the Hindu pantheon with Shiva, the destroyer of illusions, false understandings, and chimeric, empty philosophies. Yet the dogs of Sirius are also guides to the Underworld, psychopomps for those interested in exploring the mysteries of the cosmos, creation, and consciousness.

So the Wild Hunt is an invitation or an assault, depending on your soul mood. Regardless of your free-willed response, once a year the spiritual hierarchy sends a marvelous impulse through Earth to renew our soul life. During the Wild Hunt, the full spectrum of cosmic experience, embodied in the 14 Rays, is pulsed into the Earth's subtle anatomy as a gift from above, and as an open-ended invitation to participate in the development of higher consciousness.

The motif of Gabriel Hounds is surprisingly apt, for the Archangel Gabriel is involved in all this and, in a subtle sense, leads the Wild Hunt. The Crystal City, or Asgard, has a watchman and guardian, variously known as Heimdall, Pelops, Humbaba, or Gwynn ap Nudd. All are the Archangel Gabriel.

His résumé fits this. According to Judaic lore, the Archangel Gabriel smote the hosts of Sennacherib with a sharpened scythe that had been ready for this event since the Creation (see Heimdall). Gabriel was also credited with destroying the reputedly "sinful" ancient cities of Sodom and Gomorrah.

Gabriel is the Prince of Justice and chief of the angelic guards of Paradise, his name means "God Is My Strength," and he is the angel of mercy, vengeance, death, and revelation. Ultimately, Gabriel regulates the flow of Mystery revelation (having to do with the Christ) from the Crystal City into the human realm, which is perhaps why Gabriel is called God's chief ambassador to humanity.

On the day of the Wild Hunt, the Archangel Gabriel opens the floodgates, allowing a rich infusion from the Great Bear to flow through the 108 pipes.

Those wishing to participate in the Wild Hunt,

as souls to be "hunted," may find it useful to meditate expectantly at one of the 108 Crystal City pipes on that day. Selected locations of these portals include Uluru at Alice Springs, Australia; Cathedral Rock in Sedona, Arizona; Mount Shasta, California; the Tor at Glastonbury, England; Mycenae, Greece; Thomas Jefferson's Monticello in Charlottesville, Virginia; and Pyramid Lake, Nevada.

See also: Anunnaki, Bifrost, Candlemas, Da Derga's Hostel, Einherjar, Epiphany, Glass Mountain, Heimdall, Michaelmas, Seven Rishis, Shambhala, Tuatha de Danann, Valhalla.

YETI

Interdimensional guardian of the Earth grid; guide to domes, labyrinths, and tunnels; former caretaker of Earth's visionary geographic information and protocols; and one of two prototypes for humanity.

Also known as Abominable Snowman, Almas, Bigfoot, Bushman, Chewbacca, Chorti, Fsti Capcaki, Grassman, Hairy Man, Momo, Mountain Man, Nakani, Nee-Gued, Nuk-luk, Oh-mah, Old Yellow Top, Sasquatch, Skunk Ape, White Bears in their Townhouses, Wild Man of the Woods, Woods Devil, Wookie, Yowie.

Description: The Yeti (from the Sherpa *yeh-teh*) is described as an elusive, hairy, somewhat bearlike, very large humanoid dwelling in the mountains or remote areas. These bear-men (or ape-men) can be seven to eight feet tall, with bodies completely covered by thick dark hair. Himalayan mountain-climbing expeditions of 1938, 1951, and 1953 reported sighting the Yeti. The Sherpa of Nepal and Tibet, however, distinguish three types, based on size: *Dzu-teh, Meh-teh,* and *Yeh-Teh.* Occasionally, enormous physical footprints of the Yeti have been discovered in the Himalayas, as well as rust-colored skins allegedly left by them; in 1967, several Americans succeeded in filming a Yeti in Bluff Creek, California.

The English recounted sightings of the Wildman of the Woods (also called Woodwose, Woodhouse, and Wooser) in the thirteenth to sixteenth centuries. The Wildman was humanoid, huge, hairy, carried a club, wore rough skins, had green hair, and lived alone in the woods. The Hairy Man, to the Tanaina people of the subarctic region of Alaska, was a giant humanlike creature with gray hair who lived in the mountains and was known to be benevolent in interactions with humans. In Guatemala, the Chorti is an anthropoid guardian of the wilderness. For the Seminoles of Oklahoma, the Fsti Capcaki, also called Tall Man, is a gigantic, gray humanlike creature who uses tree trunks and limbs as weapons.

The Sasquatch (from the Salish *se-sxac,* "Wild Man" or "Hairy Man," one of 150 different names for this figure among the Salish of British Columbia) can be up to 15 feet tall, 900 pounds in weight, with shaggy brown hair all over his body.

The Cherokee say the Chief of the Bears, the White Bear, lives at *Kuwa'hi,* the "Mulberry Place," now known as Clingman's Dome mountain in Tennessee; they also say the Bears have "townhouses" in the mountain where they dance every autumn before hibernation. The Bears, say the Cherokee, were once human and can still talk like humans, though they seldom do; later they were transformed into White Bears who live in great townhouses inside mountains.

As Bigfoot, the Yeti has been observed in the Cascade Mountains of Washington, the coastal range of Oregon, and the Sierra Nevadas of California, often in underlit, thick forests, where they observe humans. Worldwide, 3,000 sightings have been recorded of this creature; in 1998, an American researcher reported he was telepathically contacted by a Yeti and that they are psychic.

Explanation: The Yeti is not a physically embodied creature, though it may, on occasion, seemingly appear as one in our three-dimensional realm. It has been reported widely around the world by native peoples and remembered by others in folklore accounts because its mandated function is global in scope. Primarily, the Yeti operates in the fourth dimension, at the interface between that realm and ours, but can assume a seemingly tangible ape-like form in ours.

The White Bears, for example, are half-human, half-bear, and stand 15 feet tall. They guard labyrinths (astral versions of labyrinths, which are cosmic information archives, superimposed over the landscape, sometimes at mountains, such as at Clingman's Dome). They supervise human access to the information-archive function of these labyrinths, as well as access to the past and future time frames they afford, and keep the geomantic feature intact, vital, and uncorrupted.

Only a few hundred Yetis remain on the planet, but their creation antedates humanity. They were created as a prototype for humans (another group was the Djinn) whose function was to maintain geomantic doorways. Originally, the Yetis kept the secrets of Gaia safe; these secrets pertain to the energy and consciousness functions of the planet's visionary geography and how the planet interacts with the solar system, galaxy, and subtler spiritual realms. Now these secrets and interactions are handled by the Nature spirits of the devic realm.

Yetis also guard the doorways into domes (large etheric energy canopies overlying Holy Mountains and representing different high-magnitude stars—see Holy Mountain). On a psychic level, they allow entry to humans whose intent is to interact beneficially with these important geomantic features; I was once given a twig with buttonlike white flowers as a credential to pass through to an inner realm of a dome.

Yetis may also sponsor, participate in, or help in human initiations at geomantic nodes, such as domes, facilitating access, heightening perception, or awarding swords as credentials for entry or psychic penetration. Yetis supervise human access to Light temples at the end of energy funnels (a straight-running channel for higher consciousness states with a subtle temple at the end), as formerly marked by avenues of trees. I was once greeted by a Yeti at the door of such a temple (usually offering psychic access to stars and celestial beings); he wore a gold leaf pendant on his left breast, gave it to me, and it became a sword, which I used to "penetrate" the essence and function of this feature.

Their bear-like or ape-like form is donned at the transition point between the fourth and third dimension. I have seen Yeti skins (their worldly manifestation forms as ape-like beings) hanging like suits on hooks inside domes; I have also seen Yetis dance formally and happily with humans (in their Light bodies) at holy sites; the Yetis tend to be slender, almost gangly, and intelligent and resemble Chewbacca of *Star Wars* fame.

Yetis guard Yeti Doors, grace notes in the frequency scales of Earth's energy body that resemble doorways out of the third dimension. I saw a Yeti at such a door; behind him stretched an astral tunnel into another realm. You must be very quick to slip through such a door, and you can do so only if invited by a Yeti. The Yetis also guard tunnels, whether physical or astral, linking aspects of complex sacred sites (e.g., at Glastonbury, England), and allow, or disallow, the passage of humans, even if only in consciousness, through them.

See also: Djinn, Fairy Queen, Gaia, Holy Mountain, Pan.

YGGDRASIL

The Tree of Life planted by God in the Garden of Eden, expressed geomantically as a 200-mile-tall Tree of Light in Norway.

Also known as *axis mundi*, Cosmic Tree, Etz Chayyim, Jacob's Ladder, Kalpataru ("Wish-Fulfilling Tree"), Ladder of Lights, Saeha Tree, Tree of Life, World Ash, World Tree.

Description: The term *Yggdrasil* comes from Old Norse and means "Odin's Horse" or, more precisely, "Ygg's Steed," as Ygg is Odin's name and means "the terrible one." Odin is the Norse name for God; hence Yggdrasil is God's Tree, just like in Genesis where the Tree of Life is placed in Eden by the Supreme Being (Odin). Odin's horse, called Sleipnir ("Sliding One"), has eight legs.

The Norse Yggdrasil is valuable in world myth because it elaborates the levels and beings that comprise this complex world tree. Mythographers often take Yggdrasil as an excellent cosmogonic model and metaphor. Nine dragons, all with names, gnaw at the tree's roots. A squirrel named Ratatoksr runs up and down the Tree to keep Odin informed of events down below; four stags graze in its branches; and an eagle perches high in the topmost limbs. The three roots extend into three primary domains: One goes to the Aesir, the high gods of Asgard; one to the Frost Giants of Jotunnheim; and the third to Niflheim, realm of mist.

Three springs are found at the base of Yggdrasil: Urd's Well, Mimir's Well, and Hvergelmir. Once a day, the gods from Asgard assemble at Urd's Well (*Urdarbrunnr*, also called "Well of Fate") to discuss doings in the world. The hall of the three Norns, the Norse version of the Greek Fates, is also at the well, and here the Norns determine the fate of humans. Hvergelmir ("Bubbling Cauldron") is the spring from which the rivers of the world arise, although 11 rivers are specified in Norse myth. Mimir's Well is a spring of wisdom, to which Odin resorts almost daily; Mimir is a talking head at the well.

Explanation: Yggdrasil is identical with the Tree of Life in Eden, but the Norse description of Yggdrasil is actually more accurate and *site-specific.* Although the Norse mythographers did not explicitly state where this Tree is located, and most scholars and lay readers have assumed the Tree is either symbolic or celestial, but not found on Earth, the surprising fact is that there is one actual Tree of Life, or Yggdrasil, a Tree of Light, and it is in central Norway, even today.

It is the only Tree of Life on the planet, and it is huge: As a Light form, it rises 200 miles above the surface of the Earth; its roots go down into the Earth for 150 miles; its trunk is 4.5 miles wide; and its roots extend out 15 miles in all directions from the tree. The Tree is situated in a broad open valley in and around the tiny Norwegian hamlet of Rondablikk in the Rondane Mountains; an excellent ski lodge, restaurant, and hotel sit inside the trunk of Yggdrasil, giving guests a unique opportunity to eat, sleep, and relax within the original, actual Tree of Life in Eden.

Hinduism calls this Tree the *Kalpataru*, or "Wish-Fulfilling Tree." It stands in Indra's paradise *(Svarga)* or in the abode of Vaikuntha (an aspect of Vishnu). Hindu belief says if you stand under the Tree and make a wish, the Supreme Being will grant it, and often bestow even more than you wished for. As this Tree is also situated within the heart chakra, you have the option of petitioning God from within your inner heart chakra or "outside" at Yggdrasil in Rondablikk. Often Hinduism says the Kalpataru *is* God, just as the Norse equate Yggdrasil with Odin.

The reference to the Garden of Eden is not poetic or metaphoric. The Garden of Eden was an original template and patterning for the unified field of a balanced humanity placed in 26 locations around the Earth aeons ago. Four of these 26 parts of Eden are located in the Rondane Mountains, and the primary patterning that sets the tone for all 26 and is known as Hvergelmir (one of the 26 parts) is at Rondablikk.

Mimir's Well is located at (or accessed through) the Sodorp Church in nearby Vinstra. The severed head of Mimir, to whom Odin resorted frequently for wisdom and counsel is, in fact, His own head. This is a geomantic feature called the Crown of the Ancient of Days; there are 12 large and 60 small versions of this feature around the planet. Mimir's Well is one of the large features, and it is an interactive meeting place for humans and the Supreme Being, who is expressed as a talking head, that is, a multidirectional focus of total awareness.

Urd's Well is located in a nearby deep valley called Rondvassbu, reached by a four-mile walk in open country. The Well at which the Aesir, or gods of Asgard, assemble every day to discuss affairs of the world is actually a meeting place for the Great White Brotherhood, a disembodied spiritual fellowship and conclave of post-humans, angels, and benevolent extraterrestrial intelligences.

Geomantically, Urd's Well is found at 108 locations around the Earth, and I call it a Valhalla, for it is a hall for those "slain in battle," but it is a spiritual battle: the struggle to master the inner dragon and physical world-based selfhood. The Norse myths call those slain in the spiritual battle of selfhood the Einherjar; and Hindu models of the inner heart chakra say a many-jeweled altar stands before the Kalpataru. The jeweled altar is the assembly of the Einherjar.

As for the dragon called Nidhoggr said to gnaw perpetually at the roots of Yggdrasil, I have seen this dragon, and it is the largest of the 13 primary dragons. The eight other named dragons (also called snakes or serpents) in Nidhoggr's proximity are its progeny, as each of the 13 dragons can produce 81 offspring.

Yggdrasil means "Odin's Horse," and this steed, Sleipnir, has eight legs because the Tree fundamentally resides in the inner heart chakra *(Ananda-kanda)* which has eight petals and is a subset of the main heart chakra *(Anahata)*. The outer geomantic layout mirrors the inner spiritual anatomy of the human heart chakra. The second tree of Paradise, the Tree of the Knowledge of Good and Evil, forms a hedge around the Tree of Life, which is to say, it is situated in the *Anahata* aspect, whose planetary geomantic location is at the Tor in Glastonbury, England.

In Qabala, much thought is given to the *Etz Chayyim,* the rather formal and abstract delineation of the Tree of Life. Qabala's *Etz Chayyim* consists of four complete Trees with identical structure, seen as standing one atop the other; the result is a vertical column with 40 spheres of light, called *Sefiroth,* through which the absolute, unfathomable Light is transduced in steps, eventually reaching the material realm. Qabala's abstract Tree is identical with Yggdrasil and Eden's Tree. It is an attempt to describe and structure the ineffable, for the Tree is God.

What does the Tree do? To call it a tree of course is to employ a useful physical metaphor. It is a unitive consciousness tower. It is the assembly of the 40 families of angels, the entire array of the Supreme Being's creative potency. It is Jacob's Ladder, the ladder by which one ascends to the highest heaven. It is the array of the Seven Heavens. Inside the Tree, you may experience existence before you ever incarnated, before you ever became a soul having incarnations.

The Tree of Life is a soul-making machine. The process starts at the top, at the Supreme Being's Throne (the Norse call it the *Hlidskjalf*), and works down through the Heavens, angelic tiers, Sefiroth, and stations of the Light until it congeals into an archetypal form for the soul: the Holy Grail, a golden chalice. You enter your incarnational cycle as the Holy Grail, and when you have a body, then the Grail resides within you as the perfect expression of the receptive soul.

That is why in the Western Mystery tradition the route from individuative consciousness (Tree of the Knowledge of Good and Evil) back to the unitive consciousness (Tree of Life) is called the Quest for the Holy Grail.

Why is this Tree known in the East as the Wish-Fulfilling Tree? Because it is the Supreme Being's reality creation and concept manifestation mechanism. The entire alphabet, grammar, and syntax of the creation and adjustment of reality is in it. From our embodied viewpoint, it's the field of dreams, the place where dreams come true, the source of abundance and unlimited luxury of being. It is the repository of unitive consciousness, awareness that is whole, not sundered.

The Tree of Life in Eden, though singular for Earth, is replicated 2,856 times in the form of walkable, experiential, horizontally templated miniatures distributed uniformly across the landmass of the planet. A typical landscape Tree of Life may be from 100 yards to a half-mile in length, although a few may be many miles long. Examples of this feature are found at Troy, Turkey; Teotihuacan, Mexico; Jasna Gora, Czestochowa, Poland; and Sedona, Arizona.

See also: Asgard, Avalon, Bran the Blessed, Dragon, Garden of Eden, Holy Grail, Simurgh, Tree of the Knowledge of Good and Evil.

YMIR

An anthropomorphic cosmic figure who embodies the totality of creation and out of whose body the world and all its beings were created; expressed on Earth as interactive holographic copies of the stars of the galaxy.

Also known as Adam Kadmon, Albion, Anthropos, Atman, Cosmic Man, Eternal Man, Fallen Man, Gayomart, Grand Man, Humphrey Chimpden Earwicker (HCE), Manzasiri, P'an-Ku (or Pan Gu, or Coiled Antiquity), Person, Primordial Giant, Primordial Man, Purusha, Sati, Self, Srin-mo Demoness, Universal Man *(al-insan al-kamil).*

Description: The name *Ymir* ("Groaner") comes from the Old Norse for the proto-giant of the Nordic creation account. From the sacrificial dismemberment of Ymir came all of Creation, from the physical to the spiritual.

Ymir began life in Ginnungagap (the Norse name for the void before Creation, though it is filled with creative powers) and initially fed on melting ice drops. Later he was nourished by Audhumla, the cosmic milk-rich cow. When full grown, Ymir began to take himself apart to generate various classes of beings. From Ymir came the Frost Giants of Jotunnheim; from his left armpit came the first man and woman and from these came the race of giants. Later the gods kill Ymir, and his blood drowns all the giants but one, who then carves up his body.

From Ymir's blood came the seas and all planetary water; his flesh yielded up the Earth; his bones the mountains, his teeth and bone splinters the rocks of the planet. The sky and star-filled Heaven came from his head. The trees came from his body hair, the clouds from his brain, and Midgard, or Mid-Earth, where physical life and mortal humanity reside, was fenced in by his eyebrows.

Almost the same story is told of Ymir's Chinese counterpart, P'an-Ku, with a few interesting additions. P'an-Ku begins as a speck in Hun Dun (chaos, another name for Ginnungagap), then grows at the rate of six feet per day for 18,000 years until he is a vast giant. That's 38,888,000 feet, or 7,363.6 miles high.

This line of thinking is similar to that found in Judaic lore about the size of God. Known as the mystical shape of the Godhead, or *Shi'ur Komah,* the Qabalists say the size of our Lord is 236, usually understood as 236,000,000 *parasangs;* God's height is also given as 236 myriad thousand leagues. A parasang is three miles, so this works out to be 7,008,000,000 miles tall.

Explanation: As in his many other guises, such as Albion, P'an-Ku, and Purusha, Ymir finds expression across the Earth as the centerpiece and potential culmination of 432 interactive copies of the galaxy. These are called landscape zodiacs and each, though variable in size (one mile to 200 miles in diameter, typically), consists of a hologram of the important stars and constellations of the Milky Way Galaxy, those relevant to human individuation and the process of regaining wholeness of self, mythically known as the Quest for the Holy Grail.

Ymir is also templated in 12 larger-scale expressions, each overlaying one-twelfth of the planet's surface, and as a single expression over all the Earth.

The cosmogony produced by the sacrificial dismemberment of Ymir's body is replicated through the zodiacs in the sense that his landscape body consists of numerous stars, chakras (subtle consciousness centers), and astral or Light temples that correspond to various heavenly abodes of the gods. So Ymir's galactic body is spread out across a stretch of planetary landscape, and we have the opportunity of reknitting his sundered parts by our interactions with this template.

Ymir also embodies the experience of the primordial dividing of the human wholeness in two, into duality and polarity, as experienced at the

Tree of the Knowledge of Good and Evil when humanity ate the Golden Apple that provided awareness of this reality. The dualistic aspect is copied in the landscape zodiacs, each of which, like an apple, is sliced in two and the parts laid out flat on the landscape as two slightly overlapping circles, filled with stars.

Ymir (better known as Albion in this context) is also split in two, or present twice; the halves get reunited as the zodiac is illuminated by humanity working collegially with the angelic and elemental kingdoms (Nature spirits).

See also: Adam, Albion, Cosmic Egg, Purusha, Tree of the Knowledge of Good and Evil, White Cow.

ZEP TEPI

The primordial time when Earth's visionary geography was being templated on the planet, when its cosmic rationality was readily accessible, and its living, interactive alignment with the galaxy pristine; also, the Earth grid or sacred site matrix comprehended as a total design, like a blueprint.

Also known as Dome Presence, Dreamtime, First Occasion, First Time, Golden Age, Hurqalya, Pat, Paut, Paut-taui, Satya-yuga.

Description: An Egyptian term that denotes the primordial time of the gods' first presence on Earth, similar to the Australian Aborigines' conception of the Dreamtime, Zep Tepi (from *zep,* for "first," and *tepi,* "occasion") suggests both the heavenly template for the terrestrial Egypt, and thus a time before planetary time began—a nontemporal temporality—and the actuality of the gods' first presence on the virginal Earthly template in ancient Egypt.

The world-forming events that transpired during Zep Tepi were expressions of spiritual archetypes of what would later unfold in actual, human time. It denotes a time in which only the gods existed, mythically right after the stirring of the primordial waters (in Egyptian myth, Nun) and the arising of the White Mount as the first landmass and the seat of the high god *Ta-tjenen* ("Elevated Land"), whose name refers to both the Primeval Hill and himself as the god who resided on it.

In Zep Tepi, the gods come into existence and perform their First Deeds, later recounted in their mythic résumés as fundamental acts of the cosmogony. Zep Tepi, because it is almost inconceivably long ago, and long before the advent of human or planetary time, is sacred time, the birthplace of all ritual.

It is the time we now look back to and call mythic, a puzzling intermediate realm between the real and fantasized. It is when the archetypal first events happened, when the gods performed their cosmogonic deeds in a supramundane reality that early cultures tried to invoke through ceremony and even magic.

Zep Tepi is the advent of *maat,* the expression of divine laws and order. Maat is both an Egyptian goddess and an abstract concept of right, truth, and justice, similar to the Vedic *rta,* the Buddhist Dharma, and the Sumerian *me's.* The divine world order emerges from the seeming chaos of Nun, the primordial waters, and *maat* is established as the touchstone for rationality and existence.

Maat is also portrayed as a beautiful winged goddess. She is the embodiment of divine order and cosmic rationality, and all the elements of creation—stars, planets, seasons, rivers, plants, and animals—are in harmony with her. She is the food of the gods, in that she continuously gives of herself to support the orderly functioning of the gods and the unfolding of the world.

She worked with the Egyptian kings to help them maintain *maat,* the rightful alignment of the social with the cosmic order. She helped the king resist *isfet,* the reign of disorder, falsehood, and entropy. Maat, the touchstone of order, assisted the king in continually realigning the state of social and ecological affairs with the pure, original model of perfect harmony established at Zep Tepi. Maat, in fact, is the essence and substance of Zep Tepi, its perfect order.

During Zep Tepi, the Pay Lands came into being. These are mythologic sites whose creation was credited to the original gods; they were sometimes called the Blessed Islands and were called into being by the sacred utterings (mantric speech or magical invocation) of the gods. Some of the Pay Lands included the Mansion of Isden, Island of Re, the Djed Pillar of the Earth, and Behdet (Edfu, a holy city still extant as an archeological site along the Nile River). The falcon or hawk, a god form (presumably referring to Horus), was the Pay Lands' lord.

Other Pay Lands, though harder to locate in actual ancient Egyptian geography, were called the Great Seat, Great Place, and the Throne.

Explanation: In Zep Tepi, we have a marvelous image of the original purity and organization of Earth's visionary geography or Lightgrid when its dynamics were in perfect living, interactive alignment with its celestial model.

Maat, both the personified goddess and the abstract quality of law, justice, and order, was implicit in Earth's visionary geography or what we call today the terrain of sacred sites or Earth grid. Maat is the expression of the cosmic logic and rationality implicit in this planetwide layout; it is the blueprint for our human and planetary reality, the engineer's map of all the sites.

Isfet, in contrast, is the condition of this matrix today, after millennia of entropy and inadequate maintenance. With the exception of some groups of native peoples, including a few groups in the United States, detailed knowledge of this pattern has been forgotten. Isfet is more than a metaphoric description: The Earth grid creates and maintains the etheric structure for all biological life, which, we must remember in the human case, is the foundation for consciousness.

The ancient Egyptians understood they periodically had to renew their culture's relationship to the pure and original Maat when it showed signs of slipping into disorder and isfet. In modern terms, this is like rebooting a computer when it gets stuck, frozen, or temporarily dysfunctional. In Egyptian thinking, time, and our human, material lives within it, is inherently degenerative. Thus the physical world must continually be redrawn into the conditions of Maat.

The time period indicated by Zep Tepi was about 27 million years long. That is about how long it took to get all the conditions correct and ready for life on Earth. Those conditions included installing and regulating the 100+ different features (and all their copies) of Earth's visionary geography.

During this period, the Holy Mountains were being prepared by way of their activation by extraterrestrial devices overlaid upon them, called domes. Domes were etheric energy canopies brought to Earth from elsewhere in the galaxy and distributed around the planet in accordance with star patterns as a way of creating and nourishing Earth's etheric structure.

The domes shaped Earth's etheric web by imposing upon it a conscious matrix—the overall distribution pattern and its mathematics—that would enable conscious-being evolution. The domes emitted particular sounds and lights; they all were originally 33 miles in diameter and linked by both straight-running and spirallic lines of light, usually called ley lines.

The domes, devices in between matter and light, came three times to Earth to reaffirm and energize the intended distribution pattern. Each visit was called a Dome Presence: during the first, there was no human life on Earth; during the second, there was primitive human life; during the third, some humans were able to see the domes and interact with their occupants. Zep Tepi encompasses all three Dome Presences, the time when the visionary geography was templated, nourished, and activated and made ready for human interaction.

The image of the Blessed Islands or Pay Lands created by the gods' mantric utterance points to places of heightened light and celestial access within this geography—places where information about Maat and the original design of the matrix may be accessed. It's similar to the Celtic-Irish conception of the Hollow Hills and *sidhe,* places of heightened numinosity and the gods' hidden residences accessed through certain sacred or mythologically charged hills.

Pay Lands are also similar to the Australian Aborigines' conception of dreaming places in the landscape, where, for example, at Kangaroo Dreaming, the template for the species of the kangaroo (the group animal soul) was introduced to Earth in the Dreamtime (Zep Tepi) to manifest the kangaroos as physical animals on Earth. These templates are still accessible to visionary insight today.

See also: Antichrist, Atlas, Brigit's Mantle, Dreamtime, Earth Changes, Hollow Hill, Holy Mountain, House of Atreus, Hurqalya, Hyperboreans, Land of Milk and Honey, Ley Lines, Phoenix, Wasteland, White Mount.

ZIZ

A cultural expression of the angelic family called Ofanim, emphasizing their ubiquity throughout creation and in human consciousness.

Also known as Angka, Bennu, Bialozar, Chamrosh, Eagle, Garuda, Kreutzet, Phoenix, Pyong, Renanim, Roc, Rukh, Saena Meregha, Sekwi, Semuru, Senmurv, Senmurw, Simargl, Simurgh, Thunderbird.

Description: The Ziz is a mystical bird described in the Judaic tradition as vast in size, its body spanning the distance between Earth and Heaven.

According to Judaic lore, God appointed the Ziz to be the ruler over all the birds. Its name comes from its behavior, mimicking the variety of tastes its flesh has, as in tasting like this, *zeh,* and like that, *zeh.* Hence *zeh-zeh,* or Ziz. The Ziz is as monstrous in size as Leviathan, the prodigious whale in charge of all fish. Its head reaches as far up as the Throne of Glory, where it sings to God.

The Ziz's feet are on Earth while its head reaches into the sky and its outstretched wings eclipse and darken the sun during the day. Yet these same wings protect Earth from southern storms and, without the Ziz's protection, Earth would be unable to resist the winds. Once a Ziz egg fell to Earth and cracked; its oozing fluid drowned 60 cities and the shock of the egg's crash crushed 300 cedar trees, but all that doesn't usually happen.

The Ziz is also responsible for protecting all the other birds and, without its steadfast guardianship, all bird species would have died out by now.

Another name given to the Ziz is Renanim because this bird is the celestial singer. But Ziz is also known as Sekwi, the Seer, and is called "Son of the Nest" because its young birds break out of the shell without incubation. At the end of time, the Ziz, along with Leviathan and Behemoth, will be a food delicacy for the pious at the Messianic banquet as a compensation for the privations endured during incarnation.

Explanation: The Ziz is an image that represents an aspect of the angelic family known as the Ofanim, prominent among the 40 different angelic orders. Ziz is the Judaic perception of what other cultures have called Garuda (Hinduism), Phoenix (Egyptian and Greek), Thunderbird (Native American), Simurgh (Persian), and Eagle (Toltec). It is one of many cultural forms the Ofanim take.

Like Leviathan and Behemoth, the Ziz was among the first beings created, and long before humans and Earth. Correspondingly, the Ofanim are among the oldest of angelic orders. Their age is approximately 60,480,000,000 human years, equal to one Week of Brahma (one Day of Brahma is 4.32 billion years [Day] + 4.32 billion years [Night] = 8.64 billion years), sufficient time to gain the wisdom attributed to them in their Ziz form.

The legend says the head of the Ziz reaches the Throne of Glory: This means that the Ofanim are privy to the innermost directives of the Supreme Being in His Throne room at the top of the Tree of Life, that is, the top or core of the angelic hierarchy.

In mystical language, birds usually denote

either the human soul or angels. The Ofanim are the "ruler of the birds" in the sense that other angelic orders, such as the Seraphim and Elohim, declare the Ofanim to be the teachers of the angels. Rather than ruler and the hierarchical command structure that implies, it is more accurate to say the Ofanim are mentors—Sekwi, Seer—due to their age, celestial experience, and proximity to the Supreme Being's Master Plan for Creation.

The Ziz "protects" all other "birds" (angelic orders) by way of its proximity to God and its ability to transmit information to them from that level and thereby assure other angelic orders of the authenticity of the Source.

The Ziz's extreme size, wingspan, and weight are meant to suggest the scope of the Ofanim's activity, the immensity of their commission by God, and the ubiquity of their presence through the many levels and dimensions of reality. An old Judaic text states that God created an *Ofan,* described as a type of angel, whose head reaches the Holy Hayyoth (another angelic order, very close to God) and who is the mediator between Israel (conscious humanity) and God.

The fact that the Ziz's enormous wingspan can block the sun means, as a point in universal consciousness, the Ziz (Ofanim) far predate mere suns (stars).

One interpretation of the curious *zeh-zeh* etymology for Ziz is that the Ofanim over time have assumed myriad deific or mythic forms in various cultures. Besides the bird form with its multiple expressions, the Ofanim created Ganesh, the lovable, obstacle-removing elephant god of Hinduism. So the Ofanim's "flesh," that is, their protean essence, tastes "like this and like that."

In practical terms, the Ofanim, in their various bird forms, can transport human consciousness to God, especially by way of the Son, Christ. This is more evident in Hinduism's Garuda (a celestial bird) who is Vishnu's Mount (Vishnu is the Hindu name for Christ). Ziz will carry you into Christ Consciousness.

The Ziz will be a delightful delicacy at the Messianic banquet because its essential qualities are Love from Above and transcendent consciousness. They existed before most other angelic orders, before the galaxy, solar systems, and planet Earth, which means they predate all structuring of consciousness and matter. Thus they are, in essence, a tiny point of absolute light and awareness that will be as present at the "end of time" as they are now to willing perception.

The Ofanim are also a banquet delicacy to interested humans today, even (or especially) while alive. Their point of access within human meditative experience is as a tiny blazing star two inches above the navel and two inches inside. Accessing this star is the first step in a Mystery initiation leading to the Christ.

The Messianic banquet implies a Messiah, and that is Christ Consciousness, or the point of awareness that preceded Creation and is thus always available to redeem human consciousness lost in the privations of matter.

The Ziz (the Ofanim) has a geomantic grounding point and dedicated place for human interaction on Earth at the 28.5-acre stone circle in Wiltshire, England, called Avebury.

See also: Garuda, Phoenix, Simurgh, Thunderbird, Vocub Caquix.

About the Author

Richard Leviton is the author of twelve books, including, most recently, *Signs on the Earth* (Hampton Roads, 2005). He regularly conducts workshops and field trips on the subject of myth, sacred sites, and landscape spirituality. He lives in Santa Fe, New Mexico, where he is the director of the Blue Room Consortium, which he describes as a "cosmic mysteries think tank" to do with Earth energies, mapping, and interactions. He may be contacted at blaise@cybermesa.com; see his website at: www.blueroomconsortium.com.